Managing Cisco Network Security

Michael J. Wenstrom

CISCO SYSTEMS
CISCO PRESS

Cisco Press
201 W 103rd Street
Indianapolis, IN 46290 USA

Managing Cisco Network Security

Michael J. Wenstrom

Contributing Authors: J.T. Agnello, Scott Morris, Cary A. Riddock

Copyright© 2001 Cisco Systems, Inc.

Cisco Press logo is a trademark of Cisco Systems, Inc.

Published by:
Cisco Press
201 West 103rd Street
Indianapolis, IN 46290 USA

Printed in the United States of America 1 2 3 4 5 6 7 8 9 0   04 03 02 01

First printing January 2001

Library of Congress Cataloging-in-Publication Number: 98-86504

ISBN: 1-57870-103-1

Warning and Disclaimer

This book is designed to provide information about managing Cisco network security. Every effort has been made to make this book as complete and as accurate as possible, but no warranty or fitness is implied.

The information is provided on an "as is" basis. The author, Cisco Press, and Cisco Systems, Inc. shall have neither liability nor responsibility to any person or entity with respect to any loss or damages arising from the information contained in this book or from the use of the discs or programs that may accompany it.

The opinions expressed in this book belong to the author and are not necessarily those of Cisco Systems, Inc.

Trademark Acknowledgments

All terms mentioned in this book that are known to be trademarks or service marks have been appropriately capitalized. Cisco Press or Cisco Systems, Inc. cannot attest to the accuracy of this information. Use of a term in this book should not be regarded as affecting the validity of any trademark or service mark.

Feedback Information

At Cisco Press, our goal is to create in-depth technical books of the highest quality and value. Each book is crafted with care and precision, undergoing rigorous development that involves the unique expertise of members from the professional technical community.

Readers' feedback is a natural continuation of this process. If you have any comments regarding how we could improve the quality of this book, or otherwise alter it to better suit your needs, you can contact us through e-mail at ciscopress@mcp.com. Please make sure to include the book title and ISBN in your message.

We greatly appreciate your assistance.

Publisher	John Wait
Editor-in-Chief	John Kane
Executive Editor	Brett Bartow
Cisco Systems Program Manager	Bob Anstey
Managing Editor	Patrick Kanouse
Development Editor	Kitty Wilson Jarrett
Senior Editor	Jennifer Chisholm
Copy Editor	Gayle Johnson
Course Developers	Mike Wenstrom
	Tom O'Hara
	Sean Coville
	Bob Martinez
Technical Editors	Richard Benoit
	Doug MacBeth
	Doug McKillip
	Hank Mauldin
Team Coordinator	Amy Lewis
Cover Designer	Louisa Klucznik
Production Team	Argosy
Indexer	Brad Herriman

CISCO SYSTEMS

Corporate Headquarters
Cisco Systems, Inc.
170 West Tasman Drive
San Jose, CA 95134-1706
USA
http://www.cisco.com
Tel: 408 526-4000
    800 553-NETS (6387)
Fax: 408 526-4100

European Headquarters
Cisco Systems Europe
11 Rue Camille Desmoulins
92782 Issy-les-Moulineaux
Cedex 9
France
http://www-europe.cisco.com
Tel: 33 1 58 04 60 00
Fax: 33 1 58 04 61 00

Americas Headquarters
Cisco Systems, Inc.
170 West Tasman Drive
San Jose, CA 95134-1706
USA
http://www.cisco.com
Tel: 408 526-7660
Fax: 408 527-0883

Asia Pacific Headquarters
Cisco Systems Australia,
Pty., Ltd
Level 17, 99 Walker Street
North Sydney
NSW 2059 Australia
http://www.cisco.com
Tel: +61 2 8448 7100
Fax: +61 2 9957 4350

Cisco Systems has more than 200 offices in the following countries. Addresses, phone numbers, and fax numbers are listed on the Cisco Web site at www.cisco.com/go/offices

Argentina • Australia • Austria • Belgium • Brazil • Bulgaria • Canada • Chile • China • Colombia • Costa Rica • Croatia • Czech Republic • Denmark • Dubai, UAE • Finland • France • Germany • Greece • Hong Kong • Hungary • India • Indonesia • Ireland Israel • Italy • Japan • Korea • Luxembourg • Malaysia • Mexico • The Netherlands • New Zealand • Norway • Peru • Philippines Poland • Portugal • Puerto Rico • Romania • Russia • Saudi Arabia • Scotland • Singapore • Slovakia • Slovenia • South Africa • Spain Sweden • Switzerland • Taiwan • Thailand • Turkey • Ukraine • United Kingdom • United States • Venezuela • Vietnam • Zimbabwe

About the Author

Mike Wenstrom is an education specialist at Cisco Systems, Inc., where he designs, develops, and delivers training on Cisco's virtual private network and network security products.

Mike has chosen a career in training and instruction to help people improve their knowledge and skills in communications technologies. He especially enjoys translating complex technical subjects into an easy-to-understand form. Mike has over 18 years of experience in many facets of technical training, having been an instructional designer, course developer, technical instructor, and project manager.

While a 21-year resident of Silicon Valley, Mike worked for Cisco Systems, Aspect Communications, Siemens, IBM, ROLM, Tymnet, NCR, and the U.S. Navy. He currently develops training for and teaches Cisco's VPN and network security products in Austin, Texas, where he resides with his wife and daughter. He graduated from Western Illinois University with a BA degree. He has an AS degree in electronics technology and is a CCNA.

About the Contributing Authors

J.T. Agnello has been a systems administrator in Austin, Texas, for the past 15 years, performing systems and network administration and management for companies that range in size from small-to-medium businesses (SMB) to large enterprises such as Sematech, Schlumberger, IBM, and others. He has been writing technical training courses for the past three years, producing courses that cover such topics as systems, network, security, and database management, for companies such as Tivoli Systems (an IBM company) and Pervasive Software.

Scott Morris is an instructor/consultant for Mentor Technologies, Inc. (formerly Chesapeake Computer Consultants). He has worked in many different areas involving computers and networks. Through Novell certifications, Microsoft certifications, and Cisco certifications, Scott has covered many areas, and he continues to enhance his credentials (and to relieve boredom).

Regarding Cisco pursuits, Scott is a Cisco Certified Systems Instructor (CCSI), CCIE #4713 in Routing and Switching, a CCDP in Routing and Switching, and a CCNA in WAN Switching. Scott has passed the CCIE written exams for the ISP-Dial and Design tracks, and he currently uses his little spare time to work on his next CCIE lab exam (ISP-Dial first!). Scott primarily teaches Cisco Internetwork Troubleshooting (CIT), but he tends to pick up courses on brand-new technology just for fun.

Cary A. Riddock has been a network engineer for a large Central Florida healthcare management company for the past year. His duties include monitoring the corporate LAN/WAN and troubleshooting connectivity-related problems. Currently, he is working on a system that will allow corporate executives to access private intranet applications via the public Internet utilizing PKI and token card–based authentication technology. Cary holds the following certifications: MCSE, CCNA, CCDA, CCDP, and CCA.

About the Technical Reviewers

This book's reviewers contributed their considerable practical, hands-on expertise to the entire development process for *Managing Cisco Network Security.*

Richard Benoit serves as the Network and Technology Project Manager for an international entertainment conglomerate headquartered in Orlando, Florida. Currently, his work focus is on enterprise network design, management, and security issues. Formerly, as a consultant, he worked with many customers in the design, implementation, and support of large-scale network solutions. His network certifications include CCNP + Security, CCDA, and Microsoft MCSE. He holds a BS in Management Systems from the Milwaukee School of Engineering.

Doug MacBeth is an IOS documentation manager at Cisco Systems, Inc. He has more than 15 years of experience in technical documentation and has worked for Cisco Systems since 1993. While at Cisco, Doug has been an Editor and a Project Leader for the Cisco IOS documentation set. Doug lives in San Jose, California. He holds a Bachelor's Degree in Technical and Business Communications from San Jose State University.

Doug McKillip, P.E., CCIE #1851, is an independent consultant specializing in Cisco Certified Training in association with Global Knowledge. He has more than 12 years of experience in computer networking, and for the past eight years, he has been actively involved in security and firewalls. Doug provided both instructional and technical assistance during the initial deployment of the MCNS version 1.0 training class, and he has been the Lead Instructor and Course Director for Global Knowledge, a Training Parter of Cisco Systems. Doug holds Bachelor's and Master's Degrees in Chemical Engineering from MIT and a Master's Degree in Computer Science from the University of Delaware. He resides in Wilmington, Delaware.

Hank Mauldin is a Consulting Engineer for Cisco Systems, Inc., working for the Office of the CTO. He has worked with Cisco for several years, evaluating and designing data networks. His areas of expertise include IP routing protocols, quality of service, and network security. Hank currently is Program Manager for Cisco Network Designer, which is a network design tool. Prior to joining Cisco, he worked for several different system integrators. He has more than 15 years of data networking experience. Hank resides in San Diego, California. He holds a Master's Degree in Information System Technology from George Washington University.

Dedication

I dedicate this book to my family. I could not have completed this book without the support of my wife, Virginia, and my daughter, Rosemary. They put up with the many late nights and weekends when I worked on the book. I also dedicate this book to my mother, Mary E. Wenstrom, for raising me from my childhood on and for giving me good, loving guidance to the present. And finally, I dedicate this book to my father, the late Conrad R. Wenstrom, who taught me the value of perseverance and hard work and who helped make me the man that I am.

Acknowledgments

The MCNS course was a community project with many contributors inside and outside Cisco, including Cisco course developers, course editors, and instructors. Although I was the primary course developer for the MCNS course, I would like to acknowledge the important efforts of others who made the course a success: Tom O'Hara, Sean Coville, and Bob Martinez as contributing course developers; Matt Lyons, Franjo Majstor, and Kevin Calkins as Cisco instructors, Hank Mauldin and Chris Lonvick as course consultants and architects; Doug McKillip as the key Cisco Learning Partner instructor; Brian Adams and Deborah Lewis as course editors; and Chris Berriman as the manager for the initial MCNS project.

Developing the MCNS book was a difficult yet rewarding project. I would like to acknowledge my manager, Rick Stiffler, and my workmates in the security training group, who tolerantly put up with the many times I came to work after toiling over the book until 2 the previous night. I would also like to acknowledge the Cisco Press staff, who tried to keep me on track to bring the book to a close. Kitty Jarrett and Brett Bartow deserve special commendation for patiently working with me and the other authors throughout the project. I appreciate the significant contributions made by the technical reviewers, and I thank the other authors who made this book a success.

Contents at a Glance

Contents

Foreword

Managing Cisco Network Security presents in book format all the topics covered in the challenging instructor-led certification preparation course of the same name. MCNS teaches you the knowledge and skills needed to install, configure, operate, manage, and verify Cisco network security products and Cisco IOS software security features in IP networks. You will learn how to identify network security threats, secure remote dial-in access with CiscoSecure ACS and Cisco IOS AAA features, protect Internet access using Cisco perimeter routers and PIX Firewalls, and implement secure VPNs with IPSec. Whether you are preparing for the Cisco specialization in security or are seeking to gain a practical understanding of Cisco network security solutions, you will benefit from the information presented in this book.

Cisco and Cisco Press present this material in text-based format to provide another learning vehicle for our customers and the broader user community in general. Although a publication does not duplicate the instructor-led environment, we acknowledge that not everyone responds in the same way to the same delivery mechanism. It is our intent that presenting this material via a Cisco Press publication will enhance the transfer of knowledge to a broad audience of networking professionals.

Cisco Press will present existing and future courses through these course books to help achieve Cisco Internet Learning Solutions Group's principal objectives: to educate the Cisco community of networking professionals and to enable that community to build and maintain reliable, scalable networks. The Cisco Career Certifications and classes that support these certifications are directed at meeting these objectives through a disciplined approach to progressive learning. The books Cisco Press creates in partnership with Cisco Systems will meet the same standards for content quality demanded of our courses and certifications. It is our intent that you will find this and subsequent Cisco Press certification and training publications of value as you build your networking knowledge base.

Thomas M. Kelly
Vice President, Internet Learning Solutions Group
Cisco Systems, Inc.
July 2000

Preface

Computer and network security have become front-page news due to the prevalence of attacks and the realization that the Internet revolution is here to stay and is the key to prosperity of individuals and countries. Leaders of nations and companies worldwide have been forced to pay attention to the urgent need for network security. Many have realized that their networks lack even basic security measures and that there are not enough network professionals trained to implement network security. Yet network security seems to be a complex, even esoteric subject that defies understanding by any but the most elite network professionals.

Many of us whose careers are focused on increasing the knowledge and competency level of networking professionals saw the need to create a holistic approach to teaching network security in order to help people get started in better securing their networks. We saw the need to jump-start people into the network security field so that many more people could develop security expertise, thereby increasing network security as a whole. We decided to create a new network security course to address the anticipated need.

Early in 1997, while a developer in Cisco Worldwide Training, I was assigned by my then-manager, Chris Berriman, to develop the Managing Cisco Network Security (MCNS) course. Although nobody had yet requested such a course, our group had the vision to anticipate the eventual exploding need for network security training. I performed an informal survey of competitive offerings and found that no other companies were offering an equivalent course.

The course was intended to provide a survey of Cisco network security technology, balancing breadth of technology offering with depth of coverage on each subject. Hands-on lab exercises would cement concepts and facts. The MCNS project was launched, and a team effort led to the production of the first and subsequent versions.

This book is parallel in content to the MCNS course, yet it is completely rewritten based on extensive research. The need for a comprehensive network security book is especially strong today. This book addresses the compelling need to educate many more networking professionals and associates on vital network security needs, making network security available and understandable to many more people.

Mike Wenstrom
Cisco Systems, Inc.
August 2000

Introduction

The goal of this book is to help readers implement Cisco-supported network security technologies and design and implement more-secure networks. This book is designed to supplement the MCNS course or act as a standalone reference.

This Book's Audience

The book is written for anyone who wants to learn about Cisco network security features and technologies. The main target audience is networking professionals who need to expand their knowledge beyond routing and switching technologies and improve their ability to install, configure, monitor, and verify Cisco network security products and features. This book assumes that you have a knowledge of Cisco networking equivalent to that required to pass the CCNA certification exam.

The secondary target audience is general users who need to understand network security threats and how to mitigate those threats. This book explains many network security concepts and technologies with a user-friendly approach that should appeal to readers who prefer less-technical manuals.

This Book's Features

This book has a number of unique features that will help you learn and put to work the network security topics covered in this book:

- **Concepts covered**—At the beginning of each chapter is a list of topics covered in that chapter. This provides a reference to the concepts covered and can be used as an advanced organizer.

- **Figures, examples, and tables**—This book contains figures, examples, and tables that present each chapter's content in an easy-to-use form. The figures help explain concepts and software processes, the examples provide examples of commands and output, and the tables present facts such as command syntax with descriptions.

- **Case studies**—The XYZ Company, a hypothetical enterprise, is used in each chapter to anchor configuration examples into a unified whole and to make the examples more realistic. A sample network security policy based on the XYZ Company is used throughout this book as a model of how to implement security policy directives. Case study network examples in many chapters summarize configuration information taught in the chapter based on the XYZ customer environment.

- **Command summaries**—Command summaries are included with each subject instead of in a separate section as a courtesy to you, making it easier to learn and apply the tasks being presented.

- **Chapter summaries**—At the end of each chapter is a summary of the concepts covered in that chapter. It provides a synopsis of the chapter and serves as a study aid.

- **Review questions**—After the summary in each chapter are 10 review questions that reinforce the concepts presented in that chapter. They help you test your understanding before you move on to new concepts. The answers to these questions are provided in Appendix D.

- **References**—After the review questions is a listing of references related to the topics presented in that chapter. They help you extend your knowledge beyond what is covered in the chapter.

Conventions Used in This Book

This book uses the following conventions:

- Important or new terms are *italicized*.

- All code examples appear in `monospace` type, and parts of code use the following conventions:

  — Commands and keywords are in **bold** type.

  — Arguments, which are placeholders for values the user inputs, appear in *italics*.

  — Square brackets ([ ]) indicate optional keywords or arguments.

  — Braces ({ }) indicate required choices.

  — Vertical bars (|) are used to separate required choices.

This Book's Organization

This book is divided into seven parts, including 18 chapters and four appendixes.

Part I: Establishing Network Security Policy

Chapter 1, "Evaluating Network Security Threats," answers the fundamental question "Why do we need network security?" by examining the potential threats to an enterprise network. It examines network security challenges and the three primary reasons for network security vulnerabilities. It also provides a snapshot of network intruders and addresses the four major categories of network security threats and the tools used to execute them.

Chapter 2, "Evaluating a Network Security Policy," examines the economics of protecting the network and outlines the major components of a network security policy. It also summarizes a network security survey conducted by Cisco and contains an exercise in which you evaluate a sample security policy.

Chapter 3, "Securing the Network Infrastructure," presents how to configure Cisco routers to secure the campus network environment. It covers securing the administrative interface, controlling SNMP access to network devices, ways to control routing updates from interlopers, simple methods to control network traffic, and controlling Ethernet switch port and access security.

Part II: Dialup Security

Chapter 4, "Examining Cisco AAA Security Technology," discusses the AAA architecture and technologies associated with it. It presents concepts useful for implementing AAA security solutions available in Cisco products.

Chapter 5, "Configuring the Network Access Server for AAA Security," discusses how to configure a Cisco network access server to allow AAA processes to use a local or remote security database. In addition, it covers how to troubleshoot problems with AAA processes.

Chapter 6, "Configuring CiscoSecure ACS and TACACS+/RADIUS," discusses the features and architecture of CiscoSecure ACS for Microsoft Windows NT and UNIX platforms. In addition, it describes how to configure CiscoSecure ACS for NT to perform AAA functions for Cisco network access servers, focusing on using the TACACS+ protocol.

Part III: Securing the Internet Connection

Chapter 7, "Configuring a Cisco Perimeter Router," presents how to create a perimeter security system using the security features of a Cisco router. It includes an overview of perimeter security components and Cisco IOS software features that are useful for perimeter security. It also shows you how to use each feature to secure the network perimeter.

Chapter 8, "Configuring the Cisco IOS Firewall," discusses how to use the Cisco IOS Firewall feature set on Cisco routers to enhance perimeter security. It includes an overview of context-based access control, and it shows you how to configure the IOS Firewall in a perimeter security system.

Part IV: Configuring the CiscoSecure PIX Firewall

Chapter 9, "PIX Firewall Basics," presents the capabilities, features, and configuration options of the PIX Firewall family. It shows that the PIX Firewall can provide powerful security even with a basic configuration command set.

Chapter 10, "Configuring Access Through the PIX Firewall," builds on Chapter 9, discussing how to control inbound and outbound access through the PIX Firewall with specific configuration commands. It includes configuring network address translation, static translations, and other methods of access control.

Chapter 11, "Configuring Multiple Interfaces and AAA on the PIX Firewall," discusses how to flexibly configure multiple interfaces on the PIX Firewall to create a more-secure DMZ. It also covers how to configure AAA features of the PIX Firewall to work with CiscoSecure ACS, enabling user-level access control.

Chapter 12, "Configuring Advanced PIX Firewall Features," discusses some of the more specialized features of the PIX Firewall that make it a powerful yet flexible firewall to control Internet access and features. It includes coverage of PPTP support, Java applet blocking, URL and FTP filtering, SNMP and syslog support, PIX Firewall redundancy, and maintenance features.

Part V: Configuring Cisco Encryption Technology

Chapter 13, "Cisco Encryption Technology Overview," discusses the concepts required to configure Cisco Encryption Technology on Cisco routers. It presents encryption algorithms, hashing techniques, digital signatures, and key exchange methods used with Cisco Encryption Technology.

Chapter 14, "Configuring Cisco Encryption Technology," presents the tasks and steps you must follow to configure Cisco Encryption Technology on Cisco routers. It presents the Cisco IOS commands used to configure and test Cisco Encryption Technology, organized in the order in which you would enter them to enable this feature.

Part VI: Configuring a VPN with IPSec

Chapter 15, "Understanding Cisco IPSec Support," presents an overview of IPSec and the IPSec protocols available in Cisco products used to create a VPN. Each IPSec protocol is considered. Subsequent chapters provide details on how to configure IPSec support in Cisco products.

Chapter 16, "Configuring Cisco IOS IPSec," discusses how to configure IPSec in Cisco routers for preshared key and RSA encryption authentication in a site-to-site topology. It simplifies the complex process you must follow to configure IPSec by breaking it into discreet tasks and steps.

Chapter 17, "Configuring PIX Firewall IPSec Support," discusses how to configure IPSec in PIX Firewalls for preshared key authentication in a site-to-site topology. It presents how to configure IPSec in tasks and steps, showing you all the commands necessary to enable this feature.

Chapter 18, "Scaling Cisco IPSec Networks," describes how to configure Cisco IPSec networks consisting of Cisco routers and PIX Firewalls using IPSec so that they can scale to support multiple IPSec peers while maintaining security. It covers how to configure certification authority support and remote access for Cisco VPN client access.

Part VII: Appendixes

Appendix A, "XYZ Company Case Study Scenario," describes the XYZ Company case study to help tie together the security concepts and implementation procedures discussed throughout this book. It presents the IP addresses and networking devices used in sample configurations in each chapter.

Appendix B, "An Example of an XYZ Company Network Security Policy," contains an example of a network security policy for the XYZ Company network used throughout this book. It includes policy statements that address major issues of enterprise network security for the XYZ Company.

Appendix C, "Configuring Standard and Extended Access Lists," summarizes Cisco IOS access lists, which are fundamental to many security features in Cisco routers. It includes coverage of commands used with standard and extended IP access lists.

Appendix D, "Answers to Review Questions," provides the answers to the review questions at the end of each chapter.

PART I

Establishing Network Security Policy

Chapter 1   Evaluating Network Security Threats

Chapter 2   Evaluating a Network Security Policy

Chapter 3   Securing the Network Infrastructure

Upon completing this chapter, you will be able to do the following:

- Identify the need for network security
- Identify some of the causes of network security problems
- Identify some characteristics and motivating factors of network intruders
- Identify the most significant network security threats
- Choose countermeasures to thwart network security attacks

CHAPTER 1

Evaluating Network Security Threats

This chapter examines the potential threats to an enterprise network. It considers why we need network security by examining the network security issues and challenges facing a network manager and the three primary reasons for network security vulnerabilities. The chapter attempts to provide a snapshot of network intruders so that you can understand your adversary. It addresses some of the most common types of threats, the tools used to implement them, and the tools used to thwart them. This chapter presents a summary of some of the tools and methods used to execute the four major categories of network security threats: reconnaissance, unauthorized access, denial of service, and data manipulation. The summary of attacks also gives some tips on how you can thwart the attacks. This chapter concludes with a list of resources you can access to learn more about how to protect yourself from network intruders.

Why We Need Network Security

The Internet economy is rapidly changing the way we work, live, play, and learn. It is especially affecting businesses and governments on a global scale. Business leaders recognize the strategic role that the Internet plays in their company's ability to survive and compete in the 21st century. Consumers and end users want secure methods to communicate and carry out electronic commerce. Unfortunately, because the Internet was based on open standards and ease of communication, it was initially missing some key security components such as controlling remote access, privacy of communications, and prevention of attacks that can deny services to others. The need to secure Internet-related communications has driven the growth of network security technologies.

Businesses face a daunting security problem: how to implement and constantly update defenses and practices to reduce business vulnerability to evolving hacker threats.

Security can be difficult to implement uniformly across the enterprise because some solutions work only in the campus, and others work only in the wide-area network (WAN). Some security solutions work well for smaller enterprises but are not practical as the enterprise grows in terms of effort, time, or cost to implement. This security problem is compounded by the added vulnerability created by the Internet connection, which gives a network intruder potential entry into your business infrastructure.

The security challenge that businesses face today is one of sorting through a wide range of solutions and choosing the right combination. A large number of security technologies and products exist. It is not the lack of technology that makes securing the network difficult. The problem is choosing among the many different selections available and adopting those that satisfy your unique network and business requirements while minimizing the support required with differing vendor technologies.

After the network engineer or system administrator has selected the right mix of security products for the network environment, the different products must be integrated throughout the entire enterprise to achieve a single, consistent security policy, which is a large challenge in today's environment. Cisco currently has many security products that enable a powerful security policy, and it is developing many more security products for future release. Cisco's security products are being developed under the Cisco SAFE architecture, a dynamic security framework for e-business networks.

Why We Have Security Issues

Campus, dialup, and Internet network access are being widely implemented in today's business environment. Yet each of these network environments poses network security risks and issues. The network and computing equipment used to implement access might inherently contain security exposures, might be configured incorrectly, or might be implemented and managed improperly. When you additionally consider the types and motivating factors of network intruders themselves, the need for network security becomes apparent. Each of these issues is considered in the following sections.

Three Primary Reasons for Security Issues

There are at least three primary reasons for network security threats:

- **Technology weaknesses**—Each network and computing technology has inherent security problems.

- **Configuration weaknesses**—Even the most secure technology can be misconfigured or misused, exposing security problems.

- **Policy weaknesses**—A poorly defined or improperly implemented and managed security policy can make the best security and network technology ripe for security abuse.

There are people who are eager, willing, qualified, and sometimes compensated to take advantage of each security weakness and to continually discover and exploit new weaknesses. Each weakness is explored in a bit more depth in the next few sections.

Technology Weaknesses

Computer and network technologies have intrinsic security weaknesses or vulnerabilities. Technology weaknesses considered here include TCP/IP, the operating system, and network equipment weaknesses, as illustrated in Figure 1-1.

Figure 1-1   *Networking and Computing Equipment Contains Technology Weaknesses*

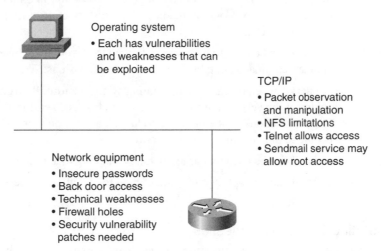

Operating system
- Each has vulnerabilities and weaknesses that can be exploited

TCP/IP
- Packet observation and manipulation
- NFS limitations
- Telnet allows access
- Sendmail service may allow root access

Network equipment
- Insecure passwords
- Back door access
- Technical weaknesses
- Firewall holes
- Security vulnerability patches needed

The Computer Emergency Response Team (CERT) archives at www.cert.org document many technology weaknesses for protocols, operating systems, and network equipment. CERT advisories address Internet-technology security problems. They offer an explanation of the problem, information that helps you determine if your site has the problem, fixes or workarounds, and vendor information.

TCP/IP Weaknesses

TCP/IP was designed as an open standard to facilitate communications. The services, tools, and utilities derived from it were each designed to also assist in open communications. Here are some examples of the intrinsic vulnerabilities of TCP/IP and its services:

- IP, TCP, and UDP packet headers and their contents can be observed, modified, and re-sent without detection.

- The Network File System (NFS) can enable insecure trusted access to hosts. NFS does not provide for user authentication and uses randomly assigned UDP ports for its sessions, making limited protocol and user access virtually impossible.

- Telnet is a powerful service that can give users access to many Internet utilities and services that might not be otherwise available. Hackers can use Telnet by specifying a port number parameter in addition to a host name or IP address to initiate an interactive dialog with a service that is known to be insecure.

- The UNIX sendmail daemon can allow access to the UNIX root, enabling unintended access to the UNIX system. sendmail is a program used to run e-mail on UNIX systems. It is a complex program that has a long history of security problems, including the following:

  — sendmail can be used to gain access to the UNIX root level by exploiting sendmail commands in fabricated e-mail transmissions.

  — Intruders can determine which operating system **sendmail** is running on by looking at the version number returned by fabricated **sendmail** messages. This information can then be used to launch attacks on vulnerabilities specific to the operating system version.

  — sendmail can be used to learn which hosts belong to a domain name.

  — sendmail can be exploited to redirect mail to unauthorized destinations.

Operating System Weaknesses

Each operating system has security problems and weaknesses that must be addressed. Linux, UNIX, Microsoft Windows 2000, Windows NT, Windows 98, Windows 95, and IBM OS/2 each have problems that have been detected and documented.

The CERT archives document many operating system weaknesses. Each operating system vendor or developer has information on specific known vulnerabilities and methods to overcome them. It is likely that many other operating system vulnerabilities exist that have yet to be detected, documented, and resolved.

Network Equipment Weaknesses

Network equipment from each vendor has security weaknesses that must be recognized and protected against. Some examples include insecure password protection, lack of authentication, routing protocols, and firewall holes. Most vendors quickly fix network equipment weaknesses when they are discovered. You can usually easily repair such weaknesses by applying a software revision or patch or by upgrading the equipment's operating system.

A hole allows unauthorized users to access or increase their level of access to a system. It can be a feature or bug in hardware or software. Most holes in network equipment and networked computers are well known and documented, such as in CERT advisories. For example, Cisco notifies users and the Internet community about potential security problems in Cisco products through Internet Security Advisories, summarized at www.cisco.com/warp/customer/707/advisory.html. This URL requires a CCO login for access. Advisories published by Cisco are usually summarized or referenced at the CERT Web site.

Note that early or limited deployment releases of Cisco IOS Software typically contain unknown holes, compared with general deployment releases, which are more thoroughly tested.

Configuration Weaknesses

Configuration weaknesses, illustrated in Figure 1-2, are a close relative of technology weaknesses. Configuration weaknesses are problems caused by not setting up or configuring networked equipment to prevent known or potential security problems. The good news about configuration weaknesses is that, once they are known, they can easily be corrected at minimal cost.

Figure 1-2   *Security Problems Caused by Configuration Weaknesses or Misuse of Equipment*

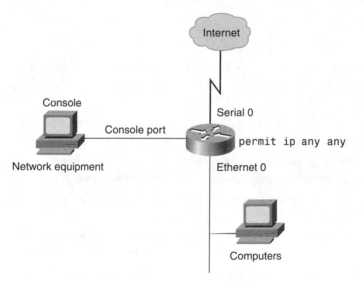

Here are some examples of configuration weaknesses:

- **Insecure default settings within products**—Many products have default settings that enable security holes. Users should consult manufacturers or user groups to identify and correct insecure default settings.

- **Misconfigured network equipment**—Misconfiguration of the equipment itself can cause significant security problems. For example, misconfigured access lists, routing protocols, or SNMP community strings can open up large security holes.

- **Insecure user accounts**—User account information may be transmitted insecurely across the network, exposing usernames and passwords to snoopers.

- **System accounts with easily guessed passwords**—This common problem is the result of poorly selected and easily guessed user passwords. For example, NetWare, UNIX, and Windows NT systems might contain legacy accounts with the username guest with the password guest.

- **Misconfigured Internet services**—A common problem is to turn on Java and JavaScript in Web browsers, enabling attacks via hostile Java applets. Network equipment or computer operating systems might enable insecure TCP/IP services that could allow remote access.

The good news about configuration weaknesses is that you can easily learn what the configuration weaknesses are and correctly configure computing and network devices to compensate by consulting CERT advisories, current documentation from network equipment vendors, and informational Requests for Comments (RFCs) that describe the best current practices for network configuration, such as RFC 2827, "Network Ingress Filtering."

Network Security Policy Weaknesses

A written, sound security policy that can readily be implemented by the organization creates a bulwark of network security. Yet some security problems can be caused by security policy weaknesses, including the following:

- **Lack of a written security policy**—An unwritten policy cannot be consistently applied or enforced.

- **Internal politics**—Political battles, turf wars, and internecine conflict will hinder the ability to have and enforce a consistent security policy.

- **Lack of business continuity**—Frequent replacement of personnel leads to an erratic approach to security.

- **Logical access controls to network equipment are not applied**—Poorly enforced and administered user password procedures allow unauthorized access to the network.

- **Security administration is lax, including monitoring and auditing**—Inadequate monitoring, auditing, and correction of problems allow attacks and unauthorized use to continue, which wastes company resources and exposes the company to legal action.

- **Lack of awareness of having been attacked**—The organization might not even be aware that it has been attacked because it does not monitor the network closely or have an intrusion detection system.

- **Software and hardware installation and changes do not follow the policy**— Unauthorized changes to the network topology or installation of unapproved applications create security holes.

- **Security incident and disaster recovery procedures are not in place**—The lack of a security incident or disaster recovery plans allows chaos, panic, and confusion to occur when someone attacks the enterprise.

Chapter 2, "Evaluating a Network Security Policy," covers how to evaluate a security policy in more depth.

Know Your Enemy: Inside the Mind of the Intruder

You can better protect your network if you know who the intruder is. The people who steal from you can be relentless. They are probably intelligent and are likely to find ways around static security implementations. For effective long-term security, you need to invest in a robust security architecture and a continuous, multistep security process. Refer to the "References" section at the end of this chapter for historical information on actual hacker exploits.

Who are network intruders? They are an extremely diverse lot who defy categorization. Yet this section attempts to help you know your enemy. Network intruder motivations are complex and numerous. The network intruder may fall under either the internal or external threat category.

In this book, we refer to an individual who attempts to access network or computer resources without authorization as a *network intruder,* or *intruder*. The intruder can be further classified as either a cracker or a hacker:

- **Cracker**—A person who uses advanced knowledge of the Internet or networks to probe or compromise network security without authorization. The cracker usually has malicious intent.

- **Hacker**—A person who investigates the integrity and security of an operating system or network. Usually a programmer, the person uses advanced knowledge of hardware and software to hack systems in innovative ways. The hacker then often freely shares his knowledge with others, usually over the Internet, which can prove an embarrassment to the victim. The hacker usually does not have malicious intent and is trying to offer a service to the Internet community. Hackers are also known as "ethical hackers" or "white hat" hackers.

Internal Threats

Internal threats are perpetrated by those inside an organization through intentional or unintentional activities such as the following:

- **Current employees with less-than-honorable intentions**—Employees who might want to test security vulnerabilities or who might even have malicious intent, hoping to exploit their employer's trust for profit or theft.

- **Current employees pursuing unintentional activities**—Employees who accidentally download a virus or other harmful program or who accidentally access a sensitive internal network or host.

- **Employees who mismanage the environment**—Employees who do not use safe passwords or who misconfigure network equipment out of ignorance.

External Threats

External threats are carried out by those outside an organization through intentional or unintentional activities such as the following:

- **Thrill seekers**—Many intruders do their work for excitement or to impress peers.

- **Competitors**—Your competition might enlist the help of a competitive analysis group to gain access to sensitive competitive information.

- **Enemies**—Many governments are concerned about information warfare from friendly or hostile countries motivated by nationalism, zealotry, or ideology. For example, during the Kosovo conflict, the NATO Web site experienced increased hacker activity.

- **Thieves**—Intruders might seek specific, valuable information for profit or some other purpose.

- **Spies**—Industrial espionage is on the increase.

- **Hostile former employees**—Employees with inside knowledge seeking revenge, thrills, or profit.

- **Others**—People might perform network intrusions for sport or for the challenge of it, to learn, or out of boredom, curiosity, or the need for acceptance from peers.

Original Intruder Skill Set and Characteristics

Network intrusion started with people gaining unauthorized access to telecommunications resources, commonly known as *phracking*. Early network intruders typically had the following skill set and characteristics:

- Knew how to code in several programming languages:

  — **C, C++**—Essential programming languages

  — **Perl**—A computer scripting language

  — **CGI (Common Gateway Interface)**—A Web server application programming interface

- — **Microsoft Visual Basic (VB)**—A user-friendly programming environment
- — **Java**—A portable derivative of C and C++
- Had in-depth knowledge of TCP/IP protocols, services, and tools.
- Was very experienced at using the Internet.
- Intimately knew at least two operating systems. For example, could use UNIX and DOS, or UNIX and VMS.
- Had a job using computers or networks. Enjoyed working with computer equipment as a way of life.
- Collected computer hardware and software. Had a variety of computers to work with.

Current Intruder Skill Set and Characteristics

Network intrusion techniques and tools are now widely known and available. The current network intruder skill set and characteristics can be typified in the following key points:

- Can download prewritten software tools from hacker Internet or bulletin board sites. Many network intrusion and testing tools exist, their source code is readily available, and more are being added daily. The only skill required is using a compiler to generate an executable from the hacker source code.
- Uses prewritten scripts and utilities in creative ways to intrude into networks and computer systems. Can use a tool to automatically probe a network for weaknesses.
- Is in an age group that has plenty of time to experiment and develop techniques. A student or hobbyist with a great interest in technology. Is also known as a "script kiddie" because his attacks are primarily carried out with scripts or programs written by someone else.

Note the shorter list for current intruders. Regardless of the type, category, or motivation of network intruders, we must find methods to thwart them.

Security Threat Types

The vast range of network security threats defies efforts to categorize them, understand what they are, and devise methods to protect against them. To help you get your arms around network security threats, we have created the following categories of network security threat types, which are considered in turn in this section of the chapter:

- Reconnaissance
- Unauthorized access
- Denial of service
- Data manipulation

The categories of security threats are generally known as *vulnerabilities*—attributes of a computer or network that permit someone to initiate exploits against the network. An *exploit* is a method to take advantage of a vulnerability by a manual procedure, a script, or an executable program. The purpose of the exploit is to collect system information (reconnaissance), deny system services to valid users, gain unauthorized access to systems or data, or manipulate data.

Vulnerabilities and exploits each have a telltale *signature*—a distinctive, recognizable state or state transition. Intrusion detection systems (IDS), such as the CiscoSecure IDS, can recognize exploit signatures as they are carried out. As soon as vulnerability and exploit signatures are known and recorded, countermeasures can be identified to either fix the vulnerability itself or somehow block the exploit from working against the vulnerability. Vulnerability science is the study of vulnerabilities and exploits.

In the following sections, we will consider the four vulnerability and exploit categories.

Reconnaissance

Reconnaissance is the unauthorized discovery, mapping, and monitoring of systems, services, or vulnerabilities in a network. Reconnaissance also includes monitoring network traffic. Reconnaissance can be carried out either actively or passively. The information gathered by reconnaissance can then be used to pose other attacks to the network or to steal vital data. Figure 1-3 illustrates where reconnaissance attacks can take place in an enterprise network.

Reconnaissance attacks can take the form of target discovery, eavesdropping, and information theft. The following sections consider reconnaissance attack types, examine exploits used to carry out the attacks, and describe countermeasures you can take to prevent reconnaissance attacks.

Target Discovery

Discovering the targets for reconnaissance includes finding out domain names and associated IP addresses, learning the IP address range of a target organization, or finding out specific IP addresses of target hosts. A specific host can then be targeted to learn of available services or host information. For example, the hacker might try to learn the IP address of a perimeter router's interface connection to an ISP so that he can attack the router. Target discovery can be carried out with common query-type network commands, **ping** sweeps, and port scans.

Figure 1-3   *Examples of Reconnaissance Attack Locations*

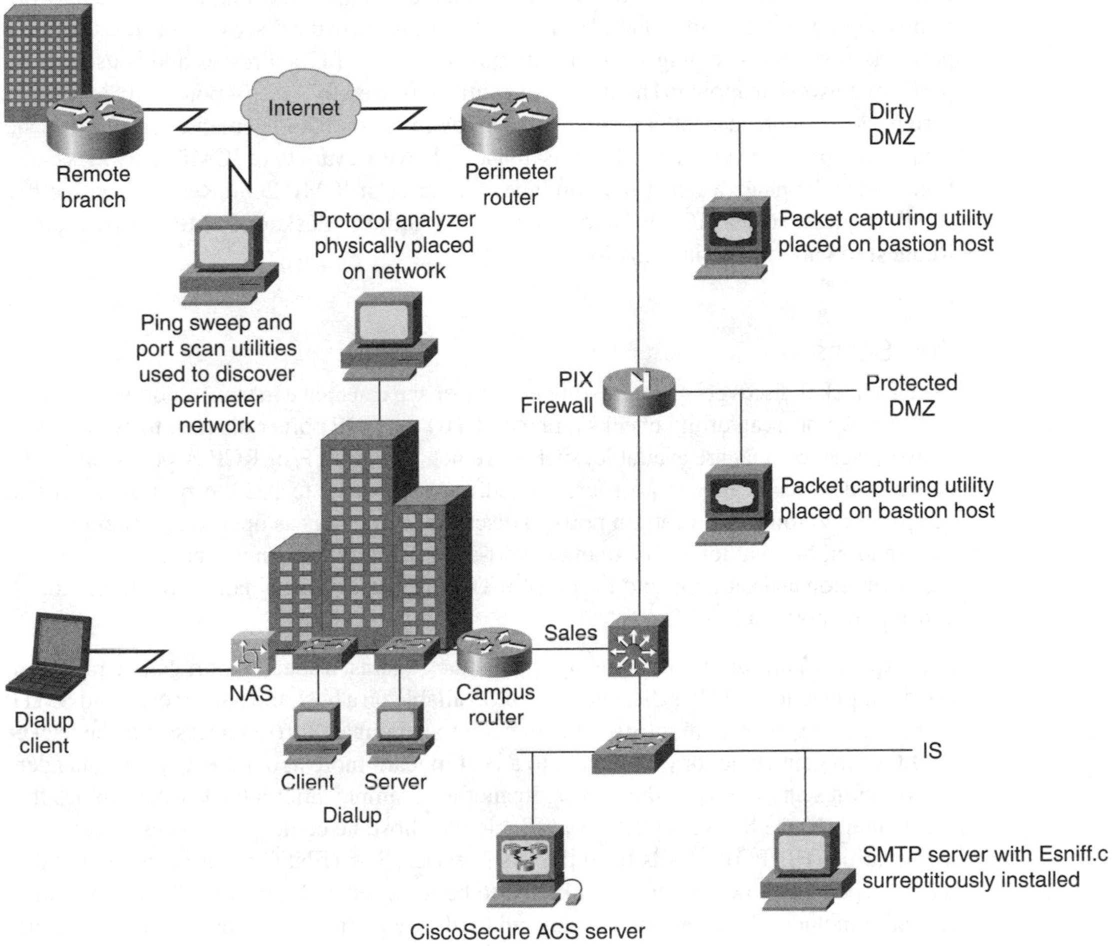

Network Commands

Reconnaissance can be accomplished using network commands readily available on UNIX, Windows, and Linux systems: **ping**, **whois**, **finger**, **rusers**, **nslookup**, **rpcinfo**, **telnet**, **dig**, **nmap**, and other commands or utilities that provide information about a host or network. The commands can be exercised individually or by using public domain utilities that combine query-type commands to accomplish a specific purpose. Some utilities can be used to gather information about network devices by exercising IP header options using synthesized packets and then gathering information sent in reply to the bogus packets.

ping Sweeps

Although individual **ping** commands can be entered to gather information about a network or hosts, ping sweep utilities have been devised to automate the discovery of hosts within a network or subnet. The ping sweep utility pings a range of IP addresses and is used to perform network mapping. The ping sweep utility is used to identify potential targets to zero in on for more in-depth reconnaissance. The **ping** command generates an ICMP Echo Request against a specific host. The host must reply with a variety of ICMP reply messages. Sometimes the ping sweep utility combines the series of ICMP Echo Requests with other ICMP requests such as ICMP Timestamp, ICMP Address Mask, or ICMP Information Request to gather more information.

Port Scans

When a hacker discovers an interesting host, he or she can then carry out a port scan against the host. A port-scan utility checks a range of TCP or UDP ports on a host to determine network services that are available, such as Telnet, FTP, HTTP, or RCP. A port scan can be general, in which a range of ports are probed, such as ports 1 to 1023. A port scan can also be specific, zeroing in on certain ports to discover such things as operating system information, host names, or usernames. Port-scanning utilities can use packet fragmentation and set SYN and FIN bits in TCP headers in combination to attempt to conceal the port scan.

After specific ports are found to be open, an attack against a specific port can be mounted. For example, after SMTP is discovered to be available on a host, the hacker can send SMTP commands to gather more information or even to gain unauthorized access. Or the hacker could try to gain Telnet or FTP access to a host to learn more about the host from header information sent in reply to the access. In another example, after a hacker determines that the Domain Name System (DNS) is available on a host, he could try to access Host Information (HINFO) records from the DNS service. The HINFO record is an optional record type that allows system information to be recorded and retrieved. This information typically includes the operating system and hardware platform that the system is running on. There is very little need to include this record in the database, and it provides attackers with valuable targeting information. Port scanners can explore an open port of insecure user accounts or vulnerability to remote access.

Examples of tools used to carry out ping sweeps and port scans include System Administrators Tool for Analyzing Networks (SATAN); security scanners made by networking vendors; **portscan.c**, nmap, and neptune (Linux port scanners that report the services running on another host); and other public-domain scanners such as Network Toolbox.

Eavesdropping

Eavesdropping (also known as information gathering) is a method of passively observing network traffic with a device or utility. The purpose of eavesdropping is to observe traffic patterns and to capture the traffic for analysis and information theft. *Network snooping* and *packet sniffing* are common synonyms for eavesdropping. The information gathered by eavesdropping can be used to pose other attacks to the network or to steal information. A common way to eavesdrop on communications is to capture TCP/IP packets and decode the contents using a protocol analyzer or a similar utility. Captured packets that are part of a session logon can be replayed to help the intruder gain access.

Network intruders can use eavesdropping to identify usernames and passwords in order to gain unauthorized access to network hosts or to identify information carried in the packet, such as credit card numbers or sensitive personal information.

An example of data susceptible to eavesdropping is SNMP version 1 community strings, which are sent in cleartext. An intruder could eavesdrop on SNMP queries and learn valuable information about network equipment configuration.

Table 1-1 describes some types of devices used for eavesdropping.

Table 1-1   *Devices Used for Eavesdropping*

Category	Type	Description
Packet-capturing utilities	**tcpdump**, **esniff.c** for UNIX **linsniffer.c** for Linux Microsoft's Network Monitor on Windows NT systems	Utility software installed on host. Requires network interface card in promiscuous mode.
Protocol analyzers	Network Associates' Sniffer or NetXray Hewlett Packard's Internet Advisor LAN Protocol Analyzers	Software installed on host or dedicated test equipment.

Information Theft

Network eavesdropping can lead to information theft. The theft can occur as data is transmitted over the internal or external network. The network intruder can also steal data from networked computers by gaining unauthorized access.

A common network intrusion is for the intruder to take files or use resources that do not belong to him. Examples include breaking into or eavesdropping on financial institutions and obtaining credit card numbers. Another example is accessing and copying a computer's password file and then using another computer to crack that file.

Table 1-2 describes methods you can take to counteract reconnaissance attacks against your network.

Table 1-2 *Methods to Counteract Reconnaissance Attacks*

Attack	Prevention
Target discovery	Turn off responses to query-type commands such as **finger** and **nslookup** on routers and network hosts. Use an IDS to detect such attempts.
ping sweep	Turn off responses to **ping**s and use IDS to detect.
Port scan	Use a port scanner to identify open ports. Turn off nonessential services on routers and network hosts and use IDS to detect port scans. Can reduce vulnerability to SYN flooding attacks.
Eavesdropping	Limit physical access to campus network equipment to prevent placement of protocol analyzers on network segments.
	Use Ethernet switches in the internal network to segment a local area network and prevent capturing of network-wide traffic from one workstation.
	Prevent unauthorized network access to hosts to prevent placement of packet-capturing utilities. Use file integrity checkers on hosts to detect any unauthorized placement.
	Use network interface cards that cannot be placed in promiscuous mode in sensitive hosts. Physically check the host for promiscuous mode interfaces.
	Run promiscuous mode-checking software such as **cpm** and **ifstatus** on each host.
	Use data encryption technology to limit the ability to observe network traffic content across insecure networks. Encryption must meet the organization's data security needs without imposing an excessive burden on the system resources or the users.

Unauthorized Access

A network intruder can gain unauthorized remote access to networked computers or networking devices through a variety of means. A common goal of the intruder is to gain root (UNIX) or administrator (Windows NT) access to a networked computer, where the intruder has great power to control the target computer or to access other networked computers. Figure 1-4 illustrates some of the points at which a network intruder might attempt to gain unauthorized access.

Figure 1-4 *Unauthorized Access Attack Points*

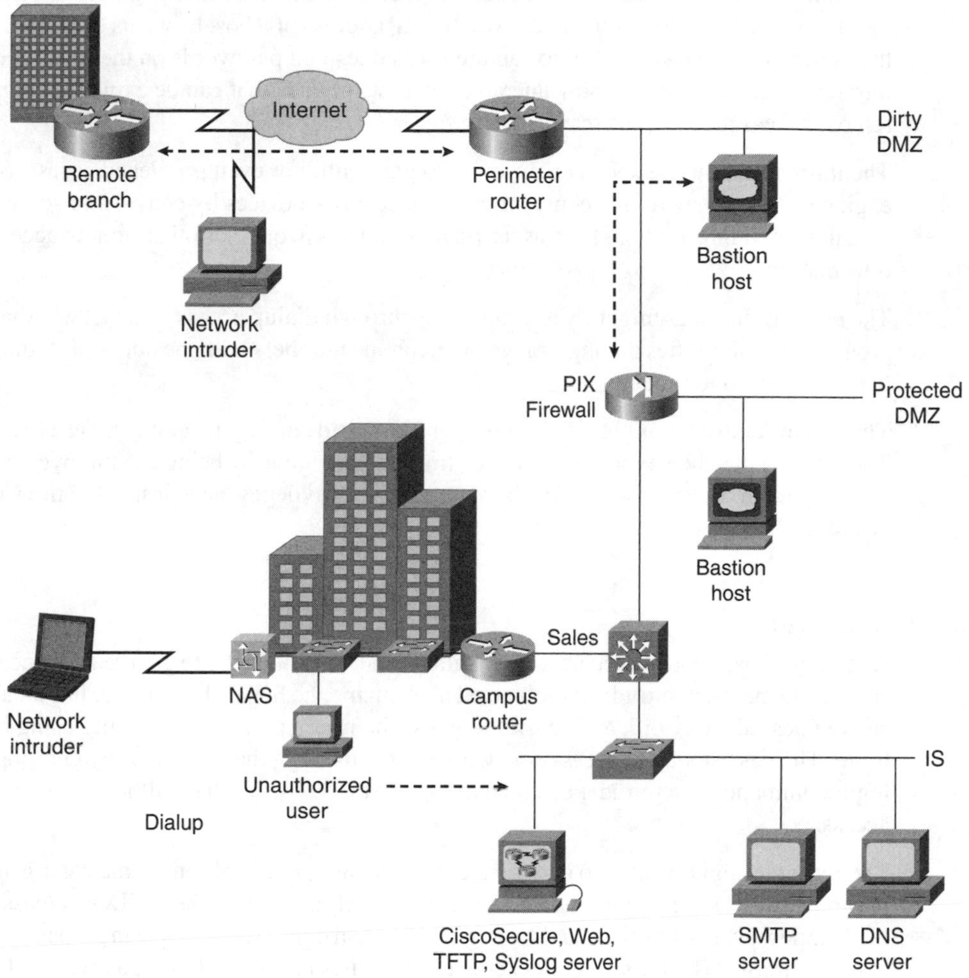

Gaining Initial Access

The network intruder usually needs to gain initial access to a networked host, and then he tries to increasingly penetrate the host and any connected networks. The intruder establishes a connection to a host without owning an account on it and can then try to find holes that allow more privileged access such as root access on UNIX systems.

The network intruder typically tries to gain as much information as possible about the target host through reconnaissance techniques and then uses the information gained to obtain initial access. The intruder might discover the IP address of a host he wants to penetrate and then might use a packet sniffer to capture usernames and passwords on the host. The intruder might attempt to find vulnerable Internet services that can be exploited to gain remote access using a port scanner.

The intruder might use social engineering to gain initial or even privileged access. Social engineering is a way to overcome information security devices by convincing someone to reveal needed information, such as usernames and passwords, or other remote access information.

The network intruder might try to gain access through dialup access using a "war dialer," a program that simplifies dialing a range of telephone numbers with the hopes of finding data ports connected to modems.

The network intruder might also be working from inside an organization, being a local user. The intruder can then exploit the trust relationship he enjoys by being an employee or other trusted person. Because the inside user has account privileges, he is inside the firewall and has fairly free rein inside the network.

Password-Based Attacks

A variety of password-based attacks can allow a network intruder to gain remote access. As soon as the network intruder has obtained a username, he hopes that the user has created an easily guessed password, and he tries to guess the user's password manually using brute force. The easiest way to access a network host is through the front door by entering the login command. The intruder can then try to enter a password that will let him gain initial access.

The intruder might be able to capture a username and password sent in the clear using a packet sniffer. Or he might obtain a host's password file such as the UNIX /etc/passwd or the Windows NT SAM hive, and he might try to learn the passwords using a password-cracking utility. The password cracker is used to guess encrypted user passwords. The utility does not really "crack" passwords. It simply guesses passwords by using computing power to match password hashes. Cracking utilities are readily available for both UNIX and NT. The intruder then uses the username and password to gain trusted access to the networked computer.

You can protect against password-based attacks by creating and enforcing a security policy that requires hard-to-crack or hard-to-guess passwords that include nonalphanumeric and capitalized characters, by not sending unencrypted passwords over an insecure network, and by carefully guarding remote access to a host's password file.

Gaining Trusted or Privileged Access

A *trusted computer* is a computer that you have administrative control over or one that you consciously make a decision to "trust" to allow access to your network.

As soon as the intruder has networked computer access, he exploits this access to gain access to more powerful privileged access or to exploit the trust relationship between networked computers to access other network hosts. The goal of gaining privileged access is to achieve root or administrator-level privileges on a host without owning a privileged account on it. The attacker can spoof a trusted user by using that person's username and password, or he can spoof a trusted host to gain access to other hosts.

The most commonly used applications in UNIX systems that use trusted host features are the **rlogin**, **rsh**, and **rcp** commands.

Intruders might also attempt to exploit operating system vulnerabilities that allow an intruder to gain unauthorized root access.

Gaining Secondary Access

After an intruder gains initial access, he might attempt to establish an inconspicuous access avenue back to the host, clear any evidence of his intrusion, and later return and use the penetrated host as a springboard to access more targets. The intruder might try some of the following means to hide the unauthorized access:

- Clean logs and remove traces of remote access
- Move accounting files to the /tmp directory, the contents of which are eventually deleted
- Install a packet sniffer to observe traffic
- Install a backdoor(s) by establishing usernames and passwords or by installing Trojan horse programs such as rootkit or BackOrifice

Attack Services Allowing Remote Access

Many IP applications and services can make your hosts and network devices very vulnerable to remote access attacks. Many applications were developed to facilitate, not prevent, communications. Some services have little or no authentication methods built in to ensure that the remote user is allowed access. You should disable unused services that can allow remote access on network hosts and equipment.

Table 1-3 summarizes some of the many IP services that are vulnerable to attack. It lists the type of service and briefly describes the service's vulnerability.

Table 1-3 *IP Applications or Services That Are Vulnerable to Remote Access Attacks*

Type	Vulnerability Description
BSD **r** commands	Authentication of remote access using the **r** commands is by source address and is easily spoofed, providing full access to remote hosts running the remote services.
FTP	Anonymous FTP allows intruders to read and possibly write files to a host. Do not use it unless absolutely necessary. Control write access.
finger	**finger** service can be used to discover information about users, a prelude to obtaining usernames.
NFS	Allows access to files on remote systems. Has weak authentication (source IP address) of requests that is easily spoofed.
Telnet	Allows a user to remotely access a command shell in cleartext. Controlled by a simple username/password authentication mechanism that can be easily spoofed.
TFTP	Intruders can easily request file transfers using TFTP because it has no authentication mechanism.
SMTP, POP, MIME, sendmail applications	Intruders can manipulate the sendmail environment to gain root privileges.
HTTP, Web servers	Vulnerabilities include bugs in server software, misconfiguration, and insecure operating systems. Java, JavaScript, and ActiveX applets can act as viruses or Trojan horses.

Program Vulnerabilities That Permit Remote Access

Many programs used for Internet communications and applications were written in the C programming language. The programs use buffers, areas of fixed length in working memory, for variable data. Buffer overflows occur when a network intruder with a knowledge of C programming deliberately tries to exceed the fixed length of program buffers to gain unauthorized access to the target host. Probably the most famous example of exploiting buffer overflow errors in programs is the Morris Worm that spread across the Internet in 1988. Buffer overflows are a common programming error. You can protect yourself from buffer overflows by installing the latest software and software patches, which you can discover by monitoring operating system advisories and vendor Web sites.

Network intruders can attempt to gain remote access by exploiting operating system vulnerabilities. Every operating system has inherent vulnerabilities that a network intruder can exploit to gain unauthorized access. You can protect yourself from operating system vulnerabilities by monitoring Web sites, network advisories, and vendor Web sites to learn which versions of operating systems are the most secure and by installing the latest operating system patches.

Misuse of Systems After Gaining Unauthorized Access

After network intruders gain access to networked computers, they can then use the hosts for unauthorized purposes. They can place unauthorized files or resources on another system for ready access by other intruders. Examples of unauthorized files include the following:

- **GIFs**—Unauthorized use of a computer to create a library of GIF and other electronic picture files. Altering GIFs and Web site content.

- **Hacker tools**—Unauthorized use of a computer to store, test, and distribute software tools that are useful for network intrusion. These tools are then widely available by associated network intruders.

- **Unlicensed versions of software for free distribution**—The term *WareZ* applies to unauthorized distribution of software.

Methods Used to Counteract Remote-Access Attacks

You can take many steps to counteract remote access attacks. Starting at the network perimeter, you can use a Cisco perimeter router to permit Internet access to only destinations you choose. You can use Cisco IOS Software features to limit access to remote services; to control user access; to filter traffic based on source and destination address, protocol, or port; or even to use the Lock and Key feature. Lock and Key couples access control lists with a challenge/response mechanism that challenges users requesting access to a corporate or campus network. At the network perimeter, you can set up a second line of defense with the CiscoSecure PIX Firewall to protect access to your internal network. Cisco routers and the PIX Firewall can interoperate with a CiscoSecure Access Control Server to control access by username, password, and service. At network hosts, you can simply turn off unneeded services; install hardened programs that offer remote-access services; ensure that operating systems and servers are correctly configured with the latest version, updates, and patches installed; and take other prudent steps to limit remote-access attacks. And you can use the CiscoSecure Intrusion Detection System to scan for and detect remote-access attack signatures and to alert you to attacks.

Table 1-4 summarizes methods you can take to counteract remote-access attacks against your network.

Table 1-4 *Methods to Counteract Remote-Access Attacks*

Attack	Prevention
Initial access	Limit points of access to your network, such as controlling setting up unauthorized dialup access by internal users.
	Use a AAA server to manage remote-access privileges, usernames, and passwords such as CiscoSecure Access Control Server.
	Use a more secure remote access protocol such as PPP, CHAP, or MS-CHAP.
	Limit or do not use a shell login that only requires a password.
	Use the Lock and Key security feature in Cisco IOS Software.
Password attacks	Enforce a hard-to-crack/hard-to-guess password policy.
	Run password crackers as an administrator to detect weak passwords.
	Use password aging features to force users to change their passwords often.
Trusted access	Ensure access security to root or administrator levels.
	Monitor and maintain trust relationships.
Secondary access	Scan for viruses and Trojan horses that might have been installed as back doors.
	Scan for open ports originating from network hosts that are not expected that might have been opened by Trojan horses.
	Install and run file integrity checkers to monitor for unauthorized file and directory tampering.
	Use encryption to secure the data on your host's hard drives.
Remote-access services	Disable all unused services and commands that you are not actively using.
	Ensure that trust relationships between hosts are secure.
	Install secure versions of programs that run Internet services such as the latest versions of Web, mail, and FTP servers.
	Change default configuration values, such as allowing Read/Write access to everyone, to values you have determined.

Denial of Service

Denial of Service (DoS) is an attempt to disable or corrupt networks, systems, or services and thereby deny network services to legitimate users. Network intruders sometimes derive pleasure from denying the use of a public service to others, similar to vandalism. Network intruders might use DoS attacks to test a system's vulnerability to attack, as a prelude to further attacks, to cover their tracks after gaining unauthorized access, or simply as retaliation. The IP protocol is vulnerable to DoS attacks, so many attack types are available and relatively easy to carry out, much as it is relatively easy to commit vandalism. DoS attacks can be launched against a perimeter router, bastion host, or firewall, as illustrated in Figure 1-5.

Figure 1-5   *DoS Attack Points*

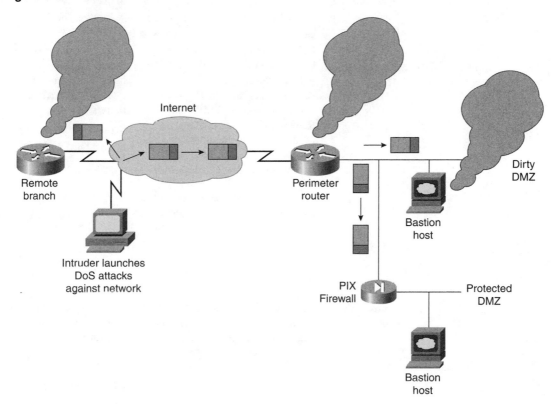

Resource Overload

Resource overload DoS exploits are an attempt to overload a target host or network equipment's resources with the result of causing the target host or network equipment to cease operating or be unavailable to legitimate users. The exploits attempt to overload target resources including bandwidth of an interface, internal memory space (buffers), CPU processing capability, or disk drive space.

Table 1-5 lists the attack type, lists typical tools used to carry out the exploit, describes the exploit, and summarizes some countermeasures you can take to mitigate the attack.

Table 1-5 *Resource Overload DoS Attacks*

Type	Exploit Name	Description	Countermeasures
ping flood	**pingflood.c**, **smurf.c**, **fraggle.c**, **papasmurf.c**	**pingflood.c** sends a large number of ICMP Echo Requests to a host. **smurf** sends a large amount of ICMP Echo Request (ping) traffic to a broadcast address, with each ICMP Echo packet containing the spoofed source address of a victim host. When the spoofed ICMP Echo Request packet arrives at the destination network, all hosts on the network send ICMP Echo Reply packets to the spoofed address. The initial ICMP Echo Request is multiplied by the number of hosts on the network. Generates a storm of replies to the victim host, tying up network bandwidth, using up CPU resources, or even crashing the victim host. **fraggle** is the UDP version of smurf.	Set perimeter routers to reject responses to ICMP Echo Request packets. Turn off directed broadcasts on all internal and external routers. Set perimeter routers to reject incoming ICMP Reply packets.
Half-open syn attack	**neptune.c**, **synk4.c**	Partially initiates numerous TCP sessions against a port so that no new connections can be initiated by legitimate users.	Use TCP Intercept features in Cisco IOS software. Use syn flooding protection in CiscoSecure PIX Firewall. Use IDS to detect.

Table 1-5 *Resource Overload DoS Attacks (Continued)*

Type	Exploit Name	Description	Countermeasures
Packet storms	**chargen**, **Pepsi5.c**, UDP Bomb	**chargen** runs on port 19. It generates a never-ending stream of ASCII characters for testing. The chargen attack consists of sending a flood of UDP packets from a spoofed source IP address to the subnet broadcast address with the destination port set to 19. The target host on the subnet running chargen responds to each broadcast, creating a flood of UDP packets in an infinite loop, which ultimately results in a Denial of Service of the host. Many variations of this attack exist.	Disable the chargen and echo services on all machines. Use syn flooding protection in CiscoSecure PIX Firewall. Install operating system patches.
		Pepsi5.c floods a target with UDP packets containing random source host addresses.	
		UDP Bomb forms UDP packets that have an incorrect length field in the packet header, causing some hosts to suffer a kernel panic.	

Out-of-Band Data DoS Attacks

Out-of-band data DoS attacks are context-based in that they manipulate the IP header (TCP or UDP) to try to exceed the normal operation of IP. The result is that the target host or network equipment ceases operating.

Table 1-6 describes some out-of-band data DoS attacks, lists typical tools used to carry out the exploit, describes the exploit, and summarizes some countermeasures you can take to mitigate the attack.

Table 1-6   *Out-of-Band Data DoS Attacks*

Type	Exploit Name	Description	Countermeasure(s)
Oversized packets	**ping** of death (**simping.c**)	Modifies the IP portion of header, indicating that there is more data in the packet than there actually is, or sends a data payload exceeding the maximum allowed packet size (larger than 65,535 bytes), causing the receiving system to crash.	Filter large or fragmented ICMP traffic from your network. Cisco Systems' IDS will detect these attacks.
Overlapped packets	**winnuke.c**	Sends out-of-band data to an established connection on a Windows 95 or Windows NT host (typically to NetBIOS, port 137), causing the host to reboot or cease operating.	Turn off NetBIOS if it isn't needed. Install operating system patches (service packs) on hosts according to CERT advisory lists.
Fragmentation	**teardrop.c**	Takes advantage of some implementations of the TCP/IP IP fragmentation reassembly code that do not properly handle overlapping IP fragments, causing a memory buffer overrun.	Discard fragmented IP packets at the perimeter router for packets coming from the outside. Install operating system patches on hosts according to CERT advisory lists.
IP source address spoofing	**land.c**	Causes a computer to create a TCP connection to itself, get caught in a loop, and have to be rebooted.	Filter IP-spoofed packets at the perimeter or host. Install operating system patches on hosts according to CERT advisory lists.
Packet headers malformed	UDP Bomb	Forms UDP packets that have an incorrect length field in the packet header, causing some hosts to suffer a kernel panic.	Install operating system patches on hosts according to CERT advisory lists.

Other DoS Attacks

Unfortunately, many other DoS attacks are used to exploit IP networks. DoS attacks can also exploit vulnerabilities in specific services or hardware not necessarily related to TCP/IP. Ultimately they prevent authorized people from using a service by using up system resources. Here is a sampling of some other DoS threats:

- **Distributed Denial of Service (DDoS)**—Uses multiple coordinated systems to attack a Web site or host. See *Strategies to Protect Against Distributed Denial of Service (DDoS) Attacks* at www.cisco.com/warp/public/707/newsflash.html for more information.

- **E-mail bombs**—Many free programs exist that send bulk e-mails to individuals, lists, or domains, monopolizing e-mail services.

- **CPU hogging**—Programs such as Trojan horses or viruses that tie up CPU cycles, memory, or other resources, denying computer resources to legitimate users.

- **Malicious applets**—Java, JavaScript, or ActiveX programs that can act as Trojan horses or viruses to cause destruction or tie up computer resources.

- **Misrouting traffic**—Disabling traffic by misconfiguring routers to reroute traffic away from the intended network or host.

- **Accidental DoS**—Legitimate users or system administrators can cause DoS attacks due to misconfiguration or misuse.

- **Buffer overflows**—Microsoft's Internet Information Server (IIS) version 4.0 is susceptible to buffer overflows that will crash the server. Known susceptibilities can be fixed by installing patches or service packs.

- **CGI exploits**—Web browsers will divulge critical information when a malicious user appends certain characters to the end of the URL that refer to a server-side include file. A remote user can recover the source code for the file, disclosing proprietary information, copyrighted source code, and even usernames and passwords used to log into databases.

- **Server DoS**—Microsoft's NT Server version 4.0 (service pack 3 or 4) will reboot or freeze, depending on the amount of memory the server has, when a character string of sufficient length appears at a certain port during a Telnet session, followed by an execution command.

Methods Used to Counteract Denial of Service Attacks

The CiscoSecure Integrated Software running in Cisco routers and the PIX Firewall contains powerful security technology to provide firewall capabilities that can prevent DoS attacks or lessen their effect, including the following:

- Context-Based Access Control (CBAC) can be used for DoS detection and prevention, such as defending against SYN attacks.

- Java blocking in the PIX Firewall can filter out Java applets.
- The TCP Intercept feature in Cisco IOS Software detects and controls SYN attacks.
- Ensure that the correct version of Cisco IOS Software is installed to prevent known vulnerabilities.

You can also use the following methods to lessen the impact of DoS attacks:

- Use audit trails to detail transactions, recording time stamp, source host, destination host, ports, duration, and total number of bytes transmitted.
- Use a real-time alerts log to generate alerts in case of Denial of Service attacks or other preconfigured conditions.

Data Manipulation

A network intruder can capture, manipulate, and replay data sent over a communication channel by using data manipulation. *Data manipulation* is also known as *impersonation*. It can take the form of IP address spoofing, session replay and hijacking, rerouting, and repudiation. Data manipulation can also include graffiti—vandalizing a Web site by accessing the Web server and altering Web pages. Data manipulation is made possible by vulnerabilities in the IP protocol and associated services and applications. Data manipulation attacks are also known as man-in-the-middle attacks because the attack usually involves a person in the middle exploiting IP session susceptibilities between two TCP/IP hosts.

Figure 1-6 illustrates where in the network data manipulation attacks can occur.

Figure 1-6   *A Data Manipulation Attack Point*

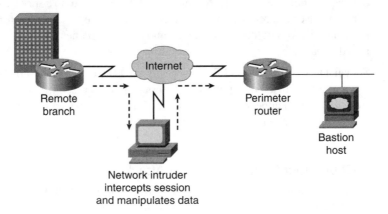

IP Spoofing

A network intruder can use IP spoofing to impersonate the identity of a host for applications or services that use source or destination addresses for authentication. An IP spoofing attack occurs when a network intruder outside your network pretends to be a trusted computer inside or outside your network. The spoof uses an IP address that is within the range of IP addresses for your network or uses an authorized external IP address that you trust and to which you want to provide access to specified resources on your network.

Spoofing usually includes manipulating TCP/IP packets to falsify IP addresses, thereby appearing to be another host. For example, the intruder could use IP address spoofing to assume the identity of a valid or trusted host and to gain the host's access privileges by falsifying the source address of a trusted host. Spoofing is also known as a masquerade attack.

An attacker can specify an arbitrary source address for a packet in an attempt to bypass address-based authentication mechanisms. This is especially effective if the arbitrary source address is that of a host behind a perimeter router or firewall.

Normally, an IP spoofing attack is limited to the injection of data or commands into an existing stream of data passed between a client and server application or a peer-to-peer network connection.

Attackers using IP spoofing might be able to bypass authentication mechanisms and, if they are improperly implemented, might subvert filters on packet-filtering routers.

Countermeasures against IP spoofing include filtering packets at the perimeter router that come from outside but claim to be from inside. The CiscoSecure IDS detects these attacks.

Session Replay and Hijacking

Session replay is an attack in which a network intruder intercepts and captures a sequence of packets or application commands, manipulates the captured data (such as to alter the dollar amount of a transaction), and then replays the data to cause an unauthorized action. Session replay exploits weaknesses in authentication of data traffic.

Session hijacking is an attack in which a network intruder takes over an IP session and inserts falsified IP data packets after session establishment. Session hijacking methods include IP spoofing, source and/or destination address manipulation over TCP/IP, and sequence number prediction and alteration. The network intruder uses a protocol analyzer or utility program to observe, predict, and then alter and retransmit TCP/IP packet sequence numbers.

An example of a documented session hijacking attack is the use of a tool that redirects Xterminal output to an intruder's terminal instead of the intended terminal.

One exploit that is a session replay attack involves the use of JavaScript to allow a network intruder to exploit a hole in Hotmail and other Web-based e-mail systems. The hole lets the malicious hacker create a piece of incriminating e-mail that can be falsely traced to another person's computer. The user is exposed to this attack by being lured to a seemingly innocent Web page into which the hacker has inserted the malicious JavaScript code.

Session replay and hijacking attacks can only be carried out by skilled programmers, so there have been few documented attacks. One session hijacking tool is the hunt-1.0 program that runs on Linux systems.

Countermeasures for session replay and hijacking include the following methods and technologies:

- Adjust the Web browser's security setting to prevent downloads of applets or make the browser notify you for permission to execute mobile code when it is encountered.
- Block corporate access to public e-mail sites to limit the risk of infection or disclosure of confidential data.
- Use access control features in the perimeter.
- Use authentication such as CiscoSecure TACACS+ or RADIUS, or SSL.
- Use encryption technologies to protect the integrity and privacy of data.
- Use digital signatures offered by certification authorities for nonrepudiation.

Rerouting

Network intruders can use rerouting by gaining unauthorized access to routers and altering the routing configuration or by spoofing the identity of routers or hosts along a network path. The consequence of rerouting is that it can allow a remote host to pose as a local host on your network. Services that rely on IP addresses as authentication might be compromised as a result.

The countermeasures for rerouting attacks are to limit access to routers to prevent reconfiguration of routes, to filter source-routed packets at the router, to use route authentication features in Cisco IOS Software, and to disable source routing on all hosts. The CiscoSecure IDS systems detect these attacks.

Repudiation

One or more users involved in a communication, such as a secure financial transaction, can deny participation, jeopardizing electronic transactions and contractual agreements. This prevents a third party from being able to prove that a communication between two other parties ever took place. This is a desirable quality if you do not want your communications to be traceable. Nonrepudiation is the opposite quality—a third party can prove that a communication between two other parties took place. Nonrepudiation is desirable if you want to be able to trace your communications and prove that they occurred.

The Security Opportunity

How do companies effectively protect their networks from security attacks? Security solutions that offer all the protection you need for your network are readily available from Cisco and other vendors.

A good security solution helps you reduce the exposure of a network to security threats and thereby saves the company money. It should also reduce the total cost of implementation and operation of network security measures.

A good security solution also enables new networked applications and services that many would consider unwise and potentially dangerous, such as business-to-business electronic commerce or extranet applications to link you more closely with your suppliers and partners.

Security is a fundamental element of networking. A good security solution does the following:

- Reduces the costs of implementation and operation of network security measures
- Enables new networked applications and services
- Makes the Internet a global, low-cost access medium

Summary

This chapter established the need for network security by focusing on the following key points:

- The great increase in network security threats makes it complicated and difficult to implement integrated network security uniformly.
- There are three primary reasons for security issues: technology, configuration, and policy weaknesses.
- Network intruders have a variety of motivations and available tools for attacking networks.
- A large number of tools are available to the network intruder, including protocol analyzers, network scanners, and tools developed by network intruders to attack networks.
- Reconnaissance is a technique for learning more about a network and its equipment with the purpose of launching further attacks.

- Unauthorized access consists of a network intruder attempting to gain access to network resources without permission. This includes initial access, privileged access, and secondary access.

- Denial of Service is similar to vandalism in that the goal of the network intruder is to deny network services or access to legitimate users.

- Data manipulation is an attempt to intercept and alter data communications between TCP/IP hosts.

- Each form of network intrusion has specific countermeasures that you can implement to prevent or lessen the attack.

- The system administrator or network engineer can implement an effective security solution that can reduce security implementation costs, enable new networked applications and services, and give your organization a competitive advantage.

Review Questions

Answer the following review questions to test your knowledge of evaluating network security threats:

1 What are two characteristics of the network security problem facing businesses today?

2 List five driving factors in the growth of network security.

3 What are the three primary reasons for network security issues?

4 What are some security policy weaknesses?

5 Who typically carries out internal attacks?

6 How is a packet sniffer used to carry out reconnaissance attacks?

7 List the four stages of unauthorized access attacks.

8 Why are DoS attacks so prevalent?

9 What is the most common data manipulation attack?

10 How can an organization benefit from having network engineers and system administrators with network security expertise?

References

The topics considered in this chapter are complex and should be studied further to more fully understand them and put them to use. Use the following references to learn more about the topics in this chapter.

Network Security and Business

T. Bernstein, A. Bismani, E. Schultz, and C. Siegel, *Internet Security for Business,* Wiley Computer Publishing, 1996. Describes how to plan for and implement network security.

D. Chapman, S. Cooper, and E. Zwicky, *Building Internet Firewalls,* Second Edition, O'Reilly and Associates Publishing, 2000. Describes how to build a firewall and explains network security vulnerabilities.

Hacking and Hacker Tools

Anonymous, *Maximum Security: A Hacker's Guide to Protecting Your Internet Site and Network,* Second Edition, Sams.net Publishing, 1998. Describes hacking from the hacker's perspective.

AntiOnline, a comprehensive security site with hacking tools, at www.antionline.com.

S. McClure, J. Scambray, et al., *Hacking Exposed: Network Security Secrets and Solutions,* McGraw-Hill, 1999. Describes hacking methods and mitigation.

Root Shell, a site that summarizes vulnerabilities and provides hacker tools, at www.rootshell.com.

T. Shimomura and J. Markoff, *Takedown: The Pursuit and Capture of Kevin Mitnick, America's Most Wanted Computer Outlaw—By the Man Who Did It,* Hyperion Books, 1996. Describes a real-life hacking drama.

The Web Site for 2600—The Hacker Quarterly, summarized hacks, vulnerabilities, and security issues, at www.2600.com.

L0pht, "The top US hackers hang out at the L0pht. But why can't they spell?" *spews.net* magazine, December 1995, at www.l0pht.com.

Security Web Sites

Computer Emergency Response Team (CERT) Coordination Center, a focal point for incident response, vulnerability analysis, and training, at www.cert.org.

Microsoft Security, the official Microsoft security home page, at www.microsoft.com/security/default.asp.

NT Bugtraq, a mailing list for Windows NT vulnerabilities and countermeasures, at www.ntbugtraq.com.

SANS (System Administration, Networking, and Security) Institute, a cooperative research and education organization with a mailing list, at www.sans.org.

SecurityFocus.com, a Web site designed to facilitate discussion on security-related topics, to create security awareness, and to provide the Internet's largest and most comprehensive database of security knowledge and resources to the public, at www.securityfocus.com. It also maintains the popular Bugtraq mailing list.

U.S. Department of Energy's Computer Incident Advisory Capability (CIAC), provides computer security services free of charge to employees and contractors of the Department of Energy, at ciac.llnl.gov.

Security Surveys and Reports

1996 Information Systems Security Survey, a summary of a security survey by WarRoom Research LLC, at www.warroomresearch.com/researchcollabor/infosecuritysurvey.htm.

1998 Annual Global Information Security Survey, Ernst & Young and Computerworld, at www.ey.com/aabs/isaas.

Accounts of Network Intruders

B. Cheswick, *An Evening with Berferd in Which a Cracker Is Lured, Endured, and Studied.* Bill Cheswick of AT&T chronicles the attacks of a cracker. This can be found at the Purdue University COAST Web site at www.cs.purdue.edu/coast/archive/data/categ40.html.

D. Farmer and W. Venema, *Improving the Security of Your Site by Breaking Into It.* This paper looks through the eyes of a potential intruder, illustrating that even seemingly harmless network services can become valuable tools in the search for a system's weak points. You can find a copy at the Advanced Laboratory Workstation System Web site at www.alw.nih.gov/Security/Docs/admin-guide-to-cracking.101.html.

Upon completing this chapter, you will be able to do the following:

- Identify the purpose of a network security policy
- Identify the components of a network security policy
- Identify how to implement a network security policy
- Evaluate the XYZ Company network security policy

Evaluating a Network Security Policy

This chapter covers the process of evaluating a network security policy in the corporate enterprise. The chapter considers the economics of protecting the network, pointing out that a balance must be struck between the level of security required and the ease of use for the user to obtain optimal network security. This chapter outlines the key components of a network security policy.

This chapter describes a network security study conducted by Cisco, where companies were surveyed about network security planning and deployment. The study grouped the surveyed companies as having either an open, a restrictive, or a closed security policy.

This chapter refers to Appendix B, "An Example of an XYZ Company Network Security Policy," and includes review questions designed to help you analyze the policy example. This chapter concludes by emphasizing the importance of testing a company's network security implementation with a security audit.

The Importance of Protecting the Network

When you analyze a network security policy with the intent of implementing its directives, you need to understand the costs of implementing and managing network security and then weigh these costs against the potential benefits of network security. You must weigh the cost in ease of use and in resources, both human and capital, to implement the security measures against the costs and likelihood of network security breaches, as illustrated in Figure 2-1. You should ensure a good return on the investment in network security compared with the potential economic loss due to possible security breaches.

Figure 2-1 *Weighing the Costs of Security Exposures Against the Cost of Security Implementation*

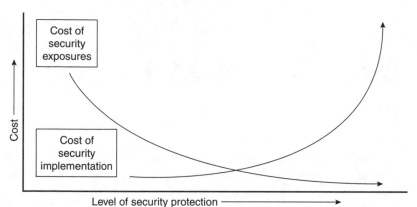

Here are some tips that might prove useful in evaluating the costs and benefits of a network security policy:

- Determine the one-time and life-cycle cost of each security control. The life cycle for most computer-related hardware is three to five years.
- Identify the reduction in exposure to loss if security controls are implemented.
- Identify the maximum possible loss if security controls are not implemented.
- Determine the lifetime savings that the security controls will enable.
- Determine the lifetime benefit of the security controls.
- Decide which security controls are most beneficial and cost effective.

The Security Posture Assessment Process

Cisco has developed a security wheel, shown in Figure 2-2, to illustrate the process of implementing network security. The process depicted in the security wheel is known as security posture assessment (SPA). It is an iterative, continual effort by the company to protect its most vital assets in the most cost-effective manner possible while reducing risk to an acceptable level.

Figure 2-2   *The Security Wheel, Which Illustrates the Process an Enterprise Should Follow to Implement Network Security*

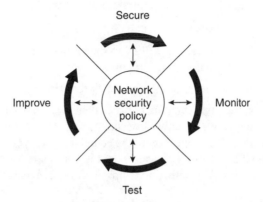

Due to the complex, iterative nature of the task of securing an enterprise, the process must never stop if the enterprise is to be protected from the latest threats. The wheel illustrates the following four phases:

- **Secure**—Protect the corporate data to the level required. In this stage, organizations typically deploy security technologies, such as firewalls and authentication systems, that increase the network's security level.

- **Monitor**—Observe the activity at critical network access points—internal as well as external. You should then continuously monitor your networks for intrusions and misuse and provide automatic, real-time response mechanisms to eliminate unauthorized activity.

- **Test**—Ensure that security measures are sufficient to resist the developing sophistication and frequency of hacker attacks. In addition, because networks are so dynamic and change frequently, you need to test your security posture and develop comprehensive assessments of the security vulnerabilities.

- **Improve**—Add or update security measures as needed. You will need to centrally manage all security products and policies to achieve maximum operational efficiency and quickly implement improvements.

The SPA process directs the development of the security measures for the entire enterprise. It defines the security-related roles and responsibilities for the IT staff and corporate management. And it ranks the corporate data and defines allowable risk for each ranking.

The center of the security wheel contains the most important element—the network security policy. The network security policy contains the instructions that communicate the desired level of security for an enterprise, and it defines the following criteria:

- The important assets that must be protected
- How much the company is willing to spend (in terms of dollars, personnel, and time) to protect what it has deemed important
- The level of risk the enterprise is willing to tolerate

A key to successfully implementing network security is to balance ease of use with the level of security presented by the network security measures, as illustrated in Figure 2-3. If the security costs are out of proportion to the actual dangers, you have done the company a disservice. And if the security measures are too restrictive for users, they might find ways to work around them, thus defeating the purpose of the measures.

Figure 2-3 *Balancing Transparent User Access with Maximum Security*

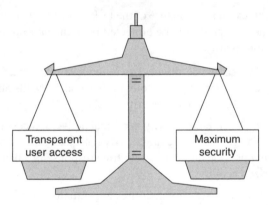

The following sections examine each step of the SPA process in more detail.

Evaluating the Network Security Policy

The most important part of controlling network security is to accurately implement the company's network security policy. You must be able to analyze the policy and then figure out how to bring it to life in the actual network. But what is a network security policy? Why should you create one? What should a network security policy contain?

According to the Site Security Handbook (RFC 2196), "A security policy is a formal statement of the rules by which people who are given access to an organization's technology and information assets must abide." It further states that "a security policy is essentially a document summarizing how the corporation will use and protect its computing and network resources."

Reasons to Create a Network Security Policy

Security policies provide many benefits and are worth the time and effort needed to develop them. The network security policy is the blueprint or architecture specification for network security, so it must be accurate and complete. Here are some reasons to develop a security policy:

- Provides a process to audit existing network security
- Provides a general security framework for implementing network security
- Defines which behavior is and is not allowed
- Often helps determine which tools and procedures are needed for the organization
- Helps communicate consensus among a group of key decision-makers and defines responsibilities of users and administrators
- Defines a process for handling network security incidents
- Enables global security implementation and enforcement: computer security is now an enterprise-wide issue and computing sites are expected to conform to the network security policy
- Creates a basis for legal action if necessary

What the Network Security Policy Should Contain

Each enterprise needs to develop a network security policy that is customized for its applications and network environment. Here are some suggested key policy components:

- **Statement of authority and scope**—This section specifies who sponsors the security policy and what areas the policy covers.
- **Acceptable use policy**—This section specifies what the company will and will not allow regarding its information infrastructure.
- **Identification and authentication policy**—This section specifies what technologies, equipment, or combination of the two the company will use to ensure that only authorized individuals have access to its data.
- **Internet access policy**—This section specifies what the company considers to be ethical and proper use of its Internet access capabilities.
- **Campus access policy**—This section specifies how on-campus users will use the company's data infrastructure.
- **Remote access policy**—This section specifies how remote users will access the company's data infrastructure.
- **Incident-handling procedure**—This section specifies how the company will create an Incident Response team and the procedures it will use during and after an incident occurs.

XYZ Company Network Security Policy

Appendix B describes an example of a network security policy for the XYZ Company. The main points of a comprehensive security policy are illustrated in the following text, which is a portion of the first section of the XYZ Company security policy (refer to Appendix B for the full text of the sample policy):

Statement of Authority and Scope

As an authorized user of the XYZ internal network, each employee has access to information with a wide range of sensitivity levels. Familiarity with and observance of XYZ's Network Security Policy ("the policy") is important so that every employee can contribute to ensuring network security and information integrity. XYZ Company follows the "need to know" principle by deliberately avoiding disclosure of information that the employee does not need to know for job performance.

The Intended Audience

The policy was written for the following intended audience:

- Network users expected to comply with the security policy
- System support personnel who implement and support the policy
- Managers who are concerned about protection of data and the associated cost of the policy
- Company executives who want to ensure network integrity balanced with ease of use and cost of implementation

---

How a Network Security Policy Is Used

A company should use a security policy to define what it considers vital, to state to what extent it is willing to go to protect that which it considers vital, and to assign responsibility for implementing the directives that the policy contains. Here are some primary ways to use a network security policy:

- **Identifying assets and threats**—A company's management can use a network security policy to locate and identify its internetworking assets and to assess threats against the corporate data.

- **Determining policy implementation**—A company's management can use a network security policy to describe how the MIS staff will implement the requirements contained in it.

- **Educating users**—A company's management can use a network security policy to inform users of their responsibilities to protect the company's information assets.

Securing the Network

The next step in using a network security policy is to select, install, and configure network security technologies. For example, a network typically has an Internet connection that needs a perimeter security system to protect this vulnerable point, a dialup network that needs access controls, and a core or backbone network that needs access and perimeter security technologies. The rest of this book is devoted to analyzing the sample network security policy for the XYZ Company and implementing security controls to meet the policy requirements.

Monitoring Network Security

A network security policy should specify technologies and procedures used to monitor the secure network. Monitoring is essential to detecting and reacting to ongoing security threats. Monitoring activities can help detect a system compromise and assist in the analysis of a system attack. Monitoring ensures compliance with the security policy. Monitoring network security may include analysis of system log messages output from a perimeter router, a firewall, or an access control system.

Monitoring can be accomplished with intrusion detection systems (IDSs). IDSs help automate the detection of network intrusions. The CiscoSecure IDS is a real-time IDS that is transparent to legitimate traffic and network usage. The CiscoSecure IDS consists of two components: sensors and directors. CiscoSecure IDS sensors, which are high-speed network appliances, analyze the content and context of individual packets to determine if traffic is considered a threat or intrusion. If a network's data stream exhibits suspicious activity, CiscoSecure IDS sensors can detect the policy violation in real time, forward alarms to a CiscoSecure IDS director management console, and shun the offender from the network, preventing further attack. The CiscoSecure IDS director is a high-performance, software-based management system that centrally monitors the activity of multiple CiscoSecure IDS sensors located on local or remote network segments.

Testing Network Security with a Security Audit

A network security policy should specify procedures used to audit, test, and maintain the secure network. Auditing and testing activities can help determine the overall health of networking components and computer systems. They can be used to test compliance with security policies and regulations.

Using auditing and testing activities is the best way to verify the effectiveness of a security infrastructure. You should perform security auditing frequently and at regular intervals, including the following:

- Audit each new system as it is installed on the network.
- Ensure that changes to network device configurations comply with the policy.
- Regularly check the system, perhaps using an automated process.
- Randomly audit the system for compliance.
- Perform nightly audit checks of special files (such as /etc/passwd) and log files.
- Do account activity audit checks.

Sample security system checklists are readily available on the Internet, such as in the "NIST Computer Security Handbook," which can be found at the URL specified in the "References" section at the end of this chapter. You should develop a site-specific checklist as well. You can automate the audit process via scripts or by using audit programs, some of which are described in the following section.

Regular System Audit Checks

Regular system audits provide a general overview of the system's security state. Most intruder break-ins can be simulated by these checks. Your intrusion prevention measures can be tested with audit tools. Illicit employee activity might also be detected. Many tools can be used for these audit checks. Some tools used for network intrusion can also be used to audit your systems. Here are a few common tools you can use to audit and test your network:

- **Cisco Secure Scanner**—A tool that automates the process of auditing a network's security posture through comprehensive network mapping and vulnerability scanning. The CiscoSecure Scanner has the following features:
  - A network mapping compiles an electronic inventory of the network.
  - A security vulnerability assessment identifies potential security holes.
  - Risk management is made easy by ready access to vulnerability data.
  - The standalone system runs on Windows NT or Solaris operating systems.

- **Computer Oracle and Password System (COPS)**—A UNIX security inspection tool that verifies that UNIX systems are configured to be less vulnerable to remote attacks.
- **Tiger**—A suite of UNIX scripts developed by Texas A&M University to check UNIX systems for vulnerabilities. It includes packet filtering, a configuration checking program, and an audit/log program. Tiger Analytical Research Assistant (TARA) is an upgrade to the Tiger program that runs on UNIX and Linux systems.
- **Tripwire**—A file system integrity monitor for UNIX alerts if key files are changed. ViperDB, Triplight, Advanced Intrusion Detection Environment (AIDE), and Sentinel are derivatives of Tripwire.
- **Simple WATCHdog (Swatch)**—A log analyzer and reducer for UNIX systems that looks through event logs for specific events.

You can find shareware versions of each of these tools at the Rootshell Web site, www.rootshell.com.

Random System Audit Checks

It is a good idea to perform random system audit checks with little or no advance notice. They can be used as a method to discover possible malicious activity of insiders. They can also be used as a method to test for the presence of a specific class of problems (such as NFS vulnerabilities). You can use them to validate conformance to specific security standards and policies. The results of random audits should be presented to management.

Improving Your Security Posture

Security monitoring and audit checks might reveal previously unknown weaknesses. Based on the results of the security audits, you must improve your company's security posture by applying the latest patches, maintenance releases, and new versions of existing software and technologies while evaluating new ones in the lab environment.

Just as eternal vigilance is the price of freedom, continual monitoring, maintenance, and modification of the enterprise are the price of network security. Because the tools and techniques attackers use change constantly, so must the security posture of the enterprise change to meet the new threats.

The risk management strategy must change as the business grows and enters new markets and leaves markets in which it no longer chooses to participate. As the risk profile changes, the security posture must change with it.

The idea that security is a "set it and forget it" effort is false. Maintaining the proper levels of security for each area of the company's business is a constant effort. Failure to expend the necessary effort at the correct time exposes the enterprise to unnecessary risk.

You can improve the security of your systems by observing the following suggestions:

- Stay current with new network attacks and vulnerabilities as they are discovered by monitoring security newsgroups and Web sites. Attend security industry events and read industry publications.

- Join security-related mailing lists such as www.sans.org, the Bugtraq list at www.securityfocus.com, and CERT advisories at www.cert.org. Each provides regular reporting of security events and patches.

- Stay current on network security technology and new techniques to secure existing equipment and systems.

- Monitor vendor Web sites for announcements about patches, maintenance releases, and new versions. Test and install security patches and bug fixes.

- Update company security policies and procedures to keep up with this dynamic field.

- Provide ongoing security-awareness training; maintain a strong information flow to other groups.

- Perform regular and frequent analysis of attack profiles. For example, the CiscoSecure IDS system contains a network security database and an attack signature list that is updated regularly and must be applied to the IDS system. The database gives you instant access to specific information about attacks and countermeasures.

- Implement new security technologies to maintain an end-to-end security posture. Evaluate product changes in the lab environment before installing them in the enterprise. Reconfigure the network as needed based on the analysis of attack profiles.

- Provide investigation, coordination, reporting, and follow-up of security incidents.

Network Security Case Studies

The following three case studies will help you understand different levels of network security policy. Part of the process of defining your security policy requires you to decide how open, restrictive, or closed you need to make your enterprise. As you move the pointer on the security dial (as shown in Figure 2-4) to make the enterprise more secure, the security policy becomes more restrictive. To make your enterprise more secure, you define a more restrictive security policy. More restrictive policies are generally more costly to implement and support.

After you have defined your security policy, you can then look for enterprise network security solutions and application security solutions that deliver the overall level of security required. You most likely will need a combination of both enterprise network and application security in order to achieve a complete solution to your required security policy.

Figure 2-4 *Classifying Network Security Policies as Either Open, Restrictive, or Closed*

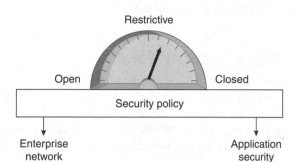

Application security is often associated with electronic commerce because much of the focus is on how to make purchasing merchandise possible on the Web without an intruder accessing your customer's credit card number.

We will focus mainly on the enterprise network part of the security solution throughout this book. In this section, we consider three case studies of network security policies with differing overall levels of network security policy.

The information used for the case studies was gathered by an independent market research company appointed by Cisco. Cisco commissioned The Registry to quantify the cost of ownership associated with current network security implementations at selected medium-size and large companies. The survey used a broad cross-section of companies in a variety of markets from financial services to public utilities to multinational consumer goods manufacturers. Some companies had Cisco networks installed.

The surveyed companies supported a total of about 70,000 managed network desktops, resulting in an adequate statistical base for determining the average cost per desktop associated with their security implementations.

The interesting finding of the study was that the cost range of security implementations was quite large—from $53 to $368 per desktop. The average amount spent on security per networked desktop per year was about $250. Cisco found that, on average, security represents 17 percent of the total cost to support each desktop.

The per-desktop cost of security consisted of the following:

- Apportioned cost of hardware and software capital equipment
- Support staff costs (60 percent of the total security costs)
- Recurring costs associated with providing the level of network security in place

Companies tended to fall into one of three security groups: open security, restrictive security, or closed security. Also, there were similarities within each group in the technologies used to implement their chosen security policy. The case study summaries generalize the companies' security solutions to protect their identity, but the information is representative of their actual implementation.

Case Study 1: An Open Security Policy

In the first case study, companies were apt to err on the side of openness when it came to their security implementations. They preferred to give users more flexibility and freedom in connectivity, performance, and ease of use. These companies are classified as having an open security policy. Figure 2-5 illustrates the balance between transparency of user access and maximum security for an open security policy.

Figure 2-5   *Case Study 1's Open Security Policy*

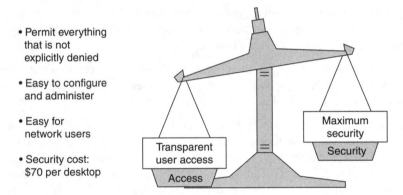

- Permit everything that is not explicitly denied

- Easy to configure and administer

- Easy for network users

- Security cost: $70 per desktop

The companies in this case study tended to permit all network connections that were not explicitly denied. This open permission policy required that the companies create specific barriers on only a select group of connections, and they could manage these "sensitive connections" using a minimum of network personnel and primarily the capabilities of their existing network equipment. As a result, the companies' security implementations were the easiest to configure and administer, and their users did not have onerous security measures to contend with, making the use of the network more transparent.

In this first case study, the companies tended to average less than $70 per desktop in security-related costs (which is at the low end of the $53 to $368 range for all companies surveyed). Generally, the companies in this group tended to be on the low end in terms of size as well.

One interesting finding was that companies in this case study had not experienced a significant financial loss resulting from a network security breach and thus had less motivation to invest more of their already-stretched IT budget in security technologies.

Company managers tended to believe they were not the "target" of possible hacker attacks, most likely because they did not perceive their proprietary information as valuable to corporate outsiders. But after a company suffered a network break-in that resulted in financial loss, it started to install additional security safeguards, which moved it into a higher security group.

Security Technologies Deployed for Minimum Enterprise Security

All companies in Case Study 1 had the kind of network connections shown in Figure 2-6. Branch offices were connected to the enterprise over ISDN lines or in a few groups over Frame Relay. Routers were used at each end of these links. The router at the headquarters end of these links is called the WAN router in this diagram.

Figure 2-6   *The Network Environment for Case Study 1—Minimum Enterprise Security*

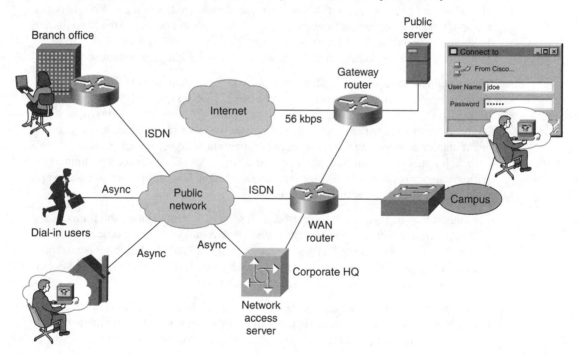

Dial-in users, whether traveling employees or from small remote offices or home, used the public telephone network to connect to the enterprise over dialup async lines. A network access server was used to aggregate these lines back at a central headquarters location.

An Internet connection existed for both outbound traffic from the enterprise and inbound traffic to the company's public server. All Internet traffic was concentrated in a single access point through a single gateway router. Remote users needed to connect to the enterprise to gain access to this Internet connection.

Remember, the companies in this group were at the low end of the security dial and had invested the least amount in their security solutions. To identify their users, these companies relied on usernames and passwords exclusively. In the campus, the passwords were administered in the directory server. Only one of the companies in this group had implemented Dynamic Host Configuration Protocol (DHCP) for dynamically assigning IP addresses.

To identify remote dial-in users, all companies relied on password entry at network login that occurred after the network access server established the dialup link. In a few groups, the user entered a separate password to establish the dialup link. This password was passed to the network access server using Password Authentication Protocol (PAP) and authenticated in the network access server. Remote users at branch office locations were also identified by password authentication when they logged in to the campus network. Remote routers used dial-on-demand routing over ISDN to connect to the headquarters WAN router. Point-to-Point Protocol (PPP) PAP was used with a fixed password programmed into the routers to authenticate the routers during link establishment.

To maintain network integrity, access lists were programmed into the WAN and Internet gateway routers to restrict access to the enterprise based on remote IP addresses. These access lists were attached to the input interface on the WAN router and the output interface on the gateway router. They were fairly simplistic and were maintained by the same technicians who managed the router network. Few standalone firewalls were used in these companies, and those that were used created security boundaries around particularly critical campus networks such as the finance department. No encryption was used to protect data confidentiality in any part of their network.

For authentication, passwords were used exclusively for both campus and remote users. PPP PAP was the extent of the authentication used on links to branch offices, and a few companies were introducing PAP on the remote clients. PAP is relatively easy to spoof because the password is sent in cleartext on these links. PAP is covered in more depth in Chapter 4, "Examining Cisco AAA Security Technology."

For access control, these companies relied almost exclusively on access lists programmed into existing routers. These access lists restricted inbound Internet access to the enterprise. These companies had predominantly unrestricted outbound Internet access.

Because these companies had experienced no significant financial loss due to security breach, there was almost no investment in standalone firewalls or encryption.

To summarize, companies in Case Study 1 implemented minimum security solutions as follows:

Open Security Policy Authentication and Access Control

Authentication

- PAP (remote clients and branch offices)
- Passwords (campus and dial-in)

Access control

- Access lists in WAN and gateway routers
- No standalone firewalls
- No encryption

Case Study 2: A Restrictive Security Policy

In Case Study 2, companies took an approach that balanced user flexibility in terms of connectivity, performance, and ease of use with the level of security in their implementations. The case study classified these companies as having a restrictive security policy. Figure 2-7 illustrates the balance between transparency of user access and maximum security for a restrictive security policy.

Figure 2-7   *Case Study 2's Restrictive Security Policy*

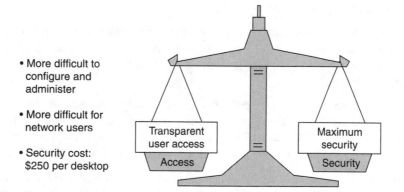

These companies used a combination of permitting some network connections and restricting others, which required that the companies create specific barriers on a select group of connections and grant specific permissions on another group of connections. As a result, these security implementations were more difficult to configure and administer, and their users needed to take extra steps to gain access to the enterprise.

These companies had more personnel assigned to security than in Case Study 1, and they tended to invest in a more detailed security policy as well. In Case Study 2, the companies tended to spend on average about $250 per desktop in security-related costs (which is near the middle of the $53 to $368 range for all companies surveyed). Most companies in this group had experienced at least one financial loss resulting from a network security breach. This group included a variety of company sizes.

Security Technologies Deployed for Medium Enterprise Security

Companies in Case Study 2 had a wide variety of network connections and topologies. Figure 2-8 shows a representative network sampling with a summary of network topologies and equipment deployed.

Branch offices were connected to the enterprise over Frame Relay lines or, in a few cases, using leased lines. Routers were used at each end of these links.

Dial-in users, including traveling employees and those in small remote offices or at home, used the public telephone network to connect to the enterprise over ISDN and dialup async lines. A network access server was used to aggregate these lines back at headquarters.

An Internet connection existed for both outbound traffic from the enterprise and inbound traffic to the company's public servers. As in the first case, all Internet traffic was still concentrated in a single access point, although redundant gateway routers were common, as were duplicate links to different ISPs. Remote users still needed to connect to the enterprise to gain access to the Internet.

To identify their users, these companies relied on usernames and passwords in the campus. For remote users in branch offices, they administered in the campus directory server. Many of the companies in this group had implemented DHCP to dynamically assign IP addresses in the campus.

To identify remote dial-in users, all but one company relied on one-time password entry, which occurred when the user dialed into the network access server before the dialup link was established. PPP and PAP were used to transmit the one-time password to the network access server. This one-time password was authenticated in the AAA/token server.

To maintain network integrity, access lists were programmed into WAN and Internet gateway routers to restrict which network addresses could access the enterprise. A stand-alone circuit-level firewall was used to further restrict Internet access to only those connections that originated inside the firewall.

Route authentication was common on the links between the branch offices and the headquarters WAN router. Several of the companies in Case Study 2 had recently started using encryption on these links to ensure data integrity.

Figure 2-8   *The Network Environment for Case Study 2—Restrictive Enterprise Security*

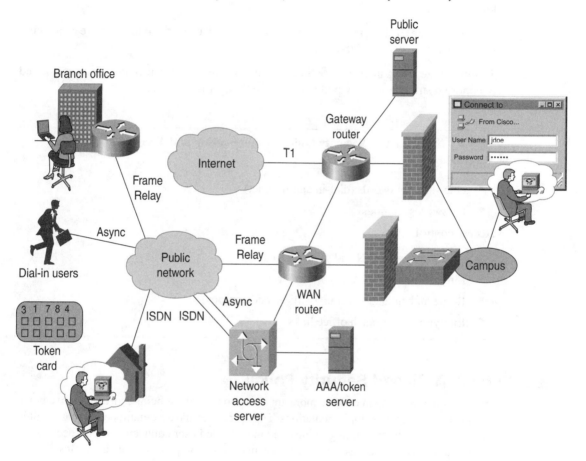

For authentication of users, passwords were used both for campus and remote branch office users. One-time passwords created by token cards were used to identify dial-in users. One of the customers in this group was experimenting with remote user access to the enterprise using the Internet. This application made use of built-in user authentication in the stand-alone firewall to identify users based on a one-time password.

To ensure access control, these companies relied on a variety of technologies, from access lists in existing routers to a standalone firewall on the Internet connection to route authentication and encryption on branch office links.

Outbound access to the Internet was restricted in a few of the companies using the circuit-level firewall.

Some companies in this group were experimenting with using the Internet to create a secure virtual private network (VPN).

To summarize, companies in Case Study 2 implemented security technologies that resulted in a more restrictive security policy than Case Study 1 as follows:

Restrictive Security Policy Authentication and Access Control

Authentication

- One-time passwords (dial-in and Internet)
- Passwords (campus)

Access control

- Access lists in WAN and gateway routers
- Firewall between Internet and enterprise
- Route authentication (branch offices and campus)
- Encryption on branch office links

Case Study 3: A Closed Security Policy

In Case Study 3, companies were more apt to err on the side of being more restrictive when it came to their security implementations. They preferred have a default policy that resulted in stronger security even though it resulted in restricted user connectivity with decreased performance and ease of use. We have classified these companies as having a closed security policy.

The companies in Case Study 3 tended to deny all network connections that were not explicitly permitted, which required a fairly detailed security policy in place that defined specific user privileges. Figure 2-9 illustrates the balance between transparency of user access and maximum security for a closed security policy.

Figure 2-9   *Case Study 3's Closed Security Policy*

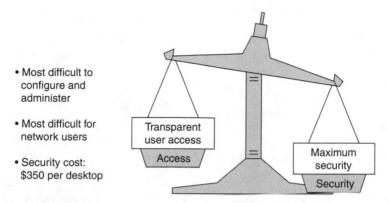

- Most difficult to configure and administer
- Most difficult for network users
- Security cost: $350 per desktop

As a result of their closed approach, these companies' security implementations were the most difficult to configure and administer and the most difficult on network users in terms of ease of use.

Not surprisingly, the companies in this group tended to average more than $350 per desktop in security-related costs (at the high end of the $53 to $368 range for all companies surveyed).

The companies in this group were the largest in terms of network size.

These companies justified the high cost of security because they had either been the victim of an expensive security breach or were required to implement a closed security policy by their auditors to prevent such a breach. These companies were all in the financial services market.

Security Technologies Deployed for Maximum Enterprise Security

Companies in Case Study 3 had network connections similar to the other groups, but far fewer connections were allowed—and users could do much less on these connections than in the other groups. Figure 2-10 shows a representative network sampling with a summary of network topologies and equipment deployed in this group.

Branch offices were connected to the enterprise over leased lines (where there was a large amount of SNA traffic) or Frame Relay lines (where there was a mix of IP and SNA). Various types of network devices were used at each end of these links, such as routers, Frame Relay access devices (FRADs), or CSU/DSUs. Routers are shown in Figure 2-10 because there were no built-in security technologies of interest in the other devices.

Figure 2-10 *The Network Environment for Case Study 3—Closed Enterprise Security*

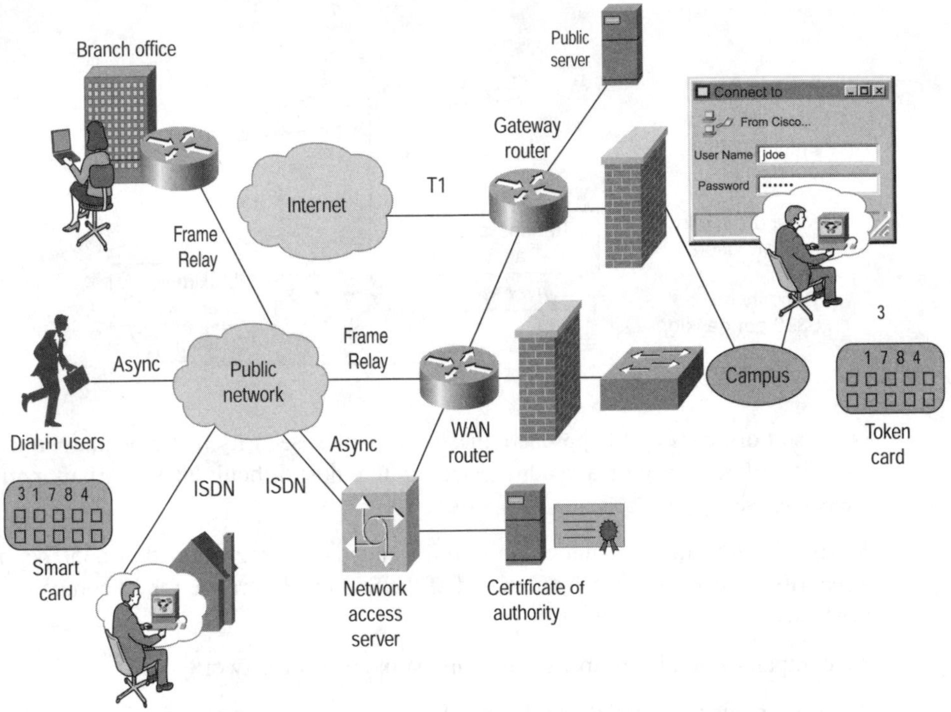

Dial-in users, including those in small remote offices or at home, used the public telephone network to connect to the enterprise over ISDN and dialup async lines. A network access server was used to aggregate these lines back at headquarters.

An Internet connection existed for both outbound traffic from the enterprise and inbound traffic to the companies' public servers. As in the other groups, all Internet traffic was still concentrated in a single access point, although redundant gateway routers were common, as were duplicate links to different ISPs. Remote users still needed to connect to the enterprise to gain access to the Internet.

To identify their users, these companies relied on usernames and passwords in the campus. For remote users in branch offices, they administered in the campus directory server. Some companies in this group had implemented DHCP to dynamically assign IP addresses in the campus. To identify remote dial-in users, all companies relied on one-time passwords but planned to convert to digital certificates (as shown in Figure 2-10) within the next six months. Digital certificates would be authenticated by a certificate authority.

Network integrity solutions implemented were similar to those in Case Study 2. Access lists were programmed into WAN and Internet gateway routers to restrict which network addresses could access the enterprise. A standalone packet-filtering firewall was used to further restrict Internet access to only those connections that originated inside the firewall.

Route authentication was common on the links between the branch offices and the headquarters WAN router (when used). All companies in this group used encryption via standalone link encryptors (not shown) on these links to protect the confidentiality of information.

To authenticate users, passwords were used for both campus and remote branch office users. One-time passwords created by token cards were used to identify dial-in users, although these companies were converting to digital certificates and smart cards because of the added security and flexibility of digital certificates.

To control access, these companies relied on a variety of technologies, from access lists in existing routers to a standalone firewall on the Internet connection to route authentication and encryption on all links outside the campus (and even some links inside the campus). Outbound access to the Internet was restricted to a select group of network users.

No companies in this group were looking at offering inbound user access via the Internet because adequate security measures are not yet available.

To summarize, companies in Case Study 3 implemented much stronger security measures than in the other two case studies as follows:

Closed Security Policy Authentication and Access Control

Authentication

- Digital certificates (dial-in, branch, and campus)

Access control

- Access lists in WAN and gateway routers
- Firewall between the Internet and the enterprise
- Route authentication (branch offices and campus)
- Encryption (dial-in, branch office, and some campus)

Summary of the Case Studies

As the case studies indicate, network security does not lend itself to a uniform approach. The security solution for each company will be different from the solution for any other company, and it might be different for a given company over time. Careful analysis, planning, and the use of tools such as the CiscoSecure Scanner will allow you to apply the correct solution in the most cost-effective manner. Table 2-1 summarizes the network security technologies deployed by companies in the case studies.

Table 2-1 *Summary of Technologies Used by Companies, Sorted by Security Policy Type*

Criteria	Open?	Restrictive?	Closed?
Passwords	Yes	Yes	Yes
Token cards	No	No	Yes
Firewalls	No	Yes	Yes
Encryption	No	Sometimes	Yes
Certificate authority	No	No	Yes

Summary

This chapter established the need for a network security policy by focusing on the following key points:

- You must weigh the cost in ease of use and in resources to establish and implement a network security policy against the costs and likelihood of network security breaches. Try to strike a balance that is acceptable to your organization.

- Security posture assessment is a process consisting of four parts that can help you iteratively and progressively enforce a network security system: secure, monitor, test, and improve.

- A security policy is a formal statement of the rules by which people who are given access to an organization's technology and information assets must abide.

- It is worth the effort to create a network security policy because it provides a basis to audit existing network security, it provides a general security framework, it defines acceptable behavior, it helps communicate security intent, it provides a basis for legal action, and it defines a process for handing security incidents.

- A security policy can be used to identify assets that must be secured and to spell out the key network security threats that the company must guard against.

- Although the security policy is not a detailed implementation plan, it can spell out the key security goals that must be achieved, making it easier for implementers to carry out its directives.

- The security policy can educate users, clarifying to them what is and is not acceptable network behavior.

- The network security policy should specify procedures and tools to be used to audit and maintain network security.

- Security audits should be frequently and regularly conducted, and they should also be conducted randomly.

- A company should have a detailed, written incident-handling procedure to ensure that incidents are handled predictably.

- The Computer Emergency Response Team (CERT) at www.cert.org/ is a good resource for determining network security threats and how to mitigate them.

- Network security policies can be classified as either open, restrictive, or closed. Often, the more restrictive the policy, the greater the cost of implementing it.

Case Study: Evaluating the XYZ Company Network Security Policy

This case study consists of analyzing the network security policy of the hypothetical XYZ Company. Read Appendix A, "XYZ Company Case Study Scenario," to become familiar with the company and then read about the company's network security policy in Appendix B. You will then be ready to answer following set of questions designed help you evaluate the XYZ Company's sample network security policy.

Case Study Scenario

The XYZ Company has developed a network security policy. The company wants you to analyze the policy with the purpose of enacting the policy in Cisco networking equipment they have purchased and installed in their network. Answer the following questions:

1 What legal authority enables the enforcement of the network security policy?

2 How is the network system administrator involved with implementing and enacting the security policy?

3 What is the security policy maintenance procedure?

4 Determine the scope of the XYZ network security policy. How restrictive is it?

5 What is the general security policy for the XYZ network campus network user and infrastructure?

6 What is the general security policy for the XYZ network for Internet access?

7 What is the general security policy for the XYZ network dial-in user?

8 What methods does the XYZ Company plan to use to detect security intrusions?

9 What is the XYZ Company's security incident-handling procedure?

10 How will the XYZ Company educate network users about acceptable uses of the network?

Answers to Case Study Scenario Questions

The following are the answers to the case study scenario questions:

1 The XYZ Company board of directors and senior executive staff have been empowered by the company shareholders to implement and enforce the policy in accordance with applicable laws under the direction of the XYZ Information Security Officer and Corporate Attorney.

2 The network administrator plays an instrumental role in ensuring the security of the XYZ enterprise. The administrator needs to ensure that all tasks performed will not reduce network security.

3 The company stakeholders shall review and update the policy at least once a year, and the IS department must conduct random system audits and document the results.

4 The policy is moderately restrictive. Authentication will be enforced by a TACACS+ server but not token servers. Outgoing Internet access is unrestricted, but incoming traffic is restricted. Campus access is controlled by trust levels. Remote access is controlled by passwords under the control of the TACACS+ server.

5 Access to campus resources and equipment is controlled by assigning a trust level to users based on their job tasks. Unauthorized access is prohibited.

6 Outgoing access to the Internet for campus and dial-in users is unrestricted for business purposes. Incoming access from the Internet is denied unless explicitly allowed. A firewall system will be implemented to enforce the Internet access policy.

7 Remote access via the dialup network is treated as an extension of the XYZ internal network, containing the same restrictions as campus access. Access is controlled by password protection or token cards and servers and a TACACS+ server.

8 The XYZ Company plans to detect security intrusions and attacks by implementing an intrusion detection system (IDS), regularly examining network equipment event logs, installing and monitoring host system logging tools, and regularly auditing network security with a network scanner.

9 The XYZ Company Security Policy stakeholders must develop a detailed incident-handling procedure containing contingency plans designed to handle all possible security incidents. CiscoSecure IDS will be used to detect intrusion attempts.

10 Security policy awareness must be incorporated as part of employee orientation. Users are required to read and sign the acceptable-use policy annually as a condition of employment. Employees will also be educated about social engineering attempts.

Review Questions

Answer the following review questions, which delve into some of the key facts and concepts covered in this chapter:

1 What two elements of network security must be balanced against each other?

2 What are the five components of the security wheel?

3 What is a network security policy?

4 Why should an organization expend the time and energy necessary to create a workable network security policy?

5 What are some key sections of a network security policy?

6 How can you use a network security policy?

7 How can a network security policy help you test and audit the network security implementation?

8 What are some Cisco tools that are useful for security testing and auditing?

9 Where can you report a serious network intrusion that has not yet been reported and resolved?

10 What is the defining characteristic of a closed security policy?

References

The topics considered in this chapter are complex and should be studied further to more fully understand them and put them to use. Use the following references to learn more about the topics in this chapter.

Developing a Security Policy

T. Bernstein, A. Bismani, E. Schultz, and C. Siegel, *Internet Security for Business,* Wiley Computer Publishing, 1996. Describes how to implement security from a business perspective.

M. Kaeo, *Designing Network Security,* Cisco Press, 1999.

"The Politics of Information Management," at www.strassmann.com/iep/info-politics.html.

RFC 2196, "Site Security Handbook." Standards document for network security policy.

Security Policy Examples and Guidelines

The Electronic Frontier Foundation Web site, at www.eff.org.

"Guidelines for the Security of Information Systems," by the Information, Computer, and Communications Policy (ICCP) Committee, at www.oecd.org/dsti/sti/it/secur/prod/e_secur.htm. A list of guidelines for writing security policies.

"Internet Security Policy: A Technical Guide NIST Special Publication 800-XX," by Barbara Guttman and Robert Bagwill, located at csrc.nist.gov/isptg. This is a great source of network security policy information because it is comprehensive, detailed, and realistic. The document chapters can be downloaded in multiple formats (Microsoft Word 97, Adobe Acrobat PDF, and HTML). If you can check only one reference, choose this one!

"Model Security Policies," at www.sans.org/newlook/resources/policies/policies.htm. Sample security policy documents compiled by Michele Crabb-Guel.

"Security Policies for the Internet," by Stephen L. Arnold, Arnold Consulting, at www.arnold.com/policies_9512_slides.html. An example of an Internet access security policy.

Incident Response Centers Useful for Security Incident Reporting

The Australian Computer Emergency Response Team (AUSCERT) home page, at www.auscert.org.au.

The Computer Emergency Response Team (CERT) home page, at www.cert.org. The principal incident response center.

The Computer Incident Advisory Capability (CIAC) home page, at www.ciac.llnl.gov.

The Defense Information Agency Center for Automated System Security Incident Support Team page for DoD sites, at www.assist.mil. The DoD CERT Web site.

"European Contact List," at www.cert.dfn.de/eng/csir/europe/certs.html. This site provides a full list of European CERTs.

Forum of Incident Response and Security Teams (FIRST), at www.first.org. International incident response team.

The German Research Network Computer Emergency Response Team (DFN-CERT) home page, at www.cert.dfn.de/eng. Designed for members of the German research network in setting up preventive measures to improve the security of participating sites.

The NASA Incident Response Center (NASIRC) home page, at nasirc.nasa.gov/NASIRC_home.html.

Other Security Web Sites

The COAST archive, at www.cs.purdue.edu/coast/hotlist. This archive at Purdue University is probably the most complete archive of security-related links on the Internet. If it has to do with security, it's probably in the COAST archive.

"InfoSec and InfoWar Portal," at www.infowar.com. A summary of security resources.

The National Security Institute's Security Resource Net, at www.nsi.org/compsec.html.

Upon completing this chapter, you will be able to do the following:

- Identify potential threats to the campus network and security methods to alleviate those threats

- Identify steps to take to increase physical device security

- Identify how to secure the administrative interface to Cisco routers

- Identify the methods and commands to secure router-to-router communications

- Identify how to configure Cisco Ethernet switches to protect the network infrastructure

CHAPTER 3

Securing the Network Infrastructure

This chapter provides a synopsis of how to configure Cisco IOS routers and Ethernet switches to protect the campus infrastructure. The chapter begins by outlining potential threats to network security that are common in the campus environment. How to increase physical access to network devices is summarized.

This chapter also covers how to secure the administrative interface to routers, how to control Simple Network Management Protocol (SNMP) access to Cisco network devices, how to control routing updates, and how to ensure that router configuration files are secure on Trivial File Transport Protocol (TFTP) servers. The use of standard and extended access lists to control network traffic through campus routers is covered. Ethernet switches are a core element of any campus network, and this chapter educates you on how to control Ethernet switch access to ports and administrative interfaces. You will gain practical knowledge by considering a case study in which a network security policy for campus security is matched up against a sample configuration for a campus router in the XYZ Company network.

Campus Security Problems and Solutions

A campus infrastructure consisting of Cisco routers and Ethernet switches is vulnerable to network security threats from a variety of internal and external intruders. Intruders that pose a threat to the campus network might include the following:

- Current employees who are curious or who want to access secure areas of the network
- Employees or users pursuing unintentional activities that might affect network security
- Hostile former employees
- Spies who want to learn internal company information

Current employees might be the most difficult to detect and protect against because of trust relationships between employees and their employers. Network intruders can use a variety of techniques to carry out their goals against the campus infrastructure. If you are aware of where the network infrastructure is vulnerable, and if you configure devices properly to provide the best possible security against these vulnerabilities, you will have made significant progress in securing the campus infrastructure. In this chapter, you will learn how to secure the campus infrastructure as much as is practical. Here are some specific threats or vulnerabilities common to campus equipment:

- Accessing device console and Telnet ports
- Accessing router configuration files and learning passwords
- Accessing device configurations and learning the internal network topology via SNMP
- Learning internal network topology by intercepting routing updates
- Misrouting traffic via spoofed routing updates
- Accessing sensitive internal networks
- Gaining Hypertext Transfer Protocol (HTTP) access to routers
- Unauthorized access to or through Ethernet switches

Figure 3-1 illustrates the campus infrastructure of the XYZ Company that is discussed in this chapter. The infrastructure consists of the Sales and Engineering internal networks. Each network has a Cisco router securing traffic to that network, and Ethernet switches. Each network has campus client computers and networked servers needing protection.

The solution to the campus infrastructure security problem is to securely configure components of the network infrastructure against vulnerabilities based on network security policy. Network infrastructure vulnerabilities that must be protected against are well known and have secure methods to counteract the vulnerabilities. Securing device configuration to protect the network infrastructure should include the following points, which are covered next:

- Securing the physical devices
- Securing the administrative interface
- Securing router-to-router communications
- Securing Ethernet switches

Figure 3-1   *XYZ's Campus Infrastructure, Including Two Internal Networks Needing Protection*

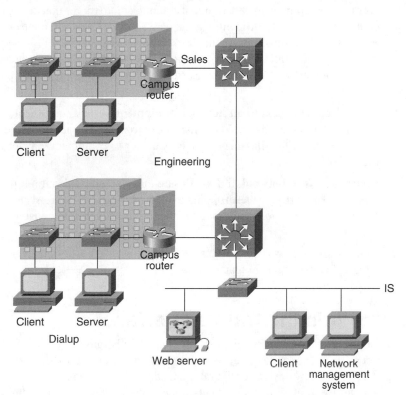

Securing the Physical Devices

Physical access to network equipment can give a fairly sophisticated user total control over that equipment. Physical access to a network link usually allows a person to eavesdrop on that link or inject traffic into it. It makes no sense to install complicated software-based security measures when access to the network equipment and communication lines is not controlled. For example, a person who can physically access a router could access the console port and reset the system password, gaining full access to the router and possibly to other network devices. You should secure your network equipment by doing the following:

- **Establish configuration and control policy**—Have a site security plan that specifies how network equipment and network links will be secured. Perform regular security audits to ensure that physical security is maintained.

- **Properly lock, power, wire, and cool equipment**—Ensure that proper site planning is done for equipment installation. Put equipment into rooms that have physical access controls such as locks or identification card readers. Carefully control who has keys or access to the rooms. Ensure that backup power is available for vital equipment. You might want to install uninterruptible power supplies (UPSs) on separate electrical circuits for your vital equipment. Ensure that air conditioning is sufficient to keep equipment cool.

- **Control direct access to all network equipment**—Lock equipment covers or put equipment into locked equipment racks. Control who has access to the equipment console port. Ensure that there is no easy access to equipment via a drop ceiling or raised floor.

- **Secure access to network links**—Ensure that all communication lines and network links are secure from eavesdropping and that wiring closets are secure. Carefully monitor equipment to ensure that no modems are attached to console ports without permission.

- **Plan for disaster recovery**—Ensure that a disaster recovery plan suitable for your geographic location is in place.

Securing the Administrative Interface

Some of the prime intruder attack points are the administrative interfaces of Cisco routers, Ethernet switches, and network access servers. If an intruder can access the administrative interface, he can view device configuration, reconfigure the device and gain control of it, or even gain access to other connected network equipment. Securing the administrative interface of Cisco routers includes the following:

- Securing console access
- Using password encryption
- Fine-tuning line parameters
- Setting multiple privilege levels
- Setting device banner messages
- Controlling Telnet access
- Controlling SNMP access

Securing Console Access

A console is a terminal attached directly to the router via the console port, as shown in Figure 3-2. Security is applied to the console by requiring users to authenticate themselves via passwords. In the router default configuration, no passwords are assigned to the console, and the initial configuration (setup) dialog box does not have you set the password, so you must do it via configuration commands. It's important to ensure the physical security of the router, because intruders can reset the password if they have physical access to the console port by pressing the Break key after forcing a reboot, enabling the password recovery process. Passwords can be configured directly in the router, or they can be controlled via a remote security database such as CiscoSecure Access Control Server (ACS), along with Cisco IOS authentication, authorization, and accounting (AAA) commands.

Figure 3-2   *A Terminal Connected to the Router's Console Port*

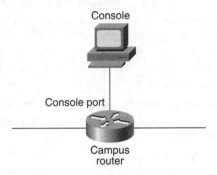

Cisco routers have many modes. You first access a console port in user EXEC (user) mode. If a user-level password (known as a login password) has been set, you are prompted to enter the login password. In user mode, the router displays the router's host name and the carat symbol as follows: router>. The user mode enables a subset of commands that you can list using the **help** or **?** commands.

You access privileged EXEC (privileged or enable) mode by typing **enable** and pressing Enter. If a privileged-level password has been configured, the router prompts you for a privileged password. The router host name and a pound sign are displayed when you are in privileged mode, as follows: router#. Privileged mode gives you access to more commands, and you can access global configuration mode, allowing you to change router configuration. You can set different levels of commands for privileged mode, enabling different command levels for administrators. Securing access to user and privileged levels is very important to router security.

Setting Console Passwords

You can set a password for both user and privileged modes. Console passwords can have from 1 to 25 uppercase and lowercase alphanumeric characters.

Here are some tips to enable console and Telnet password security, including using good passwords and password administration:

- Immediately configure passwords upon initial installation. Do not use the default.

- Make sure that the privileged password is different from the access password.

- Use passwords with mixed characters (nonalphanumeric and uppercase) to make password-cracking attempts more difficult.

- Do not write down passwords and place them where they can easily be found.

- Do not use easily guessed passwords such as pet names, addresses, or birthdays.

- Change passwords often.

- Never use cisco or san-fran or other obvious derivatives for a Cisco router password in a production environment. These will be the first passwords intruders will try if they recognize the Cisco login prompt.

User-Mode Passwords

You configure a console password for user mode by entering the commands shown in Example 3-1 in the router's configuration file. Passwords are case sensitive. In this example, the password is ruHamlet.

Example 3-1 *Configuring a Console Password for Login Mode*

```
router(config)#line console 0
router(config-line)#login
router(config-line)#password ruHamlet
```

When you log in to the router with a login password set, the router login prompt looks like what is shown in Example 3-2.

Example 3-2 *A Router Login Prompt When a Login Password Is Set*

```
User Access Verification
Password:ruHamlet
router>
```

In this example, you must enter the password ruHamlet to gain nonprivileged access to the router. The router enters user mode, as signified by the > prompt. At this point, you can enter a variety of commands to view statistics on the router, but you cannot change the router's configuration.

Privileged-Mode Passwords

You configure a password for privileged mode by entering the commands shown in Example 3-3 in the router's configuration file in global configuration mode. In this example, the password is a cleartext password of 2br!2b@?.

Example 3-3 *Configuring a Password for Privileged (Enable) Mode*

```
router(config)#enable password 2br!2b@?
```

You access privileged mode from nonprivileged mode as shown in Example 3-4. The router prompts you for an enable password. In this example, you enter the password 2br!2b@? to gain privileged access to the router. The router enters privileged mode, which is signified by the # prompt.

Example 3-4 *Accessing Privileged Mode from Nonprivileged Mode Using the Enable Password*

```
router>enable
Password:2br!2b@?
router#
```

Using Password Encryption

All console and Telnet passwords on the router are stored in cleartext in the router configuration by default and are vulnerable to being observed. They are vulnerable to eavesdropping during a Telnet session when someone is entering an enable password or if a configuration is viewed with the **write terminal** or **show running-config** privileged-mode commands. Passwords are also vulnerable if router configurations are stored on a TFTP server.

As discussed in the following sections, there are two ways to hide cleartext passwords: the **service password-encryption** command and the **enable secret** command.

The service password-encryption Command

The **service password-encryption** command stores passwords in an encrypted manner in router configuration. The encryption scheme used with this command is an unsophisticated, reversible algorithm proprietary to Cisco and based on the Vigenere cipher, a polyalphabetic cipher.

Password encryption is applied to all passwords including username passwords, authentication key passwords, the privileged command password, console and virtual terminal line access passwords, and BGP neighbor passwords. The command syntax is as follows:

```
router(config)#enable password [level level] {password |
   [encryption-type] encrypted-password}
```

The command parameters and syntax have the following meanings:

Command Syntax	Description
level *level*	(Optional) Specifies the privilege level for which the password applies. You can specify up to 16 privilege levels, using numbers **0** through **15**. Level **1** is normal privileged-mode user privileges. If this argument is not specified in the command or in the **no** form of the command, the privilege level defaults to **15** (traditional enable privileges). The same holds true for the **no** form of the command.

continues

Command Syntax	Description
password	Specifies the password for users to enter enable mode. This password should be different from the password created with the **enable** secret command.
encryption-type	(Optional) Specifies the Cisco-proprietary algorithm used to encrypt the password. Currently, the only encryption type available for this command is **7**. If you specify *encryption-type,* the next argument you supply must be an encrypted password (a password encrypted by a Cisco router using the same encryption type). If you specify **0**, you must enter an unencrypted password.
encrypted-password	Specifies the encrypted password, which you enter, copied from another router configuration.

WARNING The **service password-encryption** command does not provide a high level of network security. Many password crackers can reverse Cisco-proprietary passwords. If you use this command, you should also take additional network security measures.

When password encryption is enabled, the encrypted form of the password is displayed when a **show running-config** command is entered. The keyword password 7 indicates that password encryption is enabled, as shown in Example 3-5.

Example 3-5 *The Encrypted Form of a Password, Indicating That Password Encryption Is Enabled*

```
router#show running-config
enable password 7 14141B180F0B
!
line con 0
password 7 094F471A1A0A
!
line vty 0 4
 password 7 05080F1C2243
```

The **enable password** command allows you to specify password encryption by using the Cisco proprietary method. You would generally use this option only to reenter an encrypted password that had been misconfigured before exiting enable mode. If you specify an encryption type in the **enable password** command, you must enter the password in encrypted form, displayed by the **show running-config** command. If you enter a cleartext password, you will not be able to reenter enable mode.

NOTE If you lose or forget the encrypted password, you must clear nonvolatile random-access memory (NVRAM) and set a new password.

The enable secret Command

The **enable secret** global configuration command involves a one-way encryption scheme based on the MD5 hashing function, which is covered in Chapter 13, "Cisco Encryption Technology Overview." This method is more secure than that provided by the **service password-encryption** command. It is available in Cisco IOS Software versions 10.0(9) and later, 10.2(5) and later, and 10.3(2) and later. The enable secret password is still subject to brute force or dictionary password attacks. The command syntax is as follows:

```
enable secret [level level] {password | [encryption-type] encrypted-password}
```

The command parameters and syntax have the following meanings:

Command Syntax	Description
level *level*	(Optional) Specifies the privilege level for which the password applies. You can specify up to 16 privilege levels, using numbers **0** through **15**. Level **1** is normal privileged-mode user privileges. If this argument is not specified in the command or in the **no** form of the command, the privilege level defaults to **15** (traditional enable privileges). The same holds true for the **no** form of the command.
password	Specifies the password for users to enter enable mode. This password should be different from the password created with the **enable password** command.
encryption-type	(Optional) Specifies the Cisco-proprietary algorithm used to encrypt the password. Currently, the only encryption type available for this command is **5**. If you specify *encryption-type,* the next argument you supply must be an encrypted password (a password encrypted by a Cisco router using the same encryption type). If you specify **0**, you must enter an unencrypted password.
encrypted-password	Specifies the encrypted password, which you enter, copied from another router configuration.

An enable secret password is indicated by the numeral 5, as shown in Example 3-6.

Example 3-6 *An Encrypted Enable Secret Password Indicated by the Numeral 5*

```
router#show running-config
!
enable secret 5 $1$6cWV$inD7guHPL1D3ZmdX08MMS/
```

Although encryption is helpful, it can be compromised and thus should not be the sole method used for securing network passwords.

Cisco recommends that you use the **enable secret** command because it uses an improved encryption algorithm. Use the **enable password** command only if you boot an older image of Cisco IOS Software or if you boot older boot ROMs (prerelease 10.3, 4000, and 4000M Cisco routers) that do not recognize the **enable secret** command.

Fine-Tuning Line Parameters

Setting the login and enable passwords might not provide enough security in some cases. If the console or a Telnet session is left unattended in privileged mode, any user could modify the router's configuration. You can adjust a variety of timeouts for an unattended line to provide an additional measure of security.

Adjusting the timeout for an unattended console (which by default is a console that has not been used for 10 minutes) provides an additional measure of security. You can change the login timeout via the **exec-timeout** *mm ss* command, where *mm* is minutes and *ss* is seconds, as shown in Figure 3-3. Figure 3-3 illustrates changing the session timeout value to 2 minutes and 30 seconds on the console port.

Figure 3-3   *Fine-Tuning Line Control with the Line Command and Its Many Options*

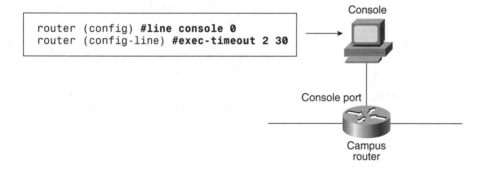

Many other parameters are useful for controlling line security. Example 3-7 shows some of the types of lines for which you can fine-tune parameters in Cisco IOS.

Example 3-7   *Some of the Types of Lines for Which You Can Fine-Tune Parameters in Cisco IOS*

```
router(config)#line ?
  <0-70>   First Line number
  aux      Auxiliary line
  console  Primary terminal line
  tty      Terminal controller
  vty      Virtual terminal
```

Example 3-8 shows some of the many parameters for controlling line security.

Example 3-8   *Parameters for Controlling Line Security*

```
router(config)#line console 0
router(config-line)#?
Line configuration commands:
  absolute-timeout             Set absolute timeout for line disconnection
  access-class                 Filter connections based on an IP access list
  exec                         Start an EXEC process
  exec-banner                  Enable the display of the EXEC banner
  exec-timeout                 Set the EXEC timeout
  exit                         Exit from line configuration mode
  full-help                    Provide help to unprivileged user
  history                      Enable and control the command history function
  login                        Enable password checking
  logout-warning               Set Warning countdown for absolute timeout of
                               line
  monitor                      Copy debug output to the current terminal line
  motd-banner                  Enable the display of the MOTD banner
  no                           Negate a command or set its defaults
  privilege                    Change privilege level for line
  refuse-message               Define a refuse banner
  session-disconnect-warning   Set warning countdown for session-timeout
  session-timeout              Set interval for closing connection when there is
                               no input traffic
  telnet                       Telnet protocol-specific configuration
  timeout                      Timeouts for the line
  vacant-message               Define a vacant banner
```

Setting Multiple Privilege Levels

As discussed earlier, Cisco IOS Software has two modes of password security by default: user EXEC mode and privileged EXEC (enable) mode. You can configure up to 16 hierarchical levels of commands for each mode, allowing you to delegate administrative authority. Cisco IOS commands can be associated with each of the levels, giving granularity of control for user access. By configuring multiple passwords, you can allow different sets of users to have access to specified commands. The following levels are predefined:

- Level 1 is predefined to enable user-mode access privileges.

- Levels 2 to 14 are customizable user-mode privilege levels.

- Level 15 is predefined to enable access at the privileged-mode level, the same access permitted by the **enable** command.

You can set the privilege level for a command using the **privilege level** global configuration command. Use the **no** form of this command to revert to default privileges for a given command. The command syntax is as follows:

```
privilege mode {level level command | reset command}
```

The command parameters and syntax have the following meanings:

Command Syntax	Description
mode	Specifies configuration mode. Includes **exec**, **configure**, **line**, **interface**, and all other router configuration modes.
level *level*	Enables setting a privilege level of **0** to **15** associated with a specified command.
command	Specifies the command to which the privilege level is associated.
reset *command*	Resets the privilege level of a designated command.

An example of the use of the **privilege level** command is to allow a system administrator to use system monitoring and testing commands (**ping**, **show**, **debug**) by assigning him to level 2, while allowing a network engineer full command access, as shown in Figure 3-4.

Figure 3-4 *Using the privilege level Command to Create Hierarchical Administrative Levels*

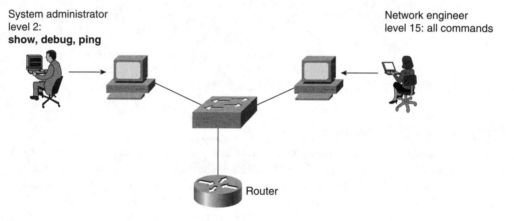

You would configure the router to enable this example as shown in Example 3-9.

Example 3-9 *Privilege Levels Allow a System Administrator to Use System Monitoring and Testing Commands*

```
router(config)#privilege exec level 2 show startup-config
router(config)#privilege exec level 2 debug ip rip
router(config)#privilege exec level 2 ping
router(config)#enable secret level 2 2kdo40d
```

You can set the default privilege level for a line by using the **privilege level** line configuration command, which has the following syntax:

```
privilege level level
```

You can log in to a privilege level by using the **enable** line privileged-mode command, which has the following syntax:

```
router>enable level
```

Setting Device Banner Messages

You can use banner messages to communicate who is or is not allowed to come into your network. Do not use the word *welcome* in any banner shown to users logging in. In court suits, intruders have been found not guilty because *welcome* indicated that the administrators were inviting them in. Make the message reflect how serious security breaches are to you. Have a legal expert review the banner messages if possible. Cite applicable civil codes and laws pertaining to network security. A simple example is "Warning: This is XYZ Company's private network. Unauthorized access to and use of the network will be vigorously prosecuted."

banner Command Options

You can configure a line activation message to be displayed when an EXEC process is begun. Banner messages can be displayed when a user enters privileged EXEC mode, upon line activation, on an incoming connection to a virtual terminal, or as a message of the day. To create a banner message, enter the following command in global configuration mode:

```
banner {exec | incoming | login | motd} d message d
```

The command parameters and syntax have the following meanings:

Command Syntax	Description
exec	Specifies a message to be displayed when an EXEC process is created (a console line is activated, or an incoming connection is made to a vty line).
incoming	Specifies a banner displayed when an incoming connection to a line (asynchronous) from a host on the network is made.
login	Specifies a message to be displayed during a login before the username and password login prompts.
motd	Specifies the display of the message of the day (MOTD) banner. This banner is displayed at login and is useful for sending messages that affect all network users.
d	Specifies a delimiting character of your choice, such as a pound sign (#). You cannot use the delimiting character in the banner message.
message	Specifies message text.

Example 3-10 shows the types of line activation for which you can set a banner message.

Example 3-10 *Example of Creating a Banner That Will Be Displayed When Users Enter an EXEC Process*

```
router(config)#banner exec $
Session activated.  Enter commands at the prompt.
$
```

Controlling Telnet Access

A fundamental security provision for Cisco routers is controlling Telnet access to the router. This type of security is important because Telnet access can lead to privileged access to the router. Users are presented with a router prompt in user mode when they Telnet into the router. The user can then enter enable mode. Here are some considerations about controlling Telnet access:

- Telnet ports on the router are called *virtual terminal* (vty) ports.

- An enable password must be configured to get enable access via Telnet.

- The default for the enable password is no enable password configured on the router. When you try to Telnet to an interface that does not have a password set, you are presented with the message Password required but none set. The console port is the only port permitted to access privileged mode when no vty password is set.

- Cisco IOS Software uses the same password security on the vty ports as on the console.

- You should restrict Telnet access with **access-class** and **access-list** commands by doing the following:

  — Restrict Telnet access from particular IP addresses.

  — Define a standard access list of allowed IP addresses.

  — Apply the access list to the vty lines via the **access-class** command.

- Configure all the configured vty ports. Ports 0 to 4 are the defaults, and more ports can be configured.

- Limit, block, or disable the AUX port with the **no exec** command in line-configuration mode.

- Disable commands such as **ip alias**, **no cdp running**, and **no cdp enable** to prevent access attacks against the router via the vty ports. See Chapter 7, "Configuring a Cisco Perimeter Router," for more details on commands to disable to prevent access attacks.

- Block connections to echo and discard via the **no service tcp-small-servers** and **no service udp-small-servers** commands.

- Limit the types of connections (secure shell, LAT, RCP) that can be made to the router using the **transport input** commands.

Examples of Telnet Configurations

The sample configurations show how to secure Telnet access. Example 3-11 shows how to configure a login (user-mode) password for vty lines 0 to 4.

Example 3-11 *Configuring a Login (User-Mode) Password for vty Lines 0 to 4*

```
router(config)#line vty 0 4
router(config-line)#login
router(config-line)#password shakespeare
```

Example 3-12 configures a privileged-mode password on a router that the user will enter after gaining Telnet access to a vty line. The example shows a Telnet session. An MOTD banner is displayed. The user enters the Telnet login password shakespeare. The user enters the **enable** command, is prompted for an enable password, enters the enable password whatlight, and gains privileged-mode access.

Example 3-12 *Configuring a Privileged-Mode Password in a Sample Telnet Session*

```
router(config)#enable password whatlight
C:\>telnet 10.1.1.2
"MOTD Banner"
User Access Verification
Password: shakespeare
router>enable
Password: whatlight
router#
```

Consider Example 3-13, which demonstrates using an access list to give only the administrator at 10.1.1.4 access to vty lines 0 to 4. Note the use of the **access-class** command to apply the list to the vty lines.

Example 3-13 *Access List 21 Gives the Administrator at 10.1.1.4 Access to vty Lines*

```
router(config)#access-list 21 permit 10.1.1.4
router(config)#line vty 0 4
router(config-line)#access-class 21 in
```

Controlling SNMP Access

SNMP can be a key source of intelligence for network intruders if it is not configured properly. You might not know when someone with an SNMP discovery tool is accessing Management Information Bases (MIBs) or trapping SNMP messages from your network equipment. It is vital to control SNMP access when securing the network infrastructure. SNMP has various access levels: Read-only (RO) allows reads of MIBs, read/write (RW) allows both reads and writes to an agent, and write (W) allows only writes to an agent.

SNMP Overview

SNMP is an application layer protocol that provides a communication conduit between SNMP managers and agents.

An SNMP system consists of the following three parts, as illustrated in Figure 3-5:

- Managed devices such as a router or switch
- SNMP agents and MIBs running on managed devices, including Remote Monitoring (RMON) MIBs
- An SNMP management application such as CiscoWorks 2000, which communicates with agents in managed devices to get statistics and alerts

NOTE An SNMP management application, together with the computer it runs on, is called a network management system (NMS).

Figure 3-5 *SNMP System Components*

NMS

SNMP manager

SNMP agent
SNMP MIBs

SNMP network management uses these SNMP agent functions:

- **MIB variable access**—This function is initiated by the SNMP agent in response to a request from the NMS. The agent retrieves the value of the requested MIB variable and responds to the NMS with that value. Access by NMS systems must be controlled to prevent network intruders from accessing MIBs in equipment and learning device configuration and status.

- **MIB variable setting**—This function is initiated by the SNMP agent in response to a message from the NMS. The SNMP agent changes the value of the MIB variable to the value requested by the NMS. Access must be controlled to prevent network intruders from altering equipment configuration.

- **SNMP trap**—This function is used to notify an NMS that a significant event has occurred at an agent. When a trap condition occurs, the SNMP agent sends an SNMP trap message to any NMS stations specified as the trap receivers. Access must be controlled to prevent network intruders from eavesdropping on equipment events.
- **SNMP community strings**—SNMP community strings authenticate access to MIB objects and function as embedded passwords.

SNMP Notifications

SNMP notifications can be sent as traps or inform requests. *Traps* are unreliable because the receiver does not send any acknowledgment when it receives a trap. The sender cannot determine whether the trap was received. *Inform requests* are more reliable because the SNMP agent sends a request that must be acknowledged by an SNMP manager with an SNMP response protocol data unit (PDU). If the manager does not receive an inform request, it does not send a response. If the sender never receives a response, the inform request can be sent again. Thus, informs are more likely to reach their intended destination.

Supported Versions of SNMP

Cisco IOS release 12.0 software supports the following versions of SNMP:

- SNMPv1, the Simple Network Management Protocol, a Full Internet Standard defined in RFC 1157
- SNMPv2C (classic), which consists of the following:
  - **SNMPv2**—Version 2 of the Simple Network Management Protocol, a Draft Internet Standard defined in RFCs 1902 through 1907
  - **SNMPv2C**—The Community-Based Administrative Framework for SNMPv2, an Experimental Internet Protocol defined in RFC 1901

SNMPv2C replaces the party-based administrative and security framework of SNMPv2Classic with the community-based administrative framework of SNMPv2C while retaining the bulk retrieval and improved error handling of SNMPv2Classic.

Both SNMPv1 and SNMPv2C use a community-based form of security. The community of managers who can access the agent's MIB are defined by an IP address access list and password. SNMPv2C support includes a bulk retrieval mechanism and more-detailed error message reporting to management stations.

Configuring the SNMP Agent

You must configure the SNMP agent to use the version of SNMP supported by the NMS. An agent can communicate with multiple NMS systems, so you can configure Cisco IOS Software to support communications with one management station using the SNMPv1 protocol and another using the SNMPv2 protocol.

To configure SNMP on the router, you define the relationship between the NMS and the agent. The SNMP agent contains MIB variables whose values the SNMP NMS can request or change. An NMS can get a value from an agent or store a value in that agent. The agent gathers data from the MIB, the repository for information about device parameters and network data. The agent can also respond to an NMS system's requests to get or set data.

Controlling SNMP Access with Community Strings

You can configure an SNMP community string to define the relationship between the SNMP manager and the agent. The community string acts like a password to permit access to the agent on the router. You can specify one or more of the following characteristics associated with the string to control access:

- An access list of IP addresses of the NMS systems that are permitted to use the community string to gain access to the agent

- A MIB view, which defines the subset of all MIB objects accessible to the given community

- Read/write or read-only permission for the MIB objects accessible to the community

To configure a community string, use the following command syntax in global configuration mode:

```
router(config)#snmp-server community string [view view-name] [ro | rw] [number]
```

The *number* field should contain the optional access list number. You can use Internet Protocol (IP) standard access lists or IP standard access lists with extended ranges in the **snmp-server community** command. You can configure one or more community strings. To remove a specific community string, use the **no snmp-server community** command.

Nonprivileged SNMP Access

You use the **ro** option of the **snmp-server community** command to provide nonprivileged access to your routers via SNMP. The configuration command shown in Example 3-14 sets the agent in the router to allow only SNMP get-request and get-next-request messages that are sent with the community string **secure**.

Example 3-14 *Allowing Selected SNMP Messages Sent with the Community String **secure***

```
router(config)#snmp-server community secure ro
```

Privileged SNMP Access

You use the **rw** option of the **snmp-server community** command to provide privileged access to your routers via SNMP. The configuration command shown in Example 3-15 sets the agent in the router to allow only SNMP set-request messages sent with the community string **semisecure**.

Example 3-15 *Allowing Selected SNMP Messages Sent with the Community String* **semisecure**

```
router(config)#snmp-server community semisecure rw
```

Access List SNMP Access

You can also specify a list of hosts at specific IP addresses that are allowed to send messages to the router by using the **access-list** option of the **snmp-server community** command. The **access-list** option can be used in both nonprivileged and privileged modes. In the configuration shown in Example 3-16, only hosts 10.1.1.4 and 10.1.1.5 are allowed privileged-mode SNMP access to the router.

Example 3-16 *Allowing Privileged-Mode SNMP Access to Hosts 10.1.1.4 and 10.1.1.5*

```
router(config)#access-list 1 permit 10.1.1.4
router(config)#access-list 1 permit 10.1.1.5
router(config)#snmp-server community private rw 1
```

Configuring SNMP Traps and Informs to Only Allowed NMS Systems

You should ensure that you configure the router to send SNMP traps to only the hosts you have designated as NMS systems. A trap is a message sent by an SNMP agent to an NMS, console, or terminal to indicate the occurrence of a significant event such as a specifically defined condition or a threshold that was reached.

You configure the router to send SNMP traps only to designated NMS hosts by using the **snmp-server host** *host* **trap** command. You configure the router to send SNMP informs only to designated NMS hosts with the **snmp-server host** *host* **informs** command.

You use the **snmp-server enable traps** command to globally enable the trap and inform production mechanism for the specified traps and informs.

Some traps and informs are not controlled by the **snmp-server enable traps** command. These items are either enabled by default or are controlled through other commands. For example, by default, SNMP link traps are sent when an interface goes up or down. For interfaces expected to go up and down during normal usage, such as ISDN interfaces, the output generated by these traps might not be useful. Use the **no snmp trap link-status** interface configuration command to disable these traps.

You can optionally specify a value other than the default trap or inform value for the number of retries, the retransmission interval, the maximum number of pending requests, or the source IP address with the optional **snmp-server informs** and **snmp-server trap-source** global configuration commands.

Securing Router-to-Router Communications

Some types of router-to-router communications are subject to eavesdropping, data manipulation, session replay, and rerouting attacks. Some examples include routing updates, router TFTP file transfers, and HTTP access to routers. Router-to-router communications can be secured as described in the following sections. The following subjects are covered:

- Routing protocol authentication
- Secure router configuration files
- Controlling traffic by using filters
- Suppressing routes received in updates from being processed
- Incoming network filters
- A simple example of security policy controlling traffic flow
- Controlling router HTTP access

Routing Protocol Authentication

Routing protocols are vulnerable to eavesdropping and spoofing of routing updates. For example, the RIP routing protocol can be spoofed merely by having a valid IP header checksum atop any arbitrary route updates; the UDP checksum is not used. Cisco IOS Software supports authentication of routing protocol updates to prevent the introduction of unauthorized or false routing messages from unknown sources. Routing protocol authentication is also known as neighbor authentication.

When neighbor authentication has been configured on a router, the router authenticates the source of each routing update packet it receives. This is done by exchanging an authenticating key or signature that is configured on both the sending and receiving router. Figure 3-6 illustrates neighbor authentication, with Routers A and B configured for neighbor authentication. Router A signs its routing update with an authentication signature and sends the routing update to Router B. Router B verifies the authentication signature to ensure that the update has not been altered in transmission.

Two types of neighbor authentication are used in Cisco IOS release 12.0: plaintext authentication and Message Digest Algorithm version 5 (MD5) authentication. Both forms work in the same way, with the exception that MD5 sends a "message digest" of the authenticating key rather than the key itself. The message digest is created using the key and a message, but the key itself is not sent, preventing it from being read while it is being transmitted. Plaintext authentication sends the authenticating key itself over the network.

We will consider how to configure MD5 authentication later in this section. MD5 is covered in more detail in Chapter 13.

Figure 3-6   *Neighbor Router Authentication Securing Routing Protocol Updates*

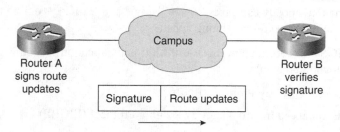

Router A signs route updates	Campus	Router B verifies signature
	Signature	Route updates

NOTE   Plaintext authentication is not recommended for use as part of a security strategy. Its primary use is to avoid accidental changes to the routing infrastructure. Using MD5 authentication, however, is a recommended practice for securing the network infrastructure.

Plaintext Authentication

Each participating neighbor router must share an authenticating key. This key is specified at each router during configuration. Multiple keys can be specified with some protocols; each key must then be identified by a key number.

In general, when a routing update is sent, the following authentication sequence occurs:

1 A router sends a routing update with a key and the corresponding key number to the neighbor router. In protocols that can have only one key, the key number is always 0.

2 The receiving (neighbor) router checks the received key against the same key stored in its own memory.

3 If the two keys match, the receiving router accepts the routing update packet. If the two keys do not match, the routing update packet is rejected.

These routing protocols are supported with plaintext authentication in Cisco IOS Software:

- DRP Server Agent
- Intermediate System-to-Intermediate System (IS-IS)
- Open Shortest Path First (OSPF)
- Routing Information Protocol (RIP) version 2

MD5 Authentication

MD5 authentication works similarly to plaintext authentication except that the key is not sent over the wire. Instead, the router uses the MD5 algorithm to produce a message digest of the key (also called a *hash*). The message digest is then sent instead of the key itself, thus ensuring that nobody can eavesdrop on the line and learn keys during transmission, or modify and retransmit the routing update.

Cisco IOS Software supports the use of MD5 authentication of routing protocol updates for the following protocols:

- Border Gateway Protocol (BGP)
- IP Enhanced Interior Gateway Routing Protocol (EIGRP)
- OSPF
- RIP version 2

MD5 Authentication for EIGRP

MD5 authentication of routing updates for the EIGRP routing protocol secures routing updates. The MD5 keyed digest in the EIGRP packet prevents the introduction of unauthorized or false routing messages from unknown sources. EIGRP route authentication uses MD5 to authenticate routing updates from the EIGRP routing protocol. The MD5 keyed digest in each EIGRP packet prevents the introduction of unauthorized or false routing messages from unapproved sources.

Before you can enable EIGRP route authentication, you must enable EIGRP. To enable authentication of EIGRP packets, follow these steps, beginning in interface configuration mode:

1 Enable MD5 authentication in IP EIGRP packets with the **ip authentication mode eigrp** *autonomous-system* **md5** command.

2 Enable authentication of IP EIGRP packets with the **ip authentication key-chain eigrp** *autonomous-system key-chain* command.

3 Exit to global configuration mode with the **exit** command.

4 Identify a key chain with the **key chain** *name-of-chain* command. Match the name configured in Step 1.

5 Identify the key number with the **key** *number* command in key chain configuration mode.

6 In key chain key configuration mode, identify the key string with the **key-string** *text* command.

7 Optionally specify the time period during which the key can be received with the **accept-lifetime** *start-time* {**infinite** | *end-time* | **duration** *seconds*} command.

8 Optionally specify the time period during which the key can be sent with the **send-lifetime** *start-time* {**infinite** | *end-time* | **duration** *seconds*} command.

Each key has its own key identifier (specified with the **key** *number* command), which is stored locally. The combination of the key identifier and the interface associated with the message uniquely identifies the authentication algorithm and MD5 authentication key in use.

You can configure multiple keys with lifetimes. Only one authentication packet is sent, regardless of how many valid keys exist. The software examines the key numbers in order, from lowest to highest, and uses the first valid key it encounters. Note that the router needs to know the time. Refer to the NTP and calendar commands in the "Performing Basic System Management" chapter of the *Configuration Fundamentals Configuration Guide*.

An Example of EIGRP Route Authentication Using MD5

Consider the sample configuration shown in Example 3-17 of route authentication for EIGRP using MD5 and refer to Figure 3-6 if needed.

Example 3-17 *Configuring Route Authentication for EIGRP Using MD5*

```
! Router A
ip authentication mode eigrp 1 md5
ip authentication key-chain eigrp 1 cbobw
key chain cbobw
  key 1
    key-string 0987654321
    accept-lifetime infinite
    send-lifetime Jan 01 2001 infinite
  key 2
    key-string 1234567890
    accept-lifetime infinite
    send-lifetime Jan 01 2002 infinite
  exit
!
router eigrp 200
 network 10.1.1.0
 network 10.1.2.0
! Router B
ip authentication mode eigrp 1 md5
ip authentication key-chain eigrp 1 cpw
key chain cpw
  key 1
    key-string 0987654321
    accept-lifetime infinite
    send-lifetime 04:00:00 Jan 01 2001
     04:00:00 Jan 01 2002
  key 2
    key-string 1234567890
    accept-lifetime infinite
    send-lifetime Jan 01 2002 infinite
```

continues

Example 3-17 *Configuring Route Authentication for EIGRP Using MD5 (Continued)*

```
   exit
router eigrp 200
 network 10.2.1.0
 network 10.2.2.0
```

In this scenario, MD5 is used to authenticate routing updates for EIGRP. Router A accepts and attempts to verify the MD5 digest of any EIGRP packet hashed with key 1 or key 2. All other MD5 packets are dropped. Router A sends all EIGRP packets with key 2. Router B accepts key 1 or key 2 and sends key 1.

CAUTION As with all keys, passwords, and other security secrets, it is imperative that you closely guard authenticating keys used in neighbor authentication. The security benefits of this feature depend on you keeping all authenticating keys confidential. Also, when performing router management tasks with SNMP, do not ignore the risk associated with sending keys using nonencrypted SNMP.

Secure Router Configuration Files

If a router regularly uploads and downloads configuration files from a TFTP or Maintenance Operations Protocol (MOP) server, anyone who can access the server can modify the router configuration files stored on the server, as illustrated in Figure 3-7. TFTP file exchanges are vulnerable to eavesdropping or interception by network intruders between the TFTP clients and servers.

Figure 3-7 *Vulnerable TFTP File Exchanges*

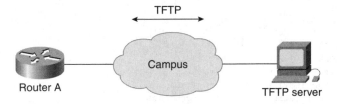

It's important to protect and limit access to TFTP servers containing router configuration files, keeping in mind the following:

- Configuration files can be stored and uploaded/downloaded to a TFTP server.
- TFTP is not a secure protocol, meaning that it does not require a password.
- Anyone with access to the TFTP server can modify the router configuration file.
- Good host security is required.

- You can use a Kerberized rcp to copy configurations encrypted across a network on Cisco routers. See Chapter 4, "Examining Cisco AAA Security Technology," for more information on Kerberized rcp.

- TFTP servers can be detected through the use of port scanning software. It might be a good idea to manually enable and disable the TFTP server software.

Limiting the TFTP Servers Used Via SNMP

You can limit access to the TFTP servers used for saving and loading configuration files via SNMP to the servers specified in an access list. Use the **snmp-server tftp-server-list** *number* command to limit TFTP servers used for configuration file copies via SNMP to the servers in an access list. Cisco routers support loading configuration and software images via FTP, which might be preferred over TFTP.

Controlling Traffic by Using Filters

Access lists are a powerful way to control router traffic such as routing updates and ordinary traffic. Access list configuration is covered in detail in Appendix C, "Configuring Standard and Extended Access Lists." Consider the following tips on using access lists to control traffic:

- Use access lists to control whether traffic is forwarded or blocked at the router interface.

- Access lists do not authenticate individual users but filter based on information in the packets, such as destination address or port, source address or port, and upper-layer protocol.

Filtering Networks in Routing Updates

Filtering networks in routing updates helps secure networks in two ways:

- **It increases security**—If a network is not advertised, no apparent route exists to that network, and intruders will have more trouble getting there. Therefore, limit the scope of advertising routes where router security is an issue.

- **It increases the network's stability**—Filtering networks in router updates provides protection against receiving false information in routing updates due to misconfiguration or intentional activity that could cause routing problems.

The following four sections describe scenarios concerning and methods for filtering routing updates. Figure 3-8 applies to the first two scenarios, showing that access lists applied to network interfaces with the **distribute-list** command are useful for filtering incoming or outgoing routing updates.

Figure 3-8 *Access Lists Filtering Routing Updates*

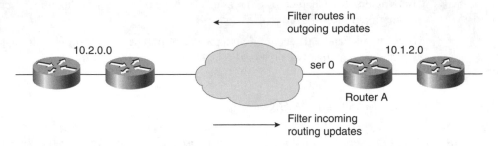

Suppressing Routes from Being Advertised in Routing Updates

To prevent potential intruders from knowing your network configuration, you should not advertise "externally" internal networks that will be accessed only by internal users. In an enterprise network, certain groups such as the Sales department of the XYZ Company might not want to advertise internal networks to network devices outside the Sales network. You suppress networks from being advertised in routing updates by using an access list, as shown in Example 3-18.

Example 3-18 *Suppressing Network Advertisement in Routing Updates with an Access List*

```
router(config)#access-list 45 deny 10.1.2.0 0.0.0.255
router(config)#access-list 45 permit any any
router(config)#router eigrp 200
router(config-router)#distribute-list 45 out serial0
```

These commands configure an access list to prevent advertisement of updates from the 10.1.2.0 network and apply the access list to outgoing EIGRP traffic on the serial 0 interface.

Suppressing Routes Received in Updates from Being Processed

You should suppress networks listed in updates from being accepted and acted upon by a routing process. Suppressing networks listed in updates keeps a router from using routes that might be spurious, helping prevent route spoofing. Access list filters are used to accept routing updates from only specific, known routers on the network to be placed into the routing table in the router. This feature does not apply to OSPF or IS-IS. You suppress routes from being processed as shown in Example 3-19.

Example 3-19 *Suppressing Routes from Being Processed*

```
router(config)#access-list 46 permit 10.2.0.0 0.0.255.255
router(config)#router eigrp 200
router(config-router)#distribute-list 46 in serial0
```

This example configures an access list to accept routing updates only from a trusted network, 10.2.0.0, and applies the access list to incoming traffic on the serial 0 interface.

Suppressing Routing Updates Through an Interface

To prevent other routers on a local network from learning about routes dynamically, you can keep routing update messages from being sent through a router interface. This feature applies to all IP-based routing protocols except BGP and EGP. You suppress the sending of routing updates through the specified router interface by using the **passive-interface** *type number* command. The interface will still listen to (accept) dynamic routing information that comes into it.

Filtering Sources of Routing Information

You can use the administrative distance parameter to allow a router to intelligently discriminate between sources of routing information. *Administrative distance* is a rating of the trustworthiness of a routing information source such as an individual router or a group of routers. The router will always pick the route whose routing protocol has the lowest administrative distance. In a large network, some routing protocols and some routers can be more reliable than others as sources of routing information. You filter sources of routing information by using the **distance** *weight* [*address mask* [*access-list-number | name*]] [*ip*] command.

Incoming Network Filters

You use access lists to filter incoming packets from inside networks to prevent spoofing attacks from outside your network. You should configure access lists to deny packets from outside your network that have a source address from inside your network. Make sure you apply filtering only on edge routers because filters reduce router performance. Consider the examples of incoming network filters, as shown in Figure 3-9. They show that you use access lists to create incoming network filters, controlling spoofing and access to internal networks and hosts.

Figure 3-9 *Incoming Network Filters Using Access Lists Control Spoofing and Access to Internal Networks and Hosts*

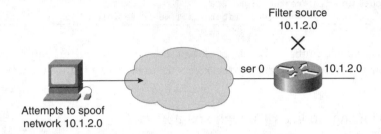

You should configure your router to never accept any internal network addresses or RFC 1918–reserved addresses from an external source (such as 192.168, 10.0, and 172. addresses). The command in Example 3-20 configures an access list to deny spoofed packets from the internal 10.1.2.0 network and logs such attempts.

Example 3-20 *Configuring an Access List to Deny Spoofed Packets from the Internal Network*

```
router(config)#access-list 102 deny ip 10.1.2.0 0.0.0.255 any log
```

The command in Example 3-21 configures the access list to allow ongoing established traffic using the **established** command option; a match occurs if the TCP header has the ACK or RST bits set.

Example 3-21 *Configuring an Access List to Allow Ongoing Established Traffic*

```
router(config)#access-list 102 permit tcp 10.1.2.0 0.0.255.255
  10.16.2.0 0.0.0.255 established
```

The commands in Example 3-22 apply the access list to the incoming portion of the interface.

Example 3-22 *Applying the Access List to the Incoming Portion of the Interface*

```
router(config)#interface serial 0
router(config-if)#ip access-group 102 in
```

A Simple Example of Security Policy Controlling Traffic Flow

Access lists should be designed to support your network security policy. Here is an example of a simple security policy that controls traffic flow in a network, as illustrated in Figure 3-10:

- Permit all outgoing traffic.
- Permit incoming traffic if originated internally to prevent spoofing.

- Allow incoming responses to established outgoing traffic.
- Deny all other incoming traffic and record any attempts at unauthorized access by logging them.

Figure 3-10 *Using Access Lists to Control Traffic Flow*

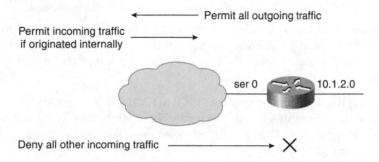

The commands in Example 3-23 enact the security policy.

Example 3-23 *Enacting a Security Policy That Controls Traffic Flow in a Network*

```
router(config)#access-list 47 permit 10.1.2.0 0.0.0.255
router(config)#access-list 103 permit tcp any any established
router(config)#access-list 103 deny ip any any log
router(config)#interface serial 0
router(config-if)#ip access-group 47 out
router(config-if)#ip access-group 103 in
```

Controlling Router HTTP Access

Cisco IOS Software now includes an HTTP server (releases 11.0(6) and later), which makes configurations easier but opens new security holes. The HTTP server is disabled by default. You can use a Web browser to issue Cisco IOS commands to your router, as illustrated in Figure 3-11.

Figure 3-11 *Controlling Router HTTP Access by Using Access Lists*

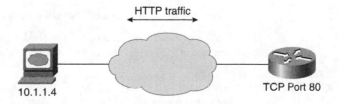

Consider the following key points about HTTP access:

- HTTP access is off by default.
- You can configure an access list to specify the addresses allowed to access TCP port 80 on the router.
- HTTP uses password security similar to console and vty access.

You can let a Cisco 1003, Cisco 1004, or Cisco 1005 router be configured from a browser using the Cisco IOS ClickStart software. You can let any router be monitored or have its configuration modified with the Cisco Web browser interface using the **ip http server** global configuration command.

You specify the port to be used by the Cisco IOS ClickStart software or the Cisco Web browser interface using the **ip http port** global configuration command to set a port used by client software, such as port 8080. To use the default port (port 80), use the **no** form of this command.

To assign an access list to the HTTP server used by the Cisco IOS ClickStart software or the Cisco Web browser interface, use the **ip http access-class** global configuration command. To remove the assigned access list, use the **no** form of this command. Assign a standard IP access list number in the range 0 to 99, as configured by the **access-list** (standard) command. You assign the access list using the **ip http access-class** command, as shown in the sample configuration in Example 3-24.

Example 3-24 *Assigning an Access List Using the **ip http access-class** Command*

```
router(config)#access-list 52 permit 10.1.1.4 0.0.0.0
router(config)#ip http access-class 52
```

You use the **ip http authentication** global configuration command to specify a particular authentication method to authenticate IP HTTP server users, providing better security if you need to use the router's HTTP server. The command syntax is as follows:

```
ip http authentication {aaa | enable | local | tacacs}
```

The command keywords have the following meanings:

Keyword	Description
aaa	Indicates that the AAA facility is used for authentication
enable	Indicates that the enable password method, which is the default method of HTTP server user authentication, is used for authentication
local	Indicates that the local user database, as defined on the Cisco router or access server, is used for authentication
tacacs	Indicates that the Terminal Access Controller Access Control System (TACACS) or XTACACS server is used for authentication

Securing Ethernet Switches

This section describes how to configure network security features on Cisco Catalyst series Ethernet switches, as well as Ethernet switch port security and Ethernet switch access security. This section covers the following topics:

- Controlling Ethernet switch management access
- Ethernet switch port security
- Ethernet switch access security

Controlling Ethernet Switch Management Access

The first step in configuring Ethernet switch security is to secure management access to the switch just as you would with a router. You can secure login access with the **set password** command to change the normal (login) mode password on the switch. You can use the **set enablepass** command to change the privileged (enable) mode password on the switch.

You can secure Telnet and SNMP access to the switch with IP permit lists. IP permit prevents inbound Telnet and SNMP access to the switch from unauthorized source IP addresses. All other TCP/IP services (such as IP **traceroute** and IP **ping**) continue to work normally when you enable the IP permit list. Outbound Telnet, Trivial File Transfer Protocol (TFTP), and other IP-based services are unaffected by the IP permit list. You need to configure and enable IP permit lists with the **ip permit list** series of commands. First you add entries of permitted Telnet clients or NMS systems, and then you apply the permit list.

You can also configure AAA features for a local or remote security database to control access to switches with the **set authentication** and **set authorization** commands.

Ethernet Switch Port Security

Secure port filtering is an access security feature on Cisco Catalyst series Ethernet switches that blocks input to an Ethernet or Fast Ethernet port from an unauthorized station. Secure port filtering is also known as Media Access Control (MAC) address lockdown.

Secure port filtering blocks input to a port when the MAC address of the station attempting to access the port is different from the MAC address specified for that port.

When a secured port receives a packet, the source MAC address of the packet is compared to the secured source address configured for the port. If the MAC address of the device attached to the port differs from the secured address, the port is disabled, the link LED for that port turns orange, and a link-down trap is sent to the SNMP manager.

You can specify the secure MAC address of the port manually, or you can have the port dynamically learn the MAC address of the connected device. After the address is specified or learned, it is stored in NVRAM and is maintained even after a reset.

NOTE Because multiple VLANs are configured to pass through a trunk port (versus the usual single station and VLAN per port), port security on the trunk port is not possible.

You use the **set port security** command to set a specified port's MAC address as the given address. If the MAC address is not given, the address is learned. The command syntax is as follows:

```
Console>set port security mod_num/port_num(s) enable [mac_addr]
```

After the address is configured or learned, it remains unchanged until the system relearns it when you reenter the command. The MAC address is stored in NVRAM and is maintained even after the reset. When a packet's source address does not match the allowed address, the port through which the packet came is disabled, and a link-down trap is sent to the SNMP manager. You can configure a port to shut down until the administrator enables it, or you can configure it to become enabled again automatically after a preset time.

The **show port** command displays all security information such as MAC addresses, the port counter values, and whether security is enabled or disabled, as shown in Example 3-25.

Example 3-25 *Displaying Port Security Information with the* **show port** *Command*

```
Console> (enable) set port security 3/1 enable 01-02-03-04-05-06
Console> (enable) set port security 3/2 enable
Console>
Console> (enable) show port 3
Port  Status  Vlan  Level  Duplex  Speed  Type
----  ------  ----  -----  ------  -----  ---------
3/1   connect  1    normal  half    10     10 BASE-T
3/2   connect  1    normal  half    10     10 BASE-T


Port   Security  Secure-Src-Addr     Last-Src-Addr       Shutdown
----   --------  ----------------    ----------------    -------
3/1    enabled   01-02-03-04-05-06   01-02-03-04-05-06   No
3/2    enabled   05-06-07-08-09-10   10-11-12-13-14-15   Yes
Console> (enable)
```

Note that the MAC address configured in the first command appears in the port security section of the **show** command. Also note that, in the last command of the **show** command, the port is shut down because the secure source address does not match the last source address.

Ethernet Switch Access Security

IP permit prevents inbound Telnet and SNMP access to the switch from unauthorized source IP addresses. All other TCP/IP services (such as IP **traceroute** and IP **ping**) continue to work normally when you enable the IP permit list. Outbound Telnet, TFTP, and other IP-based services are unaffected by the IP permit list.

You can use the IP permit list whether or not TACACS is enabled on a network. When TACACS is enabled on a network, the IP permit list provides a first level of checking based on a source IP address. The IP permit list applies only to inbound Telnet and SNMP services. You can configure up to ten entries in the permit list. Each entry consists of an IP address and mask pair in dotted-decimal format. Zeros in the mask indicate don't-care bits in the address.

When the IP permit feature is enabled, Telnet access and SNMP services are authorized only for the IP addresses of the hosts configured in the permit list. Notifications of unauthorized access attempts are available through SNMP traps and syslog options. Attempts from the same unauthorized host might trigger notifications as often as every ten minutes.

The IP permit list is disabled by default. Enable the IP permit list by entering the **set ip permit enable** command in privileged mode. You can specify an IP address to remove from the IP permit list with the **clear ip permit** command in privileged mode. You can disable an IP permit list on the switch with the **set ip permit disable** command. You can verify the IP permit list configuration with the **show ip permit** command. Example 3-26 shows how to add IP addresses to the IP permit list and verify the configuration.

Example 3-26 *Adding IP Addresses to the IP Permit List and Verifying the Configuration*

```
Console> (enable) set ip permit 172.16.1.11
Console> set ip permit 172.16.11.0 255.255.255.0
Console> set ip permit enable
Console> show ip permit
IP permit list feature enabled.
Permit List          Mask
---------------      ---------------
172.16.1.11
172.16.11.0          255.255.255.0
Denied IP Address    Last Accessed Time      Type
-----------------    ------------------      ------
172.16.1.11          01/20/2000,07:45:20     SNMP
172.16.11.3          01/21/2000,14:23:05     Telnet
Console>
```

Summary

This section summarizes the main points of the chapter:

- You should secure physical access to network devices and communications channels; otherwise, they can easily be compromised. Have sufficient contingency plans for emergencies that might affect network equipment.

- You should secure the administrative interface by configuring console and Telnet passwords and access privileges.

- You should configure device banner messages as follows: They should include a warning to potential network intruders, they should never welcome intruders, and they should be placed on any potential network access method.

- You should use the password encryption capabilities of Cisco IOS Software, but do not place too much trust in them as a sole security method. Ensure that secure passwords are used for network users.

- You can control SNMP access to network devices by configuring community strings and by using access lists to limit NMS access to SNMP agents and MIBs in network devices.

- You can use routing protocol authentication to secure routing protocol updates. Use MD5 authentication if at all possible to prevent transmission of authentication passwords that can be easily spoofed or compromised.

- You can ensure that router configuration files are secure by using host security and SNMP capabilities.

- You can use standard and extended access lists to control network traffic through routers.

- You can control router HTTP access by using access lists and **ip http** commands if a browser-based configuration tool is used to configure the router. HTTP access is turned off by default.

- You can control Ethernet switch access by securing management access to the switch and by using secure port filtering.

Case Study: Configuring Basic Network Security

This case study illustrates how to implement the facts and concepts taught in this chapter in the hypothetical XYZ Company. Read the case study scenario, examine the topology diagram, and read the security policy. Then analyze the sample configuration to see how the security policy statements are enacted for the Cisco routers.

Case Study Scenario

The XYZ Company wants to begin securing its network infrastructure by securely configuring its campus routers against internal threats. The company can easily begin to protect its network without any additional expense by having you configure the routers for basic security.

Topology

Figure 3-12 illustrates the portion of the XYZ network that will be configured in this case study. Note that the focus here is on the R2 and R3 campus routers.

Figure 3-12 *Configuring the R2 and R3 Routers According to the XYZ Company Network Security Policy*

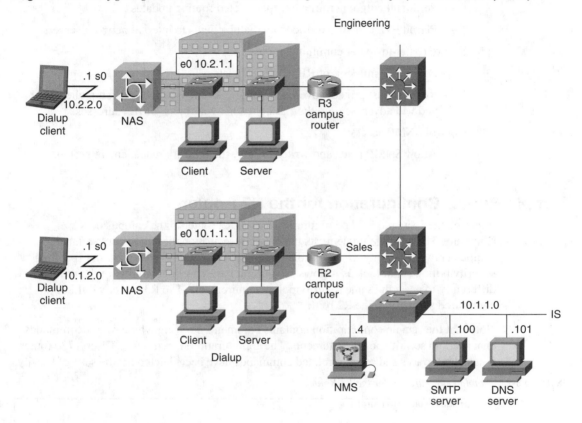

Network Security Policy

The security policy for the XYZ Company campus security contains the following details for the Sales and Engineering networks:

- Secure console and Telnet access:
    - — Secure console and Telnet access with unique passwords.
    - — Configure session timeouts to shut down EXEC mode on idle sessions.
    - — Create a router banner message to discourage intruders.
    - — Permit Telnet access to network access servers only from the NMS.

- Control router-to-router traffic:
  - Permit incoming traffic only if originated internally (established).
  - Permit any campus equipment or dialup client to ping any other campus equipment or dialup client to allow testing of connectivity.
  - Permit all outgoing traffic except selected routing updates.
  - Permit FTP and Web traffic from dialup clients to internal network servers.
- Secure router-to-router communications:
  - Permit transmission of RIP routing updates.
  - Routers must protect advertisement of internal networks to dialup clients and will advertise only their assigned network block of IP addresses.
- Control SNMP access:
  - Allow SNMP reads and writes only by the network management system.

Sample Router Configuration for the R2 Router

Examine the Example 3-27 configuration for the R2 router in the campus of XYZ Company. The example implements the network security policy statements related to campus network security. One possible configuration of the R2 router for the specified security policy might look as follows. You might have chosen to configure the router differently to enact the same security policy requirements. The R3 router would be configured similarly to the R2 router.

Note that the sample configuration contains comments showing which router commands enact certain security policy statements. The configuration shown is for a Cisco 1720 router. Unused interfaces and other unrelated commands have been deleted for the sake of brevity.

Example 3-27 *Sample Configuration for the R2 Router*

```
p1r2#show running-config

Current configuration:
!
version 12.0
service password-encryption
no service udp-small-servers
no service tcp-small-servers
!
hostname p1r2
!
! Secure console and Telnet passwords with different passwords
! The service password-encryption command encrypted the passwords

enable secret 5 $1$b4X5$7A7IUNmzGm8vOmi9nBkC1/
enable password 7 15141905172924
!
```

Example 3-27 *Sample Configuration for the R2 Router (Continued)*

```
ip host modem 2002 10.1.1.1
!
!
! Access-list 101 is applied to incoming traffic on this interface
interface FastEthernet0
 ip address 10.1.1.1 255.255.255.0
 ip access-group 101 in
 no mop enabled
!
!
interface Serial0
 physical-layer async
 ip address 10.1.2.1 255.255.255.0
 ip tcp header-compression passive
 encapsulation ppp
 bandwidth 38
 async mode interactive
 peer default ip address pool classpool
 no fair-queue
 no cdp enable
!
! Permit transmission of RIP routing updates
! Routers must protect advertisement of internal networks
!  to dialup clients and will only advertise
!  their assigned network block of IP addresses
router rip
 version 1
 network 10.0.0.0
 distribute-list 21 out Ethernet0
 distribute-list 22 out Serial2
 distance 2
!
ip local pool classpool 10.1.2.2 10.1.2.10
ip classless
access-list 20 permit 10.1.1.4
! Permit transmission of RIP routing updates
! Routers must protect advertisement of internal networks to
!  dialup clients and will only advertise
!  their assigned network block of IP addresses
access-list 21 permit 10.1.2.0 0.0.0.255
! Deny routing updates from campus to be advertised to dialup
access-list 22 deny   10.1.0.0 0.0.255.255
! Allow SNMP reads and writes only by the network management
!  system (the Windows NT server)
access-list 25 permit 10.1.1.4
! Permit Telnet access to network access servers only from the Windows NT server
access-list 101 permit tcp host 10.1.1.4 any eq telnet
! Permit incoming traffic only if originated internally (established)
! Permit all outgoing traffic except for selected routing updates
access-list 101 permit tcp any any established
! Permit any campus equipment or dialup clients to ping any other campus
!  equipment or dialup client to allow testing of connectivity
```

continues

Example 3-27 *Sample Configuration for the R2 Router (Continued)*

```
access-list 101 permit icmp 10.1.0.0 0.0.255.255 any echo
access-list 101 permit icmp 10.1.0.0 0.0.255.255 any echo-reply
! Permit FTP and Web traffic from dialup clients to internal network servers
! Permits incoming FTP and Web sessions from campus or dialup clients to the
! PC A "FTP and Web servers"
access-list 101 permit tcp 10.1.0.0 0.0.255.255 10.1.2.0 0.0.0.255 eq ftp
access-list 101 permit tcp 10.1.0.0 0.0.255.255 10.1.2.0 0.0.0.255 eq ftp-data
access-list 101 permit tcp 10.1.0.0 0.0.255.255 10.1.2.0 0.0.0.255 eq www
access-list 101 permit udp any any eq rip
! Permits RIP routing updates to be received by R2
! Permits TCP traffic from CiscoSecure server on nt1
! Deny all other IP traffic and log such traffic attempts
access-list 101 deny   ip any any log
! Allow SNMP reads and writes only by the network management
! system (the Windows NT server)
snmp-server party nt1 iso.2.3.4.10.1.4.1 udp 0.0.0.0 0 authentication snmpv1 pc
snmp-server community KingLear RW 25
! Create a router banner message to discourage intruders
banner motd ^C Warning: Unauthorized users will be prosecuted ^C
!
! Secure console and Telnet passwords with different passwords
! Configure session timeouts to shut down EXEC mode on idle sessions
line con 0
 exec-timeout 60 0
 password 7 02050D480809
 login
line 2
 password 7 13061E010803
 autoselect during-login
 autoselect ppp
 login local
 modem InOut
 modem autoconfigure type usr_sportster
 transport input all
 stopbits 1
 rxspeed 115200
 txspeed 115200
 flowcontrol hardware
line aux 0
line vty 0 4
! Permit Telnet access to network access servers only from
! the Windows NT
access-class 20 in
! Configure session timeouts to shut down EXEC mode on idle sessions
 exec-timeout 5 0
! Secure console and Telnet passwords with different passwords
 password 7 13061E010803
 login
!
end
```

Review Questions

Answer the following review questions, which delve into some of the key facts and concepts covered in this chapter:

1 What are some advantages of taking the time to ensure that the equipment that makes up your network infrastructure is as secure as possible?

2 What two Cisco IOS commands would you use to configure console and Telnet login passwords?

3 What are some key commands that are useful for securing the administrator interface in line configuration mode?

4 What command would you use to create hierarchical levels of administrator privileges?

5 What three Cisco IOS commands would you enter to restrict Telnet access to a router with five configured vty ports to a host with an address of 10.16.4.1?

6 How can you prevent an intruder NMS from accessing an SNMP agent?

7 What Cisco IOS feature would you use to secure routing updates from spoofing attacks for the EIGRP routing protocol?

8 What are four methods and their commands used to control router broadcast or processing of routing updates?

9 What three Cisco IOS commands would you enter to prevent the broadcast of IGRP (autonomous system 100) routing updates on an Ethernet 0 interface from a 16.17.1.0 network on an Ethernet 1 interface?

10 What are two methods used to control Ethernet switch security?

References

The topics considered in this chapter are complex and should be studied further to more fully understand them and put them to use. Use the following references to learn more about the topics in this chapter.

General Router Security Configuration

Refer to the chapters in the *Cisco IOS Release 12.0 Security Configuration Guide* called "Security Overview," "Traffic Filtering and Firewalls," and "Other Security Features" for an overview of how to configure general security on Cisco routers.

Refer to the chapter in the *Cisco IOS Release 12.0 Security Command Reference* called "Other Security Features," in the "Router and Network Monitoring Commands" section, for specific commands you can use to configure general security on Cisco routers.

Standard and Extended Access Lists

Refer to the chapters in the *Cisco IOS Release 12.0 Network Protocols Configuration Guide* called "Configuring IP Services," and "IP Addressing and Services," in the "Configuring IP Services" section, for information on how to configure standard and extended access lists.

Refer to the chapter in the *Cisco IOS Release 12.0 Network Protocols Command Reference* called "IP Addressing and Services," in the "IP Services Commands" section, for specific standard and extended **access-list** commands.

SNMP

Refer to the chapter in the *Cisco IOS Release 12.0 Configuration Fundamentals Configuration Guide* called "System Management," in the "Monitoring the Router and Network" section, for an overview of how to configure SNMP on Cisco routers.

Refer to the chapter in the *Cisco IOS Release 12.0 Configuration Fundamentals Command Reference* called "System Management Commands," in the "Router and Network Monitoring Commands" section, for specific commands you can use to configure SNMP on Cisco routers.

Neighbor Router Authentication

Refer to the chapter in the *Cisco IOS Release 12.0 Security Configuration Guide* called "Other Security Features," in the "Neighbor Router Authentication: Overview and Guidelines" section, for an overview of route authentication. Refer to the "Finding Neighbor Authentication Configuration Information" subsection to find configuration commands used to configure neighbor router authentication for supported protocols.

Ethernet Switch Security

Refer to the *Catalyst 6000/6500 Series Software Configuration Guide* (5.2), in the "Configuring Network Security" section, for an overview of how to configure Ethernet switch security for the Catalyst 6000/6500 series.

Refer to the software documentation for the Catalyst 5000, 4000, 2948G, 2926G, and 2926 series switches (4.5), in the chapters called "Software Configuration Guide," "Controlling Access to the Switch Using Authentication," and "Configuring Secure Port Filtering," for an overview of how to configure Ethernet switch security for that Catalyst series of switches.

Dialup Security

Upon completing this chapter, you will be able to do the following:

- Describe the components of the AAA model
- Describe access password technologies
- Describe how authentication over PPP works
- Describe the interaction of PAP and CHAP authentication
- Compare the capabilities of each of the security server types
- Describe Cisco security servers

CHAPTER 4

Examining Cisco AAA Security Technology

This chapter presents an overview of the authentication, authorization, and accounting (AAA) architecture and the security technologies associated with it. This chapter contains information required to implement the access security solutions using the Cisco products covered in Chapter 5, "Configuring the Network Access Server for AAA Security," and Chapter 6, "Configuring CiscoSecure ACS and TACACS+/RADIUS." This chapter generally avoids coverage of "generic" access security that isn't related to Cisco products.

Securing Network Access by Using AAA

Unauthorized access and repudiation in the campus, dialup, and Internet environments creates the potential for network intruders to gain access to sensitive network equipment and services. The AAA architecture gives legitimate users the ability to access networked assets while limiting unauthorized access and repudiation in the campus, dialup, and Internet environments.

The AAA Security Architecture

Network access security—whether it involves campus, dialup, or Internet access—is based on a modular architecture that has three components:

- **Authentication**—Requires users to prove that they really are who they say they are, utilizing a username and password, challenge/response, token cards, and other methods:

  "I am user student, and my password validateme proves it."

- **Authorization**—After authenticating the user, authorization services decide which resources the user is allowed to access and which operations the user is allowed to perform:

  "User student can access host NT_Server with Telnet."

- **Accounting**—Accounting records what the user actually did, what he accessed, and how long he accessed it, for accounting, billing, and auditing purposes. Accounting keeps track of how network resources are used. Auditing can be used to track network access and to detect network intrusions:

"User student accessed host NT_Server with Telnet 15 times."

Table 4-1 summarizes access security problems and shows the AAA methods that can be used to solve them. It also shows some ways in which AAA methods are accomplished.

Table 4-1 *Access Security Problems and Solutions*

Security Problem	AAA Method	How It's Accomplished
Unauthorized access: • Campus • Dialup • Internet	• Authentication • Authorization	• Passwords • Access security in network equipment • Security servers
Repudiation	Accounting	• Accounting features in network equipment • Security servers

Note that the solutions to securing network access summarized in Table 4-1 all include at least one of the three AAA methods supported in Cisco products. The solutions may also include AAA security server (remote security database) standards supported by Cisco products, including Terminal Access Controller Access Control System Plus (TACACS+), Remote Access Dial-In User Service (RADIUS), and Kerberos. Each AAA method and remote security database standard is examined in more detail in this chapter.

AAA and Access Traffic

Remote access is an integral part of the corporate mission. Traveling salespeople, executives, remote office staff, telecommuters, and others need to communicate by connecting to the main office LAN.

A remote user will have the needed application software (for example, FTP or Telnet client software), a protocol stack (for example, Transmission Control Protocol/Internet Protocol [TCP/IP], Internetwork Packet Exchange [IPX], AppleTalk), and link-layer drivers installed on the remote client to make network connections.

The application software and protocol stacks encapsulate the higher-layer data and protocols in link-layer protocols such as Serial Line Interface Protocol (SLIP) and Point-to-Point Protocol (PPP). The encapsulated packets are transmitted across the dialup line in analog or digital form, depending on the type of telecommunication line used.

The dialup networking components typically consist of a remote client system (Windows 95/98/2000 PC or Macintosh), the telephone network connections (Public Switched Telephone Network [PSTN] or Integrated Services Digital Network [ISDN]), a network access server (such as a Cisco 5300 network access server), and a remote security database running security server software (CiscoSecure Access Control Sever [ACS] running TACACS+), as shown in Figure 4-1.

Figure 4-1   *AAA Technologies Securing Character- and Packet-Mode Traffic*

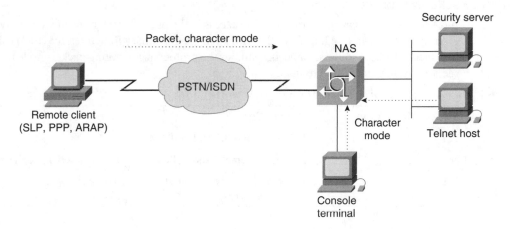

AAA technologies in the remote client system, the network access server, and the security server work together to secure dialup access. The network access server implements AAA protocols to handle the AAA services.

AAA and Character-Mode Traffic

AAA technologies are useful for protecting character-mode or line-mode access to network access servers and other network equipment. In Cisco routers, AAA secures character-mode traffic during login sessions via the line types described in Table 4-2.

Table 4-2   *Line Types Generating Character-Mode Traffic Secured by AAA*

Line Type	Description
Aux	Auxiliary EIA/TIA-232 DTE port on Cisco routers and Ethernet switches used for modem support and asynchronous access
Console	Console EIA/TIA-232 DCE port on Cisco routers and Ethernet switches used for asynchronous access to device configuration modes
tty	Standard EIA/TIA-232 DTE asynchronous line on a network access server

continues

Table 4-2 *Line Types Generating Character-Mode Traffic Secured by AAA (Continued)*

Line Type	Description
vty	Virtual terminal line and interface terminating incoming character streams that do not have a physical connection to the access server or router

AAA and Packet-Mode Traffic

AAA technologies can also protect dialup access in the packet or interface mode via async, group-async, Basic Rate Interface (BRI) ISDN lines, or Primary Rate Interface (PRI) ISDN interfaces on Cisco routers. Table 4-3 outlines the protocols generating packet-mode traffic secured by AAA on Cisco routers.

Table 4-3 *Protocols Generating Packet-Mode Traffic Secured by AAA*

Packet-Mode Type	Description
PPP	PPP on serial or ISDN interfaces
arap	AppleTalk Remote Access Protocol (ARAP) on serial interfaces
NASI	NetWare Access Server Interface (NASI) clients connecting through the access server on serial interfaces

Authentication Methods

The main authentication methods considered are username and password, S/Key, token card and server, Password Authentication Protocol (PAP), and Challenge Handshake Authentication Protocol (CHAP) authentication. Each is covered in the following sections.

Username and Password Authentication

The most common user authentication method is the use of usernames and passwords. Username/password combination methods range from weak to strong in authentication power. Simple authentication methods use a database of usernames and passwords, whereas more complex methods use one-time passwords. Consider each of the methods shown in Figure 4-2, from the weakest at the bottom of the figure to the strongest at the top. Stronger authentication methods are better able to resist attempts to gain unauthorized access. Weaker methods are often easier to use and administer, and stronger methods are often harder to use and administer. Simple authentication methods use a database of usernames and passwords, and more complex methods use one-time passwords.

Figure 4-2   *Authentication Methods and Ease of Use*

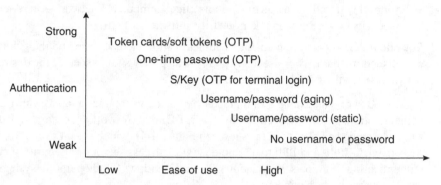

The authentication methods outlined in Figure 4-2 are as follows:

- **No username or password**—Some system administrators and users opt to not use the username/password capabilities of their network access systems. This is obviously the least-secure option. A network intruder only has to discover the access method to gain access to the networked system.

- **Username/password (static)**—Stays the same until changed by the system administrator or user. Susceptible to playback attacks and password-cracking programs.

- **Username/password (aging)**—Expires after a set time (usually 30 to 60 days) and must be reset, usually by the user, before network access is granted. Susceptible to playback attacks and password cracking but to a lesser degree than static username/password pairs.

- **S/Key one-time passwords (OTP)**—An OTP method generating multiple passwords typically used for terminal logins. In S/Key, a secret passphrase is used to generate the first password, and each successive password is generated from the previous one by encrypting it. A list of accessible passwords is generated by S/Key server software and is distributed to users.

- **One-time passwords (OTP)**—A stronger method, providing the most secure username/password method. Most OTP systems are based on a secret passphrase, which is used to generate a list of passwords. These passphrases are good for only one login and therefore are not useful to anyone who manages to eavesdrop and capture the passphrase. S/Key is an OTP method typically used for terminal logins.

- **Token cards/soft tokens**—Based on something you have (for example, a token card) and something you know (for example, a token card personal identification number [PIN]). Token cards are typically small electronic devices about the size and complexity of a credit card-size calculator. There are many token card vendors, and each has its own token card server. The PIN is entered into the card, which generates a secure password. A token server receives and validates the password. The password interplay usually consists of a remote client computer, a network access server, and a security server running token security software.

You should choose and implement an authentication method based on the guidelines established in your network security policy. The policy should specify the desired balance between strength of security and ease of use.

Figure 4-3 shows an example of dialup access using usernames and password authentication. On the client end, Windows NT Dialup Networking prompts the dialup user for a username and password (as shown in Figure 4-4), which is sent over communication lines using TCP/IP and PPP to a remote network access server or a security server for authentication. Windows 95, Windows 98, and Windows 2000 operating systems have a similar authentication window.

Figure 4-3 *A Remote Client Sending a Username and Password to a Network Access Server for Authentication*

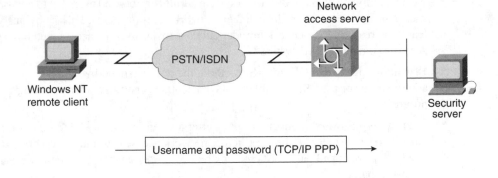

Figure 4-4 *The Windows NT Dialup Access Username and Password Authentication Dialog Box*

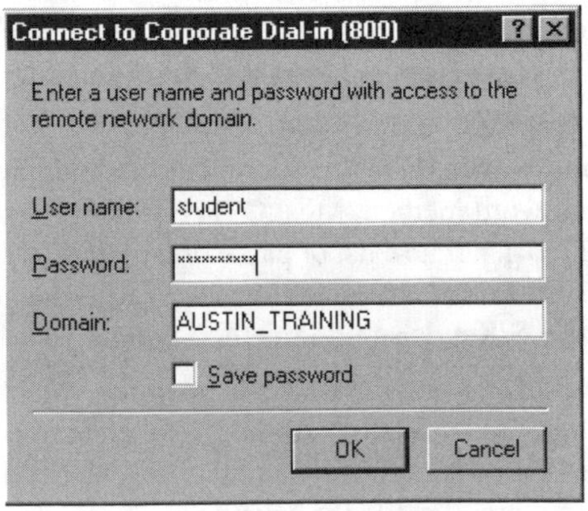

The remote user enters a username and password in the User name and Password fields and clicks the OK button to initiate a dialup connection.

After the user enters the username and password and clicks the OK button, Windows NT Dialup Networking transmits the username and password, over communication lines using TCP/IP and PPP, to a remote network access server or a security server for authentication, as shown in Figure 4-3.

Authentication of usernames and passwords is commonly used with secure Internet applications. For example, some Cisco Connection Online (CCO) applications require a user to be registered and to possess a username and password assigned by CCO. When the user accesses a secure CCO application using a Web browser, the application causes the Web browser to display a window requesting a username and password similar to that shown in Figure 4-4. The username and password may be validated using a AAA security server.

S/Key Authentication

Remote logins are vulnerable to network intruders using eavesdropping techniques to obtain the usernames and passwords. Intruders can use captured information in a replay attack to gain unauthorized access to the target system. The S/Key one-time password system was designed by Bellcore and others as a way to create passwords that can be safely sent over remote connections, thereby countering eavesdropping and replay attacks. With S/Key, only the one-time password crosses the network. The one-time password is a hash of the user's secret password, so the secret password never crosses the network, and the hashed one-time password is never used again.

Where S/Key Got Its Name

After searching available RFCs and publications to find the meaning of the name *S/Key* with no success, I decided to ask Neil Haller, one of the original developers of S/Key and coauthor of several S/Key RFCs. Here is his reply: "I made up the name. It was originally called something else, but we discovered that name was trademarked. Then came a lengthy search for a name that we could trademark. S/Key came from desperation, trying many alternatives. I suppose the words 'secure' and 'key' were in my mind."

A strong advantage of S/Key is that it protects against eavesdroppers without modification of remote client software, and it imposes little inconvenience on the users. Because S/Key is easy to integrate, many security-sensitive networks use it as their password security system. The S/Key client and host do not store any secret information. If either element is compromised, a network intruder cannot obtain secret passwords.

The S/Key system consists of three main parts, as shown in Figure 4-5: the remote client system that the user is using to gain remote access, S/Key client software installed on the remote client system that generates one-time passwords for the remote user, and S/Key host software running on the remote security server.

Figure 4-5 *S/Key Authentication System Components: Remote Client, S/Key Client Software, and S/Key Host*

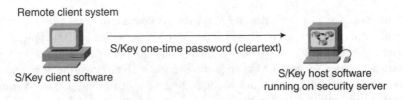

Remote client system

S/Key one-time password (cleartext)

S/Key client software

S/Key host software running on security server

S/Key Client Software

The S/Key client software that is usually installed on the remote system (also known as a *password generator*) generates a one-time password. When a one-time password is needed, the user enters a secret password into the S/Key client user interface. The S/Key client runs a one-way hashing algorithm using the secret password entered by the user and a seed value sent by the S/Key host to create the one-time password. S/Key uses either MD4 or MD5, which are one-way hashing algorithms, to create the one-time passwords. Each one-time password generated by S/Key consists of six short words. S/Key clients can have a command-line interface or a graphical user interface. An example of an S/Key password generated via a command-line interface is BONE YANK ROW RING WHOA TRUE. Figure 4-6 shows an example of the user interface of an S/Key password generator, the keyapp.exe program for Windows 95 systems.

Figure 4-6 *The S/Key Client keyapp.exe User Interface*

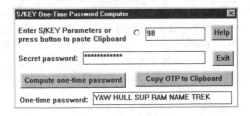

keyapp.exe has a graphical user interface that allows the user to enter the secret password, compute a one-time password, copy the password to the clipboard, and then paste the password into an authentication screen (such as Windows Dialup Networking) for the remote login. The authentication software on the remote client sends the one-time password in cleartext over the network to the S/Key host, which validates the one-time password.

After the one-time password has been used, it is no longer useful to an eavesdropper. Some S/Key password generators create a list of one-time passwords that can be printed and manually entered into the authentication screen when needed.

S/Key Hosts

The S/Key host receives an authentication request from the S/Key client and sends a challenge/response with S/Key parameters that include a sequence number and a seed value used by the client hash algorithm. The S/Key client then sends the one-time password to the S/Key host. The S/Key host receives the one-time password and validates it by running the hash algorithm against it and comparing the hashed output with the previously received one-time password. If the values match, the user request is approved, and the received one-time password is stored in a file. The S/Key client and server keep track of the number of one-time passwords generated by decrementing a sequence number so that the user must reinitialize the S/Key calculator with a new secret password when the sequence number reaches 0. The CiscoSecure ACS for UNIX security server supports S/Key authentication.

An S/Key User Example

Consider an example of how a user named Sally uses S/Key from a remote UNIX system (with a command-line interface), through a network access server, to CiscoSecure ACS:

1 Sally identifies herself to the network access server in response to a standard prompt for authentication:

```
User Access Verification
Username: sally
s/key 98 agst2359
Password:
```

2 CiscoSecure ACS issues a challenge that includes a sequence number of 98 for the one-time password expected and a seed value of agst2359. The values are displayed to Sally by the network access server.

3 Sally enters **98** and **agst2359** into her S/Key calculator program, called key, at the UNIX prompt. The secret password is any string of at least 10 alphanumeric characters generated by Sally, for Sally, and known only by Sally, as follows:

```
% key 98 agst2359
Enter secret password: secret_password
The S/Key calculator creates a one-time password, as follows:
ANNE JEAN MILK SHAW LARK NEST
```

4 Sally now returns to her interaction with the network access server. She enters the S/Key password and is authenticated, as follows:

```
Password: ANNE JEAN MILK SHAW LARK NEST
```

5 The next time Sally attempts network access, she will be prompted for the one-time password sequence number 97. The sequence number is one less than what was used for the previous authentication. When the sequence number reaches 0, Sally will not be able to log on without reinitializing the S/Key calculator with a new secret password.

Token Cards and Servers

Another one-time password authentication method that adds a new layer of security is accomplished with a token card and a token server. Each token card, about the size of a credit card, is programmed to a specific user, and each user has a unique PIN that can generate a password keyed strictly to the corresponding card. The password is then entered into the password field during a remote authentication.

The use of the token card requires the user to possess a token card or soft token software and to know a password to enable the token. This is called "something you have and something you know." This represents one of the highest commercially available security methods of authentication. One-time password authentication takes place between the specified token server with a token card database and the remote client's authentication software.

Token Card and Server Operation

Token card and server systems consist of a remote client PC, a token card, a network access server, and a token server. Token cards and servers generally work as follows:

1 The user generates a one-time password with the token card, using a security algorithm.

2 The user enters the one-time password into the authentication screen generated by the remote client (in this example, the Windows Dialup Networking screen).

3 The remote client sends the one-time password to the token server via the network and a remote access server.

4 The token server uses the same algorithm to verify that the password is correct and authenticates the remote user.

Token Card and Server Methods

Two token card and server methods are commonly used:

- **Time-based**—In this system, the token card contains a cryptographic key and generates a password (or token) through the use of a PIN entered by the user. The password is entered into the remote client, which sends it to the token server. The password is loosely synchronized in time to the token server. The server compares the token received to a token generated internally. If they match, the user is authenticated and allowed access.

- **Challenge/response**—In this system, the token card stores a cryptographic key. The token server generates a random string of digits and sends it to the remote client that is trying to access the network. The remote user enters the random string, and the token card computes a cryptographic function using the stored key and random string. The result is sent back to the token server, which has also computed the function. If the results match, the user is authenticated.

Token cards are now implemented in software for installation on the remote client. SofToken, which generates single-use passwords without the associated cost of a hardware token, is one example of software token cards.

Cisco Token Card and Server Support

Cisco supports authentication from the following four token-card servers within CiscoSecure ACS software:

- CRYPTOCard RB-1 from CRYPTOCard Corporation
- SecurID ACE/Server from RSA Security, Inc.
- SafeWord from Secure Computing Corporation, which uses the DES Gold Card token card and the SafeWord SofToken software token card
- Axent Technologies token server in CiscoSecure ACS 2.4 for Windows NT

See the "References" section of this chapter for more information about these servers.

PAP and CHAP Authentication

An important component of dialup access security is support for authentication accomplished with PAP and CHAP. The following sections look at the relative strengths of PAP and CHAP. We will examine how PAP and CHAP authentication operates. We will also consider Microsoft Challenge Handshake Authentication Protocol (MS-CHAP), an extension to CHAP.

PPP is a standard encapsulation protocol for the transport of different network layer protocols (including, but not limited to, IP) across serial, point-to-point links such as the PSTN or ISDN. PPP enables authentication between remote clients and servers using either PAP or CHAP.

NOTE PPP was designed to overcome the limitations of SLIP and to meet the need for an encapsulation protocol for serial lines based on Internet standards. PPP enhancements include encryption, error control, dynamic IP addressing, multiple protocol support, and connection negotiation and authentication.

Cisco network access servers are configured to perform authentication using the **aaa authentication** commands, which are covered in Chapters 5 and 6.

PAP Authentication Over PPP

PAP authentication, which uses PPP, provides a simple way for the remote client to establish its identity: a two-way handshake (see Figure 4-7). The handshake is done only after initial PPP link establishment. After the link establishment phase is complete, a username/password pair is repeatedly sent by the peer to the authenticator until authentication is acknowledged or the connection is terminated. Here are the messages exchanged during PAP authentication:

1 The remote client establishes the dialup link.

2 The remote client tells the network access server that it is running PPP.

3 The network access server, configured to use PAP, notifies the remote client to use PAP in this session.

4 The remote client sends the username and password in PAP format.

5 The network access server compares the username and password to that stored in its database and accepts or rejects the username and password entered.

Figure 4-7 *The Steps in PAP Authentication Over PPP*

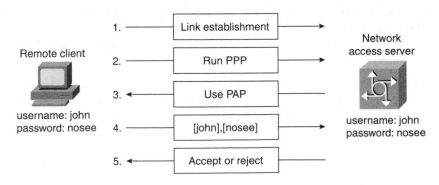

PAP is not a strong authentication method. The username and password are sent in cleartext across the link. A protocol analyzer could be used to easily capture the password in an eavesdropping attack. PAP offers no protection from playback or repeated trial-and-error attacks. The peer is in control of the frequency and timing of the attempts. PAP provides a level of security similar to the usual user login at the remote host.

Usually PAP is used if it is the only authentication method supported by the client, when a plaintext password must be available to simulate a login at a remote host, or where the communication links are secure. CHAP is the preferred authentication method. Most vendor equipment and software support PAP, enabling greater interoperability between them.

CHAP Authentication Over PPP

CHAP is a stronger authentication method than PAP because the user's actual password never crosses the communications channel. CHAP uses a three-way handshake to verify the identity of the peer. The handshake is done upon initial link establishment, and it may be repeated periodically thereafter to ensure the identity of the peer. The CHAP initiation sequence and three-way handshake occur as follows and as illustrated in Figure 4-8:

1 The PPP link is established after dialup. The network access server is configured to support PPP and CHAP.

2 The network access server tells the remote client to use CHAP.

3 The remote client responds with an OK.

4 The three-way handshake occurs as follows:

   a. The network access server sends a challenge message to the remote client.

   b. The remote client replies with a one-way hash value.

   c. The network access server processes the received hash value. If it matches the station's own calculation, authentication is acknowledged. Passwords are not sent over the link.

CHAP periodically verifies the identity of the remote client by using a three-way handshake. The network access server sends a challenge message to the remote node. The remote node responds with a value calculated using a one-way hash function (typically MD5). The network access server checks the response against its own calculation of the expected hash value. If the values match, the authentication is acknowledged. Otherwise, the connection is terminated immediately.

Figure 4-8   *CHAP Authentication Steps Over PPP*

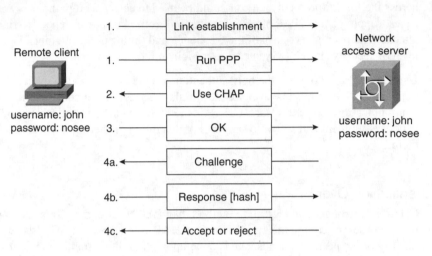

CHAP provides protection against playback attack through the use of a variable challenge value that is unique and unpredictable. The use of repeated challenges is intended to limit the time of exposure to any single attack. The network access server (or a security server such as CiscoSecure TACACS+) is in control of the frequency and timing of the challenges. A major advantage of the constantly changing challenge string is that eavesdropping cannot be used to capture the challenge value and replay it back later in order to gain unauthorized access to the network because the value constantly changes. CHAP is preferable to PAP for authentication. One problem with CHAP has been that it was not supported in Windows NT authentication systems. Windows NT now supports the Microsoft version of CHAP, MS-CHAP.

CHAP authentication depends on a "secret" known only to the authenticator and the remote client. The secret is not sent over the link. Although the authentication is only one-way, by negotiating CHAP in both directions, the same secret set may easily be used for mutual authentication.

CHAP requires that the secret be available in plaintext form. Irreversibly encrypted password databases that are commonly available (such as the Windows NT SAM hive, the NT password database) cannot be used.

Most vendor efforts have been focused on enabling and improving authentication methods, particularly password access technologies. Improvements to authorization and accounting methods are being made more slowly.

MS-CHAP Authentication

MS-CHAP is the Microsoft version of CHAP, an extension of CHAP described in RFC 1994. MS-CHAP enables PPP authentication between a PC using Microsoft Windows 95, Windows 98, Windows NT, or Windows 2000 and a network access server. PPP authentication using MS-CHAP can be used with or without AAA security services.

MS-CHAP differs from standard CHAP in the following ways:

- MS-CHAP is enabled while the remote client and the network access server negotiate PPP parameters after link establishment.

- The MS-CHAP Response packet is in a format designed for compatibility with Microsoft's Windows NT 3.5, 3.51, and 4.0 and Windows 95 networking products.

- MS-CHAP lets the network security server (authenticator) control retry and password-changing mechanisms. MS-CHAP allows the remote client to change the MS-CHAP password.

- MS-CHAP defines a set of reason-for-failure codes returned to the remote client by the network access server.

Cisco routers support MS-CHAP in Cisco IOS Release 11.3 and later releases with the **ppp authentication ms-chap** command.

Cisco routers support double authentication for PPP in Cisco IOS Release 11.3 and later. With double authentication, the remote host is authenticated with PAP or CHAP, and then the user is authenticated for remote access, potentially with one-time passwords such as token card passwords, which are not supported by CHAP. See the "Enabling Double Authentication" section in the *Cisco IOS Security Configuration Guide, Release 12.0,* for more information about double authentication.

Authorization Methods

AAA authorization lets you control the network services available to each user and helps restrict access to internal networks. Authorization also lets you specify which Cisco IOS commands a user can issue on specific network devices. It also lets mobile users connect to the closest local connection and still have the same access privileges they would have if they were directly connected to their local networks.

You can configure the network access server to control user access to the network so that users can perform only certain functions after successful authentication, such as controlling EXEC access. As with authentication, authorization can be used with either a local security database on the network access server or a remote security database, as shown in Figure 4-9. The figure also gives an example of authentication controlling network services, Cisco IOS command access, and access to specific networks. The remote security database can cause access lists configured in the network access server to be applied to the authenticated user.

Figure 4-9 *Authorization Controls User Access to Networks and Network Services*

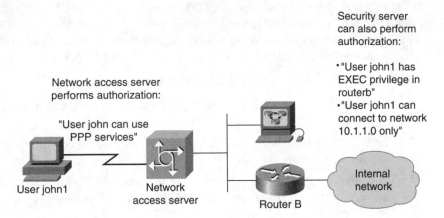

Authorization works by assembling a set of attributes describing what a user is authorized to perform. The attributes are configured in either a local security database on the network access server or a remote security database. When the user wants to gain remote access to a system, the network access server determines and enforces the user's capabilities and restrictions by gathering authentication information from the database.

Authorization can be configured to run for all network-related service requests including IP, IPX, SLIP, PPP, Telnet, and ARAP. It can also be configured to determine whether the user is allowed to run an EXEC shell in a network access server and to specify permitted commands and EXEC privilege levels. Authorization can also be configured to control or restrict access to hosts on the network by using dynamically assigned access lists.

Cisco network access servers are configured to perform authorization by using the **aaa authorization** commands, which are covered in Chapters 5 and 6. CiscoSecure can also be configured to perform authorization tasks with network access servers. The group and per-user security policies determine how authorization is configured.

Accounting Methods

AAA accounting lets you track the amount of network resources users are accessing and the types of services they are using. For example, system administrators might need to bill departments or customers for connection time or resources used on the network (for example, total time connected). Accounting tracks this kind of information. You can also use accounting to track suspicious connection attempts into the network.

When AAA accounting is configured, the network access server creates accounting records that report user activity. The accounting records are stored on the network access server or can be sent to the remote security database, as shown in Figure 4-10. The accounting records, which are similar to syslog records, can then be imported into a spreadsheet or accounting program and analyzed for network management, billing, and auditing.

Figure 4-10 *The Network Access Server, Router, and Remote Security Database Generating and Processing Accounting Information*

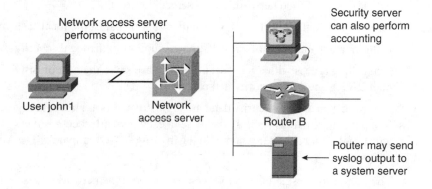

The accounting record consists of attribute/value (AV) pairs that typically contain the username, user network address, attempted service, start and stop time and date, amount of data transferred, network access server accessed, and source of the network record. The RADIUS and TACACS+ remote security database protocols each have provisions for recording and transmitting accounting records.

Cisco network access servers can be configured to capture and display accounting data by using the **aaa accounting** commands including the following: EXEC commands; network services such as SLIP, PPP, and ARA; and system-level events not associated with users, which are covered in Chapters 5 and 6.

AAA Security Servers

Cisco products support AAA access control by using either a local server database in the network access server or a remote security database running a AAA security protocol. Each security database has pluses and minuses. This section examines AAA with a local security database, AAA with a remote security database, and the remote security database standards supported by Cisco AAA features.

AAA with a Local Security Database

If only a few remote users access your network through one or two network access servers, you might want to store username and password security information on the Cisco network access server, which is referred to as *local authentication* on a local security database. Here are some characteristics of AAA on a local security database:

- Local authentication on a local security database is best for small networks of just a few remote users and network access servers.
- Usernames, passwords, and authorization parameters are stored in the local security database of the Cisco network access server.
- Remote users authenticate and gain authorization against the local security database.
- Authorization and accounting have limited support in the local security database.
- Controlling access with a local security database saves the cost of installing and maintaining a remote security database.

Authentication with a local security database typically works as shown in Figure 4-11. You must first populate the local security database in each network access server by specifying username profiles for each user who might log in using AAA commands. The AAA process is as follows:

1 The remote user establishes a PPP connection with the network access server.

2 The network access server prompts the user for a username and password.

3 The network access server authenticates the username and password in its local database.

4 The network access server authorizes the user to access network services and the destination based on authentication values in its local database.

5 The network access server tracks user traffic and compiles accounting records as specified in the local database.

Figure 4-11 *A Local Security Database Performing AAA*

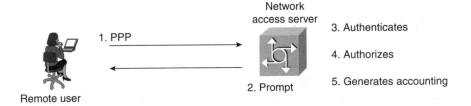

AAA with a Remote Security Database

As your network grows to more than just a few remote users and network access servers, you probably should use a remote security database that provides username and password information for each of the network access servers and routers on the network. The remote security database resides in a security server on your network.

A remote security database is convenient when you have a large number of network access servers controlling network access. A remote security database lets you centrally manage remote user profiles, preventing you from having to update each network access server with new or changed user profiles for each remote user. A remote security database helps establish and enforce consistent remote access policies throughout a corporation.

Here are some characteristics of AAA on a remote security database:

- Authentication against a remote security database is best for medium- to large-size networks with many remote users and network access servers, where the cost of a security server can be justified.

- Usernames, passwords, and authorization parameters are centrally stored in the remote security database in the security server.

- Remote users authenticate and gain authorization against the remote security database.

- Authorization and accounting are supported in the network access server and the remote security database.

- A remote security database can control access to or through a network access server. Some remote security database protocols also support access control to routers, Ethernet switches, and firewalls. The remote security database controls access to network equipment that supports standards-based remote access protocols.

- The central control enabled by a remote security database saves the cost of administering each network access server on the network. The database must be secured by ensuring that the host it runs on is as secure as possible. Chapter 1, "Evaluating Network Security Threats," contains some suggestions for improving host security.

Authentication with a remote security database typically works as shown in Figure 4-12. You must first populate the remote security database with user profiles for each remote user who might log in. You must also configure the network access server (or other network equipment) to interoperate with the remote security database for AAA services. The AAA process with a remote security database is as follows:

1 User establishes a PPP connection with the network access server.

2 The network access server prompts the user for the username and password, and the user responds.

3 The network access server passes the username and password to the security server.

4 The remote security database authenticates and authorizes the user to access the network. The database in effect configures the network access server with authentication parameters by downloading commands and activating access lists in the network access server.

5 The network access server compiles accounting records as specified in the remote security database and sends the records to the security server. The security server may also compile accounting records.

Figure 4-12 *A Remote Security Database Centralizing AAA Control*

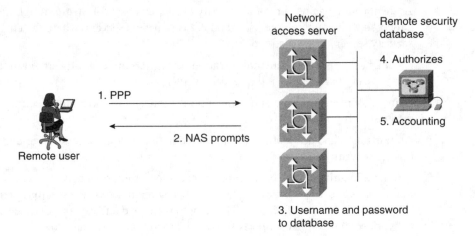

The primary benefit of a remote security database is that it simplifies management and ensures consistent administration of policies for remote access, dialup access, and router management through centralized control.

Remote Security Database Standards Supported by Cisco

Several remote security database standards have been written to provide uniform access control for network equipment and users. A variety of applications have been developed as shareware and as commercial products to conform to the standards.

Cisco network equipment supports the three primary security server protocols: TACACS+, RADIUS, and Kerberos. TACACS+ and RADIUS are the predominant security server protocols used for AAA with network access servers, routers, and firewalls. These protocols are used to communicate access control information between the security server and the network equipment. Cisco has also developed the CiscoSecure ACS family of remote security databases to support the TACACS+ and RADIUS protocols.

The Cisco family of network access servers, routers, the Cisco IOS user interface, and the PIX Firewall support interaction with security servers running TACACS+ and RADIUS.

The TACACS+ or RADIUS security server interacts with the network equipment as if they were all network access servers. In Figure 4-13, the network access server acts as a TACACS+ or RADIUS client to the TACACS+ or RADIUS security server. Communications for AAA events between the client and server use the TACACS+ or RADIUS protocol.

Figure 4-13 *TACACS+ or RADIUS Supported on Network Access Server, Router, and Remote Security Database*

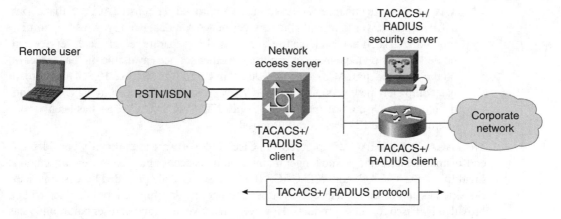

The following sections describe TACACS+, RADIUS, Kerberos, and CiscoSecure ACS in more detail.

TACACS+

TACACS+ is a security server application and protocol that enables central control of users attempting to gain access to a network access server, router, or other network equipment that supports TACACS+. TACACS+ services and user information are maintained in a database typically running on a UNIX or Windows NT computer. TACACS+ allows a single application control server (the TACACS+ daemon) to support AAA services independently.

TACACS Versions

There are three versions of TACACS security server applications:

- **TACACS**—An industry-standard protocol specification, described in RFC 1492, that forwards username and password information to a centralized server. The centralized server can either be a TACACS database or a database such as the UNIX password file with TACACS protocol support. For example, the UNIX server with TACACS passes requests to the UNIX database and sends the accept or reject message back to the access server.

- **XTACACS**—Defines the extensions that Cisco added to the TACACS protocol to support new and advanced features. XTACACS is multiprotocol and can authorize connections with SLIP, enable, PPP (IP or IPX), ARA, EXEC, and Telnet. XTACACS supports multiple TACACS servers and syslog for sending accounting information to a UNIX host, connects where the user is authenticated into the access server "shell," and can Telnet or initiate slip, PPP, or ARA after initial authentication. XTACACS has been superseded by TACACS+.

- **TACACS+**—An enhanced and continually improved version of TACACS that allows a TACACS+ server to provide the services of AAA independently. AAA support is modularized such that each feature is essentially a separate server. Each service can be tied into its own database or can use the other services available on that server or on the network. TACACS+ was introduced in Cisco IOS Release 10.3. This protocol is a completely new version of the TACACS protocol, referenced by RFC 1492 and developed by Cisco. It is incompatible with XTACACS. TACACS+ has been submitted to the IETF as a draft proposal.

The TACACS and XTACACS protocols in Cisco IOS software are officially considered end-of-maintenance and are no longer maintained by Cisco for bug fixes or enhancements. In addition, the TACACS and XTACACS freeware server code provided by Cisco is also classified as end-of-maintenance. No further engineering development or bug fixes will be provided by Cisco for these products. However, an active independent user community has been adding enhancements to the protocols.

TACACS+ Features

TACACS+ supports the following security server features:

- **TCP packets for reliable data transport**—Uses TCP as the communication protocol for TACACS+ communications between the network access server and the security server. TCP port 49 is reserved for TACACS+.

- **The AAA architecture**—Each service is separate and has its own database, yet they work together as one security server.

- **Link encryption**—The data payload of TCP packets containing TACACS+ protocol values is encrypted for security between the network access server and the security server.

- **Each TACACS+ packet has a 12-byte header sent in cleartext and a variable-length body containing TACACS+ parameters**—The body of each packet is encrypted by an algorithm that uses a pseudo-random pad (that is, fill characters) obtained with MD5. TACACS+ packets are transmitted over a network and are stored in the TACACS+ server in encrypted form. The packet is decrypted by reversing the encryption algorithm when needed by the network access server or the TACACS+ application.

- **PAP and CHAP authentication**—Provides complete control of authentication through PAP and CHAP challenge/response, as well as through the login and password dialog box, and interactive login message support.

- **LAN and WAN security**—Provides AAA support for remote dialup and LAN access for network access servers, routers, and other network equipment that supports TACACS+. Enables centralized management of network equipment.

- **Encapsulation protocols for dialup access**—Supports SLIP, PPP, and ARAP as well as TN3270 and X.121 addresses used with X.25.

- **Auto-command**—Is automatically executed for a user if it is configured in the TACACS+ database and is supported by the network access server.

- **Callback**—Reverses phone charges by commanding the network access server to call back the user. Can offer extra security for telecommuters.

- **Per-user access lists**—The TACACS+ database can instruct the network access server to assign a previously configured access list for controlling user access to network services and destinations during the authorization phase.

The TACACS+ Authentication Process

The TACACS+ packet header has a type field that identifies whether each packet is part of a AAA process. TACACS+ authentication has three packet types: START, CONTINUE, and REPLY. Consider the TACACS+ authentication process, in which the network access server exchanges user authentication packets with the TACACS+ server (see Figure 4-14) using the following steps:

1 The network access server sends a START authentication packet to the TACACS+ security server to initiate the authentication process.

2 The authentication process on the TACACS+ security server typically sends a GETUSER packet containing a username prompt to the network access server.

3 The network access server displays a username prompt to the user and sends the username entered by the user inside a CONTINUE packet to the TACACS+ security server.

4 The TACACS+ security server typically sends a GETPASS packet to the network access server, containing a prompt for a password. The network access server displays the password prompt.

5 The network access server sends a CONTINUE packet containing the password entered by the user to the TACACS+ security server.

6 The TACACS+ security server checks the password against the information stored in the TACACS+ configuration file to decide whether the user passes or fails the authentication. The server process then sends a PASS or FAIL packet back to the network access server as its final status.

Figure 4-14 *The TACACS+ Authentication Process*

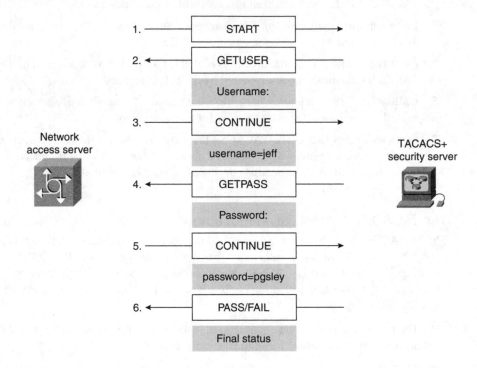

The TACACS+ Authorization Process

The TACACS+ authorization process uses two packet types: REQUEST and RESPONSE. User authorization is controlled by exchanging AV pairs from the TACACS+ security server with the network access server. Consider the TACACS+ authorization process between the network access server and the TACACS+ server, which is as follows (see Figure 4-15):

1 The access server sends an authorization REQUEST packet to the TACACS+ security server. The packet contains a fixed set of fields that describe the authenticity of the user or process, and a variable set of arguments that describe the services and options for which authorization is requested.

2 The TACACS+ security server process sends a RESPONSE packet containing a variable set of response arguments (AV pairs) back to the network access server. The AV pairs are based on the permissions previously configured for that user stored in the TACACS+ configuration file. Here are some examples of AV pairs:

service = ppp—The primary service allowed
protocol = ip—The protocol allowed for this service
addr = 172.16.10.1—An authorized network address
timeout = 12—An absolute timer for the connection in minutes

3 The network access server uses the AV pairs to deny, permit, or modify the commands and services requested by the user.

Figure 4-15 *The TACACS+ Authorization Process*

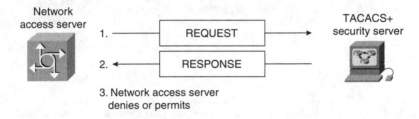

The TACACS+ Accounting Process

The TACACS+ accounting process uses two packet types—REQUEST and RESPONSE—and operates much like the authorization process. Accounting provides an audit record of user activity on specified network services. The accounting service can compile records of all activity on the network equipment and can store the record in a standard format (such as a .csv [comma-separated value] file) on the security server for later analysis.

With TACACS+, AAA accounting is not provided as a stringent security feature. It is often used merely for billing or management. However, AAA accounting provides a way to keep track of user activity, allowing you to be aware of unusual user activity with your network equipment.

Consider the TACACS+ accounting process between the network access server and the TACACS+ server, which is as follows (see Figure 4-16):

1 The network access server sends an accounting REQUEST packet to the TACACS+ security server containing a fixed set of fields that describe the authenticity of the user or process. The packet includes an accounting record consisting of a variable set of arguments (AV pairs) that describe the services and options for which accounting is being compiled based on the selected event and accounting method. The accounting AV pairs include those used for authorization plus additional pairs specifying start, stop, and the elapsed time of the accounting record.

2 The TACACS+ security server sends a RESPONSE packet to the access server and acknowledges receipt of the accounting record. The response packet indicates that the accounting function on the TACACS+ security server has completed and that the record has been recorded and stored.

Figure 4-16 *The TACACS+ Accounting Process*

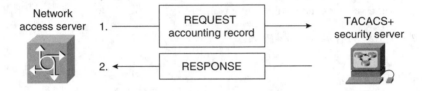

RADIUS

RADIUS is a distributed client/server protocol that secures networks against unauthorized access. Cisco supports RADIUS under its AAA security paradigm. RADIUS combines authentication and authorization rather than treating them separately, as it does with accounting. RADIUS can be used with other AAA security protocols such as TACACS+, Kerberos, and local security databases. RADIUS was initially developed by Livingston Enterprises (now a part of Lucent Technologies). The RADIUS protocol is specified in RFC 2865 and RADIUS accounting in RFC 2866.

RADIUS has been implemented in a variety of network environments that require high levels of security while maintaining network access for remote users. RADIUS is a fully open protocol, distributed in source code format that can be modified to work with any security system currently available. RADIUS is widely used in part because the protocol permits vendors to extend the AV pairs beyond those specified in RFC 2865. The RADIUS protocol specifies the vendor-specific attribute (attribute 26), allowing vendors to support their own extended attributes that aren't suitable for general use. A drawback of vendor-specific AV pairs is a lack of standardization and a fragmentation of RADIUS security server products. RADIUS security servers and clients must ignore vendor-specific AV pairs that they have not been programmed to accept.

Cisco supports RADIUS clients on a variety of network access servers, routers, Ethernet switches, PIX Firewalls, VPN 3000 Concentrators, and CiscoSecure ACS.

RADIUS Versions

Many versions of RADIUS are available. Some major versions of RADIUS are summarized in this section:

- **IETF implementation**—Developed and proposed to the IETF by Livingston Enterprises, now a division of Lucent Technologies, the IETF implementation of the RADIUS protocol is specified in RFC 2865 and RADIUS accounting in RFC 2866. It supports approximately 63 attributes.

- **Cisco implementation**—Starting in Cisco IOS release 11.2, an increasing number of attributes and functionality are included in each release of Cisco IOS Software and CiscoSecure ACS. It supports approximately 58 attributes.

- **Ascend implementation**—Ascend is constantly changing and adding vendor-specific attributes such as token caching and password changing. An application programming interface (API) allows the rapid development of new extensions, making competing vendors work hard to keep up. Although RADIUS was originally developed by Livingston Enterprises, it was championed by Ascend. It supports more than 254 attributes.

- **Other vendors**—Other versions of RADIUS are available as follows:
  - Merit, a UNIX- and LINUX-based version. See www.merit.net/radius/ for more information.
  - Internet Authentication Service for Microsoft Windows 2000 supports RADIUS. See www.microsoft.com/windows2000/library/howitworks/communications/remoteaccess/ias.asp for more information.
  - Funk Steel-Belted RADIUS by Funk Software. See www.funk.com/Default.htm for more information.

RADIUS Features

RADIUS supports the following security server features:

- **UDP packets**—Uses UDP as the communication protocol for RADIUS communications between the network access server and the security server over UDP port 1812, the officially assigned port number. Some deployments of RADIUS use UDP port 1645. UDP simplifies RADIUS client and server implementations.

- **Combined authentication and authorization, and separate accounting**—The RADIUS server receives user requests, authenticates users, and provides configuration information to the client. The RADIUS accounting server performs accounting.

- **Encrypted user passwords**—Only user passwords in RADIUS packets are encrypted, using MD5 hashing for security.

- **PAP and CHAP authentication**—Provides control of authentication through PAP and CHAP challenge/response and through login and password dialogs such as the UNIX login.

- **WAN security**—Provides AAA support for remote dialup for network access servers developed by many vendors that support RADIUS clients. Enables centralized management of remote access.

- **SLIP, PPP, and ARAP framed protocols**—Also supports Telnet, rlogin, and Local Area Transport (LAT).

- **Auto-command**—A user can automatically execute a command if it is configured in the RADIUS database and is supported by the network access server.

- **Callback**—Reverses phone charges by commanding the network access server to call back the user. Can give extra security for telecommuters.

- **Extensible**—All transactions use variable-length AV pairs. New attributes can easily be added without disturbing existing implementations of the protocol. The protocol allows vendors to develop their own attributes with the vendor-specific attribute. Vendor-specific AV pairs allow the addition of new AV pairs.

- **Ensures network security**—Transactions between the client and RADIUS security server are authenticated through the use of a shared secret.

The RADIUS Authentication and Authorization Process

The RADIUS client and RADIUS security server communicate using Access-Request, Access-Accept, Access-Reject, and Access-Challenge packets. As shown in Figure 4-17, when a user attempts to log in and authenticate to a network access server configured as a RADIUS client, the following steps occur:

1 The user initiates a PPP authentication request to the network access server.

2 The user is prompted for and enters a username and password.

3 The network access server sends an Access-Request packet containing the username and encrypted password and other attributes over the network to the RADIUS security server.

4 The RADIUS security server validates the sending client, authenticates the user, looks up the user authorization parameters, and sends one of the following responses:

Access-Accept—The user is authenticated.
Access-Reject—The user is not authenticated and is prompted to reenter the username and password by the network access server, or access is denied.
Access-Challenge—A challenge is optionally issued by the RADIUS security server. The network access server collects additional data from the user and sends it to the RADIUS security server.

5 The network access server acts on the authentication parameters, permitting selected services.

6 The Access-Accept or Access-Reject response is bundled with additional data (AV pairs) that is used for EXEC sessions or network authorization. The RADIUS authentication process must be completed before the RADIUS authorization process. Some additional data that can be included in the Accept or Reject packets consists of the following in AV pairs:

— Services that the user can access, including Telnet, rlogin, or LAT connections, and PPP

— SLIP or EXEC services

— Connection parameters including the host or client IP address, access list, and user timeouts

7 The RADIUS security server can periodically send an Access-Challenge packet to the network access server to prompt the user to reenter his username and password, send the state of the network access server, or to perform other actions determined by the RADIUS server vendor. The RADIUS client cannot send an Access-Challenge packet.

Figure 4-17 *The RADIUS Authentication and Authorization Process*

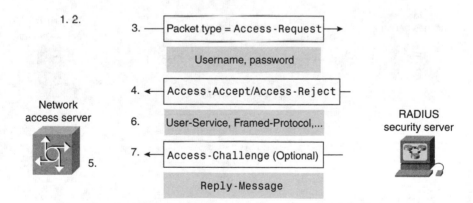

The RADIUS Accounting Process

The RADIUS protocol has been enhanced to include delivery of accounting information from a RADIUS client to a RADIUS accounting server using UDP port 1813. The RADIUS client is responsible for sending user accounting information to a designated RADIUS accounting server using an Accounting-Request packet with accounting AV values.

The RADIUS accounting server is responsible for receiving the accounting request and returning a response that it has successfully received the request. It uses an Accounting-Response packet to do so.

As shown in Figure 4-18, when a user attempts to log in and authenticate to a network access server configured as a RADIUS client, the following steps occur:

1 After initial authentication, the network access server sends an Accounting-Request start packet to the RADIUS security server.

2 The RADIUS security server acknowledges receipt of the start packet with an Accounting-Response packet.

3 At the end of service delivery, the network access server sends an Accounting-Request stop packet describing the type of service delivered and optional statistics.

4 The RADIUS security server acknowledges receipt of the stop packet with an Accounting-Response packet.

Figure 4-18 *The RADIUS Accounting Process*

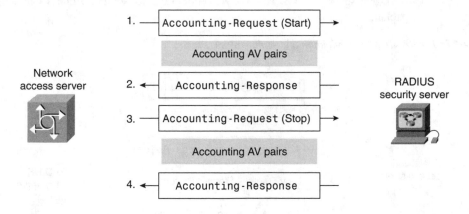

RADIUS Attributes

RADIUS attributes carry the specific authentication, authorization, information, and configuration details for the request and reply. Attributes are appended to the end of a RADIUS packet. One or more attributes can be appended. The overall length of the RADIUS packet indicates the end of the list of attributes.

Figure 4-19 summarizes the attribute format. The fields are transmitted from left to right.

Figure 4-19 *The RADIUS Attribute Format, Showing Type, Length, and Value Fields*

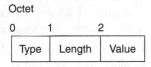

RADIUS attributes consist of a type/length/value triplet. The purpose of each field is as follows:

- **Type**—One octet in length. Indicates the overall type of the RADIUS attribute. One example of the many Type fields is 1, User-Name, which indicates that the Value field contains a username. Type 26, Vendor-Specific, indicates the RADIUS vendor or user and specifies the Length and Value fields.

- **Length**—One octet in length, this indicates the length of the attribute, including the Type, Length, and Value fields.

- **Value**—Zero or more octets in length. Contains information specific to the attribute. The Type and Length fields determine the format and length of the Value field.

A Comparison of TACACS+ and RADIUS

Although TACACS+ and RADIUS are very similar in function, they have several key differences, as listed in Table 4-4.

Table 4-4 *TACACS+ and RADIUS Comparison*

Functionality	TACACS+	RADIUS
AAA support	Separates the three services of AAA	Combines authentication and authorization and separates accounting
Transport protocol	TCP	UDP
Challenge/response	Bidirectional	Unidirectional
Protocol support	Full support	No NetBEUI
Data integrity	The entire TACACS+ packet is encrypted	Only the user password is encrypted

- **Functionality**—TACACS+ separates AAA functions according to the AAA architecture, allowing modularity of the security server implementation. RADIUS combines authentication and authorization and treats accounting separately, thus allowing less flexibility in implementation.

- **Transport protocol**—TACACS+ uses TCP. RADIUS uses UDP, which was chosen for simplification of client and server implementation, yet it makes the RADIUS protocol less robust and requires the server to implement reliability measures such as packet retransmission and timeouts instead of relying on the Layer 4 protocol.

- **Challenge/response**—TACACS+ supports bidirectional challenge/response as used in CHAP between two network access servers. RADIUS supports unidirectional challenge/response from the RADIUS security server to the RADIUS client.

- **Protocol support**—TACACS+ provides more complete dialup and WAN protocol support.

- **Data integrity**—TACACS+ encrypts the entire packet body of every packet. RADIUS encrypts only the password attribute in the Access-Request packet, which makes TACACS+ more secure.

Here are some additional points of comparison between TACACS+ and RADIUS:

- **Customizability**—The flexibility provided in the TACACS+ protocol allows for many things to be customized on a per-user basis (for example, customizable username and password prompts). Because RADIUS lacks flexibility, many features that are possible with TACACS+ are not possible with RADIUS (for example, message catalogs). However, RADIUS supports flexible customization of AV pairs.

- **Authorization process**—With TACACS+, the server accepts or rejects the authentication request based on the contents of the user profile. The client (network access server) never knows the contents of the user profile. With RADIUS, all reply attributes in the user profile are sent to the network access server. The network access server accepts or rejects the authentication request based on the attributes received.

- **Accounting**—TACACS+ accounting includes a limited number of information fields. RADIUS accounting can contain more information than TACACS+ accounting records, which is RADIUS's key strength over TACACS+.

Kerberos

Kerberos is an authentication protocol designed to validate requests for network services or resources on an open, unprotected network. Kerberos was developed at MIT to honor requests for services from hosts in the university environment that were not under organizational control. It uses the DES encryption algorithm (discussed in more detail in Chapter 13, "Cisco Encryption Technology Overview") for encryption and authentication.

Kerberos relies on a trusted third-party application, called the key distribution center (KDC), to perform secure verification of users and services, much like a title company provides escrow services for real estate transactions. Kerberos keeps a database of its clients in the KDC.

The primary use of Kerberos is to ensure that users and the network services they access are really who and what they claim to be. To accomplish this verification, the Kerberos KDC issues tickets to users. These tickets, which have a limited life span, are stored in a user's credential cache and can be used in place of the standard username-and-password authentication mechanism.

Kerberos implements the single-logon concept. This process requires authenticating a user once and then allows secure authentication (without encrypting another password) wherever that user's credential is accepted for other network services.

Kerberos software components are freely available from MIT in C source code under a copyright permission notice. The latest generally released version of Kerberos from MIT is version 5. Kerberos is also available commercially from many different vendors such as CyberSafe Corporation and WRQ Incorporated. Microsoft Windows 2000 has a built-in Kerberos server.

Cisco IOS Software version 11.2 and later (versions 11.2(6) and later are recommended) supports the Kerberos version 5 protocol specified in RFC 1510, "The Kerberos Network Authentication Service (V5)." A Cisco network access server or router configured for Kerberos acts as Kerberos client, much as a UNIX workstation would, and as a Kerberos server for Cisco IOS remote shell and Telnet daemons. Cisco considers Kerberos a legacy application that is most beneficial in networks that are already using Kerberos. Cisco routers can integrate into a Kerberos system.

Kerberos Features

Here is a summary of the Kerberos features:

- Secret-key authentication protocol
- Authentication of users and their network services
- 40- or 56-bit DES for encryption and authentication
- Trusted third-party key distribution (key distribution center)
- Single login
- Labor-intensive administration

Kerberos Components

Kerberos consists of many software components. Figure 4-20 illustrates the main Kerberos components in a network using Cisco routers and network access servers. They are summarized as follows:

- The KDC contains the user database.
- The Kerberos server software supports the server side of Kerberos.

- The Kerberos client and utilities software enable remote client features.
- Kerberized Cisco products contain client, server, and utilities.

Figure 4-20 *The Main Kerberos Components in a Cisco Environment*

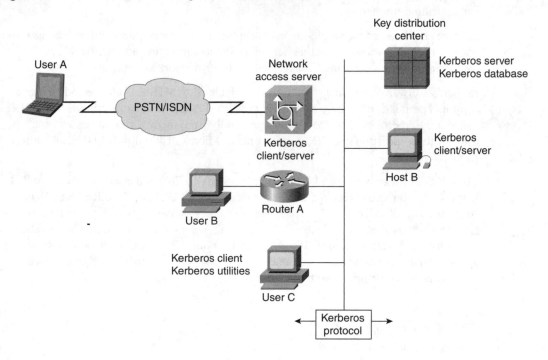

Kerberos Terminology

Kerberos uses terminology with specific meanings. The following list defines the Kerberos terminology that is used in the following section:

- **Credential**—A general term that refers to authentication tickets such as ticket granting tickets (TGTs) and service credentials.

- **KDC**—Key distribution center. A Kerberos server and database program running on a network host.

- **Kerberized**—Applications and services that have been modified to support the Kerberos credential infrastructure.

- **Kerberos realm**—A domain consisting of users, hosts, and network services that are registered to a Kerberos server.

- **KINIT**—Kerberos client software that authenticates the user to the KDC.

- **Service credential**—A credential authorizing a network service. When issued from the KDC, this credential is encrypted with the password shared by the network service and the KDC and with the user's TGT.

- **TGT**—Ticket Granting Ticket. A credential that the KDC issues to authenticated users. It lets them authenticate to network services within the Kerberos realm represented by the KDC.

Kerberos Operation

This section summarizes the complex Kerberos authentication and administration process. To help understand how Kerberos works, we will consider the operation of Kerberos components with no Cisco product involved. Kerberos can be used to authenticate PPP sessions, with the KDC operating as a remote security database, so we will consider using Kerberos for PPP authentication to a network access server. Kerberos can also be used to authenticate logins to a Cisco router or network access server, with the KDC operating as a remote security database, so we will consider using Kerberos for login authentication to a network access server. Finally, we will consider the login-type applications that Cisco has Kerberized in Cisco IOS Software. Refer to Figure 4-20 for each of the following examples.

Generic Kerberos Authentication   To help understand how Kerberos authentication works, we will consider basic transactions that occur in the Kerberos protocol without using Cisco networking products. In the this example, User C wants to Telnet into Host B. User C, Host B, and the KDC are set up to perform Kerberos authentication. The following steps describe the authentication process:

1 User C logs on and authenticates to the KDC. User C uses the KINIT program as a Kerberos client.

2 The KDC provides an encrypted TGT to User C's system. User C's system authenticates the received TGT.

3 User C attempts to Telnet to Host B. User C's system presents the TGT to the KDC and requests a service credential authorizing access to Host B.

4 The KDC provides a service credential authorizing Telnet access to Host B.

5 User C's system provides the service credential to Host B and gets Telnet access.

6 User C's system presents the service credential for subsequent access to other systems or services, enabling single logon.

Using Kerberos for PPP Authentication   Cisco IOS Software supports using Kerberos as a method to authenticate PPP access to a network access server, much as TACACS+ or RADIUS is used. The remote user does not need to run the KINIT program because the network access server acts as a Kerberos client to the KDC, proxying the authentication for the remote user. In this example, User A uses Microsoft Windows 95 dialup networking to dial into the network access server and connect to the campus network. The following steps sum up the authentication process:

1 The User A establishes a PPP session with the network access server via a dialup PPP session.

2 The network access server prompts the user for a username and password, and the user enters these. The network access server is configured to authenticate PPP sessions using Kerberos.

3 The network access server proxies the request, acts as a Kerberos client, and requests a TGT from the KDC to authenticate the access request.

4 The KDC sends an encrypted TGT to the network access server that includes the user's identity.

5 The network access server attempts to decrypt the TGT using the password the user entered. If the decryption is successful, the remote user is authenticated to the network access server. The network access server is now assured that the KDC itself is valid, and the remote user's computer is now part of the network. The remote user must still authenticate directly to the KDC to gain access to network services.

NOTE Dialup via asynchronous or ISDN access bypasses the Cisco IOS command-line interface. Instead, a network protocol (such as PPP) starts as soon as the connection is established.

Use the **aaa authentication ppp** command with the **krb5** keyword to specify Kerberos as the method of user authentication for PPP.

Kerberos login authentication works only with PPP PAP authentication.

Using Kerberos for Login Authentication   Cisco IOS Software supports using Kerberos as a method to authenticate login access to a network access server, much as TACACS+ or RADIUS is used. Just as in authenticating PPP, the remote user does not need to run the KINIT program because the network access server acts as a Kerberos client to the KDC, proxying the authentication for the remote user. In this example, User B wants to log into Router A. The following steps sum up the login authentication process:

1 User B attempts to Telnet into Router A.

2 Router A is configured to authenticate login sessions using Kerberos, so Router A prompts the user for a username, and the user enters it.

3 Router A proxies the request, acts as a Kerberos client, and requests a TGT from the KDC to authenticate the access request.

4 The KDC sends an encrypted TGT to Router A that includes the user's identity. Router A prompts User B for a password, and the user enters it.

5 Router A attempts to decrypt the TGT using the password that the user entered. If the decryption is successful, Router A is assured that the KDC is valid.

6 Router A sends the TGT and requests a service credential for the Telnet access.

7 The KDC presents a service credential for the Telnet access to Router A, and Router A stores the TGT and service credential. User B is logged into Router A and obtains a router prompt. User B can now request other services on other Kerberized hosts without having to reauthenticate.

NOTE

A remote user does not need to run the KINIT program to get a TGT to authenticate to a Cisco router configured for Kerberos because KINIT has been integrated into the login procedure in the Cisco IOS implementation of Kerberos.

Use the **aaa authentication login** command with the **krb5** method keyword to specify Kerberos as the login authentication method. For example, to specify Kerberos as the method of user authentication at login when no other method list has been defined, enter **aaa authentication login default krb5**.

The credentials forwarding feature allows forwarding of users' TGTs so that they can authenticate to multiple Kerberized hosts without having to reenter their username and password, enabling single logon.

Cisco IOS Software Kerberized Applications

Cisco IOS Release 12.0 includes Kerberos 5 support, which allows organizations that are already deploying Kerberos 5 to use existing KDCs with their routers and network access servers. The following network services are Kerberized in Cisco IOS Software:

- **Telnet**—The Telnet client (from a router to another host) and Telnet server (from another host to a router) are Kerberized.

- **rlogin**—Logs a user into a remote UNIX host for an interactive session similar to Telnet.

- **rsh**—Logs a user into a remote UNIX host and allows execution of one UNIX command.

- **rcp**—Logs a user into a remote UNIX host and allows copying of files from the host.

NOTE

You can use the **connect** EXEC command with the **/telnet** or **/rlogin** keywords to log into a host that supports Telnet or rlogin. You can use the **/encrypt kerberos** keyword to establish an encrypted Telnet session from a router to a remote Kerberos host. Or you can use the **telnet** EXEC command with the **/encrypt kerberos** keyword to establish an encrypted Telnet session.

You can use the **rlogin** and **rsh** EXEC commands to initiate rlogin and rsh sessions.

You can use the **copy rcp** EXEC or configuration command to enable obtaining configuration or image files from an RCP server.

Cisco IOS Kerberos support is described in more detail in the documents mentioned in the "References" section at the end of this chapter.

CiscoSecure ACS

Cisco has developed a scalable family of CiscoSecure ACS products to meet the remote security database needs of small to medium-size enterprise and service provider businesses. CiscoSecure ACS supports the industry-standard TACACS+ and RADIUS security server protocols.

Cisco offers CiscoSecure ACS versions that run on either the Sun Solaris or Windows NT Server operating systems. CiscoSecure uses a central database that stores user and group profiles with authentication and authorization information and to store accounting records. CiscoSecure ACS is easily managed remotely with standard Web browsers, enabling simple moves, additions, and changes to usernames, passwords, and network devices.

CiscoSecure ACS is a comprehensive and flexible platform for controlling network access. As shown in Figure 4-21, CiscoSecure controls network access for the following:

- Dialup via Cisco network access servers and routers
- Router and Ethernet switch console and vty port access for central management
- Access control through a PIX Firewall

CiscoSecure ACS closely interoperates with the network access server, router, and PIX Firewall to implement a comprehensive security policy via the AAA architecture. It interoperates with industry-leading token cards and servers. CiscoSecure ACS can also be used for access control of other vendors' equipment that supports the TACACS+ and RADIUS protocols. The CiscoSecure ACS product family includes the following:

- CiscoSecure ACS for Windows NT
- CiscoSecure ACS for UNIX
- CiscoSecure Global Roaming Server (GRS)

These products are discussed in the following sections.

Figure 4-21 *The CiscoSecure ACS Remote Security Database Controls Network Equipment AAA*

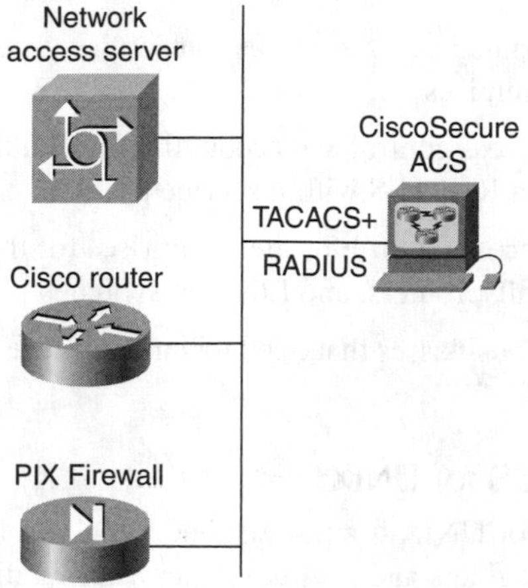

CiscoSecure ACS for Windows NT

CiscoSecure ACS for Windows NT is a powerful remote security database for enterprises and workgroups that need to scale a security policy across a Windows NT infrastructure. CiscoSecure ACS for Windows NT includes the following features:

- It is a powerful remote security database for Windows NT Server.

- It supports TACACS+ and RADIUS protocols simultaneously.

- It enables AAA support for multiple network access servers, firewalls, routers, and Ethernet switches.

- It supports authentication with leading token-card servers.

- It authenticates using the Windows NT user database using MS-CHAP or a CiscoSecure ACS database.

- Its support for the Windows NT user database enables a single login to leverage and consolidate the Windows NT username and password.

- Its Web browser-based interface simplifies the configuration of user profiles, group profiles, and CiscoSecure ACS for Windows NT itself.

- It stores accounting and audit information in comma-separated value format, which makes the import process for billing applications convenient.

- It supports the Windows NT Performance Monitor for real-time statistics viewing.

CiscoSecure ACS for Windows NT can meet the needs of enterprises with large-scale Windows NT networks, workgroups, and smaller organizations whose secure access needs have grown beyond using a local security database. These organizations will find that

CiscoSecure ACS for Windows NT is tailored to their needs. CiscoSecure ACS for Windows NT lends itself to many application solutions:

- An advanced outsourcing solution that service providers can provide for the enterprise's premises
- Centralized access control and accounting for multiple access servers running TACACS+ and RADIUS within service provider organizations
- Centralized access control for the enterprises for the management of network access servers, firewalls, routers, and Ethernet switches
- Medium-size businesses that need to support more than one network access server

CiscoSecure ACS for UNIX

CiscoSecure ACS for UNIX is a powerful access control server that meets the demanding needs of service providers and medium to large corporations. CiscoSecure ACS for UNIX includes features that extend service providers' ability to offer outsourcing services to the enterprise. It also provides the level of reliable, secure AAA that large corporate customers need to protect their networks and information assets. CiscoSecure ACS for UNIX includes the following features:

- It is a powerful remote security database for Sun Solaris.
- It supports TACACS+ and RADIUS protocols simultaneously.
- It enables AAA support for multiple network access servers, firewalls, routers, and Ethernet switches.
- It supports authentication with leading token-card servers.
- It supports Oracle and Sybase external databases, scaled to large customer needs. SQL Anywhere is included with the product.
- It includes a utility to easily import an existing RADIUS database.
- Dial VPN support is available at both Layer 2 Forwarding (L2F) tunnel points of origin and termination.
- Its Web browser-based interface simplifies the configuration of user profiles, group profiles, network access servers, and CiscoSecure ACS for UNIX itself.
- The distributed architecture of CiscoSecure ACS for UNIX allows you to scale your performance, yet allows for distributed database replication.

Cisco developed CiscoSecure ACS for UNIX to address the very powerful configuration and functionality needs of service providers and medium to large corporations. CiscoSecure ACS for UNIX includes features that extend service providers' ability to offer outsourcing services to the enterprise. It also provides the level of reliable, secure AAA that large corporate customers need to protect their networks and information assets. CiscoSecure ACS for UNIX makes the following application solutions possible:

- Enables an advanced outsourcing solution that service providers can offer to enterprise customers to manage the enterprise's premises access

- Makes possible centralized access control and service provisioning for multiple access and network devices, TACACS+, and RADIUS within the service provider organizations

- Supports enterprises using Oracle or Sybase as their strategic database application or those that need the scalable functionality of a relational database to store ACS data

CiscoSecure GRS

CiscoSecure GRS software acts as a proxy agent that translates and forwards packets between network access servers and multiple CiscoSecure ACS systems. Mobile dial VPN and Internet users can dial into a global roaming network made up of regional and Internet service providers using existing TACACS+ or RADIUS security servers and network access servers. Global roaming reduces the costs of long-distance mobile access to corporate networks and the Internet.

CiscoSecure GRS allows a regional service provider (RSP) to lease its points of presence (POPs) to customers such as ISPs. The ISP can lease the RSP's POPs to provide or expand coverage. Service providers can offer global roaming services with other service providers, extending their service offerings to include connectivity outside their local territory. Service providers can provide global roaming services to enterprises that need local connectivity available globally. Service providers can also extend their territory by leveraging the capabilities of other regional service providers without the purchase of additional equipment.

Summary

This section summarizes the main points of this chapter:

- Authentication methods range from the use of no username or password; to static usernames and passwords, aging usernames and passwords, and the S/Key one-time password system; to the strongest authentication, one-time passwords using token cards and server systems.

- CHAP authentication includes a periodic three-way handshake to verify the authenticity of the CHAP client.

- Authorization controls access to network services and destinations.

- Accounting tracks user data in the network access server or the security server.

- In AAA with a local security database, the network access server performs AAA services and contains a user database.

- In AAA with a remote security database, the security server performs AAA, enabling centralized management of multiple network access servers.

- TACACS+ separates authentication, authorization, and accounting services.

- RADIUS accounting is made more powerful with the use of extensible vendor-specific attribute-value pairs.

- Kerberos works with a key distribution center. Servers must be "Kerberized" to support Kerberos services.

- Cisco offers three remote security database products: CiscoSecure ACS for Windows NT, CiscoSecure ACS for UNIX, and CiscoSecure Global Roaming Server.

Review Questions

Answer the following review questions, which delve into some of the key facts and concepts covered in this chapter:

1 AAA protects which modes of network access?

2 An authentication method should be selected based on what criteria or standard?

3 What are the parts of the CHAP three-way handshake?

4 Network managers use authorization to accomplish what tasks?

5 When should a local security database be used?

6 Which security server protocols does Cisco IOS Software support?

7 What are the chief characteristics of TACACS+?

8 What is a strength of RADIUS compared with TACACS+?

9 Which Cisco IOS Software services have been Kerberized?

10 When should CiscoSecure ACS for Windows NT be used?

References

The topics considered in this chapter are complex and should be studied further to more fully understand them and put them to use. Use the following references to learn more about the topics in this chapter.

Token Card Servers

Axent Technologies token server in CiscoSecure ACS for Windows NT 2.4, located at www.axent.com.

CRYPTOCard token-card servers information, located at www.cryptocard.com.

SafeWord token-card and authentication servers information, located at www.securecomputing.com.

SecurID ACE/Server from RSA Security information, located at www.rsasecurity.com.

S/Key

RFC 1760, N. Haller, "The S/Key One-time Password System," February 1995.

RFC 2289, N. Haller, C. Metz, P. Nesser, and M. Straw, "A One-Time Password System," February 1998.

Refer to the following URL for more information on S/Key: medg.lcs.mit.edu/people/wwinston/skey-overview.html.

Refer to the CiscoSecure ACS for UNIX User's Guide, in the "S/Key Authentication" and "Working with S/Key Authentication" sections, for more information on S/Key.

PPP

RFC 1661, W. Simpson, editor, "The Point-to-Point Protocol (PPP)," July 1994.

CHAP

RFC 1994, W. Simpson, "PPP Challenge Handshake Authentication Protocol (CHAP)," August 1996.

MD5

RFC 1321, R. Rivest, "The MD5 Message-Digest Algorithm," April 1992.

TACACS+

draft-grant-tacacs-02.txt, D. Carrel and L. Grant, "The TACACS+ Protocol," January 1997. This Internet draft for TACACS+, proposed to IETF by Cisco Systems, Inc., can be found at search.ietf.org/internet-drafts/draft-grant-tacacs-02.txt.

RFC 1492, C. Finseth, "An Access Control Protocol, Sometimes Called TACACS," July 1993.

RADIUS

RFC 2138, C. Rigney, A. Rubens, W. Simpson, and S. Willens, "Remote Authentication Dial in User Service (RADIUS)," April 1997.

RFC 2139, C. Rigney, "RADIUS Accounting," April 1997.

Kerberos

"How to Kerberize Your Site," a Web page maintained by Jim Rome, a senior scientist. This Web page can be found at www.ornl.gov/~jar/HowToKerb.html.

"The Kerberos Network Authentication Service," a Web page maintained by USC/ISI's GOST Group. It contains lots of information and links about Kerberos. This Web page is located at gost.isi.edu/info/kerberos.

"Kerberos: The Network Authentication Protocol," a Web page supplied by MIT, located at web.mit.edu/kerberos/www.

RFC 1510, C. Neuman, "The Kerberos Network Authentication Service (V5)," September 1993.

USC/ISI Technical Report number ISI/RS-94-399, B. Neuman and T. Ts'o, "Kerberos: An Authentication Service for Computer Networks," September 1994. This document can be found at nii.isi.edu/publications/kerberos-neuman-tso.html.

CiscoSecure ACS Security Server and Cisco IOS Software

Cisco IOS Software Security Configuration Guide, Cisco IOS Release 12.0, October 1998.

Upon completing this chapter, you will be able to do the following:

- Describe network access server port types and access control methods

- Identify how to configure NAS to enable AAA processes locally, given a security policy for a case study network

- Identify how to test the NAS AAA configuration using applicable debugging and testing commands

CHAPTER 5

Configuring the Network Access Server for AAA Security

Your company's employees will typically access the company network through a network access server (NAS) device, such as the Cisco ACS5300 or the Cisco 2500. To implement your company's security policies, you need to develop authentication methods. To apply these security policies, you need to configure the NAS for access control.

Now that you understand Cisco authentication, authorization, and accounting (AAA) security methods, as well as the general security policy for your company, you will now learn how to develop authentication methods that combine security policies with AAA security.

This chapter begins with an overview of the NAS AAA configuration process. You will secure NAS and prepare it for AAA, and you will learn about the commands available to implement AAA. Examples are provided to guide you through the process. To aid in debugging the NAS configuration, troubleshooting commands are also provided.

You will then configure NAS for each of the AAA functions. A complete listing of a NAS configuration file is available for you to compare to your own configuration efforts. This configuration listing is built on similar test equipment and is annotated to link configuration commands to security policies.

The Remote Access Security Problem and Solution

The campus infrastructure typically incorporates remote access facilities, giving remote users access to the corporate LAN. Although this achieves the goal of corporate access for company users, it exposes the company to attacks on the remote access facility by intruders if a security policy is not defined and implemented. Intruders might attempt to gain access using a variety of methods, including the following:

- Discovering and gaining access to the device's console if it is unprotected
- Guessing current username/password combinations if the device is discovered to be of the dialup class of equipment
- Considering a lack of policy notifications to be permission to attempt access by any possible means

Figure 5-1 illustrates the campus infrastructure of the XYZ Company that is discussed in this chapter. The company has incorporated a NAS to allow remote dialup clients to gain dialup access to the corporate LAN. In the campus infrastructure, the NAS component is the target of security configuration for the network administrator, who wants to implement the first stage of remote access security policy.

The solution to the remote access infrastructure security problem is to securely configure the remote access components against vulnerabilities, utilizing the overall network security policy. As discussed in previous chapters, you will match configuration and policy against the threats just listed, similar to the following:

- **Block entry points**—Configure network equipment with access passwords at entry points to the NAS.
- **Control dialup access**—Use password authentication from the NAS local database.

The NAS AAA Configuration Process

As discussed in Chapter 4, "Examining Cisco AAA Security Technology," access control is how you control who is allowed access to the network server and what services they are allowed to use after they have access. AAA network security services provide the primary framework through which you set up access control on your access server.

Configuring AAA is relatively simple after you understand the basic process involved. A prerequisite is to consider access modes, port types, and other preliminary steps to securing access to the NAS. You can then proceed with the steps to configure AAA on the NAS.

The NAS should be configured to secure access to it via character mode or packet mode with AAA commands. Table 5-1 compares the NAS access modes, port types, and AAA command elements.

Table 5-1 *Access Modes, Port Types, and AAA Command Elements*

Mode	NAS Ports	AAA Command Elements
Character (line mode)	tty, vty, aux, and cty	Login, exec, NetWare Asynchronous Support Interface (NASI) connection, AppleTalk Remote Access Protocol (ARAP), and enable
Packet (interface mode)	async, group-async, Basic Rate Interface (BRI), and serial (Primary Rate Interface [PRI])	PPP, network, and ARAP

Figure 5-1   *XYZ Company Campus Infrastructure*

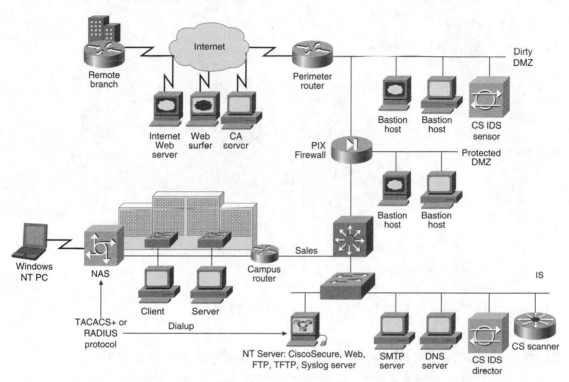

Figure 5-2 illustrates the authenticated port types and access modes for a NAS.

To configure security on a NAS using AAA, follow these general steps:

Step 1   Secure access to privileged EXEC and configuration mode (enable and enable secret) on vty, asynchronous, auxiliary, and tty ports.

Step 2   Enable AAA globally on the NAS with the **aaa new-model** command.

Step 3   Configure AAA authentication profiles. Additionally, make sure you have a last-resort access method before you are certain that your security server is set up and functioning properly.

Step 4   Configure AAA authorization for use after the user has passed authentication.

Step 5   Configure the AAA accounting options for how you want to write accounting records and what you want accounted for in them.

Step 6   Debug the configuration.

Figure 5-2 *Authenticated Port Types and Access Modes for a NAS*

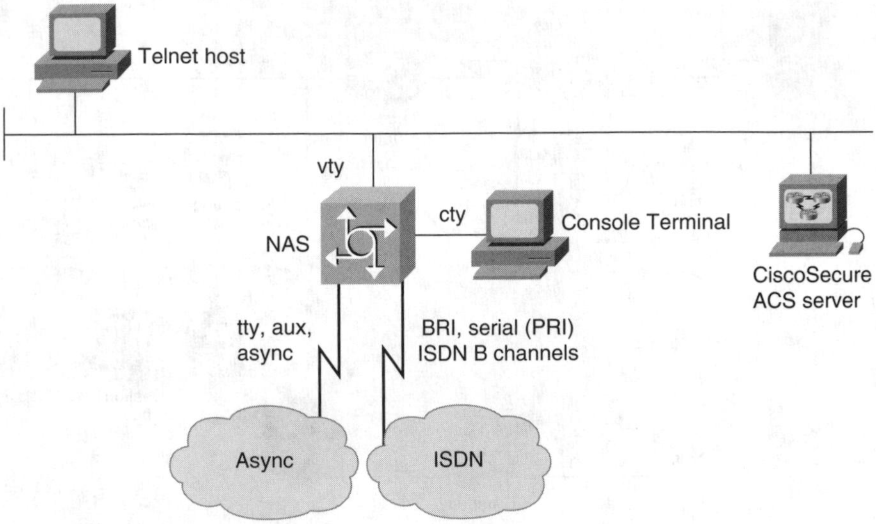

The following sections describe these steps in detail.

Step 1: Secure Privileged EXEC and Configuration Mode

The first thing to secure is access to privileged EXEC (enable) mode. Enable mode provides access to configuration mode, which enables configuration changes to the access server.

An **enable** password is defined as follows:

- It must contain from 1 to 25 uppercase and lowercase alphanumeric characters.

- It must not have a number as the first character.

- It can have leading spaces, but they are ignored. However, intermediate and trailing spaces are recognized.

The console is the only port that can access privileged EXEC mode without an **enable** password, so remote administration of the NAS is not possible without one.

Cisco recommends that you use the **enable secret** command whenever possible, for the additional security of its Message Digest 5 (MD5) hashing function. Passwords can be further protected from display by using the **service password-encryption** command.

To secure privileged EXEC mode, you use the **enable** and **service** commands. The command syntax for these commands is as follows:

```
enable password [level level] {password | [encryption-type] encrypted-password}
service password-encryption
```

As shown here, the **service password-encryption** command has no arguments or keywords. However, you can specify additional protection for privileged EXEC mode, and the **password-encryption** command is used in conjunction with the **service password-encryption** command to encrypt passwords. You use the **no** forms of these commands to cancel the action. The **enable password** command parameters and syntax have the following meanings:

Command Parameter	Description
• **level** *level*	(Optional) Specifies the level for which the password applies. You can specify up to 16 privilege levels, using numbers 0 through 15. Level 1 is normal EXEC mode user privileges. If this argument is not specified in the command or the **no** form of the command, the privilege level defaults to 15 (traditional enable privileges).
• *password*	Specifies the password that users type to enter enable mode.
• *encryption-type*	(Optional) Specifies a Cisco-proprietary algorithm used to encrypt the password. Currently, the only encryption type available is 7. If you specify *encryption-type,* the next argument you supply must be an encrypted password (a password already encrypted by a Cisco router).
• *encrypted-password*	Specifies the encrypted password that users enter, copied from another router configuration.

CAUTION　A lost encrypted password cannot be recovered. The only solution is to execute the proper password recovery routine and set a new **enable** password. Improperly executing the password recovery routine might damage the configuration file.

Also, the vulnerability of **service password-encryption** should be evaluated in your security policies, where the possibility for breaking this with hacking tools exists.

Example 5-1 shows the commands used to secure access to the NAS.

Example 5-1 *Securing Access to the NAS*

```
Router(config)#enable password changeme
Router(config)#enable secret supersecret
Router(config)#service password-encryption
```

Step 2: Enable AAA Globally on the NAS

After securing access to the NAS, you need to establish a AAA section in the configuration file. Then you need to follow these steps:

1 Configure the NAS to enable authentication for a user to access the privileged command level.

2 Create a character string used to name the list of authentication methods activated when a user logs in, and assign a username database to use for authentication (there can be more than one).

3 Specify one or more AAA authentication methods for use on serial interfaces running Point-to-Point Protocol (PPP).

Example 5-2 shows an example of enabling AAA globally on the NAS.

Example 5-2 *Enabling AAA Globally on the NAS*

```
NASx(config)#aaa new-model
NASx(config)#aaa authentication login default enable
```

The first command, **aaa new-model**, establishes a new AAA configuration. The second command, **aaa authentication login default enable**, instantly secures access to all lines (except PPP). You can now proceed to configuration and testing with the AAA commands and their application.

CAUTION Only the *first* use of **aaa new-model** establishes a *new* configuration. Subsequent uses will, by default, include previous AAA statements that have been entered.

If you intend to authenticate users via a security server, make sure you do not inadvertently lock yourself out of the access server ports after you issue the **aaa new-model** command. For example, enter line configuration mode and issue the **aaa authentication login default tacacs+ enable** global configuration command. This command specifies that if your TACACS+ (or RADIUS) server is not functioning properly, you can enter your enable password to log in to the access server.

Step 3: Configure AAA Authentication Profiles

You use the **aaa authentication** global configuration command to set parameters that determine a user's identity and to verify the information.

After enabling AAA globally on the access server, you need to define the authentication method lists and then apply them to lines and interfaces. These authentication method lists are security profiles that indicate the service (PPP, ARAP, or NASI) or login and authentication method (local, TACACS+, RADIUS, login, enable authentication, line, or none).

To define an authentication method list using the **aaa authentication** command, follow these steps:

1 Specify the service (PPP, ARAP, or NASI) or login authentication.

2 Identify a list name or default. A list name is any alphanumeric string you choose. The default indicates that the method applies to all lines or interfaces unless otherwise specified. You assign different authentication methods to different named lists. You can specify only one dial-in protocol per authentication method list. However, you can create multiple authentication method lists with each of these options. You must give each list a different name.

3 Specify the authentication method. You can specify up to four multiple methods. Note that if an error condition is encountered with a method (as shown by **debug aaa authentication**), the next method in the sequence is attempted.

After defining these authentication method lists, apply them to one of the following:

- **Lines**—tty, vty, console, aux, and async lines or the console port for login and asynchronous lines (in most cases) for ARA

- **Interfaces**—Interfaces sync, async, and virtual configured for PPP, SLIP, NASI, or ARAP

You use the **aaa authentication** command in global configuration mode to enable AAA authentication processes. The following is the syntax for the **aaa authentication** command:

```
aaa authentication {arap | enable | login | nasi | ppp} {default | list-name}
    method1 [method2] [method3] [method4]
```

The command parameters and syntax have the following meanings:

Command Parameter	Description
arap *method*	Enables an AAA authentication method for AppleTalk Remote Access (ARA) using RADIUS or TACACS+. The *method* argument includes the following parameters: • **guest**—Allows guest logins. This method must be the first method listed, but it can be followed by other methods if it does not succeed. • **autho-guest**—Allows guest logins only if the user has already logged in to EXEC. This method must be the first method listed, but it can be followed by other methods if it does not succeed. • **line**—Uses the line password for authentication. • **local**—Uses the local username database for authentication. • **tacacs+**—Uses TACACS+ authentication. • **radius**—Uses RADIUS authentication.
enable *method*	Creates a series of authentication methods that are used to determine whether a user can access the privileged command level. The *method* argument identifies the methods the authentication algorithm tries in the given sequence as follows: • **enable**—Uses the enable password for authentication. • **line**—Uses the line password for authentication. • **none**—Does not use authentication. • **tacacs+**—Uses TACACS+ authentication. • **radius**—Uses RADIUS authentication.
login *method*	Sets AAA authentication at login. The *method* argument identifies the list of methods that the authentication algorithm tries, in the following order: • **enable**—Uses the enable password for authentication. • **krb5**—Uses Kerberos 5 for authentication. • **line**—Uses the line password for authentication. • **local**—Uses the line password for authentication. • **none**—Does not use authentication. • **radius**—Uses RADIUS authentication. • **tacacs+**—Uses TACACS+ authentication. • **krb5-telnet**—Uses the Kerberos 5 Telnet authentication protocol when using Telnet to connect to the router.

Command Parameter	Description
nasi	Specifies AAA authentication for NASI clients connecting through the access server. The *method* argument identifies the list of methods that the authentication algorithm tries, in the following order: • **enable**—Uses the enable password for authentication. • **line**—Uses the line password for authentication. • **local**—Uses the line password for authentication. • **none**—Does not use authentication. • **tacacs+**—Uses TACACS+ authentication.
ppp *method*	Specifies one or more AAA authentication methods for use on serial interfaces running PPP and TACACS+. The *method* argument identifies the list of methods that the authentication algorithm tries, in the following order: • **if-needed**—Does not authenticate if the user has already been authenticated on a tty line. • **krb5**—Uses Kerberos 5 for authentication. Can be used only for PAP authentication. • **local**—Uses the line password for authentication. • **none**—Does not use authentication. • **radius**—Uses RADIUS authentication. • **tacacs+**—Uses TACACS+ authentication.
default	Uses the listed methods that follow this argument as the default list of methods when a user logs in.
list-name	Names the following list of authentication methods tried when a user logs in.

Table 5-2 illustrates configuration commands for using AAA authentication.

Table 5-2 *AAA Authentication Commands*

Command	Description
aaa authentication login tech-pubs local	Defines a login authentication profile, tech-pubs, using the local database for authentication.
aaa authentication ppp mktg if-needed local	Defines a PPP authentication profile, mktg, which requires no authentication if the user is already authenticated. Otherwise, use the local database for PPP authentication.

Example 5-3 is an example of authentication commands as they are applied to lines or interfaces.

Example 5-3 *Authentication Commands Applied to Lines or Interfaces*

```
(config)#line console 0
(config-line)#login authentication tech-pubs
(config)#interface serial 3/0
(config-line)#ppp authentication chap mktg
```

The command **line console 0** enters line console configuration mode. The command **login authentication tech-pubs** uses the tech-pubs profile for login authentication on console port 0. The command **interface serial 3/0** specifies port 0 of serial interface slot 3. The command **ppp authentication chap mktg** uses the mktg profile for PPP CHAP authentication on the interface specified in the preceding line. Use a default list for AAA "last resort" authentication.

Step 4: Configure AAA Authorization

AAA authorization lets you limit the services that are available to a user. When AAA authorization is enabled, the network access server uses information retrieved from the user's profile, which is located either in the local user database or on the security server, to configure the user's session. After this is done, the user is granted access to a requested service only if the information in the user profile allows it.

You use the **aaa authorization** global configuration command to set parameters that determine what a user is allowed to do. You configure the access server to restrict the user to only certain functions after successful authentication. You use the **aaa authorization** command in global configuration mode. Here is its syntax:

```
aaa authorization {network | exec | commands level | reverse-access}
    {default | list-name} {if-authenticated | local | none | radius |
    tacacs+ | krb5-instance}
```

The command parameters and syntax have the following meanings:

Command Parameter	Description
network	For network services (PPP, SLIP, ARAP).
exec	For starting an exec (shell).
commands	For exec (shell) commands.
level	Specifies the command level that should be authorized. Valid entries are 0 through 15.
reverse-access	Runs authorization for reverse access connections, such as reverse Telnet.

Command Parameter	Description
default	Uses the listed authorization methods that follow this argument as the default list of methods for authorization.
list-name	Character string used to name the list of authorization methods.
if-authenticated	Allows the user to use the requested function if the user is authenticated.
local	Uses the local database for authorization (with the username password commands).
none	Performs no authorization.
radius	Uses RADIUS for authorization.
tacacs+	Uses TACACS+ for authorization.
krb5-instance	Uses the instance defined by the Kerberos instance map command.

Similar to naming an authentication profile, there is a provision for naming the authorization profile after specifying the service. Also, like the **aaa authentication** command, this one can have up to four methods listed.

Named authorization lists allow you to define different methods for authorization and accounting and to apply those methods on a per-interface or per-line basis.

Table 5-3 lists AAA authorization commands that should be used in global configuration mode.

Table 5-3   *AAA Authorization Commands*

Command	Description
aaa authorization commands 1 Orion local	Uses the local username database to authorize the use of all level 1 commands.
aaa authorization commands 15 Andromeda local	Works similarly to authorize the use of all level 15 commands.
aaa authorization network Pisces local none	Uses the local database to authorize the use of all network services such as Serial Line Interface Protocol (SLIP), PPP, and ARAP. If the local server is unavailable, no authorization is performed, and the user can use all network services.
aaa authorization exec Virgo if-authenticated	Lets the user run the EXEC process if he or she is already authenticated.

Step 5: Configure the AAA Accounting Options

The AAA accounting feature lets you track the services that users are accessing as well as the amount of network resources they are consuming.

You use the **aaa accounting** global configuration command to set parameters that record what a user is doing or has done. You use accounting commands in global configuration mode for auditing and billing purposes. The following is the syntax for the **aaa accounting** command:

```
aaa accounting {system | network | exec | connection | commands level}
    {default | list-name} {start-stop | wait-start | stop-only | none}
    [method1 [method2]]
```

The command parameters and syntax have the following meanings:

Command Parameter	Description
system	Audits all system-level events such as reload.
network	Audits network service requests, SLIP, PPP, and ARAP.
exec	Audits the EXEC process.
connection	Audits all outbound connections such as Telnet and rlogin.
commands *level*	Audits all commands at the specified privilege level (0 through 15).
default	Uses the listed accounting methods that follow this argument as the default list of methods for accounting services.
list-name	Character string used to name the list of accounting methods.
start-stop	Sends a start accounting notice at the beginning of a process and a stop accounting notice at the end of a process. The start accounting record is sent in the background. The requested user process begins even if the start accounting notice was not received by the accounting server.
wait-start	As in **start-stop**, sends both a start and a stop accounting notice to the accounting server. However, if you use the **wait-start** keyword, the requested user service does not begin until the start accounting notice is acknowledged. A stop accounting notice is also sent.
stop-only	Sends a stop accounting notice at the end of the requested user process.

Command Parameter	Description
none	Disables accounting services on this line or interface.
method1, *method2*	Enables TACACS+ or RADIUS accounting using either the **radius** or **tacacs+** keywords.

The commands listed in Table 5-4 are configuration commands for AAA accounting that should be used in global configuration mode.

Table 5-4 *AAA Accounting Commands*

Command	Description
aaa accounting system wait-start local	Audits system events using the wait-start accounting method.
aaa accounting network stop-only local	Sends stop record notices when network services terminate.
aaa accounting exec start-stop local	Sends a start record notice when the EXEC process begins and a stop record when the EXEC process ends.
aaa accounting commands 15 wait-start local	Sends a start record notice and waits for acknowledgment before any level 15 command can begin. Sends a stop record notice when the command terminates.

Step 6: Debug the Configuration

The **debug aaa** commands are used to see what methods of authentication and authorization are being used, to show the results of these methods, and to show accounting events as they occur.

You use the **debug** commands shown in Table 5-5 on the NAS to monitor authentication, authorization, and accounting activities.

Table 5-5 *AAA Debug Commands*

Command Parameter	Description
debug aaa authentication	Displays information on AAA/TACACS+ authentication. Use the **no** form of the command to disable debugging output.
debug aaa authorization	Displays information on AAA/TACACS+ authorization. Use the **no** form of the command to disable debugging output.

continues

Table 5-5 *AAA Debug Commands (Continued)*

Command Parameter	Description
debug aaa accounting	Displays information on accountable events as they occur. Use the **no** form of the command to disable debugging output.

Output formats vary with each **debug** command. Some commands generate a single line of output per packet, whereas others generate multiple lines of output per packet. Some generate large amounts of output, and others generate only occasional output. Some generate lines of text, and others generate information in field format.

Summary

This section summarizes the main points of this chapter:

- The process of configuring NAS security using AAA involves six steps:
  - Secure access to privileged EXEC and configuration mode (enable and enable secret) on vty, asynchronous, auxiliary, and tty ports.
  - Enable AAA globally on the NAS with the **aaa new-model** command.
  - Configure AAA authentication profiles, ensuring that you have a last-resort access method before you are certain that your security server is set up and functioning properly.
  - Configure AAA authorization for use after the user has passed authentication.
  - Configure the AAA accounting options for how you want to write accounting records and what you want accounted for in them.
  - Debug the configuration if necessary.
- In local-server AAA, the local NAS performs AAA services.
- Character and packet modes can be secured with AAA.
- Network access server AAA configuration should follow an orderly progression.
- Use the **aaa authentication** command to specify the authentication process and method.
- Use **aaa debug** commands selectively to troubleshoot AAA.
- Use the **no aaa new-model** command to remove AAA commands from the configuration.

Case Study: Configuring the NAS for AAA Security

This case study illustrates how to configure the NAS to provide AAA services in the hypothetical XYZ Company. Read the case study scenario, examine the topology diagram, read the security policy, and then analyze the configuration example to see how the security policy statements are enacted for the Cisco routers.

Case Study Scenario

The XYZ Company wants to secure dialup access for remote employees. It wants to configure a NAS to enable AAA functions with a local security database initially and then later prepare the NAS for use in conjunction with CiscoSecure ACS for NT (CSNT) as a AAA server.

Topology

Figure 5-3 illustrates the portion of the XYZ network that will be configured in this case study. Note that the focus is on the elements involving the NAS.

Figure 5-3   *The NAS on the XYZ Company Corporate Network*

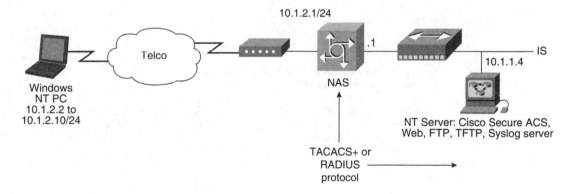

Network Security Policy

The network security policy that XYZ wants to implement is as follows:

- Network equipment will be configured with access passwords at entry points to the NAS.

- Dialup access will be strictly controlled using password authentication from the local database.

- The XYZ Company will prepare for migration to a remote security database running the TACACS+ protocol for policy enforcement of authentication.

NAS Configuration Example

Examine the configuration example for the NAS1 device of the XYZ Company shown in Example 5-4. This example implements the network security policy statements related to access security configuration on the NAS. One possible configuration of the NAS for the specified security policy might look as follows. You might have chosen to configure the router differently to enact the same security policy requirements. Note that the sample configuration contains comments showing which router commands enact particular security policy statements. Unrelated commands were deleted for the sake of brevity.

Example 5-4 *Sample Configuration for the NAS1 Device*

```
version 12.0
!
! setting up proper time reference for messages
service timestamps debug datetime msec
service timestamps log uptime
no service password-encryption
!
hostname NAS1
!

! Establish a new AAA section, and secure lines
aaa new-model
aaa authentication login default enable
aaa authentication login console-in local
aaa authentication login vty-in local
aaa authentication login tty-in line
aaa authentication ppp dial-in if-needed local
!
enable secret 5 $1$a8hM$8S2.ZmgUyGL2Ask4TVRSQ.
enable password 7 0300540C5E0B2E4B
!
username admin password 0 back door
username isgroup password 0 other door
username remotes password 0 billy8bong
clock timezone PST -8
ip subnet-zero
ip host modem 2097 10.1.1.1
!
!
!
!
!
interface BRI0/0
 no ip address
 no ip directed-broadcast
 shutdown
!
interface Ethernet0/0
 ip address 10.1.1.1 255.255.255.0
 no ip directed-broadcast
!
```

Example 5-4 *Sample Configuration for the NAS1 Device (Continued)*

```
interface Ethernet0/1
 no ip address
 no ip directed-broadcast
 shutdown
!
interface Serial3/0
 physical-layer async
 ip address 10.1.2.1 255.255.255.0
 no ip directed-broadcast
 encapsulation ppp
 ip tcp header-compression passive
 async mode dedicated
 peer default ip address pool classpool
 no fair-queue
 no cdp enable
 ppp authentication chap dial-in
!
interface Serial3/1
 no ip address
 no ip directed-broadcast
 shutdown
!
interface Serial3/2
 no ip address
 no ip directed-broadcast
 shutdown
!
interface Serial3/3
 no ip address
 no ip directed-broadcast
 shutdown
!
router rip
 network 10.0.0.0
!
ip local pool classpool 10.1.2.2 10.1.2.10
ip classless
ip route 0.0.0.0 0.0.0.0 10.1.1.3
no ip http server
!
!
line console 0
 exec-timeout 0 0
 password 7 110F0B0A19064B080B2539
 logging synchronous
 login authentication console-in
 transport input none
line 65 70
line 97
 no exec
 password 7 0825454F0554100417191F
 login authentication tty-in
```

continues

Example 5-4 *Sample Configuration for the NAS1 Device (Continued)*

```
 modem InOut
 modem autoconfigure type usr_sportster
 transport input all
 stopbits 1
 speed 115200
 flowcontrol hardware
line aux 0
 password 7 094D4A04100B5A16020D08
line vty 0 4
 password 7 121C061F1D52
 login authentication is-in
 !
end
```

Review Questions

Answer the following review questions, which delve into some of the key facts and concepts covered in this chapter:

1 What would you use the **service password-encryption** command for when preparing to implement AAA configurations?

2 Which two network access server modes can be secured by AAA commands?

3 Why is the **local** parameter needed in the command **aaa authentication ppp sales if-needed local**?

4 Which AAA commands would be useful to enable AAA globally and instantly secure all access lines?

5 What does the **aaa authorization network Pisces local none** command do?

6 What EXEC command can be used to monitor information on accountable events as they occur?

7 What three steps are used to define method lists?

8 What command might you use to ensure a proper time reference for messages as you begin a **debug aaa authentication** session?

9 What does the **aaa accounting exec start-stop local** command do?

10 When using the **aaa authentication** command to define an authentication method list, how many authentication methods can be specified?

References

This chapter summarizes the configuration process to implement security policy on your NAS. The following references will help you increase your knowledge of AAA and security policy in general.

Configuring Security Policy

The System Administration, Networking, and Security (SANS) Institute (www.sans.org) is a cooperative research and education organization for system administrators, security professionals, and network administrators.

Model Security Policies—Compiled by Michele Crabb-Guel is a collection of templates and overview information for use in crafting your own security policies. It also has reference information from the SANS course "Building an Effective Security Infrastructure." It is located at www.sans.org/newlook/resources/policies/policies.htm.

RFC 2196, "The Site Security Procedures Handbook," provides overview information on security policies and authentication procedures. It is located at ds.internic.net/rfc/rfc2196.txt.

Configuring AAA

Security Command Reference, Cisco IOS Release 12.0, October 1998.

Security Configuration Guide, Cisco IOS Release 12.0, October 1998.

Upon completing this chapter, you will be able to do the following:

- Describe the features and architecture of CiscoSecure ACS 2.4 for Windows NT

- Configure CiscoSecure ACS for Windows NT to perform AAA functions

- Describe the features and architecture of CiscoSecure ACS 2.3 for UNIX

- Configure the network access server to allow AAA processes to use a TACACS+ remote security database

CHAPTER 6

Configuring CiscoSecure ACS and TACACS+/RADIUS

This chapter explores the CiscoSecure Access Control Server (ACS) software. The CiscoSecure ACS software is designed to help ensure the security of your network and track the activity of people who successfully connect to your network. The CiscoSecure ACS software uses either the Terminal Access Controller Access Control System (TACACS)+ or the Remote Access Dial-In User Service (RADIUS) protocol to provide this network security and tracking. The CiscoSecure ACS uses authentication, authorization, and accounting (AAA) to provide network security.

You will then configure a network access server (NAS) for each of the AAA functions. A complete listing of a NAS configuration file is available for you to compare to your own configuration efforts. This configuration listing is built on similar test equipment and is annotated to link configuration commands to security policies.

CiscoSecure ACS for Windows NT and UNIX

CiscoSecure ACS is available for both the NT and UNIX operating systems. Common to both of these packages is a Web browser interface that allows you to do the following:

- Support centralization of AAA for access via NAS, routers, switches, and firewalls
- Manage Telnet access to routers and switches
- Support unlimited Cisco network access servers
- Support token cards and servers
- Manage TACACS+-enabled and RADIUS-enabled NAS clients
- Manage TACACS+-enabled and RADIUS-enabled CiscoSecure ACSs
- Set up and manage remote connections to virtual private dial-up networks (VPDNs)
- Configure a default profile to accommodate guest users or users logging in through a client NAS who are authorized by some other control system to access the network
- Assign midlevel group administrative privileges
- Configure token caching for all users logging in through a token server
- Assign group-level absolute attributes
- Administer Secure Computing token card users

Other common features of ACS include support of TACACS+ and RADIUS protocols, support for database replication, command-line interface support, and profile data caching for enhanced authentication performance.

CiscoSecure ACS software supports Cisco NASs and any third-party device that can be configured with the TACACS+ and/or RADIUS protocol. CiscoSecure ACS uses the TACACS+ and/or RADIUS protocols to provide AAA services to ensure a secure environment.

The NAS is configured to direct all user access requests to CiscoSecure ACS for authentication and authorization of privileges. Using the TACACS+ or RADIUS protocol, the NAS sends authentication requests to CiscoSecure ACS, which verifies the username and password against the selected user database. CiscoSecure ACS then returns a success or failure response to the NAS, which permits or denies user access.

When the user has successfully authenticated, a set of session attributes can be sent to the NAS to provide additional security and control of privileges. These attributes might include the IP address pool, access control list, or type of connection (for example, IP, IPX, or Telnet).

TACACS+ Support

CiscoSecure ACS conforms to the TACACS+ protocol as defined by Cisco Systems in draft 1.77. See your Cisco IOS Software documentation or www.cisco.com for more information.

RADIUS Support

CiscoSecure ACS software conforms to the RADIUS protocol as defined in draft April 1997 and in the following Requests for Comments (RFCs): RFC 2138 ("Remote Authentication Dial In User Service"), RFC 2139 ("RADIUS Accounting"), draft-ietf-radius-tunnel-auth-07.txt, and draft-ietf-radius-tunnel-acct-03.txt.

CiscoSecure ACS for Windows NT

CiscoSecure ACS for NT (CSNT) operates as a Windows NT Service and controls the AAA of users accessing networks. Each facet of AAA significantly contributes to the overall security of your network:

- *Authentication* determines the identity of users and whether they should be allowed access to the network.
- *Authorization* determines the level of network services available to authenticated users after they are connected.
- *Accounting* keeps track of each user's network activity.

AAA within a client/server architecture (in which transaction responsibilities are divided into two parts: client [front end] and server [back end]) allows you to store all security information in a single centralized database instead of distributing the information around the network in many different devices.

CSNT operates with Windows NT Server version 4.0, with at least Service Pack 4 installed. CSNT supports the centralization of access control and accounting for dialup, campus, and Internet access. It centralizes access to dialup access servers and firewalls as well as management of access to routers and switches. System administrators can quickly administer accounts and globally change levels of service offerings for entire groups of users, improving the system administrators' ability to manage dialup and networking services throughout the corporation from a central point. Because of the tight integration between CSNT and the Windows NT operating system, companies may leverage the working knowledge as well as the investment already made into building a Windows NT network.

CSNT supports the Cisco PIX Firewall and different Cisco network access servers such as the Cisco 1600 series, 2500 series, 2600 series, 3600 series, AS5200, AS5300, and AS5800. CSNT also supports authentication and authorization of network access server products developed by vendors other than Cisco that support IETF, Ascend RADIUS, or TACACS+.

You view the CSNT administration interface using a supported Web browser, which makes it easy to administer. Figure 6-1 illustrates the CiscoSecure ACS for Windows NT interface.

Figure 6-1   *The CiscoSecure ACS for NT Web Interface*

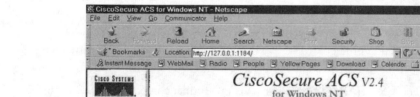

CSNT authenticates usernames and passwords against the Windows NT User Database, the CSNT ACS User Database, or a token server database.

Different levels of security can be used with CiscoSecure ACS for different requirements. The basic user-to-network security level is Password Authentication Protocol (PAP). Although it does not represent the highest form of encrypted security, PAP does offer the client convenience and simplicity. PAP allows authentication against the Windows NT database. With this configuration, users need to log in only once. Challenge Handshake Authentication Protocol (CHAP) allows a higher level of security for encrypting passwords when communicating from a client to the NAS. You can use CHAP with the CiscoSecure ACS User Database.

Comparing PAP, CHAP, and ARAP

PAP, CHAP, and ARAP are authentication protocols used to encrypt passwords. Each provides a different level of security:

- **PAP**—Uses cleartext passwords and is the least-sophisticated authentication protocol. If you are using the Windows NT User Database to authenticate users, you must use PAP password encryption.

- **CHAP**—Uses a challenge-response mechanism with one-way encryption on the response. CHAP lets CiscoSecure ACS negotiate downward from the most-secure to the least-secure encryption mechanism, and it protects passwords transmitted in the process. CHAP passwords are reusable. If you are using the CiscoSecure ACS User Database for authentication, you can use either PAP or CHAP.

- **MS-CHAP**—CiscoSecure ACS supports Microsoft Challenge Handshake Authentication Protocol (MS-CHAP) for user authentication. The differences between MS-CHAP and standard CHAP are as follows:

  — The MS-CHAP Response packet is in a format compatible with Microsoft Windows NT, Windows 95/98, and LAN Manager 2.x. The MS-CHAP format does not require the authenticator to store a cleartext or reversibly encrypted password.

  — MS-CHAP provides an authenticator-controlled authentication retry mechanism.

  — MS-CHAP provides additional failure codes in the Failure packet Message field.

  — With MS-CHAP, the NT User Database can be securely used for authentication.

- **AppleTalk Remote Access Protocol (ARAP)**—Uses a two-way challenge-response mechanism. The NAS challenges the dial-in client to authenticate itself, and the dial-in client challenges the NAS to authenticate itself.

Features of CSNT

The general features of CSNT include the following:

- You have simultaneous TACACS+ and RADIUS support. You can use TACACS+ or RADIUS between CiscoSecure ACS and a NAS.

- It allows authentication against the Windows NT User Database or the ACS User Database. Windows NT User Database support does the following:

  — Leverages and consolidates Windows NT username and password management

  — Enables a single login to the network and the Windows NT domain

  — Runs on Windows NT standalone primary domain controller (PDC) and backup domain controller (BDC) server configurations

- It supports all the leading authentication protocols including CHAP, PAP, MS-CHAP, ARAP, external token card servers, the Windows NT User Database, and Novell NDS.

- It supports the NAS callback feature for increased security.

- It disables the account after a specified number of failed logins.

AAA Product Features of CSNT

CSNT supports the following AAA features:

- It provides TACACS+ support for access lists (named or numbered), time-of-day and day-of-week access restrictions, enable privilege levels, authentication to an LDAP server, and OTP for enable passwords.

- It provides RADIUS support for IETF RADIUS, Cisco RADIUS AV-pair, proprietary RADIUS extensions, and RADIUS tunneling attributes.

- It provides a single TACACS+/RADIUS database for simultaneous support.

- Virtual private network (VPN) and VPDN support are available at the origination and termination of VPN (L2F) tunnels

- It has user restrictions based on remote address Caller Line Identification (CLID).

- You can disable an account on a specific date or after a specified number of failed attempts.

CiscoSecure ACS Release 2.4 adds the following new features and capabilities to earlier releases:

- **Encryption enhancements**—Stronger encryption for the CiscoSecure ACS database.

- **Database replication enhancements**—Enhancements to the database replication feature.

- **Directory services authentication**—Authentication to any supported version of the LDAP directory service.

- **External user database enable options**—The ability for external users to authenticate via an enable password.

- **Group-level network device groups (NDGs)**—The ability to assign user groups to an NDG.

- **NDS database group mappings**—The ability to map a Novell Directory Services (NDS) group.

- **RDBMS Synchronization enhancements**—The ability to synchronize NAS, AAA, NDG, and proxy table entries.

- **The availability of VPDNs, using the CiscoSecure ACS User Database with RADIUS tunneling attributes**—Support for IETF RADIUS tunneling attributes, which allows you to specify multiple tunnels in a single RADIUS packet.

- **VoIP accounting**—The ability to log Voice over IP (VoIP) accounting data to the normal RADIUS accounting comma-separated value (CSV) and Open Database Connectivity (ODBC) file, the additional VoIP accounting CSV or ODBC file, or both.

- **Date format control**—The ability to use either a month/day/year or day/month/year format.

- **Microsoft Callback**—Support for the Microsoft Callback feature.

- **CSV and ODBC log files**—Support for both CSV- and ODBC-compatible accounting and administration logging.

Administration Product Features

CSNT has many user-friendly administration features:

- Its HTML/JAVA GUI allows management from a Web browser via LAN or by dialing in. This simplifies and distributes configuration for ACS, user profiles, and group profiles:

  — Help and online documentation are included for quick problem solving, accessible via Web browser (not an SSL browser—it uses CSAdmin).

  — It allows group administration of users for maximum flexibility and to facilitate enforcement and changes of security policies.

  — Remote administration is permitted or denied by a unique administration username/password.

  — A remote administrator session has a timeout value.

  — You can view a logged-in user list for a quick look at who is connected.

- It supports Windows NT Performance Monitor so that you can view real-time statistics such as transactions per second.

- It creates separate TACACS+ and RADIUS files, stored in the CSV spreadsheet format for easy import into databases and spreadsheet applications.

- It has an import utility to rapidly import a large number of users.

- It offers hash-indexed flat-file database support for high-speed transaction processing (CSNT User Database).

Distributed System Features

CSNT can be used in a distributed system. Multiple CSNT servers and AAA servers can be configured to communicate with one another as masters, clients, or peers. CSNT also recognizes network access restrictions of other CSNT servers on the distributed network. CSNT allows you to use powerful features such as the following:

- **Authentication forwarding**—CSNT can automatically forward an authentication request from a NAS to another CSNT. After authentication, authorization privileges are applied to the NAS for that user authentication.

- **Fallback upon a failed connection**—You can configure the order in which the remote CSNT servers will be checked by the CSNT client if the network connection to the primary CSNT server fails. If an authentication request cannot be sent to the first listed server, the next listed server is checked in order down the list until the authentication request is handled by a CSNT server. If the CSNT client cannot connect to any of the servers in the list, authentication fails.

- **Remote and centralized logging**—CSNT can be configured to point to a centralized CSNT that will be used as the logging server. The centralized CSNT will still have all the capabilities that a CSNT server has, with the addition of being a central repository for all accounting logs that are sent.

CSNT External Database Support

CSNT can authenticate users who are defined in Network Operating System security databases or directory services, such as Novell NDS or Windows NT accounts database, and it supports authentication forwarding to LDAP servers. ODBC support is available to rapidly import a large number of users.

Database Information Management Features

The Database Replication and Remote Database Management System (RDBMS) Synchronization features are provided with CSNT to help automate the process of keeping your CSNT database and network configuration current. The CSUtil.exe utility allows database backup and restoration functionality.

Database Replication

Database Replication is a powerful feature designed to simplify the construction of a fault-tolerant AAA service environment based on CiscoSecure 2.4 for Windows NT. The primary purpose of Database Replication is to replicate various parts of the setup on a CSNT master server to one or more CSNT client systems, allowing the administrator to automate the creation of mirror systems. These mirror systems can then be used to provide server redundancy as fallback or secondary servers to support fault-tolerant operation in case of the failure of the master or primary system.

Do not confuse Database Replication with Database/System Backup. Database Replication is an incomplete replacement for Database Backup. You should still have a reliable database backup strategy to ensure data integrity.

RDBMS Synchronization

RDBMS Synchronization is an integration feature designed to simplify integration of CiscoSecure 2.4 for Windows NT with a third-party RDBMS application. RDBMS Synchronization automates synchronization with another RDBMS data source by providing the following functions:

- Specification of an ODBC data source to use for synchronization data shared by the CSNT and the other RDBMS application and to provide control of the CSNT updates to an external application

- Control of the timing of the import/synchronization process, including the creation of schedules

- Control of which systems are to be synchronized

The RDBMS Synchronization feature has two components, CSDBSync and an ODBC data store table. CSDBSync is a dedicated Windows NT Service that performs automated user and group account management services for the CSNT. The ODBC data store specifies the record format. Each record holds user or group information that corresponds with the data stored for each user in the CSNT database. Additionally, each record contains other fields, including an action code for the record. Any application can write to this table. CSDBSync reads from it and takes actions on each record it finds in the table (for example, add user, delete user, and so on) as determined by the action code.

ODBC Import Definitions

CSNT supports the import of data from ODBC-compliant databases such as Microsoft Access and Oracle. Importing is done with a single table to import user and group information into one or more ACS servers. The CSAccupdate service processes the table and updates local and remote ACS installations according to its configuration.

CSNT System Requirements

Before installing CSNT, you need to ensure that the system that will run it meets the following minimum requirements (to improve performance of services, you should increase the RAM, CPU speed, and hard drive speed and capacity as appropriate for your environment):

- IBM PC or compatible with a Pentium 200 MHz processor or better.

- 64 MB of RAM minimum. 128 MB recommended.

- CD-ROM support.

- At least 150 MB free space. Typical installations might require at least twice this much free space.

- Windows NT Server 4.0 (with SP5 or SP6).

- A minimum monitor resolution of 256 colors at 800×600 lines.

- One of the following browsers must be installed on the PC running CSNT and on remote administration systems: Microsoft Internet Explorer 4.x or 5.x, Netscape Navigator 4.0.x, or Netscape Communicator 4.x. Also, Java and JavaScript support must be enabled.

- Cisco IOS Software Release 11.1 or later on the NAS. IOS 11.1 is required for RADIUS support.

- PIX Firewall version 4.24 or later.

CSNT Architecture

CSNT provides AAA services to multiple NASs. It includes the administration service and the six service modules described here:

- **Administration service (CSAdmin)**—The service for the internal Web server. CSNT is equipped with its own internal server. After CSNT is installed, you must configure it from its HTML/Java interface, which requires CSAdmin to always be enabled.

- **The CSAuth module**—The primary responsibility of CSNT is the authentication and authorization of requests from devices to permit or deny access to a specified user. CSAuth is the service responsible for determining whether access should be granted and defining the privileges associated with that user. CSAuth is the database manager.

- **The CSTacacs and CSRadius modules**—Services communicate between the CSAuth module and the access device requesting the authentication and authorization services. CSTacacs is used to communicate with TACACS+ devices, and CSRadius is used to communicate with RADIUS devices. Both services can run at the same time. When only one security protocol is used, only the respective service needs to run.

- **The CSLog module**—The service used to capture and place logging information. CSLog gathers data from the TACACS+ or RADIUS packet and CSAuth and manipulates the data to be put into the CSV files. The CSV files are created daily, starting at midnight. CSV files are stored in the default subdirectory \Program Files\CSNT v2.4\Logs\.

- **The CSDBSynch module**—Used to perform automated user and group account management services for CiscoSecure ACS.

- **The CSMonitor module**—CiscoSecure ACS monitors itself and corrects system problems.

Each of these modules can be started and stopped individually from within the Microsoft Service Control Panel or as a group from within the CSNT browser interface. These can also be controlled using the Windows NT Task Manager.

Using the ACS Database

Using either the RADIUS or TACACS+ protocol, the NAS directs all dial-in user access requests to the CSNT for authentication and authorization of privileges, which verifies the username and password. The CSNT then returns a success or failure response to the NAS to permit or deny user access. When the user has been authenticated, CSNT sends a set of authorization attributes to the NAS, and the accounting functions take effect.

When the CSNT User Database is selected, the following service and database interactions occur:

- TACACS+ or RADIUS directs a request to the CSNT Authentication and Authorization NT Service, where the request is authenticated against the CSNT User Database, associated authorizations are assigned, and accounting information is logged to the CSNT Logging service.

- The Windows NT User Database does not authenticate the user to permit dial-in. The user must log in to Windows NT when the dialup AAA process is complete.

The CSNT uses a built-in user database that is a hash-indexed flat file. This type of file is not searched from the top of a text file, as is typically associated with the term *flat file*. Instead, it is indexed like a database. The hash-indexed flat file builds an index and tree structure that optimize the search process, allowing the CSNT User Database to rapidly authenticate users.

Using the CSNT User Database requires you to manually enter the usernames. However, after the names exist in the CSNT User Database, administration is easier than with using the Windows NT User Database. The CSNT User Database supports authentication for both PAP and CHAP.

Figure 6-2 illustrates the interaction between the NAS and the ACS database of CSNT.

Figure 6-2   *Interaction Between the NAS and the ACS Database*

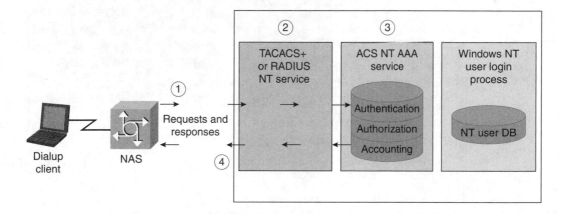

The steps in the authentication process are as follows:

1 Requests and responses, such as username and password, authentication confirmation, and authorization information, are passed to the CSNT.

2 The NT Service directs the request to the appropriate administrative service.

3 The request is authenticated against the ACS NT database, associated authorizations are assigned, and accounting information is logged.

4 The NT User Database does not authenticate the user to permit dial-in. The user must log in to NT after the dialup AAA process is complete.

Using the NT Database

When the CSNT uses the Windows NT User Database for AAA, TACACS+ or RADIUS directs a request to the CSNT Authentication and Authorization service, where the username and password are sent to the Windows NT User Database for authentication.

An added benefit of using the Windows NT User Database is that the username and password used for authentication are the same as those used for network login. Therefore, you can require users to enter their username and password once, for the convenience of a single, simple login.

Figure 6-3 illustrates the interaction between the NAS and the NT Security Accounts Manager.

Figure 6-3 *Interaction Between the NAS and the NT Security Accounts Manager*

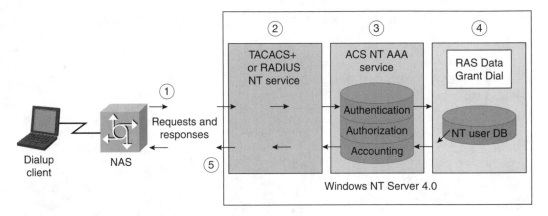

The steps in the authentication process are as follows:

1 Requests and responses, such as username and password, authentication confirmation, and authorization information, are passed to the CSNT.

2 The TACACS+ or RADIUS NT Service directs the request to the appropriate administrative service.

3 The username and password are sent to the NT User Database for authentication. If they are approved, confirmation and the associated authorization assigned in ACS NT for that user are sent to NAS. Accounting information is logged.

4 The username and password are submitted to NT and grant dial-in as a local user. A response is returned to ACS NT and authorizations are assigned, which makes a single login for dialup and network login possible.

5 Responses are sent back to NAS.

CSNT Token Card Support

CSNT includes the CryptoCard token card server software and supports the Security Dynamics, Inc. (SDI), SafeWord, and Axent token card servers for authentication. CSNT can authenticate against any hexadecimal X.909-compliant token cards such as the DES

Gold Card. The CSNT is configured as a client to the token card server. As when using the Windows NT User Database, when that username is located in the CSNT User Database, CSAuth sees the token card server selected to compare the username and token card password against. The token card server then provides a response, approving or denying validation. If validation is approved, CSAuth knows that authentication should be granted for the user.

In the case of using a token card server, the CSNT manages communications, via TACACS+ or RADIUS, with the device where the client is requesting network access. Although token servers might offer some support for TACACS+ or RADIUS, that function is not used because the CSNT maintains that communication. Therefore, TACACS+ or RADIUS should be disabled at the token card server.

CSNT supports token caching for ISDN terminal adapters (TAs). When token caching is enabled, ISDN users can connect a second B channel through bandwidth-on-demand (multilink), using the same one-time password entered during the original authentication (this token is cached and remains valid for only a limited time). The risk of the second B channel being hijacked is reduced by using CHAP for the password cached for the second channel and by limiting the duration of time that the second B channel can use the cached token.

Figure 6-4 illustrates token card support between the NAS, CSNT, and the token server.

Figure 6-4   *Token Card Support*

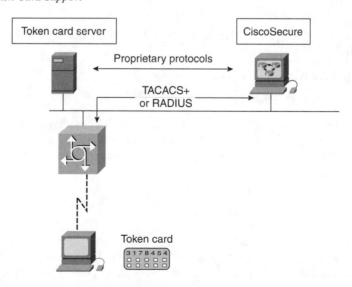

Installing CSNT

CSNT is easy to install and configure. This section presents a brief overview of the essential installation steps. The following discussion assumes that a PPP dialup user is authenticated against CSNT using the Windows NT User Database via the TACACS+ protocol.

The CSNT installation can be condensed to the following steps:

Step 1 Configure the Windows NT Server to work with CSNT.

Step 2 Verify a basic network connection from Windows NT to the client PC, network access server, or PIX using ping and Telnet.

Step 3 Install CSNT on the Windows NT Server. CSNT uses an InstallShield-based setup.

Step 4 Initially configure CSNT via the Web browser interface.

Step 5 Configure the network access server, PIX, and the client PC for AAA.

The following sections describe these steps in more detail. After completing these steps, you can verify or troubleshoot operations using the information in the section "Administering and Troubleshooting CSNT."

Step 1: Configure the NT Server

To configure Windows NT for CSNT, you need to do the following:

1 Determine the Windows NT Server type, based on the design of the company's Windows NT Server architecture.

2 Configure Windows NT User Manager.

3 Use Windows NT Services to control ACS.

When running CSNT on a PDC/BDC and using multiple domains, you can make authentication requests across interdomain trusts, given that local login is enabled for the user on that domain, grant dial-in permission does not cross the trust with CSNT, and the user authenticates on domain 1 CSNT.

Step 2: Verify Connections

You need to verify that the dialup client, the network access server, and/or the PIX Firewall can ping the Windows NT server that will host CSNT. This verification simplifies installation and eliminates problems when you configure CSNT and devices that interface with it.

Step 3: Install CSNT on the Server

CSNT is easy to install from a CD-ROM. It installs like any other Windows application, using an InstallShield-based setup program. Before you begin the installation, ensure that you have network access server information such as host name, IP address, and TACACS+ key.

Follow these InstallShield instructions:

1 Select and configure the database.

2 Configure CSNT for NAS using the Web browser.

3 Configure NAS and PIX for CSNT.

4 Configure CSNT using the Web browser.

Step 4: Configure CSNT via the Web Browser

After you successfully install CSNT, an ACSNT Admin icon appears on the NT desktop. You need to continue initially configuring CSNT with the Web browser interface. CSNT is HTML only, so using a Web browser is the only way to configure it. You can launch the browser by using http://127.0.0.1:2002, http://*<ip address>*:2002, or http://*<host name>*:2002.

Step 5: Configure the Remaining Devices for AAA

You must configure the NAS, PIX Firewall, routers, and switches to work with CSNT. Specific configuration of these devices is covered in later chapters.

You might also need to configure a token card server to work with CSNT to perform AAA. Here are some of the possible configuration combinations when CSNT is used to perform AAA. In each configuration, each of the devices must be configured to work with CSNT:

- Dialup using the Windows NT User Database with TACACS+

- Dialup using the CSNT User Database with TACACS+

- Dialup using a token card server with TACACS+

- Dialup using the CSNT User Database with RADIUS (Cisco)

- Dialup for an ARAP client using the CSNT User Database with TACACS+

- Router management using the CSNT User Database with TACACS+

- PIX Firewall authentication/authorization using the Windows NT User Database with TACACS+

- VPDN using the CSNT User Database with TACACS+

Administering and Troubleshooting CSNT

The Web browser interface is the key to the administration and configuration of CSNT. This interface provides access to all the product's features, from any location accessible by the browser. The ability to access reports on the activity of CSNT via the Web browser is a starting point for troubleshooting. The following sections describe these administration and troubleshooting tasks and list typical debugging commands.

Administering CSNT

The CSNT Web browser interface makes administering AAA features easy. Each of the nine buttons on the navigational bar represents a particular area or function that you can configure. Depending on your configuration, you might not need to configure all the areas. Select one of these buttons to begin configuring:

- **User Setup**—Adds, edits, and deletes user accounts and lists the users in the databases.

- **Group Setup**—Creates, edits, and renames groups and lists all users in a group. You can configure authorization to give different users and groups different levels of service.

- **Network Configuration**—Configures and edits network access server parameters, adds and deletes network access servers, and configures AAA server distribution parameters.

- **System Configuration**—Starts and stops CSNT services, configures logging, controls database replication, and controls RDBMS synchronization.

- **Interface Configuration**—Configures user-defined fields that will be recorded in accounting logs, configures TACACS+ and RADIUS options, and controls the display of options in the user interface.

- **Administration Control**—Controls the administration of CSNT from any workstation on the network.

- **External User Databases**—Configures the unknown users policy, configures authorization privileges for unknown users, and configures external database types.

- **Reports and Activity**—Finds the following information, which you can import into most database and spreadsheet applications:

  — **RADIUS Accounting Reports**—Lists when sessions stop and start, records network access server messages with the username, provides caller line identification information, and records the duration of each session.

  — **Failed Attempts Report**—Lists authentication and authorization failures, with an indication of the cause.

— **List Logged in Users**—Lists all users currently receiving services for a single network access server or all network access servers that have access to the CSNT.

— **List Disabled Accounts**—Lists all user accounts that are currently disabled.

— **Admin Accounting Reports**—Lists configuration commands entered on a TACACS+ (Cisco) network access server.

— **TACACS+ Accounting Reports**—Lists when sessions stop and start, records network access server messages with the username, provides caller line identification information, and records the duration of each session.

- **Online Documentation**—Gives more-detailed information about the configuration, operation, and concepts of CSNT.

The order of this list follows the default order of the buttons in the navigational bar. The order to follow for configuration depends on your preferences and needs.

Troubleshooting CSNT

If you need to troubleshoot CSNT-related AAA problems, begin by examining the Failed Attempts Report under the Reports and Activity section of the CSNT GUI. This report shows several types of failures.

A variety of Cisco IOS **debug** commands are useful for troubleshooting CSNT. Table 6-1 is a partial listing of these commands and their usage.

Table 6-1   *debug Commands for CSNT*

Command	Description
debug aaa authentication	Enabling this **debug** command displays authentication information with TACACS+ and RADIUS client/server interaction.
debug aaa authorization	Enabling this **debug** command displays authorization information with TACACS+ and RADIUS client/server interaction.
debug tacacs	Enabling this **debug** command displays TACACS+ interaction between the IOS client and the AAA server.
debug radius	Enabling this **debug** command displays RADIUS interaction between the IOS client and the AAA server.

Table 6-2 provides further troubleshooting assistance for CSNT, in the form of common problems and resolutions.

Table 6-2 *Common CSNT Problems and Troubleshooting*

Common Problem	Troubleshooting
Authentication failure—Assume that CSNT and NAS are communicating and that you are authenticating against the Windows NT User Database.	Check the following: • Are the username and password being entered correctly? (The password is case sensitive.) • Do the username and password exist in the Windows NT User Database? (Check User Manager.) • Is the box User must change password at next login checked in Windows NT? (Uncheck it if it is.) • Does the username have the rights to log on locally in the Windows NT Server window (Trust Relationship/Domain)? • Is CSNT configured to authenticate against the Windows NT User Database? • Is CSNT configured to reference the **grant dial-in permission to user**? • If the username could authenticate before and cannot now, is the account disabled on Windows NT or CSNT? • Has the password expired on Windows NT? • Does the username contain an illegal character?
Authorization failure—The dial-in user is authenticating, but authorization is failing.	Check the following: • Are the proper network services checked in the Group Settings? • If IP is checked, how is the dial-in user obtaining an IP address? • Is an IP pool configured on the network access server? • Is the name of the IP pool entered in the Group Settings? (Leave it blank if a default IP pool has been configured.) • If you're authorizing commands, has the appropriate command-level AAA authorization statement been entered into the Cisco IOS configuration? • Has the Permitted radio button for the command been selected? • Has the Permitted radio button for the argument been selected?

Table 6-2   *Common CSNT Problems and Troubleshooting (Continued)*

Common Problem	Troubleshooting
No Entry in the Failed Attempts Report—If authentication or authorization is failing, but there is no entry in the Failed Attempts Report, there is an invalid setup between CSNT and the network access server.	Check the following: • Can the network access server ping the Windows NT server? • Can the Windows NT Server ping the NAS? • Is the TACACS+ host IP address correctly configured in the NAS? • Is the identical TACACS+ host key entered on both the NAS and CSNT? • Is TACACS+ accounting configured on the NAS?
Dial-in client PC problems—The dial-in user is a Windows 95 PC using Dial-Up Networking.	Check the following: • Are connection properties configured to require an encrypted password under Server Type? • Is the connection configured to use the correct protocol? • Is the selected Dial-Up Server type PPP: Windows 95, Windows NT 3.5, Internet? • Is the user authorized to use a specific command?
Remote administration	Check the following: • Is the Web browser configured correctly? Is enough cache allocated, and is Java enabled? • Is Remote Administration configured to allow remote Web browser access (IP address, username/password)?

CiscoSecure ACS for UNIX

CiscoSecure ACS 2.3 for UNIX (CSUNIX) integrates seamlessly into enterprise networks. ACS is used to authenticate users and to determine which internal networks and services they may access. By authenticating users against a database of user and group profiles, CSUNIX effectively secures enterprise and service provider networks from unauthorized access.

CSUNIX incorporates a new, multiuser, Web-based Java configuration and management tool that simplifies server administration and lets multiple system administrators simultaneously manage security services from multiple locations. The GUI supports Microsoft and Netscape Web browsers, providing multiplatform compatibility and offering secure administration via the industry-standard Secure Sockets Layer (SSL) communication mechanism.

CSUNIX includes CryptoCard token card server software and supports Secure Computing Corporation and Security Dynamics Technologies token card servers. Token cards are the strongest available method for authenticating users dialing in. They prevent unauthorized users from accessing proprietary information.

CSUNIX now supports industry-leading relational database technologies from Sybase and Oracle, removing earlier limitations of scalability, redundancy, and nondistributed architecture, and simplifying storage and management of user and group profile information.

Features of CSUNIX

Security is an increasingly important aspect of the growth and proliferation of LANs and WANs. You want to provide easy access to information on a network, but you also want to prevent access by unauthorized personnel. CSUNIX is designed to help ensure the security of the network and track the activity of people who successfully connect to it.

CSUNIX uses the TACACS+ protocol to provide this network security and tracking. TACACS+ uses AAA to provide network access security and to let you control access to your network from a central location.

CSUNIX has a browser-based interface that lets you do the following:

- Manage TACACS+-enabled and RADIUS-enabled NAS clients
- Manage TACACS+-enabled and RADIUS-enabled CiscoSecure ACSs
- Set up and manage remote connections to virtual private dial-up networks (VPDNs)
- Configure a default profile to accommodate guest users or users logging in through a client NAS who are authorized by some other control system to access the network
- Assign mid-level group administration privileges
- Configure token caching for all users logging in through a token server
- Assign group-level absolute attributes
- Administer Secure Computing token card users

Other features include the following:

- Session management support. If you have the optional CiscoSecure Distributed Session Manager (DSM) module licensed, installed, and enabled, you can have the CiscoSecure ACS limit the number of concurrent sessions that are available to a specific user, group, or VPDN. If you install CiscoSecure without the DSM module licensed or installed, CiscoSecure ACS 2.3 for UNIX still provides limited-feature max sessions support, allowing you to set per-user session limits for individual users or groups of users.
- UNIX command-line interface support.
- Profile data caching for enhanced authentication performance.

- Support for database replication among multiple Oracle or Sybase database sites that contain the profile data for multiple CiscoSecure ACS sites.

You can use CSUNIX to make changes to the database that administers security on your network on a few security servers instead of making changes to every NAS in your network.

Using CSUNIX, you can expand your network to accommodate more users and to provide more services without overburdening system administrators with security issues. As new users are added, system administrators can make a small number of changes in a few places and still ensure network security.

CSUNIX can be used with the TACACS+ protocol, the RADIUS protocol, or both. Some features are common to both protocols, and others are protocol-dependent.

CSUNIX System Requirements

Before installing CSUNIX, ensure that the system that will run it meets the following minimum requirements (to improve performance of services, you should increase the RAM, CPU speed, and hard drive speed and capacity as appropriate for your environment):

- UltraSPARC 1 or compatible (without DSM installed)
- UltraSPARC 10 or compatible (with DSM and Oracle or Sybase installed)
- 128 MB of RAM required; 256 MB of RAM for Oracle or Sybase
- 256 MB swap space (SQL Anywhere; 512 MB for Oracle or Sybase)
- At least 256 MB of free disk space (SQL Anywhere)
- At least 2 GB of free disk space (Oracle or Sybase)
- CD-ROM drive
- Solaris 2.6, or Solaris 2.5.1 with patches

Configuring TACACS+ for CiscoSecure ACS

To configure TACACS+ on your Cisco router or access server, you must follow these steps:

1 Use the **aaa new-model** global configuration command to enable AAA. AAA must be configured if you plan to use TACACS+. Use the **tacacs-server host** command to specify the IP address of one or more TACACS+ daemons. Use the **tacacs-server key** command to specify an encryption key that will be used to encrypt all exchanges between the network access server and the TACACS+ daemon. This same key must also be configured on the TACACS+ daemon.

2 Use the **aaa authentication** global configuration command to define method lists that use TACACS+ for authentication.

3 Use line and interface commands to apply the defined method lists to various interfaces.

If needed, use the **aaa authorization** global configuration command to configure authorization for the network access server. Unlike authentication, which can be configured per line or per interface, authorization is configured globally for the entire network access server.

You use the **tacacs-server** command, with the **host** and **key** options, to configure TACACS+ for CiscoSecure ACS. The syntax is as follows:

```
tacacs-server host hostname [single-connection] [port number]
  [timeout seconds] [key string]
tacacs-server key key
```

The command parameters and syntax have the following meanings:

Command Parameter	Description
hostname	Name or IP address of the host.
single-connection	(Optional) Specifies that the router maintain a single open connection for confirmation from a AAA/TACACS+ server (CiscoSecure Release 1.0.1 or later). This command contains no autodetect and fails if the specified host is not running a CiscoSecure daemon.
port number	(Optional) Specifies a server port number. This option overrides the default, which is port 49. Valid port numbers range from 1 to 65535.
timeout seconds	(Optional) Specifies a timeout value in seconds. This option overrides the global timeout value set with the **tacacs-server timeout** command for this server only.
key string	(Optional) Specifies an authentication and encryption key. This must match the key used by the TACACS+ daemon. Specifying this key overrides the key set by the global command **tacacs-server key** for this server only.
key	Key used to set authentication and encryption. This key must match the key used on the TACACS+ daemon.

To begin global configuration, enter the commands shown in Example 6-1, using the correct IP address of the CiscoSecure ACS servers and your own encryption key.

Example 6-1 *Enabling TACACS+*

```
Router(config)#aaa new-model
Router(config)#tacacs-server host 10.1.1.4
Router(config)#tacacs-server key 2bor!2b@?
```

In Example 6-1, the key **2bor!2b@?** is the encryption key that is shared between the NAS and the CiscoSecure ACS server. The encryption key you choose for your environment should be kept secret in order to protect the privacy of passwords that are sent between the CiscoSecure ACS server and the network access server during the authentication process. The NAS automatically encrypts this key when sent over the wire but does not store it encrypted.

When configuring a TACACS+ key for use on multiple TACACS+ servers, remember that the key must be the same for all TACACS+ servers listed for a given NAS.

You can specify multiple CiscoSecure ACS servers by repeating the **tacacs-server host** command.

AAA Configuration Commands

After enabling AAA globally on the access server, define the authentication method lists and then apply them to lines and interfaces. These authentication method lists are security profiles that indicate the service (PPP, ARAP, or NASI) or login and authentication method (local, TACACS+, RADIUS, login, or enable authentication).

To define an authentication method list using the **aaa authentication** command, follow these steps:

1 Specify the service (PPP, ARAP, or NASI) or login authentication.

2 Identify a list name or default. A list name is any alphanumeric string you choose. You assign different authentication methods to different named lists. You can specify only one dial-in protocol per authentication method list. However, you can create multiple authentication method lists with each of these options. You must give each list a different name.

3 Specify the authentication method. You can specify up to four methods.

After defining these authentication method lists, apply them to one of the following:

- **Lines**—tty, vty, console, aux, and async lines or the console port for login and asynchronous lines (in most cases) for ARA

- **Interfaces**—Interfaces sync, async, and virtual configured for PPP, SLIP, NASI, or ARAP

NAS AAA Configuration Example for TACACS+

Example 6-2 is an example of NAS configuration for TACACS+. It has been edited to show only the commands that are important to AAA security.

Example 6-2 *NAS AAA Configuration for TACACS+*

```
aaa new-model
aaa authentication login default tacacs+
aaa authentication login no_tacacs enable
aaa authentication ppp default tacacs+
aaa authorization exec tacacs+
aaa authorization network tacacs+
aaa accounting exec start-stop tacacs+
aaa accounting network start-stop tacacs+
enable secret 5 $1$x1EE$33AXd2VTVvhbWL0A37tQ3.
enable password 7 15141905172924
!
username admin password 7 094E4F0A1201181D19
!
interface Serial2
ppp authentication pap
!
tacacs-server host 10.1.1.4
tacacs-server key ciscosecure
!
line con 0
login authentication no_tacacs
```

Table 6-3 lists the NAS AAA configuration commands for TACACS+ that are used in Example 6-2.

Table 6-3 *NAS AAA Configuration Commands for TACACS+*

Command	Description
aaa new-model	Enables the AAA access control model. You use the **no** form of this command to disable this functionality. You can subsequently restore previously configured AAA commands by reissuing this command.
aaa authentication login default tacacs+ enable	Specifies that, if the TACACS+ server fails to respond, you can log in to the access server by using your enable password. If you do not have an enable password set on the router, you can't log in to it until you have a functioning TACACS+ UNIX daemon or Windows NT Server process configured with usernames and passwords. The enable password in this case is a last-resort authentication method. You also can specify none as the last-resort method, which means that no authentication is required if all other methods failed.
aaa authentication login default tacacs+	Sets AAA authentication at login using the default list against the TACACS+ server.

Table 6-3 *NAS AAA Configuration Commands for TACACS+ (Continued)*

Command	Description
aaa authentication login no_tacacs enable	Sets AAA authentication at login to use the enable password for authentication.
aaa authentication ppp default tacacs+	Sets AAA authentication for PPP connections using the default list against the TACACS+ database.
aaa authorization exec tacacs+	Sets AAA authorization to determine if the user is allowed to run an EXEC shell on the NAS against the TACACS+ database.
aaa authorization network tacacs+	Sets AAA authorization for all network-related service requests, including SLIP, PPP, PPP NCPs, and ARAP, against the TACACS+ database. The TACACS+ database and the NAS must be configured to specify the authorized services.
aaa accounting exec start-stop tacacs+	Sets AAA accounting for EXEC processes on the NAS to record the start and stop time of the session against the TACACS+ database.
aaa accounting network start-stop tacacs+	Sets AAA accounting for all network-related service requests, including SLIP, PPP, PPP NCPs, and ARAP, to record the start and stop time of the session against the TACACS+ database.
username admin password 7 094E4F0A1201181D19	Sets a username and password in the local security database for use with the **aaa authentication local-override** command.
interface Serial2 ppp authentication pap	Sets PPP authentication to use PAP. CHAP, or both CHAP and PAP, can also be specified.
ppp authentication if-needed	Causes the NAS to not perform CHAP or PAP authentication if the user has already provided authentication. This option is available only on asynchronous interfaces.
tacacs-server key	Sets the shared key as a default key to be used if a per-host key was not set. It is a better practice to set specific keys per tacacs-server host. It is possible to configure TACACS+ with no shared key at both the client device (for example, NAS) and the security server (for example, CiscoSecure) if you want the connection to not be encrypted. This might be useful for a lab or training environment, but it is highly discouraged in a production environment.
line con 0 login authentication no_tacacs	Specifies that the AAA authentication list called **no_tacacs** is to be used on the console.

Testing and Troubleshooting TACACS+

You use the **debug** commands to trace TACACS+ packets. Table 6-4 lists some of the important TACACS+ debugging commands.

Table 6-4 *debug Commands for Testing TACACS+*

Commands and Parameters	Description
debug tacacs	Displays debugging messages for TACACS+ packet traces.
debug tacacs events	Displays information from the TACACS+ helper process.
debug aaa authentication	Use this command to see what methods of authentication are being used and what the results of these methods are.

You can get more meaningful output from the **debug** command if you first configure the router using the following syntax:

```
service timestamps type [uptime]
service timestamps type datetime [msec] [localtime] [show-timezone]
```

The command parameters and syntax have the following meanings:

Command Parameters	Description
type	Specifies the type of message to timestamp: debug or log
uptime	(Optional) Specifies the timestamp with the time since the system was rebooted
datetime	Timestamp with the date and time
msec	(Optional) Specifies to include milliseconds in the date and timestamp
localtime	(Optional) Specifies the timestamp relative to the local time zone
show-timezone	(Optional) Specifies to include the time zone name in the timestamp

Example 6-3 is sample **debug tacacs events** output, showing the opening and closing of a TCP connection to a TACACS+ server as well as the bytes read and written over the connection and the connection's TCP status.

Example 6-3 *Sample **debug tacacs events** Output*

```
router#debug tacacs events
%LINK-3-UPDOWN: Interface Async2, changed state to up
00:03:16: TAC+: Opening TCP/IP to 10.1.1.4/49 timeout=15
00:03:16: TAC+: Opened TCP/IP handle 0x48A87C to 10.1.1.4/49
00:03:16: TAC+: periodic timer started
00:03:16: TAC+: 10.1.1.4 req=3BD868 id=-1242409656 ver=193 handle=0x48A87C
 (ESTAB)
expire=14 AUTHEN/START/SENDAUTH/CHAP queued
00:03:17: TAC+: 10.1.1.4 ESTAB 3BD868 wrote 46 of 46 bytes
00:03:22: TAC+: 10.1.1.4 CLOSEWAIT read=12 wanted=12 alloc=12 got=12
00:03:22: TAC+: 10.1.1.4 CLOSEWAIT read=61 wanted=61 alloc=61 got=49
00:03:22: TAC+: 10.1.1.4 received 61 byte reply for 3BD868
00:03:22: TAC+: req=3BD868 id=-1242409656 ver=193 handle=0x48A87C (CLOSEWAIT)
 expire=9 AUTHEN/START/SENDAUTH/CHAP processed
00:03:22: TAC+: periodic timer stopped (queue empty)
00:03:22: TAC+: Closing TCP/IP 0x48A87C connection to 10.1.1.4/49
00:03:22: TAC+: Opening TCP/IP to 10.1.1.4/49 timeout=15
00:03:22: TAC+: Opened TCP/IP handle 0x489F08 to 10.1.1.4/49
00:03:22: TAC+: periodic timer started
00:03:22: TAC+: 10.1.1.4 req=3BD868 id=299214410 ver=192 handle=0x489F08 (ESTAB)
expire=14 AUTHEN/START/SENDPASS/CHAP queued
00:03:23: TAC+: 10.1.1.4 ESTAB 3BD868 wrote 41 of 41 bytes
00:03:23: TAC+: 10.1.1.4 CLOSEWAIT read=12 wanted=12 alloc=12 got=12
00:03:23: TAC+: 10.1.1.4 CLOSEWAIT read=21 wanted=21 alloc=21 got=9
00:03:23: TAC+: 10.1.1.4 received 21 byte reply for 3BD868
00:03:23: TAC+: req=3BD868 id=299214410 ver=192 handle=0x489F08 (CLOSEWAIT)
expire=13 AUTHEN/START/SENDPASS/CHAP processed
00:03:23: TAC+: periodic timer stopped (queue empty)
```

Most of the TACACS messages are self-explanatory or are intended to be for consumption by service personnel only. However, a couple of the messages are briefly explained here. Example 6-4 indicates that a TCP open request to host 10.1.1.4 on port 49 will time out in 15 seconds if it gets no response.

Example 6-4 *Sample **debug tacacs events** Output: TCP Open Request*

```
00:03:16: TAC+: Opening TCP/IP to 10.1.1.4/49 timeout=15
```

Example 6-5 indicates a successful open operation and provides the address of the internal TCP handle for this connection:

Example 6-5 *Sample **debug tacacs events** Output: Successful Open Operation*

```
00:03:16: TAC+: Opened TCP/IP handle 0x48A87C to 10.1.1.4/49
```

Example 6-6 is part of the **debug aaa authentication** command output for a TACACS login attempt that was successful. The information indicates that TACACS+ is the authentication method used. Also, note that the AAA/AUTHEN status indicates that the authentication has passed.

Example 6-6 *Debug Output of a Successful TACACS+ Login*

```
14:01:17: AAA/AUTHEN (567936829): Method=TACACS+
14:01:17: TAC+: send AUTHEN/CONT packet
14:01:17: TAC+ (567936829): received authen response status = PASS
14:01:17: AAA/AUTHEN (567936829): status = PASS
```

An AAA session has three possible results: pass, fail, and error.

Example 6-7 is part of the **debug aaa authentication** command output indicating a failure result.

Example 6-7 *A debug Session Indicating a Failure Result*

```
13:53:35: TAC+: Opening TCP/IP connection to 10.1.1.4/49
13:53:35: TAC+: Sending TCP/IP packet number 416942312-1 to 10.1.1.4/49
(AUTHEN/START)
13:53:35: TAC+: Receiving TCP/IP packet number 416942312-2 from 10.1.1.4/49
13:53:35: TAC+ (416942312): received authen response status = GETUSER
13:53:37: TAC+: send AUTHEN/CONT packet
13:53:37: TAC+: Sending TCP/IP packet number 416942312-3 to 10.1.1.4/49
(AUTHEN/CONT)
13:53:37: TAC+: Receiving TCP/IP packet number 416942312-4 from 10.1.1.4/49
13:53:37: TAC+ (416942312): received authen response status = GETPASS
13:53:38: TAC+: send AUTHEN/CONT packet
13:53:38: TAC+: Sending TCP/IP packet number 416942312-5 to 10.1.1.4/49
(AUTHEN/CONT)
13:53:38: TAC+: Receiving TCP/IP packet number 416942312-6 from 10.1.1.4/49
13:53:38: TAC+ (416942312): received authen response status = FAIL
13:53:40: TAC+: Closing TCP/IP connection to 10.1.1.4/49
```

Example 6-8 is part of the **debug aaa authentication** command output indicating a pass result.

Example 6-8 *A debug Session Indicating a Pass Result*

```
14:00:09: TAC+: Opening TCP/IP connection to 10.1.1.4/49
14:00:09: TAC+: Sending TCP/IP packet number 383258052-1 to 10.1.1.4/49
 (AUTHEN/START)
14:00:09: TAC+: Receiving TCP/IP packet number 383258052-2 from 10.1.1.4/49
14:00:09: TAC+ (383258052): received authen response status = GETUSER
14:00:10: TAC+: send AUTHEN/CONT packet
14:00:10: TAC+: Sending TCP/IP packet number 383258052-3 to 10.1.1.4/49
 (AUTHEN/CONT)
14:00:10: TAC+: Receiving TCP/IP packet number 383258052-4 from 10.1.1.4/49
14:00:10: TAC+ (383258052): received authen response status = GETPASS
14:00:14: TAC+: send AUTHEN/CONT packet
```

Example 6-8 *A **debug** Session Indicating a Pass Result (Continued)*

```
14:00:14: TAC+: Sending TCP/IP packet number 383258052-5 to 10.1.1.4/49
(AUTHEN/CONT)
14:00:14: TAC+: Receiving TCP/IP packet number 383258052-6 from 10.1.1.4/49
14:00:14: TAC+ (383258052): received authen response status = PASS
14:00:14: TAC+: Closing TCP/IP connection to 10.1.1.4/49
```

For more detailed information, refer to the Cisco *Debug Command Reference*.

Configuring RADIUS for CiscoSecure ACS

The configuration of a RADIUS server resembles that of the TACACS+ server presented earlier in this chapter. It is one of the method options available in the AAA commands. To configure RADIUS on your Cisco router or access server, you must follow these steps:

1 Use the **aaa new-model** global configuration command to enable AAA. AAA must be configured if you plan to use RADIUS.

2 Use the **aaa authentication** global configuration command to define method lists for RADIUS authentication.

3 Use line and interface commands to enable the defined method lists to be used.

If needed, use the **aaa authorization** global command to authorize specific user functions. If needed, use the **aaa accounting** command to enable accounting for RADIUS connections.

Enabling and Configuring AAA

You use the **radius-server** command, with the **host** and **key** options, to configure RADIUS for CiscoSecure ACS. The syntax is as follows:

```
radius-server host {hostname | ip-address} [auth-port port-number]
[acct-port port-number]
radius-server key string
```

The command parameters and syntax have the following meanings:

Command Parameters	Description
hostname	DNS name of the RADIUS server host.
ip-address	IP address of the RADIUS server host.
auth-port	(Optional) Specifies the UDP destination port for authentication requests.
port-number	(Optional) Port number for authentication requests. The host is not used for authentication if this is set to 0.

continues

Command Parameters	Description
acct-port	(Optional) Specifies the UDP destination port for accounting requests.
port-number	(Optional) Port number for accounting requests. The host is not used for accounting if this is set to 0.
string	The key used to set authentication and encryption. This key must match the encryption used on the RADIUS daemon.

The **radius-server host** command specifies the IP address or the host name of the remote RADIUS server host. The **radius-server key** command specifies the key used by the router and RADIUS server for encrypting passwords and exchanging responses.

These two commands are mandatory for RADIUS; other commands (such as **radius-server directed-request** and **radius-server retransmit**) add optional functions and settings. Example 6-9 shows the enablement of AAA for RADIUS on the NAS.

Example 6-9 *Enabling and Configuring AAA for RADIUS*

```
Router(config)#aaa new-model
Router(config)#radius-server host 10.1.1.4
Router(config)#radius-server key 2bor!2b@?
```

In Example 6-9, the key **2bor!2b@?** is the encryption key that is shared between the NAS and the CiscoSecure ACS server. The encryption key you choose for your environment should be kept secret in order to protect the privacy of passwords that are sent between the CiscoSecure ACS server and the network access server during the authentication process. The NAS automatically encrypts this key when it is sent over the wire but does not store it encrypted.

AAA Configuration Commands

After enabling AAA globally on the access server, define the authentication method lists and then apply them to lines and interfaces. These authentication method lists are security profiles that indicate the service (PPP, ARAP, or NASI) or login and authentication method (local, TACACS+, RADIUS, login, or enable authentication).

To define an authentication method list using the **aaa authentication** command, follow these steps:

1 Specify the service (PPP, ARAP, or NASI) or login authentication.

2 Identify a list name or default. A list name is any alphanumeric string you choose. You assign different authentication methods to different named lists. You can specify only one dial-in protocol per authentication method list. However, you can create multiple authentication method lists with each of these options. You must give each list a different name.

3 Specify the authentication method. You can specify up to four methods.

After defining these authentication method lists, apply them to one of the following:

- **Lines**—tty, vty, console, aux, and async lines or the console port for login and asynchronous lines (in most cases) for ARA

- **Interfaces**—Interfaces sync, async, and virtual configured for PPP, SLIP, NASI, or ARAP

NAS AAA Configuration Example for RADIUS

In Example 6-10, an ISP offers only PPP service to its customers. The **aaa authentication ppp dialins radius local** command configures the line to do RADIUS authentication for lines that automatically detect incoming PPP packets.

Example 6-10 *Radius Configuration: PPP Service Only*

```
radius-server host 123.45.1.2
radius-server key myRaDIUSpassWoRd
username root password ALongPassword
aaa authentication ppp dialins radius local
aaa authorization network radius local
aaa authentication login admins local
aaa authorization exec local if-authenticated
aaa accounting network start-stop radius
line 1 16
autoselect ppp
login authentication admins
modem ri-is-cd
interface group-async 1
encapsulation ppp
ppp authentication pap dialins
```

Table 6-5 describes the command parameters used in the RADIUS configuration shown in Example 6-10.

Table 6-5 *Commands Used in the RADIUS Configuration Shown in Example 6-10*

Commands	Description
ppp authentication pap dialins	Configures PAP to be used for dial-in authentication.
aaa authorization network radius local	Assigns an address and other network parameters to the RADIUS user.
aaa accounting network start-stop radius	Tracks PPP usage.
aaa authentication login admins local	Sets the administrator's access to use the internal username and password database. This is intended to be used by network administrators when debugging problems with the network.

Testing and Troubleshooting RADIUS

Debugging authentication and accounting for RADIUS and other services is accomplished using **debug** and **show** commands. Table 6-6 describes some of the common **debug** and **show** commands.

Table 6-6 *Common **debug** and **show** Commands*

Command	Description
debug aaa authentication	Debugs AAA authentication
debug aaa authorization	Debugs AAA authorization
debug aaa accounting	Debugs AAA accounting
show accounting	Not RADIUS-specific but displays accounting activities

Example 6-11 shows part of the **debug radius** command output that shows a successful login attempt, as indicated by an access-accept message.

Example 6-11 *Debug Output for a Successful Login*

```
Router#debug radius
13:59:02: Radius: IPC Send 0.0.0.0:1645, Access-Request, id 0xB, len 56
13:59:02:        Attribute 4 6 AC150E5A
13:59:02:        Attribute 5 6 0000000A
13:59:02:        Attribute 1 6 62696C6C
13:59:02:        Attribute 2 18 0531FEA3
13:59:04: Radius: Received from 171.69.1.152:1645, Access-Accept, id 0xB,
 len 26
13:59:04:        Attribute 6 6 00000001
```

You should use a RADIUS Attribute-Value dictionary, such as the one found in the CSUNIX documentation, to sort out the debug information.

The RADIUS debugging output in Example 6-12 shows the sequence when the secret does not match the secret configured on the RADIUS server. It shows a login attempt that failed because of a key mismatch (a configuration problem).

Example 6-12 *Debug Output for a Key Mismatch*

```
Router#debug radius
22:15:45: RADIUS: IPC Send 0.0.0.0:1645, Access-Request, id 0xB, len 52
22:15:45:         Attribute 4 6 AC150E5A
22:15:45:         Attribute 5 6 0000000E
22:15:45:         Attribute 1 2 0212D2C3
22:15:45:         Attribute 2 18 D2C36202
22:15:45: RADIUS: Received from 171.69.1.152:1645, Access-Reject, id 0xB,
 len 20
22:15:45: RADIUS: Reply for 11 fails decrypt
```

In Example 6-13, **debug aaa authentication** and **debug radius** are turned on. The output shows an unsuccessful login attempt that failed because of an incorrect password.

Example 6-13 *Debug Output for a Failed Login*

```
Router#debug aaa authentication
22:13:34: AAA/AUTHEN: create_user user='' "user='' port='tty14'
rem_addr='172.21.14.90' authen_type=1 service=1 priv=1
22:13:34: AAA/AUTHEN/START (0): local override set: GETUSER
Username: mar
Password:
22:13:37: AAA/AUTHEN/CONT (0): continue_login
22:13:37: AAA/AUTHEN (0): status = GETUSER
22:13:37: AAA/AUTHEN/CONT (0): local_override. Call start_login again
22:13:37: AAA/AUTHEN/START (0): port='tty14' list='boo' action=LOGIN
service LOGIN
22:13:37: AAA/AUTHEN/START (5295640): found list
22:13:37: AAA/AUTHEN/START (591331466): Method=RADIUS
22:13:37: AAA/AUTHEN (591331466): status = GETPASS
22:13:37: AAA/AUTHEN (591331466): METHOD=radius
22:13:37: RADIUS: IPC SEND 0.0.0.0 :1645, ACCESS-REQUEST, ID 0X9, LEN 55
22:13:37:    ATTRIBUTE    4  6   AC150E5A
22:13:37:    ATTRIBUTE    5  6   0000000E
22:13:37:    ATTRIBUTE    5  6   6D617202
22:13:37:    ATTRIBUTE    2  18  AC150E5A
22:13:37: RADIUS: received from 171.69.1.152:1645 Access-Reject, id 0x9,
len 20
22:1:41:  AAA/AUTHEN  (5913331466( : status = FAIL
# Authentication failed.
Username:
```

Example 6-14 shows sample output from the **show accounting** command.

Example 6-14 *show accounting Command Output*

```
Router#show accounting
Active Accounted actions on tty0, User chard Priv 1
 Task ID 4425, EXEC Accounting record, 0:04:53 Elapsed
 task_id=4425 service=exec port=0
 Task ID 3759, Connection Accounting record, 0:01:06 Elapsed
 task_id=3759 service=exec port=0 protocol=telnet address=171.19.3.78
cmd=grill
Active Accounted actions on tty10, User chard Priv 1
 Task ID 5115, EXEC Accounting record, 0:04:07 Elapsed
 task_id=5115 service=exec port=10
 Task ID 2593, Connection Accounting record, 0:00:56 Elapsed
 task_id=2593 service=exec port=10 protocol=tn3270 address=172.21.14.90
cmd=tn snap
Active Accounted actions on tty11, User mary Priv 1
 Task ID 7390, EXEC Accounting record, 0:00:25 Elapsed
 task_id=7390 service=exec port=11
 Task ID 931, Connection Accounting record, 0:00:20 Elapsed
 task_id=931 service=exec port=11 protocol=telnet address=171.19.6.129
cmd=coal
```

The information displayed by the **debug aaa accounting** command is independent of the protocol used to transfer the accounting information to a server. You use the **debug tacacs** and **debug radius** protocol-specific commands to get more detailed information about protocol-level issues.

Example 6-15 is sample **debug aaa accounting** command output.

Example 6-15 *debug aaa accounting Command Output*

```
router#debug aaa accounting
AAA Accounting debugging is on
16:49:21: AAA/ACCT: EXEC acct start, line 10
16:49:32: AAA/ACCT: Connect start, line 10, glare
16:49:47: AAA/ACCT: Connection acct stop:
task_id=70 service=exec port=10 protocol=telnet address=171.69.3.78 cmd=glare
bytes_in=308 bytes_out=76 paks_in=45 paks_out=54 elapsed_time=14
```

Double Authentication

Double Authentication provides additional authentication for PPP sessions. Previously, PPP session authentication was limited to CHAP or PAP. With Double Authentication, you essentially require remote users to pass a second stage of user authentication—after CHAP or PAP authentication—before they can gain network access.

Problems with Using Only CHAP or PAP for Authentication

A remote user dialing in to a local host (NAS or router) over PPP can be authenticated via CHAP or PAP. However, both CHAP and PAP rely on a secret password that must be stored on the remote user host and on the local host. If either host ever comes under the control of a network attacker, the secret password is compromised.

For example, Bob often uses his laptop computer to log in to his company's enterprise network, which uses only CHAP for authentication. If Bob's laptop computer is stolen, the thief has the computer's CHAP password. This password (with or without Bob's laptop computer) can now be used to gain access to the company network.

In addition, with CHAP or PAP authentication, you cannot assign different network access privileges to different remote users who use the same remote host. Because one set of privileges is assigned to a specific host, everybody who uses that host will have the same set of privileges.

The Solution of Double Authentication

To configure a local host (NAS or router) for Double Authentication, remote users are required to complete a second stage of authentication to gain network access. This second (double) authentication requires a password that is known to the user but is not stored on the user's remote host. Therefore, the second authentication is specific to a user, not to a host. This provides an additional level of security that will be effective even if the remote host is stolen.

This also provides greater flexibility by allowing customized network privileges for each user. Moreover, the second-stage authentication can use one-time passwords such as token card passwords, which are not supported by CHAP. If one-time passwords are used, a stolen user password is useless to the perpetrator.

Double Authentication has two authentication/authorization stages. These two stages occur after a remote user dials in and a PPP session is initiated. In the first stage, CHAP (or PAP) authenticates the remote host, and then PPP negotiates with AAA to authorize the remote host (this assigns network access privileges). When this stage is complete, the remote user has limited network access, restricted to allow only Telnet to the local host.

In the second stage, the remote user must Telnet to the local host (NAS) to be user-authenticated. When the remote user logs in, he is authenticated with AAA login authentication. The user then must enter the **access-profile** command to be reauthorized using AAA. When this authorization is complete, the user has been double-authenticated, and he can access the network according to his per-user network privileges.

The system administrator determines what network privileges remote users will have after each stage of authentication by configuring appropriate parameters on an AAA server. Configure two sets of AAA parameters: one for the CHAP (or PAP) authentication/

authorization stage and another for the second user authentication/authorization stage. Define these parameters using appropriate attribute/value pairs on the AAA server.

Prerequisites for Double Authentication

These are the prerequisites for the network and for the administrator:

- A local device (NAS or router) and an AAA server accessible to the local device. The local device and AAA server should be appropriately configured and keyed to communicate with each other.

- A basic understanding of AAA, PPP, and CHAP (or PAP) and a basic understanding of how to configure a AAA server.

You can specify multiple CiscoSecure ACS servers by repeating the **tacacs-server host** command.

You can use multiple **tacacs-server host** commands to specify additional hosts. The Cisco IOS Software searches for hosts in the order in which you specify them. Use the **single-connection**, **port**, **timeout**, and **key** options only when running a AAA/TACACS+ server.

Because some of the parameters of the **tacacs-server host** command override global settings made by the **tacacs-server timeout** and **tacacs-server key** commands, you can use this command to enhance security on your network by uniquely configuring individual routers.

Summary

This section summarizes the main points of this chapter, as follows:

- CiscoSecure ACS is available for both the NT and UNIX operating systems. Common to both of these packages is a Web browser interface for ease of administration.

- CSNT can be used in a distributed system, supporting authentication forwarding, fallback on failed connection, and centralized logging.

- CSNT setup consists of configuring the Windows NT platform support, verifying network connectivity between CSNT components, installing CSNT on Windows NT, supplying an initial configuration via the Web browser interface, and configuring AAA for all CSNT components.

- CSUNIX incorporates multiuser, Web-based Java configuration and management tools, simplifying server administration and allowing the management of security services from multiple locations.

- The CiscoSecure ACS uses authentication, authorization, and accounting (AAA) to provide network security.

- The CiscoSecure ACS software uses either the Terminal Access Controller Access Control System (TACACS)+ or the Remote Authentication Dial-In User Service (RADIUS) protocol to provide this network security and tracking.

- TACACS+ configuration involves enabling TACACS+, specifying the list of CiscoSecure ACS servers that will provide AAA services, and configuring the encryption key between the NAS and the CiscoSecure ACS server.

- RADIUS configuration involves configuring communication between the router and the RADIUS server, using AAA global configuration commands to define method lists containing RADIUS, and using **line** and **interface** commands that implement authentication and authorization methods.

- Double Authentication support allows implementation of security policies that require all external access to be authenticated with strong (two-part) authentication.

- Use the variety of **show** and **debug** commands to view configuration information, verify operations, and troubleshoot TACACS+ or RADIUS.

Case Study: Configuring CSNT

This case study illustrates how to configure CSNT to provide AAA services for the hypothetical XYZ Company network. Read the case study scenario, examine the topology diagram, read the security policy, and then analyze the configuration example to see how the security policy statements are enacted for the Cisco routers.

Case Study Scenario

The XYZ Company has decided to increase its security by adding ACS software for its NT servers. Your task is to install and configure CiscoSecure on the server to use RADIUS and TACACS+ authentication, authorization, and accounting features.

Topology

Figure 6-5 illustrates the portion of the XYZ network that will be configured in this case study. Note that the focus is on the elements that involve the NAS and CSNT server.

Figure 6-6 illustrates the network topology map.

Figure 6-5 *CSNT on the XYZ Corporate Network*

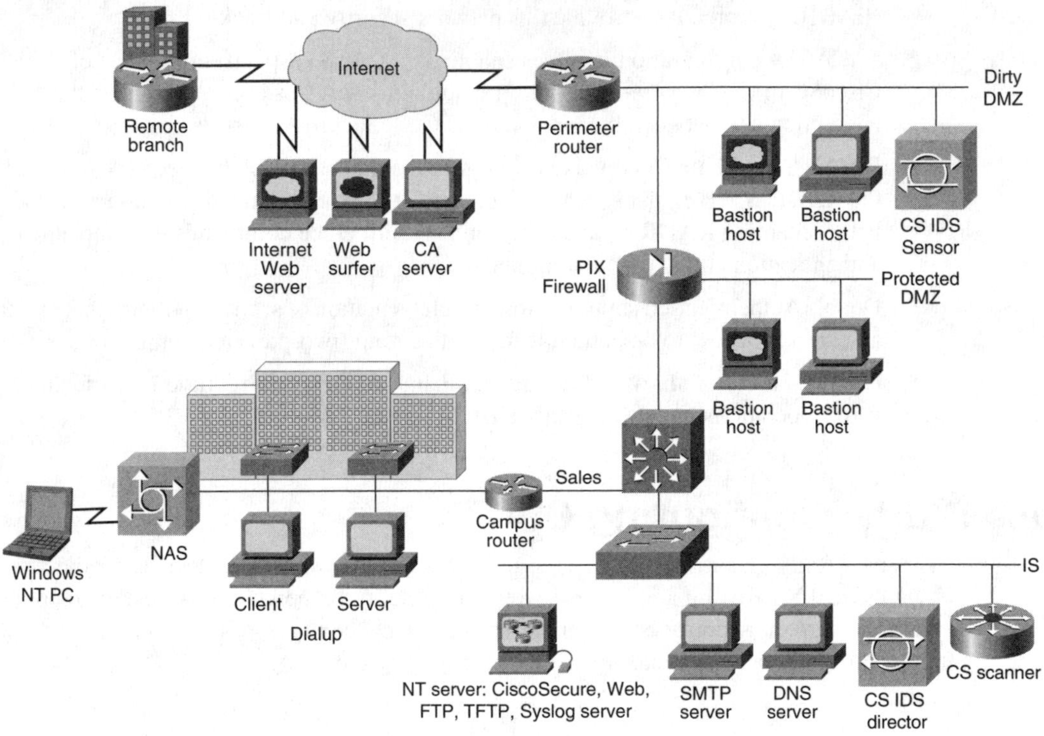

Network Security Policy

The network security policy that XYZ wants to implement is as follows:

- Use CiscoSecure ACS running the TACACS+ protocol for policy enforcement of authentication and authorization.

- Dialup access will be controlled using aging passwords authentication.

- Home office workers will use PAP or CHAP authentication.

The following features need to be configured in CSNT for each security policy statement:

- Use CiscoSecure ACS running the TACACS+ protocol for policy enforcement of authentication and authorization.

- Dialup access will be controlled using aging passwords authentication.

- Home office workers will use PAP or CHAP authentication.

Figure 6-6 *XYZ Network Topology*

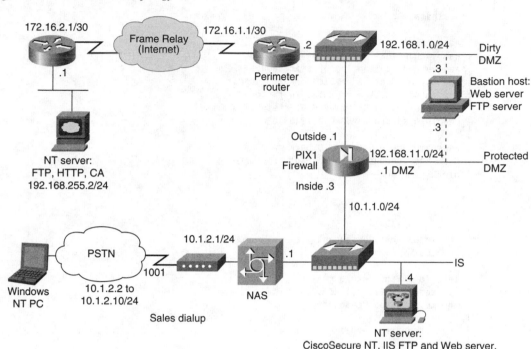

CSNT Configuration Example

Examine the configuration example for the NAS device of the XYZ Company shown in Example 6-16. This example implements the network security policy statements related to access security configuration on the NAS and in the CSNT. One possible configuration of the NAS for the specified security policy might look like Example 6-16. You might choose to configure the router differently to enact the same security policy requirements. Note that the sample configuration contains comments showing which router commands enact particular security policy statements. Unrelated commands have been deleted for the sake of brevity.

Example 6-16 *NAS Configuration for Implementing the XYZ Company Security Policy*

```
!
version 12.0
service timestamps debug datetime msec localtime
service timestamps log uptime
no service password-encryption
!
```

continues

Example 6-16 *NAS Configuration for Implementing the XYZ Company Security Policy (Continued)*

```
hostname NASx
!
aaa new-model
aaa authentication login default tacacs+
aaa authentication login is-in tacacs+ local
aaa authentication enable default tacacs+
aaa authentication ppp dial-in tacacs+
enable secret 5 $1$QZUR$r5/03JrSetB2viWswKom./
enable password 7 050F09087948410E
!
username admin password 0 back door
username isgroup password 0 other door
clock timezone PST -8
!
!
interface BRI0/0
 no ip address
 no ip directed-broadcast
 shutdown
!
interface Ethernet0/0
 ip address 10.1.1.1 255.255.255.0
 no ip directed-broadcast
!
interface Ethernet0/1
 no ip address
 no ip directed-broadcast
 shutdown
!
interface Serial3/0
 physical-layer async
 ip address 10.1.2.1 255.255.255.0
 no ip directed-broadcast
 encapsulation ppp
 ip tcp header-compression passive
 async mode dedicated
 peer default ip address pool classpool
 no fair-queue
 no cdp enable
 ppp authentication pap ms-chap dial-in
!
interface Serial3/1
 no ip address
 no ip directed-broadcast
 shutdown
!
interface Serial3/2
 no ip address
 no ip directed-broadcast
```

Example 6-16 *NAS Configuration for Implementing the XYZ Company Security Policy (Continued)*

```
 shutdown
!
interface Serial3/3
 no ip address
 no ip directed-broadcast
 shutdown
!
router rip
 network 10.0.0.0
!
ip local pool classpool 10.1.2.2 10.1.2.10
ip classless
ip route 0.0.0.0 0.0.0.0 10.1.1.3
!
ip access-list extended testblock
 deny    ip 10.1.2.0 0.0.0.255 172.19.16.0 0.0.0.255
 permit ip any any
tacacs-server host 10.1.1.4 key ciscosecure
tacacs-server key default
privilege exec level 5 reload
privilege exec level 5 show startup-config
privilege exec level 5 show
privilege exec level 5 clear line
privilege exec level 5 clear
!
line con 0
 exec-timeout 0 0
 password front door
 logging synchronous
 login authentication is-in
 transport input none
line 65 70
line 97
 no exec
 password 7 00001A0708161E150A335F
 modem InOut
 modem autoconfigure type usr_sportster
 transport input all
 stopbits 1
 speed 115200
 flowcontrol hardware
line aux 0
 no exec
line vty 0 4
 password 7 02030753045F
 login authentication is-in
!
end
```

Review Questions

Answer the following review questions, which delve into some of the key facts and concepts covered in this chapter:

1 List the pros and cons of using the Windows NT User Database with CSNT.

2 What do you need in order to configure CSNT in the Windows NT User Manager?

3 What is configured using the CiscoSecure ACS Web interface?

4 How is AAA accounting information reported in CiscoSecure ACS?

5 Where should you start when troubleshooting CiscoSecure ACS problems?

6 Name and describe the features of CiscoSecure ACS for NT that make it valuable in a distributed security system.

7 CiscoSecure ACS for NT supports which three types of token servers?

8 What is the purpose of the **tacacs-server key** *your_key_string* command?

9 List the three basic steps of NAS configuration for a RADIUS security server.

10 What are the two stages of Double Authentication authentication/authorization?

References

This chapter summarizes the configuration process needed to implement a security policy utilizing CiscoSecure ACS for NT (CSNT). For the exact command syntax for the version of IOS you are using, refer to the appropriate documentation release for that version of Cisco IOS. Specifically, review the *Security Configuration Guide* and *Security Command Reference* that matches your version of the Cisco IOS.

The following references will help you increase your knowledge of CSNT and CiscoSecure ACS for UNIX (CSUNIX) concepts and security policy in general.

Configuring Security Policy

The SANS (System Administration, Networking, and Security) Institute is a cooperative research and education organization for system administrators, security professionals, and network administrators. Located at www.sans.org.

Security Policy Templates, Model Security Policies—compiled by Michele Crabb-Guel. This is a collection of templates and overview information for use in crafting your own security policies. It also has reference information from the SANS course "Building an Effective Security Infrastructure." Located at www.sans.org/newlook/resources/policies/policies.htm.

RFC 1661, "The Point-to-Point Protocol (PPP)," provides specific information about PPP. Located at ds.internic.net/rfc/rfc1661.txt.

RFC 1994, "PPP Challenge Handshake Authentication Protocol (CHAP)," provides specific information about CHAP. Located at ds.internic.net/rfc/rfc1994.txt.

RFC 2196, "The Site Security Procedures Handbook," provides overview information on security policies and authentication procedures. Located at ds.internic.net/rfc/rfc2196.txt.

Configuring TACACS+/RADIUS

Security Command Reference, Cisco IOS Release 12.0, October 1998.

Security Configuration Guide, Cisco IOS Release 12.0, October 1998.

CiscoSecure ACS

CiscoSecure ACS 2.4 for Windows NT User Guide, 1999.

CiscoSecure ACS 2.3 for UNIX User Guide, 1998.

CiscoSecure ACS 2.3 for UNIX Reference Guide, 1998.

Securing the Internet Connection

Upon completing this chapter, you will be able to do the following:

- Define perimeter security
- Identify perimeter system components that secure the Internet connection
- Describe Cisco IOS Software perimeter security features
- Identify how to configure a Cisco router as a perimeter router to protect Internet access from common security threats

CHAPTER 7

Configuring a Cisco Perimeter Router

This chapter covers how to create a security perimeter system using a Cisco router. This chapter initially presents an overview of perimeter security components and Cisco IOS Software features that are useful for protecting a network. It then delves into each feature, showing you how to use the feature for perimeter security. This chapter ends with a case study demonstration lab based on the XYZ Company case study, showing one possible implementation of a Cisco router for perimeter security.

Cisco Perimeter Security Systems

Perimeter security is the intelligent selection and deployment of networking technologies to secure the edge of a network from intruders. Perimeter security typically is used to secure the Internet connection to the corporate network, although the same technologies and techniques can be used to secure one part of a network from another.

Like a wall and moat around a medieval castle, perimeter security builds the equivalent of a wall around your network to protect against network intruders. Missing or weak perimeter security opens up a network security hole for network intruders to exploit.

Perimeter security is primarily established with a perimeter router, the demarcation point between an insecure and a secure network. For example, a perimeter router can be used to create a demarcation between the insecure Internet and a semisecure demilitarized zone (DMZ), shown as the "dirty" DMZ in Figure 7-1. The perimeter router is a general-purpose router that acts as a first line of defense. This router often has a serial interface to the Internet on the outside domain and a LAN interface on the inside domain. We will focus on implementing perimeter security with a Cisco router in this chapter, as illustrated in Figure 7-1.

An important part of perimeter security is identifying the edge of the network by specifying a network's inside and outside domains. In Figure 7-1, the inside domain is the corporate network below the PIX Firewall, and the outside domain is the Internet. The outside domain could also be a link to a business partner or supplier.

Perimeter security devices are used to implement the part of the network security policy that specifies how the internal network will be connected to the outside network.

Figure 7-1 *A Perimeter Security System*

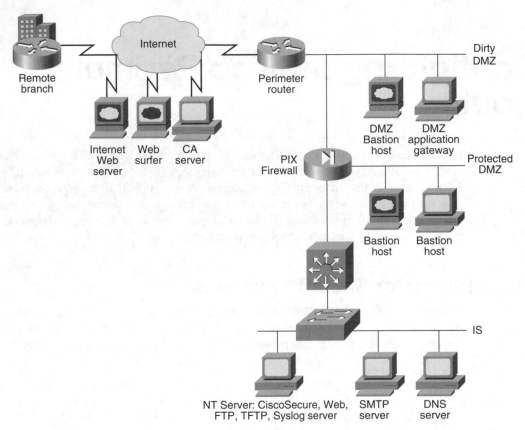

Perimeter security can be implemented in many different ways depending on the security policy, what must be protected, the level of security needed, the security budget, and many other factors. Perimeter security is accomplished using commonly available networking devices. The devices can be combined in numerous ways to protect the inside network. For example, a Cisco router could be used by itself to create a perimeter security system. This chapter implements perimeter security in a topology commonly referred to as *screened subnet architecture,* in which a perimeter (or *screening*) router is used to provide one line of defense, and a firewall provides a second line of defense. The following sections consider the functions of each device used to implement perimeter security.

Cisco Perimeter Routers

The perimeter router is usually a general-purpose router such as a Cisco 1720 with a serial connection to the Internet and an Ethernet connection to a DMZ. Cisco routers have many powerful perimeter security features that secure the Internet connection. A Cisco router performs the following functions and has the following features:

- It acts as a first line of defense, defines the DMZ (or dirty DMZ, as shown in Figure 7-1), protects the bastion hosts on the DMZs, protects the PIX Firewall from directed attacks, and acts as an alarm system in case anyone tries to break into the perimeter router itself or the bastion host.

- It has a flexible feature set that can be reconfigured to adapt to new security threats and new Internet applications.

- It costs less than dedicated, specialized firewalls.

- It harnesses the power of Cisco IOS Software including specific firewall and perimeter security features.

The perimeter router primarily uses packet-filtering rules to restrict access to TCP/IP services and applications. Access lists are used to implement the packet-filtering rules derived from the network security policy. The perimeter router creates a dirty DMZ or screened subnet. The PIX Firewall can be used to create a "protected" DMZ by placing the bastion hosts on a third PIX Firewall interface (see Figure 7-1).

Cisco Perimeter Router Features

Cisco engineers have developed many core perimeter security capabilities into Cisco IOS Software, allowing Cisco customers to use their routers as a primary point of network access control to their internal networks. The core security features enable user authentication and authorization, protect against unknown or unwelcome source/ destination addresses, hide internal IP addresses from public view, track activity within and across a router, and let administrators implement policy-based security at perimeters.

Table 7-1 lists these core perimeter security features (organized by feature), the vulnerability that the feature protects against, and a description of the feature. Refer to Chapter 1, "Evaluating Network Security Threats," for more information about network vulnerabilities.

Table 7-1   *Perimeter Router Features That Protect Against Security Threats*

Feature	Vulnerability	Description
Control of TCP/IP services	Reconnaissance, Denial of Service (DoS), unauthorized access	General and interface-specific commands provide protection.
Control of route advertisement	Data manipulation	Static routes, controlling route advertisement, and peer router authentication prevent rerouting attacks.

continues

Table 7-1 *Perimeter Router Features That Protect Against Security Threats (Continued)*

Feature	Vulnerability	Description
Packet filtering	Data manipulation, unauthorized access, DoS	Standard access lists and extended IP access lists are used to filter incoming and outgoing traffic.
Rate limiting	DoS	Controls ICMP and SYN flood attacks.
TCP intercept	DoS	Controls SYN flood attacks.
Network layer encryption	Data manipulation, reconnaissance	CET and IPSec protocols help ensure the integrity and confidentiality of data between perimeters.
Network Address Translation	Data manipulation	NAT helps hide internal addressing schemes and simplifies readdressing.
Port Address Translation	Data manipulation	PAT helps hide internal addressing schemes and helps extend the use of limited registered IP addresses.
Lock-and-key (dynamic) access lists	Unauthorized access	Provides additional user access security.
Firewall feature set	Unauthorized access	Provides a rich set of additional firewall features for Cisco routers.
Event logging	Data manipulation	Helps provide tracking data to aid in detecting and analyzing attack patterns.

The Cisco IOS Firewall Feature Set

Cisco has developed a low-cost, advanced firewall solution with the Cisco IOS Firewall feature set (Cisco IOS Firewall, also known as CiscoSecure Integrated Software), available in Cisco IOS Software images deployed in Cisco routers. The Cisco IOS Firewall adds practical, state-of-the-art firewall technology to the core security capabilities of Cisco IOS-based routers. The Cisco IOS Firewall introduces several enhancements to existing security services in Cisco IOS Software. The most significant feature is Context-Based Access Control (CBAC), which enables many other new features such as Java applet blocking, DoS detection and prevention, and audit trails.

The Cisco IOS Firewall is covered in more depth in Chapter 8, "Configuring the Cisco IOS Firewall." It is summarized in Table 7-2.

Table 7-2 *Cisco IOS Firewall Feature Summary*

Feature	Vulnerability	Description
CBAC	Data manipulation, remote access	Provides secure, per-application access control for all IP traffic across perimeters (for example, between private enterprise networks and the Internet). CBAC inspection rules can trigger alerts and audit trail information by application protocol.
Java blocking	Data manipulation	Protects against identified malicious Java applets.
DoS detection and prevention	DoS	Defends and protects router resources against half-open TCP and UDP attacks. Checks packet headers and drops suspicious packets based on configured thresholds. Incompatible with the TCP intercept feature.
Audit trail	Data manipulation	Details connections. Records time stamp, source host, destination host, ports, and total number of bytes transmitted. Detects unaccounted-for activity.
Real-time alerts	Data manipulation	Logs alerts in case of DoS attacks or other undetected suspicious conditions.
Intrusion detection system	All	Acts as an in-line intrusion detection sensor. Watches packets and sessions as they flow through the router and scans each to match any of the IDS signatures. When it detects suspicious activity, it responds before network security can be compromised and logs the event through Cisco IOS syslog. Works with CiscoSecure IDS Director.
Authentication proxy	Unauthorized access	Allows you to apply specific security policies on a per-user basis. Authenticates and authorizes users via HTTP session to an external security database.
ConfigMaker support	N/A	A Windows 95/Windows NT wizard-based network configuration tool that offers step-by-step guidance through network design, addressing, and firewall feature set implementation.

The DMZ

The DMZ, or isolation LAN, is a buffer between the corporate network and the outside world. The DMZ has a unique network number that is different from the corporate network number. Generally, the DMZ network is the only network visible to the outside.

The DMZ is created by the perimeter security devices working together to make up a firewall system that includes the perimeter router, the bastion host, and the firewall.

In Figure 7-1, the perimeter router creates a dirty DMZ, which is a partially protected environment for a bastion host, which provides services to outside and inside users such as a corporate Web site and an application gateway, which provides TCP/IP services such as e-mail relay.

The Bastion Host

A bastion host is a secure server (typically UNIX, Windows NT, or Linux based) that resides on the DMZ. It provides essential services to the outside world:

- Anonymous FTP server services
- World Wide Web server services
- Domain Name Service (DNS) services
- Incoming e-mail (SMTP) services to deliver e-mail to the company
- Internet proxy services for internal hosts

The bastion host must be highly secured: It is vulnerable to attack because it is exposed to the Internet and is usually the main point of contact from the Internet to the corporate network. The bastion host may also be accessed by internal users.

Sometimes the bastion host provides proxy services by running specialized application or server programs. Proxy services take users' requests for Internet services (such as sending e-mail, FTP, or Telnet) and forward them to the actual services based on the network security policy.

If the bastion host provides proxy services, it is inherently aware of the applications it will proxy. It monitors its TCP or UDP ports for the services it will proxy: Telnet, FTP, HTTP, gopher, Wide Area Information Service (WAIS), Network Time Protocol (NTP), Network News Transfer Protocol (NNTP), and SMTP.

A bastion host may also be configured as a *dual-homed host* if it has two network interfaces—one on the internal network and one on the outside network. Bastion hosts can provide firewall features in the dual-homed host configuration. You should closely monitor the bastion host to detect attempts to compromise it because the dual-homed host configuration can make your network highly vulnerable. A PIX Firewall provides much stronger security than a dual-homed host and is the recommended solution for firewall implementations.

The Firewall

A firewall is a special-purpose networking device specially designed to protect an internal network from an external network. A firewall uses a variety of features, which collectively have the following properties:

- There is a traffic choke point: All traffic from inside to outside and from outside to inside must pass through the firewall.
- Only authorized traffic, as defined by the local security policy, is allowed to pass.
- The firewall itself is configured to be immune to penetration.
- The firewall makes the inside network invisible to the outside.

Firewalls can be implemented in several ways:

- **Packet filter**—This firewall device inspects each packet for user-specified parameters such as an IP address or a TCP or UDP port, but it does not keep track of the sessions. General-purpose routers such as a Cisco 7500 can be configured to provide firewall features using packet filtering and Cisco IOS Firewall features.
- **Application gateway**—A firewall that examines application-level data in all packets passing through it before allowing a connection. Only valid application-level data is allowed through the firewall. An FTP application gateway, for example, examines FTP application-level packets and allows only valid FTP access.
- **Circuit-level gateway**—A firewall that validates TCP and UDP sessions before opening a connection, or circuit, through the firewall. The gateway examines TCP or UDP session data to ensure that legitimate packets are allowed through the firewall. After a session is established, the firewall maintains a table of valid session connections and lets data pass through when session information matches an entry in the table. When the session is over, the table entry is removed, and the circuit is closed until another process begins.
- **Proxy server**—A firewall process that shields the internal (protected) network by replacing the IP address of a host on the internal network with its own IP address for all traffic passing through it. Most application and circuit-level gateways now available include a built-in proxy function for added security. Firewall vendors often term such products *application proxies* and *circuit-level proxies*. The PIX Firewall includes the cut-through proxy feature that offers secure proxying and high performance.

The firewall market is growing quickly. Many vendors and security associations have developed firewalls. In the context of this book, we will consider the following firewalls:

- **Cisco IOS Firewall**—A set of powerful firewall features for Cisco routers.
- **Cisco PIX Firewall**—A specialized hardware and software firewall with a secure operating system. This firewall will be considered in future chapters.

Controlling TCP/IP Services

Cisco IOS Software includes specific commands to control TCP/IP services offered by routers, allowing you to reduce susceptibility to eavesdropping, DoS attacks, and unauthorized access attacks (see Table 7-3). You should enter these commands only if the service is specifically needed. Many of the TCP/IP services are turned on by default and must be manually disabled with the commands listed in Table 7-3. These commands are useful for controlling TCP/IP services in global configuration mode. Commands that are in the default router configuration are noted.

Table 7-3 *Commands for Controlling TCP/IP Services Offered by Routers*

Command	Description
no service tcp-small-servers	Disables access to minor TCP services available from hosts on the network for the Echo, Discard, Chargen, and Daytime ports.
	By default, the TCP servers for Echo, Discard, Chargen, and Daytime services are enabled.
	When they are disabled, access to the Echo, Discard, Chargen, and Daytime ports causes the Cisco IOS Software to send a TCP RESET packet to the sender and discard the original incoming packet.
no service udp-small-servers	Disables access to minor UDP services available from hosts on the network for the Echo, Discard, Chargen, and Daytime ports.
	By default, the UDP servers for Echo, Discard, Chargen, and Daytime services are enabled.
	When they are disabled, access to the Echo, Discard, Chargen, and Daytime ports causes the Cisco IOS Software to send an "ICMP port unreachable" packet to the sender and discard the original incoming packet.
no service finger	Prevents **finger** protocol requests (defined in RFC 742) from being made of the router, stopping remote queries of users.
no ip domain-lookup	Disables the IP DNS-based host name-to-address translation on the perimeter router.

Table 7-3   *Commands for Controlling TCP/IP Services Offered by Routers (Continued)*

Command	Description
no ip source-route	Disables IP source routing.
no ip tcp selective-ack	Disables TCP selective acknowledgment (as specified in RFC 2018). Reduces performance but increases protection against DoS attacks.
no ip bootp server	Disables the BOOTP service available from hosts on the network.
no mop enabled	Disables the Maintenance Operations Protocol (MOP). Can also be applied to a specific interface.
no cdp run	Disables Cisco Discovery Protocol globally.
no ip rsh-enable	Configures the router to disallow remote users to execute commands on it using **rsh**.
no ip rcmd rcp-enable	Configures the router to disallow remote users to copy files to and from the router using **rcp** commands.
no ip identd	Disables identification support, preventing the return of identification information about a TCP port.

The commands listed in Table 7-4 are useful for controlling TCP/IP services in interface configuration mode.

Table 7-4   *Commands for Controlling TCP/IP Services in Interface Configuration Mode*

Command	Description
no ip proxy-arp	Disables proxy ARP on an interface.
no ip redirects	Disables the sending of redirect messages if the Cisco IOS Software is forced to resend a packet through the same interface on which it was received. Limits information sent by the router in the case of a port scan.
no ip tcp path-mtu-discovery	Disables Path MTU Discovery for all new TCP connections from the router for an interface. Enabling Path MTU Discovery can increase susceptibility to DoS attacks.
no ip unreachable	Disables the generation of ICMP Unreachable messages on a specified interface.
no ip route-cache	Disables autonomous switching and/or fast switching caches for IP routing.
no ip mroute-cache	Disables IP multicast fast switching, sending packets at the process level. Required to enable logging of debug messages and access list processing. Default command.

continues

Table 7-4 *Commands for Controlling TCP/IP Services in Interface Configuration Mode (Continued)*

Command	Description
no cdp enable	Disables CDP on an interface.
no ip directed-broadcast	Turns off IP directed broadcasts, preventing the router from becoming a broadcast amplifier in a distributed DoS attack. Default command.

Example 7-1 shows a partial **show running-config** that controls the SNMP TCP/IP service by blocking SNMP access from the outside. The access list is applied to the incoming portion of an interface connected to an insecure network.

Example 7-1 *Controlling the SNMP TCP/IP Service by Blocking SNMP Access from the Outside*

```
interface serial 0
 access-group 101 in
access-list 101 deny udp any any eq snmp
```

Preventing Rerouting Attacks

Perimeter routers are particularly susceptible to an eavesdropper trying to examine routing updates to learn the composition of a DMZ or an inside network. You can configure static routes to tell the router where to forward traffic into and out of a perimeter router and to point to the next-hop router, usually a router inside the ISP's network. If you must use a routing protocol to communicate with other perimeter routers, such as at an extranet partner or a remote branch in a site-to-site topology, you can control route advertisement with standard access lists and **distribute-list** commands, and you can use peer router authentication to secure routing traffic and to prevent route traffic spoofing. This section provides a summary of how to protect perimeter router routing.

You can secure router-to-router communications as described in the following sections.

Static Routes

Static routes are used on a perimeter router to send all traffic destined for the Internet to the ISP's router. Static routes used to send all traffic to a specific destination are also known as default routes. The ISP router is then responsible for forwarding packets to the correct destinations. The perimeter router then does not have to exchange dynamic routing information and possibly reveal details about the internal network topology. Static routes have some drawbacks including the inability to adapt when a data circuit goes down or when the network topology changes.

Configuring static routes is performed by the **ip route** command in global configuration mode. You can specify where the router should send packets destined for that network as either the next-hop IP address of the ISP router (the preferred method), the network address of another route in the routing table to which packets should be forwarded (useful when you have multiple redundant paths to the ISP), or a specific IP address of the next router in the path (not recommended because IP addresses have to be resolved to the Interface data link layer). Example 7-2 shows a static route forwarding all packets to the ISP's router at 172.16.100.2.

Example 7-2 *Forwarding All Packets to the ISP's Router at 172.16.100.2*

```
ip route 0.0.0.0 0.0.0.0 172.16.100.2
```

Controlling Route Advertisement

You might choose to use a routing protocol between your perimeter router and the ISP router or another perimeter router at a remote location. Route filters can be set up on any interface to prevent learning or propagating routing information inappropriately. Some routing protocols (such as Enhanced IGRP) allow you to insert a filter on the routes being advertised so that certain routes are not advertised in some parts of the network. Routing protocols also let you filter incoming routes so that that the router learns routes from only trusted networks.

You might choose to use Enhanced IGRP between Cisco perimeter routers because it is available only on Cisco routers. This reduces the chances of accidental or malicious routing disruption caused by hosts in a network.

Refer to Chapter 3, "Securing the Network Infrastructure," for more information on controlling route advertisement.

Route Authentication

If you choose to use a routing protocol between perimeter routers, you might choose to use route authentication. Authentication mechanisms are protocol-specific and generally weak. In spite of this, it is worthwhile to take advantage of the techniques that exist. Authentication can increase network stability by preventing unauthorized routers or hosts from participating in the routing protocol, whether those devices are participating accidentally or deliberately. Refer to Chapter 3 for more information on peer router authentication.

Controlling Access

A perimeter router is typically positioned at the edge of a network, between your internal network and an external network such as the Internet. The router can be configured to be a powerful tool to control access of data and users between the networks. Access lists are the primary tool for controlling access. Cisco IOS Software supports standard and extended access lists. Refer to Appendix C, "Configuring Standard and Extended Access Lists," for more details about access lists. Access lists provide packet filtering of incoming and outgoing packets.

Controlling access includes filtering inbound and outbound traffic, controlling administrator access to the perimeter router, using lock-and-key security, and performing user authentication using the authentication proxy feature.

Inbound Packet Filtering

You can use packet filtering with access lists to control incoming traffic through a perimeter router. Some typical rules or policies for inbound traffic to the perimeter might include the following:

- Filter packets with internal addresses as source to prevent IP address spoofing attacks.
- Filter packets with RFC-reserved addresses as source to prevent IP address spoofing attacks.
- Filter bootp, TFTP, SNMP, and traceroute as incoming to prevent against remote access and reconnaissance attacks.
- Allow TCP connections initiated from internal networks to prevent IP spoofing attacks.
- Prevent direct pings against the PIX Firewall outside the interface to prevent reconnaissance attacks.
- Allow all other incoming connections to DMZ servers only to prevent remote access attacks.

Table 7-5 summarizes typical IP addresses you would want to filter on incoming packets.

Table 7-5   *IP Addresses to Filter on Incoming Packets*

IP Address and Mask Bits	IP Address Use
0.0.0.0/8	Historical broadcast
10.0.0.0/8	RFC 1918 private network
127.0.0.0/8	Local loopback
169.254.0.0/16	Link local networks
172.16.0.0/12	RFC 1918 private network

Table 7-5   *IP Addresses to Filter on Incoming Packets (Continued)*

IP Address and Mask Bits	IP Address Use
192.0.2.0/24	TEST-NET
192.168.0.0/16	RFC 1918 private network
224.0.0.0/4	Class D multicast
240.0.0.0/5	Class E reserved
248.0.0.0/5	Unallocated
255.255.255.255/32	Broadcast

Example 7-3 shows incoming filtering of RFC 1918 addresses as source.

Example 7-3   *Incoming Filtering of RFC 1918 Addresses as Source*

```
interface serial 0
    ip access-group 101 in
access-list 101 deny ip 10.0.0.0     0.255.255.255 any
access-list 101 deny ip 192.168.0.0 0.0.255.255 any
access-list 101 deny ip 172.16.0.0  0.15.255.255 any
access-list 101 permit ip any any
```

Outbound Packet Filtering

You can use packet filtering with access lists to control outbound traffic through a perimeter router. Typically, you should ensure that your perimeter routers and firewalls are configured to forward IP packets only if those packets have the correct source IP address for the network to prevent your network devices from being used for distributed DoS (DDoS) attacks against other networks. The correct source IP address(es) would consist of the IP network addresses that have been assigned to the site.

Some typical rules or policies for outbound traffic from the perimeter might include the following:

- Allow only packets with a source address from the internal network (or translated address) to the Internet.
- Allow only packets with a source address from the bastion host to the Internet.
- Filter any IP addresses that are not allowed out as defined by the security policy.

Lock-and-Key Security

A useful security solution is the lock-and-key security feature, which is available with IP extended access lists. Standard, extended, and static access lists require the assignment of an access list to an interface permanently. When an access list is assigned statically to an interface, it operates as configured, regardless of the hosts on that interface network. This type of access list does not take into account the host that might be accessing information beyond the firewall, and it cannot authenticate the host.

An improved security solution in Cisco IOS Release 11.1 and later is the lock-and-key security feature. Lock-and-key uses dynamic access lists that grant access per user to a specific source/destination host through a user authentication process. You can allow user access through a firewall dynamically without compromising security restrictions.

Lock-and-key is activated after the user has been authenticated, through the router or a network security server such as the TACACS+ server, which is then responsible for altering the access list for the incoming interface to enable the privileges allowed to that user. Figure 7-2 illustrates the operation of lock-and-key.

Figure 7-2 *Lock-and-Key Security Operation*

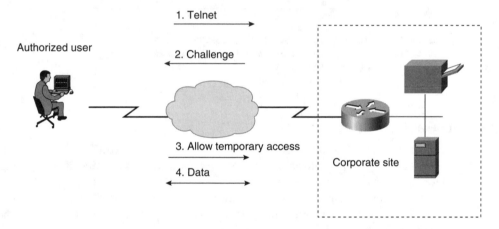

In a typical environment, lock-and-key puts in place an access list that filters all traffic until the remote user has authenticated with the configured security mechanism. A remote host can execute a Telnet session and open the corporate site firewall after authentication. Until then, the firewall is configured to disallow all traffic except Telnet.

In this manner, no access lists exist for any port except for the Telnet access list. Until the remote user authenticates, access is denied on the port. After authentication, a specific access list is applied for that port only, allowing the authenticating user/network access beyond the firewall.

Configuring Lock-and-Key Security

To configure lock-and-key, follow these steps, beginning in global configuration mode:

1 Configure a dynamic access list, which serves as a template and place holder for temporary access list entries with the **access-list** *access-list-number* [**dynamic** *dynamic-name* [**timeout** *minutes*]] {**deny** | **permit**} **telnet** *source source-wildcard destination destination-wildcard* [**precedence** *precedence*] [**tos** *tos*] [**established**] [**log**] command. The **timeout** *minutes* argument is an absolute timeout value for the dynamic access list.

2 Enter interface configuration mode for the interface where you will apply the access list with the **interface** *type number* command.

3 Apply the access list to the interface with the **ip access-group** *access-list-number* command in interface configuration mode.

4 Define one or more virtual terminal (vty) ports you will use with lock-and-key with the **line vty** *line-number* [*ending-line-number*] command in global configuration mode. If you specify multiple vty ports, they must all be configured identically because the software hunts for available vty ports on a round-robin basis. If you do not want to configure all your vty ports for lock-and-key access, you can specify a group of vty ports for lock-and-key support only.

5 Configure user authentication to either an external authentication server or the internal user database with the **login tacacs**, **username** *name* **password** *secret*, **password** *password*, or **login local** command.

6 Enable the creation of temporary access list entries with the **autocommand access-enable** [**host**] [**timeout** *minutes*] command. The **timeout** *minutes* argument is an idle timeout value. If the host argument is not specified, all hosts on the entire network are allowed to set up a temporary access list entry. The dynamic access list contains the network mask to enable the new network connection.

Lock-and-key allows an external event (that is, a Telnet session) to place an opening in the perimeter router. While this opening exists, the router is susceptible to source address spoofing.

DoS Protection

Perimeter routers can provide a first line of defense against DoS attacks. You can use a perimeter router to reduce the chances that your network is used as the source of a DDoS attack against another network by taking a few essential steps. You can also limit the effect of SYN-flooding attacks with the TCP intercept feature.

Preventing DDoS

Here are some actions you can take to prevent DDoS attacks:

- Prevent your network equipment from being a participant in a DDoS attack. Ensure that you have taken all steps possible to prevent unauthorized access to the bastion host to prevent placement of DDoS software. Turn off all unneeded IP services. And use the **no ip directed-broadcast** command on interfaces to prevent your perimeter router from becoming a broadcast amplifier for DDoS attacks.

- Filter all incoming traffic for private (per RFC 1918) and reserved addresses using access control lists. (See RFC 2827, "Network Ingress Filtering.")

- Filter all outgoing traffic to prevent source IP address spoofing. You should only permit packets to exit the perimeter with source addresses from the DMZ or other permitted addresses. You can use access lists and the **ip verify unicast reverse-path** interface command to filter outgoing traffic.

- Use committed access rate (CAR) to rate-limit ICMP packet floods. Rate limiting or policing can be applied on the inbound, outbound, or both interfaces. The limiting action is available only with CAR, so the devices must be running IOS version 11.1cc or 12.0+. For example, traffic can be limited or policed at the input interface of the perimeter router. First, the packet is classified using an access list as ICMP traffic. After the traffic is classified, CAR can selectively limit classified traffic flows to specific levels of bandwidth. If the rate is exceeded, the policy action is triggered, and the packets are dropped. The rate limit interface configuration command is used to configure CAR. CEF must be enabled on the interface before you configure CAR.

  In the following example on the serial 0 interface of the perimeter router, access list 105 selects the CAR traffic to be ICMP ECHOREPLY. The average rate is 1544 Kbps, with a burst rate of 512 Kbps and a peak of 786 Kbps. If the rate limit is exceeded, packets are dropped:

  ```
  interface serial 0
     rate-limit output access-group 105 1540000 512000 786000
       conform-action
     transmit exceed-action drop
     access-list 105 permit icmp any any echo-reply
  ```

- Configure rate limiting for SYN packets. Measure the amount of normal SYN traffic using the **show interfaces rate-limit** command to display the conformed and exceeded rates for the interface to help set a benchmark for normal traffic rates. Your objective should be to rate-limit the SYNs as little as necessary. Here is a sample configuration for Web traffic through the perimeter router:

  ```
  interface serial 0
     rate-limit output access-group 150 1540000  512000 786000
       conform-action
     transmit exceed-action drop
  ```

```
access-list 150 permit tcp any host eq www
access-list 150 permit tcp any host eq www established
```

- Enable logging on the perimeter devices, especially the perimeter router, to help trace DDoS attacks.

Using TCP Intercept to Control SYN Attacks

The TCP intercept feature in Cisco IOS Software protects TCP servers from SYN-flooding attacks, a type of DoS attack. TCP intercept can be deployed in a perimeter router to protect DMZ or other hosts from SYN attacks. TCP intercept tracks and optionally intercepts and validates TCP connection requests from a TCP client to a TCP server. TCP intercept helps prevent SYN-flooding attacks by intercepting and validating TCP connection requests from a TCP client to a TCP server. TCP intercept operates in two modes: intercept mode and monitor mode. Figure 7-3 shows how TCP intercept works.

Figure 7-3   *Protecting Against TCP SYN Attacks with TCP Intercept*

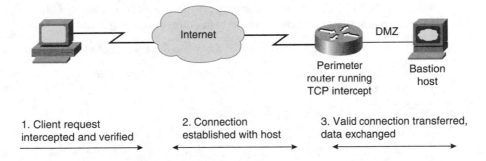

In intercept mode (the default setting), TCP intercept software intercepts TCP synchronization (SYN) packets from clients to servers that match an extended access list. TCP intercept proxy-answers the client for the destination server and validates the connection before connecting the client to the server. If the client request is valid, TCP intercept establishes the connection with the server on behalf of the client and knits the two half-connections together into a source-destination flow. TCP intercept continues to intercept and forward packets throughout the duration of the connection.

In monitor mode, TCP intercept software passively watches the connection requests flowing through the router. If a connection fails to get established in a configurable interval, the software intervenes and terminates the connection attempt.

TCP intercept goes into aggressive mode in the case of a SYN flood in which the number of half-open connections exceeds configurable threshold values. In aggressive mode, the connection threshold values are reduced, and half-open connections exceeding the thresholds are reset, while valid requests are still allowed.

TCP options that are negotiated on handshake (such as RFC 1323 for window scaling, for example) are not negotiated because the TCP intercept software does not know what the server can do or will negotiate.

TCP intercept connections are fast-switched except on the RP/SP/SSP-based C7000, which supports process switching only.

When establishing a security policy using TCP intercept, you can choose to intercept all requests or only those coming from specific networks or destined for specific servers. You can also configure the connection rate and threshold of outstanding connections. Configuring TCP intercept consists of following these steps:

1 Define an IP extended access list with the **access-list** *access-list-number* {**deny** | **permit**} **tcp any** *destination destination-wildcard* command. Identify the destination in order to protect destination servers.

2 Enable TCP intercept with the **ip tcp intercept list** *access-list-number* command.

3 Set the intercept mode with the **ip tcp intercept mode** {**intercept** | **watch**} command.

4 Verify TCP intercept by displaying incomplete connections and established connections with the **show tcp intercept connections** command.

5 Display TCP intercept statistics with the **show tcp intercept statistics** command.

6 Tune TCP intercept values by performing the following optional tasks by entering associated commands:

— Set the TCP intercept drop mode.

— Change the TCP intercept timers.

— Change the TCP intercept aggressive thresholds.

Refer to the chapter "Configuring TCP Intercept (Preventing Denial-of-Service Attacks)" in the *Cisco IOS Security Configuration Guide, Release 12.1* for more details.

Example 7-4 defines extended IP access list 101, causing the software to intercept packets for all TCP servers on the 192.168.1.0/24 subnet.

Example 7-4 *Extended IP Access List 101 Blocks Private IP Addresses*

```
ip tcp intercept list 101
!
access-list 101 permit tcp any 192.168.1.0 0.0.0.255
```

NOTE   You can also use the **ip tcp intercept** commands available with the CBAC feature in Cisco IOS Software images supporting Cisco IOS Firewall software to prevent DoS SYN attacks. If you use CBAC, you cannot also use TCP intercept.

Using Network Layer Encryption

Network layer encryption can be used at a perimeter router to provide protection between perimeter systems. Network layer encryption encrypts traffic on a flow-by-flow basis between specific source/destination user-application pairs or subnets, as illustrated in Figure 7-4.

Figure 7-4 *Network Layer Encryption*

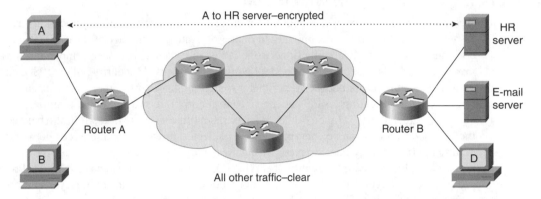

Network encryption encrypts only payload information, leaving network layer headers in the clear. This makes encrypted payload information transparent to intermediary network layer devices.

Because it operates at the network layer, network encryption is protocol-specific but media- and interface-independent, which also makes it topology-independent.

Cisco IOS Software offers Cisco Encryption Technology (CET) and IPSec support to enable network layer encryption between a perimeter router and another router.

Network Layer Encryption with CET

CET is a proprietary security solution introduced in Cisco IOS Release 11.2. It provides network data encryption at the IP packet level and implements the following standards: Digital Signature Standard (DSS), Diffie-Hellman (DH) public key algorithm, and Data Encryption Standard (DES).

CET can be configured at perimeter routers to provide secure communications between two secured networks that are physically separated. The actual encryption and decryption of IP packets occur only at routers that you configure for CET. Such routers are considered to be peer encrypting routers. Intermediate hops do not participate in encryption/decryption. Packets are encrypted at one peer router's outbound interface and decrypted at the other peer router's inbound interface.

Cleartext (that is, unencrypted) traffic that enters a peer router from the secure network side is encrypted and forwarded across the unsecure network. When the encrypted traffic reaches the remote peer router, the router decrypts the traffic before forwarding it to the remote secure network. See Part V, "Configuring Cisco Encryption Technology," for more detailed coverage of how to configure CET.

Network Layer Encryption with IPSec

IPSec is a framework of open standards for ensuring secure private communications over IP networks. IPSec ensures confidentiality, integrity, and authenticity of data communications across a public IP network. IPSec provides a necessary component of a flexible, standards-based solution for deploying a network-wide security policy. IPSec can be used to secure traffic between a perimeter router and another perimeter router in a site-to-site topology, creating a VPN between a central corporate site and either a remote corporate site, a remote branch office, or an extranet (partner) network. All traffic between the perimeter routers can be encrypted, or only selected flows between hosts or networks behind the routers may be encrypted. Businesses enjoy the same policies as a private network, including security, quality of service (QoS), manageability, and reliability. IPSec provides more flexibility in the choice of encryption algorithms and supports many more IPSec peers than does CET. See Chapters 15 through 18 for detailed coverage of how to configure IPSec.

Managing IP Addresses with NAT and PAT

Perimeter routers help organizations alleviate depletion of IP address space, hide internal IP addresses from the outside, enhance scaling in routing inside to outside networks, and simplify system administration by allowing discontinuous or nonroutable IP addresses to be converted to routable IP addresses. Perimeter routers use Network Address Translation (NAT) and Port Address Translation (PAT) to enable these capabilities.

Using NAT

NAT is a feature of perimeter routers and packet-filtering firewalls that translates inside local IP addresses to outside global addresses, usually IP addresses assigned by the Network Information Center. NAT is described in RFC 1631, and it can be used in the perimeter to do the following:

- It alleviates depletion of relatively scarce NIC-registered IP addresses.
- It hides the IP addresses used in the internal network and internal devices from network intruders on the outside.

- It allows you to connect your campus network to the Internet without worrying about Internet address limitations, about duplicate addresses, or that your IP addresses are not legal, officially assigned IP addresses.

Cisco IOS Software uses the following terminology for NAT:

- **Inside local address**—The IP address that is assigned to a host on the inside network. The address is probably not a legitimate IP address assigned by the NIC or a service provider.

- **Inside global address**—A legitimate IP address (assigned by the NIC or service provider) that represents one or more inside local IP addresses to the outside world.

- **Outside local address**—The IP address of an outside host as it appears to the inside network. Not necessarily a legitimate address, it was allocated from address space routable on the inside.

- **Outside global address**—The IP address assigned to a host on the outside network by the host's owner. The address was allocated from globally routable addresses or network space.

Figure 7-5 illustrates a router that is translating a source address from inside a network of 10.1.1.2 to an inside global address of 172.16.1.100.

Figure 7-5   *An Example of NAT*

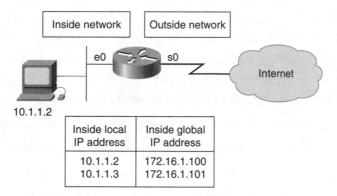

NAT can be configured to perform either static or dynamic address translation. With static translation, an inside local address is statically mapped to an inside global address. For example, in Figure 7-5, a host with an address of 10.1.1.2 is statically mapped to an inside global address of 172.16.1.100.

With dynamic translation, a pool of inside global addresses is defined and assigned to an interface, and the router dynamically maps an inside local address to an available address in the global pool. In Figure 7-5, a dynamic address pool is assigned to the router's s0 interface.

NAT maintains a table of translated IP addresses. To the outside world, the network appears to have a certain IP address range. These addresses are mapped into the actual addresses used within the campus. When a packet comes into the firewall from the Internet, the IP address is translated, and the packet goes to the correct destination. Likewise, outgoing messages are given the "public" IP addresses; the real ones are hidden.

NAT can provide additional capabilities:

- **Overloading an inside global address**—You can conserve addresses in the inside global address pool by allowing the router to use one global address for many local addresses. This feature is also called PAT.

- **Translating overlapping addresses**—NAT can translate a mixture of legal, officially assigned IP addresses, private IP addresses as specified in RFC 1918, and public IP addresses used illegally inside the network.

Configuring Dynamic NAT

To configure dynamic inside source address translation, use the following commands, beginning in global configuration mode:

1 Define a pool of global addresses to be allocated as needed with the **ip nat pool** *name start-ip end-ip* {**netmask** *netmask* | **prefix-length** *prefix-length*} command.

2 Define a standard access list permitting those addresses that are to be translated with the **access-list** *access-list-number* **permit** *source* [*source-wildcard*] command.

3 Establish dynamic source translation, specifying the access list defined in the prior step with the **ip nat inside source list** *access-list-number* **pool** *name* command.

4 Specify the inside interface with the **interface type number** command.

5 Mark the interface as connected to the inside with the **ip nat inside** command.

6 Specify the outside interface with the **interface type number** command.

7 Mark the interface as connected to the outside with the **ip nat outside** command.

Consider Example 7-5, which shows dynamic inside source address translation for the XYZ Company. This example dynamically translates all source addresses passing access list 1 (having a source address from 10.1.1.0/24) to an address from the pool named net-182. The pool contains addresses from 172.16.1.100 to 172.16.1.199.

Example 7-5 *Dynamic Inside Source Address Translation for the XYZ Company*

```
ip nat pool net-182 172.16.1.100 172.16.1.199 netmask 255.255.255.0
ip nat inside source list 1 pool net-182
!
interface serial 0
 ip address 172.16.1.1 255.255.255.0
 ip nat outside
```

Example 7-5 *Dynamic Inside Source Address Translation for the XYZ Company (Continued)*

```
!
interface ethernet 0
 ip address 10.1.1.1 255.255.255.0
 ip nat inside
!
access-list 1 permit 10.1.1.0 0.0.0.255
```

Using PAT

Many internal addresses can perform NAT to only one or a few external addresses by using PAT, which is sometimes referred to as *NAT overloading*. PAT provides additional IP address expansion, although it is less flexible than NAT, as the following examples show:

- With PAT, one IP address can be used for up to 64,000 hosts (theoretically and practically, it can be used for up to 4,000 hosts). PAT makes economical use of IP addresses and physical connections.

- PAT remaps different TCP or UDP port numbers to a single IP address.

- PAT provides some security. It hides clients' source addresses by using a single IP address from the perimeter router.

- Address pool density affects performance.

PAT lets you conserve public IP addresses allocated by the Internet Network Information Center (InterNIC) by using one InterNIC-assigned IP address in the global address pool for all outgoing connections to the Internet. The source IP address of outgoing packets is translated to the single PAT address.

Ports are service specifiers inside a UDP or TCP packet. With PAT enabled, the perimeter router chooses a unique source port number for each outbound connection, thereby permitting many connections to use a single IP address.

PAT does not use well-known or assigned port numbers for translation. Destination TCP or UDP ports are not translated. Different local addresses then map to the same global address, with port translation providing the necessary uniqueness of source ports.

NOTE   Do not use PAT when running multimedia applications through the firewall. Multimedia applications need access to specific ports and can conflict with port mappings provided by PAT.

Configuring PAT

Consider the example of PAT for the XYZ Company illustrated in Figure 7-6. In the example, a user at Workstation A needs to establish Telnet sessions to Host A and Host B.

Figure 7-6 *An Example of PAT*

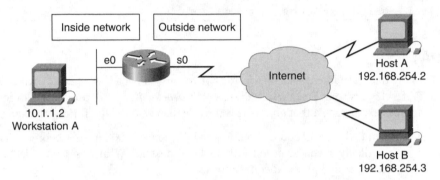

Protocol port	Inside local IP address:port	Inside global IP address:port	Outside global IP address:port
TCP/Telnet	10.1.1.1:1026	172.16.1.200:1026	192.168.254.2:23
TCP/Telnet	10.1.1.2:1027	172.16.1.200:1027	192.168.254.3:23

PAT is configured on the perimeter router, and it dynamically translates all source addresses selected by access list 1 (having a source address from 10.1.1.0/24) to an address from the pool named net-183. The pool contains one IP address of 172.16.1.200.

The **overload** command lets the router use one global address for many local addresses. When overloading is configured, each inside host's TCP or UDP port number distinguishes between multiple conversations using the same local IP address. Consider the example of PAT for the XYZ Company shown in Example 7-6.

Example 7-6 *An Example of PAT for the XYZ Company*

```
ip nat pool net-183 172.16.1.200 172.16.1.200 netmask 255.255.255.0
ip nat inside source list 2 pool net-184 overload
!
interface serial 0
 ip address 172.16.1.1 255.255.255.0
 ip nat outside
!
interface ethernet 0
 ip address 10.1.1.1 255.255.255.0
 ip nat inside
!
access-list 2 permit 10.1.1.0 0.0.0.255
```

Logging Perimeter Router Events

Typically, you will want to log every event on the perimeter router to the syslog server. You do this by using the **logging trap debugging** command. You can optionally control time stamps applied to log entries with the **service timestamps** command. Configure logging of perimeter router events by following these steps:

1 Specify the debugging level of messages logged to the syslog server with the **logging trap** *level* command.

2 Specify that syslog packets contain the IP address of a particular interface, regardless of which interface the packet uses to exit the router, using the logging source-interface type number command.

3 Log messages to a syslog server host using the **logging host** command.

4 Enable message logging using the **logging on** command.

5 Enable timestamps on log messages with the **service timestamps** {**log** | **debug**} **datetime** [**msec**] [**localtime**] [**show-timezone**] command.

Example 7-7 is an example of configuring the logging of perimeter events.

Example 7-7 *Configuring the Logging of Perimeter Events*

```
service timestamps log datetime msec
service timestamps debug datetime msec
logging trap informational
logging source-interface FastEthernet 0
logging 192.168.1.10
logging on
Perimeter1# show logging
Syslog logging: enabled (0 messages dropped, 0 flushes, 0 overruns)
    Console logging: level informational, 0 messages logged
    Monitor logging: level informational, 0 messages logged
    Buffer logging: disabled
    Trap logging: level informational, 4583 message lines logged
        Logging to 192.168.1.10, 4038 message lines logged
```

In this example, log events are sent to the PIX Firewall global address of 192.168.1.10, which is statically mapped to a syslog server on the inside network with an IP address of 10.1.1.4.

Summary

This section summarizes the main points of this chapter:

- Cisco IOS Software has a powerful set of perimeter security and firewall features that are useful for creating a perimeter security system. These features are constantly being enhanced.

- Cisco IOS Software has a variety of general and interface commands that are useful for controlling TCP/IP services, reducing susceptibility to reconnaissance and remote access attacks.

- You can use a perimeter router to control DoS attacks by filtering incoming and outgoing traffic for IP address spoofing, controlling ICMP-flooding attacks through rate limiting, and controlling SYN-flooding attacks by using the TCP intercept feature.

- Network layer encryption provided by Cisco Encryption Technology and IPSec support in Cisco routers are useful to ensure secure communication between perimeter routers, preventing eavesdropping, information theft, and data manipulation attacks.

- You can control rerouting attacks by using default or static routes to point traffic to the ISP's router, by controlling advertisement of routing updates, and by using route authentication between routers using routing protocols.

- Cisco IOS Software access lists enable powerful yet flexible implementation of network security policy. Access lists can be used to filter packets, controlling incoming and outgoing traffic access.

- Lock-and-key security enables dynamic reconfiguration of access lists upon user authentication, helping secure remote user access.

- NAT enables maximum use of IP addresses registered with InterNIC and serves to hide internal addressing from the public Internet.

- PAT enables maximum use of individual connections to the Internet and hides internal addressing from the public Internet.

- You should log every event on the perimeter router to a syslog server to help analyze attacks on the perimeter security system.

Case Study: Configuring a Cisco Perimeter Router

This case study illustrates how to configure a perimeter router in the hypothetical XYZ Company. Read the case study scenario, examine the topology diagram, read the security policy, and then analyze the sample configuration to see how the security policy statements are enacted for the perimeter router.

Case Study Scenario

The XYZ Company wants you to configure a Cisco router to function as a perimeter router, creating a DMZ. The XYZ Company has asked you to implement a moderately restrictive security policy for its network.

Topology

Figure 7-7 illustrates the portion of the XYZ network that will be configured in this case study. Note that the focus here is on the perimeter router.

Network Security Policy

The moderately restrictive network security policy that the XYZ Company wants to implement is as follows:

- Control TCP/IP services:
  - Protect exposed services with Cisco IOS Software commands.
- Control Admin access:
  - Allow Telnet to the perimeter router only from the Windows NT server inside the network.
  - Specifically prevent SNMP access from the Internet to anywhere in the XYZ Company network.
  - Authenticate Telnet sessions with usernames and passwords entered into the perimeter router's local security database.
  - Log all Admin attempts to the syslog server.
- Prevent source address spoofing:
  - Deny incoming IP traffic if the source address is from the DMZ or internal network.
  - Deny outgoing IP traffic with the campus internal address as the source address.
  - Deny packets with local host or with broadcast or multicast (or both) source addresses.
  - Deny packets without any source address.
  - Control incoming traffic.
  - Permit incoming TCP traffic that is part of an established TCP session.
  - Permit SMTP traffic to the mail gateway on the bastion host.
  - Permit HTTP traffic only to the Web server on the bastion host.

Figure 7-7 *XYZ Company's Perimeter Router, Controlling Network Access*

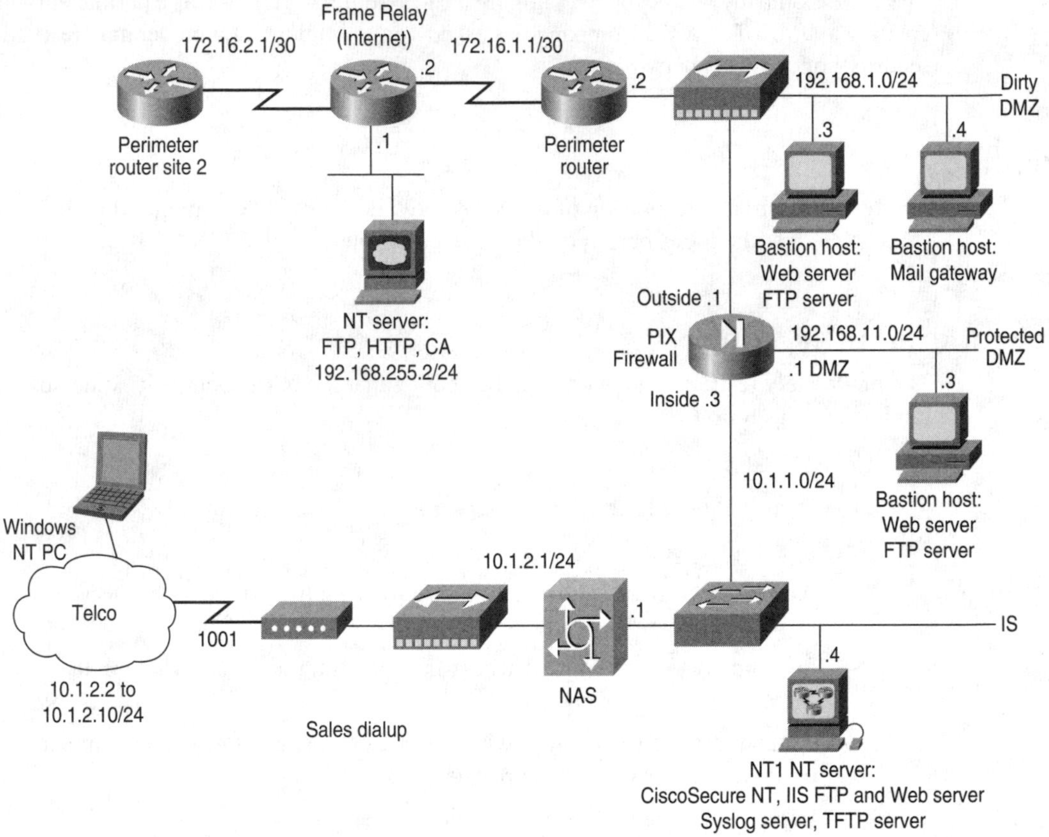

— Permit SHTTP traffic only to the Web server on the bastion host.

— Permit FTP traffic only to the FTP server on the bastion host.

— Permit FTP traffic to ports 1024 and above on the FTP server on the bastion host.

— Permit DNS requests to the DNS server on the bastion host.

— Permit Network News Transfer Protocol (NNTP) and Network Time Protocol (NTP) traffic from registered servers to the bastion host.

— Deny all other incoming traffic unless specifically allowed.

— Log all disallowed connections to the syslog server.

- Control ping access:
  - — Deny direct access (ping or Telnet) to the outside interface of the PIX Firewall.
  - — Allow incoming pings to the external interface of the perimeter router only from the ISP host.
- Log perimeter router events:
  - — Send perimeter router syslog output to the internal syslog server on the NT server.
  - — Log every event on the perimeter router to the syslog server.
  - — Set accurate time-stamping for log and debug messages.
  - — Control access into the router from the console, aux ports, and vty lines.

Sample Configuration for the Perimeter Router

Examine the sample configuration for the perimeter router of the XYZ Company shown in Example 7-8. This example implements the network security policy statements related to perimeter security. One possible configuration of the perimeter router for the specified security policy might look like Example 7-8. You might choose to configure the router differently to enact the same security policy requirements. Note that the sample configuration contains comments showing which router commands enact particular security policy statements. The configuration shown is for a Cisco 1720 router. Unused interfaces and other unrelated commands were deleted for the sake of brevity.

Example 7-8 *A Sample Configuration for the Perimeter Router of the XYZ Company*

```
Current configuration:
!version 12.0
! Set accurate time-stamping for log and debug messages
service timestamps debug datetime msec localtime show-timezone
service timestamps log datetime msec localtime show-timezone
no service password-encryption
! Control TCP/IP services
no service udp-small-servers
no service tcp-small-servers
!
hostname Perimeter1
!
logging buffered 4096 debugging
no logging console
!
! Authenticate Telnet sessions with usernames and passwords entered
! into the perimeter router's local security database
aaa new-model
aaa authentication local-override
aaa authentication login no_tacacs enable
```

continues

Example 7-8 *A Sample Configuration for the Perimeter Router of the XYZ Company (Continued)*

```
aaa authentication login default local
!
username student password 0 cisco
memory-size iomem 25
clock timezone PST -8
clock summer-time zone recurring
ip subnet-zero
! Control TCP/IP services
no ip source-route
no ip finger
ip tcp selective-ack
ip tcp path-mtu-discovery
no ip domain-lookup
!
no ip bootp server
!
 interface Serial0
 ip address 172.16.1.1 255.255.255.252
 ip access-group 101 in
! Control TCP/IP services
 no ip redirects
 no ip unreachables
 no ip directed-broadcast
 no ip proxy-arp
 encapsulation frame-relay
 no ip route-cache
 no ip mroute-cache
 frame-relay lmi-type cisco
!
interface Serial1
 no ip address
 no ip directed-broadcast
 shutdown
!
interface FastEthernet0
 ip address 192.168.1.2 255.255.255.0
 ip access-group 102 in
! Control TCP/IP services
 no ip redirects
 no ip unreachables
 no ip directed-broadcast
 no ip proxy-arp
 no ip route-cache
 no ip mroute-cache
!
ip classless
!
! Use static routes to the ISP router
ip route 0.0.0.0 0.0.0.0 192.168.255.4
! Control TCP/IP services
no ip http server
!
```

Example 7-8 *A Sample Configuration for the Perimeter Router of the XYZ Company (Continued)*

```
! Log every event on the perimeter router to the syslog server.
logging trap debugging
! Send perimeter router syslog output to the internal syslog server on the
! NT server. Syslog server at 10.1.1.4 is statically mapped to 192.168.1.10
! by PIX Firewall.

logging source-interface FastEthernet0
logging 192.168.1.10
!
! Allow Telnet to the perimeter router only from the Windows NT server
! inside the network
access-list 1 permit 192.168.1.10
! Filter incoming traffic for spoofed or illegal addresses
access-list 101 deny    ip 127.0.0.0 0.255.255.255 any log
access-list 101 deny    ip 255.0.0.0 0.255.255.255 any log
access-list 101 deny    ip 224.0.0.0 7.255.255.255 any log
access-list 101 deny    ip host 0.0.0.0 any log
! Deny incoming IP traffic if source address is from the DMZ or
! internal network
access-list 101 deny    ip 192.168.1.0 0.0.0.255 any log
access-list 101 deny    ip 10.0.0.0 0.255.255.255 any log
access-list 101 deny    udp any any eq snmp
! Permit incoming TCP traffic that is part of an established TCP session
access-list 101 permit tcp any 192.168.1.0 0.0.0.255 established
! Permit SMTP traffic to the mail gateway on the bastion host on protected DMZ
access-list 101 permit tcp any host 192.168.1.4 eq smtp
! Permit HTTP traffic only to the Web server on the bastion host
! Port 444 is HTTPS
access-list 101 permit tcp any host 192.168.1.3 eq www
access-list 101 permit tcp any host 192.168.1.3 eq 443
! Permit FTP traffic only to the FTP server on the bastion host
access-list 101 permit tcp any host 192.168.1.3 eq ftp
access-list 101 permit tcp any host 192.168.1.3 eq ftp-data
! Permit FTP traffic to ports 1024 and above on the FTP server
! on the bastion host
access-list 101 permit tcp any host 192.168.1.3 gt 1023
! Allow ICMP echo-replies to reach XYZ hosts and network devices
access-list 101 permit icmp any 192.168.1.0 0.0.0.255 echo-reply
access-list 101 permit icmp any host 172.16.1.1 echo-reply
! Allow incoming pings to the external interface of the perimeter router only
! from the ISP host
access-list 101 permit icmp host 192.168.255.2 host 172.16.1.1 echo
! Permit DNS requests to the DNS server on the bastion host
access-list 101 permit udp any host 192.168.1.3 eq domain
! Permit NNTP and NTP traffic to the bastion host
access-list 101 permit tcp host 192.168.255.2 host 192.168.1.3 eq nntp
access-list 101 permit udp host 192.168.255.2 host 192.168.1.3 eq ntp
! Deny direct access (ping or Telnet) to the outside interface of
! the PIX firewall
access-list 101 deny    icmp any host 192.168.1.1 echo log
access-list 101 deny    tcp any host 192.168.1.1 eq telnet log
```

continues

Example 7-8 *A Sample Configuration for the Perimeter Router of the XYZ Company (Continued)*

```
! Deny direct Telnet access to the perimeter router
access-list 101 deny   tcp any host 172.16.1.1 eq telnet log
access-list 101 deny   tcp any host 192.168.1.2 eq telnet log
! Deny all other incoming traffic unless specifically allowed
! Log all disallowed connections to the syslog server
access-list 101 deny   ip any any log
! Deny outgoing IP traffic with the campus internal address as the
! source address
access-list 102 permit ip 192.168.1.0 0.0.0.255 any
access-list 102 deny   ip any any log
! Control TCP/IP services
no cdp run
!
line con 0
 exec-timeout 0 0
 logging synchronous
 login local
 transport input none
line aux 0
 no exec
 login local
line vty 0 4
 access-class 1 in
 login local
!
end
```

Review Questions

Answer the following review questions, which delve into some of the key facts and concepts covered in this chapter:

1 List three purposes of a perimeter security system.

2 List the components that make up a perimeter security system and briefly identify the functions they perform.

3 What is the purpose of a Cisco perimeter router?

4 Consider the following IOS command: **ip route 0.0.0.0 0.0.0.0 172.16.100.2**. Where and why would you use this command on a perimeter security system?

5 Which Cisco IOS Software commands would you use to control TCP/IP services on a perimeter router to block echo and finger inquiries from the Internet?

6 Which Cisco IOS command could be used to prevent a perimeter router from becoming a broadcast amplifier in a distributed DoS attack?

7   What types of IP address spoofing would you filter on the incoming traffic of a perimeter router?

8   What type of access list is used with lock-and-key security?

9   List the six commands you would use to set up dynamic NAT on a perimeter router.

10   Why is it important to log perimeter router events to a syslog server?

References

The topics considered in this chapter are complex and should be studied further to more fully understand them and put them to use. Use the following references to learn more about the topics in this chapter.

General Perimeter Security References

Chapman and Zwicky, *Building Internet Firewalls,* O'Reilly Publishing, 1995. Comprehensive coverage of building a perimeter firewall.

Rubin, Geer, and Ranum, *Web Security Sourcebook,* John Wiley, 1997.

Simson, Garfinkel, and Spafford, *Practical UNIX and Internet Security,* Second Edition, O'Reilly & Associates, 1996.

Simson, Garfinkel, and Spafford, *Web Security and Commerce,* O'Reilly & Associates, 1997.

Cisco IOS Firewall

Cisco Web page containing a list of product literature for the Cisco IOS Firewall feature set, located at www.cisco.com/warp/public/cc/cisco/mkt/security/iosfw/prodlit/fire_ds.htm.

Data Sheet, Cisco Secure Integrated Software, presents a detailed overview of the Cisco IOS Firewall feature, located at www.cisco.com/warp/public/cc/pd/iosw/ioft/iofwft/prodlit/fire_ds.htm.

Fact sheet discussing the Cisco 1605-R Dual Ethernet Router and the Cisco IOS Firewall feature set, located at www.cisco.com/warp/public/cc/cisco/mkt/access/1600/index.shtml.

DoS Protection and Packet Filtering

"The Cisco IOS TCP Intercept Product Bulletin number 576," a Cisco product bulletin describing the TCP intercept feature, located at www.cisco.com/warp/public/cc/cisco/mkt/ios/rel/prodlit/576_pp.htm.

"Improving Security on Cisco Routers," an informal discussion of some Cisco configuration settings that network administrators should consider changing on their edge routers to improve security, located at www.cisco.com/warp/public/707/21.html#self-flood.

RFC 2827, P. Ferguson and D. Senie, "Network Ingress Filtering: Defeating Denial of Service Attacks Which Employ IP Source Address Spoofing," May 2000. Located at www.ietf.org/rfc/rfc2827.txt.

"Security Technical Tips: Internetworking," a security internetworking technical tips page with tips directly from Cisco's Technical Assistance Center (TAC) engineers to help you with security internetworking issues, located at www.cisco.com/warp/public/707/.

"Strategies to Protect Against Distributed Denial of Service (DDoS) Attacks," a Cisco white paper dated February 17, 2000, located at www.cisco.com/warp/public/707/newsflash.html#overview.

NAT and PAT

The "Configuring Network Address Translation" section of the "Configuring IP Addressing" chapter in the *Cisco IOS IP and IP Routing Configuration Guide, Release 12.1*.

Security Mailing Lists

Academic Firewalls. Send subscription requests to majordomo@net.tamu.edu.

CERT Advisories. Send subscription requests to cert-advisory-request@cert.org.

Firewalls Digest List. Send subscription requests to www.gnac.net/firewalls.

Intrusion Detection Systems (IDSs). Send subscription requests to majordomo@uow.edu.au.

The RISKS Forum. Send subscription requests to risks-request@csl.sri.com.

Upon completing this chapter, you will be able to do the following:

- Identify Cisco IOS Firewall features
- Identify how to configure Cisco IOS Firewall features to secure a case study network
- Test Cisco IOS Firewall and verify that it works properly

CHAPTER 8

Configuring the Cisco IOS Firewall

This chapter introduces the configuration of the Cisco IOS Firewall, also known as CiscoSecure Integrated Software (CSIS). The Cisco IOS Firewall feature set is a security-specific option for Cisco IOS Software. It integrates robust firewall functionality and intrusion detection for every perimeter of the network and enriches existing Cisco IOS security capabilities.

After presenting an overview of the configuration process, this chapter shows you each major step of the configuration, with examples. To help you debug the Cisco IOS Firewall configuration, troubleshooting commands are also provided.

This chapter explores in detail the Context-Based Access Control (CBAC) feature of the Cisco IOS Firewall. The configuration of CBAC is covered as a high-level overview. This chapter also covers the Cisco ConfigMaker application, a wizard-based configuration building tool that helps you develop Cisco IOS Firewall security policy configuration.

You will gain practical knowledge of the Cisco IOS Firewall as you continue to work with the fictional XYZ Company case study network, configuring it to meet the requirements of the XYZ Company security policy by securing the network against application layer attacks.

Cisco IOS Firewall Security Problems and Solutions

The campus infrastructure typically incorporates Internet access facilities. Although this achieves the goal of public Internet access for company users and services, it exposes the company to attacks on network resources by intruders if the security policy is not defined and implemented. Intruders might attempt to gain access or impede business using methods such as mobile code in the form of Java applets and Denial of Service (DoS) attacks.

To be aware of and repel future attacks of these types, you need to implement application layer filtering and real-time alerts. If you want stronger security without using additional hardware, you might choose to implement the Cisco IOS Firewall. The primary component of the Firewall feature set is CBAC. You would then install CBAC on your perimeter routers.

As discussed in previous chapters, you need to match configuration and policy against potential threats. For example, to block malicious applets, you would configure CBAC; to set activity thresholds, you would monitor real-time alerts with Cisco IOS Firewall.

CAUTION CBAC will not work with IPSec unless it is on the IPSec endpoint routers. This is because the protocol number in the IP header of the IPSec packet is not TCP or UDP, and CBAC inspects only TCP and UDP packets.

Configuring Cisco IOS Firewall

Cisco IOS Firewall is designed to prevent unauthorized external individuals from gaining access to an internal network and to block attacks on the network while at the same time allowing authorized users to access network resources. You can use Cisco IOS Firewall to configure your router as an Internet firewall, a firewall between groups in your internal network, or a firewall between your company's network and your company's partners' networks.

The Cisco IOS Firewall has an extensive feature set designed to help you secure your network. In addition to CBAC, another key feature is intrusion detection. Both the feature set and intrusion detection are covered in detail in this chapter.

The Cisco IOS Firewall Feature Set

The Cisco IOS Firewall delivers integrated firewall functionality for Cisco networks and increases the flexibility and security of Cisco routers. The following is an overview of key features:

- **CBAC**—Provides internal users with secure, per-application-based access control for all traffic across perimeters, such as between private enterprise networks and the Internet.

- **Intrusion detection**—Provides real-time monitoring, interception, and response to network misuse with a broad set of the most common attack and information-gathering intrusion detection signatures.

- **Authentication proxy**—Dynamic, per-user authentication and authorization for LAN-based and dial-in communications. Authenticates users against industry-standard TACACS+ and RADIUS authentication protocols. Network administrators can set individual, per-user security policies.

- **DoS detection and prevention**—Defends and protects router resources against common attacks. Checks packet headers, dropping suspicious packets.

- **Dynamic port mapping**—Allows network administrators to run CBAC-supported applications on nonstandard ports.

- **Java applet blocking**—Protects against unidentified, malicious Java applets.

- **Virtual private networks (VPNs), IPSec encryption, and quality of service (QoS) support**—Operate with Cisco IOS Software encryption, tunneling, and QoS features to secure VPNs. Provide scalable encrypted tunnels on the router while integrating strong perimeter security, advanced bandwidth management, intrusion detection, and service-level validation. Standards-based for interoperability.

- **Real-time alerts**—Log alerts for Denial of Service attacks or other preconfigured conditions. Can be configured on a per-application, per-feature basis.

- **Audit trail**—Details transactions. Records time stamp, source host, destination host, ports, duration, and total number of bytes transmitted for detailed reporting. Can be configured on a per-application, per-feature basis.

- **Event logging**—Allows administrators to track potential security breaches or other nonstandard activities in real time by logging system error message output to a console terminal or syslog server, setting severity levels, and recording other parameters.

- **Firewall management**—A wizard-based network configuration tool that offers step-by-step guidance through network design, addressing, and Cisco Firewall feature set implementation.

- **Secure IS security policy configuration**—Available on Cisco 1600, 1720, 2500, 2600, and 3600 routers. Also supports NAT and IPSec configurations.

- **Integration with Cisco IOS Software**—Interoperates with Cisco IOS features, integrating security policy enforcement into the network.

- **Basic and advanced traffic filtering**—Standard and extended access control lists (ACLs). Apply access controls to specific network segments and define which traffic passes through a network segment. Lock-and-key-dynamic ACLs grant temporary access through firewalls upon user identification (username/password).

- **Policy-based multi-interface support**—Provides the ability to control user access by IP address and interface as determined by the security policy.

- **Redundancy/failover**—Automatically routes traffic to a backup router if a failure occurs.

- **Network Address Translation (NAT)**—Hides the internal network from the outside for enhanced security.

- **Time-based access lists**—Defines the security policy by the time of day and the day of the week.

- **Peer router authentication**—Ensures that routers receive reliable routing information from trusted sources.

Intrusion Detection

The Cisco IOS Firewall's Intrusion Detection System (IDS) acts as an inline intrusion detection sensor, watching packets and sessions as they flow through the router, scanning each to match any of the IDS signatures. When it detects suspicious activity, it responds before network security can be compromised and logs the event through Cisco IOS syslog. The network administrator can configure the IDS to choose the appropriate response to various threats.

The Cisco IOS Firewall's IDS identifies 59 of the most common attacks using signatures to detect patterns of misuse in network traffic. A partial listing of these intrusion signatures is shown in Table 8-1. The intrusion detection signatures included in the Cisco IOS Firewall IDS were chosen from a broad cross section of intrusion detection signatures.

Table 8-1 *Examples of Cisco IOS Firewall Intrusion Signatures*

Signature ID	Short Title	Description
3045	Queso Sweep	This signature triggers after having detected a Fin, SynFin, or Push sent from a specific host to a specific host.
3450	Finger Bomb	This signature fires when it detects a finger bomb attack. Such an attack attempts to crash a finger server by issuing a finger request that contains multiple @ characters. If the finger server allows forwarding, the multiple @s cause the finger server to recursively call itself and use up system resources.
4053	Back Orifice	Back Orifice is a Windows 95/98 back door that allows a remote attacker to control a computer across a TCP/IP connection using a simple console or GUI application.
4600	IOS UDP Bomb	Some Cisco IOS systems are unable to parse dataless UDP packets bound for port 514. If these types of packets are received, the router either hangs or reboots.

Cisco IOS Firewall IDS is not available on all routers. Models supported include 2600, 3600, 7100, and 7200.

For a complete description and listing of the intrusion detection signatures of Cisco IOS Firewall, refer to the Cisco IOS Firewall documentation or obtain the latest updates from the Cisco Web site at www.cisco.com.

Planning for Cisco IOS Firewall

To maximize security with Cisco IOS Firewall, you need to do the following:

- **Determine the necessary security server support**—The Cisco IOS Firewall feature set can be a client of TACACS+, RADIUS, or Kerberos security servers.

- **Determine which types of access lists to use and where to use them**—The Cisco IOS Firewall feature set works with standard, dynamic, static extended, and reflexive access lists.

- **Decide whether to use CBAC**—CBAC is available only in the Cisco IOS Firewall feature set. If you decide to use CBAC, do not use reflexive access lists, WebSense, or TCP intercept.

- **Decide whether to use NAT**—The Cisco IOS Firewall feature set works with NAT. NAT does not work with the application layer protocols RPC, VDOLive, or SQL*Net Redirected. (NAT does work with SQL*Net Bequeathed.)

- **Decide whether to use TCP Intercept**—If you decide to use TCP intercept (software that helps prevent SYN-flooding attacks by intercepting and validating TCP connection requests), do not use it in conjunction with CBAC.

- **Determine whether encryption is needed**—Cisco IOS Firewall works with encryption programs such as Cisco Encryption Technology (CET) and IPSec.

CBAC Operation

CBAC creates temporary openings in access lists at firewall interfaces when specified traffic exits the internal network through the firewall. The openings allow returning traffic (which would normally be blocked) and additional data channels to enter the internal network back through the firewall. CBAC allows the traffic back through the firewall only if it is part of the same session as the original traffic that triggered CBAC when exiting the firewall.

Figure 8-1 illustrates the operation of CBAC, with the following activity occurring:

1 User 1 initiates a Telnet session.

2 CBAC permits return traffic from User 1's Telnet session.

3 CBAC blocks other externally generated Telnet traffic.

Figure 8-1 shows Telnet, but CBAC can monitor single-channel, or generic, TCP or UDP protocols.

Figure 8-1 *CBAC Operation*

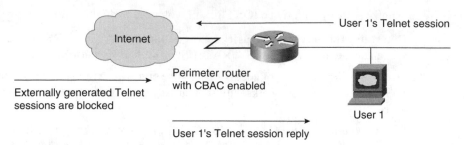

CBAC can inspect certain application layer protocols, including the following:

- CU-SeeMe (only the White Pine version)
- FTP
- H.323 (such as NetMeeting and ProShare)
- HTTP (Java blocking)
- Java
- Microsoft NetShow
- UNIX **r** commands (such as **rlogin**, **rexec**, and **rsh**)
- RealAudio
- RPC (Sun RPC, not DCE RPC)
- Microsoft RPC
- SMTP
- SQL*Net
- StreamWorks
- TFTP
- VDOLive

When a protocol is configured for CBAC, CBAC inspects all the packets for this protocol and maintains the state information. In general, packets are allowed back through the firewall only if they belong to a permissible session.

CBAC Restrictions

CBAC is restricted in the following ways regarding compatibility with other technologies:

- CBAC is available only for IP traffic. Only TCP and UDP packets are inspected. (Other IP traffic, such as ICMP, cannot be inspected with CBAC and should be filtered with basic access lists instead.)

- If you reconfigure access lists when you configure CBAC, be aware that, if access lists block TFTP traffic into an interface, you will not be able to netboot over that interface. (This is not a CBAC-specific limitation. It is part of the existing access list functionality.)

- Packets with the CBAC host device as the source or destination address are not inspected by CBAC or evaluated by access lists.

- CBAC ignores ICMP Unreachable messages.

- With FTP, CBAC does not allow third-party connections (three-way FTP transfer).

- When CBAC inspects FTP traffic, it allows only data channels with the destination port in the range of 1024 to 65535.

- CBAC will not open a data channel if the FTP client/server authentication fails.

- CET and CBAC compatibility involves the following:

  If encrypted traffic is exchanged between two routers and a firewall running CBAC is located between the two routers, CBAC cannot accurately inspect the encrypted packet payloads.

  Also, if both CET encryption and CBAC are configured at the same firewall, configure CBAC only for the following protocols: Generic TCP and UDP, CU-SeeMe, and StreamWorks.

- IPSec and CBAC compatibility involves the following:

  When CBAC and IPSec are enabled on the same router and the firewall router is an endpoint for IPSec for the particular flow, IPSec is compatible with CBAC (that is, CBAC can do its normal inspection processing on the flow).

  If the router is not an IPSec endpoint but the packet is an IPSec packet, CBAC will not inspect the packets because the protocol number in the IP header of the IPSec packet is not TCP or UDP. CBAC inspects only TCP and UDP packets.

  In other words, IPSec and CBAC can coexist on the perimeter router so long as the inspection of packets is done on the internal interface and the encryption termination is done on the external interface. In this manner, the inspection is done on unencrypted traffic.

CBAC Memory and Performance

A few parameters affect CBAC memory and performance:

- CBAC uses 600 bytes of memory per connection.

- CBAC uses additional CPU resources during packet inspection.

- CBAC uses CPU resources during ACL inspection, although it minimizes its consumption by efficient storage of the access list (hashing the access list and then evaluating the hash).

Configuring CBAC

This section describes how to configure CBAC. CBAC provides advanced traffic inspection functionality and can be used as an integral part of a network's firewall. The configuration examples in this chapter are based on the XYZ Company case study.

The general steps used to configure CBAC encryption on Cisco routers are summarized as follows:

Step 1 **Choose an interface**—Decide whether to configure CBAC on an internal or external interface of the firewall. CBAC blocks externally originated sessions. If encryption will be used on the same perimeter router, you should have the external interface be the encryption endpoint and the internal one be the CBAC inspection interface.

Step 2 **Configure IP access lists at the interface**—Use an extended access list. Ensure that the access list permits traffic that will be inspected by CBAC. If the firewall service has only two connections, one internal and one external, using all inbound access lists works well because they stop packets before they affect the router. The access list used for outbound traffic (traffic destined for the Internet) permits traffic inspected by CBAC.

Step 3 **Configure global timeouts and thresholds**—Timeouts and thresholds determine how long to manage state information for a session and when to drop sessions that do not become fully established. They apply globally to all sessions.

Step 4 **Define an inspection rule**—An inspection rule specifies what IP traffic (which application layer protocols) CBAC will inspect. The rule specifies each desired application layer protocol as well as generic TCP or generic UDP.

Step 5 **Apply the inspection rule to an interface**—For an external interface, use outbound rules; for an internal interface, use inbound rules.

Step 6 **Test and verify CBAC**—Use **show**, **debug**, and related commands to test and verify that CBAC works and to troubleshoot problems.

Step 1: Choose the Interface for CBAC

You must decide whether to configure CBAC on an internal or external interface of your firewall. *Internal* refers to the side where sessions must originate for their traffic to be permitted through the firewall. *External* refers to the side where sessions cannot originate (sessions originating from the external side are blocked). Designate one port as internal (where the sessions originate). The other port is the external port.

For CBAC to work properly, ensure that the IP access lists are configured appropriately at the interface. For temporary openings to be created in an access list, it must be an extended access list. Wherever the access lists will be applied to returning traffic, use extended access lists. Remember that all access lists that evaluate traffic leaving the protected network should permit traffic that will be inspected by CBAC.

If you will be configuring CBAC in two directions, you should configure CBAC in one direction first, using the appropriate "internal" and "external" interface designations. When you configure CBAC in the other direction the interface designations are swapped. (CBAC is rarely configured in two directions, and usually only when the firewall is between two networks that need protection from each other, such as with two partners' networks connected by the firewall.)

Step 2: Configure IP Access Lists at the Interface

Consider the following information if you will be configuring CBAC on an external interface:

- If you have an outbound IP access list at the external interface, the access list can be a standard or extended access list. This outbound access list should permit traffic that you want to be inspected by CBAC. If traffic is not permitted, it is not inspected by CBAC. It is simply dropped.

- The inbound IP access list at the external interface must be an extended access list. This inbound access list should deny traffic that you want to be inspected by CBAC. (CBAC will create temporary openings in this inbound access list as appropriate to permit only return traffic that is part of a valid, existing session.)

Figure 8-2 illustrates the configuration of the external interface.

Consider the following information if you will be configuring CBAC on an internal interface:

- If you have an inbound IP access list at the internal interface or an outbound IP access list at the external interface(s), these access lists can be either standard or extended access lists. These access lists should permit traffic that you want to be inspected by CBAC. If traffic is not permitted, it is not inspected by CBAC. It is simply dropped.

- The outbound IP access list at the internal interface and the inbound IP access list at the external interface must be extended access lists. These outbound access lists should deny traffic that you want to be inspected by CBAC. (CBAC will create temporary openings in these outbound access lists as appropriate to permit only return traffic that is part of a valid, existing session.) You do not necessarily need to configure an extended access list at both the outbound internal interface and the inbound external interface, but at least one is necessary to restrict traffic flowing through the firewall into the internal protected network.

Figure 8-2   *Configuration of the External Interface*

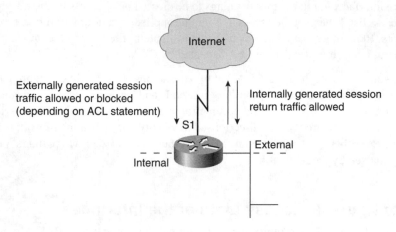

Figure 8-3 illustrates the configuration of the internal interface.

Figure 8-3   *Configuration of the Internal Interface*

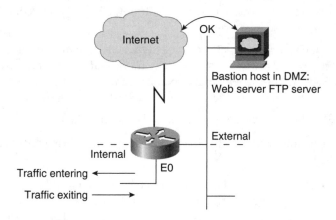

Step 3: Configure Global Timeouts and Thresholds

CBAC uses timeouts and thresholds to determine how long to manage state information for a session and to determine when to drop sessions that do not become fully established. These parameters apply globally to all sessions.

Figure 8-4 illustrates the flow of session state information that is monitored by CBAC.

Figure 8-4 *Flow of Session State Information Monitored by CBAC*

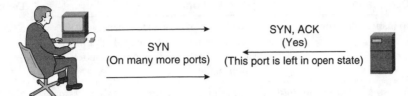

Table 8-2 describes the common commands used to manage state information for sessions and gives the default values or ranges of values associated with them.

Table 8-2 *Commands to Manage State Information for Sessions*

Command	Description	Default
ip inspect tcp synwait-time *seconds*	The length of time the software waits for a TCP session to reach the established state before dropping the session.	30 seconds.
ip inspect name *inspection-name* **rpc program-number** *number* [**wait-time** *minutes*] [**timeout** *seconds*]	An RPC program number specified to allow all traffic associated with that number through the firewall. The global TCP and UDP idle timeouts can be overridden for specified application layer protocols' sessions. This is discussed in the **ip inspect name** (global configuration) command description found in the "Context-Based Access Control Commands" chapter of the *Security Command Reference*. The **wait-time** keeps a hole in the firewall to allow subsequent connections from the same source address and to the same destination address and port.	The default wait-time is 0 minutes.
ip inspect tcp finwait-time *seconds*	The length of time a TCP session will still be managed after the firewall detects a FIN-exchange.	5 seconds.
ip inspect tcp idle-time *seconds*	The length of time a TCP session will still be managed after no activity (the TCP idle timeout).	3600 seconds (1 hour).
ip inspect udp idle-time *seconds*	The length of time a UDP session will still be managed after no activity (the UDP idle timeout).	30 seconds.

continues

Table 8-2 *Commands to Manage State Information for Sessions (Continued)*

Command	Description	Default
ip inspect dns-timeout *seconds*	The length of time a DNS name lookup session will still be managed after no activity. See the following section for more information.	5 seconds.
ip inspect max-incomplete high *number*	The number of existing half-open sessions that will cause the software to start deleting half-open sessions. See the following section for more information.	500 existing half-open sessions.
ip inspect max-incomplete low *number*	The number of existing half-open sessions that will cause the software to stop deleting half-open sessions.	400 existing half-open sessions.
ip inspect one-minute high *number*	The rate of new unestablished sessions that will cause the software to start deleting half-open sessions.	500 half-open sessions per minute.
ip inspect one-minute low *number*	The rate of new unestablished sessions that will cause the software to stop deleting half-open sessions.	400 half-open sessions per minute.
ip inspect tcp max-incomplete host *number* **block-time** *seconds*	The number of existing half-open TCP sessions with the same destination host address that will cause the software to start dropping half-open sessions to the same destination host address. When the **max-incomplete host** threshold is exceeded, CBAC drops half-open sessions differently, depending on whether the **block-time** timeout is 0 or a positive nonzero number. If the **block-time** timeout is 0, CBAC deletes the oldest existing half-open session for the host for every new connection request to the host and lets the SYN packet through. If the **block-time** timeout is greater than 0, CBAC deletes all existing half-open sessions for the host and then blocks all new connection requests. CBAC continues to block all new connection requests until the **block-time** expires.	50 existing half-open TCP sessions. 0 seconds. Range is 1 to 250.

Half-Open Sessions

An unusually high number of half-open sessions (connection requests that are not completed) could indicate that a DoS attack is occurring or that someone is conducting a port scan. CBAC measures both the total number of half-open sessions and the rate of session establishment attempts. It counts total TCP and UDP half-open sessions (UDP sessions are approximated) and measures the rate of half-open session establishment once per minute. When the number of existing half-open sessions exceeds the max-incomplete high number, CBAC deletes half-open sessions as required to accommodate new connection requests. The software continues to delete half-open requests until the number of existing half-open sessions drops below the max-incomplete low number.

When the rate of new connection attempts rises above the one-minute high number, the software deletes half-open sessions to accommodate new connection attempts. The software continues to delete half-open sessions until the rate of new connection attempts drops below the one-minute low number. The rate thresholds are measured as the number of new session connection attempts detected in the last one-minute sample period. The router reviews the rate of new connection attempts more frequently than one minute and does not keep deleting half-open sessions for one minute after a DoS attack has stopped—it will stop deleting the sessions when the rate drops below the high threshold.

Step 4: Define an Inspection Rule

After the global timeouts and thresholds have been configured, the next step in configuring CBAC is to define an inspection rule. This rule specifies what IP traffic (which application layer protocols) CBAC will inspect at an interface. An inspection rule specifies each desired application layer protocol as well as generic TCP or generic UDP if desired. The inspection rule consists of a series of statements, each listing a protocol and specifying the same inspection rule name.

You define the inspection rules as follows:

1 Configure application layer protocol inspection.

2 Configure Java inspection.

3 Configure generic TCP and UDP inspection.

Inspection rules are mandatory components of CBAC. If a protocol (or Java) does not have an inspection rule created for it, CBAC ignores it. In addition, Java has a two-step configuration process in which you configure a Java access list in addition to the inspection rule. The application rules have optional components that can be applied as needed.

Configuring Application Layer Protocol Inspection

In general, if you configure inspection for an application layer protocol, packets for that protocol are permitted to exit the firewall, and packets for that protocol are allowed back in through the firewall only if they belong to a valid existing session. Each protocol packet is inspected to maintain information about the session state and to determine if that packet belongs to a valid existing session.

Follow these guidelines when configuring application layer protocol inspection:

- Use a global configuration command.

- Configure CBAC inspection for an application layer protocol (except for RPC and Java).

- The **timeout** option refers to the idle time to use instead of TCP or UDP timeouts.

To configure CBAC inspection for an application layer protocol, use one or both of the following global configuration commands:

```
ip inspect name inspection-name protocol [timeout seconds]

ip inspect name inspection-name rpc program-number number
  [wait-time minutes] [timeout seconds]
```

The first command, **ip inspect name** *inspection-name protocol* [**timeout** *seconds*], configures CBAC inspection for an application layer protocol (except for RPC and Java). Use one of the protocol keywords defined in Table 8-3. Repeat this command for each desired protocol. Use the same *inspection-name* to create a single inspection rule.

Table 8-3 *Application Protocol Keywords* (inspection-name protocol) *for the* **ip inspect name** *Command*

Application Protocol	*protocol* Keyword
Transport Layer Protocols:	
TCP	**tcp**
UDP	**udp**
Application Layer Protocols:	
CU-SeeMe	**cuseeme**
FTP commands and responses	**ftp-cmd**
FTP tokens (enables tracing of the FTP tokens parsed)	**ftp-tokens**
H.323	**h323**
HTTP (Java applets)	**http**
Microsoft NetShow	**netshow**
UNIX **r** commands (**rlogin, rexec, rsh**)	**rcmd**
RealAudio	**realaudio**

Table 8-3 *Application Protocol Keywords* (inspection-name protocol) *for the* **ip inspect name** *Command (Continued)*

Application Protocol	*protocol* Keyword
RPC	**rpc**
SMTP	**smtp**
SQL*Net	**sqlnet**
StreamWorks	**streamworks**
TFTP	**tftp**
VDOLive	**vdolive**

The second command, **ip inspect name** *inspection-name* **rpc program-number** *number* [**wait-time** *minutes*] [**timeout** *seconds*], enables CBAC inspection for the RPC application layer protocol. Specify multiple RPC program numbers by repeating this command for each program number. Use the same *inspection-name* to create a single inspection rule.

The command parameters and syntax have the following meanings:

Command Parameter	Description
inspection-name	Names the set of inspection rules. If you want to add a protocol to an existing set of rules, use the same *inspection-name* as the existing set of rules.
protocol	Specifies one of the protocol keywords listed in Table 8-3.
timeout *seconds*	(Optional) To override the global TCP or UDP idle timeouts for the specified protocol, specifies the number of seconds for a different idle timeout.
java-list *access-list*	(Optional) Specifies the access list (name or number) to use to determine "friendly" sites. This keyword is available only for the HTTP protocol, for Java applet blocking. Java blocking works only with standard access lists.
rpc program-number *number*	Specifies the program number to permit. This keyword is available only for the RPC protocol.
wait-time *minutes*	(Optional) Specifies the number of minutes to keep a small hole in the firewall to allow subsequent connections from the same source address and to the same destination address and port. The default **wait-time** is 0 minutes. This keyword is available only for the RPC protocol.

NOTE For CBAC inspection to work with NetMeeting 2.x traffic (an H.323 application layer protocol), configure inspection for TCP, as described later in the section "Configuring Generic TCP and UDP Inspection." This requirement exists because NetMeeting 2.x uses an additional TCP channel not defined in the H.323 specification.

Configuring Java Inspection

Java inspection has additional considerations. With Java, you must protect against the risk of users inadvertently downloading destructive applets into your network. You can use CBAC to filter Java applets at the firewall, which allows users to download only applets residing within the firewall and trusted applets from outside the firewall.

Java inspection enables Java applet filtering at the firewall. Java applet filtering distinguishes between trusted and untrusted applets by relying on a list of external sites that you designate as "friendly." If an applet is from a friendly site, the firewall allows the applet through. If the applet is not from a friendly site, it is blocked. Alternatively, you could permit applets from all sites except those specifically designated as "hostile."

CAUTION CBAC does not detect or block encapsulated Java applets. Therefore, Java applets that are wrapped or encapsulated, such as applets in .zip or .jar format, are not blocked at the firewall. CBAC also does not detect or block applets loaded from FTP, gopher, HTTP on a nonstandard port, and other irregular configurations.

To block all Java applets except those from friendly locations, follow these steps:

Step 1 Create a standard access list that permits traffic only from friendly sites and that denies traffic from hostile sites using either of the following commands:

```
ip access-list standard name
    permit...
    deny... (Use statements as needed)
```

or

```
access-list access-list-number {deny | permit} source [source-wildcard]
```

The following example shows a standard access list that allows access for only those hosts on the three specified networks:

```
access-list 1 permit 192.5.34.0   0.0.0.255
access-list 1 permit 128.88.0.0   0.0.255.255
access-list 1 permit 36.0.0.0   0.255.255.255
! (Note: all other access implicitly denied)
```

The wildcard bits apply to the host portions of the network addresses. Any host with a source address that does not match the access list statements is rejected.

For all internal users to be able to download friendly applets, use the **any** keyword for the destination as appropriate—but be careful to not misuse the **any** keyword to inadvertently allow all applets through.

Step 2   Block all Java applets except those from the friendly sites defined previously in the access list using the following:

```
ip inspect name inspection-name [http java-list access-list] [timeout
seconds]
```

Java blocking works only with standard access lists. Use the same *inspection-name* here as when you specified other protocols, to create a single inspection rule.

Configuring Generic TCP and UDP Inspection

You can configure TCP and UDP inspection to permit TCP and UDP packets to enter the internal network through the firewall, even if the application layer protocol is not configured for inspection. TCP and UDP inspection do not recognize application-specific commands and might not permit all return packets for an application if the return packets have a different port number than the previous exiting packet.

Any application layer protocol that is inspected takes precedence over the TCP or UDP packet inspection. For example, if inspection is configured for FTP, all control channel information is recorded in the state table. All FTP traffic is permitted back through the firewall if the control channel information is valid for the state of the FTP session. The fact that TCP inspection is configured is irrelevant to the FTP state information.

With TCP and UDP inspection, packets entering the network must exactly match the corresponding packets that previously exited the network. The entering packets must have the same source/destination addresses and source/destination port numbers as the exiting packets (but reversed); otherwise, CBAC blocks the entering packets at the interface. CBAC drops all TCP packets with a sequence number outside the window.

With UDP inspection configured, replies are permitted back in through the firewall if they are received within a configurable time after the last request was sent out. This time is configured with the **ip inspect name udp idle-timeout** command.

The commands for configuring CBAC inspection for TCP or UDP packets have the following syntax:

```
ip inspect name inspection-name tcp [timeout seconds]
ip inspect name inspection-name udp [timeout seconds]
```

Again, you should use the same *inspection-name* as specified for other protocols to create a single inspection rule.

Step 5: Apply the Inspection Rule to an Interface

If you are configuring CBAC on an external interface, apply the rule to outbound traffic by using the **out** keyword. If you are configuring CBAC on an internal interface, apply the rule to inbound traffic by using the **in** keyword. The phrase identified as *inspection-name* identifies which set of inspection rules to apply. It allows the administrator to create a set of unique inspection rules for each interface and to rapidly identify them in the configuration file.

To apply an inspection rule to an interface, use the following interface configuration command:

```
ip inspect inspection-name {in | out}
```

Example 8-1 applies a set of inspection rules named **outboundrules** to an external interface's outbound traffic. This causes inbound IP traffic to be permitted only if the traffic is part of an existing session and to be denied if the traffic is not part of an existing session.

Example 8-1 *Applying a Set of Inspection Rules to an External Interface's Outbound Traffic*

```
Perimeterx(config)# ip inspect outboundrules out
Perimeterx(config-if)# interface serial0 ip inspect outboundrules out
```

The first command is a global configuration command to use the named inspection rule. The second command applies the named rule to an interface.

Step 6: Test and Verify CBAC

The **ip inspect audit trail** and **debug** commands provide the means to monitor, test, and verify the CBAC configuration. This section describes the commands that provide information about the most common problems.

Monitoring CBAC

To assist with CBAC debugging, you can turn on audit trail messages that will be displayed on the console after each CBAC session closes. Example 8-2 shows a global configuration command that enables audit trail messages.

Example 8-2 *Enabling Audit Trail Messages*

```
Perimeterx(config)# ip inspect audit trail
```

Audit trail information can be configured on a per-application basis using the CBAC inspection rules.

Debugging CBAC

You use the **debug ip inspect** EXEC command to display messages about CBAC events. The **no** form of this command disables debugging output. Three categories of **debug** commands are typically used to debug CBAC: generic, transport level, and application protocol. The syntax is as follows:

```
debug ip inspect {function-trace | object-creation | object-deletion |
  events | timers | protocol | detail}
debug ip inspect detail
```

The syntax for the **debug** commands is as follows:

Command Parameter	Description
function-trace	Displays messages about software functions called by CBAC.
object-creation	Displays messages about software objects being created by CBAC. Object creation corresponds to the beginning of CBAC-inspected sessions.
object-deletion	Displays messages about software objects being deleted by CBAC. Object deletion corresponds to the closing of CBAC-inspected sessions.
events	Displays messages about CBAC software events, including information about CBAC packet processing.
timers	Displays messages about CBAC timer events such as when a CBAC idle timeout is reached.
protocol	Displays messages about CBAC-inspected protocol events, including details about the protocol's packets. Refer to Table 8-3 for a list of *protocol* keywords.
detail	Enables the detailed option, which can be used in combination with other options to get additional information.

You can turn off debugging for each of the commands discussed in this section by using the **no** form of the command. To disable all debugging, use the privileged EXEC commands **no debug all** or **undebug all**.

Cisco IOS Firewall Administration

There are two methods for administering Cisco IOS Firewall: through the command-line interface (CLI) and using ConfigMaker.

Administering Cisco IOS Firewall Through the CLI

The CLI has been the means for configuring Cisco products since they were first available. Here are the advantages of CLI:

- It is powerful.
- Commands exist for every parameter across products, in the version of IOS for your family of products.
- Variables allow configuration of timers and counters to meet the specific needs of every enterprise.

Here are the disadvantages of CLI:

- The numerous, complex commands are difficult to remember.
- More commands appear with every new release of IOS software.

The CLI is the best choice for an enterprise that has a staff with enough expertise and experience to use all the power and flexibility it offers.

ConfigMaker

With the growth of the product line and the increasing number of installations in the small and medium business market that have occurred in the past few years, Cisco identified the need for a tool that would create a workable configuration for this type of enterprise: ConfigMaker. Figure 8-5 shows the ConfigMaker interface, which steps users through building configurations.

Here are the advantages of ConfigMaker:

- It has a graphical user interface.
- It is a familiar windowed environment with supporting dialog boxes.
- Its wizards provide guidance during configuration.

Here are the disadvantages of ConfigMaker:

- It offers limited product support.
- It has limited configuration parameters.

ConfigMaker meets the security and configuration needs of the small and medium business market while minimizing the administrative burden. The latest version adds NAT, DHCP, and CSU/DSU support and has well-integrated wizards.

Figure 8-5   *The ConfigMaker Interface*

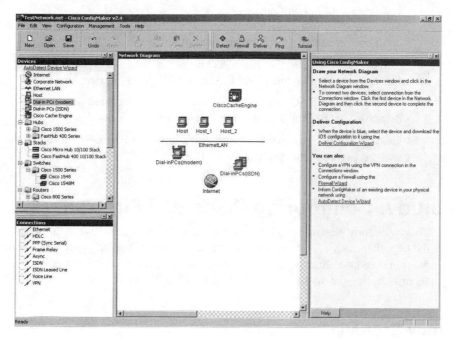

Summary

This section summarizes the main points of this chapter, as follows:

- The Cisco IOS Firewall makes you aware of and allows you to repel attacks on network resources by intruders by allowing you to implement application layer filtering and real-time alerts.

- CBAC is one of the key features of Cisco IOS Firewall. It can provide per-application-based access control for all traffic across perimeters between private enterprise networks and the Internet.

- Intrusion detection is another of the key features of Cisco IOS Firewall. It can provide real-time monitoring, interception, and response to network misuse with a broad set of the most common attack and information-gathering intrusion detection signatures.

- Planning for Cisco IOS Firewall consists of determining the necessary security server support; determining which types of access lists to use and where to use them; deciding whether to use CBAC, NAT, and TCP intercept; and determining whether encryption is needed.

- The methodology to configure CBAC consists of choosing an interface upon which to configure CBAC, configuring IP access lists at the interface, configuring global timeouts and thresholds, defining an inspection rule, applying the inspection rule to an interface, and testing and verifying CBAC.

- You can use the variety of **ip inspect debug** commands to display messages about CBAC events and to test or verify your CBAC configuration.

- To assist with CBAC debugging, you can turn on audit trail messages that will be displayed on the console after each CBAC session closes.

- Cisco provides two powerful methods to administer your Cisco IOS Firewall: the CLI and the ConfigMaker application.

Case Study: Configuring Cisco IOS Firewall

This case study illustrates how to configure Cisco IOS Firewall as taught in this chapter for the hypothetical XYZ Company. Read the case study scenario, examine the topology diagram, read the security policy, and then analyze the sample configuration to see how the security policy statements are enacted for Cisco IOS Firewall.

Case Study Scenario

The XYZ Company has implemented all the standard security features in IOS software. Recently, it was attacked by an external party using mobile code in the form of Java applets and DoS attacks. To repel future attacks of these types, it needs application layer filtering and real-time alerts. The company wants stronger security without using additional hardware, so it has chosen to implement the Cisco IOS Firewall. The primary component of the firewall feature set is CBAC. XYZ has chosen to install CBAC on its perimeter routers.

Figure 8-6 illustrates the campus infrastructure of the XYZ Company that is discussed in this chapter.

The company has implemented CBAC on its perimeter routers to provide enhanced security functionality. These routers are also the endpoints for the company's IPSec encryption implementation. This is vital because CBAC will not work with IPSec unless it is on the IPSec endpoint routers.

Figure 8-6   *Cisco IOS Firewall in the Campus Infrastructure*

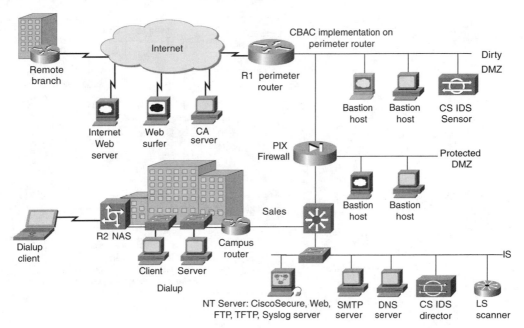

Topology

Figure 8-7 illustrates the portion of the XYZ network that will be configured in this case study.

Network Security Policy

The network security policy that XYZ wants to implement is as follows:

- Outbound access to the Internet can be openly used by XYZ employees for company research. Dial-in users can gain outbound access to the Internet.

- A firewall system consisting of a perimeter router and a bastion host at a minimum shall be used to prevent unauthorized access to the campus and branch networks from the Internet.

- Inbound access from the Internet to the campus and branch networks shall be severely restricted unless network layer encryption is employed over the Internet. Inbound access shall be restricted to the bastion host for e-mail, HTTP, and FTP traffic.

Figure 8-7 *Cisco IOS Firewall on the XYZ Corporate Network*

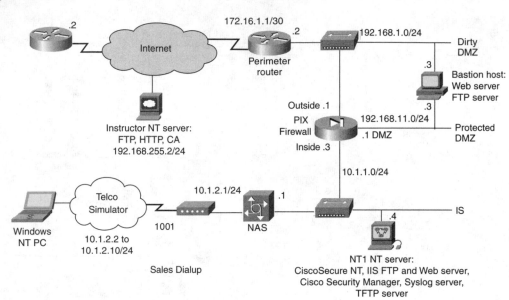

Cisco IOS Firewall Configuration Example

Example 8-3 approximates what you should have in your router after properly configuring it for Cisco IOS Firewall operation.

Example 8-3 *Configuring a Router for Cisco IOS Firewall Operation*

```
Current configuration:
!
version 12.0
service timestamps debug datetime msec localtime show-timezone
service timestamps log datetime msec localtime show-timezone
no service password-encryption
!
hostname Perimeter1
!
logging buffered 4096 debugging
no logging console
!
username student password 0 cisco
memory-size iomem 25
clock timezone PST -8
clock summer-time zone recurring
ip subnet-zero
no ip source-route
no ip finger
```

Example 8-3   *Configuring a Router for Cisco IOS Firewall Operation (Continued)*

```
ip tcp selective-ack
ip tcp path-mtu-discovery
no ip domain-lookup
!
no ip bootp server
ip inspect audit-trail
ip inspect max-incomplete low 800
ip inspect max-incomplete high 1000
ip inspect one-minute high 600
ip inspect tcp synwait-time 20
ip inspect tcp max-incomplete host 50 block-time 1
ip inspect name mcns rpc program-number 100003 wait-time 2 timeout 5
ip inspect name mcns rcmd timeout 10
ip inspect name mcns cuseeme timeout 10
ip inspect name mcns smtp timeout 45
ip inspect name mcns tftp timeout 10
ip inspect name mcns http java-list 16 timeout 60
ip inspect name mcns tcp
ip inspect name mcns udp
!
!
 !
 !
 !
interface Serial0
 ip address 172.16.1.1 255.255.255.252
 ip access-group 101 in
 no ip redirects
 no ip unreachables
 no ip directed-broadcast
 encapsulation frame-relay
 no ip route-cache
 no ip mroute-cache
 frame-relay lmi-type cisco
!
interface Serial1
 no ip address
 no ip directed-broadcast
 shutdown
!
interface FastEthernet0
 ip address 192.168.1.2 255.255.255.0
 ip access-group 102 in
 no ip redirects
 no ip unreachables
 no ip directed-broadcast
 no ip proxy-arp
 ip inspect mcns in
 no ip route-cache
 no ip mroute-cache
!
```

continues

Example 8-3 *Configuring a Router for Cisco IOS Firewall Operation (Continued)*

```
ip classless
ip route 0.0.0.0 0.0.0.0 172.16.1.2
no ip http server
!
logging trap debugging
logging source-interface FastEthernet0
logging 192.168.1.10
access-list 1 permit 192.168.1.10
access-list 16 permit 192.168.255.2
access-list 16 deny    any log
access-list 101 deny    ip 127.0.0.0 0.255.255.255 any log
access-list 101 deny    ip 255.0.0.0 0.255.255.255 any log
access-list 101 deny    ip 224.0.0.0 7.255.255.255 any log
access-list 101 deny    ip host 0.0.0.0 any log
access-list 101 deny    ip 192.168.1.0 0.0.0.255 any log
access-list 101 deny    ip 10.0.0.0 0.255.255.255 any log
access-list 101 deny    udp any any eq snmp
access-list 101 permit tcp any host 192.168.1.4 eq smtp
access-list 101 permit tcp any host 192.168.1.3 eq www
access-list 101 permit tcp any host 192.168.1.3 eq 443
access-list 101 permit tcp any host 192.168.1.3 eq ftp
access-list 101 permit tcp any host 192.168.1.3 gt 1023
access-list 101 permit icmp any 192.168.1.0 0.0.0.255 echo-reply
access-list 101 permit icmp any host 172.16.1.1 echo-reply
access-list 101 permit icmp host 192.168.255.2 host 172.16.1.1 echo
access-list 101 permit udp any host 192.168.1.3 eq domain
access-list 101 permit tcp host 192.168.255.2 host 192.168.1.3 eq nntp
access-list 101 permit udp host 192.168.255.2 host 192.168.1.3 eq ntp
access-list 101 deny    icmp any host 192.168.1.1 echo log
access-list 101 deny    tcp any host 192.168.1.1 eq telnet log
access-list 101 deny    tcp any host 172.16.1.1 eq telnet log
access-list 101 deny    tcp any host 192.168.1.2 eq telnet log
access-list 101 deny    ip any any log
access-list 102 permit ip 192.168.1.0 0.0.0.255 any
access-list 102 deny    ip any any log
no cdp run
!
line console 0
 exec-timeout 0 0
 logging synchronous
 login local
 transport input none
line aux 0
 no exec
 login local
line vty 0 4
 access-class 1 in
 login local
!
end
```

Review Questions

Answer the following review questions, which delve into some of the key facts and concepts covered in this chapter:

1 What are four features of CBAC?

2 What are the steps in the CBAC configuration process?

3 What command would you use to verify application protocol inspection of packets?

4 Is CBAC capable of inspecting TCP, UDP, and ICMP IP protocol traffic?

5 What command would you use to turn on audit trail messages that will be displayed on the console after each CBAC session closes?

6 Does CBAC block malicious Java applets that are in .jar format?

7 Are inspection rules mandatory components of CBAC?

8 What command would you use to define the number of half-open sessions (250, for example) that would cause CBAC to start deleting half-open sessions above this number?

9 What three categories of **debug** commands are typically used to debug CBAC?

10 If CBAC is installed on a firewall located between two routers that are IPSec endpoints, can CBAC inspect the IPSec packets?

References

This chapter summarized the configuration process to implement security policy utilizing Cisco IOS Firewall. For the exact command syntax for the version of IOS you are using, refer to the appropriate documentation release for that version of Cisco IOS. Specifically, review the *Security Configuration Guide* and *Security Command Reference* that matches your version of the Cisco IOS.

The following references will help you increase your knowledge of Cisco IOS Firewall concepts and security policy in general.

Configuring Firewalls

The Computer Emergency Response Team (CERT) Web site (www.cert.org) contains security practices and implementations. It also has published warnings and downloadable files of solutions for defeating various types of attacks that have been reported to CERT, among other relevant information.

The FAQS Organization Web site (www.faqs.org/faqs/firewalls-faq) contains firewall and related Frequently Asked Questions (FAQs) listings.

The Cisco white paper "Building a Perimeter Security Solution" provides a detailed technical overview of the specific features offered by the Cisco IOS Firewall feature set (formerly known as CiscoSecure Integrated Software). It also has configuration examples. Located at www.cisco.com/warp/public/cc/pd/iosw/ioft/iofwft/tech/firew_wp.htm.

RFC 2196, "The Site Security Procedures Handbook," provides overview information on security policies and authentication procedures. Located at ds.internic.net/rfc/rfc2196.txt.

Configuring Cisco IOS Firewall

Security Command Reference, Cisco IOS Release 12.0, October 1998.

Security Configuration Guide, Cisco IOS Release 12.0, October 1998.

For complete details on the features of and enhancements to Cisco IOS Firewall and the ConfigMaker application, along with product release notes and user guides, refer to the product documentation sets on your Cisco Product Documentation CD-ROM or on the Web at www.cisco.com.

PART IV

Configuring the CiscoSecure PIX Firewall

Chapter 9   PIX Firewall Basics

Chapter 10   Configuring Access Through the PIX Firewall

Chapter 11   Configuring Multiple Interfaces and AAA on the PIX Firewall

Chapter 12   Configuring Advanced PIX Firewall Features

Upon completing this chapter, you will be able to do the following:

- Identify PIX Firewall features and components
- Configure a PIX Firewall to work with a Cisco router
- Configure basic PIX Firewall features to protect Internet access to an enterprise
- Test and verify basic PIX Firewall operation
- Verify correct operation using the management features of the PIX software

CHAPTER 9

PIX Firewall Basics

This chapter presents the fundamental features and configuration options of the CiscoSecure PIX Firewall (PIX Firewall). It covers the basics of the architecture and configuration tasks associated with the predeployment of the PIX Firewall.

This chapter also covers suggested implementation strategies as well as security features and how they can protect your network. You will get a more in-depth look at the inner workings of the PIX Firewall in later chapters.

The sections in this chapter cover various topics, including security concepts, command syntax, and configuration guidelines, as well as a case study that gives you a real-world look at a PIX Firewall deployment scenario in which the PIX is operational with a basic set of commands.

What Is the PIX Firewall?

The Private Internet Exchange (PIX) Firewall is a stateful firewall that delivers high security and fast performance to corporate networks. It provides feature-rich protection that completely conceals the architecture of an internal network from the outside world. The PIX Firewall acts as a gatekeeper between a corporate network and the Internet—sort of a border patrol agent.

Keeping prowlers out of a corporate network is its full-time job. The keepers of corporate networks must implement a means of ensuring the safety of networks connected to the Internet. It is in this capacity that the PIX Firewall functions. Some network engineers have chosen to deploy router-based solutions as an alternative to deploying task-specific firewall devices. These devices, through a software (and sometimes hardware) upgrade, function similarly to a firewall. The thought behind this decision is that dedicated firewall products are too expensive and are very difficult to implement. But routers are designed to route packets, not act as full-featured firewalls. Consequently, the ability of the router to provide real-time notification of intruder activity and extensive packet examination is frequently lacking.

Sophisticated routers can duplicate some of the same functions of a firewall through the use of access lists, filters, and configuration tricks. Although this might prove effective at first, the long-term management tasks related to this kind of solution are daunting as well as limited in terms of scalability.

Companies that use router-centric designs have found them to be very effective against casual weekend hackers, but as technology has evolved, the weekend hacker has become more sophisticated and resilient, has started reading technical bulletins, and has begun to share information instantly via e-mail, Web sites, and chat rooms. It has become common for network security experts to frequent known hacker groups' Web sites in an effort to keep current on the latest means of attack and penetration.

Recently, international hackers have demonstrated the ability to launch Distributed Denial of Service attacks that use hundreds of unwitting accomplices. These distributed attacks can run unattended 24 hours a day from hundreds of different machines after a target has been identified.

When you consider what modern hackers are capable of, it becomes clear that a firewall is a necessary addition to any network. The PIX Firewall provides the following features:

- The PIX Firewall utilizes stateful filtering, which is the collection of extensive information about a data packet into a table. In order for a session to be established, information about the connection must match information stored in the table.

- The technique of IP "session hijacking" has been well-known since the mid-1980s. Essentially, spoofing IP addresses requires the ability to guess the sequence numbers of TCP packets. Most TCP/IP implementations use a simple additive algorithm to increment sequence numbers, making it a trivial matter for an intruder to guess the next number in a connection (from even a single intercepted packet) and subsequently hijack that session. Cisco's PIX Firewall series makes the process of guessing TCP sequence numbers extremely difficult, if not impossible, by using a randomizing algorithm for their generation for each session.

- The PIX Firewall operates from a secure, real-time, embedded operating system without any UNIX or Windows NT security holes. The operating system on the PIX Firewall has been specifically hardened against attacks. It was designed with security in mind.

- The PIX Firewall's Adaptive Security Algorithm (ASA) and cut-through proxy allow the PIX Firewall to deliver outstanding performance for more than 256,000 simultaneous connections (on a PIX 520 with 128 MB RAM), which is greater than any UNIX- or Windows NT–based firewall.

- The PIX Firewall is Intel Pentium–based, enabling lower cost of ownership.

The PIX Firewall provides the following security enhancement features:

- Inbound connections (that is, through the Internet) are denied unless they are specifically authenticated or mapped. The methods used for access and authentications are discussed in the next section.

- The PIX Firewall security model is two-tiered whenever possible, with a perimeter router, a DMZ for public servers, the PIX Firewall, and an internal network router.
- The PIX Firewall employs secure conduits on inbound/outbound static translations.
- Outbound connections (connections originating from inside the protected network) are allowed as soon as global address pools are configured unless they are specifically denied.

PIX Firewall Features and Operation

The PIX Firewall has a formidable set of security features that make it one of the highest-rated security solutions on the market today. When used in conjunction with a perimeter router, the PIX Firewall sets up a virtually impenetrable barrier between your private network and the outside world.

Deciding what your network security needs are is usually the first thing that comes to mind when you're developing a network security plan. After you have given careful consideration to exactly what will be expected of the firewall solution, you can begin the task of deciding which PIX Firewall will meet your needs. The recommended configuration involves the use of a Cisco router as the primary defense layer, followed by the PIX Firewall. Getting through the first line of defense would mean that the intruder would have to circumvent access lists and route authentication rules implemented by the network administrator. Even if the intruder were sophisticated enough to bypass these security measures, he would still have to contend with the PIX Firewall.

Getting Through the PIX Firewall from the Outside

Consider a firewall that is so secure that it does not allow any traffic in or out. Not much of a solution, is it? In order for a firewall to be of benefit to a network, it must have a secure and manageable way for user traffic to pass in and out.

The PIX Firewall has great aptitude for traffic management. Allowing traffic inbound access through the PIX Firewall involves more than just opening up a hole and letting packets flow freely in and out. Steps must be taken to ensure that only authorized traffic can traverse from the public segment to the private segment and vice versa.

The PIX Firewall is designed to allow only three ways for traffic to travel through it:

- The ASA examines all the traffic flowing into and out of the PIX Firewall and maintains a database of session state information for each connection. Any packet that doesn't match its recorded entry in the ASA's session state database is rejected immediately.
- The network administrator can configure a static tunnel or conduit that bypasses the ASA to provide an access portal though the PIX Firewall.

- Cut-through proxy authentication allows users to be validated via RADIUS or TACACS+ database entries in order to access the Internet or other outside networks.

The following sections describe these three ways through the PIX Firewall from the outside in more detail.

The PIX ASA

The ASA is the brains behind the PIX Firewall's secure operation. The ASA records characteristics associated with a connection, stores that information in a table, and then checks the packets flowing in and out to make sure that the "session state" information previously recorded when the connection first took place stays the same. If everything checks out, the traffic flows freely. If anything fails the check, the transmission is terminated.

When a connection request is initiated, the ASA records the source and destination IP addresses, source ports, and TCP sequence numbers related to the interface making the request. An encrypted signature based on this information is created and is used by the PIX Firewall to recognize this host in the future. This signature is valid only for the duration of the connection. When the connection ceases, the signature becomes invalid. Each time a connection request is made, the signature is re-created for that host.

In order for intruders to penetrate the PIX Firewall and reach a host on the inside, they would need to duplicate the working of the ASA and generate packets in a real-time stateful manner that would exactly match the randomized TCP sequence numbers, IP addresses, and port numbers that have been recorded in the ASA's connection database. It would be a gargantuan task to do this, and the hacker would quickly conclude that there are more inviting targets elsewhere.

To understand how the ASA operates, imagine you purchase a new monitor from a computer store. Before you leave the store, a store employee takes your picture and makes you sign a form that states when and where you made the purchase. The store then files these items away for later use. If you decide to return the monitor, the clerks at the return counter retrieve the form and compare your signature and photograph to make sure that you were the one who made the purchase. If everything matches, you get your refund.

Advantages of the PIX ASA

The PIX Firewall has many advantages over other firewall products on the market. The most notable feature that stands out against the competition is the fact that ASA provides a secure stateful connection and does so in an extremely efficient, high-performance manner.

The following are some of the other advantages of the ASA:

- No packets can traverse the PIX Firewall without connection and state information that matches the table maintained by the ASA.

- Outbound connections or states are allowed, except those specifically denied by outbound access lists. An outbound connection is one in which the originator or client is on a higher-security interface than the receiver or server. The highest-security interface is always the inside interface, and the lowest is the outside interface. Any additional (multiple DMZ type) interfaces can have security levels between the inside and outside values.

- Inbound connections or states are denied, except those specifically allowed by conduits. An inbound connection or state is one in which the originator or client is on a lower-security interface or network than the receiver or server. You can apply multiple exceptions to a single address translation, which lets you permit access from an arbitrary machine, network, or any host on the Internet to the host defined by the translation.

- All attempts to circumvent the previous rules are dropped, and a message is sent to syslog.

- All ICMP packets are denied unless specifically permitted using the **conduit permit icmp** command.

The Operation of the PIX ASA

In the following example, the PIX Firewall contains two interfaces—one on the inside (protected network) with a high security value and the other on the outside (the Internet) with a lower security value.

In this example, we will also see the PIX Firewall perform dynamic Network Address Translations (NAT). The PIX Firewall will take the private (internal) address and convert it to a registered (external) address. The external address will be provided from a pool of available addresses that we will designate in a later step.

The following are the steps in the process:

1 An outbound packet arrives at the inside (more secure) interface on the PIX Firewall. (The default security rules state that a connection can take place only when the source is of a higher security value than the destination. Exceptions to this rule are made only when a **conduit** command is present that allows this to happen.)

2 The PIX Firewall examines the destination address and determines that it is bound for a host located outside the protected network.

3 A determination is made regarding the security value of the requesting interface. Is it a lower or higher security value than the destination?

4 The requesting interface has a high security value, and it is destined for an outside interface, which has a lower security value.

5 Based on the comparison of the security values, the PIX Firewall determines that this connection is okay.

6 The PIX Firewall checks to see if any translation instructions need to be executed. These translations can be either static or dynamic in nature. This is done to see whether there are any specific paths that the traffic should take.

7 The PIX Firewall checks to see if previous packets have come from the host making the connection request. If not, the PIX Firewall records the session information, creates an encrypted signature that is exclusive to the requesting host, and creates a dynamic translation slot that will let the requestor have access to the outside world.

8 The packet is stripped of its original IP address and is assigned a randomly selected address maintained by the PIX Firewall's global address pool. This is done to let the PIX route the data back to the host making the request and to further hide the identity of the internal network. The PIX then changes the dynamically assigned IP address to the reserved address assigned to the organization and forwards the packet to the outside network for processing.

9 When the translated packet is received and processed by the Web site or other Internet destination, and the destination sends a packet back to the PIX outside network interface, the packet is processed by the ASA, is checked for validity against the table of session data computes, and compares the signatures. (Did this packet come from a valid inside address? Does it match the information in the session table? and so on.)

10 If all the security metrics match the information that the PIX Firewall recorded on the way out, the packet is readdressed to the host on the inside and is forwarded to the inside host, which completes the transaction.

The beauty of this procedure is that it is extremely fast as well as transparent to the users. They have no idea how much is going on behind the scenes thanks to the high-speed nature of the ASA.

Using Conduits and Statics for Inbound Access

Creating conduits and statics for inbound access through a PIX Firewall might be required when an asset on the protected network needs to be available to users on the outside network. For example, consider the case of using a virtual private network (VPN) concentrator on the inside, protected network. The VPN concentrator terminates IP Security (IPSec) tunnels originated by VPN client software installed on notebook computers used by mobile users.

The PIX Firewall must be deliberately configured to permit the IPSec traffic to securely transit the PIX from the outside to the inside network because the PIX's default security policy is to deny all incoming traffic. A static and conduit are configured to allow the IPSec traffic through. The static maps the IP address of VPN concentrator's public interface to a global IP address on the outside. The conduit acts as an access list on a Cisco router, filtering the type of traffic permitted through the static translation (IPSec traffic, in this example).

Selectively permitting VPN traffic through the PIX Firewall via conduits makes it possible for the VPN concentrator to handle VPN traffic independent of the PIX Firewall.

You might wonder why this kind of arrangement is necessary when the VPN concentrator could easily be placed outside the PIX Firewall and still provide termination of VPN tunnels. The answer is simple. Placing the VPN concentrator on the public network would expose it unnecessarily to risk of attack and penetration.

Placing the VPN concentrator on the protected network (note that it could have been placed on a PIX Firewall DMZ interface such as Ethernet 2) protects the VPN concentrator and makes administrative tasks (such as backups and configuration changes) a great deal easier and more secure.

Permitting traffic through a PIX Firewall in this way could be a recipe for disaster because there is a risk of an inbound connection being hijacked or exploited by an unwanted party. However, careful planning can mitigate this risk and provide flexibility for network administrators and their users. And the PIX Firewall's ASA provides stateful security to VPN traffic through the conduit.

Advantages of Using Conduits and Statics for Inbound Access

Statics and conduits can be configured to allow for special situations that might require an inbound connection to directly access an asset on the protected network.

Before we dive too deeply into the subject of inbound access, it is important to understand what statics and conduits are. Static translation is often used when an asset on the protected network needs to have a constant IP address assigned to it so that it can be reached from the outside on a regular basis.

Conduits permit access through the PIX Firewall if certain conditions are met. A typical **conduit** command specifies that access be granted when the source address, port address, and protocol type match a predefined criterion. The **conduit** command circumvents the PIX Firewall's ASA measures, so be careful when considering putting it to use.

Normally, you would allow the PIX Firewall to manage inbound connections automatically (if deemed necessary), but circumstances might arise that require the creation of specific paths in order to route traffic in a desired direction for the purposes of traffic shaping, content inspection, or some other administrative need.

The Process of Using Conduits and Statics for Inbound Access

The PIX Firewall, by default, prevents hosts outside the PIX Firewall from accessing hosts or servers inside the private network. The **static** command, when used in conjunction with the **conduit** command, allows inbound traffic to flow through the PIX Firewall and reach the protected assets. This chapter covers only the basics of these commands; a more detailed look is provided in Chapter 10, "Configuring Access Through the PIX Firewall."

It is important to remember that a security value, or "sec value," needs to be assigned to interfaces on the PIX Firewall before inbound access is allowed. The assignment of security values is accomplished with the **nameif** command, which is covered later in this chapter. Any interface that connects to a network located behind the PIX Firewall has a higher (more secure) value than an interface connecting to the Internet (or other network segment) outside the PIX Firewall (less secure).

The logic behind assigning this value is to establish connectivity rules for purposes of security. Typically, lower-value interfaces are denied connectivity to higher-value interfaces. The one exception to this rule is through the use of the **conduit** command. The **conduit** command overrides the ASA and allows the connection to occur. We will cover the assigning of security values later in this chapter.

In Figure 9-1, the PIX Firewall has a DMZ interface on which resides the primary (externally available) Web server for the enterprise. In the event that the primary Web server becomes unavailable, you can shift traffic (via a change in the **conduit** and **static** statements) to the emergency backup Web server on the inside interface using the following steps.

CAUTION This example places the backup Web server on the inside interface purely for purposes of illustration and training. This model is unsuitable as a template for an actual deployment. In a production environment, an additional DMZ interface (DMZ2) would be a more realistic location for the backup Web server.

---

1 The user types **www.secureweb.web** in the address line of the Web browser. This domain name is resolved to IP address 192.168.1.11.

2 The IP address 192.168.1.11 has been assigned to a low security value (less secure) outside the interface on the PIX Firewall.

3 The PIX Firewall sees that a **static** has been defined to translate traffic with a destination of 192.168.1.11 to the private address of 192.168.11.3:

```
Pixfirewall(config)# static (inside,outside) 192.168.1.11 192.168.11.3
```

Figure 9-1 *Example of Statics and Conduits*

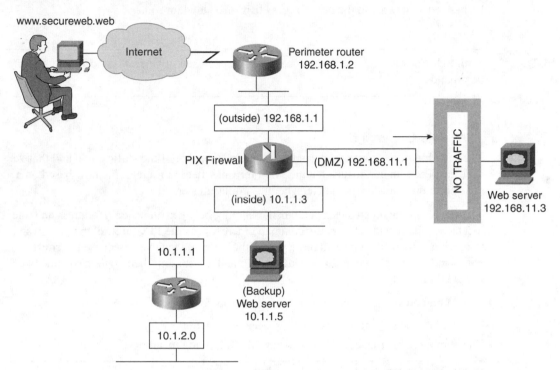

4   In the event of an equipment failure, the preceding **static** statement can be modified as shown here to point the traffic to the backup Web server until repairs can be performed on the primary server:

    Pixfirewall(config)# **static (inside,outside) 192.168.1.11 10.1.1.5**

5   The PIX Firewall does a quick check of the security values assigned to the interfaces involved, and it sees that the external interface has a lower security value than the internal interface. At this point, the connection attempt is normally refused, unless a corresponding **conduit** statement is found that will permit the access to take place.

6   The PIX Firewall sees that a corresponding **conduit** command has been created to permit Web traffic (TCP port 80):

    Pixfirewall(config)# **conduit permit tcp host 192.168.1.11 eq 80 any**

7   The PIX Firewall sees that connections to IP address 192.168.1.11 (statically mapped to the Web server address) through port 80 are permitted and are translated and sent to the internal Web server at 192.168.11.3.

8   The user accesses the Web server, and the page loads successfully.

As you can see from this example, the whole process is very simple in its execution. It can be likened somewhat to the use of access lists on a standard router.

NOTE With PIX Firewall Release 5.1.2, access lists can be used in place of **conduit** and **static** commands.

The route Command

The function of the **route** command is very similar to that of the **static** command that we used earlier. Both commands tell the PIX Firewall where to route traffic flow based on a series of command-line parameters, but the similarities end there.

The **static** command creates a permanent mapping between an inside IP address and one located on the outside. The **route** command merely tells the PIX Firewall that, if it wants to reach a certain IP address, it needs to use the specified gateway. Because the **route** command can be of benefit to the **static** command, discussing them together seems like a logical thing to do.

The command syntax for the **route** command is as follows:

```
route if_name ip_address netmask gateway_ip [metric]
```

The command parameters and syntax have the following meanings:

Command Parameter	Description
if_name	Specifies the network interface name.
ip_address	Specifies the internal or external network IP address. Use 0.0.0.0 to specify a default route. The 0.0.0.0 IP address can be abbreviated as 0.
netmask	Specifies a network mask to apply to *ip_address*. Use 0.0.0.0 to specify a default route. The 0.0.0.0 netmask can be abbreviated as 0.
gateway_ip	Specifies the IP address of the gateway router (the next-hop address for this route).
metric	Specifies the number of hops to *gateway_ip*. If you are not sure, enter **1**. Your network administrator can supply this information, or you can use a **traceroute** command to obtain the number of hops. The default is 1 if a metric is not specified.

If your PIX Firewall has two interfaces, you should specify a default route for the inside and outside interfaces. If there are more than two interfaces, specify a single default route for the outside interface only. You must do this because the PIX Firewall is not a router and can't route traffic in any capacity above what is possible using the **static** and **route** commands. Specifying a single default route to the outside interface ensures that packets destined as outbound will be sent to the outside interface from the interior network. In Example 9-1, the **route inside** command tells the PIX Firewall that all traffic destined for the 10.1.2.0 network should be reachable via a next-hop router at 10.1.1.1 with a hop count of 1, which means that it's the next hop away.

Example 9-1   *Using the **route inside** Command to Direct Traffic*

```
Pixfirewall(config)# route inside 10.1.2.0 255.255.255.0 10.1.1.1 1
Pixfirewall(config)# route outside 0 0 192.168.1.2 1
```

Cut-Through Proxy User Authentication

The PIX Firewall cut-through proxy feature challenges a user initially at the application layer (just like a standard proxy server can do), but as soon as the user is authenticated against a security database server such as TACACS+ or RADIUS, the PIX Firewall takes a different approach. After the user is authenticated and the security policy is checked, the PIX Firewall shifts the connection back to the high-performance ASA engine, which operates at the much faster network layer, all the while maintaining the TCP/IP session state.

NOTE   It is important to mention at this point that, after the user authenticates successfully, he has until the **uauth** timer expires to continue his authenticated session. After the **uauth** timer expires, he must repeat the login process. This is a security measure designed to prevent users from leaving workstations logged in and unattended.

The use of standard proxy server–based authentication can hamper the performance of the transactions because of the reliance on the application layer. (A standard proxy server intercepts requests for heavily accessed Web pages, retrieves the Web pages, stores them in its cache, and then uses this cache to service all future requests for the pages in question. If the pages requested by the user are unavailable in the Web cache, it drops the current connection and attempts to retrieve the pages before continuing.) The application layer is totally dependent on the processing speed of the host computer and is subject to the speed limitations imposed by the host PC's CPU. This cut-through proxy user authentication capability allows the PIX Firewall to perform significantly faster than proxy servers without compromising security.

Advantages of Using Cut-Through Proxy User Authentication

Authenticating users via the cut-through proxy method has significant advantages—most notably, the speed at which the session flow takes place. After the user is authenticated against an existing TACACS+ or RADIUS user database, the PIX Firewall can shift this process from the application layer to the faster-operating network layer. This means that overall packet flow is accelerated, thus realizing performance gains for the users of the protected network.

The PIX Firewall also offers features not offered by traditional proxy servers, such as the following:

- The PIX Firewall initially performs authentication and authorization at the application layer. After authentication takes place, the session flow is shifted to the ASA for high performance.

- The PIX Firewall can authenticate users against a security database server such as TACACS+ or RADIUS. This is a feature that proxy server vendors are finally adding to their products.

- After authentication takes place, the PIX Firewall cuts through to a transparent, high-performance session.

- The PIX Firewall authenticates both inbound and outbound connections in a stateful manner.

The Operation of Cut-Through Proxy User Authentication

Let's take a closer look at a real-world example of cut-through proxy authentication. The following steps (as illustrated in Figure 9-2) show how the session flow is shifted to the network layer and continues between the user and the Web server:

1 The user attempts to access a protected network asset.

2 The PIX Firewall intercepts the connection setup request and checks its session table in the ASA to see if this user has been previously authenticated. If he has been previously authenticated and his session timer has not expired, he is allowed to proceed. If his session timer (the session timer's official name is **uauth timer**) has expired, he is required to authenticate again.

3 The PIX Firewall issues an authentication prompt appropriate to the connection type (for Web connections, this would be a standard HTTP authentication challenge), and the user enters his username and password (this occurs at the application layer).

4 The PIX Firewall forwards the user's credentials to the authentication authority, such as a TACACS+ or RADIUS server. (The PIX Firewall can authenticate Telnet, FTP, and HTTP traffic.)

5 After the user is authenticated, the PIX Firewall shifts the session flow to the network layer for the duration of the connection directly between the two parties while still maintaining a stateful connection.

Figure 9-2   *The Cut-Through Proxy User Authentication Process*

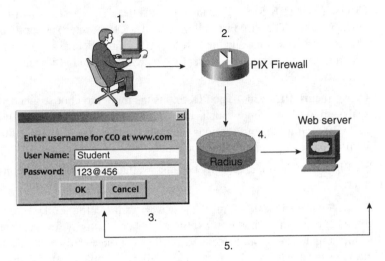

The cut-through capability allows the PIX Firewall to perform dramatically faster than other firewall solutions that require all packets to flow up to the application layer even after authentication is complete.

PIX Firewall Models and Components

Selecting the proper model of PIX Firewall can be very easy, provided that you have a clear understanding of the answers to these questions:

- How does implementing a PIX Firewall solution meet the requirements of the security policy?
- What benefit do I hope to gain from having a PIX Firewall in place?
- Will the PIX Firewall be used to protect the entire network, or just a part of it?
- What kinds of threats have been encountered, and against what part of the network were they launched?
- How does this solution scale if the network expands at a rapid pace?
- Will this solution protect me from current and future threats?
- Will this solution work with my current network topology?

- Is this product easily upgraded?
- Is this product easy to configure and deploy?

Cisco offers PIX Firewall models 515 and 520, which scale to fit the following customer profiles and beyond:

- **Cisco Secure PIX 515**—This model is just the right size for small-to-medium business users. The PIX Firewall Model 515-R (restricted) supports up to 64,000 simultaneous sessions, and the PIX 515-UR (unrestricted) supports up to 128,000 simultaneous sessions. Cisco recently lowered the price of these models to make them more affordable.

- **Cisco Secure PIX 520**—The PIX 520 is the model to choose when your network scales up to a larger, more sophisticated, enterprise-level topology. It can support up to 256,000 simultaneous sessions (upgrades are required to handle this volume) with no noticeable depreciation in throughput.

Another PIX Firewall model recently became available to the security-conscious consumer:

- **Cisco Secure PIX 506**—This is the newest addition to the PIX Firewall family. It is aimed at companies that want to utilize VPN connectivity for their employees. It can connect up to four simultaneous VPN clients at once. This model is designed to provide standards-based IPSec connectivity with sophisticated data encryption to protect sensitive data.

The model 506 is excluded from the remainder of this discussion because its main focus is VPN connectivity and data encryption. That puts it outside the scope of this chapter.

Cisco has designed the PIX Firewall product line to be scalable and upgradeable in an effort to provide the longest life possible for whatever configuration you choose. The next portion of this chapter covers the configuration options available to PIX Firewall models 515 and 520 only.

Table 9-1 gives you a good start in determining which PIX model you need. You must consider current and future security needs, possible topology upgrades, increases in the number of users generating traffic that the PIX Firewall will handle, and the performance you expect from your PIX Firewall solution.

Table 9-1 *Selecting a PIX Firewall Model*

Question	Answer	PIX Firewall Model	Reason
How many network segments will connect to the PIX Firewall?	Four or more	PIX 520 or 515-U	PIX Firewall model 520 has two additional PCI expansion ports for future expansion. Model 515-U can accommodate a four-port Ethernet interface to provide similar functionality.

Table 9-1   *Selecting a PIX Firewall Model (Continued)*

Question	Answer	PIX Firewall Model	Reason
How many users will connect to the Internet via the PIX Firewall?	No more than 1000	PIX 515	The 515 can handle up to 50,000 connections in the 515-R model.
What is your network's topology?	Ethernet only	PIX 515	The basic 515 models provide connectivity for networks utilizing Ethernet-only topology.
Will a Token Ring segment be connected?	Use Token Ring and Ethernet	PIX 520	Model 520 is currently the only model that can accommodate Token Ring and Ethernet simultaneously.
What kind of throughput will you need?	Your network is 100 Mb switched	PIX 515 or 520	PIX Firewall models 515 and 520 can handle up to 170 Mbps throughput (rated speed).
What is the expected growth of the network being protected by the PIX Firewall?	Unknown growth potential	PIX 520	Model 520 is the best choice when potential growth is unknown. It has the capacity for extreme scalability and can integrate with the widest range of network topologies.

If you are still unsure as to what PIX Firewall model you will need after reading this chapter, take some time to research what other network administrators are using and in what capacity they are deploying the solution. You will find that there are a variety of opinions as to which PIX Firewall model is best in certain circumstances.

Cisco also provides hardware bundles that include network interfaces and the appropriate license to activate them. You should visit the Cisco home page for more information regarding the complete PIX Firewall product line.

NOTE   The PIX Firewall Model 525 is also available for large enterprise business. Consult www.cisco.com for the current list of available PIX Firewall models.

CiscoSecure PIX 515

PIX Firewall model 515 is an excellent choice for small-to-medium businesses that need a reliable security solution that meets the budgetary and performance constraints of an entry-level campus network. The options available to the model 515 are designated by the suffixes U (unrestricted—170 Mbps and up to 100,000 concurrent connections) and R (restricted— 170 Mbps and up to 50,000 concurrent connections). Table 9-2 outlines the limitations imposed by the two licensing models. It also lists the configuration choices that Cisco PIX Firewall model 515 allows.

Table 9-2 *PIX Firewall Model 515 Features and Options*

Feature Description	Configuration Option(s)
Processor	200 MHz Pentium Pro
PCI local bus card slots	Two internal
Memory (DRAM)	32 MB (515-R)
	64 MB (515-UR)
Ethernet	Two (515-R)
	Six (515-UR)
Token Ring interface	Not supported
FDDI interface	Not supported
Connections	50,000 (515-R)
	100,000 (515-UR)
Performance	Up to 45 Mbps, up to 50,000 simultaneous connections, and up to 2000 connections per second
Flash (contains the operating system and the configuration file)	8 MB (515-R)
	16 MB (515-UR)
Software options	PIX Firewall version 5.02
Power options	None

CiscoSecure PIX 520

When your security solution requires a more robust platform than is possible with PIX model 515 (that is, additional interfaces, Token Ring or FDDI interfaces, and more simultaneous connections), the PIX Firewall Model 520 is the perfect choice. The model 520 easily handles the load for companies that require enterprise-level protection. See Table 9-3.

Table 9-3 *PIX Firewall Model 520 Features and Options*

Feature Description	Configuration Option(s)
Processor	Either the 233 or 350 MHz Intel Pentium II, depending on the serial number: • For 18005000 through 18013334, use the 233 MHz PII (minimum PIX release is 4.0.7). • For the 18013335 onward, use the 350 MHz PII (minimum PIX release is 4.2.4 for slot numbering capability).
PCI local bus card slots	Four internal
Memory (SDRAM)	128 MB (standard)
Ethernet	Six configurable
Token Ring interface	Four configurable
FDDI interface	Two configurable
Connections	50,000 (515-R) 100,000 (515-UR)
Performance	Up to 170 Mbps, up to 256,000 simultaneous connections, and up to 6,500 connections per second
Flash (contains the operating system and configuration file)	2 MB
Software options	PIX Firewall version 5.02
Power options	PIX 520 DC. PIX Firewall 520 is also available with a -48 VDC power supply that is NEBS Level 3-compliant as tested to Bellcore GR-63 and GR-1089 standards.

NOTE   PIX Firewall model 520 Pentium II MB contains three DIMM slots. The PIX software cannot address amounts of memory greater than 128 MB, even though the **show version** command will display amounts greater than 128 MB.

PIX Firewall–Supported Network Interfaces

As demonstrated by the configuration options in the preceding section, the PIX Firewall supports a variety of network interface configurations. Installation and usage of these interfaces (such as Ethernet, Token Ring, and FDDI) are based entirely on the licensing plan you purchase.

If your configuration requires you to have two Ethernet cards and one Token Ring card installed, you will need a licensing plan that supports this. The licensing plan you purchase will also stipulate a limit on the number of concurrent connections allowed by the network interfaces. The total number of connections is based on the amount of installed RAM (IOS version 5.x and above) and the software license option. A connection is similar to a session socket in that it has a source and destination IP address and a source and destination TCP or UDP port number. You can upgrade connection licenses by purchasing an upgrade license and entering a secure activation key (provided by Cisco) into the PIX Firewall configuration.

The following sections contain more-detailed licensing breakdowns for PIX Firewall models 515 and 520 (as presented in the Cisco Systems product catalog).

Available Software Licensing Choices

For PIX 515 (version 4.4), licensing is feature based. All PIX 515 software comes with an unrestricted user license, and the number of simultaneous outbound TCP/IP connections is governed by the hardware limits set by each box.

The entry-level PIX 515-R (restricted) provides up to 50,000 connections. (The PIX 515-R is further restricted by not providing failover and being limited to only two 10/100 Ethernet interfaces.) The midrange PIX 515-UR provides up to 100,000 connections, failover, and up to six 10/100 Ethernet interfaces.

Pricing for the PIX 520 will remain the same, with entry-level, midrange, and unrestricted licenses available. The PIX 520 provides more than a quarter of a million connections, failover, and up to six 10/100 Ethernet connections or up to four Token Ring or two FDDI interfaces.

NIC Support

The PIX Firewall supports the following quantities and types of network interface cards (NICs):

Single-port 10/100BaseT Ethernet—Up to four NICs per PIX Firewall chassis. Not available for the PIX 515 with restricted software.

Four-port 10/100BaseT Ethernet—May be combined with one or more single-port 10/100 Ethernet NICs. Not available for the PIX 515 with restricted software.

4/16 Mbps Token Ring—Up to four NICs per PIX Firewall chassis. Not available for the PIX 515.

FDDI—Limited to two NICs per PIX Firewall chassis. Not available for the PIX 515.

NOTE Only NICs purchased from Cisco or its authorized resellers can be used in the CiscoSecure PIX Firewall. Attempts to use other cards will void the warranty.

NOTE HTTP sessions are temporary, lasting only as long as it takes to download an object. Between downloads, when the user is not using the client software, no sessions are active.

With the recent addition of an optional Cisco four-port Ethernet interface card, the PIX Firewall now has more flexibility in its network connectivity capability. This component provides four 10/100 Ethernet connections and has auto-sense capability. Connectors on the four-port card are numbered left to right sequentially when installed in the model 515. The ports are numbered 2 through 5, starting from the left when facing the rear of the unit.

The four-port Ethernet card top port number is dependent on the slot number in which the card is installed (see Table 9-4).

Table 9-4 *Port Number Assignment*

Slot 0 Contains	Slot 1 Contains	Slot 2 Contains	Four-Port Top Connector Is
Four-port	Any	Any	Ethernet0
Ethernet	Four-port	Any	Ethernet1
Ethernet	Ethernet	Four-port	Ethernet2
Token Ring	Four-port	Any	Ethernet0
Token Ring	Token Ring	Four-port	Ethernet0
Token Ring	Ethernet	Four-port	Ethernet1
Ethernet	Token Ring	Four-port	Ethernet1

NOTE With the four-port card, having a card in slot 3 makes the number of interfaces greater than six. The card in slot 3 cannot be accessed, but its presence does not cause problems with the PIX 520 Firewall.

Configuring the PIX Firewall

Configuring the PIX Firewall involves the following steps:

- Setting the interfaces' security levels to ensure that security policies are adhered to
- Naming each interface in a way that describes the interface's function
- Assigning IP addresses to each interface
- Setting CLI and Telnet access passwords
- Creating statics and conduits (if needed)
- Creating a global pool of addresses if NAT functionality is required
- Saving the configuration to memory or disk

We will use the **nameif**, **interface**, and **ip address** commands to configure the PIX Firewall so that it can safely and securely communicate with the outside world.

The **global** command allows you to create pools of IP addresses that will be used by the **nat** command to obscure the packet's source address by assigning the packet a new IP address as it exits the PIX Firewall.

Finally, and importantly, we will use the **write** command to save all the configuration settings to memory, floppy disk, or network file server so that we have a backup in case of emergency. Overall, this is one of the most informative sections in this chapter.

The command-line syntax of all these commands is covered in more detail in later sections of this chapter.

Which method you use to initially configure the PIX Firewall depends on which version of PIX Firewall software you are installing and the type of workstation you will use to access the PIX Firewall. If you are installing PIX Firewall software version 4.2 or later and you have a Windows-based PC available, there are two ways to configure it:

- You can plug the console cable into your PC's serial cable and configure the PIX Firewall using the CLI.
- You can install the PIX Firewall Setup wizard and use it to create an initial configuration and download that configuration to the PIX Firewall.

If you are running version 4.2 or later and you have a UNIX or other non-Windows workstation, you can use a terminal emulator and the PIX Firewall CLI to configure the unit.

NOTE   The sample configuration at the end of this chapter can be modified and used as a template for entering the commands via the CLI.

The PIX Command-Line Interface

The PIX Firewall command-line interface (CLI) provides a command set that is very similar in structure and appearance to the Cisco IOS commands found on Cisco product routers.

Various command functions can be performed at only certain command mode levels. Remembering what command can be performed at what level can be very confusing if this is your first exposure to the Cisco IOS CLI paradigm. The best way to remember where you are and what you can do in that mode is to think about the operation you are trying to perform:

- **Unprivileged mode**—Also called user mode. You can only view administrative items.

- **Privileged mode** Also called enable mode. You can view and change administrative items.

- **Configuration mode**—Also called config mode. You can change the physical configuration of the PIX Firewall. Unlike the config mode in Cisco IOS Software, you can issue interactive commands while in this mode.

The following sections cover the three command modes and give a high-level view of the capabilities of each command level.

Unprivileged Mode

When you log in to a router via console cable or Telnet session, the first mode you encounter is unprivileged mode, the default, low-security level. If you want to reenter unprivileged mode regardless of the current mode you are in, you can press Ctrl+Z to immediately be brought back.

Unprivileged mode has the following characteristics:

- It is identified by the greater-than sign (>) at the command prompt (for example, Pixfirewall>).

- It allows a limited view of the current running settings.

- Commands that can affect the operation of the PIX Firewall cannot be performed at this level.

- It is the console's default setting.

- No password is initially assigned to this level.

Commands available at this level are the **enable** command (requests access to privileged mode) and a limited number of operational commands. Table 9-5 lists examples of operational commands available at the unprivileged mode command level.

Table 9-5 *Unprivileged Mode Commands*

Command	Function
show checksum	Displays the configuration checksum, which is useful for troubleshooting configuration problems and recovering a lost password. The user can bypass the start-up configuration if this value is changed.
show version	Allows the user to view the Cisco IOS release version and various configuration parameters (such as installed interfaces and licensing options).
help	Displays help information available for commands and related options.
who	Displays active administrator Telnet sessions.

Because unprivileged mode is so restrictive, you probably will not spend much time at this command level. You will need to enter privileged mode in order to make any modifications to the PIX Firewall.

Privileged Mode

Privileged mode, which you enter by typing **enable** and pressing the Enter key, is the gateway to the inner workings of the PIX Firewall. You can access all the commands dealing with the operation and configuration of the PIX Firewall after you have entered this mode, so privileged mode needs to be protected by a password. Setting the password is relatively easy to do. You enter the **enable password** command. If no password is actively configured, you can enter one by invoking the **enable** command and entering a password when you see the Pixfirewall# password prompt. If you are at this stage in the deployment of your PIX Firewall, be very careful that you configure an enable mode password before proceeding any further.

NOTE   Unlike the enable password on a standard Cisco router (versus the hashed enable secret password), the enable password on the PIX is automatically encrypted.

Privileged mode has the following characteristics:

- It is identified by the pound sign (#) at the command prompt (for example, Pixfirewall#).
- It lets you change current settings and write them to Flash memory. When you are finished configuring the PIX Firewall, change the password with the **enable password** command.

- Unprivileged mode commands work here also.
- It can be accessed by entering the **enable** command from the unprivileged mode command prompt.

While you are in privileged mode, you have access to all command modes, access to configuration mode if configuration changes are needed, and access to commands that can affect the current "running config" of the PIX Firewall.

Table 9-6 lists examples of commands available at the privileged mode command level.

Table 9-6 *Privileged Mode Commands*

Command	Function
disable	Exits privileged mode and returns the user to unprivileged mode.
configure terminal	Puts the user in config mode. This is **config t** on a standard Cisco router.
kill *telnet_id*	Allows the user to kill a Telnet session based on session id.
clear configure primary	Resets the default values for the **interface**, **ip**, **mtu**, **nameif**, and **route** commands.

After you begin the task of configuring your PIX Firewall, you will become very familiar with privileged mode as well as config mode, which is the subject of the next section.

Configuration Mode

Even though privileged mode is the one with the secret encrypted password assigned to it, nothing compares to the power that configuration mode holds. This command mode allows you to make configuration changes to any part of the PIX Firewall. You can enter configuration mode by typing **config t** and pressing Enter.

Privileged mode has the following characteristics:

- It is identified by (config) at the command prompt (for example, Pixfirewall(config)#).
- It lets you make changes to the current running configuration of the PIX Firewall.
- Unprivileged mode commands do not work here. You must exit configuration mode in order to execute these commands.
- All privileged mode and configuration mode commands work here.

While you are in configuration mode, you have access to all command modes, you have access to all configuration-altering commands, and you have access to commands that can affect the current running config of the PIX Firewall.

Table 9-7 lists examples of commands available at the configuration mode command level.

Table 9-7 *Examples of Configuration Mode Commands*

Command	Function
access-list	Allows the user to create access lists permitting or denying specific types of traffic flow
clear arp	Clears the current ARP cache
clear conduit	Removes conduits from the current configuration
copy tftp flash	Allows the user to copy a configuration file from TFTP server to Flash memory for configuration tasks

This mode has by far the most potential for disaster if misused. Only someone familiar with the PIX CLI should use this command mode. The commands related to configuring the PIX Firewall that you'll see later in this chapter need to be entered while in this mode.

Implementing Interface Security

The PIX Firewall is, by definition, a security appliance. As mentioned earlier in this chapter, you enable interface security through the assigning of a security value to a network interface. Connections between two interfaces can occur only if the higher-to-lower rule is observed.

Even though the PIX Firewall's main function is to protect a network from intruders attacking via the Internet, it also protects the internal network from intruders attacking from inside the network. It is for these reasons that we assign the security values to all interfaces that make up the PIX Firewall.

Consider the building you work in. There is undoubtedly some kind of security mechanism at the front door, whether it is a badge reader or a security guard. The security mechanism's job is to protect the building from unauthorized access. After you enter the building, you might find locks on closets and meeting rooms that perform the same function. This kind of segmented security model is present inside the PIX Firewall as well.

The PIX Firewall model that you purchase may contain four or more separate interface cards, and those interfaces may connect different segments of the network. To keep those segments from accessing each other, you need to set different levels of security at each interface.

Using the nameif Command to Implement Interface Security

You use the **nameif** command to assign a name and security value to the interfaces on the PIX Firewall. The names you assign to the interfaces will be used as parameters in a variety of other PIX Firewall commands such as the **ip address** and **ping** commands. Be sure to make the names descriptive and, if possible, make them relevant to the job they will perform. Later in this section, we will cover the rules for connecting interfaces with differing security levels. We will also examine the relationship that exists between interfaces with the same security levels.

The **nameif** command syntax is as follows:

```
nameif hardware_id if_name security_level
```

The command parameters and syntax have the following meanings:

Command Parameter	Description
hardware_id	Specifies the hardware name for the NIC and the order in which the NICs are numbered, according to the model in which they are installed. These names can be abbreviated with leading characters in the name—for example, ether1, e2, FDDI1, F1, token0, or t0.
if_name	Specifies a name for the internal or external network interface of up to 255 characters. This name can be uppercase or lowercase.
security_level	Specifies how you want to protect the network and the relationship between interfaces. A possible choice is **security**n. The names can be abbreviated as **sec**n or just **s**n, as in **s0**.

NOTE   The first two interfaces have the default names outside and inside. The inside interface has default security level 100; the outside interface has default security level 0. The inside and outside interfaces cannot have their default security levels changed; however, although the inside interface cannot have its default name changed, the outside interface can.

Security Levels

The concept of assigning security levels to interfaces is the heart of the secure infrastructure through which sensitive network information will flow. Not all networks are created equal, and communication between segments or networks might not be desired. Segmenting networks by assigning security levels has the advantage of providing a network engineer who might not be familiar with the security model as a method for determining which sections of the network are a higher security risk than others.

Keep in mind that the **conduit** and **static** commands can circumvent any security measures that may be put in place with the **nameif** command.

Security Level Rules

Traffic originating from the inside network with a security level of 100 to the outside network with a security level of 0 uses the following rule: Allow all IP-based traffic unless restricted by access lists, authentication, or authorization. Also take into account that the

nat needs to be engaged in order to specify which interface host communication can start, and the **global** command needs to be engaged in order to specify what externally available addresses are made available for the network translation taking place in the **nat** command.

Traffic originating from the outside network with a security level of 0 to the inside network with a security level of 100 uses the following rule: Drop all packets unless specifically allowed by the **conduit** command. Furthermore, restrict the traffic if authentication and authorization are used.

The **conduit** and **static** commands are required to enable traffic flowing from outside to inside.

No communication is allowed between two networks with the same security level, except in an instance where **conduit** and **static** commands are present to mitigate the restriction. If the perimeter networks were configured with the same security level, no traffic could flow between the networks. This rule is more significant when the PIX Firewall supports up to 16 network interfaces.

Security level 100 is

- The highest security level. (Only one network should have a security level of 100.)
- Usually assigned only to an interface connected to an inside network.
- Usually assigned to the interface that connects the greatest number of networks to the PIX Firewall.

Security level 0 is

- The lowest security level.
- Usually assigned only to an outside interface.
- Usually assigned to the interface connected to the Internet.

If a command requires two interface names, always specify the more-secure network first and the less-secure network second, as shown in Example 9-2.

Example 9-2 *Specifying the More-Secure Network First and Then the Less-Secure Network*

```
Pixfirewall(config)# static (inside,outside)
Pixfirewall(config)# static (inside,dmz1)
```

Communication Between Interface Security Levels

Communication between PIX Firewall interfaces is based on the comparison of security levels between the two interfaces. See Table 9-8 for an explanation of the following security level comparison examples:

- An interface is considered the outside interface when comparing a *lower value to a higher value* security level.

- An interface is considered the inside interface when comparing a *higher value to a lower value* security level.

Table 9-8   *Connectivity Pair Configuration Guide*

Interface Pair	Relative Interface Relationship for Ethernet 2 (DMZ1) Interface	Configuration Guidelines
Outside sec 0 to DMZ1 sec 50	DMZ1 is considered inside.	Globals, statics, and conduits must be configured to enable sessions originated from the outside interface to the DMZ1 interface.
Inside sec 100 to DMZ1 sec 50	DMZ1 is considered outside.	Globals and NAT are configured to enable sessions originated from the inside interface to the DMZ1 interface. Statics may be configured for the DMZ1 interface to ensure that service hosts have the same source address.

When you compare the security levels of two interfaces, try to visualize the interface with the lower security level as always being outside the PIX Firewall, whether it actually is or not. This emphasizes the point that you should always take into account an interface's security level when making configuration decisions. Table 9-9 illustrates the visualization technique described here.

Table 9-9   *Security Value Connection Visualization*

Connecting from A	Connecting to B	Consider A as
Security value 0	Security value 50	Outside
Security value 100	Security value 50	Inside
Security value 50	Security value 100	Outside

Using the interface and ip address Commands

Now it is time to go over the assigning of names and IP addresses to the interfaces we have installed in the PIX Firewall. We have been using the console cable solely for connectivity purposes up to this point. However, this method of connection is not always practical or even possible if the network topology is spread out over a city or maybe even separated by an ocean.

Eventually, we will want to connect to the PIX Firewall via a Telnet application, and that will require us to have an IP address assigned to the interface we are targeting. The two commands that we will cover in this section are the **interface** and **ip address** commands. These commands set values that we will be using throughout the remainder of this chapter to test connectivity and check for configuration errors.

PIX Telnet Passwords

Using the Telnet program is the most widely used method of connecting to a router or firewall and performing maintenance and configuration tasks. It is important to note that the PIX Firewall cannot be accessed via Telnet from the outside interface, so all configuration tasks need to be done from an inside interface connection. By default, the Telnet password is set to the word *cisco* at the factory. Because this password is published in the PIX Firewall literature, it makes sense to change it right away. Follow these steps to change the Telnet password:

1 Connect to the PIX Firewall via your console port.

2 Enter the **enable** command in unprivileged mode.

3 Enter the enable mode password.

4 Check to make sure that you are in privileged mode by examining the command prompt (it should look like this: Pixfirewall#).

5 After you have verified that you are at the correct command prompt, issue the **passwd** command followed by the desired password. This password is used by both Telnet and the PIX Firewall Manager interface, so be sure that the appropriate personnel are informed of the password after it has been installed.

Be very careful that you accurately annotate what the new password is because you will have no way of knowing what the password has been set to after you press the Enter key. The PIX Firewall stores the password in encrypted form. Even blank spaces appear as an encrypted string when you issue the **show passwd** command.

After a password has been encrypted, there is no way to turn it back into plain text. If the password becomes lost or forgotten, the only way to gain access again is to boot the PIX Firewall into ROM monitor mode and set the configuration register to bypass the startup configuration.

The interface Command

The **interface** command is used to assign a recognizable name to the various interfaces. It also designates the speed and duplex settings of the factory-installed NICs. The **show interface** command lets you view network interface information. This is one of the first commands you should use when establishing network connectivity after installing a PIX Firewall.

The **interface** command syntax is as follows:

```
interface hardware_id [hardware_speed] [shutdown]
```

The command parameters and syntax have the following meanings:

Command Parameter	Description
hardware_id	Identifies the network interface type. Possible values are **ethernet0**, **ethernet1** to **ethernet**n, **token-ring0**, **token-ring1** to **token-ring**n, and **fddi1** to **fddi2**, depending on how many network interfaces are in the PIX Firewall.
hardware_speed	Indicates the network interface speed. Possible Ethernet values are **10baset**, **100basetx**, **100full**, **aui**, **auto**, and **bnc**. Possible Token Ring values are **4mbps** and **16mbps** (the default).
shutdown	Disables an interface.

Example 9-3 is an example of the usage of the **interface** command that identifies the network interface as ethernet1 and sets the hardware speed to auto configure mode.

Example 9-3 *An Example of Using the **interface** Command*

```
Pixfirewall(config)# interface ethernet1 auto
```

The ip address Command

After you have given an interface a logical name, the next step is assigning it an IP address.

The **ip address** command assigns IP addresses to PIX Firewall interfaces. The **ip address** command syntax is as follows:

```
ip address if_name ip_address [netmask]
```

The command parameters and syntax have the following meanings:

Command Parameter	Description
if_name	Specifies the interface name designated by the **nameif** command.
ip_address	Specifies the PIX Firewall's network interface IP address.
netmask	Specifies the network mask of *ip_address*. A subnet mask can be associated with an IP address with PIX Firewall version 4.2.

The write Command

You use the **write** command to store, view, or erase the current configuration. The command syntax for the **write** command is as follows:

```
write erase
write floppy
write memory
```

```
write standby
write terminal
write net [[server_ip]:[filename]
```

The command parameters and syntax have the following meanings:

Command Parameter	Description
erase	Clears the Flash memory configuration. To refresh the Flash memory without erasing information, use the **groom** command.
floppy	Stores the current configuration on disk. The disk must be DOS formatted or a PIX 520 boot disk. The disk you create can only be read or written by the PIX 520. (Note that the PIX 515 does not have a floppy drive.)
memory	Stores the current configuration in Flash memory. Use **configure memory** to merge the current configuration with the image you saved in Flash memory.
standby	Stores configuration to the failover standby unit from RAM to RAM. When the primary unit boots, it automatically writes the configuration to the secondary unit. Use the **write standby** command if the primary and secondary units' configurations have different information.
terminal	Displays the current configuration on the terminal. You can also display the configuration stored in Flash memory using the **show configure** command.
net *server_ip:*	Stores the current configuration at a host available across the network. If you specify the full path and filename in the **tftp-server** command, specify only a colon (:) in the **write** command.
filename	Specifies a filename used to qualify the location of the configuration file on the TFTP server named in *server_ip*. If you set a filename with the **tftp-server** command, do not specify it in the **write** command; instead, just use a colon (:) without a filename. Many TFTP servers require the configuration file to be world-writable to write to it.

PIX Firewall Translations Using Global and NAT Commands

The dictionary defines the word *translate* as "to change from one form, function, or state to another; convert or transform." When the PIX Firewall strips the source IP address off a packet from an inside network and assigns it a new one maintained by the global address pool, it is making an address translation, or an *xlate,* that obscures or hides that packet's true identity from the outside world.

The combination of **nat** and **global** commands is what makes possible the process of giving the user's connection a "new identity." In this section, we will discuss the different kinds of translations that take place and the commands used to implement them.

The global and nat Commands

NAT is responsible for mapping one address class to another for outbound traffic while it maintains a table of the mappings that allows the traffic coming back through the PIX Firewall to be routed back to the original requestor address. It typically allows an organization to use one set of IP addresses for internal traffic and a second set of addresses for external traffic.

At this point, you might be wondering why you need to do this. The answer is simple: conservation of registered address space. If your organization has purchased a single registered IP address from your ISP, you can use NAT to allow your entire enterprise to use that single address.

Traditionally, private networks have used the RFC Reserved address schemes (10.0.0.0, 192.168.0.0) for their network implementation in conjunction with NAT to give the interior network hosts the ability to connect to the outside world. When a host initiates an outbound session, that connection appears to have originated from a publicly registered IP address retrieved from the globally available address pool. Although this "security through obscurity" approach does provide a modest level of protection, NAT should be considered *part* of the overall security model and not the *only* security you have in place.

You use the **global** and **nat** commands to control network address assignments and NAT for outgoing connections.

Let's examine the flow of a NAT transaction to better understand what actually takes place. The network in Figure 9-3 shows how the PIX Firewall changes the IP address on the way out.

NAT is really a very simple process in concept: The requestor's source address is recorded and stripped off by the PIX Firewall. After the PIX Firewall makes a note of the "old" address, it assigns the connection a new one from the pool of globally available addresses and sends the packets on their way. Look at the following list and walk through the process step by step:

1 Address 10.1.2.2 makes a request for a Web page to the Web server at 192.168.255.2.

2 The request reaches the PIX Firewall and is processed for delivery to the external interface.

3 The PIX Firewall strips the original source address (10.1.2.2) and assigns it one of the IP addresses available from the global pool (192.168.1.10).

4 The PIX Firewall makes an entry in its NAT translation table (source address, TCP sequence number, and so on) to remember that it originally took the request from 10.1.2.2.

Figure 9-3 *Global and NAT Example*

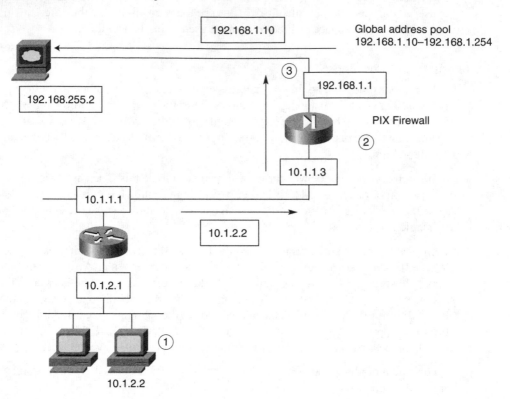

5 The request is processed by the Web server (or whatever external asset was requested) and starts its trip back to the original location.

6 The PIX Firewall reads the packet and checks its NAT table to identify the internal address of the original requestor.

7 The packet makes its way back to the host that originally made the request.

The **global** command defines a pool of global addresses. The global pool provides an IP address for each outbound connection and for inbound connections that result from outbound connections. The **global** command syntax is as follows:

```
global [(if_name)] nat_id global_ip[-global_ip] [netmask global_mask]
```

The command parameters and syntax have the following meanings:

Command Parameter	Description
if_name	Specifies the external network interface name where you use these global addresses.

Command Parameter	Description
nat_id	Specifies a positive number shared with the nat command that groups the nat and global statements. A valid ID number can be any positive number up to 2,147,483,647.
global_ip	Specifies one or more global IP addresses that the PIX Firewall shares among its connections. If the external network is connected to the Internet, each global IP address must be registered with the Network Information Center. You can specify a range of IP addresses by separating the addresses with a dash (-).
netmask	Prefaces the network *global_mask* variable. Allows you to extend the pool of global entries across network boundaries.
global_mask	Specifies the network mask for *global_ip*.

NAT shields IP addresses on the inside network from the outside network. The **nat** command enables NAT on the PIX Firewall. The **nat** command associates a network with a pool of IP addresses specified with the **global** or **static** commands. The **nat** command lets you enable or disable address translation for one or more internal addresses.

When you initially configure the PIX Firewall, you can let all inside hosts start outbound connections with the **nat inside 1 0.0.0.0 0.0.0.0** command. The **nat inside 1 0.0.0.0 0.0.0.0** command enables NAT and lets all hosts (specified as 0.0.0.0) start outbound connections. The **nat** command can also specify single hosts or ranges of hosts to make access more selective.

NOTE   If you omit the interface name in the **nat** command syntax, the default will be whatever name is chosen for the outside interface.

The **nat** command syntax is as follows:

```
nat [(if_name)] nat_id local_ip [netmask [max_conns [em_limit]]] [norandomseq]
```

The command parameters and syntax have the following meanings:

Command Parameter	Description
if_name	Specifies the internal network interface name.
nat_id	Specifies an arbitrary positive number between 0 and 2 billion. This number is specified by the **global** command and can be the same as the ID used with the **outbound** and **apply** commands. Use 0 to indicate that no address translation should be used with *local_ip*. All *nat* statements with the same *nat_id* are in the same **nat** group.

continues

Command Parameter	Description
local ip	Specifies the internal network IP address to be translated. You can use 0.0.0.0 to allow all hosts to start outbound connections. The 0.0.0.0 *local_ip* can be abbreviated as 0.
netmask	Specifies the network mask for *local_ip*. You can use 0.0.0.0 to allow all outbound connections to translate with IP addresses from the global pool.
max_conns	Specifies the maximum TCP connections permitted from the interface you specify, with the interface being the one specified by the *if_name* parameter at the beginning of the command. Set this value to less than or equal to your connection license. Use **show conn** to view the maximum number of connections for your PIX Firewall. To accurately gauge the total number of connections you will allow to be used, add the *max_conns* value from the **nat** and **static** statements in your configuration. The total number must be less than or equal to your connection license.
em_limit	Specifies the embryonic connection limit. The default is 0, which means unlimited connections. The maximum depends on your connection license, and the minimum is 1. A general rule for the limit is the maximum number of connections on your connection license minus 30 percent. For example, on a 1024-session license, set it to at least 715. Set it lower for slower systems and higher for faster systems.
norandomseq	Specifies not to randomize the TCP packet's sequence number. Use this option only if another inline firewall also is randomizing sequence numbers and the result is scrambling the data. Use of this option opens a security hole in the PIX Firewall.

Examples 9-4 and 9-5 are simple examples of using the **global** and **nat** commands upon initial PIX Firewall configuration. The **global** command, shown in Example 9-4, creates a global pool of IP addresses starting at 192.168.1.10 and ending at 192.168.1.254 for connections to the outside.

Example 9-4 *Configuring the Global Pool of Addresses to be Used by the **nat** Command*

```
Pixfirewall(config)# global (outside) 1 192.168.1.10-192.168.1.254
    netmask 255.255.255.0
```

The **nat** command, shown in Example 9-5, causes the translation of all inside addresses into addresses specified by the **global** command. The *nat_id* field points to the global pool specified in the same field of the **global** command.

Example 9-5 *Configuring the **nat** Command for Use by the Inside Interface*

```
Pixfirewall(config)# nat (inside) 1 0.0.0.0 0.0.0.0
```

NOTE The PIX Firewall assigns addresses from the global pool, starting from the low end and going to the high end of the range specified in the **global** command.

Testing the Basic PIX Firewall Configuration

Now that we have covered the basics of configuring the PIX Firewall, it is important to test and verify the work that has been done. The commands in this section test different portions of the configuration and point out any flaws in the design.

You should never assume that your work is finished just because you have done preliminary configuration tests. The tests that we will run in this section are only operational tests, designed to determine if the PIX Firewall is operating properly. If possible, you should deploy your PIX Firewall in a lab environment that is similar to your operating network. In a lab setting, you can perform some real-world testing that might reveal a weakness you might not have considered.

The show ip address Command

You use the **show ip address** command to ensure that the IP address you assigned to an interface is correct. Example 9-6 is an example of using the **show ip address** command.

Example 9-6 *Using the **show ip address** Command*

```
Pixfirewall# show ip address
inside ip address 10.1.1.3 mask 255.255.255.0
outside ip address 192.168.1.1 mask 255.255.255.0
```

The show interface Command

Use the **show interface** command to ensure that the interface is functioning and that the cables are connected correctly. If the display contains the phrase "line protocol is up," the cable type used is correct and is connected to the PIX Firewall. If the display states that each interface "is up," the interface is ready for use. If both of these phrases appear, check "packets input" and "packets output." If packets are being received and transmitted, the PIX

Firewall is correctly configured, and a cable is attached. Example 9-7 is an example of using the **show interface** command.

Example 9-7 *Using the **show interface** Command*

```
Pixfirewall# show interface
ethernet outside is up, line protocol is up
Hardware is i82557 ethernet, address is 00a0.c90a.eb4d
IP address 192.168.1.1, subnet mask 255.255.255.0
MTU 1500 bytes, BW 10000 Kbit half duplex
798 packets input, 35112 bytes, 0 no buffer
Received 0 broadcasts, 0 runts, 0 giants
0 input errors, 0 CRC, 0 frame, 0 overrun, 0 ignored, 0 abort
798 packets output, 35112 bytes, 0 underruns
ethernet inside is up, line protocol is up
Hardware is i82557 ethernet, address is 00a0.c90a.eb43
IP address 10.1.1.3, subnet mask 255.255.255.0
MTU 1500 bytes, BW 10000 Kbit half duplex
1071 packets input, 71410 bytes, 0 no buffer
Received 232 broadcasts, 0 runts, 0 giants
0 input errors, 0 CRC, 0 frame, 0 overrun, 0 ignored, 0 abort
1071 packets output, 71410 bytes, 0 underruns
```

The show arp and clear arp Commands

You use the **show arp** command to see if the PIX Firewall has connectivity by determining if entries are in the ARP cache. If there are entries, clear the ARP cache with the **clear arp** command and check to see if new entries appear by repeating the **show arp** command. Example 9-8 is an example of using the **show arp** command.

Example 9-8 *Using the **show arp** Command*

```
Pixfirewall# show arp
inside 10.1.1.1 02020.cd29.72c0
```

Before starting to test your configuration, flush the ARP caches on any routers that feed traffic into or from the PIX Firewall and between the PIX Firewall and the Internet. For Cisco routers, use the **clear arp** command to flush the ARP cache. This command does not display output. Example 9-9 is an example of the **clear arp** command.

Example 9-9 *Using the **clear arp** Command*

```
Pixfirewall(config)# clear arp
Pixfirewall(config)#
```

The ping *if_name ip_address* Command

You can **ping** interfaces by name to test the PIX Firewall's ability to reach hosts on each network interface. This is especially useful if you doubt an interface's connectivity status. The **ping** command, when used with the PIX Firewall interfaces, does not return "extended ping" information such as is normally possible with routers. However, you can get very similar results with the **debug** command, as we'll see later in this chapter. Example 9-10 is an example of using the **ping** command.

NOTE   The PIX Firewall's **ping** command cannot test its global addresses. You do not have to use the *if_name* argument on PIX Firewall 5.1.2 and later versions.

Example 9-10 *Using the **ping** Command*

```
Pixfirewall(config)# ping inside 10.1.2.2
10.1.2.2 response received - 20Ms
10.1.2.2 response received - 20Ms
10.1.2.2 response received - 20Ms
```

The debug icmp trace Command

You use the **debug icmp trace** command to view pings and to ensure that traffic is moving through the PIX Firewall correctly. Example 9-11 is an example of using the **debug icmp trace** command.

Example 9-11 *Using the **debug icmp trace** Command*

```
Pixfirewall(config)# debug icmp trace
ICMP trace on
Pixfirewall(config)# ping inside 10.1.2.2
ICMP echo request (len 32 id 1 seq 512) 10.1.1.3 > 10.1.2.2
ICMP echo reply (len 32 id 1 seq 256) 10.1.2.1 > 10.1.1.3
```

The debug packet Command

You can use the **debug packet** command to view ICMP, TCP, and UDP packet traffic. You can view the output of this command only from the console port connection. Although this command can be useful in troubleshooting network connectivity problems, it should be used with care due to the sheer volume of data that is generated and the fact that the overhead has the potential to disrupt any users who might be logged in via Telnet sessions. Example 9-12 is an example of using the **debug packet** command that captures all the traffic destined for the Web server located at IP address 10.1.1.5 inside the PIX Firewall.

Example 9-12 *Using the* **debug packet** *Command*

```
Pixfirewall# debug packet outside dst 10.1.1.5 proto tcp dport 80 bot
```

Example 9-13 is an example of the output from a **debug packet** command that is watching NetBIOS traffic.

Example 9-13 *Using* **debug packet** *to Watch NetBIOS Traffic*

```
--------- PACKET ---------
-- IP --
10.1.2.2 ==>      192.168.2.11
  ver = 0x4       hlen = 0x5      tos = 0x0        tlen = 0x60
  id = 0x3902     flags = 0x0     frag off=0x0
  ttl = 0x20      proto=0x11      chksum = 0x5885
  -- UDP --
        source port = 0x89      dest port = 0x89
        len = 0x4c        checksum = 0xa6a0
  -- DATA --
    00000014:                         00 01 00 00¦....
    00000024: 00 00 00 01 20 45 49 45 50 45 47 45 47 45 46 46¦ . EIEPEGEGEFF
    00000034: 43 43 4e 46 41 45 44 43 41 43 41 43 41 43 41 43¦ CC
    NFAEDCACACACAC
    00000044: 41 43 41 41 41 00 00 20 00 01 c0 0c 00 20 00 01¦ AC
    AAA.. ..... ..
    00000054: 00 04 93 e0 00 06 60 00 01 02 03 04 00¦ .\Q......
--------- END OF PACKET ---------
```

Testing Methodology

The previous sections explored the commands needed to perform troubleshooting. We will now take all those individual pieces and use them in one concerted effort. Follow these steps to determine whether the PIX Firewall is functioning correctly:

1 Start the debugging commands. Enter configuration mode and start the **debug icmp trace** command to monitor ping results through the PIX Firewall. In addition, start syslog logging with the **logging buffered debugging** command to check for denied connections or **ping** results. The **debug** messages display directly on the console session. You can view syslog messages with the **show logging** command.

Before using the **debug** command, use the **who** command to see if there are any Telnet sessions to the console. If the **debug** command finds a Telnet session, it automatically sends the **debug** output to the Telnet session instead of the console. This causes the serial console session to seem as though no output is appearing, when it is really going to the Telnet session.

2 Ping around the PIX Firewall. Ping from the PIX Firewall to a host or router on each interface. Then go to a host or router on each interface and ping the PIX Firewall's interface. For the example, you would use these commands from the PIX Firewall to ping other network devices:

```
ping inside 10.1.1.1
ping dmz 192.168.11.3
ping outside 192.168.1.2
```

Then ping the PIX Firewall interfaces from a PC or another router connected to the PIX Firewall (leave out the interface name when doing this from anywhere else). If the pings from the hosts or routers to the PIX Firewall interfaces are not successful, check the **debug** messages, which should be displayed on the console.

If you were to ping the outside interface from host 192.168.255.2, on the outside network, you would see the following **debug** output:

```
ICMP echo request (len 32 id 1 seq 512) 192.168.255.2> 192.168.1.1
ICMP echo reply (len 32 id 1 seq 256) 192.168.1.1 > 192.168.225.2
```

Both the request and reply statements should appear to show that the PIX Firewall and the host responded. If none of these messages appeared while you pinged the interfaces, there is a routing problem between the host or router and the PIX Firewall that caused the ping (ICMP) packets to never arrive at the PIX Firewall.

Also try the following to fix unsuccessful pings:

a. Make sure you have a default **route** command statement for the outside interface, such as the following, which points to the next-hop router:

```
Pixfirewall(config)# route outside 0 0 192.168.1.2 1
```

b. Use the **show conduit** command to ensure that the **conduit permit icmp any any** command is in the configuration. Add this command if it is not present.

c. Except for the outside interface, make sure that the host or router on each interface has the PIX Firewall as its default gateway. If so, set the host's default gateway to the router and set the router's default route to the PIX Firewall.

d. Check to see if there is a router between the host and the PIX Firewall. If so, make sure the default route on the router points to the PIX Firewall interface. If there is a hub between the host and the PIX Firewall, make sure that the hub does not have a routing module. If there is a routing module, configure its default route to point to the PIX Firewall.

e. Go to the PIX Firewall and use the **show interface** command to ensure that the interface is functioning and that the cables are connected correctly. If the display contains the phrase "line protocol is up," the cable type used is correct and is connected to the PIX Firewall. If the display states that each interface "is up," the interface is ready for use. If both of these phrases appear, check "packets input" and "packets output." If packets are being received and transmitted, the PIX Firewall is correctly configured, and a cable is attached.

f. Check that network cables are attached.

3 Ping through the PIX Firewall. After you can ping the PIX Firewall's inside interface, try pinging through the PIX Firewall to a host on another interface, such as the outside. If there is no host on the interface, ping the router. If the ping is not successful, check the debug messages on the PIX Firewall console to be sure both inbound and outbound pings were received. If you see the inbound message without the outbound, the host or router is not responding. Check that the **nat** and **global** command statements are correct and that the host or router is on the same subnet as the outside interface.

4 As soon as you can ping successfully across interfaces of higher security levels to lower security levels, such as inside to outside and inside to DMZ, add **static** and **conduit** command statements as needed so that you can ping from the lower security level interfaces to the higher security level interfaces.

A PIX Firewall Configuration Example

You can get the PIX Firewall up and running, providing security for your network, with just a few basic commands. Additional features can then be enabled according to the security policy.

The network diagram shown in Figure 9-4 includes two user networks to help you visualize how internal networks are masked by the **nat** commands that are part of this configuration example.

Example 9-14 walks through entering commands in configuration mode to enable the basic configuration. The commands are numbered in the order they should be entered on the command line so that they can more easily be described here.

Example 9-14 *Configuring a PIX Firewall for Basic Operation*

```
1. nameif ethernet0 outside sec0
2. nameif ethernet1 inside sec100
3. interface ethernet0 auto
4. interface ethernet1 auto
5. ip address inside 10.1.1.3 255.255.255.0
6. ip address outside 192.168.1.1 255.255.255.0
7. global (outside) 1 192.168.1.128-192.168.1.254 netmask 255.255.255.0
8. nat (inside) 1 0.0.0.0 0.0.0.0
9. route outside 0.0.0.0 0.0.0.0 192.168.1.2 1
10. route inside 0.0.0.0 0.0.0.0 10.1.1.1 1
```

Figure 9-4   *A Basic PIX Firewall Configuration Example*

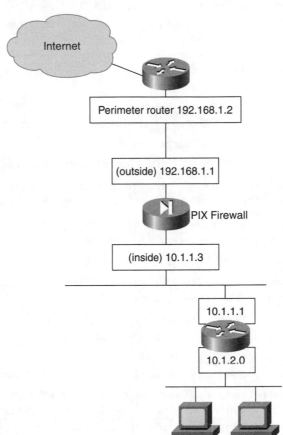

In the previous example, lines 1 and 2 name the Ethernet 0 (outside) and Ethernet 1 (inside) interfaces and specify the security level for each interface. Lines 3 and 4 identify the speed and duplex settings of the network interfaces. Lines 5 and 6 assign the IP addresses to the inside and outside network interface cards. Line 7 assigns a pool of NIC-registered IP addresses for use by outbound connections. Line 8 allows any packets entering the PIX through the inside interface to have their source address translated into an address from the pool referenced by tag 1. If the packets are exiting the PIX through the outside interface, this would be the global pool defined in Line 7. Lines 9 and 10 let you assign default routes to the inside and outside network interfaces. The *metric* field is the number of hops from the PIX Firewall to the default router—usually 1.

CAUTION The default route inside should not be used on a PIX Firewall with more than two interfaces. In an instance that has more than two interfaces, it is better to install static routes to the inside networks instead.

Summary

This chapter established the need for network security by focusing on the following key points:

- The PIX Firewall provides stateful inspection, thanks to the ASA.

- There are only three ways through the PIX Firewall from the outside: cut-through proxy authentication, the creation of statics and conduits, and the ASA.

- Cut-through proxy eliminates application layer bottlenecks by shifting the session flow to the network layer after authentication.

- PIX Firewall model 515 supports up to six Ethernet interfaces (Ethernet only).

- PIX Firewall model 520 supports up to six Ethernet interfaces, up to four Token Ring interfaces, up to two FDDI interfaces, and a combination of Ethernet and Token Ring.

- Three levels of command access are available to the PIX Firewall administrator: unprivileged, privileged, and configuration modes.

- Assigning security level values to interfaces in the PIX Firewall allows administrators to "compartmentalize" the segments of their networks based on risk assessment.

- Using the **nat** and **global** commands gives networks the luxury of using RFC reserved addressing schemes inside, at the same time allowing the reserved address networks to connect to the Internet via a single registered address outside.

- The PIX Firewall has a rich set of **debug** commands that let administrators troubleshoot connectivity problems on a granular level.

Case Study: Configuring NAT on the PIX Firewall to Protect the Identity of the Internal Network

This case study illustrates how to configure, test, and verify the PIX Firewall in the hypothetical XYZ Company. Read the case study scenario, examine the topology diagram, read the security policy, and then analyze the configuration examples to see how the security policy statements are enacted for the Cisco routers.

Case Study Scenario

XYZ Company has purchased the Cisco PIX Firewall to protect its internal network from intruders. Your task initially is to provide a basic configuration for the PIX.

After you have finished entering the commands in the sample XYZ Company PIX Firewall configuration in the section "Configuring the PIX Firewall," it's important to test your design using the commands covered in the section "Testing the Basic PIX Firewall Configuration." Basically, you need to do the following:

- Start debugging commands.
- Ping around the PIX Firewall.
- Make sure you have a default **route** command statement for the outside interface.
- Use the **show conduit** command to ensure that the **conduit permit icmp any any** command is in the configuration.
- Except for the outside interface, make sure that the host or router on each interface has the PIX Firewall as its default gateway.

Topology

Figure 9-5 illustrates the portion of the XYZ network that will be configured in this case study. The focus here is to implement a security policy that protects the network via NAT and the placement of publicly accessible servers on an internal segment using the **static** and **conduit** commands.

Network Security Policy

The network security policy that XYZ Company wants to implement is as follows:

- Use NAT to translate internal IP addresses for the XYZ network to registered external IP addresses.
- Place servers offering public Internet services on a physically isolated network (DMZ) for maximum security.
- Permit inside users to access the public Internet and the public Internet server on the DMZ.

Figure 9-5 *Network Topology for the XYZ Company PIX Firewall*

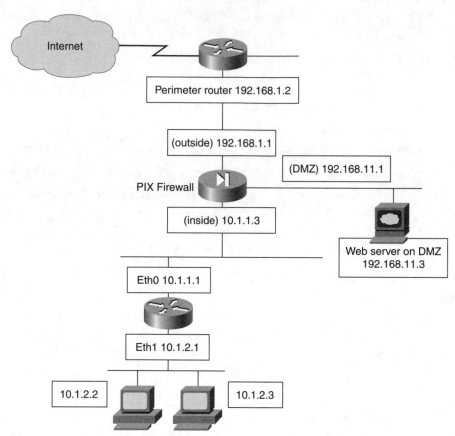

Sample PIX Firewall Configuration

The configuration in Example 9-15 contains the command set that allows you to configure the PIX Firewall to accomplish the goals of the case study.

Example 9-15 *XYZ Company Case Study Sample PIX Configuration*

```
nameif ethernet0 outside security0
nameif ethernet1 inside security100
nameif ethernet2 dmz security50
enable password 6RD5.96v/eXN3kta encrypted
passwd 2KFQnbNIdI.2KYOU encrypted
hostname PIX1
interface ethernet0 auto
interface ethernet1 auto
interface ethernet2 auto
```

Example 9-15 *XYZ Company Case Study Sample PIX Configuration (Continued)*

```
ip address outside 192.168.1.1 255.255.255.0
ip address inside 10.1.1.3 255.255.255.0
ip address dmz 192.168.11.1 255.255.255.0
conduit permit icmp any any
conduit permit tcp host 192.168.1.10 eq www any
static (dmz,outside) 192.168.1.10 192.168.11.3 netmask 255.255.255.255
nat(inside) 1 0 0
global (dmz) 1 192.168.11.10-192.168.11.20 netmask 255.255.255.0
global (outside) 1 192.168.1.10-192.168.1.254 netmask 255.255.255.0
route outside 0.0.0.0 0.0.0.0 192.168.1.2 1
route inside 10.1.2.0 255.255.255.0 10.1.1.1
```

Review Questions

Answer the following review questions to test your knowledge of evaluating network security threats:

1 What is stateful filtering?

2 What kind of operating system does the PIX Firewall use?

3 What internal processor does the PIX Firewall use?

4 What happens to inbound connections on a PIX Firewall?

5 Why is cut-through proxy user authentication better than standard proxy servers?

6 What does ASA stand for?

7 How many interfaces can a PIX Firewall have?

8 What operation are you trying to perform if you type the following commands?

```
PIXx(config)# interface ethernet0 auto
PIXx(config)# interface ethernet1 auto
PIXx(config)# interface ethernet2 auto
```

9 Which command mode allows you to issue the **show version** command?

10 An interface with the lowest security value in a pair is considered to be what?

References

The topics considered in this chapter are complex and should be studied further to more fully understand them and put them to use. Use the following references to learn more about the topics in this chapter.

NAT

IP Fundamentals: What Everyone Needs to Know About Addressing & Routing, by Thomas A. Maufer, provides an excellent background on the history of TCP/IP. It also covers advanced topics, from general knowledge of the TCP/IP suite to obscure facts about the protocol and its operation.

Hackers and Hacking

Law and Disorder on the Electronic Frontier, by Bruce Sterling, details the means and methods by which hackers operate. It gives the history of some of the more famous exploits of hackers and how they were brought to justice.

Network Intrusion Detection, by Stephen Northcutt, gives real-world examples of how hackers sneak into systems and wreak havoc. Contains a detailed account of the Kevin Mitnik story and provides advice for understanding what your intrusion detection system is trying to tell you.

CLI

www.ccprep.com contains labs and a wide variety of training on the proper usage of the PIX Firewall command modes.

Network Security

Cisco IOS Network Security approaches network security topics from the view of the enterprise network administrator outward. It contains great overviews of planning security policies and fixing existing ones.

firewall.com offers firewall security-related forums, tools, and links to other informational Web sites dealing with firewalls and general security topics.

knowcisco.com is a Web site dedicated to general network-related topics. It has a great section on network security.

Other Security-Related Resources

The World Wide Web Consortium site (www.w3.org/Security) tells you everything you always wanted to know about the Internet, Web security, and more.

The Entrust Technologies (www.ecerts.com) site's Knowledge Center section covers various aspects of the technology being used to conduct e-commerce via the Internet. It also contains an extensive white paper section dedicated to subjects such as PKI, cryptography, and general computer security.

Upon completing this chapter, you will be able to do the following:

- Configure inbound and outbound access control on a PIX Firewall
- Administratively restrict incoming traffic from the Internet
- Allow traffic from one host on a given network to access a host on a different network (extranet)
- Verify that the PIX Firewall performs the way it needs to in order to meet a company's security objectives

CHAPTER 10

Configuring Access Through the PIX Firewall

Restricting access into a protected network is only part of the overall security equation. Many security experts will tell you that in order to maintain security in an environment—whether it is an office building, a military base, or a corporate network—the traffic flow out of the environment is just as important as the traffic flowing inbound.

This chapter covers how to configure the PIX Firewall to perform more stringent control than was discussed in Chapter 9, "PIX Firewall Basics." It explains how to configure the PIX Firewall to allow access from a specific outside host to an inside host.

Configuring Outbound Access Control

Determining the correct method for configuring outbound access control can sometimes be as difficult as finding the proverbial needle in a haystack. Today's modern network engineers are faced with the unenviable task of securing corporate networks against penetration and attack by unauthorized users. At the same time, they must make the security policy flexible enough to let authorized users perform their job functions with a minimum of inconvenience. A network engineer whose design fails to provide protection and user access flexibility will find himself out of a job.

The PIX Firewall provides features that make controlling outbound access relatively easy to implement, change, and—if necessary—remove altogether. These features include dynamic Network Address Translation (NAT) and dynamic Port Address Translation (PAT) running simultaneously, the use of **conduit** statements that give outside networks special access to hosts behind the firewall, and the ability to give multimedia applications dynamic access through the firewall in order to retrieve full-motion video and Internet-based broadcasts.

Paying careful attention to the behind-the-scenes technology and weighing those capabilities against the users' wants and needs facilitates the process of determining whether the solution fits the need. The PIX Firewall is unique in that it can fit many needs all at once. This chapter gives you a behind-the-scenes look at the PIX Firewall. You will see firsthand how the PIX Firewall handles the demands of today's corporate users. We will also look at the commands used to configure the PIX Firewall in a real-world environment.

PIX NAT Overview

The PIX Firewall NAT feature gives private networks connected to the Internet the ability to utilize IP classes they ordinarily wouldn't have access to. NAT enables Internet access from unregistered clients without the need to reassign a campus IP addressing scheme. It also gives the organization the luxury of a significantly larger addressing space.

Using NAT means that, when a host starts an outbound connection, the IP addresses on the internal network are translated into addresses specified in the **global** or **static** commands.

Address translation lets your protected network have any IP addressing scheme you want. The PIX Firewall protects these addresses from visibility on the external network. The PIX Firewall supports true NAT as specified in RFC 1631.

The basics of the PIX Firewall are covered in Chapter 9. This chapter is devoted to the actual creation and implementation of bidirectional communication strategies through a PIX Firewall. The method employed by the PIX Firewall to accomplish this task is NAT.

As discussed in Chapter 9, in NAT, an internal address is mapped to an external registered address assigned to the PIX Firewall. All the traffic flowing in and out is then managed by the Cisco Internetwork Operating System (IOS) on the PIX Firewall.

Three types of NAT are available. Each has features that allow a very fine level of configuration and flexibility:

- **Static NAT**—Static NAT is when each host on the internal network is permanently or statically mapped to an address on the external network. Because this is not a dynamic assignment process, a certain amount of administrative overhead is involved with this method.

- **Dynamic NAT**—Dynamic NAT intercepts traffic from a host on the internal network and maps it to an externally registered Internet Protocol (IP) address available from a pool of addresses maintained by the PIX Firewall. All translations are stored in a table to allow the traffic to make its way back to the internal host.

- **PAT**—Think of PAT as the port traffic version of NAT. Traffic is identified and routed through a single IP address assigned to an external interface on the firewall. PAT maps the source address of internal host connections to a single IP address on the external interface. The PIX Firewall selects and assigns the packets a new (TCP or UDP) source port number. The port remapping is tracked by the PIX Firewall to ensure that traffic has a circuitous route.

Configuring NAT for Outbound Access Control

This section deals specifically with NAT and the outbound direction of traffic flow. Two commands—**global(outside)** and **nat(inside)**—need to be issued in order for the PIX Firewall to translate the internal address of the requestor to an externally registered address assigned to the firewall.

The syntax for the **global** command is as follows:

```
global [(if_name)] nat_id global_ip[-global_ip] [netmask global_mask]
```

The command parameters have the following meanings:

Command Parameter	Description
if_name	Specifies the external network where you use these global addresses.
nat_id	Specifies a positive number shared with the **nat** command that groups the **nat** and **global** command statements together. Valid ID numbers include any positive number up to 2,147,483,647.
$global\_ip$	Specifies one or more global IP addresses that the PIX Firewall shares among its connections. If the external network is connected to the Internet, each global IP address must be registered with the Network Information Center. You can specify a range of IP addresses by separating the addresses with a dash (-).
	You can create a PAT global command statement by specifying a single IP address. You can have one PAT global command statement per interface. A PAT can support up to 65,535 xlate objects.
netmask	Prefaces the network $global\_mask$ argument.
$global\_mask$	Specifies the network mask for $global\_ip$. If subnetting is in effect, use the subnet mask such as 255.255.255.128. If you specify an address range that overlaps subnets, **global** will not use the broadcast or network addresses in the pool of global addresses. For example, if you use 255.255.255.224 and an address range of 209.165.201.1 to 209.165.201.30, the 209.165.201.31 broadcast address and the 209.165.201.0 network address will not be included in the pool of global addresses.

The syntax for the **nat** command is as follows:

```
nat [(if_name)] nat_id local_ip [netmask [max_conns [em_limit]]] [norandomseq]
```

The command parameters have the following meanings:

Command Parameter	Description
if_name	Specifies the internal network interface name. If the interface is to be associated with an access list, *if_name* is the higher security level interface name.
nat_id	Specifies that all **nat** command statements with the same *nat_id* are in the same **nat** group. *nat_id* is an arbitrary positive number between 0 and 2,000,000,000. This number can be the same as the ID used with the **outbound** and **apply** commands. Specify **0** with IP addresses and netmasks to identify internal networks that want only outbound identity address translation.
local_ip	Specifies an internal network IP address to be translated. You can use **0.0.0.0** to allow all hosts to start outbound connections. **0.0.0.0** *local_ip* can be abbreviated as **0**.
netmask	Specifies a network mask for *local_ip*. You can use **0.0.0.0** to allow all outbound connections to translate with IP addresses from the global pool.
max_conns	Specifies the maximum TCP connections permitted from the interface you specify.
em_limit	The embryonic connection limit. The default is 0, which means unlimited connections. Set this lower for slower systems and higher for faster systems.
norandomseq	Does not randomize the TCP packet's sequence number. Use this keyword only if another inline firewall is also randomizing sequence numbers and the result is scrambling the data. Use of this keyword opens a security hole in the PIX Firewall.

The first step in a NAT implementation is to configure the **global** command, which specifies the addresses that will be part of the global pool of outside addresses managed by the PIX Firewall for purposes of address translation (see Example 10-1).

Example 10-1 *Configuring the **global** Command*

```
Pix(config)# global (outside) 1 192.168.1.128-192.168.1.254
```

The number **1** that comes after the **outside** command is known as the *global_id,* which tells the firewall how many internal networks will be using the global pool of addresses. In this case, only a single internal network is translated, so this value can be set to 1. If there were more networks to be translated, this value would be set to a number between 2 and 2,147,483,647 as a means of tracking the **global** command as it relates to the **nat** command statement.

The next step in this process is to issue the **nat** command itself, as shown in Example 10-2.

Example 10-2 *Configuring **nat** for Inside Addresses*

```
Pix(config)# nat (inside) 1 10.1.0.0 255.255.0.0
```

In Example 10-2, all internal network addresses in the 10.1.0.0 network are translated to global addresses specified by the **global** command with the *global_id* of 1. If additional addresses need to be translated, it is important to know the *global_id* number that corresponds to the global pool of addresses being utilized for each **nat** instance. The netmask of 255.255.0.0 tells the firewall to honor requests for this translation only if they originate from the 10.1.*x.x* network.

The next step is really understanding how the **nat** and **global** commands work together in a real-world application. Figure 10-1 shows at what points the following translation steps take place:

1 A user on the internal network with the IP address 10.1.2.2 requests an asset that's available on the Internet.

2 The user's request is mapped to IP address 192.168.1.128, which is an IP address selected from the available pool of addresses specified by the **global** command.

3 A connection from the internal address 10.1.2.2 now appears to have come from IP address 192.168.1.128.

Figure 10-1 *Translating Internal Network Addresses to Global Addresses*

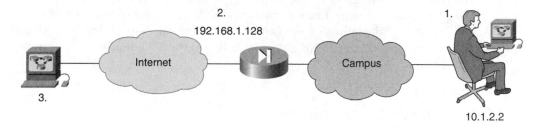

NAT Configuration Example

In the next scenario, a company has purchased the network address 192.168.1.0/24 from its local ISP, enabling up to 254 individual IP addresses. The total number of internal hosts exceeds 600, but at any given time, it is estimated that no more than 100 hosts will access the network.

NAT translates inside IP addresses to addresses specified in the **global** command while maintaining firewall security for connection. The **nat** command works with the **global** command to enable NAT functionality.

Example 10-3 first creates a global pool of 106 registered IP addresses that will be used for NAT. (You can specify up to 256 global pools of IP addresses. The maximum is one Class B network worth of IP addresses, or 255 Class C addresses—that is, 65,535 addresses.) Then it proceeds to use that pool of addresses further on down when it gets to the actual **nat** command statements. The **nat** commands specify which selected internal network addresses will be translated.

Example 10-3 *Creating a Global Pool of 106 Registered IP Addresses for NAT*

```
global (outside) 3 192.168.1.10-192.168.1.115
nat (inside) 3 10.1.0.0 255.255.255.0
nat (inside) 3 10.1.1.0 255.255.255.0
nat (inside) 3 10.1.2.0 255.255.255.0
nat (inside) 3 10.1.3.0 255.255.255.0
```

Example 10-4 is a more concise way of configuring the same NAT.

Example 10-4 *Concisely Creating a Global Pool of Registered IP Addresses for NAT*

```
global (outside) 3 192.168.1.10-192.168.1.115
nat (inside) 3 10.1.0.0 255.255.252.0
```

The first line of this example has the same configuration information as Example 10-3. The line **global (outside) 3 192.168.1.10-192.168.1.115** uses a range of IP addresses to express the global addresses instead of listing them individually.

Example 10-4 uses a more precise method of representing the subnet ranges that we are allowing to use NAT. This example uses a single entry with a mask of 255.255.252.0 by using bit pattern matching. Example 10-3 uses four entries, each with a mask of 255.255.255.0. Both methods are correct and will match any host address from networks 10.1.0.0 through 10.1.3.0. However, Example 10-4 allows for a smaller and easier configuration.

NAT 0 Configuration Example

The **nat 0** command lets you disable address translation so that certain inside IP addresses are visible to the outside world without address translation, provided that their routes are advertised properly. You should use this feature when you have registered IP addresses on the protected network that you want made accessible to Internet users.

A good example of when you might want to use **nat 0** would be if you had a Web or mail server that needed to be accessible from the Internet. You could also use **nat 0** in conjunction with an access list on a perimeter router to allow only certain types of port traffic to enter the protected network (for example, a certificate authority server for a VPN that uses secure certificates for authentication).

The **nat 0** command can potentially cause problems if you are using non-RFC reserved addresses on a private network, so be sure to take into account your current network schema before implementing this command.

NOTE

Both forms of the **nat 0** command can potentially cause problems if the IP address or addresses are registered addresses belonging to someone else and are advertised by internal routing protocols. The **nat 0** command alone does not bypass the ASA's functionality; it only allows internal addresses to potentially be seen by the outside world. The only way to circumvent the ASA for an inbound connection is through the proper use of **conduit** statements.

When you're deploying a PIX Firewall with more than two interfaces, it is important to remember that **nat 0** does not translate the source address, regardless of on which interface the packet exits.

In Figure 10-2, the server PC located at 172.16.1.4 needs to be made visible to users on the outside. Ordinarily, you would use **conduit** and **static** statements to hide the address from Internet users. However, because the 172.16.1.x network is "owned" by the corporation in this example, you can proceed with the task of revealing it to the Internet with the **nat 0** command. The first step is to issue the command shown in Example 10-5.

Example 10-5 *Specifying NAT 0 for One Inside Address with Resultant Output*

```
Pix(config)# nat (inside) 0 172.16.1.4 255.255.255.255
nat 0 172.16.1.4 will be non-translated
```

This first command tells the firewall that only the address specified on the command line (172.16.1.4) will be exempt from translation services. You can also use the **nat 0** command to specify that no inside addresses will be translated, as shown in Example 10-6.

Figure 10-2 *Configuring NAT 0*

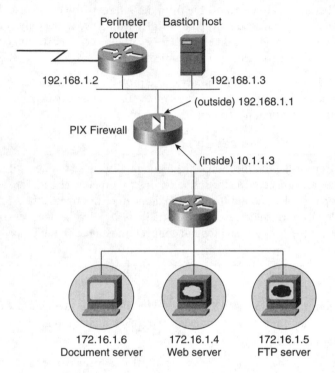

Example 10-6 *Specifying That No Inside Addresses Will Be Translated*

```
Pix(config)# nat (inside) 0 0 0
```

If you instructed the firewall to use the **nat (inside) 0 0 0** command, would the FTP server (172.16.1.5) and the document server (172.16.1.6) in Figure 10-2 also be visible to the outside? The answer is yes.

It all has to do with the 0s that come after the **nat** command just shown. As you already know, the first 0 in the **nat 0** command lets you disable address translation so that inside IP addresses are visible on the outside without the benefit of translation services. When a single 0 is shown as the value for the *local ip* and *netmask* parameters, it can be interpreted the same as if the value 0.0.0.0 had been entered. Think of the 0 as shorthand for 0.0.0.0, which means that you should consider everything a match.

If you have a single address that you want made visible, you would enter that address and netmask on the command line, as shown in Example 10-7.

Example 10-7 *Making a Single Address Visible Using NAT 0*

```
Pix(config)# nat (inside) 0 172.16.1.5 255.255.255.255
```

This **nat 0** command tells the firewall to reveal the 172.16.1.5 address to the outside.

Port Address Translation

Often referred to as *many-to-one* address translation, PAT takes all traffic on the internal network and maps it to a single externally available IP address.

When a host on the protected network makes a request for an asset available via the Internet, an entry is added to a NAT table in the PIX Firewall. This NAT table entry records two things about the request:

- The translation from the local host address to the globally available address assigned by the PIX Firewall

- The translation from the host-assigned port number to a random port number assigned by the PIX Firewall

The PIX Firewall keeps this data and uses the mapping information to ensure that the request originated from inside the protected network. It discards the information when the session is completed. These concepts are illustrated in more depth later in this chapter.

The PIX PAT feature expands a company's address pool by doing the following:

- It uses one outside IP address for approximately 4,000 inside hosts. Theoretically, the limit is greater than 64,000, but 4,000 is the practical limit.

- It maps specific TCP port numbers to a preselected IP address and port number, unless otherwise specified by a **static** command.

- It hides an inside source address by using a single IP address available from a global pool maintained by the PIX Firewall.

PAT can be used with NAT, and a PAT address is a virtual address different from the port address on the outside interface.

You shouldn't use PAT when running multimedia applications through the PIX Firewall. Multimedia applications need access to specific ports and can conflict with port mappings provided by PAT. In cases where port traffic needs to keep its original configuration, you might want to consider using **nat 0**.

Figure 10-3 shows a network diagram in which PAT can be implemented with a minimum of configuration: XYZ Company has three registered IP addresses. The perimeter router, the PIX Firewall, and the bastion host take one address each. (A bastion host is typically the only host accessible via the Internet, such as a Web or mail server.)

Figure 10-3 *PAT Example*

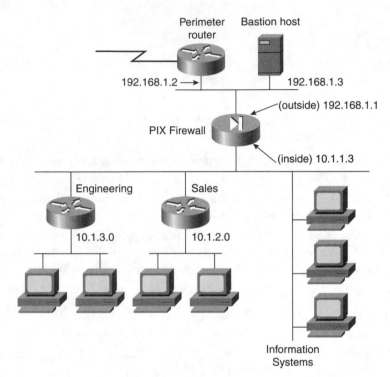

Configuring PAT for deployment in Figure 10-3 requires that you enter the five command lines shown in Example 10-8.

Example 10-8 *Configuring PAT for an Inside Network of 10.0.1.0*

```
Pix(config)# ip address (inside) 10.1.1.3 255.255.252.0
Pix(config)# ip address (outside) 192.168.1.1 255.255.252.0
Pix(config)# route (outside) 0 0 192.168.1.2 1
Pix(config)# nat (inside) 2 10.1.0.0 255.255.0.0
Pix(config)# global (outside) 2 192.168.1.4 netmask  255.255.252.0
```

Let's examine what has been configured here. The first line assigns the IP address 10.1.1.3 to the PIX Firewall interface known as "inside" (the interface that connects to the protected network). The second line assigns the IP address 192.168.1.1 to the PIX Firewall interface known as "outside" (the interface that is outside the protected network, exposed to the Internet). The third line tells the firewall which traffic qualifies for routing through the 192.168.1.2 interface on the perimeter router. It takes traffic leaving the interface known as "outside" (IP address 192.168.1.1) and checks to make sure that it matches the values entered for the *ip address* and *netmask* command-line parameters. In this case, all traffic is eligible because a single 0 was entered as the value for both *ip address* and *netmask*.

(Remember, the single 0 is the abbreviated form of 0.0.0.0.) The fourth line assigns the NAT ID 2 to the internal hosts on the 10.1.0.0 network. The last line puts the address 192.168.1.4 into the global address pool and tells the firewall that only NAT entries identified as being members of the NAT ID 2 grouping (the next-to-last line shows which network addresses are in this grouping) will use the IP address 192.168.1.4 for outbound NAT translation services.

NOTE   The nat_id parameter shown in Example 10-8 tells the firewall to treat all **nat** command entries that use the same nat_id number as a single entity and to apply the translation rules found in the companion global command containing the corresponding nat_id number.

If you issue the commands shown in Example 10-9, the PIX Firewall will see that the first three lines all contain the same nat_id number and will consider them part of the same **nat** group (nat_id group 3).

Example 10-9 *Using the* nat_id *Argument to Bind **nat** to **global** Commands*

```
Pix(config)# nat (inside) 3 10.1.0.0 255.255.0.0
Pix(config)# nat (inside) 3 10.2.0.0 255.255.0.0
Pix(config)# nat (inside) 3 10.3.0.0 255.255.0.0
Pix(config)# global (outside) 3 192.168.1.4-192.168.1.5 netmask  255.255.252.0
```

The firewall then looks at the **global** command that follows and sees that it is associated with whatever **nat** commands are members of **nat** group 3. The firewall will provide outbound translation services for only members of that group.

It is very important to keep track of the order in which you issue configuration statements. Commands that rely on a configuration argument (such as the nat_id requirement for the **global** command) can be ignored if other referenced parameters are not configured properly.

NetBIOS Translation

NetBIOS is a particularly difficult protocol for the PIX Firewall to work with because of its reliance on English language-based naming conventions. TCP/IP, on the other hand, requires the use of dotted-decimal notation, so it is easier for the PIX Firewall to work with. NetBIOS is not routable by nature and needs to be encapsulated for transport when used over an IP network.

NetBIOS implementation is a complicated issue when using NAT because, in addition to the IP header, the IP source address is part of the NetBIOS header. At the network layer, the NetBIOS header is part of the data portion of the IP packet.

Figure 10-4 shows that the source and destination IP addresses (the last two items in the header packet) are buried deep inside the NetBIOS packet header. This is the primary reason that NetBIOS translation can become difficult to configure. The PIX Firewall not only changes the IP header, it also changes the IP source that is part of the NetBIOS packet header itself. If any part of this packet gets corrupted or damaged during the translation, the destination host simply discards the packet altogether.

Figure 10-4 *The NetBIOS Packet Header Structure*

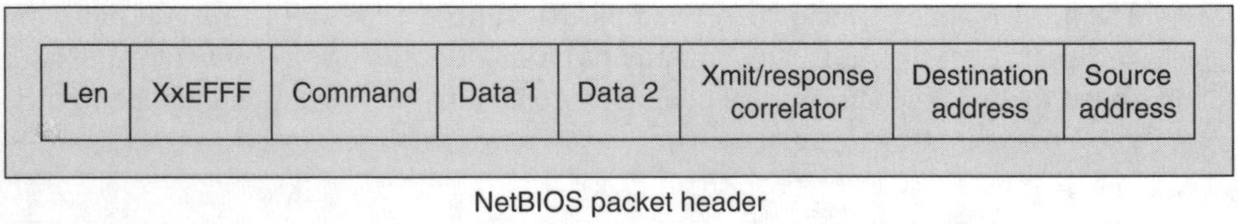

Len	XxEFFF	Command	Data 1	Data 2	Xmit/response correlator	Destination address	Source address

NetBIOS packet header

Firewalls using NAT without built-in NetBIOS support only translate the IP address in the IP header to a new global address. When the packet reaches the Windows NT Server, the server compares the two addresses. If it finds a discrepancy, it drops the packet. However, upon determining that a NetBIOS packet has been received, the PIX Firewall translates the IP addresses in the IP header and the NetBIOS header.

In the next example, we examine how the PIX Firewall handles NetBIOS translations. NetBIOS packets are unique because the source address is present in both the IP packet header and the NetBIOS data payload. The PIX Firewall must replace the original source address information with the source address that is assigned to the firewall interface. This operation is transparent to the user and usually doesn't pose a problem. Windows NT can sometimes have a problem with modified packets. It will reject them and request a retransmission if problems are detected.

Let's take a quick look at what happens:

1 The network is configured to allow NetBIOS over IP.

2 The user at address 10.1.1.14 sends data to an outside server that gets routed through the PIX Firewall.

3 The PIX Firewall sees the NetBIOS packet from 10.1.1.14, changes the source address on both the IP header and the NetBIOS data packet to 192.168.1.12, and sends out the packet.

The translation that occurs during this process is recorded in the NAT database so that the requested data makes its way back to the requestor. NetBIOS over IP is a very handy thing to have running as a network service, but due to its exacting nature, it can be a bit of a liability. The NetBIOS protocol is also very susceptible to being hacked, so you should carefully consider its use before deploying it.

Controlling Outbound and Inbound Access

Suppose a large company decides to increase its security by revising its established inbound/outbound security policy. This measure not only will make the network more secure, it will also afford the company some measure of bandwidth control. Here are some of the questions that need to be answered in order to create this security policy:

- Which outside IP addresses will you permit outbound connections to access?
- Are there any services or URLs you want to restrict outbound users from accessing?
- Do any inside hosts need to be restricted from starting outbound connections?

Before you get started configuring inbound and outbound access methods, it is important to decide how much freedom you will allow users to have when it comes to network access. This section discusses two access models or policies—closed and open.

The *open model* gives users the maximum network access freedom that is prudent. Generally, an open model lets the users have free reign when it comes to Web, FTP, and POP3 or SMTP mail access. This kind of model is favored by "power users" who have specific access needs and who are technically savvy enough to implement supplemental security measures of their own (for example, personal firewalls or setting proper file permissions). Most members of the "power user" community consider this extra responsibility to be part of the "trade-off" required for additional network freedom and will happily comply. By default, the PIX Firewall implements the open model for all outgoing traffic.

The *closed model* is the most aggressive security posture a company can maintain. It is basically a "deny all except that which is specified" attitude. In this type of environment, access to the Web and FTP are funneled through a proxy server that maintains a separate access control list. You will likely also find that a Web content control filter is in place. By default, the PIX Firewall implements the closed model for all incoming traffic.

These examples are very generic in nature. They are not intended to provide a complete picture of access control methodologies. When any kind of access control restriction is instituted, users might complain that their freedom is being too heavily curtailed. The best way to handle this situation is to lock down everything at first and then gradually loosen things up (as users makes requests for more freedom).

Configuring Outbound Access Control

In this example, you will configure outbound access for the private network that will be translated into a publicly registered IP address. You will use the **global** command to establish which addresses will be available to the global translation pool and the **nat** command to specify which networks will use the globally assigned address pool.

Follow these steps to configure PIX Firewall global address pools and routing:

1 Configure NAT for the XYZ Company to use the range of IP addresses specified in the **global (outside) 1** statement:

```
Pix(config)# global (outside) 1 192.168.1.10-192.168.1.254
   netmask 255.255.255.0
Pix(config)# nat (inside) 1 10.1.0.0 255.255.0.0
```

2 Enter the **route (outside) 0.0.0.0 0.0.0.0 192.168.1.2 1** command to configure default routing.

3 Display the currently configured NAT by using the **show nat** command. You get the following output:

```
nat (inside) 1 10.1.0.0 255.255.0.0 0 0
```

4 Write the current configuration to Flash memory with the **write memory** command.

5 Write the current configuration to the terminal with the **write term** command.

6 Use the **clear xlate** command after configuring with the **nat** and **global** commands to make the global IP addresses available in the translation table. (See the following Caution.)

CAUTION The **clear xlate** command invoked without parameters destroys the entire nat table. If you want to clear a specific xlate to make the IP addresses available in the translation table again, be sure to include the xlate parameters *local_ip* and *global_ip* on the **clear xlate** command line, as shown here:

```
Pix# clear xlate 10.1.1.4 192.168.1.10
```

Configuring Inbound Access Control

This scenario's configuration deals with giving the outside world access to the private network. This feat will be accomplished through the use of the **conduit** command to open a secure passageway through the firewall and the **static** command to make sure that the passageway you have opened leads to only one destination.

You should configure a static translation and conduit statement so that traffic originating from the internal server always has the same source address on the outside interface of the PIX Firewall. After you enter the commands listed next, you'll test the **static** and **conduit** commands you've entered by pinging the Windows NT Server (IP address 10.1.1.4) located behind the firewall from the perimeter router (located at IP address 192.168.2.2). This will let you see if the ICMP replies are making their way through the firewall in response to your ping requests.

Follow these steps:

1 Clear the translation table by using the **clear xlate** command.

2 Create a static translation from the outside PIX Firewall interface to the internal host by issuing the **static (inside, outside) 192.168.1.10 10.1.1.4 netmask 255.255.255.255** command. This static command makes access to the host address 10.1.1.4 possible by mapping it through a global address on the outside interface of 192.168.1.10.

3 Create a conduit to allow the ping from the perimeter router to reach the Windows NT Server by issuing the **conduit permit icmp host 192.168.1.10 host 192.168.2.2 echo-reply** command. This command will create a portal that permits the ping of global address 192.168.1.10 to reach the inside address of 10.1.1.4. The static command in Step 2 provides the mapping between the two addresses. Ping access is permitted only from the perimeter router. Other outside hosts will not receive a reply to their ping requests.

4 Turn on ICMP monitoring at the PIX Firewall and perimeter router by using the **debug icmp trace**, **debug ip packet**, and **debug ip icmp** commands.

5 Ping your Windows NT Server from the perimeter router to test the translation. Example 10-10 shows the display that the PIX Firewall would give.

Example 10-10 *Examining the Result of debug icmp trace*

```
Perimeter1> ping 192.168.1.10
PIX#
Inbound ICMP echo request (len 32 id 1 seq 9216)
192.168.1.2 > 192.168.1.10 > 10.1.1.4
Outbound ICMP echo reply (len 32 id 1 seq 9216)
10.1.1.4 > 192.168.1.10 > 192.168.1.2
Inbound ICMP echo request (len 32 id 1 seq 9216)
192.168.1.2 > 192.168.1.10 > 10.1.1.4
Outbound ICMP echo reply (len 32 id 1 seq 9216)
10.1.1.4 > 192.168.1.10 > 192.168.1.2
Inbound ICMP echo request (len 32 id 1 seq 9216)
192.168.1.2 > 192.168.1.10 > 10.1.1.4
Outbound ICMP echo reply (len 32 id 1 seq 9216)
10.1.1.4 > 192.168.1.10 > 192.168.1.2
```

Take a close look at the output of the **icmp debug** commands that were entered. The **debug icmp trace** command lets you see the address translations in progress. Notice how the PIX Firewall takes the **ping** request and processes from the source through the external interface and then on the Windows NT Server (see Example 10-11).

Example 10-11 *Seeing Inbound Address Translation*

```
192.168.1.2 > 192.168.1.10 > 10.1.1.4
```

The traffic flows from the perimeter router (192.168.1.2) to the external interface (192.168.1.10). There, **conduit** checks to see who sent the traffic, what kind it is, and where is it directed. **static** then tells the firewall to redirect this traffic to the Windows NT Workstation (10.1.1.4) on the internal network. The traffic reverses itself on the way back out (see Example 10-12).

Example 10-12 *Seeing Address Translation of Return Traffic*

```
10.1.1.4 > 192.168.1.10 > 192.168.1.2
```

PIX-Supported Multimedia Applications

The PIX Firewall supports a growing list of multimedia applications including the following:

- **Real Networks' RealAudio**—Streaming audio
- **Xing Technologies' Stream Works**—Streaming video
- **White Pines' CuSeeMe**—Video teleconferencing
- **Vocal Tec's Internet Phone**—Transmitting voice over an IP network
- **VDOnet's VDOLive**—Streaming video
- **Microsoft's NetShow**—Streaming video
- **VXtreme's Web Theatre 2**—Streaming video
- **Intel's Internet Video Phone**—Video teleconferencing
- **Microsoft's NetMeeting**—Video teleconferencing
- **Oracle's SQL*Net**—Client/server communication

The PIX Firewall offers advantages that other firewall solutions don't provide for multimedia applications, such as the ability to dynamically open and close User Datagram Protocol (UDP) ports for secure multimedia connections. Other vendors must open a large range of UDP ports, which creates a security risk, or they must configure one port for inbound multimedia data, which requires client reconfiguration. The PIX Firewall supports multimedia with or without NAT. Some firewalls cannot simultaneously support NAT and multimedia, which limits multimedia usage to registered addresses and requires exposure of inside addresses to the Internet. Multimedia applications need access to specific ports and can conflict with port mappings provided by PAT. This is due to the fact that the streaming audio/video player software expects the data stream to be on an established port and can become confused if it is presented on any other port number.

If a multimedia application fails to function properly after traversing the firewall, you can use the **established** command to shed some light on the problem. When this command is invoked, the firewall allows all TCP or UDP traffic between the client and the media server to return but only for the duration of the current TCP connection.

CAUTION   The **established** command can open some very large and easily exploited holes in your firewall, so be sure to use the **permitto** and **permitfrom** keywords. They will minimize the risks of opening these holes to port access that is enabled through the use of the **conduit** and **static** commands.

The **established** command lets you debug an application that requires multiple TCP or UDP port connections. It is recommended only for use with Web Theater 2 and NetShow. The PIX Firewall supports other multimedia applications without the need for the **established** command, including RealAudio, VDO, Xing/VocalTech, H.323, and CuSeeMe. The PIX Firewall supports these applications using its enhanced multimedia ASA, which does not in any way compromise security.

Here is the syntax of the **established** command:

```
established protocol dst_port_1 [permitto protocol [dst_port_2[-dst_port_2]]]
    [permitfrom protocol [src_port[-src_port]]]
```

The command parameters have the following meanings:

Command Parameter	Description
protocol	Specifies the IP protocol type—either UDP or TCP.
dst_port_1	Specifies the destination port to which you want to establish a connection.
dst_port_2	Specifies the destination port that you want the PIX Firewall to permit the connection to return on.
src_port	Specifies the source port on the server from which the return connection will originate.
permitto	Permits inbound connections to the specified port or protocol. This keyword opens only the destination port.
permitfrom	Permits inbound connections from the specified port or protocol. Used with the **permitto** keyword, the **permitfrom** keyword provides a more specific source port. If the **permitfrom** keyword is used by itself, it requests access from a specific port to any port.

Example 10-13 shows an example of using the **established** command.

Example 10-13 *Using the **established** Command*

```
Pix(config)#established tcp 1464 permitto tcp 1465 permitfrom tcp 3039
```

Controlling Access to Inside Hosts

An important task in the development of a network security strategy is examining the procedures for allowing the outside world to access the private network. In reality, this isn't as grand a contradiction as it might immediately seem because anyone who has deployed a Web or mail server on a DMZ (demilitarized zone) has done exactly that. The use of a DMZ has until now been the traditional method for allowing access to an asset protected by a firewall. The PIX Firewall enhances this relationship by providing features that further harden the protection afforded by the firewall-DMZ configuration.

Static Translation

If your security policy requires that outside users access servers inside the protected network, use the **static** command to specify which IP addresses are available to the outside world and use the **conduit** command to permit or deny access to those assets based on port, protocol, and/or IP address requirements. When these two commands are used in conjunction with each other, they create an access tunnel that permits traffic only when conditions imposed by the **conduit** statement have been met.

The **static** command creates a permanent mapping (called a static translation slot, or an xlate) between a local IP address and a global IP address. Due to the nature of this type of translation, it is not necessary for the PIX Firewall to maintain a database of the connections' "statefulness," or specific session-related metrics. This means less processing overhead for the firewall.

The static Command

The **static** command is very flexible and can be configured to meet a variety of needs. A static address is a permanent mapping (a one-to-one mapping between two addresses for purposes of translation) of a registered IP address to a local IP address inside the private network. Static addresses are recommended for hosts on the private network that are required to have a specific IP address. The **static** command can create a single translation function (regular static) and can provide translations for a range of addresses (net static). The **static** command is analogous to a static route in a routing table in that it is manually configured and inflexible.

Let's look at some of the possible configuration options and then walk through the actual implementation of these options:

- For outbound connections, you can use **static** to specify an address in the pool of global addresses that is always used for translation between the local host and the global address. (For example, address 10.1.1.16 on the internal network always uses external address 192.168.1.15 for outbound access.)

- For inbound connections, you can use **static** along with the **conduit** command to identify addresses visible on the external network. (For example, when Internet users need access to a server on the internal network, they are given an external address that is translated to an internal address and that travels to the server via the portal created by the **conduit** statement.)

- The PIX Firewall, by design, has the ability to automatically manage all inbound and outbound traffic requests. If ranges of statics are needed, a net static provides the mapping for that range. A net static can create 256 statics simultaneously, provided that the host addresses in the *global_ip* and *local_ip* addresses are set to 0.

NOTE For inbound connections, you should not use a global IP address created with the **global** command because this will not allow the traffic to reach its designated host.

The syntax for the **static** command is as follows:

```
static [(internal_if_name, external_if_name)] global_ip local_ip
  [netmask network_mask] [max_conns [em_limit]] [norandomseq]
```

The command parameters have the following meanings:

Command Parameter	Description
internal_if_name	Specifies the internal network interface name.
external_if_name	Specifies the external network interface name.
global_ip	Specifies a global IP address for the outside interface. This address cannot be a PAT IP address.
local_ip	Specifies the local IP address from the inside network.
netmask	Acts as a reserve word that is required before the network mask is specified.
network_mask	Specifies that the network mask pertains to both *global_ip* and *local_ip*.
max_conns	Specifies the maximum connections permitted across all interfaces. Set this value to less than or equal to your connection license. Use **show conn** to view the maximum number of connections for your PIX Firewall. To accurately gauge the total number of connections you will allow to be used, add the *max_conns* value from the **nat** and **static** statements in your configuration. The total number must be less than or equal to your connection license.

continues

Command Parameter	Description
em_limit	Specifies the embryonic connection limit. The default is 0, which means unlimited connections. The maximum depends on your connection license, and the minimum is 1. A general rule for the limit is the maximum number of connections on your connection license minus 30 percent. For example, on a 1024-session license, set this to at least 715. Set it lower for slower systems and higher for faster systems.
	The *em_limit* argument specifies the total number of partially completed connections allowed, helping prevent Denial of Service attacks such as the SYN attack. A SYN attack occurs when a sender transmits a large number of faked or "spoofed" connection requests that by design cannot be completed. This causes the destination network's IP stack connection queues to fill up, causing a DoS, or Denial of Service. See the section "DoS Attack Prevention: Controlling SYN Flood DoS Attacks" for more information on this topic.
norandomseq	Specifies that the TCP/IP packet's sequence number is not optimized. Use this keyword only if another inline firewall also is randomizing sequence numbers and the result is scrambling the data. Use of this keyword opens a security hole in the PIX Firewall.

The **static** command used in conjunction with the **netmask** keyword determines the scope of addresses that will be permanently mapped between the local and global IP ranges. The **netmask** keyword overrides the number in the first octet, as shown in Example 10-14.

Example 10-14 *The **netmask** Keyword Overriding the Number in the First Octet*

```
Pix(config)# static (inside, outside) 192.168.0.0 10.1.0.0 netmask 255.255.0.0
```

If the address is all 0s where the netmask is 0, the address is a net address (also called a net static). Statics take precedence over **nat** and **global** command pairs, which means that **nat 1 0 0** grants outbound access to only hosts not specified in the static statement. Think of this procedure as being similar to the "anding" exercises that are performed when you do subnet calculations.

CAUTION   Do not create statics with overlapping IP addresses because this can cause translation problems.

The **static** and **conduit** commands must be configured to allow traffic to originate from an interface with a lower security value specified with the **nameif** command through the PIX

Firewall to an interface with a higher security value. For example, **static** and **conduit** must be configured to allow incoming sessions from the outside interface to the DMZ interface or from the outside interface to the inside interface. The security value, or *sec value,* is a numeric value between 0 and 100 that is specified with the **nameif** command. The higher the number, the higher the security level, as illustrated in Example 10-15.

Example 10-15 *Establishing the Security Level with the **nameif** Command*

```
Pix(config)# nameif eth02 inside security100
```

Choosing the correct command to use when accessing disparate security value interfaces can be confusing. The following list helps you remember which command to use in each circumstance:

- When connecting from a higher security value interface to a lower security value interface, use the **nat** command in combination with the **global** command.

- When connecting from a lower security value interface to a higher security value interface, use the **static** command.

NOTE   To handle multiple perimeter interface changes, you can optionally specify an interface name for the following commands: **alias**, **apply**, **conduit**, **global**, **mailhost**, **nat**, and **static**. For each of these commands, the interface name *must* be enclosed in parentheses.

An Example of Static Mapping

What does a static mapping look like? Can you see what is taking place? An example should provide some insight into answering these questions.

This example assumes that the following command has been entered:

```
Pix(config)# ip address (outside) 192.168.1.1 netmask 255.255.255.0
```

This command line assigns the name "outside" to the exterior interface of the PIX Firewall and assigns it IP address 192.168.1.1. It is important to understand where the source address comes from when you read through the following example.

In the example shown in Figure 10-5, whenever a packet from client station 10.1.1.101 goes out through the PIX Firewall, it appears (to the outside world) to have come from IP address 192.168.1.1.

Figure 10-5 *Static Mapping Example*

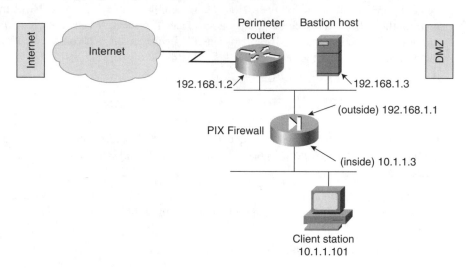

The **static** command creates a permanent mapping (that is, a static translation slot, or an xlate) between a local IP address and a NIC-registered IP address. You can create a single mapping or create a range of statics known as a net static. This type of static is recommended for internal service hosts such as a DNS, mail server, or Web server. Connection limit options limit the maximum number of connections, and the embryonic limit, or *em_limit,* controls the number of uncompleted connections. The *max_conns* value that limits the number of connections across all interfaces applies to both inbound and outbound.

An example of the **static** command is shown in Example 10-16.

Example 10-16 *Using the **static** Command*

```
Pix(config)#static (inside, outside) 192.168.1.11 10.1.1.101
```

This tells the firewall to map all traffic from 10.1.1.101 through the registered address of 192.168.1.11 as it leaves the outside interface of the PIX Firewall. You display currently configured statics as shown in Example 10-17.

Example 10-17 *Displaying Currently Configured Statics*

```
Pix# show static
static (inside,outside) 10.1.1.101 192.168.1.11 netmask 255.255.255.255 0 0
```

Net Static Configuration

In Figure 10-6, XYZ Company wants to enable many contiguous statics for the 10.1.1.0 network. It will use what is known as a net static to accomplish this without needing to manually enter every static route for the inside network.

Figure 10-6 *Net Static Configuration Example*

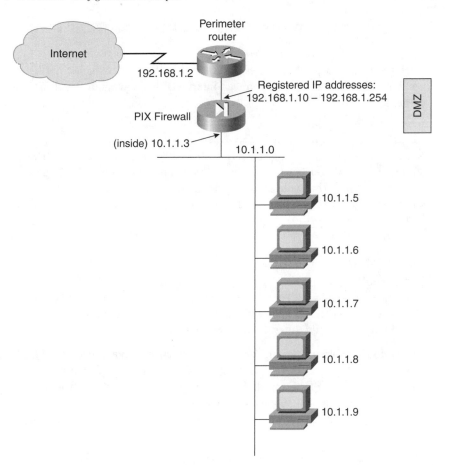

Net statics permit up to 256 statics to be created simultaneously. If both *global_ip* and *local_ip* are network addresses (the host ID is 0), net statics are created for the full number of IP addresses available in the class. Each address is mapped one-to-one between the global and local addresses.

The **static** command, when used in the creation of a net static, encompasses all the IP addresses available to the specified class, provided that the host ID is set to 0 in both the global IP address and the local IP address. The **static** command provides address summarization by default.

In Figure 10-6, each address of the inside network 10.1.1.0 is statically mapped to each address of outside network 192.168.11.0. Example 10-18 shows an example of the command needed to achieve the mappings.

Example 10-18 *Displaying a Configured Net Static*

```
Pix(config)# static 192.168.11.0 10.1.1.0 netmask 255.255.255.0
```

Because the host address of 0 is used in both IP addresses and the netmask is also a 0 in the corresponding octets, the PIX Firewall interprets this to mean that you want a net static created.

NOTE Remember that regular static translations and net static translations use the same command structure. The difference between the two is that net statics use a host address that is set to 0, which indicates that a range of host addresses will be used, while a regular static uses a single specified source and single destination address.

The conduit Command

The **conduit** command opens a designated port in the firewall and allows traffic to flow from the outside into a selected subnet or host on the inside (typically a host found on a DMZ). This can come in handy when you have a Web or mail server on a DMZ that you would like users on the Internet to access for various reasons.

The **conduit** command permits or denies connections from outside the PIX Firewall to access TCP/IP services on hosts inside the network. The **conduit** command syntax creates an exception to the PIX Firewall ASA by permitting connections from one PIX Firewall network interface to access hosts on another. Starting with PIX Firewall version 4.2, the **conduit** command can work with a global address created with either the **global** or **static** command.

You can associate a **conduit** command with a **global** or **static** command to the global address, specifically to a single global address, to a range of global addresses, or to all global addresses. A conduit can be created for a range of addresses specified by a single static statement representing a range of host addresses, otherwise known as a net static.

You can have as many conduits as needed. When the **static** and **conduit** commands are used in conjunction with each other, the conduits can be used only by the host IDs specified by the **static** command. You can also remove a conduit by using the **no** form of the **conduit** command.

The syntax for the **conduit** command is as follows:

```
conduit {permit | deny} protocol global_ip global_mask
    [operator port [port]] foreign_ip foreign_mask
    [operator port [port]] operator
conduit permit | deny icmp global_ip global_mask foreign_ip
    foreign_mask icmp_type
```

The command parameters have the following meanings:

Command Parameter	Description
permit	Permits access if the conditions are met.
deny	Denies access if the conditions are met.
protocol	Specifies the transport protocol for the connection. Possible literal values are **eigrp, gre, icmp, igmp, grp, ip, ipinip, nos, ospf, tcp, udp,** or an integer in the range 0 to 255 representing an IP protocol number. Use **ip** to specify all transport protocols.
icmp	Permits or denies ICMP access to one or more global IP addresses. Specify the ICMP type in the *icmp_type* argument or omit it to specify all ICMP types.
global_ip	Specifies the IP address from the global pool to associate with this conduit. This address can be Class A, B, or C.
operator	Specifies a port or a port range. Possible values are **eq, lt, any, gt, neq,** and **range**. Use the **no** operator and port to indicate all ports.
global_mask	Specifies a network mask of *global_ip*. The *global_mask* is a 32-bit four-part dotted decimal such as 255.255.255.255. Use 0s to indicate bit positions to be ignored. Use subnetting if required. If you use 0 for *global_ip*, use 0 for the *global_mask*; otherwise, enter the *global_mask* appropriate to *global_ip*.
port	Specifies the service(s) you permit to be used while accessing *global_ip*. Specify a service by the port that handles it, such as 25 for SMTP, 80 for HTTP, and so on. 0 means any port. The port values are defined in RFC 1700. Permitted literal names are **dns, esp, ftp, h323, http, ident, nntp, ntp, pop2, pop3, pptp, rpc, smtp, snmp, snmptrap, sqlnet, tcp, telnet, tftp,** and **udp.** You can specify literals in port ranges, such as **ftp-h323**. You can also specify numbers.
foreign_ip	Specifies an external IP address (host or network) that can access *global_ip*. You can specify 0.0.0.0 or 0 for any host. If both *foreign_ip* and *foreign_mask* are 0.0.0.0 0.0.0.0, you can use the shorthand **any** command, which applies to all interfaces. If *foreign_ip* is a host, you can omit *foreign_mask* by specifying the host command before *foreign_ip*.

continues

Command Parameter	Description
foreign_mask	Specifies a network mask of *foreign_ip*. The *foreign_mask* is a 32-bit four-part dotted decimal such as 255.255.255.255. Use 0s in a part to indicate bit positions to be ignored. Use subnetting if required.
	If you use 0 for *foreign_ip*, use 0 for the *foreign_mask*; otherwise, enter the *foreign_mask* appropriate to *foreign_ip*.

Figure 10-7 shows that a proxy server needs to have access to the application server on the inside network.

Figure 10-7 *Conduit Configuration for Outside-to-Inside Connections*

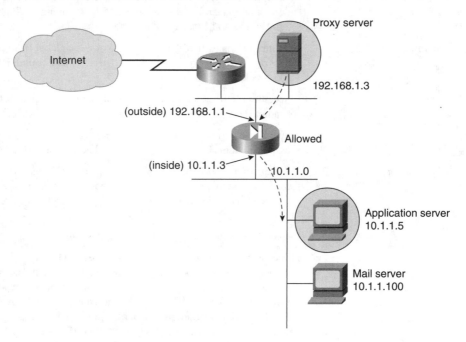

The commands in Example 10-19 accommodate the need to reach the application server.

Example 10-19 *Configuring **static** and **conduit** Commands to Permit TCP Port 5190 Traffic*

```
Pix(config)# static 192.168.1.11 10.1.1.5
Pix(config)# conduit permit tcp host 192.168.1.11 eq 5190 host 192.168.1.3
```

The first command in Example 10-19 instructs the PIX Firewall to create a static mapping between 192.168.1.11 (the outside interface on the PIX) to IP address 10.1.1.5 (the application server on the inside). The second command line allows TCP traffic that is sent on port 5190 to be permitted if the source host has the IP address of 192.168.1.3 and the destination host is 192.168.1.11.

To view all configured conduits in the current configuration and to see how many times the conduit statement has been matched and utilized, issue the **show conduit** command. The **show conduit** command provides the information shown in Example 10-20.

Example 10-20 *Using the **show conduit** Command*

```
Pix# show conduit
conduit 192.168.1.11 5190 tcp 192.168.1.3
```

By default, all ports are denied until they are explicitly permitted. The **conduit** command cannot be utilized when translating addresses through PAT because PAT randomizes the port assignments, which would cause the **conduit** statements to be inaccurate.

If you want internal users to be able to **ping** external hosts, you must create an ICMP conduit for echo reply. For example, to give **ping** access to all hosts, use the **conduit permit icmp any any echo-reply** command.

When issuing the **ping** command to test interface reachability, be sure to specify on the command line which interface you will be testing, as shown in Example 10-21.

Example 10-21 *Specifying Which Interface to Test*

```
Pix# ping outside 192.168.1.3
```

Using the conduit Command for Outside-to-Inside Connections

It might be hard to understand why someone would want to create a conduit that pokes a hole in the firewall, but specific access needs might arise that would warrant this action. In Figure 10-7, a proxy server needs to communicate with an application server on the inside for a precise reason.

In Figure 10-7, XYZ Company wants to permit the proxy server on the outside DMZ network (192.168.1.3) to access the application server (10.1.1.5) on the inside network. In order to control access in situations like this, you can incorporate **conduit permit** and **conduit deny** statements into your configuration. The command to allow this type of access looks like Example 10-22.

Example 10-22 *Configuring a Conduit to Permit TCP Port 80 Traffic to the Inside Server*

```
Pix(config)# conduit permit tcp host 192.168.1.11 eq 80 host 10.1.1.5
```

NOTE	In PIX Firewall Release 5.1.2, the **access-list** and **access-group** commands can be used instead of the **conduit** command along with the **static** command to control inbound access. The **conduit** command is still supported. The **access-list** and **conduit** commands have counter values that show the number of hits against the access list or conduit.

Configuring PIX Mail Guard

The PIX Firewall's Mail Guard feature removes the need for an external mail relay in the perimeter or DMZ network. Mail Guard is an integrated component of the PIX OPERATING SYSTEM. The main function of Mail Guard is to allow only seven common SMTP commands (**HELO, MAIL, RCPT, DATA, RSET, NOOP,** and **QUIT**) to be used on an SMTP server that is protected by a PIX Firewall. The commands supported by Mail Guard represent the minimum RFC821 SMTP commands.

If the Mail Guard feature set has been previously disabled (it is turned on by default) on the PIX Firewall, you first need to issue the **fixup protocol** command, which is described in the next section.

The command **fixup protocol smtp 25** activates Mail Guard capabilities. All commands besides the seven that are allowed are rejected or are treated as noop (which means "do nothing") and are discarded, and a response of OK is sent back to the requester. Any attempt to use commands besides those that are allowed proves futile for the hacker. To disable the Mail Guard feature set, simply issue the **no** form of the command, as you would in normal Cisco router syntax.

If you use a **static** command in conjunction with Mail Guard, you must also use a **conduit** command. The **static** command makes the mapping, and the **conduit** command lets users access the static mapping.

Example 10-23 enables access to an inside server running Mail Guard (see Figure 10-7).

Example 10-23 *Enabling Access to an Inside Server Running Mail Guard*

```
Pix(config)# static (inside, outside) 192.168.1.14 10.1.1.100
  netmask 255.255.255.0
Pix(config)# conduit permit tcp host 192.168.1.14  eq smtp any
Pix(config)# fixup protocol smtp 25
```

In this example, the static command uses the global address 192.168.1.14 to permit outside hosts access to the 10.1.1.100 mail server host on the (**inside**) interface. The **conduit** command lets any outside users (the **any** keyword) access the global address 192.168.1.100 through SMTP port number 25.

In addition to using the **conduit** and **static** methods for SMTP mail server access, you can also elect to issue the **mailhost** command in PIX if you have a PIX Firewall running releases earlier than 4.2. The **fixup protocol** command has made the **mailhost** command obsolete in PIX Firewall Release 4.2 and later.

After you have entered all the appropriate commands to enable Mail Guard, the final task is to register the external global mail address with InterNIC (MX Record) so that your mail domain points to that address.

As you can see in Figure 10-8, the implementation of the PIX Mail Guard removes the need for a mail relay server to be placed outside the firewall. This not only affords the network administrator a simpler design, it also removes the need to manage an additional server that could prove to be a security risk if not carefully hardened against possible attack.

Figure 10-8 *Configuring PIX Mail Guard*

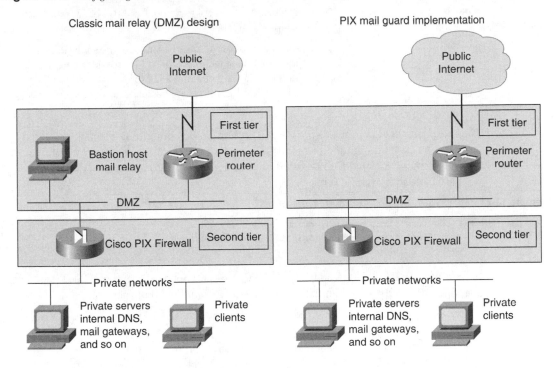

The fixup protocol Command

The **fixup protocol** command lets you view, change, enable, or disable application level protocol analysis through the PIX Firewall. This is a very powerful feature of the PIX Firewall because it allows the PIX Firewall to actually change the contents of the packet to suit a configuration need. Some PIX Firewall security features are based on checking and changing or fixing up information in packets sent over a network. Different network protocols, such as SMTP for mail transfer, include protocol-specific information in the packets. Protocol fix-up for SMTP packets includes changing addresses embedded in the payload of packets, checking for supported commands, and replacing bad characters.

By default, the PIX Firewall is configured to fix up the following protocols: FTP, SMTP, HTTP, RSH, SQLNET, and H.323.

The syntax for the **fixup protocol** command is as follows:

```
fixup protocol protocol [port[-port]
no fixup protocol protocol [port[-port]]
show fixup [protocol protocol]
```

The command arguments have the following meanings:

Command Argument	Description
protocol	Specifies the protocol to fix up: **ftp**, **http**, **h323**, **rsh**, **smtp**, or **sqlnet**.
port	Specifies the port number or range for the application protocol. The default ports are **23** for **ftp**, **80** for **http**, **1720** for **h323**, **25** for **smtp**, and **1521** for **sqlnet**. The default port value of **514** for **rsh** cannot be changed.

The **fixup protocol** commands are always present in the configuration and are enabled by default. You can add multiple commands for each protocol. You can specify multiple ports for one protocol. Example 10-24 specifies ports 1521 and 1523 and gets SQLNET to work with NAT on both of these ports.

Example 10-24 *Specifying Multiple Ports for One Protocol*

```
Pix(config)# fixup protocol sqlnet 1521
Pix(config)# fixup protocol sqlnet 1523
```

In Example 10-25, global IP address 192.168.1.14 is mapped to the internal SMTP gateway at address 10.1.1.100 through the use of the **static** command that follows it.

Example 10-25 *Mapping Global IP Address 192.168.1.14 to an Internal SMTP Gateway*

```
Pix(config)# fixup protocol smtp 25
Pix(config)# static (inside, outside) 192.168.1.14 10.1.1.100
  netmask 255.255.255.255
Pix(config)# conduit permit tcp host 192.168.1.14  eq smtp host 192.168.1.3
```

The xlate Command

The two commands that are covered in this section are very important administrative and troubleshooting commands:

- The **clear xlate** command clears the contents of the translation slots and recycles back into the global pool IP addresses that have been used for translations.

- The **show xlate** command displays a detailed list of the translation and connection information related to that translation.

You should use the **clear xlate** command after removing, changing, or adding an alias, a **conduit** statement, a **global** statement, a **nat** statement, or a **route** command. Translation slots can persist indefinitely after key changes have been made. If the translation slots are not cleared by **clear xlate**, you should save your configuration and reboot the PIX Firewall. Be sure to include the IP address or interface name that you want to clear because invoking this command without a target name might cause undesired results including corruption of your connection table.

The syntax for the **xlate** command is as follows:

```
show xlate [global_ip [local_ip]]
clear xlate [global_ip [local_ip]]
```

The command arguments have the following meanings:

Command Argument	Description
global_ip	The registered IP address to be used from the global pool
local_ip	The local IP address from the inside network

The **clear xlate** command, which clears the translation between the *global_ip* 192.168.1.11 and the *local_ip* 10.1.1.101, is shown in Example 10-26.

Example 10-26 *Clearing an Xlate*

```
Pix(config)# clear xlate 192.168.1.11 10.1.1.101
```

Example 10-27 is an example of the **show xlate** command.

Example 10-27 *Using the **show xlate** Command*

```
Pix> show xlate
Global 192.168.1.11 Local 10.1.1.101 static nconns 0 econns 0 flags s
PAT Global 192.168.1.11(2065) Local 10.1.1.101 out 192.168.1.3:80
    in 10.1.1.5:1883 idle 0:00:08 Bytes 0 flags 0x0
```

Permitting ping Access

Because the PIX Firewall explicitly denies all port traffic by default, you cannot use **ping** to test connectivity outside the protected network. However, you can use the **conduit** command to open a doorway or conduit that gives the ICMP reply a route back through the firewall.

As we explored in the section "Configuring Inbound Access Control," regarding the ability to allow inbound pings to reach a host on the protected network, you can achieve a more granular level of control by specifying that only **echo-reply** port traffic is acceptable, but the benefit gained by this discretion is still overshadowed by the security risks.

NOTE The command that we are discussing in this section should be used only for testing purposes. You should remove it immediately after testing has been successfully completed. The **conduit** command opens holes in the firewall, and hackers could possibly exploit these holes.

If we dissect the command line shown in Example 10-28, the security compromise becomes very apparent.

Example 10-28 *Using a Conduit to Permit ICMP Traffic for Testing*

```
Pix (config)# conduit permit icmp any any echo-reply
```

The **conduit** keyword tells the PIX Firewall to prepare a communications pipeline based on the arguments that will follow. The **permit** keyword tells the PIX Firewall to allow the traffic specified in the following keyword the ability to travel through the static at will. The **icmp** keyword informs the PIX Firewall that ICMP (or ping) protocol from all global IP addresses will be allowed free passage. The **any** keyword specifies that all global IP addresses can be accessed from the outside via ICMP traffic. The **any echo-reply** keyword tells the firewall that all foreign IP addresses that are pinged will have their responses allowed back through the firewall as an echo-reply ICMP type.

Opening a bidirectional port in the firewall can have unwanted results, especially if the hole is an indiscriminate one such as the one needed to allow ICMP traffic passage through a security perimeter.

CAUTION Recent network security advisories have detailed the efforts of hackers utilizing automated random ping generation to gather information about private networks based on the replies received from these "ping assaults."

PIX DNS Guard and Denial of Service Protection Features

DNS Guard identifies an outbound DNS resolve request and allows only a single DNS response. A host may query several servers for a response (in case the first server is slow in responding), but only the first answer to the specific question is allowed. All additional answers from other servers are dropped (see Figure 10-9).

Figure 10-9 *DNS Guard in Action*

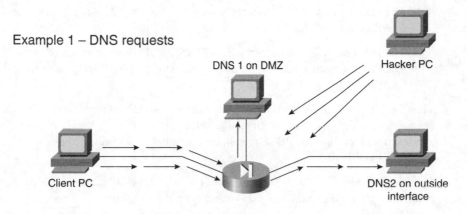

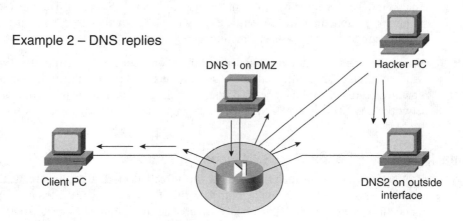

To illustrate more fully how DNS Guard works, we will break it into two sections—the DNS request and the DNS reply.

The DNS request (Example 1 in Figure 10-9) happens like this:

1 The client makes DNS resolve requests to the DNS servers it knows about.

2 The PIX Firewall records the requests and prepares to allow only one reply from each DNS server.

3 The intruder watches for traffic on port 53 (DNS) and begins a DoS attack when traffic is seen.

The DNS reply (Example 2 in Figure 10-9) happens like this:

1 The intruder hijacks the DNS reply session from DNS2 and floods the outside interface with replies.

2 The PIX Firewall sees the reply from DNS 1 and allows it to return to the client PC. The PIX checks the session state information on the bogus DNS requests and discards them in kind.

The PIX Firewall's ASA, working in conjunction with DNS Guard, maintains a stateful connection, which prevents hijacking and permits only one session. It also prevents DoS attacks to and through the PIX Firewall, even against UDP multimedia sessions, DNS services, and e-mail.

The PIX Firewall opens a dynamic conduit to allow the UDP packets to come in from the requesting client. When the request is completed, the PIX Firewall determines that the last response packet for the request has been sent. Then it closes the dynamic conduit, even if the UDP timer has not expired, which prevents the open UDP port from being hijacked. Hijacking UDP session ports is one of the most popular DoS attacks. The software used in streaming multimedia presentations is usually not very sophisticated, and this lack of protocol sophistication makes an inviting target for resourceful hackers.

Although some of the newer multimedia applications, such as RealAudio/RealVideo and Windows Media Player, offer advanced users some configuration flexibility, DNS Guard is typically geared toward the fidelity of the streaming media, not the protection of the network client. This is why DNS Guard is so important in ensuring network security.

DoS Attack Prevention: Controlling SYN Flood DoS Attacks

A SYN (synchronize segment) flood attack is a DoS attack that attempts to block one or more TCP ports from receiving legitimate traffic. The hacker sends faked incomplete connection packets (complete with faked source address) to the designated ports, causing the ports to wait for these connections to complete. This is known as an ACK (acknowledge connection). The faked packets cause the TCP/IP stack's "listen queue" to fill up and wait for the connection attempts to complete. While the queue is filling up, the operating system devotes system resources to the management of the bogus packets until the connection queues time out.

Figure 10-10 shows the normal connection process between a host and a server, in which the following occurs:

1 Host A sends a SYN packet to Server B to inform it that a connection is being requested.

2 Server B receives and acknowledges the SYN packet with a SYN ACK. The server knows how to reach the requestor because the SYN packet contains the source address.

3 Host A sends an ACK packet to finalize the connection process.

Figure 10-10 *The Normal Connection Process*

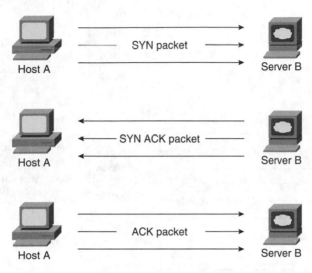

Figure 10-11 shows a SYN flood attack, which involves the following:

1 Hacker Host A sends multiple SYN packets with faked source addresses to Server B.

2 Server B attempts to respond to Host A with a SYN ACK. The problem is that the address the SYN ACK is going to doesn't exist. Server B continues to send SYN ACK packets until the connection timeout limit is reached.

3 Hacker Host A continues to send multiple SYN packets with faked source addresses to Server B. Server B queues them and tries to respond to each one.

In Figure 10-11, the futile attempts of the server to answer the bogus SYN packets cause the DoS. The server that is being attacked continues to send SYN ACKs until the connection timer limit is reached. The server then considers the connection attempt a failure and proceeds to process the backlog queue, which causes the process to repeat. It's like answering the phone and repeatedly saying "Hello," thinking someone is there when he is not. You stay on the line for only so long before you hang up. While you are saying "Hello," no one else can call you because your line is busy.

The PIX Firewall uses *em_limit* as a component of the **static** and **nat** commands (among others) to help stop SYN attacks. This setting instructs the PIX Firewall to keep track of the number of incomplete connections and to not accept any more when the threshold has been reached. This keeps the "listen queues" from continually accepting connection attempts to the point of service denial.

Figure 10-11 *The SYN Flood Attack Process*

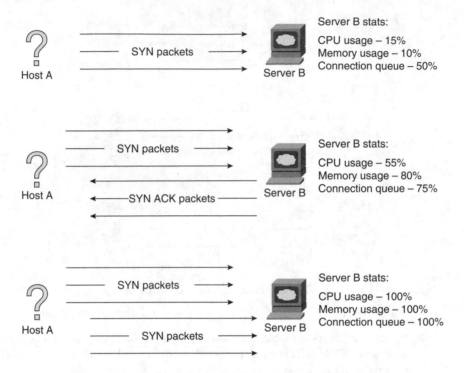

Example 10-29 shows how the *em_limit* argument is used in conjunction with the **static** command to protect a mail server.

Example 10-29 *Using* em_limit *in Conjunction with* **static** *to Protect a Mail Server*

```
Pix(config)# static (inside, outside) 192.168.1.14 10.1.1.100
  netmask 255.255.255.255 10 40
```

This command tells the firewall to let the outside host (IP address 192.168.1.14) communicate with the inside mail host (IP address 10.1.1.100). The total number of completed connections allowed (*max_cons*) is set to 10, and the total number of incomplete connection attempts (*em_limit*) is set to 40. You will need to experiment and fine-tune these values in a production environment to enable a secure connection without denying service to legitimate users.

Because Denial of Service (DoS) attacks are targeted at mostly service providers (mail and Web service providers), careful attention should be paid to the protection of these asset servers.

Summary

This section summarizes the main points of this chapter, as follows:

- The PIX Firewall and its operating system were designed to give an enterprise the ability to employ only a single network appliance to secure the network.

- The PIX's security features do not interfere with network TCP/IP services (Web browsers, mail, FTP, Telnet, and so on) unless your corporate security policy dictates their restriction.

- The PIX Firewall supports multimedia applications such as RealAudio, VDO Live, StreamWorks, CuSeeMe, and many others.

- The PIX Firewall's operating system upgrades are accomplished entirely with software (via Flash memory), making functionality upgrades available for purchase and download via the Internet. (Features available via new versions might require additional memory before they can be installed.)

- The PIX Firewall is a secure, embedded, real-time operating system running from Flash memory that was designed from the ground up for maximum stability.

- The PIX Firewall, through the use of NAT, gives you access to the Internet no matter what IP class you are currently using.

- The PIX Firewall does not affect existing LANs or users; it is totally transparent.

- The ability to run dynamic/static NAT and PAT, as well as the ability to perform both simultaneously, means that the PIX Firewall is versatile enough for any situation.

Case Study: Configuring the PIX Firewall for Secured Bidirectional Communication

This case study illustrates how to configure the PIX Firewall in the hypothetical XYZ Company. Read the case study scenario, examine the topology diagram, read the security policy, and then analyze the configuration examples to see how the security policy statements are enacted for the Cisco routers.

Case Study Scenario

The XYZ Company has purchased the Cisco PIX Firewall to work with the existing perimeter router and bastion hosts to protect its internal network from intruders. You must configure the firewall to restrict unwanted access while still giving the network analysis staff the unrestricted access they'll need to get their jobs done.

Topology

Figure 10-12 illustrates the portion of the XYZ network that will be configured in this case study. Note that the focus here is on creating a security policy that protects the network's internal assets while allowing enough access so that the employees can do their jobs. This seemingly impossible feat will be accomplished by the careful application of the following security policy.

Figure 10-12 *Controlled Internet Access for the XYZ Company*

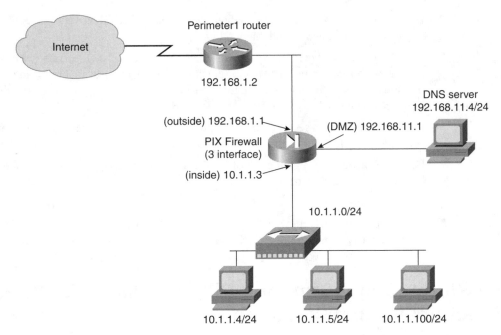

Network Security Policy

The network security policy that the XYZ Company wants to implement must do the following:

- Use the PIX Firewall to perform NAT for the company networks
- Configure statics for outgoing traffic from the DNS host
- Configure statics and conduits for incoming traffic
- Configure the firewall to allow **telnet** access
- Configure the firewall to allow **ping** access

Sample Configuration for Implementing the PIX Firewall

The configuration in Example 10-30 contains the command set that will allow you to set up a PIX Firewall to accomplish the goals of this case study. Be sure to remove **conduit permit icmp any any echo-reply** after you have finished testing by issuing the **no conduit permit icmp any any echo-reply** statement.

Example 10-30 *Sample Configuration for Access Through the PIX Firewall*

```
nameif ethernet0 outside security0
nameif ethernet1 inside security100
nameif ethernet2 DMZ security50
enable password 6RD5.96v/eXN3kta encrypted
passwd 2KFQnbNIdI.2KYOU encrypted
hostname PIX1
fixup protocol ftp 21
fixup protocol http 80
fixup protocol smtp 25
fixup protocol h323 1720
fixup protocol rsh 514
fixup protocol sqlnet 1521
fixup protocol telnet 11
names
pager lines 24
no logging timestamp
no logging standby
no logging console
no logging monitor
no logging buffered
no logging trap
logging facility 20
logging queue 512
interface ethernet0 auto
interface ethernet1 auto
interface ethernet2 auto
mtu outside 1500
mtu inside 1500
mtu DMZ 1500
ip address outside 192.168.1.1 255.255.255.0
ip address inside 10.1.1.3 255.255.255.0
ip address DMZ 192.168.11.1 255.255.255.0
no failover
failover timeout 0:00:00
failover ip address outside 0.0.0.0
failover ip address inside 0.0.0.0
failover ip address DMZ 0.0.0.0
arp timeout 14400
global (outside) 1 192.168.1.10-192.168.1.254 netmask 255.255.255.0
nat (inside) 1 10.1.0.0 255.255.0.0 0 0
static (inside,outside) 192.168.1.11 10.1.1.4 netmask 255.255.255.255 0 0
static (inside,outside) 192.168.1.12 10.1.1.5 netmask 255.255.255.255 0 0
static (inside,outside) 192.168.1.13 192.168.11.4 netmask 255.255.255.255 0 0
static (inside,outside) 192.168.1.14 10.1.1.100 netmask 255.255.255.255 0 0
```

continues

Example 10-30 *Sample Configuration for Access Through the PIX Firewall (Continued)*

```
conduit permit icmp any any echo-reply
conduit permit tcp host 192.168.1.12 eq telnet host 192.168.1.2
conduit permit tcp host 192.168.1.11 eq www any
conduit permit udp host 192.168.1.11 eq syslog host 192.168.1.2
conduit permit tcp host 192.168.1.14 eq smtp any
no rip outside passive
no rip outside default
rip inside passive
rip inside default
no rip DMZ passive
no rip DMZ default
route outside 0.0.0.0 0.0.0.0 192.168.1.2 1
timeout xlate 3:00:00 conn 1:00:00 half-closed 0:10:00 udp 0:02:00
timeout rpc 0:10:00 h323 0:05:00
timeout uauth 0:05:00 absolute
aaa-server TACACS+ protocol tacacs+
aaa-server RADIUS protocol radius
no snmp-server location
no snmp-server contact
snmp-server community public
no snmp-server enable traps
telnet timeout 5
terminal width 80
Cryptochecksum:377f6e0f8d9ac2f00141ef827bb4f9e6
: end
[OK]
```

Review Questions

Answer the following review questions for this chapter to test your knowledge of configuring access through the PIX Firewall:

1 The PIX Firewall NAT feature allows networks connected to the Internet to be which of the following?

   a. Free from Internet port limitations

   b. Free from Internet address limitations

   c. Independent networks

   d. Totally stealthy and secure

2 All internal network addresses in the 10.1.0.0 network are translated to global addresses specified by which global command?

   a. global (outside) 1 192.168.1.128-192.168.1.254 netmask 255.255.255.0
   nat (inside) 1 10.1.0.0 255.255.0.0

   b. global (inside) 1 192.168.1.128-192.168.1.254
   nat (outside) 1 10.1.0.0 255.255.0.0

    c. inside 1 192.168.1.128-192.168.1.254
       nat 1 10.1.0.0 255.255.0.0

    d. outside 1 192.168.1.128-192.168.1.254
       inside 1 10.1.0.0 255.255.0.0

3 What does the **nat 0** command allow you to do?

4 Should you use PAT when you run multimedia applications through a PIX Firewall?

5 How is NetBIOS translation different from TCP/IP address translation?

6 What does the **established** command do?

7 What does the **static** command do?

8 What command limits the number of partially completed connections allowed?

9 What does the **conduit** command do?

10 In what order are **conduit permit** and **deny** statements processed?

References

The topics considered in this chapter are complex and should be studied further to more fully understand them and put them to use. Use the following references to learn more about the topics in this chapter.

Configuring Conduit Commands

Refer to PIX Firewall Release Notes for the latest changes to the command syntax as well as information on possible configuration problems and their respective fixes. You might also want to consider reading the PIX Firewall *Configuration Guide* and *Command Reference,* available at Cisco's Web site.

DoS Attacks

The U.S. Government Computer Incident Advisory Capability, located at ciac.llnl.gov.

The Computer Emergency Response Team Coordination Center, located at www.cert.org.

The Department of Defense Computer Emergency Response Team, located at www.assist.mil.

The SANS Institute Online, located at www.sans.org/newlook/home.htm.

Xlates and Command Structure

See the *Configuration Guide* for the PIX Firewall, Release 4.2, for a description of the **xlate** and **conn** fields displayed with the **show xlate** command.

Upon completing this chapter, you will be able to do the following:

- Identify how to configure multiple interfaces on the PIX Firewall

- Identify how to protect a bastion host based on a case study network

- Identify how to configure AAA features of the PIX Firewall to work with CiscoSecure ACS based on a case study network

- Identify how to test and verify PIX Firewall operation

CHAPTER 11

Configuring Multiple Interfaces and AAA on the PIX Firewall

This chapter covers how to configure the PIX Firewall to handle multiple interface configurations as well as how to provide access control to services through the PIX Firewall.

You will learn additional ways to expand on the basic commands you learned in earlier chapters to enhance your use of the PIX Firewall in more advanced networks. Network design ideas for creating a DMZ, which is a network for bastion hosts, are discussed in this chapter and are integrated into the case study.

Many companies that connect to the Internet do so without fully creating and implementing a security policy. A security policy for a network is a set of guidelines that should be logically thought out and documented in some fashion so that they can be adhered to over time. One of the most important pieces of a security policy is to separate the necessary systems, physically or logically.

This chapter discusses the logical separation of systems by need or design. When a network designer begins to view systems or services as separate from others, designing and implementing a more complete security policy is easier to do.

Configuring Access to Multiple Interfaces

At this point, you have learned some of the basic configuration tasks and other things you need to do to properly configure the PIX Firewall. Now we will expand on some of these concepts and apply them to some real-world scenarios for firewall design.

Our first scenario involves the configuration of multiple interfaces on the PIX Firewall. "Multiple" in this case means a number beyond the generic inside and outside interfaces, as we have discussed previously. One common usage for an additional interface in firewall design is to set up a DMZ (demilitarized zone) area on a network with a collection of servers or services that will be publicly accessible, while the "private" inside network is more heavily guarded. This is illustrated in Figure 11-1. Another advantage of using multiple interfaces on a PIX Firewall is that you can use the PIX Firewall as a policy enforcement tool to control access to networks or hosts connected to the additional interfaces.

Figure 11-1 *An Example of Network Design with the DMZ or Bastion Host Network*

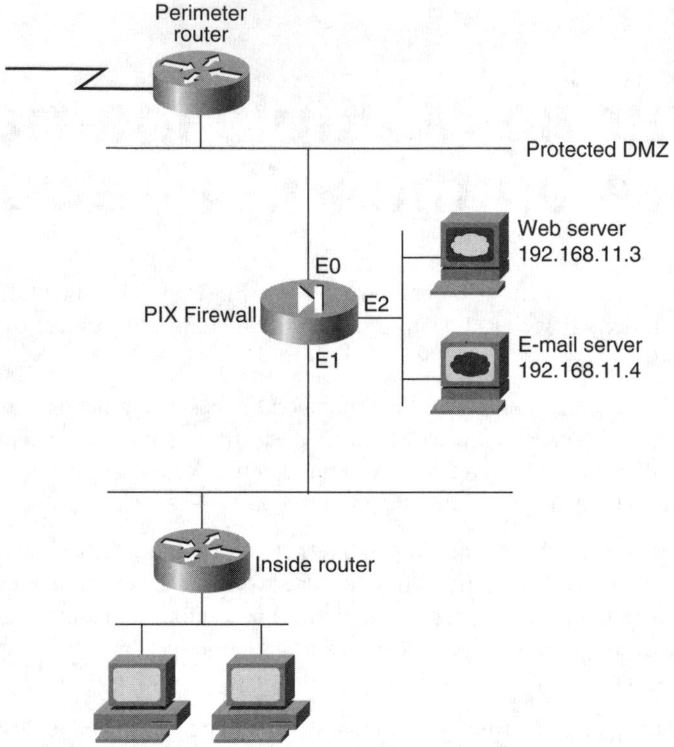

In the case study examples in Chapters 9 and 10, you configured the inside and outside Ethernet interfaces, so some parts of this chapter should seem very familiar.

Configuring Multiple Interface Support

The examples in this chapter deal with three interfaces on the PIX Firewall. Various PIX Firewall models can support multiple interface cards. Currently, some single cards have four interfaces, so different PIX Firewall configurations might contain a significant number of interfaces. Current models also support a variety of interface types including Ethernet, Fast Ethernet, Gigabit Ethernet, Token Ring, and FDDI interfaces.

As in other chapters, the ethernet0 interface is shown in this chapter as the outside interface and ethernet1 as the inside interface.

NOTE Any interface can be named anything the designer wants and can be set to any security level. Therefore, when you configure a PIX Firewall on a network, you don't need to feel constrained to the logic that is used throughout this book.

The two exceptions to that open-ended naming scheme are the inside (security 100) and outside (security 0) interfaces. Anything beyond those two interfaces is fair game for custom naming.

In Figure 11-1, note that the DMZ area uses a different network numbering scheme than the inside network. In the examples in this book, all the addresses used are private address spaces per RFC 1918, but in real life, the outside world is all of the Internet addresses, and the DMZ would be public IP addresses. This book uses private addresses to protect the innocent.

To begin with, let's briefly review the **nameif**, **interface**, and **ip address** commands, which are discussed in Chapter 9, "PIX Firewall Basics." Then we'll discuss the configuration of the three interfaces.

To name the interface, you use the **nameif** command, whose syntax is as follows:

```
nameif interface name security-level
```

The command parameters and syntax have the following meanings:

Command Parameter	Description
interface	Specifies the name of the interface to be configured, such as **ethernet0**.
name	Specifies a name for the internal or external network interface. Can be up to 48 characters in length. Indicates the port's usage, such as **inside**, **outside**, or **serverfarm**.
security-level	Specifies the interface's security level. This should be a different number than all the other interfaces (in the range 0 to 100).

After defining the name of the interface on the PIX Firewall, you need to add some technical details. Specifically, the PIX Firewall must be told information about the interface, such as speed and duplex (for Ethernet) or ring speed (for Token Ring).

The **interface** command has a very straightforward syntax that describes the port speed:

```
interface hardware_id [hardware_speed] [shutdown]
```

The command parameters and syntax have the following meanings:

Command Parameter	Description
hardware_id	Specifies the name of the interface to be configured, such as **ethernet0**.
hardware_speed	Specifies the speed of the link and duplex, such as **10baset**, **100full**, and so on. **auto** is also a valid setting to allow the PIX Firewall to test on power-up.
shutdown	Disables the interface.

When you're sitting in front of a PIX Firewall console with multiple interfaces, your screen will look similar to Example 11-1.

Example 11-1 *A PIX Firewall Console with Multiple Interfaces*

```
Pixfirewall(config)#nameif ethernet0 outside security0
Pixfirewall(config)#nameif ethernet1 inside security100
Pixfirewall(config)#nameif ethernet2 dmz security 50
Pixfirewall(config)#interface ethernet0 10baset
Pixfirewall(config)#interface ethernet1 100full
Pixfirewall(config)#interface ethernet2 10baset
```

NOTE

Remember that, if two interfaces have the same security level, they can't talk with each other.

When you are concerned with multiple interfaces, you might also consider restricting Telnet access directly to the PIX Firewall. By default, the PIX Firewall doesn't allow anyone from any interface to Telnet directly in. Although this is a good security practice, it makes ongoing maintenance (particularly from faraway places) difficult.

The syntax to allow direct Telnet access to the PIX Firewall is as follows:

```
telnet ip_address [netmask] [if_name]
```

telnet *ip_address* allows a single host to have Telnet access. **telnet** *ip_address netmask* allows a range of host IPs to have Telnet access. You can also limit from which direction a Telnet session is allowed by specifying the interface name. It is recommended that you allow Telnet access from a static management station IP inside your network or a known, trusted IP elsewhere. The command parameters and syntax have the following meanings:

Command Parameter	Description
ip_address	Specifies either the host IP (single) or network IP number.
netmask	Specifies the netmask associated with the network IP number.
if_name	Specifies an unsecure interface name if IPSec is operating. Typically, this is the outside interface.

You should not allow the external router to have direct Telnet access, nor should you allow a range of IP addresses from an ISP's dialup pool to have direct Telnet access. If an ISP modem pool is the only method of accessing the firewall, you should research other options of access, simply from a security viewpoint (for example, you could use a modem attached to the AUX port of the inside router).

Now that the interfaces are defined, they can be referred to simply by name. Inside, outside, and DMZ are the three names discussed in this chapter:

- **Inside**—This is the private network, containing user workstations that might need access to the Internet. Access directly from the Internet to these stations is unnecessary and unwanted. You want to keep the private network private.

- **DMZ**—This is the network containing services that are publicly accessible and that help the internal network users. Examples might include DNS servers (where inside clients might need to perform name lookups and where external users might need to look up necessary information about the company), WWW servers (both inside and outside users need access), and SMTP (e-mail) servers (both inside and outside users need access). This zone is for *any* service that will be accessed by outside (Internet) users, so the particular applications might vary.

- **Outside**—This is the rest of the world. You don't know who they are, and you don't really trust who they are, but they still want or need to access some of your services. This is the interface where publicly accessible Internet IP addresses are used. These IPs are assigned through the Internet Assigned Numbers Authority (IANA, located at www.iana.org) or through an Internet service provider (ISP).

Figure 11-2 shows the layout of the PIX Firewall and the appropriate interfaces. When looking at the three interfaces, be sure to look at their needs, their purpose, and their configuration.

Figure 11-2 *A PIX Firewall with Multiple Interfaces and a Basic Network Design*

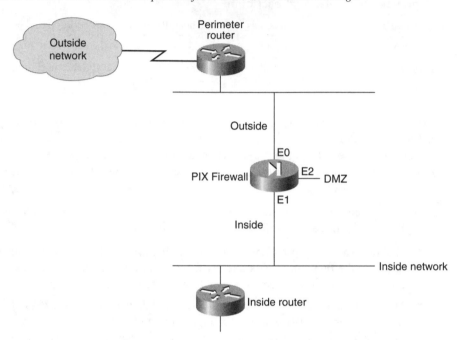

Configuring Inside to the World: Using global and nat

At this point, it is necessary to look at some design issues and how different interfaces on the PIX Firewall should be defined. Feel free to go through Chapter 10, "Configuring Access Through the PIX Firewall," to review the **nat** and **global** commands. As discussed in Chapter 10, the assignment of addresses to hosts is handled through Network Address Translation (NAT).

Now that the foundation is laid, other building blocks can be placed on top to help you learn the finer points of firewall design.

NOTE	In this chapter, the network 10.0.0.0/8 represents the private address space for an inside network. The 172.16.0.0/12 represents a publicly accessible Internet address space. In real life, the 172.16.0.0/12 space is another set of private addresses per RFC 1918 and is not to be used publicly.

The first thing to decide is which workstations will have access through the firewall and which pool of "real" public IP addresses will be assigned to that group of workstations.

The basic commands are simple, but we will go through some more-advanced applications of those commands. To assign addresses to be "allowed" access through the firewall, the command syntax is as follows:

`nat [(if_name)] nat_id local_ip [netmask [max_conns [em_limit]]] [norandomseq]`

The command parameters and syntax have the following meanings:

Command Parameter	Description
if_name	Specifies the internal interface name (from the **nameif** command) that is being configured.
nat_id	Associates **nat** commands with global pools specified with the **global** command.
local_ip	Specifies the internal network IP address to be translated. You can use **0.0.0.0** or **0** to allow all hosts to start outbound connections.
netmask	Specifies the IP network mask associated with the network specified in the local_ip argument.
max_conns	Specifies the maximum TCP connections permitted from the interface specified with the if_name argument.
em_limit	Sets the embryonic connection limit. The default is **0**, which means unlimited connections. Set this lower for slower systems and higher for faster systems.
norandomseq	Does not randomize the TCP packet's sequence number. This is used when other firewalls inline with the PIX Firewall are randomizing sequence numbers.

Example 11-2 shows a NAT configuration that allows a subnet of IP addresses to be translated from the inside interface. This allows 62 devices (in the range 10.1.2.1 through 10.1.2.62) to be translated in Pool 1.

Example 11-2 *A Sample NAT Configuration Allowing a Subnet in a Pool*

```
Pixfirewall(config)#nat (inside) 1 10.1.2.0 255.255.255.192
```

After the pool of inside addresses is configured with the **nat** command, you next configure a pool of public IP addresses used for the translation with the **global** command. The command syntax is as follows:

`global [(if_name)] nat_id global_ip[-global_ip] [netmask global_mask]`

The command parameters and syntax have the following meanings:

Command Parameter	Description
if_name	Specifies the name of the interface (from the **nameif** command) that is being configured
nat_id	Specifies the logical pool currently being configured that corresponds to the *nat_id* of the **nat** command
global_ip-global_ip	Specifies a range of consecutive IP numbers to be used in the pool
netmask *global_mask*	(Optional) Specifies the network mask for *global_ip* arguments for subnetting

Example 11-3 shows a NAT configuration whose global address pool has a range of individual addresses to be used by the addresses specified with the **nat** command.

Example 11-3 *A NAT Configuration with a Specific Address Pool*

```
Pixfirewall(config)#global (outside) 1 172.16.1.3-172.16.1.64
```

Notice that the numbers do not directly correlate (that is, 10.1.2.1 doesn't map to 172.16.1.1), but there are still 62 viable numbers for translation based on the previous **nat** command example. So a 1:1 ratio exists for translations. On the other hand, sometimes in network design, the needs do not line up quite so well. The PIX Firewall can also do Port Address Translation (PAT), in which many workstations inside share a single IP or a limited number of public IPs.

PAT utilizes all 65,536 TCP/UDP ports available to the IP protocol stack in order to allow sharing. Remember that, in a normal networking scenario, all workstations use port 80 to process HTTP requests. If more than one workstation were to share a single IP and attempt to share port 80, things would get very complicated very quickly because the firewall device or the individual workstations would have no way to tell whose response was whose. It would be similar to delivering mail to a large apartment complex that has one address. If the name and apartment number were taken off every piece of mail, it would be difficult to determine the recipient. PAT translates the port numbers in order to help maintain some sanity in the network needs.

You need to consider a few things when allowing PAT on your firewall. First, the IP address (or the range) used for PAT cannot overlap with or be a part of another global address pool configured. It must also be different from the IP address of the outside interface. Second, PAT does not work correctly with a number of applications that require a particular port address. Some of these applications include H.323, many multimedia applications, and caching name servers. PAT does work with other common applications such as FTP, HTTP, SMTP, RPC, **telnet**, and **traceroute**.

Finally, in order for PAT to work efficiently, you need to have a reverse-DNS mapping for the PIX Firewall box. Many applications (particularly FTP servers) use reverse-DNS lookups to log who is doing what. Many times, systems become confused or concerned when a client suddenly uses a port mapping they do not consider normal. Without reverse-DNS entries, many applications will be slowed down, and you might have intermittent connectivity issues. FTP requests will consistently fail.

NOTE   For more information on Domain Name Services (DNS), including the maintenance of reverse DNS, see *DNS and BIND* from O'Reilly & Associates.

The same commands are used for PAT as for NAT, but Example 11-4 contains a mathematical inaccuracy on purpose.

Example 11-4 *A NAT Configuration for PAT*

```
Pixfirewall(config)#nat (inside) 2 10.1.2.64 255.255.255.192
Pixfirewall(config)#global (outside) 2 172.16.1.65
```

This tells the firewall that 62 devices on network 10.1.6.64 will share a single IP (172.16.1.65) for accessing the Internet.

Hosts are translated on a first-come, first-served basis. So, out of the global pool assigned to a group of inside workstations, they are not translated in numerical order. Furthermore, because it is possible to give a larger group of private workstations access to a smaller pool of global addresses, you might witness translation errors if a global IP is not available for use.

To overcome this pool depletion, there are translation timeout intervals. How long will an address keep a translation if no traffic activity is occurring?

You can change the IP translation timeout by issuing the following command:

> **timeout xlate** *hh:mm:ss*

hh is the hours, *mm* is the minutes, and *ss* is the seconds. A timeout is a period of inactivity from the host that is translated. After the timer expires, the translation is deleted, and that global IP is available for use by another station (see Example 11-5).

Example 11-5 *NAT Timeout Value*

```
Pixfirewall(config)#nat (inside) 3 10.1.2.128 255.255.255.128
Pixfirewall(config)#global (outside) 3 172.16.1.66-172.16.1.126
Pixfirewall(config)#timeout xlate 1:00:00
```

This example allows 128 private IP addresses to be translated into 61 public IP addresses. This example also shows that the translation timeout value has changed to expire in 1 hour.

The default translation timeout is 12 hours. The **timeout xlate** command is a global command on the PIX Firewall, so be sure not to set the value *too* small, or you will create extra work for the PIX Firewall if your workstations have intermittent access needs.

Global groups can also be assigned to be translated. Whether you are setting a pool for every user in your organization or just a pool for users outside the ranges already specified, you can use the 0.0.0.0 network designation to specify everyone. Network translations are matched on the most-specific values, just like routing tables. So even though 0.0.0.0 encompasses the other networks already specified, the more-specific entries will be activated. Example 11-6 shows a blanket NAT pool configuration.

Example 11-6 *A Blanket NAT Pool Configuration*

```
Pixfirewall(config)#nat (inside) 4 0.0.0.0 0.0.0.0
Pixfirewall(config)#global (outside) 4 172.16.1.127
```

This allows every other IP on the internal network that was not matched elsewhere to be translated via PAT through that one specific IP. Without a command like this in place, if you had inside private addresses outside the ranges you already specified that were trying to use the Internet, you would see error messages regarding no translation existing for the request being made.

Now it's time to look at the overall command list created and get a sense of the combination of commands and how they relate to the network (see Example 11-7).

Example 11-7 *Multiple NAT Configurations Within a PIX Firewall Configuration*

```
Pixfirewall(config)#nat (inside) 1 10.1.2.0 255.255.255.192
Pixfirewall(config)#global (outside) 1 172.16.1.3-172.16.1.64
Pixfirewall(config)#nat (inside) 2 10.1.2.64 255.255.255.192
Pixfirewall(config)#global (outside) 2 172.16.1.65
Pixfirewall(config)#nat (inside) 3 10.1.2.128 255.255.255.128
Pixfirewall(config)#global (outside) 3 172.16.1.66-172.16.1.126
Pixfirewall(config)#nat (inside) 4 0.0.0.0 0.0.0.0
Pixfirewall(config)#global (outside) 4 172.16.1.127
```

The following is a review of what was done with each pool number:

- **Pool 1**—Maps 62 device IPs to a pool of 62 global addresses (1:1 ratio)
- **Pool 2**—Maps 62 device IPs to a single IP address (PAT)
- **Pool 3**—Maps 128 device IPs to a pool of 61 global addresses (overlap translation)
- **Pool 4**—Maps every other device IP to a single IP address (PAT)

When a device on a higher-security network (the inside network, in this example) tries to access something on a lower-security network, one of the steps a PIX Firewall goes through is checking the translation table for an entry. If there is no current entry, the PIX Firewall goes through the various pools (or statics) that are configured. It processes the pools in order, so in the configuration shown in Example 11-7, the 0.0.0.0 should always be last since that includes every device.

NOTE The inside and outside names used in the examples are default names. These names are set up with the **nameif** command, as discussed in the earlier section "Configuring Multiple Interface Support." With regard to this statement, they are simply a global representation, indicating what the PIX Firewall should do with a particular interface.

show and Other Useful Commands

There are a number of useful commands as you configure and use the PIX Firewall. **show** will likely be the most useful command to see the current state of operation. **clear** will be the next-favorite command. The following are some of the most useful commands for dealing with NAT. They are covered from the inside network to the outside network:

- **show nat**—Shows all NAT pools currently assigned. You can limit by interface or by pool for details.
- **show xlate**—Shows the current translation table, both static and NAT-assigned IPs.
- **show conn**—Shows the current state of connections through the PIX Firewall as well as a maximum count reached since the last reload.

NOTE Connections are important for licensing a PIX Firewall. Only outbound connections count against the PIX Firewall, so if you have thousands of users internally, purchasing a PIX Firewall with only 128 simultaneous connections licensed is unwise. Inbound connections do not count against the count, so if you are an ISP with no internal clients, you can purchase a low-number license and be just fine.

- **clear xlate**—Clears the current translation table. This command should be executed any time you change the NAT pools after saving the configuration. A variety of parameters can be exercised in order to clear select groups or individual addresses from the local or global IP pools. This command entered by itself clears the entire translation table.
- **write memory**—Saves the configuration.

Configuring Outside to the DMZ: Using static and conduit

There are a couple of things to think about when configuring outside to the DMZ, including any addressing rules (address translation) and permissions. On the PIX Firewall, by default, a higher-security interface (inside) is permitted to send anything and everything to a lower-security interface (outside).

Also by default (and as discussed earlier in this chapter), address translations are set up from the inside and are handled on a first-come, first-served basis. With this rule in mind, a user on the Internet would have no reliable way to determine the IP address of a server he needed to access, and no default permissions to do so either.

To resolve the addressing/translation problems, first assume that you have some servers you would like the outside world to get to, such as an e-mail server and a Web server. Next, you will set up static addresses (meaning that the translation never changes) so that people will always know how to reach those servers.

The following is the syntax:

```
static [(internal_if_name, external_if_name)] global_ip local_ip
    [netmask network_mask][max_conns [em_limit]]] [norandomseq]
```

The command parameters and syntax have the following meanings:

Command Parameter	Description
internal_if_name	Specifies the internal interface name (from the **nameif** command) that is being configured. This should be the higher security level interface.
external_if_name	Specifies the external interface name (from the **nameif** command) that is being configured. This should be the lower security level interface.
global_ip	Specifies the global (outside) IP address to be translated. An IP address on the lower security level interface. Cannot be a PAT address.
local_ip	Specifies the local (inside) IP address to be translated. An IP address on the higher security level interface.
netmask *network_mask*	Specifies the IP network mask associated with both the *global_ip* and *local_ip* arguments.
max_conns	Specifies the maximum TCP connections permitted through the static.
em_limit	Sets the embryonic connection limit. The default is **0**, which means unlimited connections. Set this lower for slower systems and higher for faster systems.
norandomseq	Does not randomize the TCP packet's sequence number. Used when other firewalls inline with the PIX Firewall are randomizing sequence numbers.

Example 11-8 shows an example of creating a static address map.

Example 11-8 *An Example of Creating a Static Address Map*

```
Pixfirewall(config)#static (dmz,outside) 172.16.1.1 10.1.5.47
Pixfirewall(config)#static (dmz,outside) 172.16.1.2 10.1.5.172
```

When the addresses are set up and the rest of the world knows which IP address is designated as a particular server, those in the outside world need permission to get there. Remember that, by default, the outside world is not allowed to initiate any contact whatsoever.

The following is the syntax for setting up permissions with the **conduit** statement:

```
conduit {permit | deny} protocol global_ip global_mask [operator port [port]]
    foreign_ip foreign_mask [operator port [port]]
```

The command parameters and syntax have the following meanings:

Command Parameter	Description
permit	Permits access if the conditions are matched.
deny	Denies access if the conditions are matched.
protocol	Specifies the transport protocol for the connection. Possible literal values are **eigrp, gre, icmp, igmp, grp, ip, ipinip, nos, ospf, tcp, udp,** or an integer in the range 0 to 255 representing an IP protocol number. Use **ip** to specify all transport protocols. Valid protocol numbers are online at www.isi.edu/in-notes/iana/assignments/protocol-numbers.
global_ip	Specifies a globally accessible IP address (public) specified in a **static** command elsewhere. If you are referencing a single specific IP, you can precede the IP with the word **host** and avoid specifying a netmask.
global_mask	Specifies the IP netmask for the *global_ip* range.
operator	Specifies a comparison operand that lets you specify a port or a port range. Possible values are **eq, lt, any, gt, neq,** and **range**. Use the **no** operator and **port** to indicate all ports.
port	Specifies service(s) you permit to be used while accessing *global_ip*. Specify services by the port that handles it, such as **25** for SMTP, **80** for HTTP, and so on. **0** means any port. The port values are defined in RFC 1700. Permitted literal names are **dns, esp, ftp, h323, http, ident, nntp, ntp, pop2, pop3, pptp, rpc, smtp, snmp, snmptrap, sqlnet, tcp, telnet, tftp,** and **udp**. You can specify literals in port ranges, such as **ftp-h323**. You can also specify numbers.

continues

Command Parameter	Description
foreign_ip	Specifies an external IP address (host or network) that can access the *global_ip*. You can specify **0.0.0.0** or **0** for any host.
foreign_mask	Specifies the IP netmask clarifying the *foreign_ip* range.

Example 11-9 shows a **conduit** command to specify permissions from a lower-security interface to a higher-security interface.

Example 11-9 *A **conduit** Command to Specify SMTP Permissions*

```
Pixfirewall(config)#conduit permit tcp host 172.16.1.2 eq smtp any 0 0
```

This statement permits any TCP connection going to the e-mail server as long as it's directed to the SMTP port, originating from anyone using any port. Because the **conduit** statement allows both protocol specification and port specification, when designing a firewall, you can be as relaxed or as restrictive as necessary. If you had an FTP server running on the same machine as the e-mail system, you would need a separate conduit for permissions. Example 11-10 shows another example of a **conduit** command.

Example 11-10 *A Conduit Command to Grant FTP Permissions*

```
Pixfirewall(config)#conduit permit tcp host 172.16.1.2 eq
  ftp host 199.199.199.37 0 0
```

This statement permits TCP traffic going to the e-mail server's FTP port only from a specific host on the Internet, originating from any port. Remember that, although information to well-known ports is destined for specific ports, the source ports are usually a randomly picked number in the range above 1024. Keep this in mind while setting up a firewall so that you don't make up rules that will never be met.

Example 11-11 is another example of a **conduit** command.

Example 11-11 *A Conduit Command to Allow Web Access from Any Host*

```
Pixfirewall(config)#conduit permit tcp host 172.16.1.1 eq www any 0 0
```

This permits all standard HTTP traffic, originating from anybody, to go to the Web server.

NOTE   The **nat** and **global** commands are one-way translations to allow internal traffic to get out (return "conversation" traffic is allowed). Static translations are a two-way reference, and the **conduit** command allows permissions for lower-security interface members to access the higher-security devices set up with static translations.

Permitting Ping Access and Filtering ICMP

Another important piece of security to think about is ICMP messages. ICMP is a valuable tool for testing network connectivity and reachability issues. It is also a tool that allows hackers to probe your network to see which devices are live.

The **conduit** command can be used to permit or deny ICMP messages from lower-security interfaces to higher-security interfaces. Because private hosts (higher-security) can send anything and everything unchecked, it is wise to watch things on the way in.

There are a number of different types of ICMP messages, and the PIX Firewall **conduit** command allows the filtering of 18 of them. Logically, although your business needs might vary, you will want to deny any request ICMP types while permitting any message or reply ICMP types. This will allow your inside stations to receive the replies of any ICMP queries they send but prohibit unknown people from scanning your network with ICMP messages. Or, to make things simple, permit the ones you want and deny the rest.

Example 11-12 is an example of a group of **conduit** commands working toward the same goal. This example shows a method of combining different ICMP types to achieve part of a security policy.

Example 11-12 *An Example of a Group of **conduit** Commands Working Toward the Same Goal*

```
Pixfirewall(config)#conduit permit icmp any any echo-reply
Pixfirewall(config)#conduit permit icmp any any unreachable
Pixfirewall(config)#conduit permit icmp any any redirect
Pixfirewall(config)#conduit permit icmp any any time-exceeded
Pixfirewall(config)#conduit deny icmp any any
```

Table 11-1 shows the different types of ICMP packets that the PIX Firewall allows filtering on. Remember that any packets are allowed from a higher-security interface (inside) going to a lower-security interface (outside), so at this point, you're only concerned with packets coming back in.

Table 11-1 *ICMP Type Codes Allowed in PIX Firewall **conduit** Commands*

ICMP Type Code	Literal ICMP Name
0	echo-reply
3	unreachable
4	source-quench
5	redirect
6	alternate-address
8	echo
9	router-advertisement
10	router-solicitation

continues

Table 11-1 *ICMP Type Codes Allowed in PIX Firewall* **conduit** *Commands (Continued)*

ICMP Type Code	Literal ICMP Name
11	time-exceeded
12	parameter-problem
13	timestamp-reply
14	timestamp-request
15	information-request
16	information-reply
17	network mask-request
18	network mask-reply
31	conversion-error
32	mobile-redirect

NOTE   As with any particulars of a command, be sure to check the release notes of the software version being used on the PIX Firewall. Options can change as new features become available.

Another thing to remember when building huge **conduit** lists is that the **conduit** commands are processed in order of appearance in the configuration. When removing or adding **conduit** command statements, you can greatly alter the logic (and functionality) of your PIX Firewall if you are not careful with placement. Also, the PIX Firewall supports up to 8000 separate **conduit** statements within a configuration. Hopefully, your business needs are not more complicated than that.

Configuring Syslog Output

Now that you have set up some interfaces, translated addresses, and set up **conduit**s for permissions, you will likely want to enable logging to watch for potential hacks or problems with the PIX Firewall itself. Another reason to log messages is to check the configuration to make sure it is working as it was intended to. For example, if you set up a new mail server for one department within your company and you set up all the necessary translations, but you are receiving complaints that nobody can reach the new mail server, you can examine the logs to see that a myriad of hosts are being denied access to your new mail servers' SMTP port.

By reviewing the configuration with the logs in hand, you can quickly determine that the cause of the problem was a mistyped IP address within the **conduit** statement. Or perhaps it was because you added a **conduit** statement without paying attention to the statements already in place, so your new **permit** statement occurred after a large **deny** statement.

Setting up logging on a PIX Firewall is a simple process. The first thing to make sure of is that there is a functioning syslog server someplace on the network and that you know which interface of the PIX Firewall the syslog server resides on. All UNIX boxes are capable of being (and are by default) a syslog server. In addition, Cisco Connection Online (CCO) offers a free PIX Firewall Syslog Server (PFSS) for Microsoft Windows NT machines.

To turn on logging to a syslog server, you need to tell the PIX Firewall where to send things. To configure initial logging, use the following syntax:

```
logging host interface ipaddress [protocol/port]
```

The command parameters and syntax have the following meanings:

Command Parameter	Description
interface	Specifies the name of the PIX Firewall interface as configured with the **nameif** command
ipaddress	Specifies the IP address of the syslog server
protocol	The protocol over which the syslog message is sent—either **tcp** or **udp**
port	The port from which the PIX Firewall sends either TCP or UDP syslog messages (514 is the default)

There are other features to make your logs say what you need them to say.

To change how many messages are buffered in memory until they are sent to a syslog server, use the following syntax:

```
logging queue messages
```

The command parameter has the following meaning:

Command Parameter	Description
messages	Specifies the number of messages that are buffered before being transmitted over the network. The default is 512 messages. 0 indicates unlimited messages.

You use the **no** form of this command to prevent log entries from being sent to the console port of the PIX Firewall.

To adjust the highest level of messages to be logged (see Table 11-2), use the following:

```
logging trap level
```

Table 11-2 *Syslog Message Levels*

Severity Level	Type of Message	Description
1	Alert messages	Hardware errors, failover errors, interface errors
2	Critical messages	Denied/attempted connections
3	Error messages	Exceeded connections, no free pool IPs for net, and so on
4	Warning messages	IPSec errors, PPP errors, and so on
5	Notification messages	Authentication sessions ended, URL/Java/ActiveX denied
6	Informational messages	Authentication denied, TCP denied, security association setup (IPSec, PPP)
7	Debugging messages	URL lookups, deny inbound (no xlate)

To log messages to a buffer that can be viewed by **show logging**, use the following:

```
logging buffered level
```

To adjust the queue size for buffered logging, use the following:

```
logging queue messages
```

To make sure your logs reflect the exact times things are occurring, use the following:

```
clock set hh:mm:ss month day year
logging timestamp
```

NOTE   By default, syslog messages are sent as UDP packets with a port number of 514. With the Cisco PFSS program, you can also use TCP to send syslog messages. This gives you higher reliability that your messages are being logged, but it also creates other complications. For example, suppose you're using TCP for syslog messaging to a PFSS server and the NT box runs out of disk space. After you run out of disk space, the PIX Firewall stops allowing new connections because it is unable to log information. This is a defensive response! The reason for this functionality is to prevent your system from being compromised in the middle of the night. If a good hacker can fill up the disk space of a syslog server and then launch an attack, there will be no hard record of the occurrence. Although this is a good response to have, it is something that every administrator should be aware of prior to enabling TCP message transfer.

Now let's look at some sample syslog messages. CCO and your documentation CD contain a full list of all syslog messages and their meanings so that you can spend some time going through your logs and characterizing the information.

In reviewing the syslog file (a plaintext file stored by day on the syslog server), you will find many different messages about events happening on the network. Here are a few examples. Example 11-13 shows someone attempting to access a port that was not configured by a **conduit** to allow access.

Example 11-13 *A Denied TCP Access Attempt*

```
<162>May 07 2000 08:16:44: %PIX-2-106001: Inbound TCP connection denied from
202.105.111.13/1160 to 208.158.37.5/8080 flags SYN
```

The message in Example 11-14 says that someone attempted to access a Web server at that address. (Perhaps a mistake in the **conduit** command prevented access to a Web server that should have been accessed.)

Example 11-14 *A Denied Attempt at Web Server Access*

```
<162>May 07 2000 12:35:27: %PIX-2-106001: Inbound TCP connection denied from
209.86.158.174/1108 to 208.158.37.28/80 flags SYN
```

The message in Example 11-15 shows that someone attempted an Internet Relay Chat (IRC) connection to a machine that has no conduit (permission) to allow that kind of connection. This probably means that no IRC server is running on the home network.

Example 11-15 *A Message Showing a Denied Connection to the Common IRC Port*

```
<162>May 07 2000 12:36:59: %PIX-2-106001: Inbound TCP connection denied from
24.49.167.76/39401 to 208.158.37.10/6667 flags SYN
```

The message in Example 11-16 indicates that someone attempted to find a Remote Procedure Call (RPC) server and then potentially exploit an older system (if indeed there was such a system).

Example 11-16 *A Message Saying That Someone Attempted to Find an RPC Server*

```
<162>May 07 2000 21:24:04: %PIX-2-106001: Inbound TCP connection denied from
211.34.149.1/1633 to 208.158.37.10/111 flags SYN
```

Example 11-17 indicates that someone scanned the network with a series of NetBIOS commands from his computer. Because a firewall was set up, the administrator was able to verify that this kind of connectivity was not allowed and found a methodical scan for potential machines to exploit.

Example 11-17 *Syslog Messages Indicating a Series of NetBIOS Commands*

```
<162>May 07 2000 21:36:40: %PIX-2-106001: Inbound TCP connection
  denied from 216.77.240.61/2402 to 208.158.37.10/139 flags SYN
<162>May 07 2000 21:36:40: %PIX-2-106001: Inbound TCP connection
  denied from 216.77.240.61/2402 to 208.158.37.10/139 flags SYN
<162>May 07 2000 21:36:40: %PIX-2-106001: Inbound TCP connection
  denied from 216.77.240.61/2404 to 208.158.37.12/139 flags SYN
<162>May 07 2000 21:36:40: %PIX-2-106001: Inbound TCP connection
  denied from 216.77.240.61/2405 to 208.158.37.13/139 flags SYN
<162>May 07 2000 21:36:40: %PIX-2-106001: Inbound TCP connection
  denied from 216.77.240.61/2406 to 208.158.37.14/139 flags SYN
<162>May 07 2000 21:36:40: %PIX-2-106001: Inbound TCP connection
  denied from 216.77.240.61/2412 to 208.158.37.20/139 flags SYN
<162>May 07 2000 21:36:40: %PIX-2-106001: Inbound TCP connection
denied from 216.77.240.61/2413 to 208.158.37.21/139 flags SYN
<162>May 07 2000 21:36:40: %PIX-2-106001: Inbound TCP connection
denied from 216.77.240.61/2423 to 208.158.37.31/139 flags SYN
<162>May 07 2000 21:36:40: %PIX-2-106001: Inbound TCP connection
denied from 216.77.240.61/2424 to 208.158.37.32/139 flags SYN
```

Ports 137, 138, and 139 are used by Microsoft systems for NetBIOS connectivity. You will probably want to restrict this kind of connectivity from the Internet into your private network. If you do need to allow this type of connectivity, make sure that your NT/Windows systems are secure in and of themselves.

There are also firewalls designed for particular machines to assist in this type of scenario. If Internet-based access to Windows NT services is necessary, if the administration for the network firewall and the individual NT system is performed by separate entities, or if you have another reason, as long as someone is thinking of security and verifying that systems are secure, the goal is being met. BlackIce Defender and BlackIce Pro are very good per-system firewalls. More information can be found at www.networkice.com.

Logs are also necessary when someone hacks into the network (if a hole in the conduit permissions and/or a hole in an old revision of software on a machine was accidentally left). Being able to demonstrate a pattern of a scan, and then a hack to a system, is very important if law enforcement needs to become involved. Different countries have different laws regarding these actions, so check with your local law enforcement if this is an area that concerns you in implementing a firewall solution.

NOTE A network firewall is not always the *only* or last step in making sure your network is secure. As you've seen throughout this book, different security solutions can be put together in any way you need. Your network might need many pieces, or it might not.

Whatever your business needs, make sure you address all appropriate areas for security. Implementing a firewall is not the end of the line. The traffic you allow through can be exploited as well. For instance, if you have some older UNIX machines running DNS services, you allow DNS requests and traffic through your firewall in order to implement this. Let's say some exploits of older DNS/BIND systems allowed a hacker to gain access to your system. Because you allowed the traffic to come through your firewall, the PIX Firewall system would think everything was fine at that point, even though it wasn't. Keep up-to-date on the systems you are running and make sure you are aware of the current exploits and patches. Check out www.cert.org or www.sans.org for ongoing lists.

Configuring User Authentication

Oftentimes, besides setting up specific conduits and static address mappings to configure a security policy, you will want to have further authentication or authorization throughout your network.

In order to help centrally manage a user pool and the associated rights of those users, there are applications to allow a global configuration to serve multiple devices. This saves any administrator from making changes on every device when necessary.

Configuring the PIX Firewall AAA Server

As discussed in Part II, "Dialup Security," the authentication, authorization, and accounting (AAA) server provides three basic services:

- **Authentication**—For basic access rights where sessions are controlled in terms of who's allowed or who's not allowed.

- **Authorization**—For more extended service-related functions where some users might be able to use the Web and others might not.

- **Accounting**—To bill for services, or simply monitor services, you can enable accounting for certain services. When AAA accounting is turned on, the PIX Firewall reports user activity to the appropriate TACACS+ or RADIUS server in the form of database accounting records.

Back on the TACACS+ or RADIUS server, the data can be analyzed or compiled for network management, billing, or auditing purposes.

The first step in this security method is to let the PIX Firewall know where to reach a AAA server and how to talk with it.

The following is the command syntax for beginning a AAA configuration:

```
aaa-server group_tag (if_name) host server_ip key timeout seconds
aaa-server group_tag protocol auth_protocol
```

The command parameters and syntax have the following meanings:

Command Parameter	Description
group_tag	Specifies a name to represent the group of authentication partners
if_name	Specifies the name of the PIX Firewall interface that can reach the AAA server (from the **nameif** command)
host *server_ip*	Designates the IP address of the AAA server
key	Specifies the password shared with the AAA server
timeout *seconds*	Specifies the timeout value for the PIX Firewall awaiting a response from the AAA server before trying to contact the next AAA server in a list (if others are configured)
protocol *auth_protocol*	Specifies the security protocol as **radius** or **tacacs+**

The *group_tag* argument is important in more complicated configurations where you might want to authenticate different services or source addresses through different types of services (RADIUS, TACACS+, and so on). You can have a maximum of 16 *group_tags,* each consisting of 16 AAA servers. That gives you 256 total usable AAA servers, which should be far more than you'll ever need. The **aaa server-group** command replaced the **aaa-tacacs** and **aaa-radius** commands in PIX Firewall version 4.4(1).

Before you begin the configuration of AAA services, there are a few pieces of information you need to know:

- The IP address of the AAA server (for example, 10.1.1.4).
- The AAA protocol that will be used. In these examples, we are using CiscoSecure ACS on the server, so the choice will be the TACACS+ protocol.
- The shared key or password to talk to the AAA server, which will be cisco.

Figure 11-3 shows a placement relationship of the AAA server to the PIX Firewall.

The commands to be used on the PIX Firewall are shown in Example 11-18.

Example 11-18 *Configuration to Start AAA Service Configuration*

```
Pixfirewall(config)#aaa-server main protocol tacacs+
Pixfirewall(config)#aaa-server main (inside) host 10.1.1.4 cisco timeout 20
```

Figure 11-3 *The PIX Firewall Depicted in a Network Adding AAA Security Services*

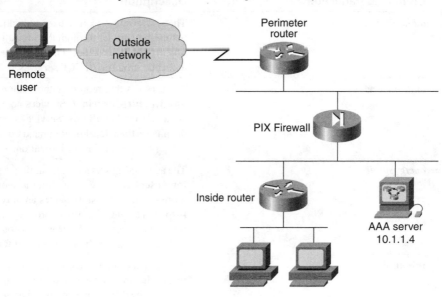

AAA Examples

Now that the PIX Firewall is aware of the AAA server on the network, the specific AAA security policy can be specified. The commands used to configure AAA services are as follows:

```
aaa authentication {include | exclude} authen_service
  {inbound | outbound | if_name} local_ip local_mask
  foreign_ip foreign_mask group_tag
aaa authorization {include | exclude} author_service
  {inbound | outbound | if_name} local_ip local_mask
  foreign_ip foreign_mask
aaa accounting {include | exclude} acctg_service
  {inbound | outbound | if_name} local_ip local_mask
  foreign_ip foreign_mask group_tag
```

The command parameters and syntax have the following meanings:

Command Parameter	Description
include	Creates a new rule to include the specified service.
exclude	Creates an exception to a previously stated rule by excluding the specified service from authentication to the specified host. Allows you to specify an excluded port to a specific host or hosts.

continues

Command Parameter	Description
authen_service	The services that require user authentication before they are let through the firewall. Use **any**, **ftp**, **http**, or **telnet**. The **any** value enables authentication for all TCP services.
author_service	The services that require authorization. Use **any**, **ftp**, **http**, or **telnet**. Services not specified are authorized implicitly. Services specified in the **aaa authentication** command do not affect the services requiring authorization.
acctg_service	The accounting service. Accounting is provided for all services, or you can limit it to one or more services. Possible values are **any**, **ftp**, **http**, and **telnet**. Use **any** to provide accounting for all TCP services. To provide accounting for UDP services, use the protocol/port form.
inbound	Authenticates inbound connections. Inbound means that the connection originates on a lower security level interface and is being directed to a higher security level interface.
outbound	Authenticates outbound connections. Outbound means that the connection originates on a higher security level interface and is being directed to a lower security level interface.
if_name	The interface name from which users require authentication. Use *if_name* in combination with the *local_ip* address and the *foreign_ip* address to determine from where access is sought. The *local_ip* address is always on the interface with the highest security level, and *foreign_ip* is always on the lowest.
local_ip	The IP address of the host or network of hosts that you want to be authenticated. You can set this address to **0** to mean all hosts and to let the authentication server decide which hosts are authenticated.
local_mask	The network mask of *local_ip*. Always specify a specific mask value. Use **0** if the IP address is **0**. Use **255.255.255.255** for a host.
foreign_ip	The IP address of the hosts you want to access the *local_ip* address. Use **0** to mean all hosts.

Command Parameter	Description
foreign_mask	The network mask of *foreign_ip*. Always specify a specific mask value. Use **0** if the IP address is **0**. Use **255.255.255.255** for a host.
group_tag	The group tag set with the **aaa-server** command.

As in most PIX Firewall commands, 0 is a shortcut for 0.0.0.0 in IP addresses and netmasks. Some examples of AAA authentication command configuration on a PIX Firewall follow. Example 11-19 shows an example of getting authorization for any outbound Telnet session to any destination from the AAA server named main.

Example 11-19 *Authorization for an Outbound Telnet Session to a Destination from the AAA Server main*

```
Pixfirewall(config)#aaa authorization telnet outbound 0 0 0 0 main
```

Example 11-20 is an example of obtaining authorization for all sessions that can be tracked and monitored to any destination from the AAA server named main.

Example 11-20 *An Example That Authorizes All Outbound Sessions*

```
Pixfirewall(config)#aaa authorization any outbound 0 0 0 0 main
```

Example 11-21 obtains the necessary authentication information to log on to the console port of a PIX firewall from the AAA server called main.

Example 11-21 *An Example That Uses AAA Services to Authenticate Any Console Access to the PIX Firewall*

```
Pixfirewall(config)#aaa authentication any serial console main
```

All three of these AAA examples can also be used to control outbound Internet access from people and devices within the network. You can use this to track who uses what or to allow certain people to use certain services.

AAA services allow for a high degree of granularity in the security policy that can be implemented for a large network. The possibilities are vast and should be handled with care. Overauthorization or overauthentication makes more work for the PIX Firewall, the AAA server, the network, and the users. A balance must be achieved.

PIX Firewall Authentication Example

As stated earlier, the type of AAA service (in this case, authentication) is selected with the appropriate command-line criteria. Example 11-22 is another example of the authentication configuration.

Example 11-22 *An Example That Authenticates Any Inbound Session Through the PIX Firewall*

```
Pixfirewall(config)#aaa authentication any inbound 0 0 0 0 main
```

This command authenticates any inbound flow to any server from any host. It authenticates through the TACACS+ server main. The process works like this:

1 On inbound traffic, after the conduit test is passed, if authentication is required, the PIX Firewall sends a username prompt back to the station initiating traffic. When the PIX Firewall receives a reply, it opens a session with the configured server and passes along the information.

2 The AAA server looks up the supplied username and determines the type of authentication it needs, such as token card, CiscoSecure password, or generic password. After this information is given to the PIX Firewall, the PIX Firewall requests the appropriate password type from the initiating user.

3 The returned password is sent back to the AAA server for verification. A yes or no answer is given to the PIX Firewall at this point; the requested session is either allowed or denied. Other than supplying the username and password, all other functions are transparent to the end user.

PIX Firewall Authorization Example

As stated earlier, the type of AAA service (in this case, authorization) is selected with the appropriate command-line criteria. Example 11-23 is an example of AAA authorization command configuration on a PIX Firewall.

Example 11-23 *An Example That Authorizes Any Inbound FTP Sessions Through the PIX Firewall*

```
SecurePIX(config)#aaa authorization ftp inbound 0 0 0 0 main
```

This command checks authorization for any inbound FTP flow to any server from any host. It authorizes off the TACACS+ server main.

After authentication is complete, if the service being requested requires authorization, the PIX Firewall sends the operation information back to the AAA server. The AAA server looks in the user profile and verifies whether the requested operation is allowed. If it is allowed, the requested service session is established transparently to the user.

A sample user profile on the CiscoSecure ACS server might look as shown in Example 11-24.

Example 11-24 *A Sample User Profile on the CiscoSecure ACS Server*

```
{
Profile_cycle = 11
Profile_id = 8
Password = clear "cisco"
Set Server current failed_login = 0
Service = Shell {
Cmd = ftp {
Permit 10.1.1.6
}
}
}
```

PIX Firewall Accounting Example

As stated earlier, the type of AAA service (in this case, accounting) is selected with the appropriate command-line criteria. Example 11-25 is an example of the AAA accounting command configuration on a PIX Firewall.

Example 11-25 *A AAA Accounting Command Configuration on a PIX Firewall*

```
Pixfirewall(config)#aaa accounting any inbound 0 0 0 0 main
```

This command turns on statistical accounting (for example, username, service, time, time stamp) for all inbound connections. It sends the appropriate information to the TACACS+ server main, where statistics can be compiled and reports generated.

Summary

This section summarizes the main points of this chapter, as follows:

- Configuring multiple interfaces enhances the design of secure networks.
- You secure the network from the "outside world" using a DMZ and multiple interfaces.
- You configure the PIX Firewall from the inside interface to the DMZ using **global** and **nat** commands, including multiple advanced methods.
- You configure the PIX Firewall from the outside interface to the DMZ using **static** and **conduit** statements to build the security policies on the PIX Firewall.
- You configure the PIX Firewall to allow ping access and to filter multiple varieties of ICMP messages.
- You configure syslog output to monitor the ongoing performance and status of the PIX Firewall.
- You configure user authentication, authorization, and accounting services through a AAA server for additional security controls.

Case Study: Configuring Multiple Interfaces and AAA on the PIX Firewall

This case study illustrates how to configure multiple interfaces and AAA on the PIX Firewall in the hypothetical XYZ Company. Read the case study scenario, examine the topology diagram, read the security policy, and then analyze the configuration examples to see how the security policy statements are enacted for the PIX Firewall.

Case Study Scenario

The XYZ Company needs to set up a PIX Firewall for its main campus building. Within this building, XYZ sublets office space to extranet partners and also provides Internet connectivity as an added benefit for its partners. XYZ uses two Internet service providers for redundancy. XYZ wants to use a PIX Firewall with multiple interfaces to secure the network connections to each network segment and to the public Internet.

Topology

Figure 11-4 illustrates the basic design of the XYZ network that will be configured in this case study.

Figure 11-4 *The Network Design of the XYZ Company's Office Network*

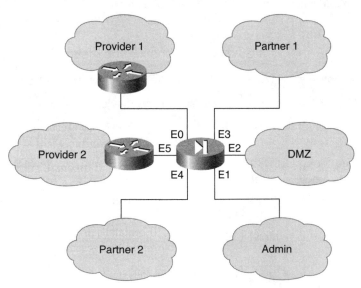

Network Design and Security Policy

The network design and security policy specifics that XYZ Company wants to implement are as follows:

- IP address allocation:
  - Admin LAN: 10.1.1.0/24
  - Client 1 LAN: 10.2.1.0/24
  - Client 2 LAN: 10.3.1.0/24
  - DMZ LAN: 192.168.11.0/24
  - Provider 1 WAN: 192.168.1.0/24
  - Provider 2 WAN: 192.168.2.0/24

- Network Address Translation:
  - One of the management Class Cs uses PAT through 192.168.1.127.
  - One of the management Class Cs shares a range of global IP addresses from 192.168.1.10 through 192.168.1.126.
  - Client 1 uses global addresses from 192.168.1.128 through 192.168.1.254.
  - Client 2 uses global addresses from 192.168.2.128 through 192.168.2.254.
  - All remaining (or additional) management and client internal IPs will share all remaining global addresses for pool translation.
  - Internal clients are connected with full-duplex 100BaseTX Ethernet connections.
  - Internet providers are connected with half-duplex 10BaseT Ethernet connections.

- Some addresses on the DMZ will be statically mapped.

- Limit ICMP access from the outside world but permit replies from internally generated traffic.

- Enable syslog services and configure options:
  - Enable the perimeter router to send syslog to 10.1.1.5 on the admin LAN.
  - Establish the syslog service to 10.1.1.5.
  - Syslog messages should include information about sessions being denied.
  - The syslog buffer size should be 1 KB of information.

- Set up a AAA server at 10.1.1.4 on the admin LAN.

- Set up AAA for authentication and accounting of access to a private Web site.

Sample Configuration for the XYZ Company PIX Firewall

Examine Example 11-26, which is a configuration example for the PIX Firewall of the XYZ Company. This example implements the security design and policy considerations as outlined in the case study. One possible configuration for that policy might look like Example 11-26. You might choose to configure the PIX Firewall differently to enact the same design and policy requirements. Note that the sample configuration contains comments showing which commands affect which particular design or policy statements.

Example 11-26 *A Sample Full PIX Firewall Configuration for the XYZ Company*

```
pix1#write terminal
Building configuration...
: Saved
:
PIX Version 5.1(2)
! nameif commands to delineate the interface configurations and security levels.
! Remember that equal weight interfaces aren't allowed to talk to each other.
nameif ethernet0 provider1 security0
nameif ethernet1 admin security100
nameif ethernet2 dmz security60
nameif ethernet3 client1 security50
nameif ethernet4 client2 security50
nameif ethernet5 provider2 security10
enable password AOywFtG5fs3ljpjx encrypted
passwd FSbblTfmfXKC.viH encrypted
hostname pix1
fixup protocol ftp 21
fixup protocol http 80
fixup protocol smtp 25
fixup protocol h323 1720
fixup protocol rsh 514
fixup protocol sqlnet 1521
names
pager lines 24
! Sets up the logging information to a syslog server
logging timestamp
no logging standby
no logging console
no logging monitor
logging buffered errors
logging trap informational
logging facility 20
logging queue 1024
logging host admin 10.1.1.5
! Additional information configuring the Ethernet interfaces
interface ethernet0 10baset
interface ethernet1 100full
interface ethernet2 100full
interface ethernet3 100full
interface ethernet4 100full
interface ethernet5 10baset
mtu provider1 1500
```

Example 11-26 *A Sample Full PIX Firewall Configuration for the XYZ Company (Continued)*

```
mtu admin 1500
mtu client1 1500
mtu client2 1500
mtu dmz 1500
mtu provider2 1500
! Additional information configuring the Ethernet interfaces
ip address admin 10.1.1.1 255.255.254.0
ip address client1 10.2.1.1 255.255.0.0
ip address client2 10.3.1.1 255.255.0.0
ip address dmz 192.168.11.1 255.255.255.0
ip address provider1 192.168.1.1 255.255.255.252
ip address provider2 192.168.2.1 255.255.255.252
! Note: provider addresses are typically assigned by the provider
! and not necessarily a part of the IP address range used for globals.
no failover
failover timeout 0:00:00
failover ip address outside 0.0.0.0
failover ip address inside 0.0.0.0
arp timeout 14400
!  Configuration information for Client NAT pools
nat (admin) 1 10.1.1.0 255.255.255.0
nat (admin) 2 10.1.4.0 255.255.255.0
nat (client1) 3 10.2.1.0 255.255.255.0
nat (client2) 4 10.3.1.0 255.255.255.0
nat (admin) 5 0.0.0.0 0.0.0.0
nat (client1) 5 0 0      !(which is the same as 0.0.0.0)
nat (client2) 5 0 0
global (provider1) 1 192.168.1.10-192.168.1.126
global (provider1) 2 192.168.1.127
global (provider1) 3 192.168.1.128-192.168.1.253
global (provider2) 4 192.168.2.128-192.168.2.254
global (provider1) 5 192.168.1.254
!  Static NAT configuration and conduits
static (dmz,provider1) 192.168.1.10 10.1.1.4 netmask 255.255.255.255 0 0
static (dmz,provider1) 192.168.1.13 10.1.1.5 netmask 255.255.255.255 0 0
static (dmz,provider1) 192.168.1.11 192.168.11.3 netmask 255.255.255.255 0 0
static (dmz,provider1) 192.168.1.12 192.168.11.4 netmask 255.255.255.255 0 0
conduit permit tcp host 192.168.1.12 eq smtp any 0 0
conduit permit tcp host 192.168.1.11 eq www any 0 0
conduit permit tcp host 192.168.1.11 eq ftp any 0 0
conduit permit tcp host 192.168.2.11 eq ftp any 0 0
conduit permit tcp host 192.168.1.13 eq syslog any 0 0
!  Conduit permissions for ICMP filtering
conduit permit icmp any any echo-reply
conduit permit icmp any any unreachable
conduit permit icmp any any redirect
conduit permit icmp any any time-exceeded
conduit deny icmp any any
rip provider1 passive
no rip provider1 default
no rip admin passive
no rip admin default
```

continues

Example 11-26 *A Sample Full PIX Firewall Configuration for the XYZ Company (Continued)*

```
no rip client1 passive
no rip client1 default
no rip client2 passive
no rip client2 default
no rip dmz passive
no rip dmz default
no rip provider2 passive
no rip provider2 default
timeout xlate 24:00:00 conn 12:00:00 half-closed 0:10:00 udp 0:02:00
timeout rpc 0:10:00 h323 0:05:00
timeout uauth 0:05:00 absolute
!Configuration of client authentication
aaa-server TACACS+ protocol tacacs+
aaa-server RADIUS protocol radius
aaa-server admin protocol tacacs+
aaa-server admin (admin) host 10.1.1.4 AdminKey timeout 30
aaa authentication http inbound host 0 0 0
aaa accounting http inbound 0 0 0 0 admin
snmp-server location Lexington, KY
snmp-server contact Scott Morris
snmp-server community emanon
snmp-server enable traps
telnet 10.1.1.4 255.255.255.0 admin
telnet timeout 5
terminal width 80
Cryptochecksum:dc2a867907ccf77cb25d142d34fb3449
: end
```

Review Questions

Answer the following review questions, which delve into some of the key facts and concepts covered in this chapter:

1 What are two advantages of using multiple perimeter interfaces?

2 What command replaced the **aaa-tacacs** and **aaa-radius** commands?

3 How many group tags does the PIX Firewall software allow, and how many servers are allowed in each AAA group?

4 When adding, changing, or removing a global statement, what is the next command to enter after saving the configuration?

5 How many **conduit** statements can the PIX Firewall support?

6 What protocol and port number are syslog messages sent to in a default configuration?

7 How many different types of ICMP packets does the PIX Firewall allow filtering on?

8 Where are log messages sent by default?

9   How many different security levels are there to be assigned to interfaces?

10 When users outside on the Internet initiate a "ping scan" of a network, what type of
    packet is seen (and perhaps denied) coming in through the PIX Firewall?

References

The topics considered in this chapter are complex and should be studied further to more
fully understand them and put them to use. Refer to the *PIX Firewall Release 5.11
Configuration Guide*, in the chapter "IP Security and Encryption Overview," for an
overview of how NAT and related protocols are supported on PIX Firewalls.

General PIX Firewall Information Online

The CiscoSecure PIX Firewall Series Support page has a variety of support links, including
sample configurations. Located at www.cisco.com/cgi-bin/Support/PSP/
psp_view.pl?Product_Name=PIX.

The CiscoSecure PIX Firewall Software Information page also can be found on the
documentation CD, but the most up-to-date information is on the Web site. Located at
www.cisco.com/univercd/cc/td/doc/product/iaabu/pix/index.htm.

AAA Information Online

The general AAA information page at www.cisco.com/univercd/cc/td/doc/product/
software/ios120/12supdoc/dsqcg3/qcsecur.htm has specifics pertaining to access servers,
but its discussion of the relationships in and concepts of using AAA apply equally well to
a firewall.

General Security Online

The Computer Emergency Response Team (www.cert.org) offers useful information on
viruses, worms, DoS attacks, and other security concerns.

SANS (www.sans.org) is another security-oriented group. This site also contains references
to known bugs in software and operating systems as well as a plethora of vendor links.

www.cisco.com/kobayashi/sw-center/internet/netsonar.shtml is part of the Software Center
on Cisco's Web site, where you can download an evaluation copy of CiscoSecure Scanner
(formerly NetSonar), a program to test your network vulnerabilities.

www.networkice.com is the home of the BlackIce Defender and BlackIce Pro software for
the Windows and Windows NT systems' firewall software.

PIX Firewall Software Information Online

www.cisco.com/cgi-bin/tablebuild.pl/pix contains the software updates for the PIX Firewall itself as well as other utilities such as the PIX Firewall Syslog Server (PFSS) for Windows NT. Note that CCO access is required for access to downloads.

Upon completing this chapter, you will be able to do the following:

- Configure PIX Firewall advanced features to protect an enterprise network from Internet access

- Configure a PIX Firewall to protect a network even where Network Address Translation is not needed

- Configure additional options to further manage PIX Firewall installations

- Test and verify correct PIX Firewall operation

CHAPTER 12

Configuring Advanced PIX Firewall Features

This chapter covers Cisco's advanced PIX Firewall features and configuration information, including some additional options for NAT, building on what was learned in Chapter 11, "Configuring Multiple Interfaces and AAA on the PIX Firewall." This chapter also discusses methods to control outbound access, which builds on the inbound access controls learned in Chapter 11. This chapter describes the PIX Firewall features for specialized traffic blocking, handling of syslog messages, and special e-mail handling. This chapter also covers how a PIX Firewall can use failover to another connected PIX Firewall and how PIX Firewalls operate in a virtual private network (VPN). Furthermore, this chapter covers CiscoSecure Policy Manager (CSPM), which replaces the PIX Firewall Manager.

Advanced Network Address Translation: NAT 0

The basic theories of network address translation (NAT) were discussed in earlier chapters. You have learned about using the **nat** command to look at the local IPs and the **global** command to specify the outside address pool for translation. Now we will look at some advanced features with these commands. First, we will review the commands themselves and add to the options. As a review, here is the basic syntax for **nat**:

```
nat [(if_name)] nat_id local_ip [netmask [max_conns [em_limit]]] [norandomseq]
```

The command parameters and syntax have the following meanings:

Command Parameter	Description
if_name	Provides the name of the interface where the devices reside.
nat_id	Acts as a reference number for the pool.
local_ip	Specifies an IP number or network IP number to be translated.
netmask	Shows the netmask associated with the *local_ip* network.
max_conns	Specifies the maximum number of TCP connections from the interface specified.
em_limit	Limits the number of embryonic (half-open) connections. Embryonic connections are connections in which the three-way TCP handshake has started but has not completed. They represent a popular place for DoS attacks.

continues

Command Parameter	Description
nonrandomseq	Forces a change in TCP handling. By default, the PIX Firewall randomizes the TCP sequence numbers. If another firewall is inline, this can cause problems for connections due to mismatched sequence numbers that TCP connections rely on to establish validity and detect missed packets. **nonrandomseq** turns off this feature. Technically, by not randomizing, you are opening up a security hole, so be aware of the application before using this option.

Some other options included for further tweaking were discussed in Chapter 11. In addition to that, there is a reserved NAT_ID (pool) as well.

NAT 0 is a reserved ID to specify addresses that are not to be translated. You might use NAT 0 when acquiring a company, for example. Say you come across a company that "owns" its own public IP range and also uses those IP addresses as local device IP addresses. If you wanted to place these IP addresses behind a firewall, the command structure might look like Example 12-1. No global command would be associated with this command.

Example 12-1 *NAT 0 Configuration*

```
Pixfirewall(config)#nat (inside) 0 200.200.200.0 255.255.255.0 0 0
Pixfirewall(config)#^Z
Pixfirewall#
```

Example 12-1 allows internal addresses 200.200.200.0/24 (a Class C address space) to be the same as inside and outside addresses. Table 12-1 shows that the internal and external addresses match. The PIX Firewall is translating addresses into themselves, or essentially is not translating those addresses.

Table 12-1 *Sample NAT Xlate Table Using NAT 0*

Inside Address	Outside Address
200.200.200.1	200.200.200.1
200.200.200.2	200.200.200.2
200.200.200.53	200.200.200.53

Notice in Table 12-1 that there is a large gap—not all of the 254 available IP addresses are reflected. Translations are added to the table when there is activity either inbound or outbound. Without any activity present, no entry is built.

Another option you have is to use NAT 0 between particular interfaces. For instance, say you have one interface with 10.1.1.0/24 (inside) and another interface with 10.2.2.0/24 (inside2). In order to establish access between these two inside networks without utilizing global addresses, you might want to use NAT 0. NAT 0's pass-through translation can coexist with other pools of addresses that are being translated, as shown in Example 12-2.

Example 12-2 *An Example of Coexisting Pass-Through Translation and Regular NAT Pools*

```
Pixfirewall(config)#access-list nonat permit ip 10.1.1.0 255.255.255.0
  10.2.2.0 255.255.255.0
Pixfirewall(config)#nat (inside) 0 access-list nonat
Pixfirewall(config)#nat (inside) 1 10.1.1.0 255.255.255.0 0 0
Pixfirewall(config)#global (outside) 1 172.16.22.1-172.16.22.254
Pixfirewall(config)#^Z
Pixfirewall#
```

Controlling Outbound Access

Earlier in this book, you learned about setting up NAT and static translations. You also set up conduit statements for inbound permission control. Now we will discuss outbound access control. If you remember, in the discussion of NAT issues, you learned that, by default, internal hosts have rights to send anything and everything to lower-security interfaces. As an administrator, you might not always want this. Particularly when you have multiple interfaces on your PIX Firewall, and potentially multiple clients attached, you might want to place limitations on outbound access.

The two commands that are important for controlling outbound access are **outbound** (to create a list) and **apply** (to apply the list to an interface). The command syntax for outbound access lists is different than for router-based ACLs. It uses the **outbound** command, which has the following syntax:

```
outbound list_ID {permit | deny} ip_address [netmask [java | port[-port]]]
  [protocol]
outbound list_ID except ip_address [netmask [java | port[-port]]] [protocol]
```

The command parameters and syntax have the following meanings:

Command Parameter	Description
permit	Allows the type of connections described in the following parameters.
deny	Denies the type of connections described in the following parameters.
list_ID	Specifies the identifying number of the access list. It is arbitrary, so make it whatever you want it to be.
ip_address	Shows the specific host IP or network number IP.
netmask	Reflects the associated mask for the IP number.
port	Specifies the TCP/UDP port number or range of port numbers for the statement.

continues

Command Parameter	Description
java	Indicates port 80 traffic. When used with the **deny** option, the firewall blocks Java applets. Java applets are permitted by default and do not need to be specifically mentioned if permitting.
protocol	Limits the list to TCP, UDP, or ICMP. The default is TCP if nothing is specified.
except	Creates exceptions to previously established rules of **outbound** **permit** or **deny** statements. Otherwise, parameters for **except** statements are the same as those listed here.

After you have created an outbound access list, you should apply it to an interface. The command syntax for the **apply** command is as follows:

```
apply [(if_name)] list_ID {outgoing_src | outgoing_dest}
```

The command parameters and syntax have the following meanings:

Command Parameter	Description
if_name	Reflects the name of the interface as specified in **nameif** commands. As with most commands, the parentheses are included.
list_ID	Indicates a number matching an outgoing access list that exists on the PIX Firewall.
outgoing_src	Reflects that the **permit** or **deny** statements of the access list were geared toward the source IP address of hosts inside the PIX Firewall (inside interfaces).
outgoing_dest	Reflects that the **permit** or **deny** statements of the access list were geared toward destination IP addresses located on the outside interfaces (or other lower-security interfaces).

Again, like most commands on the PIX Firewall, the **outbound** and **apply** commands give the administrator a tremendous amount of opportunity to make a very confusing configuration. A computing device works in a black-and-white world of 1s and 0s. Something either is or is not one thing or another. For example, a packet either is or is not TCP. If it is a TCP packet, it either is or is not destined for port 23 (Telnet). If it is a Telnet packet, it either is or is not originating from a network that is trusted. The logic to configure the firewall exactly as needed, or the logic to make a network unusable, is under the administrator's control. As always, great care should be taken when implementing a security policy.

Outbound access lists create a set of rules. The **apply** statement binds the access list to an interface, as a source or destination-based list, and activates it. When the **apply** statement is entered with **outgoing_src**, the source IP address, destination port, and protocol are filtered. When the **apply** statement is entered with **outgoing_dest**, the destination IP address, port, and protocol are filtered. The reasoning behind this is that most applications use random (and changing) source ports, so filtering them would be ineffective.

When the PIX Firewall utilizes lists of **outbound** statements, the "best match" criteria is used. The best match is based on the IP address mask and the port range check. More-strict IP address masks (longest bit match) and smaller port ranges are considered a better match. In case of a tie, a **permit** statement wins over a **deny** statement.

The **except** rules work within a list of other **permit** and **deny** statements. If you create a list with only a single **except** statement, you are logically doing nothing, so the list has no effect.

NOTE   PIX Firewall software Releases 5.0(1) and later let you use access lists similar to routers' access lists. Through named access lists, the same statements and formatting used on a router can be used on the PIX Firewall in an inbound or outbound direction.

The **access-list** and **access-group** statements from the Cisco router IOS are now a part of the PIX Firewall software. These "new" access list formats can coexist with the types of access controls listed throughout this book. This is something to pay careful attention to when maintaining a single or multiple PIX Firewalls. The PIX Firewall will always be able to determine what the rules are according to the configuration statements, but often, administrators increase the confusion in supporting complex scenarios by mixing and matching command sets that are completely different. Pay careful attention to this.

Examples of Controlling Outbound Access

This section gives a few examples of outbound access lists and their application to interfaces. The list in Example 12-3 prevents any inside host from initiating any session.

Example 12-3 *Preventing an Inside Host from Initiating a Session*

```
Pixfirewall(config)#outbound 1 deny 0 0 0 0
Pixfirewall(config)#apply (inside) 1 outgoing_src
Pixfirewall(config)#^Z
Pixfirewall#
```

The list in Example 12-4 denies everything except Telnet and HTTP traffic generated from host 200.200.200.11.

Example 12-4 *Allowing Only Telnet and HTTP Traffic from a Particular Host*

```
Pixfirewall(config)#outbound 2 deny 0 0 0 0
Pixfirewall(config)#outbound 2 except 200.200.200.11 255.255.255.255 23 tcp
Pixfirewall(config)#outbound 2 except 200.200.200.11 255.255.255.255 80 tcp
Pixfirewall(config)#apply (inside) 2 outgoing_src
Pixfirewall(config)#^Z
Pixfirewall#
```

The general **deny** statement often comes first in the list (which is much different from a router's access list) because the best match is a more specific match. This works much like route selection in a router. You can also apply multiple lists in order to help sort your logic. Be aware that applying a large number of lists to the same interface delays packet processing due to the increased number of steps the firewall must go through.

Example 12-5 shows multiple lists applied to the same interface.

Example 12-5 *Multiple Lists Applied to the Same Interface*

```
Pixfirewall(config)#outbound 3 deny 0 0 0 0
Pixfirewall(config)#outbound 3 except 200.200.200.0 255.255.255.0 23 tcp
Pixfirewall(config)#outbound 4 deny 0 0 0 0
Pixfirewall(config)#outbound 4 permit 10.1.1.21 255.255.255.255 0 0
Pixfirewall(config)#outbound 4 permit 10.1.1.22 255.255.255.255 0 0
Pixfirewall(config)#outbound 4 permit 10.1.1.64 255.255.255.192 0 0
Pixfirewall(config)#outbound 4 permit 0 0 21 tcp
Pixfirewall(config)#apply (inside) 3 outgoing_src
Pixfirewall(config)#apply (inside) 4 outgoing_src
Pixfirewall(config)#^Z
Pixfirewall#
```

The list outbound 3 denies all traffic other than Telnet traffic originating from the Class C network 200.200.200.0. The list outbound 4 permits specific hosts 10.1.1.21 and 10.1.1.22 as well as 64 hosts beginning at 10.1.1.64 and ending at 10.1.1.127. In addition, it permits any host to have FTP sessions. Both of these lists are applied to the same interface and are checked in order as each flow starts. Although this might logically be easier for the administrator, it is not easier for the PIX Firewall.

Configuring Java Applet Blocking and URL Filtering

At any company, employee use (and potential misuse) of corporate Internet connectivity and work time is a major concern. Even if employees spend their time on the Internet efficiently, the applications they come in contact with are also a concern. Every company with Internet connectivity needs to protect its assets, whether against misused company or employee time or against malicious applets being inadvertently accessed on a Web page. URL filtering mechanisms and Java applet blocking are two technologies used by the PIX Firewall.

There have been many reports in the news in the past year of malicious Java applications that can be unwittingly run by users with inadequate security settings on their browsers. Java is a very powerful programming language. By allowing unchecked applications to be run, network or security administrators might inadvertently allow malicious destruction.

Java Applet Blocking

The Java applet block removes Java applets that come in through the HTTP protocol port. The PIX Firewall removes any applet containing a Java signature anywhere in the message. This doesn't work for applets that are archived (ZIP, LHA, ARJ, and so on). However, it does work for legitimate, harmless Java files, so users might complain of incomplete pages. This is an all-or-nothing block of Java.

In order to filter Java applets, you need to create an outgoing access list and apply it to the interfaces that you want to protect. In doing so, you prevent all Java applets from initiation by the protected interfaces.

Again, it is much more work for the PIX Firewall to use multiple lists in the same direction than if all necessary logic is thought out ahead of time and programmed into the same list of **outbound** restrictions. Yet in Example 12-6, you add yet another access list.

Example 12-6 *Java Blocking Through an* ***outbound*** *List*

```
Pixfirewall(config)#outbound 5 deny 0 0 java
Pixfirewall(config)#apply (inside) 1 outgoing_src
Pixfirewall(config)#^Z
Pixfirewall#
```

This list prevents all inside users from executing Java applets on the inside network. All other traffic is permitted by default. The application of access lists on a firewall is logically opposite that of a router, so take care when designing these controls. This means that, most often, access lists on a router are applied in an inbound direction to the appropriate interface. This becomes especially important if you're mixing technology types now that **access-list** and **access-group** commands are supported on newer revisions of PIX Firewall software.

URL Filtering

To provide further security to your users, as well as to enforce a corporate policy on Web usage, you can have the PIX Firewall interact with a URL filtering and accounting system. WebSENSE is a product that enhances access management and content filtering needs. WebSENSE consists of an extensive database of URLs arranged in 29 categories of Internet content. The network or security administrator (typically acting on HR policy) can determine which of these categories should be allowed or blocked during different time periods.

NOTE Be aware that WebSENSE is not free. You must subscribe to the service and purchase software to install on a Windows NT box residing on your network.

Two commands are associated with setting up WebSENSE: **url-server** and **filter**. In order to specify interaction with a content manager (URL server), you use the **url-server** command, which has the following syntax:

```
url-server [(if_name)] host local_ip [timeout seconds]
```

The command parameters and syntax have the following meanings:

Command Parameter	Description
if_name	Specifies the interface where the URL server resides. As with other interface commands, parentheses are included.
local_ip	Shows the local IP address (not a NAT address) of the machine on the interface specified.
seconds	Specifies the number of seconds to wait for a timeout.

To specify the type of URL filtering to use, you use the **filter** command, which has the following syntax:

```
filter url {http | except} local_ip local_mask foreign_ip foreign_mask [allow]
filter java port[-port] local_ip mask foreign_ip mask
filter activex port local_ip mask foreign_ip mask
```

The command parameters and syntax have the following meanings:

Command Parameter	Description
url	Specifies the filtering of URLs.
port	Details the port number to be monitored for filtering. Typically, the entry is **http**, but other specific ports can be allocated as well if you know of off-normal Web servers. Another option is to control access to specific Web addresses through outgoing access list port control.
http	Filters HTTP (World Wide Web) URLs.
except	Creates exceptions to previously established rules of **filter permit** or **deny** statements.
local_ip	Shows the local IP number or network number to filter.
local_mask	Specifies the netmask associated with the local IP number.
foreign_ip	Shows the foreign IP number or network number to filter against.

Command Parameter	Description
foreign_mask	Reflects the netmask associated with the foreign IP number.
allow	If the URL server becomes unavailable (timeouts occur), this specifies that you will allow traffic to proceed unchecked. Without this command, all HTTP requests are dropped if the URL server becomes unavailable.
activex	Specifies the filtering of ActiveX controls.
java	Specifies the filtering of Java applets.

The commands for allowing the PIX Firewall to begin filtering URLs are relatively simple, as shown in Example 12-7.

Example 12-7 *Setting up a URL Filter Server for All Outgoing Web Requests*

```
Pixfirewall(config)#url-server (dmz) host 192.168.1.42 timeout 10
Pixfirewall(config)#filter url http 0 0 0 0 allow
Pixfirewall(config)#^Z
Pixfirewall#
```

One advanced issue with the filtering commands is the caching of the requests. If a number of people are attempting to access www.cisco.com or www.ciscopress.com at close to the same time, the PIX Firewall does not need to issue separate requests and responses from every HTTP session.

In addition, it is possible to set up a cache for URL requests and responses by using the **url-cache** command, which has the following syntax:

```
url-cache {dst | src_dst} size
```

The command parameters and syntax have the following meanings:

Command Parameter	Description
dst	Caches responses based on destination Web sites
src_dst	Caches responses based on destination Web sites specific to each source station requesting them
size	Specifies the memory buffer size allocated to caching the URL request information

For example, to set up a cache of 16 KB for URL filter requests based on destinations, you'd use the command shown in Example 12-8.

Example 12-8 *Specifying URL Request Cache Buffer Space*

```
Pixfirewall(config)#url-cache dst 16
Pixfirewall(config)#^Z
Pixfirewall#
```

NOTE   By using the **url-cache** command, the PIX Firewall checks the cache before issuing a request to the URL server. This action bypasses the URL server's ability to log good or bad Web requests. Make sure that you are aware of the implications of this command versus what you are trying to accomplish with your HR Internet Usage Policy.

Configuring FTP and URL Logging

There are additional ways to use commands you already know to manage the PIX Firewall and the network it protects. To log URL and FTP access, you apply the knowledge of logging you gained in Chapter 11. Chapter 11 described the details of setting up a syslog server and configuring the options on the PIX Firewall to log messages to that server. The PIX Firewall spends time diving into each FTP and HTTP packet. It does this by using the **fixup** commands, which are enabled by default.

HTTP and FTP are two protocols that inherently do not follow standards of RFCs, and they cause problems with NAT. They do this by logging specific machine information (IP) in the upper layers of the OSI model. Because NAT works only at Layer 3, things can go wrong. When your browser makes a request, your machine's IP address is put into the Layer 7 (application) information *and* the Layer 3 (source address) information. If your network is using NAT, it changes only the address at Layer 3. So by the time the HTTP packet gets to the other end, two different IP numbers are referenced at different layers of the same packet.

The **fixup protocol** command helps alleviate these discrepancies with well-known protocol types. Here is the syntax:

```
fixup protocol type port-num
```

The command parameters and syntax have the following meanings:

Command Parameter	Description
type	Specifies the protocol type for the PIX Firewall to further fix. Options are **http**, **ftp**, **h323**, **rsh**, **rtsp**, **smtp**, and **sqlnet**.
port-num	Specifies the port number that will be used by the protocol type specified. You might need to configure multiple statements if, for example, you have Web servers at port 80 (normal) and port 8000.

Some commands, such as those shown in Example 12-9, are in the PIX Firewall configuration by default.

Example 12-9 *Using the fixup protocol Command*

```
Pixfirewall(config)#fixup protocol http 80
Pixfirewall(config)#fixup protocol ftp 21
Pixfirewall(config)#^Z
Pixfirewall#
```

Other protocols, including many custom protocols, do not correctly adhere to RFC standards and might cause problems. Cisco programmers may add more protocol fixups, but only in response to general customer usage. They may not make code changes for a customer's specific protocol.

Because the PIX Firewall is already diving into the upper layers with those packets, logging specifics about FTP and HTTP is quite easy.

All URL information generates syslog messages with a severity of 7 (debugging messages). So if you want to log those types of messages, all you need to do is set the appropriate logging type (through a syslog trap or console buffer) to that level.

NOTE   Specifying a debug level for syslog generates a *lot* of information on a populated network. I don't want to scare you away from implementing log messages of this nature, but be aware of the need before you implement this feature.

Some companies need to log outgoing URL access and perhaps charge back to various departments, or simply monitor what sites the users are going to, or whatever the reason within policy.

If your security policy dictates this detail of logging, be aware of the effect it will have. For each message logged, there is CPU time on the PIX Firewall, packets with syslog message information are sent to the syslog server, there is a huge increase in syslog text file size each day, and there is an increase in the time and effort it takes to analyze those collected syslog files.

If you are aware of the consequences, there's nothing wrong with implementing these features.

An added bonus to the logging features on the PIX Firewall is the **logging message** command. You can start to control the specific information that you want to have populating your logs, or you can turn off those you do not want to see. To turn off specific syslog message logging, you use the **no** form of this command. The following is the syntax for the **logging message** command:

```
logging message syslog_id
```

The command parameter has the following meaning:

Command Parameter	Description
syslog_id	The ID number of the syslog message type that you do or do not want to have processed. This command is typically used with the **no** option in front of the command to turn off a particular message type.

The various *syslog_id* numbers each refer to a certain type of message. They can be found on the Cisco Connection Online or on your documentation CD. Each version of PIX Firewall software has its own set of syslog "Messages Listed by Severity Level" documents as the specifics change.

In the following examples, and in appropriate real-life logs, the syslog messages reflect action by a source to a destination. Example 12-10 shows an example of a URL log message. In this example, 192.168.69.71 is the source machine that is accessing the file secrets.gif from destination machine 10.0.0.1.

Example 12-10 *An Example of a URL Log Message*

```
%PIX-5-304001: 192.168.69.71 accessed URL 10.0.0.1/secrets.gif
```

Example 12-11 shows an example of an FTP log message. Source 192.168.69.42 retrieved a file, and source 192.168.42.54 stored a file.

Example 12-11 *An Example of an FTP Log Message*

```
%PIX-5-304001:  192.168.69.42 Retrieved 10.0.0.42:feathers.tar
%PIX-5-304001:  192.168.42.54 Stored 10.0.42.69:privacy.zip
```

You can find a detailed list of the *syslog_id* messages for the latest version of PIX Firewall software on Cisco's documentation CD or on Cisco Connection Online (CCO).

Configuring SNMP

When you have a PIX Firewall working in a production environment and you are monitoring its status messages through syslog, you need to configure some further monitoring ability. Under network management software, you have the ability to proactively monitor the PIX Firewall (as well as other devices in the network).

Simple Network Management Protocol (SNMP) allows a network device to participate in a network management setup. Each device can be polled for information ("get" requests), and each device can also send information to a management station ("trap" information) to monitor problems as they occur.

Some of the traps that are allowed are basic and security-related traps. Basic traps include the following:

- Interface up
- Interface down
- PIX Firewall reboot (cold start)

Security-related traps include the following:

- Global access denied
- Failover syslog messages (redundancy failure)
- Any syslog messages

SNMP programs use a Management Information Base (MIB) file to refer to specific messages and abilities of each type of device on a network. With MIB files, SNMP programs know what each device really means with its messages and what features each has for network management.

You can use the CiscoWorks family of products, or any other SNMP V1 MIB-II-compliant program, to receive traps or browse the MIB. SNMP traps occur at UDP port 162, so be aware of this for any conduits necessary to access the network management workstation.

You must configure a few SNMP commands in order to enable basic access.

To begin the setup of SNMP, you use the **snmp-server** command, which has the following syntax:

```
snmp-server {community key | contact text | location text}
```

The command parameters and syntax have the following meanings:

Command Parameter	Description
community *key*	Specifies the SNMP community name. If you are working with SNMP over the Internet, or any other unsecured interface, avoid using "public" or "private" community names. Pick something more meaningful and harder to guess to prevent unauthorized monitoring or changes.
contact *text*	Provides basic information for the contact to administer the device.
location *text*	Provides basic information on the device's location. In larger networks, this can prevent much "hunting."

Notice while configuring the **snmp-server** community string that there is no designation for read-only (RO) or read-write (RW) variables. The PIX Firewall, as part of its intention to be as secure as possible, does not support read-write network management. It treats any community variable as read-only.

The **snmp-server host** command specifies a host to send trap information to; it uses the following syntax:

```
snmp-server host [if_name] local_ip
```

The command parameters and syntax have the following meanings:

Command Parameter	Description
if_name	Specifies the name of the interface where an SNMP management station resides to send trap information to. There are no parentheses around this value.
local_ip	Reflects the local (untranslated) IP of the management station on this interface.

To enable the use of traps sent to the management workstation, you use the **snmp-server enable table** command. This will enable or disable sending SNMP trap notifications via syslog.

Example 12-12 shows how you put together many of these commands to enable SNMP configurations on the PIX Firewall. It gives some basic reference information so that the network management software knows the particular PIX Firewall as something other than just "PIX Firewall."

Example 12-12 *PIX Firewall SNMP Configuration*

```
Pixfirewall(config)#snmp-server location 1212 First Street South, Room 12A
Pixfirewall(config)#snmp-server contact Bob Jones (800)555-1212 ext 4893
Pixfirewall(config)#snmp-server community supersecure
Pixfirewall(config)#snmp-server host 10.2.6.5
Pixfirewall(config)#snmp-server enable traps
Pixfirewall(config)#^Z
Pixfirewall#
```

Configuring PIX Firewall Failover

Failover allows two separate PIX Firewall boxes on a network to provide redundancy to the security infrastructure. In the event that one unit fails, the other picks up. This might seem familiar from the router commands revolving around Hot Standby Router Protocol (HSRP), and it is very similar.

The PIX Firewall can perform two types of failover monitoring: basic and stateful. In all versions of PIX Firewall software, basic failover can be monitored. In such a case, there is a special serial cable between two PIX Firewall units (active and standby) to exchange basic information such as active IP addresses and MAC addresses of the active unit. In addition, each unit sends hello packets every 15 seconds over every interface to talk with the other PIX Firewall. This means that packets go over the special serial cable and every LAN interface as well.

Basic Failover

The failover code in the PIX Firewall monitors all failover communications, the power status of the remote unit, and all hello packets received over each interface. If two consecutive hello packets are missed during the time determined by the failover communication, the failover code starts testing the interfaces to determine which unit failed and where it failed, and active control is passed to the standby unit.

When a failover occurs, the active unit (formerly the standby unit) assumes all IP and MAC addresses of the previously active unit. This makes everything simple on LAN interfaces where there is no need for any routers or hosts to re-ARP in order to rediscover the new gateway.

The failover cable is a proprietary cable that must be purchased. This cable has a primary end and a secondary end (much like DCE/DTE). Be sure that the correct end of the cable is plugged in to the correct PIX Firewall (active or standby) because it is crucial for initial failover configuration.

Stateful Failover

Beginning with PIX Firewall Software version 5.0, there is a stateful failover option. If stateful failover has been configured, all connection states are relayed between the two units, so there is minimal interruption in services. If stateful failover is not configured, all active connections are dropped when failover occurs, and all client systems must reestablish connections and translations.

In order to accommodate the extensive amount of information needed to handle all translations and connection states being passed between the active and standby PIX Firewalls, a dedicated Ethernet interface is required. The amount of information to be transferred would far exceed the transfer capabilities of the serial failover cable.

This dedicated interface must be operating at 100 Mbps and over Ethernet only. The interface can be connected with the following:

- CAT 5 crossover cable directly between the units
- 100BaseTX half-duplex hub
- 100BaseTX full-duplex switch or VLAN ports

NOTE   Although the PIX Firewall supports multiple media types in general, it does not support Token Ring or FDDI for the stateful failover dedicated interface. No other hosts or devices should be on the same link as the stateful failover interfaces.

If you have a PIX 515, obtain a PIX-515-UR feature license key that lets you add the failover option. Then purchase the failover option, which includes the secondary unit. If you have a PIX 520 or older model, purchase a second unit with the same connection license as the primary unit. Cisco's pricing structure does allow for a large discount on the second unit in a failover scenario because one unit would be largely unused.

When a PIX Firewall boots up, it defaults to **no failover active**. If the cable is not present, the PIX Firewall automatically assumes it is the active unit. If the cable is present, the PIX Firewall that has the primary end of the failover cable plugged into it becomes the primary (active) unit by default.

The failover cable is much like serial cables, in which one end is DTE and the other end is DCE determined by pinouts. One end must be connected to the primary (active by default) PIX Firewall and the other end to the secondary (standby by default) PIX Firewall.

Failover Operation

You need to consider a number of issues with failover and stateful failover. The following events cause a failover to occur:

- Power off or power down of active PIX Firewall
- Reboot of active PIX Firewall
- An interface of the active PIX Firewall going down for more than 30 seconds
- The **failover active** command being issued on the standby PIX Firewall
- Out-of-memory errors on the active PIX Firewall for 15 consecutive seconds

The following information is assumed by the newly active PIX Firewall during stateful failover (remember that normal failover resets all connections and tables):

- Configuration of the PIX Firewall (includes IP and MAC addresses)
- TCP connection table and timeout values (this does not include the HTTP connections)
- NAT translation (xlate) table
- System clock (useful for maintaining logs)

The following information is not synchronized, even during stateful failover:

- User authentication table (uauth)
- HTTP connection table
- ISAKMP and IPSec SA tables
- ARP table
- Learned routing information

Configuring Failover

To configure the failover, after appropriate licensing and/or cabling is complete, you use the **failover** command, whose syntax is as follows:

```
failover ip address if_name ip_address
failover timeout hh:mm:ss
```

The command parameters and syntax have the following meanings:

Command Parameter	Description
if_name	Provides the name of the PIX Firewall interface as specified in the **nameif** command.
ip_address	Reflects the IP address of the other PIX Firewall unit as known through the interface specified. This is used for stateful failover, and it reflects the IP address of the other unit on the dedicated Ethernet interface. Similar to HSRP on a router, it must know what IP to send the various hello packets and state information to.
hh	Shows the time in hours.
mm	Shows the time in minutes.
ss	Shows the time in seconds.

These commands specify which interface to monitor and the IP address of the other PIX Firewall (they will share one). Remember that, in failover, the standby PIX Firewall assumes the IP and MAC addresses of the active PIX Firewall.

To specify the interface for communication, you use the **failover link** command, which has the following syntax:

```
failover link if_name
```

The command parameter has the following meaning:

Command Parameter	Description
if_name	Name of the interface to be used for the failover messages. Specified with the **nameif** command.

If you are configuring stateful failover, this command specifies the Fast Ethernet interface to be used.

You can manually manipulate the status of active and standby. The **failover reset** command forces PIX Firewalls back to the initial primary and secondary roles. Remember that the failover cable pinouts signify which end is which. This is assumed after an administrator has rectified whatever problem caused failover to begin with. The **failover active** command forces PIX Firewalls to initiate a failover. This can be used to test the architecture and network effect.

Both the active and standby units must have the same version of PIX Firewall software in order to work correctly. Remember this when you upgrade your PIX Firewall software. In addition, both units need to have the same interfaces installed in the same slots of a like-model PIX Firewall. In order to update configuration information to a standby PIX Firewall, you can issue a command from the active PIX Firewall. **write standby** pushes all configuration information to the standby PIX Firewall. When using this, note that the failover cable is a serial port connection, so larger configurations take longer to complete. The **write memory** command should still be used to write configuration to the active PIX Firewall.

Configuring VPN Features

The PIX Firewall supports a number of different VPN methods. Some are hardware-related, and others are software-related. Older versions of PIX Firewall (and some current ones) supported only hardware-based encryption methods; this involved purchasing a PIX Firewall Private Link card to handle the encryption needs. More recent versions of PIX Firewall software support IPSec tunnels. Security policies can be implemented to support Microsoft's PPTP tunnel technology.

VPNs are often maintained between sites (PIX Firewall to PIX Firewall or router to PIX Firewall) as well as from a specific client machine (such as a laptop), as in the case of PPTP. PIX Firewalls, although they are very robust, are not designed for large-scale VPN tunnel termination.

Currently, the VPN 3000 series (Altiga acquisition) and VPN 5000 series (Compatible Systems acquisition) handle this job much better. Also, for large-scale PPTP or IPSec client tunnel termination, the Cisco 7206 router has an Integrated Services Module (ISM) card specifically designed to terminate up to 2000 tunnels per card. So, as with any rule of network design, select the appropriate equipment to do the necessary job rather than trying to make one piece of equipment perform many tasks in a mediocre manner.

Private Link Encryption

Private Link is the legacy version of encryption that took place between two PIX Firewalls over a shared public infrastructure with a hardware-based encryption engine. This was proprietary technology that allowed only PIX Firewall-to-PIX Firewall VPN tunnels. This type of encryption is no longer supported in PIX Firewalls as of software version 5.0. PIX Firewall version 4.x still supports this card and these links if they are still needed in a network.

Please be aware that the following commands are valid only for the PIX Private Link card and are valid only on PIX Firewall software versions previous to 5.0. Since version 5.0 of the PIX Firewall software, the command structures have changed to support industry-standard IPSec tunnels, which are explained beginning in Chapter 16, "Configuring Cisco IOS IPSec."

The Private Link feature allowed incoming Private Link packets to bypass the NAT and ASA (Adaptive Security Algorithm) features and terminate on an inside interface. You use the **link** command for private linking. To set the basic information for the remote peer, including private key values, you use the following syntax:

```
link (interface) remote_peer_ip key_id key_text
link remote_peer_ip md5
```

The command parameters and syntax have the following meanings:

Command Parameter	Description
interface	Shows the interface where the tunnel terminates on the local PIX Firewall, such as (**inside**)
remote_peer_ip	Gives the IP address of the remote PIX Firewall
key_id	Gives the value of the key information (sequenced number)
key_text	Provides the value of that particular key (password text)

To set information for the remote network range for private communications, you use the **linkpath** command, which has the following syntax:

```
linkpath remote_network_ip remote_netmask remote_peer_ip
```

The command parameters and syntax have the following meanings:

Command Parameter	Description
remote_network_ip	Gives the network IP address of the remote network
remote_netmask	Provides the netmask of the remote network's IP address
remote_peer_ip	Gives the IP address of the remote PIX Firewall

To specify the length of activity allowed per tunnel link, you use the **age** command, which has the following syntax:

```
age minutes
```

The command parameter has the following meaning:

Command Parameter	Description
minutes	Specifies the age, in minutes, that the tunnel can be active on each key value.

The **linkpath** command works much like an **ip route** statement in terms of establishing multiple tunnels and directing traffic where it needs to go. Figure 12-1 illustrates the network topology described in Example 12-13.

Figure 12-1 *A Network with a Private Link*

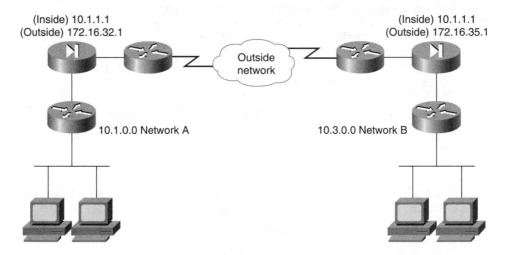

On Firewall A, the Private Link configuration would be as shown in Example 12-13.

Example 12-13 *Sample Private Link Configuration*

```
Pixfirewall(config)#link 172.16.35.1 1 aaaaaaaaaa
Pixfirewall(config)#link 172.16.35.1 2 bbbbbbbbbb
Pixfirewall(config)#link 172.16.35.1 3 cccccccccc
Pixfirewall(config)#link 172.16.35.1 4 dddddddddd
Pixfirewall(config)#link 172.16.35.1 5 eeeeeeeeee
Pixfirewall(config)#linkpath 10.3.0.0 255.255.255.0 172.16.35.1
Pixfirewall(config)#^Z
Pixfirewall#
```

On Firewall B, the Private Link configuration would be as shown in Example 12-14.

Example 12-14 *Remote End Sample Private Link Configuration*

```
Pixfirewall(config)#link 172.16.32.1 1 aaaaaaaaaa
Pixfircwall(config)#link 172.16.32.1 2 bbbbbbbbbb
Pixfirewall(config)#link 172.16.32.1 3 cccccccccc
Pixfirewall(config)#link 172.16.32.1 4 dddddddddd
Pixfirewall(config)#link 172.16.32.1 5 eeeeeeeeee
Pixfirewall(config)#linkpath 10.1.0.0 255.255.255.0 172.16.32.1
Pixfirewall(config)#^Z
Pixfirewall#
```

At this point, all traffic from 10.1.0.0/24 destined for 10.3.0.0/24 and vice versa would be sent encrypted through the Private Link.

Notice that each **link** statement is configured with multiple preshared keys for tunnel setup. This provides a rotation of encrypted keys. For additional information on shared keys and encryption, see Chapter 16.

If the statements in Example 12-15 were added, the algorithm used would be Message Digest 5 encryption.

Example 12-15 *Changing Key Encryption to MD5 Hash*

```
Firewall A: link 172.16.35.1 md5
Firewall B: link 172.16.32.1 md5
```

Both sides *must* match when changing standards like this. Otherwise, one side will be speaking a language the other is not set to understand.

Configuring PPTP Support

Many companies that maintain a large Windows NT network domain have implemented Microsoft's Point-to-Point Tunneling Protocol (PPTP) on their networks. The initial configuration of this technology is that PPTP is a client-initiated encryption scheme.

Because PPTP is client-initiated, it is referred to as a "voluntary" tunnel. The service provider between the laptop user and the home network does not need to be aware of the tunneling that is occurring.

Because PPTP is software-based encryption, there is a performance hit when you implement this type of VPN, particularly en masse. PPTP requires software on the client PC (typically a laptop traveling around). Windows Dial-Up Networking (DUN) version 1.3 is the preferred version to minimally support PPTP and all other options.

The options allowed are Microsoft Point-to-Point Encryption (MPPE) and Microsoft Point-to-Point Compression (MPPC) on the packets. These options are selected through checkboxes, as shown in Figure 12-2.

Figure 12-2 *Microsoft Dial-Up Networking Configuration Screen*

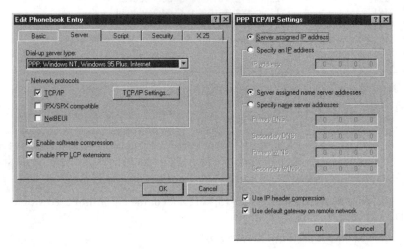

The client initiates a tunnel back to a server, referred to as a PPTP Network Server or "home gateway." In recent versions of IOS, select routers have been able to terminate PPTP sessions themselves. In the past, the only box to terminate PPTP sessions was a Microsoft Windows NT Server running Remote-Access Services (RAS). Beginning with PIX Firewall software version 5.1, the PIX Firewall supports inbound termination of PPTP sessions from a Microsoft Windows device.

The PPTP technology is an endpoint solution only, meaning that the PIX Firewall does not directly support PPTP tunneling. It supports the use of PPTP tunneling on the network only insofar as the security policy allows.

Some configuration steps are required to change the security policy to allow PPTP tunnels through. First, the end device where the PPTP tunnels are to be terminated must be set up with a static translation. This makes sense only from a rollout perspective. Each client needs to know the end address to set up its laptop correctly.

After the static translation is covered, a **conduit** command must be added, as shown in Example 12-16.

Example 12-16 *Conduit Examples for PPTP Pass-Through*

```
conduit permit tcp global_ip global_mask eq 1723 foreign_ip foreign_mask
conduit permit gre global_ip global_mask foreign_ip foreign_mask
```

TCP port 1723 is where tunnel maintenance packets take place. Other than that, **gre** is the Generic Route Encapsulation type packet that indicates the tunneled packets themselves.

The same parameters are necessary for newer technologies such as Layer 2 Forwarding (L2F) and Layer 2 Tunneling Protocol (L2TP). There are technology differences, but PIX Firewall support and requirements are identical.

The newer technologies involving client-based IPSec support can offer tunnel termination on the PIX Firewall. These technologies are discussed in greater detail later in this book.

The following steps allow PPTP tunnels to pass through a PIX Firewall:

1 The tunnel termination device (NT Server or other hardware) must have a static Network Address Translation entry to a known global address.

2 A conduit must be set up for tunnel control (TCP port 1723) to the tunnel termination device.

3 A conduit must be set up for the tunnels themselves (GRE protocol) to the tunnel termination device.

Beginning with PIX Firewall software version 5.1, the PIX Firewall itself can serve as the tunnel termination device for PPTP tunnels. Again, using the global address of a PIX Firewall interface to configure on the Microsoft Windows devices, you can set up the PIX Firewall to authenticate and terminate PPTP tunnels.

CiscoSecure Policy Manager

CiscoSecure Policy Manager (CSPM) allows you to centrally manage the security policy of up to 500 Cisco devices. CSPM works with the PIX Firewall and other Cisco IOS devices, particularly those configured with the IOS Firewall feature set.

CSPM allows you to define a security policy independent of device command-line interfaces, using an intuitive template and flowcharting interface. CSPM automatically creates the correct command-line code from the policy you have determined and distributes the security policy for high-level security and VPN-oriented features to the network devices.

CSPM makes centralized management of enterprise security and VPN policies much easier. It also enhances monitoring capabilities beyond a standard manual approach, but it offers fewer capabilities than Cisco Works network management software systems. CSPM includes reporting and monitoring features for studying basic network activity and alerts for possible security breaches in the network.

You can download an evaluation version of CSPM from the CCO Web site. The evaluation version is fully featured for managing one network device. Purchase of a software license key is required to manage additional devices.

PIX Firewall Maintenance

Even when a security policy is defined and the configuration is tested and working, PIX Firewall tasks are not complete. You need to perform ongoing PIX Firewall maintenance because needs, attacks, and policies change in today's dynamic environment. Two important components of maintenance are password recovery and software upgrades.

PIX Firewall Password Recovery

Chances are you will never need to know how to recover a password. But as companies grow and merge and IS department personnel change, there are times when the PIX Firewall enable password is lost or forgotten, making the PIX Firewall enable mode inaccessible.

PIX Firewall password recovery involves a different procedure than Cisco routers. All standard password recovery techniques for the various Cisco routers and switches can be found in documentation on Cisco's Web site, and you only need physical access to the unit to perform them. PIX Firewall password recovery requires you to obtain a special software image (see the next section for details on changing software images) so that you can recover from a lost PIX Firewall enable password. To obtain this image and install it, follow these steps:

1 Go to the Software Center on Cisco's Web site. Within the CiscoSecure PIX Firewall Software section, look for the image pix*xxx*.bin, where *xxx* represents the software version number currently running on the PIX Firewall.

2 If you don't know the current software version, simply enter the **show version** command at the PIX Firewall prompt. Part of the information returned will contain the software image version number. The **show version** command can be executed from any privilege level.

3 Download the password recovery image and load it onto a disk using the RAWRITE.EXE utility.

4 Power off the PIX Firewall, place the newly created disk into the PIX Firewall, and power the unit back on.

5 Follow the on-screen directions for recovering the password. The specific steps vary according to the software image, so they are not detailed here.

NOTE   The PIX Firewall 515 does not have a floppy disk drive. You must copy the password recovery image to the PIX Firewall's Flash memory using TFTP by following the PIX Firewall software upgrade procedure outlined in the next section.

PIX Firewall Software Upgrades

Updating a PIX Firewall's software is a relatively simple and painless task. The firewall on a network performs many important tasks, so the operating system should be kept up-to-date. Cisco Systems is also constantly enhancing PIX Firewall software, so you will want to make use of the latest features.

You follow different steps to upgrade the PIX Firewall software depending on which hardware platform you have and the software version you are planning to run. There are basically two methods of upgrading PIX Firewall software images:

- Creating a bootable disk containing the image for PIX Firewalls with floppy disk drives and then booting the PIX Firewall with the disk installed

- Copying the PIX Firewall software image file to PIX Firewall Flash memory using TFTP

Before you upgrade the PIX Firewall image, enter the **show version command** and write down the activation key.

Upgrading PIX Firewall Software Images Using Disks

The following are the basic steps involved in upgrading a PIX Firewall image using disks. You can modify these steps as necessary for the specific setup of your network:

1 The first step, regardless of platform, is to download the necessary version of the PIX Firewall software. This software is available through the Software Center on CCO. You must have a login and password (usually tied to a support contract) to gain access to the files.

NOTE   When you download files, image names will be PIX*xxx*.BIN or BH*xxx*.BIN, depending on the revision, where the *xxx* indicates the specific version number. For example, PIX403.BIN indicates version 4.03 of the PIX Firewall software. PIX503.BIN and BH503.BIN both are needed for version 5.03 of the PIX Firewall software.

---

2 Next you need to create a new boot disk for the PIX Firewall (versions 10000, 510, and 520). You need a blank, formatted floppy disk (1.44 MB, double-sided, high-density) and a program called RAWRITE.EXE, which is also available from CCO. The RAWRITE program is a sector-level imaging program that creates functional floppy disks independent of the operating system.

3 From a DOS prompt or a UNIX command prompt, execute RAWRITE from within the directory to which the image files were downloaded. You are prompted for the destination disk drive (typically A for the A: drive) and the image name

(corresponding to what was downloaded). The system formats the disk for the PIX Firewall's operating system, creates a bootable disk, and copies the software image to the disk.

With older versions of PIX Firewall software (5.0 and earlier), only one image file needs to be downloaded and transferred to a floppy disk.

With newer versions of PIX Firewall software, the main image itself doesn't fit on a floppy disk because it is larger than 1.44 MB. In order to copy these newer images into the Flash memory of the PIX Firewall, a BootHelper image is needed. This is a stripped-down version of the operating system that gives TFTP support to the box and allows basic configuration information to be entered manually. It segments the image into two disks.

4 Place the book disk in the PIX Firewall's disk drive. Perform a reload of the PIX Firewall. This loads the new software image into memory (and copies it into NVRAM/Flash for later use) and updates the configuration to match command-line changes.

Upgrading PIX Firewall Software Images Using TFTP

The following are the basic steps involved in upgrading a PIX Firewall image using TFTP. This procedure should be followed for PIX Firewall model 515. You can modify the steps as necessary for the specific setup of your network:

1 The first step, regardless of platform, is to download the necessary version of the PIX Firewall software, just as in Steps 1 and 2 in the preceding section.

2 Next, ensure that your PIX Firewall can connect to a TFTP server. Ensure that the software image files are copied onto the TFTP server.

3 For PIX Firewalls with version 5.0 and earlier images currently installed, reboot the PIX Firewall and enter monitor mode by pressing the Esc or Break key before the boot sequence completes. Specify the interface you will use to connect to the TFTP server (typically the inside interface, number 0), the interface's IP address, the IP address of the TFTP server, and the software image name. You can use the Help function to identify the necessary commands. Establish a TFTP session with the **tftp** command, and the PIX Firewall will download the new image file directly to Flash memory.

4 For PIX Firewalls with version 5.1.2 and later images currently installed, you can use the **copy tftp flash** command to upgrade the image without using monitor mode. The command prompts you for the TFTP server's IP address and the image filename.

Check all Release Notes for size limitations of new PIX Firewall images. Bear in mind that older PIX Firewall units have only 2 MB of Flash memory, which at some time in the near future might become too small for new software images.

See the *PIX Firewall Configuration Guide,* in the chapter "Configuring the PIX Firewall," for more information about software image upgrades.

Summary

This section summarizes the main points of this chapter, as follows:

- You configure advanced Network Address Translation through the NAT 0 feature to control a range of addresses that are not translated by the PIX Firewall.

- You control outbound access through applied outbound statements based on source or destination addresses.

- You can control security policies through Java applet blocking and URL filtering.

- You specify logging options for more-precise monitoring.

- You can set up SNMP for remote network management.

- You can configure various levels of PIX Firewall failover for redundancy in network firewall devices.

- You can configure basic VPN functionality, including the use of the Private Link encryption card.

- You can allow Microsoft Point-to-Point Tunneling Protocol access through the PIX Firewall.

Case Study: Configuring Advanced PIX Firewall Features

This case study illustrates how to configure Advanced PIX Firewall features in the hypothetical XYZ Company. Read the case study scenario, examine the topology diagram, read the security policy, and then analyze the configuration examples to see how the security policy statements are enacted for the PIX Firewall(s).

Case Study Scenario

The XYZ Company wants to add some new features and policies to its office network. Remember from Chapter 11 that XYZ had connections to two Internet providers and provided service to two extranet partners.

Topology

Figure 12-3 illustrates the pending design of the XYZ network that will be configured in this case study.

Figure 12-3 *The Design of the XYZ Company's Office Network*

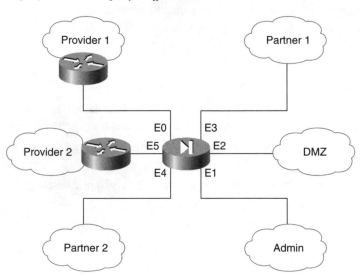

Network Design and Security Policy Additions

The additions that XYZ Company wants to make to its network design and security policy are as follows:

- Restrict the access of internal clients' networks to the Lotus Notes server (192.168.11.44 on the DMZ network).

- Add a WebSENSE server (10.1.1.77 on the administration/management LAN) that restricts HTTP access for users of the administration/management LAN.

- Set up an additional LAN for Client 2 that does not get translated. The XYZ Company has obtained the network 208.155.233.0/24.

- Set up basic SNMP, passing traps to a CiscoWorks system at 10.1.1.99 of the admin/ management LAN.

Sample Configuration for the XYZ Company PIX Firewall

Examine the configuration example for the PIX Firewall of the XYZ Company, shown in Example 12-17. This example implements the security design and policy considerations as outlined in the case study. One possible configuration for that policy might look like Example 12-17. You might choose to configure the PIX Firewall differently to enact the same design and policy requirements. Example 12-17 contains comments showing which commands affect which particular design or policy statements.

Example 12-17 *Advanced PIX Firewall Features Configuration for XYZ Company*

```
pix1#write terminal
Building configuration...
: Saved
:
PIX Version 5.1(2)
! nameif commands to delineate the interface configurations and security levels.
! Remember that equal weight interfaces aren't allowed to talk to each other.
nameif ethernet0 provider1 security0
nameif ethernet1 admin security100
nameif ethernet2 dmz security60
nameif ethernet3 client1 security50
nameif ethernet4 client2 security50
nameif ethernet5 provider2 security10
enable password AOywFtG5fs3ljpjx encrypted
passwd FSbblTfmfXKC.viH encrypted
hostname pix1
fixup protocol ftp 21
fixup protocol http 80
fixup protocol smtp 25
fixup protocol h323 1720
fixup protocol rsh 514
fixup protocol sqlnet 1521
names
pager lines 24
! Sets up the logging information to a syslog server
logging timestamp
no logging standby
no logging console
no logging monitor
logging buffered errors
logging trap informational
logging facility 20
logging queue 1024
logging host admin 10.1.1.5
! Additional information configuring the Ethernet interfaces
interface ethernet0 10baset
interface ethernet1 100full
interface ethernet2 100full
interface ethernet3 100full
interface ethernet4 100full
interface ethernet5 10baset
mtu provider1 1500
mtu admin 1500
mtu client1 1500
mtu client2 1500
mtu dmz 1500
mtu provider2 1500
! Additional information configuring the Ethernet interfaces
ip address admin 10.1.1.1 255.255.254.0
```

continues

Example 12-17 *Advanced PIX Firewall Features Configuration for XYZ Company (Continued)*

```
ip address client1 10.2.1.1 255.255.0.0
ip address client2 10.3.1.1 255.255.0.0
ip address dmz 192.168.11.1 255.255.255.0
ip address provider1 192.168.1.1 255.255.255.252
ip address provider2 192.168.2.1 255.255.255.252
! Note: provider addresses are typically assigned by the provider
! and not necessarily a part of the IP address range used for globals.
no failover
failover timeout 0:00:00
failover ip address outside 0.0.0.0
failover ip address inside 0.0.0.0
arp timeout 14400
!  Configuration information for Client NAT pools
nat (admin) 0 208.155.233.0 255.255.255.0
nat (admin) 1 10.1.1.0 255.255.255.0
nat (admin) 2 10.1.4.0 255.255.255.0
nat (client1) 3 10.2.1.0 255.255.255.0
nat (client2) 4 10.3.1.0 255.255.255.0
nat (admin) 5 0.0.0.0 0.0.0.0
nat (client1) 5 0 0     !(which is the same as 0.0.0.0)
nat (client2) 5 0 0
global (provider1) 1 192.168.1.10-192.168.1.126
global (provider1) 2 192.168.1.127
global (provider1) 3 192.168.1.128-192.168.1.253
global (provider2) 4 192.168.2.128-192.168.2.254
global (provider1) 5 192.168.1.254
!  Static NAT configuration and conduits
static (dmz,provider1) 192.168.1.10 10.1.1.4 netmask 255.255.255.255 0 0
static (dmz,provider1) 192.168.1.13 10.1.1.5 netmask 255.255.255.255 0 0
static (dmz,provider1) 192.168.1.11 192.168.11.3 netmask 255.255.255.255 0 0
static (dmz,provider1) 192.168.1.12 192.168.11.4 netmask 255.255.255.255 0 0
conduit permit tcp host 192.168.1.12 eq smtp any 0 0
conduit permit tcp host 192.168.1.11 eq www any 0 0
conduit permit tcp host 192.168.1.11 eq ftp any 0 0
conduit permit tcp host 192.168.2.11 eq ftp any 0 0
conduit permit tcp host 192.168.1.13 eq syslog any 0 0
!  Conduit permissions for ICMP filtering
conduit permit icmp any any echo-reply
conduit permit icmp any any unreachable
conduit permit icmp any any redirect
conduit permit icmp any any time-exceeded
conduit deny icmp any any
!Restrict access to the Lotus Notes server from internal Clients' LANs
outbound 1 deny 192.168.11.44
apply (client1) 1 outgoing_dest
apply (client2) 1 outgoing_dest
! Set up and use URL filtering server for admin HTTP access
url-server (admin) host 10.1.1.77
filter url http 10.0.0.0 255.255.255.0 0 0
rip provider1 passive
no rip provider1 default
no rip admin passive
```

Example 12-17 *Advanced PIX Firewall Features Configuration for XYZ Company (Continued)*

```
no rip admin default
no rip client1 passive
no rip client1 default
no rip client2 passive
no rip client2 default
no rip dmz passive
no rip dmz default
no rip provider2 passive
no rip provider2 default
timeout xlate 24:00:00 conn 12:00:00 half-closed 0:10:00 udp 0:02:00
timeout rpc 0:10:00 h323 0:05:00
timeout uauth 0:05:00 absolute
!Configuration of client authentication
aaa-server TACACS+ protocol tacacs+
aaa-server RADIUS protocol radius
aaa-server admin protocol tacacs+
aaa-server admin (admin) host 10.1.1.4 AdminKey timeout 30
aaa authentication http inbound host 0 0 0
aaa accounting http inbound 0 0 0 0 admin
! SNMP configuration information
snmp-server location Wiring Closet #2
snmp-server contact John Doe 555-1212
snmp-server community Kookookachoo
snmp-server host admin 10.1.1.99
snmp-server enable traps
telnet 10.1.1.4 255.255.255.0 admin
telnet timeout 5
terminal width 80
Cryptochecksum:dc2a867907ccf77cb25d142d34fb3449
: end
telnet 10.0.0.0 255.255.255.0 admin
telnet timeout 5
terminal width 80
Cryptochecksum:dc2a867907ccf77cb25d142d34fb3449
: end
Pixfirewall#
```

Review Questions

Answer the following review questions, which delve into some of the key facts and concepts covered in this chapter:

1 What is the name for TCP connections that have not completed the three-way handshake?

2 How do you upgrade a PIX Firewall model 515's software image for Release 5.1.2 and later?

3 Does WebSENSE allow FTP filtering?

4 What severity level is listed for URL and FTP syslog messages?

5 How often do PIX Firewall failover units send hello messages?

6 What three things are required to make stateful failover work between two PIX Firewall units?

7 Which version of PIX Firewall software first supported IPSec VPN tunnels?

8 What two port numbers do SNMP packets use?

9 What conduit permission(s) is/are necessary to permit PPTP sessions to pass through the PIX Firewall to a Microsoft Windows NT Server inside?

10 How many different protocols are covered by the **fixup** feature? What are they?

References

The topics considered in this chapter are complex and should be studied further to more fully understand them and put them to use. Use the following references to learn more about the topics in this chapter.

URL Filtering

WebSENSE (www.websense.com) provides links to specific product information for the WebSENSE URL filtering software, pricing, and updates. Currently the PIX Firewall supports only WebSENSE URL servers.

Private Link Encryption

Cisco lists the Private Link encryption card under its End-of-Life materials online (www.cisco.com). It is no longer possible to purchase this card. Specifics were included in this chapter due to the large number of current installations of this technology.

Point-to-Point Tunneling Protocol

At the Microsoft Web site (support.microsoft.com), you can search links for configuration information for PPTP and VPNs on various Microsoft Windows 95, 98, NT, and 2000 machines.

TFTP Server

Go to www.cisco.com/pcgi-bin/tablebuild.pl/tftp to set up a TFTP server to load new releases of PIX Firewall software.

Cisco Secure Policy Manager

Follow the link at www.cisco.com/public/sw-center/sw-ciscosecure.shtml to register for a single-device evaluation version of the CiscoSecure Policy Manager software.

Cisco Secure Software Center

Follow the links at www.cisco.com/public/sw-center/sw-ciscosecure.shtml for PIX Firewall software updates, maintenance releases, password recovery, and TFTP bootloader files.

Managing Cisco Network Security 2.0 course materials.

Cisco Connection Online documentation CD.

PIX Firewall 520, software version 5.1(2).

PART V

Configuring Cisco Encryption Technology

Chapter 13   Cisco Encryption Technology Overview

Chapter 14   Configuring Cisco Encryption Technology

Upon completing this chapter, you will understand the following:

- The types of security problems that can be solved by using encryption
- What encryption is and how it works
- How encryption technology is used in Cisco products
- How DES encryption works
- How the MD5 message hash function works
- How DSS encryption works
- How the Diffie-Hellman key exchange works

CHAPTER **13**

Cisco Encryption Technology Overview

Encryption technologies enable the secure transmission of data over insecure networks. This chapter explores the encryption technologies that make up Cisco Encryption Technology (CET), which is used in Cisco routers.

Encryption Solutions

Encryption can solve some significant threats to the integrity of network traffic. Customers can use CET to ensure that data remains private and confidential as it transits a network. This chapter explores the encryption technologies used with CET.

Data Integrity Problems and Solutions

A major problem for network managers and users is that network traffic is vulnerable to various threats. One solution to this problem is CET. The following are some of the threats that can be solved with encryption technology:

- Eavesdropping:
  - Intruders can use packet sniffers to capture and decode traffic, obtaining usernames, passwords, and sensitive data.
  - Intruders can launch information-gathering attacks to gain knowledge of network devices so that they can launch further attacks.
  - Intruders can use eavesdropping to capture and steal information traversing the network.
- Data manipulation:
  - Intruders can construct bogus Internet data messages and send them to a destination host. UDP traffic is easier to forge than TCP traffic, yet it is still possible to forge TCP traffic.
  - Intruders can eavesdrop on traffic, capture the traffic, modify selected portions of the traffic, and then replay it to the recipient.

— Intruders can intercept a message, make subtle changes to the message header and data payload, and then send them to the recipient, taking over the session. Encryption can partially prevent this type of session hijacking attack because the data payload is encrypted and cannot easily be deciphered.

- A network user can deny having performed a transaction (repudiation).

One solution to these vulnerabilities is CET, which employs industry-standard encryption technologies to provide data privacy and integrity.

What Is Encryption?

Encryption is the process of taking data in readable or usable (cleartext) form and converting it into unreadable or unusable form. Then the data can be transmitted or stored securely. The data is decrypted and converted back into usable form. Encryption is also known as *enciphering*. Encryption can be accomplished in software or in hardware by specialized integrated circuits such as digital signal processors (DSPs) or application-specific integrated circuits (ASICs). Encryption provides the following services:

- Data privacy
- Data integrity
- Nonrepudiation

Data Privacy

Encryption in data communications is used to change a digital message from its original form to an encrypted form so that it can be transmitted securely over an insecure network. The encrypted message can be read only by intended parties, ensuring data privacy. The data privacy feature protects against eavesdropping.

Data Integrity

Encryption can also ensure the integrity of stored, transmitted, and received data, protecting against data manipulation. Data integrity can involve device authentication, which ensures that the peer network device you are communicating with is legitimate and is not part of a session hijacking attack. Data integrity can also involve data authentication, ensuring that the message has not been modified without the sender's knowledge during transmission. An authentication check of data can produce one of three results. The data can be

- **Authentic**—It really is from the person it claims it is from, and it has not been altered.
- **Forged**—It is not authentic.

- **Unverifiable**—You cannot check whether it is authentic because you do not have the sender's public key.

Data authentication is handled by encryption schemes that combine several encryption technologies, such as CET for key exchange and peer authentication, or Pretty Good Privacy (PGP) for e-mail security. Authentication can be added with a separate algorithm such as Digital Signature Standard (DSS) (as described later in this chapter), which is used by CET for authentication.

Nonrepudiation

Some encryption schemes enable *nonrepudiation,* a feature used to prove that a message has been sent and received. Nonrepudiation works by attaching a digital signature to the sent message that proves the identity of the sender, the time the message was sent, and the authenticity of the data in the message. ("I did not authorize that credit card transaction!" "Yes you did! Here is proof that you did.") Nonrepudiation is similar to using witnesses or a notary public to attest that someone signed a binding contract so that the signer cannot later deny having done so. It is useful for financial transactions such as credit card debits. CET can be used to enable nonrepudiation.

How Does Encryption Work?

Broken down into its essential elements, encryption consists of data to be encrypted, a key that is a sequence of digits, and an encryption algorithm, as illustrated in Figure 13-1.

Figure 13-1 *Data, a Key, and an Encryption Algorithm Are the Essential Encryption Elements*

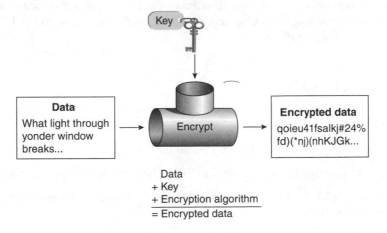

The combination of the three essential encryption elements results in an encrypted message that can be transmitted securely over a network as follows:

- **Data**—A message in cleartext form that needs to be encrypted. The data may consist of a credit card transmission, a banking transaction, confidential company data, a patient's medical record, or any other data deemed sensitive and requiring privacy.

- **Key**—A sequence of digits of a certain length used to encrypt and decrypt data. Keys are similar to passwords. Keys can be either public or private. The standard key length of DES is 56 bits. CET uses both 56-bit DES and a 40-bit variant of DES. Newer standards such as IPSec are implementing longer keys (such as 168 bits). The longer the key length, the less likely it is that someone can determine the key and decrypt the data. Longer key lengths require more CPU utilization in a Cisco router for encryption and decryption.

- **Encryption algorithm**—A mathematical formula designed to scramble input data to the point where an observer cannot determine the content of the original input data. DES, described later in this chapter, is the encryption algorithm used by CET.

- **Encrypted data**—Data that has been run through an encryption algorithm. The encrypted message is undecipherable to the observer. The encrypted message is useless unless it can be decrypted and restored to its original cleartext state.

Encryption can take place in the originating host or in a router at a strategic point in the network. The encryption process in a Cisco router is executed either in router software or on a hardware-assist module. Cisco routers accomplish encryption in Cisco IOS Software called crypto engines. The crypto engine can run in router CPUs and memory or in hardware-assist circuit boards. Hardware-assist boards enable higher encryption throughput. For example, the 7500 series routers can have the crypto engine run in the second-generation Versatile Interface Processor (VIP2) processor card or in software. Chapter 14, "Configuring Cisco Encryption Technology," covers how CET runs in Cisco routers in more detail.

Encryption Applications

Figure 13-2 shows some examples of applications where encryption can be used to secure communications over an IP network.

The applications shown in Figure 13-2 do the following:

1 Secure virtual private networks (VPNs) between business partners over the Internet.

2 Secure VPN gateways from remote company branches or sites to the campus site over the Internet.

3 Protect WAN traffic over leased lines or the Internet.

4 Secure transactions between Web browsers and servers.

Figure 13-2 *Six Sample Applications Where Encryption Can Be Used*

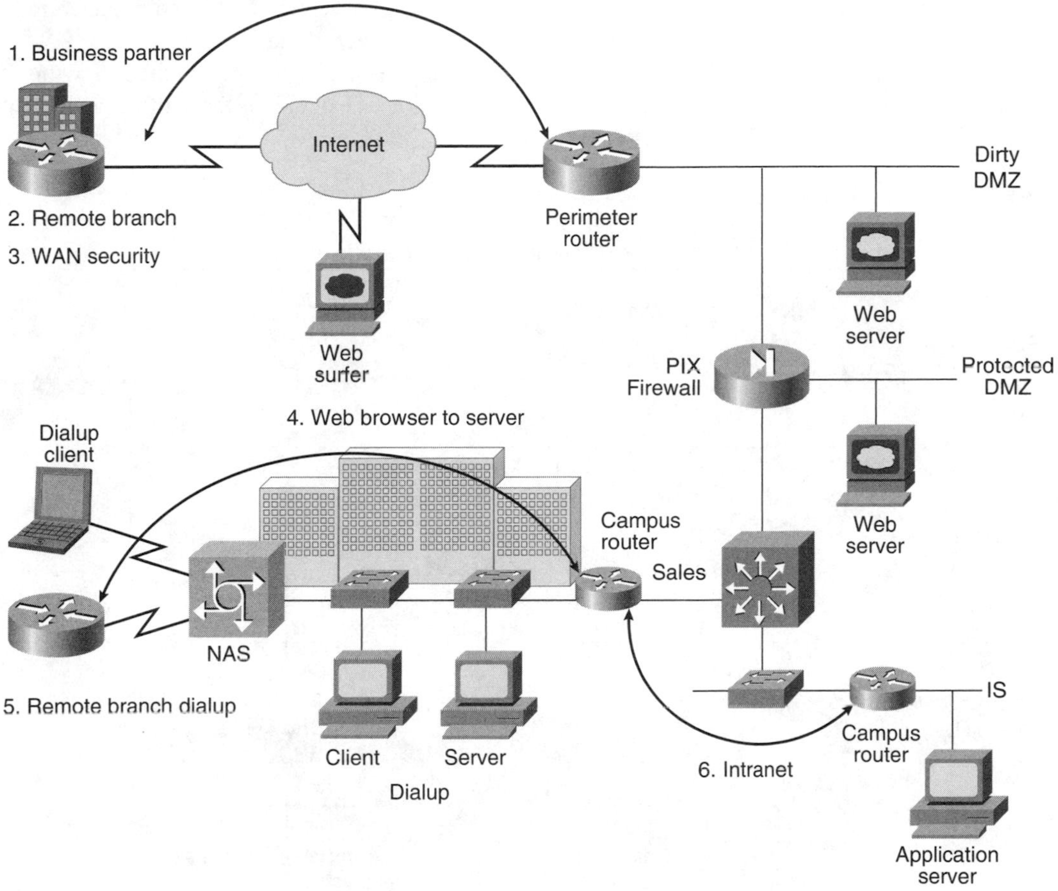

1. Business partner
2. Remote branch
3. WAN security
4. Web browser to server
5. Remote branch dialup
6. Intranet

Internet

Web surfer

Perimeter router

Dirty DMZ

Web server

PIX Firewall

Protected DMZ

Web server

Dialup client

Campus router

Sales

NAS

Client   Server

Dialup

Campus router

IS

Application server

5 Secure dialup communications from a remote company site to the campus site if a suitable router is used at the remote site.

6 Secure intranet traffic to protect sensitive traffic from internal eavesdroppers.

You should determine whether encryption is the proper solution to your communication problem after careful investigation and research. Encryption can require additional router CPU usage and can slow data transmission. Your network security policy should clearly state where, when, and how encryption is used in your network.

Encryption Alternatives

Network managers have the choice of implementing encryption in data communications at either the application, the data link, or the network layer of the Open Systems Interconnection (OSI) model, as shown in Figure 13-3. As described in the following sections, there are advantages to placing encryption at any one of these three layers, with associated implementation issues and costs.

Figure 13-3 *Encryption Implemented at Any of Three Layers*

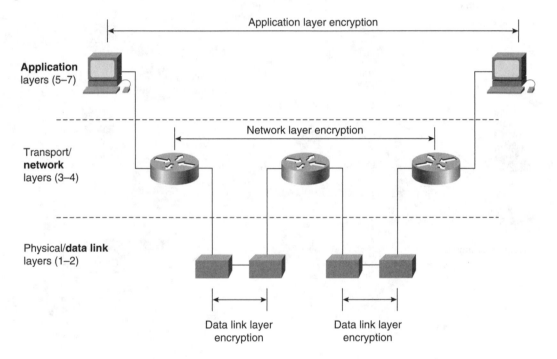

Application Layer Encryption

Application layer encryption requires each application on a host that is generating sensitive data to support encryption. All hosts that communicate with the application must use the same encryption algorithms, even if they reside on different platforms. Web browsers and servers are one example of application layer encryption. Web browsers and servers perform encryption and decryption of data using Secure Sockets Layer (SSL) and Secure Hypertext Transport Protocol (HTTPS), enabling secure Internet transactions. E-mail client and server applications supporting PGP are another example of application layer encryption.

Application layer encryption has the advantage of operating from end to end and can be invoked only when needed by the user. Decentralized user control and the need to install and configure encryption on each host make it difficult for the system administrator to control security policy company-wide.

Data Link Layer Encryption

Data link layer encryption can be implemented in devices outside the router on sensitive links, as shown in Figure 13-3. Link layer encryption encrypts all traffic on a given link, including network layer headers and protocol type information. The utility of link layer encryption is extremely dependent on network topology. The encryption/decryption process must be repeated on every link where security is a concern. Because this method does not leave IP addresses in the clear for routing, decryption and reencryption might need to occur several times, leading to increased delay in the network and possibly compromising security because these routers need to be trusted with cleartext.

An example of a link layer encryption device is an IRE Model HS Remote Encryptor, which is a hardware device about the size of an external modem. The Model HS has two ports. One port always handles cleartext data, and the other port handles encrypted data.

Network Layer Encryption

Network layer encryption can be done anywhere in the network. It can be implemented on all traffic without upgrading all the host applications. It also leaves appropriate Layer 3 and 4 information in the clear for use in routing. So, while adding to the overall security throughout the network, users can continue to enable quality of service (QoS) end to end.

Network layer encryption has the advantage of operating transparently between subnet boundaries and being reliably enforceable from a network administrator's perspective. Examples of network layer encryption technology are CET on Cisco routers enabled by Cisco IOS Software and IP security (IPSec) encryption on the PIX Firewall.

The IPSec protocol was developed to provide network layer encryption and secure key establishment. IPSec is discussed in more detail in Chapter 15, "Understanding Cisco IPSec Support."

Network Layer Encryption and Cisco Encryption Technology

CET, Cisco's implementation of network layer encryption, lets a network manager smoothly integrate the security of encryption into a network. The integration is transparent to end users and their applications as well as to all intermediate routers and other network media and devices. Encryption need only happen at the edge of the network, on the LAN where the sensitive data originates. Decryption is not necessary until the data reaches the router on the far-end LAN where the destination host resides.

Network managers retain the option of enabling encryption anywhere in the data path with network layer encryption. By encrypting after the UDP or TCP headers so that only the TCP or UDP data is encrypted, CET allows all intermediate routers and Layer 3 switches to forward the traffic as they would any other IP packets. This payload-only encryption allows flow switching and list features to work with the encrypted traffic just as they would with plaintext traffic, thereby preserving the desired QoS for all data. Users can send encrypted data over the Internet transparently.

Here are some characteristics of network layer encryption:

- It encrypts traffic on a flow-by-flow basis—between specific user/application pairs or subnets.
- It is specific to a protocol but is media/interface independent.
- It need not be supported by intermediate network devices.
- It is topology independent.
- Cisco IOS Software supports network layer encryption.

In Figure 13-4, the encrypting peer routers encrypt only traffic between Host A and the HR server. All other traffic is unencrypted.

Figure 13-4 *Network Layer Encryption Is Routable*

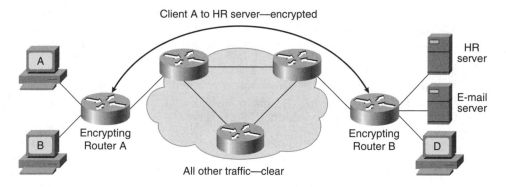

Cisco IOS Cryptosystem Overview

Cisco performs encryption with CET using four encryption technologies to form an integrated *cryptosystem,* a combination of encryption technologies to solve communications problems (see Figure 13-5):

Figure 13-5 *DES, MD5, DSS, and Diffie-Hellman Make Up the CET Cryptosystem*

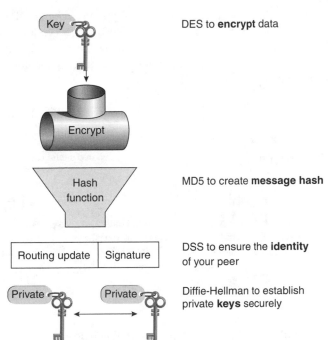

- **Digital Encryption Standard (DES)**—The most popular of several methods used to encrypt and decrypt data, ensuring that it is kept private.

- **Message Digest 5 (MD5)**—A one-way encryption method that produces a fixed-length output from a variable-length input. MD5 is used with DSS to create digital signatures.

- **Digital Signature Standard (DSS)**—An encryption method that produces an encryption checksum attached to a message as a signature. DSS ensures the identity of peer encrypting routers.

- **Diffie-Hellman key agreement**—A secure method of establishing public keys used to create the shared secret keys used for a DES session between peer encrypting routers.

Many standards have emerged to protect the secrecy of keys and to facilitate the changing of these keys. One of these, DSS, uses a public/private key system to ensure the identity of another party and also to prove a user's own identity when communicating via electronic means. Diffie-Hellman is used to do key exchange without exchanging keys. This is the most well-known and widely used algorithm for establishing session keys to encrypt data. However, because it does not guarantee the peer's identity, CET necessarily includes DSS. DES, DSS, and Diffie-Hellman are integral parts of Cisco IOS Release 11.2 and later releases that support CET.

DES Encryption

DES is one of the most widely used encryption standards. DES turns cleartext into ciphertext via an encryption algorithm. The DES decryption algorithm on the remote end restores cleartext from ciphertext. Keys enable the encryption and decryption. The keys are identical (or shared) in each peer, yet they are never transmitted over the wire. Figure 13-6 illustrates this process.

Figure 13-6 *Encryption Turns Cleartext into Ciphertext, Decryption Reverses the Process, and Keys Are Enablers*

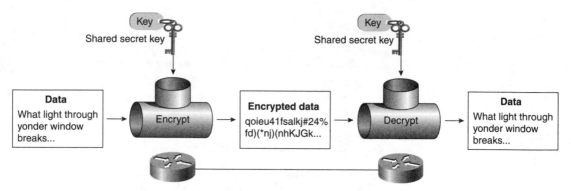

DES is a block-cipher algorithm that is publicly available. The DES algorithm takes the cleartext data to be encrypted, breaks it into 64-bit blocks, performs its encryption operation, and outputs encrypted data in 64-bit blocks. An 8-bit block option is also available.

As you will learn later in this chapter, the strength of DES lies in the key that is plugged into the encryption algorithm. The standard DES key length is 56 bits and can be any 56-bit number. Cisco IOS Software randomly generates the DES key using Diffie-Hellman.

The DES Encryption Process

DES encrypts data in five main steps:

1 DES does an initial permutation of the cleartext block, making it easier to handle the text in byte-sized chunks.

2 The key is transformed into a form suitable for the primary encryption algorithm.

3 The permutated 64-bit block is broken into two 32-bit halves.

4 One of the halves is run through a complex, table-specified substitution that is dependent on the transformed key. The output is exclusive ORed (XOR) with the other 32-bit half. This function takes place in 16 cycles, called rounds. After each round, the two 32-bit halves are swapped.

5 Following the final round, a final permutation is applied. The resulting ciphertext block is a series of 64 bits, each of which depends on every bit of the input and every bit of the key.

Block ciphers further guarantee the integrity of the data received by using feedback. Cisco's encryption algorithm incorporates cipher feedback (CFB), which does an XOR of the plaintext data with each block of encrypted data. CFB provides a means to verify that all data was received as transmitted.

DES is a symmetric algorithm, meaning that the same algorithm works for both encryption and decryption. The same encryption key is used to both encrypt and decrypt data.

DES is fairly easily implemented in both hardware and software. IBM developed DES initially to run in hardware. CET uses the DES algorithm to encrypt and decrypt data.

DES Keys

The most important feature of a cryptographic algorithm is its security against being compromised. The security of a cryptosystem, or the degree of difficulty for an attacker to determine the contents of the ciphertext, depends on several key areas. In most protocols, the cornerstone of security lies in the secrecy of the key used to encrypt data. The DES algorithm was designed so that it would be too difficult for anyone to be able to determine the cleartext without having the key.

In any cryptosystem, strong measures are taken to protect the secrecy of the encryption key. Cisco recognizes the importance of key secrecy; two of the three encryption technologies used by CET have more to do with key distribution and secrecy than with the actual encryption of data (DSS and Diffie-Hellman).

After peer encrypting routers obtain their shared secret key used with DES via Diffie-Hellman, they can use it to communicate with each other using the DES encryption algorithm. Key length is important because it is more difficult to guess more digits than fewer. Even DES encrypted data can be decrypted by an attacker, given enough computing power and time dedicated to finding the key. If a key were to be discovered, every packet that was encrypted with that key would easily be decrypted by the attacker. Frequently changing shared secret keys makes it less likely that attackers can decrypt the data because there is less time to launch a key attack, discover a key, and decrypt data before the key is changed again. The longer the key length, the more secure the encrypted data. Also, the shorter the encrypted session, the less likely a hacker can break into it.

CET uses the standard 56-bit DES key and a 40-bit key variant of DES for compliance with export laws. Triple DES (used in IPSec) uses a 168-bit key length for stronger security.

Attacks Against DES

DES is vulnerable to brute-force attacks and cryptanalysis. With brute-force attacks, network intruders use software to attempt to determine the encryption key by running the DES algorithm against an encrypted block of data using every possible key, one by one, until the encrypted data is deciphered. Cryptanalysis is the art and science of using mathematics to determine the encryption key. For more information about efforts to crack DES, see www.distributed.net/des.

MD5 Message Hashing

Message hashing is an encryption technique that can be used to ensure that a message has not been altered. The MD5 algorithm takes as input a cleartext message of arbitrary length. The message could be a username and password pair, or a Cisco routing update. The MD5 algorithm is run on the input, which produces as output a fixed-length, 128-bit "message digest" or "hash" of the input. Figure 13-7 illustrates this process.

Figure 13-7 *MD5 Produces a Fixed-Length Hash of a Variable-Length Input Useful for Data Integrity*

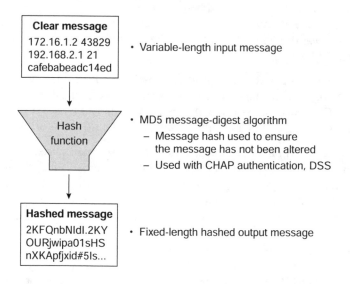

It is considered computationally infeasible to reverse the hash process or to produce two messages having the same message digest. The MD5 algorithm is useful for digital signature applications. Cisco IOS Software uses the MD5 message-digest algorithm to perform message hashing with CHAP password authentication and with DSS. MD5 was developed by Ronald Rivest and is described in RFC 1321. See the "Hashed Message Authentication Codes" section in Chapter 15 for more information about hashing algorithms.

DSS Encryption

DSS encryption is a mechanism that protects data from undetected change. Digital signatures use a private key to produce an encrypted checksum. Anyone with the public key of the message signer can verify the digital signature, but only the message signer can generate the signature.

DSS verifies the identity of a person or a computer with whom a user is communicating electronically, just as a signature verifies the identity of a check issuer. DSS uses the concept of a public key/private key pair. The public key is derived from the private key by a one-way transformation. Each user or device has a public key (which is known by everyone who wants to communicate with that user) and a private key. It is computationally infeasible to determine the private key from the public key. The algorithm relies on the MD5 hash function to verify the authenticity of the data sent. The hash function is a way of taking a message's "fingerprint." The idea is that, if two fingerprints match, the message has not been altered. The hash is then run through a function that uses the private key to "sign" the message. The values are reversible only if someone has the public key. The other party then runs the same hash and verifies the signature to ensure the identity and content of the message.

DSS is a very secure way of exchanging data with the assurance that it has not been changed because the other person's identity is verified by that person's possession of his or her private key, the only key that could be used to generate the signature verified by that same person's public key. All users keep their private key secret but share the public key with everyone who might want to communicate with them. Ideally, these public keys would be held in a known and trusted repository such as a certificate authority (CA). DSS uses message hashing technology to ensure data authenticity.

DSS Signature Generation

Figure 13-8 shows how a DSS signature is generated.

One example of how DSS is used is routing update authentication performed in Cisco IOS Software. Actually, DSS will work with any type of data that needs authentication.

1 Router A hashes the routing update using MD5.

2 Router A encrypts the hashed routing update using its own private key, creating a digital signature.

3 Router A appends the signature to the routing update and sends both to Router B.

Figure 13-8 *DSS Signature Generation at Router A Creates a Digital Signature of a Routing Update*

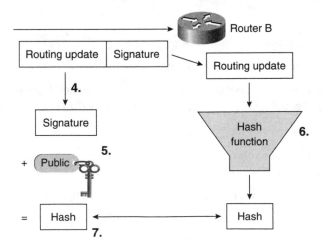

DSS Signature Verification

The digital signature is verified on the receiving router, as shown in Figure 13-9.

Figure 13-9 *DSS Is Used at Router B to Ensure the Integrity of the Received Routing Update*

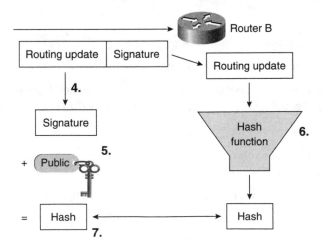

The digital signature is verified on the receiving router as follows:

4 Router B separates the digital signature from the routing update.

5 Router B decrypts the digital signature using Router A's public key and obtains the hash that was generated by Router A.

6 Router B hashes the received routing update.

7 Router B compares the hash it received from Router A with the hash it just generated. If the hashes match, it can be assured that the routing update is legitimate and that it was not spoofed by a network intruder.

Diffie-Hellman Key Agreement

Diffie-Hellman is used to securely exchange public keys so that shared secret keys can be securely generated for use as DES keys. When DSS is used to ensure the identity of a peer for establishment of the session key, users need a way to securely generate and exchange the session key. Because it is very important that this key remain secret, key exchange must ensure that a third party cannot determine the session key, even if the exchange takes place over what is suspected to be an insecure link—generally the link currently in use. The Diffie-Hellman algorithm (among others) was designed for just this purpose.

Cisco selected the Diffie-Hellman key exchange agreement protocol and process, which is one of the oldest, most trusted, and most used key exchange methods. It is very secure because at no time is the key actually transmitted (transmission would allow it to be viewed by a third party), nor can a third party determine the key. Diffie-Hellman prevents key interception by using two known prime numbers (for example, p and q). These shared numbers have a special mathematical relationship with one another that makes it possible to agree on a common secret key and makes it impossible for eavesdroppers to determine what this secret key is, even if they know the shared primes. CET uses fixed numbers for p and q.

The end result of the Diffie-Hellman exchange is the generation of a shared secret key. The keys are the same in each peer but are never revealed or exchanged over the wire. The shared secret key is used to encrypt messages using DES.

Someone intercepting the Diffie-Hellman public keys cannot easily compute the shared secret key and also cannot easily decrypt the message with the public key. It is very important to keep the shared secret key secure.

An advantage of the CET implementation of key exchange with Diffie-Hellman is that the shared secret keys are never entered manually and cannot be accessed, increasing security. A disadvantage of the implementation is that a system administrator is required at each peer router to initiate and verify the Diffie-Hellman exchange. IPSec automates the Diffie-Hellman exchange.

See the "Diffie-Hellman Key Agreement" section in Chapter 15 for more a more detailed discussion of Diffie-Hellman.

Summary

This section summarizes the main points of this chapter, as follows:

- Encryption helps reduce vulnerability to eavesdropping, information theft, data manipulation, session hijacking, and message repudiation threats.

- Encryption is the process of converting cleartext data into enciphered data using encryption algorithms and keys so that only intended parties can observe the data through decryption.

- Encryption provides data privacy, data integrity, data authentication, and nonrepudiation.

- Cisco routers accomplish encryption in Cisco IOS Software running in routers or in hardware-assist circuit boards inside the routers.

- Encryption can be used to create a VPN between business partners or remote company sites, protect WAN traffic, secure Web traffic, secure dialup communications, and secure intranet traffic.

- Cisco uses DES, MD5, DSS, and Diffie-Hellman technology in its products.

- DES is used to encrypt data, and it uses private keys of 40 or 56 bits in length.

- The MD5 message hash provides a fixed-length hash of the input message that cannot be reversed. It is used for digital signatures.

- DSS creates a digital signature of a message to ensure data authenticity.

- Diffie-Hellman enables secure key exchange of public keys used to generate DES keys.

Review Questions

Answer the following review questions to test your knowledge of the topics covered in this chapter:

1 What are two security problems that encryption technology helps solve?

2 What four essential elements make up encryption?

3 How does encryption technology enable secure communications over the Internet, an extranet, or an intranet?

4 What three features does encryption provide?

5 What four encryption technologies does Cisco use to make up CET?

6 What is the purpose of DES in CET?

7 What DES key lengths are supported in CET, and why is key length important?

8 How is the MD5 message hash used in Cisco products?

9 How is DSS used in CET?

10 How is Diffie-Hellman used in CET?

References

Each of the topics considered in this chapter is complex and should be studied further to more fully understand them and put them to use. Use the following references to learn more about the topics in this chapter.

CET Operation

White paper, "Cisco IOS Software Feature: Network Layer Encryption," 1997. Contains an overview of the technologies used in CET, and application, design, implementation, and configuration guidelines. Located at www.cisco.com/wacrp/customer/732/Security/ encrp_wp.htm.

Encryption Algorithms and Operation

B. Schneier, *Applied Cryptography,* Second Edition, Wiley, 1996.

R. E. Smith, *Internet Cryptography,* Addison-Wesley, 1997.

MD5

RFC 1321, R. Rivest, "The MD5 Message-Digest Algorithm," April 1992.

DSS

"Announcing the Standard for Digital Signature Standard (DSS)," Federal Information Processing Standards (FIPS) Publication 186, May 19, 1994.

Other Encryption References

Security Command Reference, Cisco IOS Release 12.0, October 1999.

Security Configuration Guide, Cisco IOS Release 12.0, October 1999.

Upon completing this chapter, you will be able to do the following:

- Identify the Cisco products that support CET

- Configure CET in Cisco routers to create a secure communications environment based on a case study network design

- Identify how to implement and troubleshoot CET

CHAPTER 14

Configuring Cisco Encryption Technology

This chapter presents the concepts, processes, and procedures needed to configure Cisco Encryption Technology (CET). This chapter summarizes which platforms CET runs on, and it contains useful tips on where to use, how to implement, how to order, and how to troubleshoot CET.

Cisco Encryption Technology Basics

CET is a form of network layer encryption in which the data payload of IP packets is encrypted (minus UDP and TCP headers), allowing the encrypted packets to be routed on an IP network. CET can be performed on multiple Cisco routers ranging from the 800 series access routers to 7500 core routers.

CET has the following features and functions:

- It controls encryption policy by network, subnet, or address and port pairs using extended IP access lists.
- It uses the Digital Signature Standard (DSS) for device authentication.
- It uses Diffie-Hellman for session key management.
- It uses the Data Encryption Standard (DES) for bulk encryption.
- It uses a software crypto engine running in a router or on hardware assist circuit cards—VIP2 service adapter and ESA.

CET Crypto Engines

CET is accomplished by a Cisco IOS Software service called a *crypto engine*. Depending on the hardware configuration of the encrypting router, different crypto engines govern different router interfaces. There are three types of crypto engines: the Cisco IOS crypto engine, the second-generation Versatile Interface Processor (VIP2) crypto engine, and the Encryption Service Adapter (ESA) crypto engine. Table 14-1 summarizes crypto engine support for Cisco routers.

Table 14-1 *Cisco Router Crypto Engine Support*

Router	Crypto Engine	Software Support
All Cisco routers supporting CET with no VIP2-40 or ESA	Cisco IOS crypto engine	Depends on the router
7500 series with VIP2-40 7000 series using RSP7000 or RSP7000CI with VIP2-40	VIP2-40 crypto engine on interfaces supported by VIP2-40 Cisco IOS crypto engine on other interfaces	11.2(7)P or later
7500 series with VIP2-40 and ESA 7000 series using RSP7000 or RSP7000CI with VIP2-40 and ESA	ESA crypto engine on interfaces supported by VIP2-40 Cisco IOS crypto engine on other interfaces	11.2(7)P or later
7200 series with ESA installed and active	ESA crypto engine	11.2(7a)P or later

The Cisco IOS Software Planner, at www.cisco.com/kobayashi/sw-center/sw-ios.shtml, lists the exact Cisco IOS release, platform, and software features supporting CET. The CET software feature is indicated with the digits 40 and 56. For example, the Enterprise Plus 56 software feature supports 56-bit bit DES encryption using CET. You must be a registered Cisco Connection Online (CCO) user to access the Software Center on CCO.

The Cisco IOS Crypto Engine

Every router with Cisco IOS encryption software has a Cisco IOS crypto engine. If a router has no additional crypto engines, the Cisco IOS crypto engine governs all the router interfaces. For many Cisco routers, the Cisco IOS crypto engine is the only crypto engine available. The only exceptions are the Cisco 7200, RSP7000, and 7500 series routers, which can also have additional crypto engines, as described in the next two sections.

A crypto engine is associated with the Cisco IOS Software residing in the Route Switch Processor (RSP), and a crypto engine is associated with the VIP2 (in the VIP2 IOS) and the VIP2 ESA. The advantages of using the VIP2 or VIP2 ESA encryption solutions are as follows:

- The VIP2 software (available on the 7500/VIP platform) provides encryption services per slot. Encryption operations typically execute faster because they occur on the VIP2, which also off-loads CPU cycles from the RSP Cisco IOS Software.

- Cisco 7200, RSP7000, and 7500 series routers can support an ESA to increase encryption performance.

- The VIP2 ESA (available on the 7500/VIP platform) provides encryption services on a slot basis, improves encryption performance, and has added tamper-proof qualities for all keys. (In this chapter, VIP2 is used to refer to VIP2 software and VIP2 ESA.)

The VIP2 Crypto Engine

Cisco RSP7000 and 7500 series routers with a VIP2-40 have two crypto engines: the Cisco IOS crypto engine and the VIP2 crypto engine.

The VIP2 crypto engine governs the port interfaces supported by the VIP2. The Cisco IOS crypto engine governs all remaining router interfaces. These rules assume that no ESA is installed in the VIP2. If the VIP2 has an installed ESA, the interfaces are governed differently, as explained in the next section.

The Encryption Service Adapter Crypto Engine

The ESA is a port adapter for the VIP2-40 card or a standalone port adapter for the Cisco 7200. The ESA runs the crypto engine, providing hardware assistance to encrypt and decrypt data that comes into or leaves through the interfaces on the Cisco 7500 VIP2 card, or traffic for any interfaces on the Cisco 7200 chassis. The ESA saves CPU cycles that can be used to support other Cisco IOS Software features.

Cisco 7200 Series Routers with Multiple ESAs

The ESA plugs into the Cisco 7200 chassis. When a Cisco 7200 router has an active ESA, the ESA crypto engine—not the Cisco IOS crypto engine—governs all the router interfaces.

With an inactive ESA, the Cisco IOS crypto engine governs all the router interfaces. On the Cisco 7200, you can select which engine is active; only one engine is active at a time.

Cisco RSP7000 and 7500 Series Routers with ESAs

In Cisco 7500 and RSP7000-equipped Cisco 7000 systems, the ESA requires a VIP2-40 for operation, and it must be installed in port adapter slot 1. The ESA and an adjoining port adapter plug into a VIP2 board. The ESA crypto engine—not the VIP2 crypto engine—governs the adjoining VIP2 port interfaces. The Cisco IOS crypto engine governs all remaining interfaces.

Cisco Encryption Technology Operation

Cisco routers perform network layer encryption in five general steps:

Step 1 Plan for encryption by gathering information and choosing an encryption policy.

Step 2 Prepare routers to perform encryption through a series of configuration steps. This preparation must be done by the system administrator on each peer encrypting router.

Step 3 Establish an encryption session with the appropriate peer-encrypting router.

Step 4 Encrypt and decrypt data.

Step 5 Terminate the encryption session.

The following sections discuss each of these encryption steps in more detail.

NOTE The network layer encryption process is documented in the *Cisco IOS Security Configuration Guide,* which can be found at www.cisco.com/univercd/cc/td/doc/product/software/ios120/12cgcr/secur_c/index.htm.

Step 1: Plan for Encryption

It is recommended that you plan your encryption implementation to reduce misconfiguration of the peer routers. Planning includes two areas:

- **General planning**—This refers to defining the overall encryption need based on the security policy, including the following:

  - **Identifying your security requirements**—For example, do you need to encrypt data traffic between your USA-based office and your UK-based office? Identifying security requirements should be based on your network security policy.

  - **Determining which applications need to be encrypted**—Traffic generated by applications can be encrypted on a per-port basis in TCP or UDP. For example, you might need to encrypt TCP-type packets of port 21.

  - **Determining which encryption algorithms to use for the encryption**—For example, what DES algorithm will the peer routers use to encrypt the data?

- **Per-site planning**—This refers to defining specific router and packet information that you will need to configure. Peer router configurations need to be mirror images (symmetrical) in order to operate properly. Therefore, you should determine and verify the following information for all identified peer encrypting routers:

  - ☐ Each router's name

  - ☐ Source host or subnet from which packets should be encrypted

  - ☐ Router interfaces through which encrypted packets must be sent and received

  - ☐ The public key of local and peer encrypting routers

  - ☐ Encryption algorithms to use between peer encrypting routers

Figure 14-1 illustrates the network topology and components of the XYZ Company used in the examples in this chapter. Refer to this figure to help understand the examples.

Figure 14-1 *Network Topology and Components of the XYZ Company Used in the Examples in This Chapter*

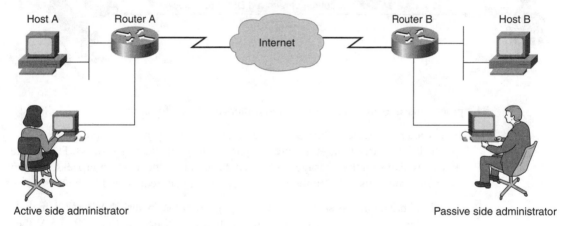

Step 2: Prepare Cisco Routers for Encryption

You must ensure that the peer router with which the local router is exchanging encrypted data is authenticated before encryption can occur. Figure 14-2 illustrates the process used to ensure that the paired routers are ready for encryption.

Figure 14-2 *System Administrators Prepare Each Peer Cisco Router for Encryption While in Voice Contact*

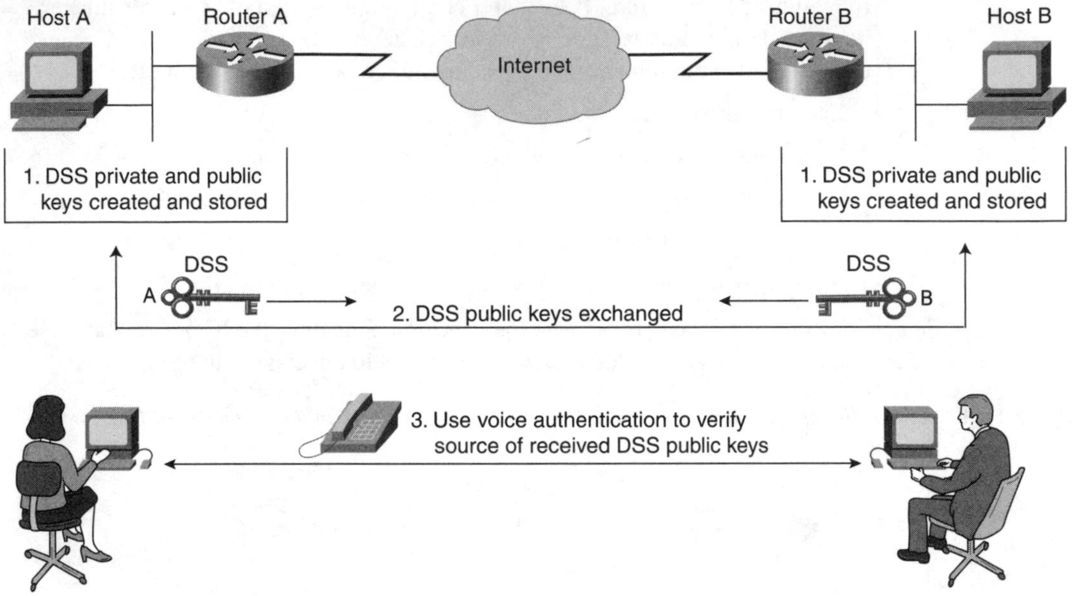

The process used to ensure that the paired routers are ready for encryption is as follows:

1 Peer routers generate Digital Signature Standard (DSS) private and public keys. The public key is shared with peer routers as part of the authentication process. The private key is used to sign the message exchanged during the authentication process, and the receiving router uses the public key to verify the signature attached to the message.

The DSS private key is stored in a private portion of the router's NVRAM, which cannot be viewed. This key is not shared with any other device. In a VIP2 ESA, the private key is stored in a tamper-proof area of the ESA. Remember that stored configurations on a TFTP server do not contain the private key information.

2 System administrators of peer routers must agree on an encryption policy and exchange DSS public keys between peer routers. Although DSS public numbers are not secret or confidential, you need to follow Step 3 to make certain of the origin and integrity of each public key received.

3 The system administrator verifies a peer router's DSS public key by verbally verifying the exchange with the administrator of the remote peer router. This verification is called voice authentication. Voice authentication requires that the network administrators of the peer routers trust each other and that they can recognize each other's identity over the phone.

The public keys received from peer routers are stored in the local router's public key list. Each router can encrypt messages only to peers that appear in the public key list.

NOTE	The detailed process for performing voice authentication is outlined in the section "Step 1: Establish Voice Contact" of this chapter.

Step 3: Establish an Encrypted Session

An encrypted session must be established between peer routers before they can exchange encrypted data. An encrypted session is established whenever a router detects an IP packet that should be encrypted and no encrypted session already exists, as shown in Figure 14-3.

Figure 14-3 *Routers Dynamically Establish an Encrypted Session*

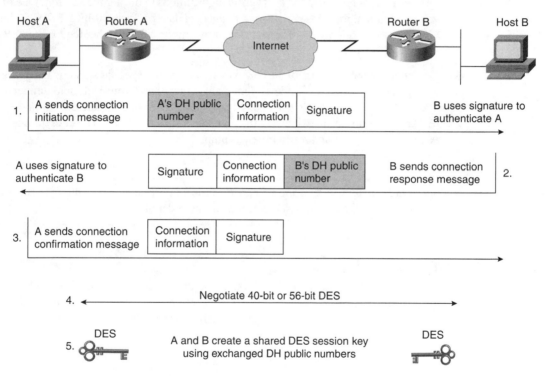

The process to establish an encryption session is as follows:

1 The peer routers exchange connection messages to establish an encrypted session. Router A authenticates with its peer router using a connection initiation message that includes a Diffie-Hellman number and a DSS signature.

2 Router B responds with a connection response message that has its own DSS signature. The DSS signatures sent in the connection messages are hexadecimal strings created by each router using their DSS private key. They are verified by the other router using the corresponding DSS public key exchanged when preparing the routers for encryption. The signature is always unique to the sending router and cannot be forged by any other device. Steps 1 and 2 are pass-or-fail steps. If the peers authenticate successfully, they continue to the next step. If the operation fails, the session is terminated.

3 Router A sends a connection confirmation message, indicating that the peer routers have authenticated.

4 The peer routers negotiate the encryption algorithm used during the session. One of two encryption algorithms can be used to encrypt data packets: 40-bit DES or 56-bit DES. Each encryption algorithm uses one of two modes: 8-bit cipher feedback (CFB) or 64-bit CFB.

5 The routers generate a temporary DES key to use for the specific session. The DES key is generated using the Diffie-Hellman algorithm. The Diffie-Hellman numbers were exchanged as part of connection setup and are used to compute the common DES key that will be shared during the given encryption session. The encryption session is now set up and ready for encrypting data.

NOTE   The *Cisco IOS Security Configuration Guide* describes the session establishment process and how to configure the encryption algorithms in more detail.

Step 4: Encrypt and Decrypting Data

After peer routers have authenticated each other and created a session DES key, they can exchange encrypted data. The negotiated DES encryption algorithm is used with the DES session key to encrypt and decrypt the data and then terminate the session, as illustrated in Figure 14-4.

Step 5: Terminate a Session

The encrypted communication session continues until the session timeout is reached, even if data exchange is not completed before the timeout is reached. The connection terminates when the configurable timeout value expires, not when the connection is idle. When the timeout is reached, the DES session key and Diffie-Hellman numbers are deleted.

If data still needs to be sent when the timeout is reached, a new session must be established. The default session timeout is 30 minutes. You can change the timeout to any value up to 24 hours.

Figure 14-4 *Data Is Encrypted and Decrypted Using DES Session Keys*

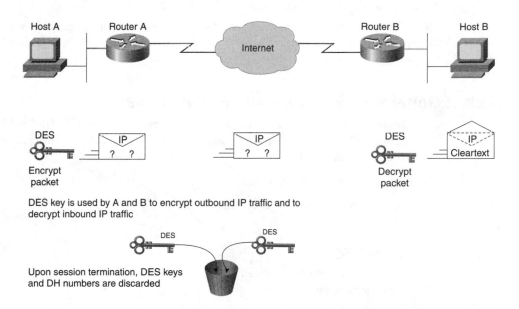

Configuring Cisco Encryption Technology

CET can be difficult to configure. It requires coordination between the system administrators of the peer encrypting routers. The major tasks you follow to configure CET are as follows. Each task consists of steps, which are detailed in subsequent sections.

- Task 1: Generate each peer router's DSS public and private key and save them to NVRAM.

- Task 2: Exchange the DSS public key with the peer router(s). Verify encryption policy details that the peer routers will use.

- Task 3: Define global encryption policy options that are usable by the router by configuring the encryption algorithms supported by the router.

- Task 4: Configure per-session encryption policy details by configuring crypto maps.

NOTE   Some of the listed tasks need to be performed only when you initially set up encryption. Refer to the details outlined on subsequent pages to determine when a step is unnecessary.

Ensure that basic network connectivity has been achieved between Cisco devices before configuring Cisco router encryption.

This chapter discusses job aids that you can use when configuring encryption. See the sections "Planning for Encryption Job Aid" and "Configuration Procedures Job Aid."

Task 1: Generate DSS Public and Private Keys

You begin configuring CET by generating the peer encrypting router's DSS public and private keys. The following steps and examples show how to generate a DSS public key pair between routers A and B:

Step 1 Generate the DSS key pair.

Step 2 Save the key pair to NVRAM.

Step 1: Generate the DSS Key Pair

Generate and save the key pair on each peer router with the following Cisco IOS command in global configuration mode:

```
crypto key generate dss key-name [slot | rsm | vip]
```

The command parameters and syntax have the following meanings:

Command	Description
key-name	A name assigned to the crypto engine to name either the Cisco IOS Software crypto engine, a VIP2 crypto engine, or an ESA crypto engine. Any character string is valid. Using a fully qualified domain name might make it easier to identify public keys.
slot	This optional argument identifies the crypto engine. This argument is available only on Cisco 7200, RSP7000, and 7500 series routers with ESA or VIP2 adapters. If no slot is specified, the Cisco IOS crypto engine is selected. Use the chassis slot number of the crypto engine location.
	For the Cisco IOS crypto engine, this is the chassis slot number of the route switch processor (RSP). For the VIP2 crypto engine, this is the chassis slot number of the VIP2. For the ESA crypto engine, this is the chassis slot number of the ESA (Cisco 7200) or the VIP2 (Cisco RSP7000 and 7500).
rsm	This optional keyword is available only on the Cisco Catalyst 5000 series switch. Identifies the Route Switch Module on the Cisco Catalyst 5000 series switch.
vip	This optional keyword is available only on the Cisco Catalyst 5000 series switch. Identifies the Versatile Interface Processor on the Cisco Catalyst 5000 series switch.

The **crypto key generate dss** command replaces the **crypto gen-signature-keys** command in Cisco IOS Release 12.0.

You can view your public keys by using the **show crypto key mypubkey dss** command. The private keys generated on both routers are saved to NVRAM and are inaccessible. Anyone who could gain access to the private key could masquerade as the legitimate owner of the key, so Cisco has taken much care to ensure that the private keys cannot be accessed or compromised.

NOTE If you are using a Cisco 7200, RSP7000, or 7500 series router or a Cisco Catalyst 5000 series switch with an ESA, you will be prompted to enter a password when you generate DSS keys for the ESA crypto engine.

Example 14-1 shows the generation of DSS keys on Routers A and B. Refer to Figure 14-1 for this example. The key names used are *routerAkey* and *routerBkey*. The crypto engines would have the names *routerAkey* and *routerBkey*.

Example 14-1 *Generating DSS Keys on Router A*

```
routerA(config)#crypto key generate dss routerAkey
Generating DSS keys ....
 [OK]
routerB(config)#crypto key generate dss routerBkey
Generating DSS keys ....
 [OK]
```

Step 2: Save the Key Pair to NVRAM

Next, you need to save the key pair on each peer router running a Cisco IOS crypto engine to a private portion of NVRAM with the **copy running-config startup-config** command. You need to keep in mind the following when using this command:

- You must perform the **copy running-config startup-config** command to save Cisco IOS crypto engine DSS keys to a private portion of NVRAM.

- If you are using a Cisco 7200, RSP7000, or 7500 series router or a Cisco Catalyst 5000 series switch with an ESA, DSS keys generated for the ESA crypto engine are automatically saved to tamper-resistant memory of the ESA during the DSS key generation process.

You can delete a DSS key pair of a crypto engine with the **crypto key zeroize dss** global configuration command. You must then regenerate the DSS keys with the **crypto key generate dss** command.

CAUTION DSS keys cannot be recovered after they have been removed. Use this command only after careful consideration. You will have to regenerate and exchange the DSS keys to establish an encrypted session if you zeroize them.

Configuring VIP2 ESA for DSS

Before you can configure the VIP2 ESA for DSS keys and encryption, you must follow these steps when installing the VIP2 ESA:

1 After you plug in the VIP2 ESA, get the ESA's status:

```
router#show crypto card
```

2 If the ESA is latched, clear the latch with the following command, which resets the ESA by clearing a hardware extraction latch that is set when an ESA is removed and reinstalled in the chassis:

```
router(config)#crypto card clear-latch {slot | vip}
```

3 As soon as the latch is clear, you can generate your DSS keys for the crypto engine as shown in Example 14-1. For additional password protection on the ESA, you are prompted for a password the first time you run the **crypto key generate dss** command.

The following steps illustrate the process for generating DSS keys for the VIP2 crypto engine:

1 Use the following command to generate DSS keys for the VIP2 crypto engine:

```
Router(config)#crypto key generate dss key-name [slot | rsm | vip]
```

When initially installed after a "zeroize" operation, the crypto card password must be initialized. You will need this password to generate new signature keys or to clear the crypto card extraction latch. You are prompted for the password, as shown in the following example:

```
router(config)# crypto key generate dss p1r3-vip 2
 % Initialize the crypto card password. You will need
   this password in order to generate new signature
   keys or clear the crypto card extraction latch.
 Password: <passwd>
 Re-enter password: <passwd>
 Generating DSS keys .... [OK]
```

2 Every other time the crypto card password is entered, a new password key must be generated, as follows:

```
p1r3(config)# crypto key generate dss p1r3-vip 2
 % Generating new DSS keys will require re-exchanging
```

```
        public keys with peers who already have the public key
        named p1r3-vip!
Generate new DSS keys? [yes/no]: yes
% Enter the crypto card password.
Password: <passwd>
Generating DSS keys .... [OK]
```

Generating new DSS keys requires re-exchanging public keys with peers who already have a public key from a previous key exchange.

Task 2: Exchange DSS Public Keys

The second task in configuring CET is for the administrators of the peer routers to exchange the DSS public keys between the routers so that they can authenticate each other. This task includes verifying through the use of voice authentication that the DSS public key received from the peer is authentic. Exchanging DSS public keys consists of the following steps:

Step 1 Establish voice contact.

Step 2 Enable the exchange connection from the passive side.

Step 3 Enable the exchange connection from the active side.

Step 4 Authenticate and accept the active side's DSS public key.

Step 5 Prompt the passive side to send a DSS key.

Step 6 Send a DSS key from the passive side.

Step 7 Authenticate and accept the passive side's DSS key.

Step 8 Verify encryption policy details and end the voice session.

The following sections detail each of the steps you must perform to exchange DSS keys. These steps require coordination between peer router administrators.

Step 1: Establish Voice Contact

First you need to call the remote peer router's administrator and decide whose router will assume the passive role and whose will be the active side. This procedure requires you to remain on the phone with the remote peer router's administrator until the key exchange is completed and the DSS keys are verified.

NOTE Both routers can be preconfigured by one person before they are put into active service. If the routers are not at the same site and under the control of one person, a system administrator must be present at both sites and in voice communication to manage the key exchange. This is the scenario presented here. Remember that, if the network over which you perform the key exchange can be eavesdropped on, intruders could spoof and substitute their own public key in the exchange, thereby compromising the encrypted connection before it has even been established. Both system administrators should verbally verify the public key fingerprints to ensure that they have not been tampered with.

Step 2: Enable the Exchange Connection from the Passive Side

The passive-side administrator enables an exchange connection by using the following command:

```
router(config)#crypto key exchange dss passive [tcp-port]
```

The command's optional parameter has the following meaning:

Command	Description
tcp-port	Cisco IOS Software uses a TCP port number of 1964 to designate a key exchange by default. You may use this optional keyword to select a different number to designate a key exchange if your system already uses port number 1964 for a different purpose.
	TCP port number 1964 has not been preassigned by the Internetworking Engineering Task Force (IETF.)

NOTE If the active-side administrator does not successfully connect, the wait can be terminated using the defined escape character, usually Shift+Ctrl+6 followed by X.

The **crypto key exchange dss passive** command replaces the **crypto key-exchange passive** command in Cisco IOS Release 12.0.

Consider Example 14-2, which shows the passive-side administrator (Router B) enabling the exchange of DSS keys. Refer to Figure 14-1 for this example.

Example 14-2 *Passive-Side Administrator Enabling DSS Key Exchange*

```
routerB(config)#crypto key-exchange passive
```

Step 3: Enable the Exchange Connection from the Active Side

The active administrator initiates an exchange connection and sends a DSS public key using the following Cisco IOS command:

```
router(config)#crypto key exchange dss ip-address key-name [tcp-port]
```

The command parameters and syntax have the following meanings:

Command	Description
ip-address	The IP address of the peer router (designated passive) participating with you in the key exchange.
key-name	Identifies the crypto engine. This name must match the key-name argument assigned when you generated DSS keys using the **crypto key generate dss** command.
tcp-port	Cisco IOS Software uses a TCP port number of 1964 to designate a key exchange by default. You may use this optional keyword to select a different number to designate a key exchange.

Here are some additional points to consider when enabling the exchange session:

- Peer encrypting routers must exchange DSS public keys before any encrypted communication can occur.

- If a particular TCP port was chosen on the passive side with the tcp-port optional keyword, you must choose the same port on the passive side. If you have a Cisco 7200, RSP7000, or 7500 series router, you need to exchange DSS public keys for each crypto engine you plan to use.

If the IP connection is successful, the active peer's DSS public key is exchanged with the passive router's key automatically. The serial number and fingerprint of the active's DSS public key display on the administrator's console on both the active and passive sides. The serial number and fingerprint are values generated from the active's DSS public key.

The **crypto key exchange dss** command replaces the **crypto key-exchange** command in Cisco IOS Release 12.0.

Example 14-3 shows the active-side administrator (Router A) initiating the DSS key exchange. Refer to Figure 14-1 for this example.

Example 14-3 *Active-Side Administrator Initiating DSS Key Exchange*

```
routerA(config)#crypto key exchange dss 10.1.1.2 routerAkey
```

Step 4: Authenticate and Accept the Active Side's DSS Public Key

The system administrators on both sides observe the serial number and fingerprint of the active side's DSS public key. Example 14-4 shows the output of Router A (see Figure 14-1) for this step. Router B would have similar output.

Example 14-4 *Router A's Serial Number and Fingerprint Used to Authenticate the DSS Key Exchange*

```
Public-key for RouterA:
 Serial Number 0514588
 Fingerprint
  ED0B F279 B0C4 152B DB8E
```

The system administrators perform voice authentication of active's public key sent to the passive router. The active administrator asks the passive administrator to authenticate and accept the DSS key. If the DSS key numbers match, the passive administrator agrees to accept the active side's DSS key and add the public key to the configuration by typing **y** at the prompt.

Peer public keys are stored in normal NVRAM and are associated with the peer's name and serial number. Because the keys are stored in the configuration after you enter the **copy running-config startup-config** command, you don't need to exchange public keys again unless you or the peer generates a new DSS key pair.

Step 5: Prompt the Passive Side to Send a DSS Key

At this point, a prompt appears on the passive router's console, asking the passive administrator to send the active administrator a DSS public key. The passive administrator presses Enter to continue. Example 14-5 shows the output of Router B at this step of the DSS public key exchange process.

Example 14-5 *Router B's Serial Number and Fingerprint Used to Authenticate the DSS Key Exchange*

```
The public-key for routerB is:
 Serial Number 05614636
  Fingerprint 5698 D554
   B55D EED5 741D
```

Step 6: Send a DSS Key from the Passive Side

The passive administrator is prompted for a public key name. When the passive administrator enters and accepts the name by pressing Enter, the DSS public key is sent to the active administrator.

Step 7: Authenticate and Accept the Passive Side's DSS Key

The serial number and fingerprint of the passive side's DSS public key appear on the console of both sides.

Both administrators authenticate the passive router's DSS key over the voice connection. The active administrator agrees to accept the passive's DSS key by typing **y** at the prompt.

Step 8: Verify Encryption Policy Details, and End the Voice Session

Both administrators verify encryption policy details, end the voice session, and continue configuring encryption.

An Example of DSS Key Exchange

This section contains an example of a DSS key exchange session between Router A (the active router) and Router B (the passive router). This section shows an example of Steps 2 through 7, organized into groups of steps. The commands are entered in the step order. Refer to Figure 14-1 for this section.

In Example 14-6, the administrators have authenticated each other (Step 1). They complete Step 2, enabling the exchange, and Step 3, initiating the exchange.

Example 14-6 *Administrators Complete Steps 2 and 3 of the DSS Key Exchange*

```
routerB(config)#crypto key exchange dss passive
Enter escape character to abort if connection does not complete.
Wait for connection from peer[confirm]<Return>
Waiting ....

routerA(config)#crypto key exchange dss 10.1.1.2 routerAkey
Public key for routerAkey:
   Serial Number 05614558
   Fingerprint   9C7D 6371 ED4E 9183 F3FE
Wait for peer to send a key[confirm] <Return>
Waiting ....
```

Example 14-7 shows Step 4 of the DSS key exchange process, in which Router B receives a DSS public key and fingerprint, and then the passive administrator authenticates the key with the active administrator and sends Router B's key to Router A.

Example 14-7 *Administrators Complete Step 4 of the DSS Key Exchange*

```
router B session: Passive

Public key for routerAkey:
   Serial Number 05614558
   Fingerprint   9C7D 6371 ED4E 9183 F3FE

Add this public key to the configuration? [yes/no]: yes
```

continues

Example 14-7 *Administrators Complete Step 4 of the DSS Key Exchange (Continued)*

```
Send peer a key in return[confirm] <Return>
Which one?
routerBkey? [yes]: yes
Public key for routerBkey:
   Serial Number 05614636
   Fingerprint   649E D4E1 4A78 DEE5 2762
routerB(config)#
```

Example 14-8 shows Steps 5, 6, and 7 of the DSS key exchange process. The Router A administrator authenticates the fingerprint of Router B's DSS key and accepts the key, and then both administrators view their peer's DSS public keys, complete Step 8, and move on to Task 3.

Example 14-8 *Administrators Complete Steps 5 Through 7 of the DSS Key Exchange*

```
routerA#
Public key for routerBkey:
   Serial Number 05614636
   Fingerprint   649E D4E1 4A78 DEE5 2762

Add this public key to the configuration? [yes/no]: yes
routerA(config)#exit

routerA#show crypto key pubkey-chain dss
Codes: M - Manually configured

Code Usage   Serial Number    Name
M    Signing 05614636         routerBkey

routerB(config)#exit

routerB#show crypto key pubkey-chain dss
Codes: M - Manually configured

Code Usage   Serial Number    Name
M    Signing 05614558         routerAkey
```

Alternative Key Exchange Methods

From a configuration perspective, each router requires the public DSS key for each encrypting peer router. The voice authentication method described earlier is the method recommended by Cisco for exchanging public DSS keys.

Obtaining and Exchanging DSS Key Data for Peer Routers

If voice authentication is not possible, you must obtain the exact DSS values for each peer router crypto engine, including the key name, serial number, and DSS key (in hexadecimal).

You can then manually enter them into the router configuration using the **crypto key pubkey-chain dss** command.

The administrator of the peer router can obtain these values for each crypto engine by performing the **show crypto key mypubkey dss** command at the peer router, recording the DSS key values, and exchanging the key data through a secure alternative method such as the following:

- Sending the public key data using a PGP-signed e-mail message. PGP stands for Pretty Good Privacy and is a well-known, application level encryption tool.

- Sending hard copy of the public key data by trusted courier.

Manually Configuring the DSS Key Data

You enter a DSS public key for each peer router's crypto engine by using the following commands starting in global configuration mode:

```
router(config)#crypto key pubkey-chain dss
named-key key-name [special-usage]
serial-number [special-usage]
key-string [hex hex hex ...]
quit
```

The command parameters and syntax have the following meanings:

Command	Description
key-name	Identifies the crypto engine of the peer encrypting router. If the device is a Cisco router, the name should be a fully qualified domain name.
special-usage	(Optional) If this parameter is not specified, the key is considered a general-purpose key.
serial-number	The serial number of the peer encrypting router's public DSS key.
hex	The DSS public key of the peer encrypting router, in hexadecimal format.
quit	When you are done entering the public key, type **quit** to exit hex input mode.

Example 14-9 shows the Router A administrator manually configuring a DSS key. Manually configuring the DSS key requires entering the peer router's DSS public key.

Example 14-9 *Manually Entering the Peer's DSS Public Key*

```
routerA#configure terminal
routerA(config)#crypto key pubkey-chain dss
routerA(config-pubkey-chain)#named-key routerBkey
routerA(config-pubkey-key)#special-usage 05614636
routerA(config-pubkey-key)#key-string
```

continues

Example 14-9 *Manually Entering the Peer's DSS Public Key (Continued)*

```
Enter a public key as a hexidecimal number ....
FFFD0891 7A3C176C 1A83BC49 68B00B24
E5A9700C BA782232 CE719B90 A7D4B3C6
B8E59BB3 D9CAA349 F7F03664 A4188A64
6EEDD7F8 F215EF6B 53F04A05 7E98278B
routerA(config-pubkey-key)#quit
routerA(config)#
```

Note the following points in Example 14-9:

- Entering the **crypto key pubkey-chain dss** command places you in an interactive command dialog. Enter the **?** character to refresh your memory of the subcommands.

- The **crypto key pubkey-chain dss** command replaces the **crypto public-key** command.

- The DSS public key is very long. It is recommended that you use a terminal emulator such as HyperTerminal to copy and paste the public key if possible.

- Verify that you have accurately entered the DSS key information using the **show crypto key pubkey-chain dss** command.

CAUTION Regardless of which authentication method you chose, it is very important to verify the source of the public DSS key you receive. Do not accept or configure a DSS public key unless you have some basis for trusting that it is for the correct peer router. Otherwise, you can compromise encryption security.

Task 3: Define the Global Encryption Policy

The third task in configuring encryption is to define the global encryption policy, determining the DES encryption algorithms and DES keys to encrypt and decrypt data. The DES encryption algorithms should be chosen based on the overall network security policy.

You must globally enable (that is, turn on) all the DES encryption algorithms that your router will use during encrypted sessions. If a DES algorithm is not enabled globally, you will not be able to use it. To conduct an encrypted session with a peer router, you must enable at least one DES algorithm that the peer router also has enabled. You must configure the same DES algorithm on both peer routers for encryption to work.

CET supports the following four types of DES encryption algorithms:

- DES with 8-bit CFB
- DES with 64-bit CFB

- 40-bit variation of DES with 8-bit CFB
- 40-bit variation of DES with 64-bit CFB

The 40-bit variations use a 40-bit DES key, which is easier for attackers to crack than basic DES, which uses a 56-bit DES key. However, some international applications might require you to use 40-bit DES because of export laws. Also, 8-bit CFB is more commonly used than 64-bit CFB but requires more CPU time to process. Other conditions might also exist that require you to use some type of DES.

If you do not know whether your image is exportable, you can use the **show crypto cisco algorithms** command to determine which DES algorithms are currently enabled.

You must follow these steps to complete this task. Each step is covered in more detail in the following sections.

Step 1 Configure the global encryption policy.

Step 2 Confirm the encryption policy details.

Step 1: Configure the Global Encryption Policy

Configuring the global encryption policy consists of enabling one or more DES algorithms with options that can be used when configuring per-session encryption policies. Two encryption algorithms with options can be specified with CET by using one or more of the following commands in global configuration mode:

```
crypto cisco algorithm des [cfb-8 | cfb-64]
crypto cisco algorithm 40-bit-des [cfb-8 | cfb-64]
```

The command parameters and syntax have the following meanings:

Command	Description
des	Globally enables 56-bit DES algorithm types. This is the default method if **40-bit-des** is not specified.
40-bit-des	Globally enables 40-bit DES algorithm types.
cfb-8	(Optional) Selects the 8-bit CFB mode of the specified DES algorithm. If no CFB mode is specified when you issue the command, 64-bit CFB mode is the default.
cfb-64	(Optional) Selects the 64-bit CFB mode of the specified 40-bit DES algorithms. If no CFB mode is specified when you issue the command, 64-bit CFB mode is the default.
quit	When you are done entering the public key, type **quit** to exit hex input mode.

Note the following configuration points:

- If you are running a nonexportable image, the basic DES algorithm (56-bit DES key) with 8-bit CFB is enabled by default.

- If you are running an exportable image, the 40-bit DES algorithm with 8-bit CFB is enabled by default.

- 8-bit CFB is more commonly used than 64-bit CFB but requires more CPU processing time. If you do not specify 8-bit or 64-bit CFB, 64-bit CFB is selected by default.

- Use the **show crypto cisco algorithms** command to determine which DES algorithms are currently enabled.

Example 14-10 shows how global encryption policy can be configured at each peer router.

Example 14-10 *Configuring Global Encryption Policy*

```
routerA(config)#crypto cisco algorithm des cfb-8
routerA(config)#crypto cisco algorithm 40-bit-des cfb-8
routerB(config)#crypto cisco algorithm des cfb-8
routerB(config)#crypto cisco algorithm des cfb-64
routerB(config)#crypto cisco algorithm 40-bit-des cfb-8
```

Note the following points in Example 14-10:

- You must globally enable all DES algorithms that will be used in crypto maps to communicate with any other peer encrypting router.

- Enabling a DES algorithm type once allows it to be used by all of a router's crypto engines.

- Common DES algorithms must be enabled at both peer routers for the encrypted session to proceed.

- The **show crypto cisco algorithms** command displays the global encryption algorithms currently enabled on your router.

Step 2: Confirm Encryption Policy Details

While you are still in voice contact with the administrator of the peer router, you should confirm encryption policy details. This information should have been gathered during the planning process. It is recommended that you confirm the following details to minimize configuration errors:

- Peer router's name
- Global encryption policy that will be used
- IP addresses of hosts that will encrypt packets
- Packet type(s) to be encrypted

Table 14-2 summarizes encryption policy details for peer routers and encrypting hosts for the XYZ Company that will be configured in examples in subsequent sections.

Table 14-2   *Encryption Policy Details for the XYZ Company*

Parameter	Router A Value	Router B Value
Peer router's host name	routerB	routerA
Encryption policy	des cfb-8	des cfb-8
IP address of hosts to be protected	10.1.2.0	10.1.3.2
Traffic (packet) type to be encrypted	TCP	TCP

Task 4: Configure the Per-Session Encryption Policy

The fourth task in configuring CET is to configure per-session encryption policies. In this step, you tell your router which interfaces should encrypt or decrypt traffic, which IP packets to encrypt or decrypt at those interfaces, and which DES encryption algorithm to use when encrypting or decrypting the packets. Three steps are required to complete this task:

Step 1   Configure access lists to specify which hosts and which packet types will be encrypted.

Step 2   Configure crypto maps to support defined encryption policy.

Step 3   Apply the crypto maps to the interfaces over which encryption will take place.

Step 1: Configure Encryption Access Lists

IP extended access lists are used to define which packets are encrypted. These access lists function as if they were outgoing access lists. The access list syntax is as follows:

```
access-list access-list-number {permit | deny} protocol source
source-wildcard destination destination-wildcard
```

Refer to Appendix C, "Configuring Standard and Extended Access Lists," for more details on how to configure extended IP access lists. Access lists used for encryption are used as follows:

- **permit** instructs the router to encrypt packets.
- *source* and *destination* are subnets or hosts.
- Source and destination TCP or UDP ports can be specified.
- When a router receives encrypted packets back, it uses the same access list to determine which inbound packets to decrypt by viewing the source and destination addresses in the access list in reverse order.

- Encryption access lists are applied to an interface as an outbound access list.
- Peer routers must have access lists that mirror each other.
- See the *Cisco IOS Security Configuration Guide* and the *Cisco IOS Security Command Reference* for complete details on the extended IP access list commands as they are used with encryption.

Example 14-11 shows how to configure access lists for encryption in the XYZ Company network based on the security policy.

Example 14-11 *Configuring Access Lists for Router A and Router B*

```
routerA(config)#access-list 101 permit tcp 10.1.2.0 0.0.0.255 host 10.1.3.2
routerB(config)#access-list 110 permit tcp host 10.1.3.2 0.0.0.255
 10.1.2.0 0.0.0.255
```

Note the following points in Example 14-11. They match the security policy in Table 14-2.

- Router A encrypts all TCP traffic from the 10.1.2.0 network only to host 10.1.3.2.
- Router B encrypts all TCP traffic from the 10.1.3.2 host to the 10.1.2.0 network.
- The routers have mirror-image access lists.

NOTE   Although the extended IP access list syntax is unchanged when used for encryption, the meanings are slightly different. **permit** specifies that matching packets must be encrypted, and **deny** specifies that matching packets need not be encrypted.

Step 2: Define Crypto Maps

Crypto maps define and control policy for encryption on a per-session basis. The Cisco router encrypts only outbound packets and decrypts inbound packets on an interface.

Crypto maps link the traffic selection criteria in the access list, peer routers, and DES algorithms. The **crypto map** command defines per-session policy. To define a crypto map, do the following:

1 Define a crypto map and enter crypto map configuration mode:

```
router(config)#crypto map map-name seq-num [cisco]
```

The command parameters and syntax have the following meanings:

Command	Description
map-name	The name you assign to the crypto map.

Command	Description
seq-num	The sequence number for the crypto map, an individual block of a complete crypto map. It identifies the order of a particular crypto map sequence within the entire crypto map. Each sequence-numbered crypto map describes an individual encrypted connection. It describes which packets to match and which encryption policy to apply to them. A default number of 10 is assigned if you do not specify the sequence number.
cisco	Default value that indicates the crypto map is used for CET instead of IP Security (IPSec) encryption.

NOTE   Always specify a sequence number. If you do not, the router will assign one. The default is 10. To add entries to a previously defined crypto map, you must always specify the entire crypto map name including the sequence number. If you do not specify the sequence number, the router assumes that you want a new crypto map with the same tag but a different sequence number. Adding additional crypto map entries with different sequence numbers creates a crypto map set. This is useful when you must encrypt traffic to multiple destinations via one interface to the insecure network.

2 In crypto map configuration mode, specify the remote peer router's name:

```
routerA(config-crypto map)#set peer key-name
```

Specify the crypto engine name of the remote peer router with the *key-name* parameter.

3 Define the encryption algorithm(s) that the router can negotiate to use for the session in crypto map configuration mode:

```
router(config-crypto map)#set algorithm des [cfb-8 | cfb-64]
router(config-crypto map)#set algorithm 40-bit-des [cfb-8 | cfb-64]
```

You can specify any of the encryption algorithms that you configured at the global level. If an encryption algorithm does not appear in the global list, you cannot specify it in a crypto map. The algorithms are negotiated with the peer in the order specified here.

4 Assign one access list to each crypto map sequence:

```
router(config-crypto map)#match address access-list
```

The **match** statement is used to describe packets *leaving* an interface. The *access-list* parameter specifies which access list is applied to the crypto map. When multiple crypto map sequences exist in a crypto map, each sequence number is checked in order for a match. When a match is found, the **set** statements (shown in Step 3) within the sequence are used to control the encryption and connection setup.

5 Assign the crypto map to a router interface:

```
router(config)#interface type slot/port
router(config-if)#crypto map map-name
```

The *map-name* parameter specifies which crypto map is applied to the interface.

NOTE No encrypted session can be established between encrypting peer routers if the encryption policy is incompatible—and, in most cases, identical——between the routers. For example, the peers must negotiate the same encryption algorithm for a given session.

Examples 14-12 and 14-13 show how to configure crypto maps and apply them to interfaces on Routers A and B. Example 14-12 is for Router A.

Example 14-12 *Configuring and Applying Crypto Maps for Router A*

```
routerA(config)#crypto map routerAmap 10 cisco
routerA(config-crypto-map)#set peer routerBkey
routerA(config-crypto-map)#match address 101
routerA(config-crypto-map)#set algorithm des
routerA(config-crypto-map)#exit
routerA(config)#interface serial 0
routerA(config-if)#crypto map routerAmap
routerA(config-if)#^Z
routerA#configure terminal
routerA(config)#access-list 101 permit tcp 10.1.2.0 0.0.0.255
 host 10.1.3.2
```

Note the key points of Example 14-12 for Router A:

- The crypto map name is *routerAmap*.
- The des cfb-8 crypto algorithm is used.
- The peer router name is *routerBkey*.
- The match address is access list 101. Access list 101 determines the traffic to be encrypted.
- Crypto map *routerAmap* is applied to interface serial 0.

Example 14-13 is for Router B.

Example 14-13 *Configuring and Applying Crypto Maps for Router B*

```
routerB(config)#crypto map routerBmap 10 cisco
routerB(config-crypto-map)#set peer routerAkey
routerB(config-crypto-map)#match address 110
routerB(config-crypto-map)#set algorithm des
routerB(config-crypto-map)#exit
routerB(config)#interface serial 0
```

Example 14-13 *Configuring and Applying Crypto Maps for Router B (Continued)*

```
routerB(config-if)#crypto map routerBmap
routerB(config-if)#^Z
routerB#configure terminal
routerB(config)#access-list 110 permit tcp host 10.1.3.2 0.0.0.255
 10.1.2.0 0.0.0.255
```

Note the key points of Example 14-13 for Router B:

- The crypto map name is *routerBmap*.
- The des cfb-8 crypto algorithm is used.
- The peer router name is *routerAkey*.
- The match address is access list 110. Access list 110 determines the traffic to be encrypted.
- Crypto map *routerBmap* is applied to interface serial 0.

Optional Encryption Commands

You can use two optional commands when defining per-session encryption policy: **crypto cisco key-timeout** *minutes* and **crypto cisco pregen-dh-pairs** *count* [*slot* | *rsm* | *vip*]. (The *count* argument specifies how many DH public numbers to pregenerate and hold in reserve, from **0** to **10**.)

Controlling the Time Duration of Encrypted Sessions

The **crypto key-timeout** command allows you to set a timeout value for crypto keys. Session keys are valid only for the amount of time set by an administrator. When the key timeout occurs, a connection setup is forced to reauthenticate the peer and determine a new session key. The command syntax is as follows:

```
crypto key-timeout minutes
```

The default timeout value is 30 minutes. The range of definable values is 1 minute to 1400 minutes (a 24-hour period).

NOTE   Using short time periods can affect router performance, such as incoming packets being dropped during the session key exchange process. Recalculation of keys during the Diffie-Hellman exchange can take several seconds, during which packets are dropped.

Pregenerating Diffie-Hellman Numbers

Use the **crypto pregen-dh-pairs** command to pregenerate Diffie-Hellman keys. Authentication and connection setup can be slow on the low-end routers because of the processing required of public key technology. To speed up the connection time, Diffie-Hellman public numbers can be pregenerated and made readily available. You can specify in the configuration how many pairs of Diffie-Hellman numbers should be precalculated at one time. Shortly after a pair is used for a connection, another pair is pregenerated, so specifying more than one or two is usually unnecessary. By default, no pairs are pregenerated. The command syntax is as follows:

```
crypto pregen-dh-pairs slot
```

On a Cisco 7500 series router or a 7200 series with chassis slots, the *slot* argument can be used to indicate which crypto engine should pregenerate the Diffie-Hellman key pairs. If no chassis slot is specified, the slot containing the main processor is assumed.

Changing Encryption Access List Limits

By default, the maximum number of distinct sources (hosts or subnets) that you can define in an encryption access list is 100. The maximum number of distinct destinations that you can define for any given source address is 10. You can change the maximum number of sources (hosts or subnets) that you can define in encryption access list statements with the following global configuration command:

```
crypto cisco entities number
```

The command parameter has the following meaning:

Command	Description
number	Specifies the maximum number of sources. Use a value from 3 to 500.

You can change the maximum number of destinations (hosts or subnets) per source that you can define in encryption access list statements with the following command in global configuration mode:

```
crypto cisco connections number
```

The command parameter has the following meaning:

Command	Description
number	Specifies the maximum number of destinations per source. Use a value from 3 to 500.

Task 5: Test and Verify Encryption

Cisco IOS Software has a wide variety of powerful commands for testing and verifying encryption operation. This section considers the commands used to test the encryption operation and commands used to verify correct encryption configuration.

Testing the Configuration

If you want to test the encryption setup between peers, you can manually initiate session establishment using the following command:

```
test crypto initiate-session src-ip-addr dst-ip-addr map-name seq-number
```

The command parameters and syntax have the following meanings:

Command	Description
src-ip-addr	IP address of the source host. Should be included in an encryption access list definition as a valid IP address source address.
dst-ip-addr	IP address of the destination host. Should be included in an encryption access list definition as a valid IP address destination address.
map-name	Names the crypto map to be used.
seq-num	Names the crypto map sequence number.

Note the following associated commands you can use:

- A session is established if the crypto maps have been set up, DSS keys generated, and public keys exchanged.

- After issuing this command, use the **show crypto cisco connections** command to verify the status of the connection just created.

NOTE   The **test crypto initiate-session** command verifies session establishment. To verify that correct packets are being encrypted, use the **show crypto engine connections active** command after issuing this command.

Example 14-14 shows an example of testing an encryption session. Router A sets up a test encryption session with Router B.

Example 14-14   *Configuring and Applying Crypto Maps for Router A*

```
routerA#test crypto initiate-session 10.1.1.1 10.1.1.2 routerAmap 10
Sending Crypto Connection Message to: 10.1.1.2 from: 10.1.1.1.
Connection id: -1
```

Note the Connection id value of −1. A negative value indicates that the connection is being set up.

Clearing an Encrypted Session Connection

When clearing an encrypted session connection, remember that, if an encrypted connection appears to be in question, you can manually clear it using the following command:

```
clear crypto connection connection-id [slot]
```

In this syntax, *connection-id* is determined by using the **show crypto cisco connections** command, discussed in Table 14-4.

Verifying Encryption Operation

You can use a variety of **show** commands to view encryption configuration information. Use the commands listed in Table 14-3 to view the local router's crypto engine status.

Table 14-3 *Crypto Engine show Commands*

Command	Description
show crypto engine brief	Displays the configuration of all crypto engines within a Cisco 7200, RSP7000, or 7500 series router
show crypto engine configuration	Displays the configuration of all Cisco crypto engines within a Cisco router

You can use the commands listed in Table 14-4 to view the local router's encrypted session connections.

Table 14-4 *Crypto Connection show Commands*

Command	Description
show crypto cisco connections	Displays the status of current and pending crypto connections. This command replaces the **show crypto connections** command used in Cisco IOS Release 11.2.
show crypto engine connections active	Displays the current active encrypted session connections for all router crypto engines.

Examples of Verifying Encryption Operation

This section contains several examples of verifying encryption operation. Example 14-15 shows the active crypto engine connections based on a session previously set up with the **test crypto initiate-session** command.

Example 14-15 *Showing Active Crypto Engine Connections*

```
router#show crypto engine connections active
Connection  Interface  IP-Address  State  Algorithm    Encrypt  Decrypt
1           Ethernet0  10.1.1.1    set    DES 56 CFB64  0        0
```

The command fields have the following meanings:

Field	Description
Connection	Identifies the connection by its number. Each active encrypted session connection is identified by a positive number from 1 to 299. These connection numbers correspond to the table entry numbers.
Interface	Identifies the local interface involved in the encrypted session connection. This displays only the actual interface, not a subinterface (even if a subinterface is defined and used for the connection).
IP-Address	Identifies the IP address of the interface. Note that, if a subinterface is used for the connection, this field displays "unassigned."
State	The state "set" indicates an active connection.
Algorithm	Identifies the DES algorithm used to encrypt and decrypt packets at the interface.
Encrypt	Shows the total number of encrypted outbound IP packets.
Decrypt	Shows the total number of decrypted inbound IP packets.

Example 14-16 shows the current crypto connections based on a session previously set up with the **test crypto initiate-session** command.

Example 14-16 *Showing CET Connections*

```
router#show crypto cisco connections
Connection Table
PE          UPE       Conn_id  New_id  Alg          Time
10.1.1.1    10.1.1.2  1        0       DES_56_CFB64  Feb 29 2000 23:41:11
            flags:TIME_KEYS
```

The command fields have the following meanings:

Command	Description
PE	Protected entity. This shows a representative source IP address as specified in the crypto map's encryption access list. This IP address can be any host that matches a source in the encryption access list being used in the connection.

continues

Command	Description
UPE	Unprotected entity. This shows a representative destination IP address as specified in the crypto map's encryption access list. This IP address can be any host that matches a destination in the encryption access list that is being used in the connection.
Time	Identifies the time when the connection was initiated for pending connections.
Timestamp	Identifies the time when the connection was initiated for completed connections.
Conn_id	A number used to identify and track the connection. This can be a positive integer value from 1 to 299 or any negative integer value. Each connection is assigned a negative connection ID when the connection is pending (being set up). After the connection is established, a positive connection ID is assigned to the connection.
New_id	Lists the connection ID number that is assigned to a connection after the connection is set up. The New_id value is a positive number from 0 to 299. If New_id value is 0, there is no pending connection. If New_id value is a positive integer, a connection is pending. As soon as the pending connection has been established, the New_id value is transferred to Conn_id for the established connection, and New_id is reset to 0.
Alg	Identifies the DES encryption algorithm used for the current connection.
Time	Identifies the time when the connection was initiated.
flags	Identifies additional information about the connection state: • PEND_CONN identifies the table entry as a pending connection. • XCHG_KEYS means that the connection has timed out. For encrypted communication to occur again, the router must first exchange Diffie-Hellman numbers and generate a new session (DES) key. • TIME_KEYS means that the encrypted communication session is currently in progress (a session key is currently installed, and the session is counting down to timeout). • BAD_CONN means that no existing or pending connection exists for this table entry. • UNK_STATUS means that invalid status (error) or connection status could not be determined

Viewing Stored Peer DSS Public Keys

Peer public keys may be displayed by any user because they are not sensitive information. They can be displayed in a number of ways using the following command:

```
show crypto key pubkey-chain dss [name key-name | serial serial-number]
```

The command parameters and syntax have the following meanings:

Command	Description
key-name	The name assigned when the DSS public key was created with the **crypto key pubkey-chain dss** command
serial-number	The serial number of the encrypting router's public DSS key

The **show crypto key pubkey-chain dss** command replaces the **show crypto pubkey**, **show crypto pubkey name**, and **show crypto pubkey serial** commands.

An Example of Viewing Stored DSS Public Keys

Example 14-17 shows an example of viewing DSS public keys on Router A and viewing DSS public key details:

Example 14-17 *Viewing DSS Public Keys on Router A*

```
routerA#show crypto key pubkey-chain dss
Codes: M - Manually configured

Code Usage    Serial Number    Name
M    Signing 05614636         routerBkey

routerA#show crypto key pubkey-chain dss name routerBkey
Key name: routerBkey
 Serial number: 05614636
 Usage: Signature Key
 Source: Manually entered
 Data:
  F03C3B12 A3282C5A 81AF0512 CDBCF6E1 508A76AE 3640D019 AFF6EB65 35349453
  6933FEDD 4991856B 565FB494 30401D5E E7D10AE1 34EBEA81 612E6D24 03F2A525
```

Example 14-18 is an example of viewing DSS public keys on Router B.

Example 14-18 *Viewing DSS Public Keys on Router B*

```
routerB#show crypto key pubkey-chain dss
Codes: M - Manually configured

Code Usage    Serial Number    Name
M    Signing 05614558         routerAkey

routerB#show crypto key pubkey-chain dss name routerAkey
```

continues

Example 14-18 *Viewing DSS Public Keys on Router B (Continued)*

```
Key name: routerAkey
 Serial number: 05614558
 Usage: Signature Key
 Source: Manually entered
 Data:
  F4D16300 CAD4C1EF 1454A194 42CD4D4A D1C1C931 F6C1FA30 24C46E21 D4BCEAB9
  646A9A18 0A2831F8 674E48A1 FD399363 B5A36DB2 9CDE7FCC 9C7CFA14 B332E820
```

Verifying the Local Router's Encryption Policy Details

The command shown in Table 14-5 lets you view the local router's own DSS public keys for all crypto engines.

Table 14-5 *DSS Public Key **show** Command for Your Router*

Command	Description
show crypto key mypubkey dss	Displays all DSS public keys for all your router crypto engines in hexadecimal form. Replaces the **show crypto mypubkey** command.

The commands shown in Table 14-6 display each map sequence for a given crypto map and show any current connection ID assigned to that sequence. They also display statistics and the protected and unprotected entity values.

Table 14-6 *Crypto **show** Commands*

Command	Description
show crypto map	Displays the crypto map configuration.
show crypto map interface *interface*	Displays only the crypto map set applied to the specified interface.
show crypto map tag *map-name*	Displays only the crypto map set that has the specified *map-name*, including all sequences.
show crypto cisco algorithms	Displays the DES algorithm types that are globally enabled for your router. To view which DES algorithms are defined for specific crypto maps, use the **show running-config** command. Replaces the **show crypto algorithms** command.
show crypto cisco pregen-dh-pairs	Shows how many Diffie-Hellman pairs are currently pregenerated.
show crypto cisco key-timeout	Displays the current setting for the duration of encrypted sessions. Replaces the **show crypto key-timeout** command.

Turning Off Encryption

If you choose to stop using encryption, you can turn off encryption on an interface or for the entire router by following these guidelines:

- To turn off encryption at all the interfaces governed by a single crypto engine, delete DSS keys for that engine with the **crypto key zeroize dss** command, described in this section.

- To turn off encryption at specific interfaces, you can remove the crypto maps from the interfaces with the **no crypto map** command.

- To turn off encryption completely for a router, delete the DSS keys for all the router's crypto engines with the **crypto key zeroize dss** command, described in this section.

Deleting DSS keys deconfigures encryption for the crypto engine. This action is recommended because it reduces security risk by ensuring that the keys cannot be misused if you lose physical control of the router or ESA.

After you delete DSS keys for a crypto engine, you will not be able to perform encryption on the interfaces governed by that crypto engine.

CAUTION   DSS keys cannot be recovered after they have been deleted. Delete DSS keys only after careful consideration.

Use the following command to delete DSS keys:

```
crypto key zeroize dss [slot]
```

Only Cisco 7200 and 7500 series routers need the *slot* argument.

Diagnosing and Troubleshooting Cisco Encryption Technology

This section discusses **show** and **debug** commands that are useful for diagnosing and troubleshooting problems.

If you need to verify the state of a connection, you can use the **show crypto cisco connections**, **show crypto map**, and **show crypto engine connections active** commands to check the status of encryption connections and crypto maps.

The following are some common problems and suggested solutions:

- When a connection is first attempted, the Cisco IOS Software signs a pending connection ID value, which is a negative number. This pending connection ID value is used as a placeholder until the connection is complete and a connection ID, which is a positive value, is assigned. If both routers have assigned a positive connection ID to the connection, the connection setup has succeeded. Check the connection ID with the **show crypto connections** command.

- If connection setup has completed, check the status of the crypto map using the **show crypto map** command. If it has a positive connection ID, it also is prepared to encrypt packets.

- Encryption is not enabled until at least one set of DSS keys is generated using the **crypto key generate dss** command. If a crypto map is assigned to an interface and is incomplete or encryption has not yet been enabled, no traffic will pass into or out of that interface. An error message is issued to the console when the crypto map is configured and when packets start matching that entry.

Debug Commands

Several debug commands aid in tracing packet flows and events associated with the crypto engine and crypto subsystem. They are outlined in Table 14-7.

Table 14-7 *Debug Commands for CET*

Command	Description
debug crypto key-exchange	Displays DSS public key exchange debugging messages.
	If the process of exchanging DSS public keys with a peer router by means of the config **crypto key-exchange** command is unsuccessful, try to exchange DSS public keys again after enabling the **debug crypto key-exchange** command to help you diagnose the problem.
debug key-exchange	Displays Diffie-Hellman key exchange messages.
debug crypto sesmgmt	Displays connection setup messages and their flow through the local router.
	When crypto connections are not completing, use the **debug crypto sesmgmt** command to follow the progress of connection messages as a first step in diagnosing the problem.

NOTE Enabling debugging severely impacts the overall performance of a router.

Examples of debug crypto sesmgmt Messages

Consider two examples of debug messages for both sides of an encryption session. The encryption session is initiated at Router A by making a Telnet connection to Router B. Example 14-19 shows debug messages for Router A. Note that the Telnet session completes successfully at the end of the example.

Example 14-19 *Debugging Encryption Session Management at Router A*

```
routerA#debug crypto sesmgmt
routerA#telnet 10.1.1.2
Trying 10.1.1.2 ...
01:49:59: CRYPTO-SDU: Key Timeout, Re-exchange Crypto Keys
01:49:59: CRYPTO: Dequeued a message: Initiate_Connection
01:50:00: CRYPTO: DH gen phase 1 status for conn_id 3 slot 0:OK
01:50:01: CRYPTO: Sign done. Status=OK
01:50:01: CRYPTO: ICMP message sent: s=10.1.1.1, d=10.1.1.2

01:50:01: CRYPTO-SDU: send_nnc_req:   NNC Echo Request sent
01:50:06: CRYPTO: Dequeued a message: CRM
01:50:07: CRYPTO: DH gen phase 2 status for conn_id 3 slot 0:OK
01:50:07: CRYPTO: Syndrome gen status for conn_id 3 slot 0:OK
01:50:08: CRYPTO: Verify done. Status=OK
01:50:09: CRYPTO: Sign done. Status=OK
01:50:09: CRYPTO: ICMP message sent: s=10.1.1.1, d=10.1.1.2
01:50:09: CRYPTO-SDU: recv_nnc_rpy:   NNC Echo Confirm sent
01:50:09: CRYPTO: Create encryption key for conn_id 3 slot 0:OK
01:50:09: CRYPTO: Replacing -3 in crypto maps with 3 (slot 0)Open
Warning! Unauthorized users will be prosecuted!

User Access Verification

Password:
routerB>
```

Example 14-20 shows debug messages for Router B caused by Router A initiating a Telnet session, as shown in Example 14-19.

Example 14-20 *Debugging Encryption Session Management at Router B*

```
routerB#debug crypto sesmgmt
01:43:48: IP: s=10.1.1.1 (Ethernet0), d=10.1.1.2, len 328, Found an ICMP conn.
01:43:48: CRYPTO: Dequeued a message: CIM
01:43:48: CRYPTO-SDU: Key Timeout, Re-exchange Crypto Keys
01:43:49: CRYPTO: Verify done. Status=OK
01:43:50: CRYPTO: DH gen phase 1 status for conn_id 3 slot 0:OK
01:43:52: CRYPTO: DH gen phase 2 status for conn_id 3 slot 0:OK
01:43:52: CRYPTO: Syndrome gen status for conn_id 3 slot 0:OK
01:43:53: CRYPTO: Sign done. Status=OK
01:43:53: CRYPTO: ICMP message sent: s=10.1.1.2, d=10.1.1.1
01:43:53: CRYPTO-SDU: act_on_nnc_req: NNC Echo Reply sent
01:43:53: CRYPTO: Create encryption key for conn_id 3 slot 0:OK
01:43:56: CRYPTO: Dequeued a message: CCM
01:43:56: CRYPTO: Syndrome gen status for conn_id 3 slot 0:OK
01:43:57: CRYPTO: Verify done. Status=OK
01:43:57: CRYPTO: Replacing -3 in crypto maps with 3 (slot 0)
```

Encryption Implementation Considerations

This section contains some CET design and configuration tips. These tips are designed to help you successfully implement CET.

Design Considerations

You should examine the considerations illustrated in Figure 14-5 and the following text before implementing encryption.

Figure 14-5 *Example of Invalid Configuration*

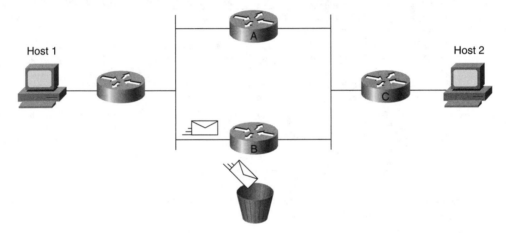

Be careful in choosing the network topology between encrypting routers. In particular, remember to set up the network so that a stream of packets must use exactly one set of encrypting routers at a time. Consider the invalid configuration shown in Figure 14-5:

- Packets from Host 1 are routed through both encrypting Routers A and B to Host 2.

- Encrypting Router C negotiates different encryption keys with Routers A and B.

- When data is encrypted for Host 1, only one of the keys is chosen, and either Router A or B receives packets encrypted under the wrong key.

- The router receiving packets encrypted under the wrong key is likely to drop the packet, and it might initiate another connection setup exchange with Router C.

- There should be exactly one stable route between a pair of encrypting routers at any one time. For example, constant routing changes, including intentional load balancing, between encrypting routers causes excessive numbers of connections to be set up, so very few data packets will be delivered. Load balancing can still be used, but it must be done on endpoint routers that are not peer encrypting routers. Peer encrypting routers can be within the load-balanced path but cannot be the endpoints.

Here are some additional design considerations:

- A common network topology used for encryption is a hub-and-spoke arrangement between an enterprise router and branch routers. Also, perimeter routers are often designated as peer encrypting routers.

- Routers that have slower CPUs and minimum memory always perform more slowly than routers with RISC processors and extra memory configurations. Encryption is very CPU intensive.

- There will be performance impacts when encryption is heavily used. In software-only configurations, encryption places the entire system under a load and might limit throughput. In systems that have hardware assist for encryption, encryption doesn't add a significant burden to the main CPU, but it might cause traffic for certain interfaces to slow and congestion to occur.

- You cannot put one set of encrypting routers between another set of encrypting routers (referred to as nesting) because encryption does not work properly in this topology.

- Select the specific traffic that you really want to encrypt so that you do not waste router resources encrypting less-important traffic.

- With dial-on-demand routing (DDR), you must make ICMP traffic interesting, or the dialup connection will never be made.

- CET is compatible with GRE tunneling. You can configure encryption so that all traffic through the GRE tunnel is encrypted when GRE tunnel endpoints are located at the peer encrypting routers. With tunnels, you need to apply the crypto maps to both the physical and tunnel interfaces.

- Only two pairs of routers may share a Diffie-Hellman session key. That is, one router cannot exchange encrypted packets with two peers using the same session key. Each pair of routers must have a session key that was the result of a Diffie-Hellman exchange between them.

- Encrypted multicast is not supported.

- CET supports a maximum of 300 encryption sessions, a prime limiting factor in scaling CET.

- CET supports only IP traffic.

Tips on Configuring CET

Here are some tips that might help you configure CET so that it operates properly and efficiently:

- As soon as the crypto map is applied to an interface, the first packet that matches the access list causes an encryption connection setup to happen. This takes a few seconds because of the processing required by the public key technology. At the conclusion of connection setup, both routers will have authenticated each other (using the previously exchanged DSS public keys), will have generated a Diffie-Hellman shared secret, and will have derived a DES encryption key from that shared secret. When both routers have successfully completed these steps, packets are encrypted between them until one of the router's key timeout values is reached.

- You might need to extend the keepalive intervals on your serial connections if the connections terminate before the DSS key exchange occurs. You can determine if this is necessary by observing encryption session setup with the **debug crypto key exchange**, **debug crypto sesmgmt**, and **show serial** commands.

- Make sure you have alternative access to the router when applying crypto maps to the router interface for the first time. If you make a mistake, you might lock yourself out of the router.

- The cfb-64 option should be faster and more efficient than CFB 56.

- The router needs to run the algorithm you want to use with the CFB you select. Defaults for each image are the image name (that is, 56) with cfb-64.

- The **test crypto initiate** command might not be the best way to test the connection. Try Telnet or generate traffic that will be allowed by the access list.

- You might want to change the *key-timeout* time limit. The 30-minute default is very short. You can increase it to 1 day (1440 minutes). The impact on security is minimal, and you can have the router renegotiate in a nonpeak time every day. Traffic is dropped during renegotiation.

- The router uses the inverse of the access list to decrypt, so make sure that the encrypting and decrypting router access lists are mirror images.

- After you have configured your routers for encryption, it is recommended that you make a backup of your configuration, perhaps on a secure TFTP site. Be sure to suitably protect the backup from modification.

NOTE   Refer to Cisco's *Security Configuration Guide* and *Security Configuration Command Reference* for more details on configuring encryption.

The Encryption Export Policy

Cisco's Export Compliance and Regulatory Affairs (ECRA) group reviews all orders that contain encryption controlled for export by the U.S. government. There are no special order policies or export restrictions for 40- and 56-bit CET software images.

Delivery of Cisco cryptographic products does not imply third-party authority to import, distribute, or use encryption. Importers, distributors, and users are responsible for compliance with all local country laws. Cisco strongly recommends that importers, distributors, and users investigate import regulations prior to encryption product ordering and deployment.

NOTE This information was obtained from the Cisco ECRA Web site, located at www.cisco.com/wwl/export. See this Web site for more details.

Planning for Encryption Job Aid

Use the following planning sheet to help define your encryption requirements and gather appropriate configuration information.

General Planning

Answer the following questions about your security requirements:

- What are your security needs?
- What is the IP packet type?
- Which global encryption algorithms will you use?

Per-Site Planning

Complete the following chart to assist you with router configuration. During the voice authentication process, verify the information you have documented about the peer router. This will minimize configuration errors.

Task	Router 1 (Your Local Router)	Router 2 (Peer Router)
What is each router's name?		
What is your source host or subnet?		
What are the peer router's destination hosts or subnet?		

continues

Task	Router 1 (Your Local Router)	Router 2 (Peer Router)
What is the interface of the local router from which the packets of the source exit (outbound)?		
What is the name of the public key associated with the remote router?		
What DES algorithm should be used by the routers?		

The policy for encryption and decryption on a router is symmetrical, which means that defining one gives you the other automatically. With the crypto map, only the encryption policy is explicitly defined. The decryption policy uses the identical information, but when matching packets, it reverses source and destination addresses and ports. Thus, the data is protected in both directions of a duplex connection.

Configuration Procedures Job Aid

You might find the configuration procedures job aid shown in Figure 14-6 helpful when configuring CET.

Summary

This section summarizes the main points of the chapter:

- CET operates in four overall steps: preparing routers to perform encryption, establishing an encryption session, encrypting and decrypting data, and terminating the encryption session.

- Configuring CET includes four general steps: generating the router's DSS public and private keys, exchanging DSS public keys with peer routers and verifying policy details, defining global encryption policy by configuring encryption algorithms, and configuring crypto maps to control per-session encryption policy.

- The system administrator must generate DSS public and private keys before exchanging them with peer encrypting routers.

- Routers can be preconfigured by one person before they are shipped to remote sites, or they can be configured by two system administrators at remote sites maintaining voice communications.

- You must define the global encryption policy with the **crypto algorithm** command to chose the encryption algorithms and modes used by per-session policies.

Figure 14-6 *CET Configuration Procedures Job Aid*

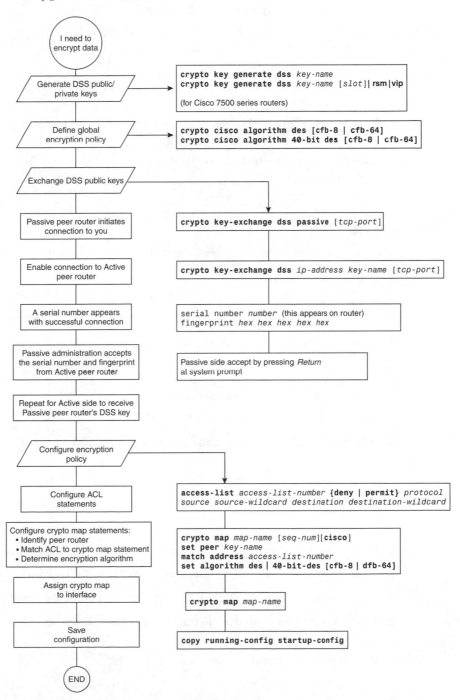

- Enable a per-session encryption policy by configuring access lists and crypto maps, and then apply the crypto maps to interfaces.
- Extended IP access lists are used to define which packets must be encrypted as they exit an interface based on source and destination address, protocol, and TCP or UDP port.
- Crypto maps are assigned to an encrypting interface with the **crypto map** command in interface configuration mode.
- Use the **test crypto initiate-session command** to set up a test encryption session.
- Use the variety of **show crypto** and **debug crypto** commands to view encryption configuration information, verify the local router's encryption policy details, and troubleshoot CET.

Review Questions

Answer the following review questions, which delve into some of the key facts and concepts covered in this chapter:

1 What are the three types of encryption engines used in Cisco routers?

2 What command is used to generate the peer router's public and private keys?

3 Which of the following commands should be entered first on peer routers when exchanging DSS public keys?

```
crypto key exchange dss ip-address key-name [tcp-port]
crypto key exchange dss passive
```

4 What command do you use to define global encryption policy?

5 Which of the following commands defines and controls per-session encryption policy?

```
crypto key generate dss
crypto key exchange dss
crypto map
access-list
```

6 How do you control the traffic, hosts, and subnets that trigger an encrypted session?

7 What command would you use to test encrypted connection setup between routers?

8 What command would you use to verify that packets are actually being encrypted?

9 What command should you use to examine the DSS key hexadecimal values of public DSS keys in a router?

10 What three debug commands are available for CET?

References

The topics considered in this chapter are complex and should be studied further to more fully understand them and put them to use. Use the following references to learn more about the topics in this chapter.

CET Technology, Design, and Configuration Overview

White paper, "Cisco IOS Software Feature: Network Layer Encryption," 1997. Contains an overview of the technologies used in CET as well as application, design, implementation, and configuration guidelines. Located at www.cisco.com/warp/customer/732/Security/encrp_wp.htm.

ESA and VIP2-40 Information

Documentation number 78-3279-01, Cisco Systems, Inc., "Data Encryption Service Adapter (ESA) Installation and Configuration," 1997. Describes how to install and configure the ESA. Located at www.cisco.com/univercd/cc/td/doc/product/core/7204/.

Configuring Cisco Encryption Technology

Security Command Reference, Cisco IOS Release 12.0, October 1998.

Security Configuration Guide, Cisco IOS Release 12.0, October 1998.

Configuring a VPN with IPSec

Upon completing this chapter, you will be able to do the following:

- Identify the encryption protocols Cisco uses to implement IPSec support in Cisco products

- Explain the purpose and operation of each IPSec protocol supported by Cisco products

- Identify how IPSec works

- Explain how certificate authorities (CAs) work and are used

- List the general task and step procedure for configuring IPSec

- Explain how Cisco IOS Software processes IPSec

CHAPTER 15

Understanding Cisco IPSec Support

This chapter presents an overview of IP security (IPSec) and the IPSec protocols available in Cisco products that are used to create a virtual private network (VPN). Each IPSec protocol is considered here, and subsequent chapters provide details on how to configure IPSec support in Cisco products.

This chapter first considers what a VPN is, and it surveys some of the protocols used to enable a VPN. This chapter also explains what IPSec is and summarizes the protocols and security algorithms that make up IPSec. It next looks at each protocol and algorithm in more depth, considering how each works and how IPSec uses it. It includes a summary of the tasks you must perform to configure IPSec and examines the first task in detail because it is common to all IPSec methods. This chapter concludes with a quick look at how IPSec is processed and configured in Cisco IOS Software.

Using IPSec to Enable a Secure VPN

There is much interest in the networking industry concerning VPNs—how to enable them and how they fit into the enterprise network architecture. A *VPN* is an enterprise network deployed on a shared infrastructure employing the same security, management, and throughput policies applied in a private network. VPNs are an alternative wide-area network (WAN) infrastructure that can be used to replace or augment existing private networks that utilize leased lines.

VPNs fall into three categories:

- **Remote-access**—Remote-access VPNs connect telecommuters, mobile users, or even smaller remote offices with minimal traffic to the enterprise WAN and corporate computing resources.

- **Intranets**—An intranet VPN connects fixed locations, branch offices, and home offices within an enterprise WAN.

- **Extranets**—An extranet extends limited access of enterprise computing resources to business partners such as suppliers or customers, enabling access to shared information.

A variety of protocols can be used to enable each type of VPN.

VPN Protocols

Many protocols have been developed to create VPNs. Each protocol has characteristics that enable specific VPN features. For example, IPSec (the focus of this chapter) is an industry-standard network layer encryption method that enables the establishment of authentication and encryption services between endpoints over a shared IP-based network. Other protocols enable VPN features by using tunneling, the ability to enclose or encapsulate data or protocols inside other protocols. The following are the most common tunneling protocols used to enable VPNs:

- **Generic Routing Encapsulation (GRE)**—A tunneling protocol developed by Cisco that encapsulates a wide variety of protocol packet types inside IP tunnels, creating a virtual point-to-point link to Cisco routers at remote points over an IP network.

- **Layer 2 Forwarding (L2F)**—A tunneling protocol developed by Cisco that enables a virtual private dialup network (VPDN), a system that permits dial-in networks to exist remotely to home networks while giving the appearance of being directly connected to an enterprise network.

- **Point-to-Point Tunneling Protocol (PPTP)**—A network protocol developed by Microsoft that enables the secure transfer of data from a remote client to a private enterprise server by creating a VPN across IP-based networks. PPTP supports on-demand, multiprotocol, virtual private networking over public networks such as the Internet.

- **Layer 2 Tunneling Protocol (L2TP)**—A tunneling protocol developed by Cisco and Microsoft that enables a VPDN. L2TP is an extension to the Point-to-Point Protocol (PPP) used for VPNs, merging the best features of two existing tunneling protocols: PPTP and L2F.

- **Microsoft Point-to-Point Encryption (MPPE)**—A means of converting PPP packets into an encrypted form. Enables a secure VPN over a dialup or remote network. MPPE uses the RSA RC4 encryption algorithm to provide data confidentiality.

What Is IPSec?

Cisco VPN products use the industry-standard IPSec protocol suite to enable advanced VPN features. IPSec provides a mechanism for secure data transmission over IP networks, ensuring confidentiality, integrity, and authenticity of data communications over unprotected networks such as the Internet. IPSec enables the following VPN features in Cisco products:

- **Data confidentiality**—The IPSec sender can encrypt packets before transmitting them across a network.

- **Data integrity**—The IPSec receiver can authenticate IPSec peers (devices or software that originate and terminate IPSec tunnels) and packets sent by the IPSec peer to ensure that the data has not been altered during transmission.

- **Data origin authentication**—The IPSec receiver can authenticate the source of the IPSec packets sent. This service is dependent on the data integrity service.

- **Anti-replay**—The IPSec receiver can detect and reject replayed packets, helping prevent spoofing and man-in-the-middle attacks.

IPSec is a standards-based set of security protocols and algorithms. IPSec and related security protocols conform to open standards promulgated by the Internet Engineering Task Force (IETF) and documented in Requests for Comments (RFCs) and IETF-draft papers. IPSec acts at the network layer, protecting and authenticating IP packets between participating IPSec devices (peers) such as Cisco routers, PIX Firewalls, the Cisco VPN Client, Cisco VPN Concentrators, and other IPSec-compliant products. IPSec can be used to scale from small to very large networks.

Security Associations

IPSec offers a standard way of establishing authentication and encryption services between IPSec peers. IPSec uses standard encryption and authentication algorithms (that is, mathematical formulas) called *transforms* to facilitate secure communications. IPSec uses open standards for encryption key negotiation and connection management to promote interoperability between peers. IPSec provides methods to allow negotiation of services between IPSec peers. IPSec uses security associations to specify negotiated parameters.

A Security Association (SA) is a negotiated policy or an agreed-upon way of handling the data that will be exchanged between two peer devices. An example of a policy detail is the algorithm used to encrypt data. Both peers must use the same algorithm for encryption and decryption. The active SA parameters are stored in an SA Database (SAD) in the peers.

Internet Key Exchange (IKE) is a hybrid protocol that provides utility services for IPSec: authentication of the IPSec peers, negotiation of IKE and IPSec security associations, and establishment of keys for encryption algorithms used by IPSec. IKE is based on the Internet Security Association and Key Management Protocol (ISAKMP) and Oakley, which are protocols used to manage the generation and handling of encryption keys used by IPSec transforms. IKE is also the protocol used to form SAs between potential IPSec peers. In this book, and in Cisco router and PIX Firewall configuration, IKE is synonymous with ISAKMP; IKE is the term used for both.

Both IKE and IPSec use SAs to specify parameters. The components of IPSec, SAs, and IKE are covered in more detail later in this chapter.

IPSec Equipment Infrastructure

IPSec VPN solutions can be built using multiple Cisco devices—Cisco routers, the CiscoSecure PIX Firewall, the CiscoSecure VPN client software, and the Cisco VPN 3000 and 5000 series concentrators—as building blocks. Cisco routers integrate VPN features with the rich feature set provided by Cisco IOS software, reducing network complexity and total cost of ownership of the VPN solution while enabling layered security services. The PIX Firewall is a high-performance network appliance that provides high-capacity tunnel endpoints with strong firewall features. The CiscoSecure VPN client software supports the remote-access VPN requirements for e-commerce, road warrior, and telecommuting applications, offering a complete implementation of IPSec standards and interoperability with Cisco routers and the PIX Firewall.

How IPSec Works

IPSec involves many component technologies and encryption methods, but its operation can be broken into five main steps (see Figure 15-1):

Step 1   IPSec process initiation—Traffic to be encrypted as specified by the IPSec security policy configured in the IPSec peers starts the IKE process.

Step 2   IKE Phase 1—IKE authenticates IPSec peers and negotiates IKE SAs during this phase, setting up a secure channel for negotiating IPSec SAs in Phase 2.

Step 3   IKE Phase 2—IKE negotiates IPSec SA parameters and sets up matching IPSec SAs in the peers.

Step 4   Data transfer—Data is transferred between IPSec peers based on the IPSec parameters and keys stored in the SA database.

Step 5   IPSec tunnel termination—IPSec SAs terminate through deletion or by timing out.

The following sections describe these steps in more detail.

Figure 15-1 *The Five Steps of IPSec*

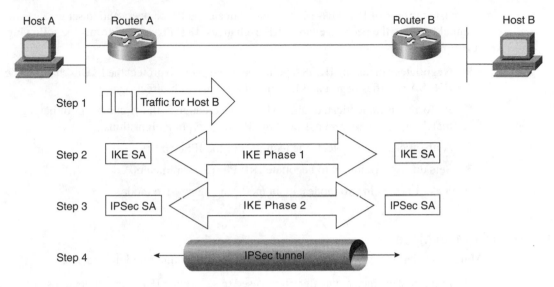

Step 1: IPSec Process Initiation

You determine what type of traffic must be protected by IPSec as part of formulating a security policy for use with a VPN. The policy is then implemented in the configuration interface for each particular IPSec peer. For example, in Cisco routers and the PIX Firewall, access lists are used to determine which traffic to encrypt. The access lists are assigned to a crypto policy such that permit statements indicate that the selected traffic must be encrypted, and deny statements indicate that selected traffic must be sent unencrypted. With the Cisco VPN client, you use menu windows to select connections to be secured by IPSec. When traffic to be encrypted is generated or transits the IPSec client, the client initiates the next step in the process, negotiating an IKE Phase 1 exchange.

Step 2: IKE Phase 1

The basic purpose of IKE Phase 1 is to authenticate the IPSec peers and to set up a secure channel between the peers to enable IKE exchanges. IKE Phase 1 performs the following functions:

- Negotiates a matching IKE SA policy between peers to protect the IKE exchange. The IKE SA specifies negotiated IKE parameters and is bidirectional.

- Performs an authenticated Diffie-Hellman exchange with the end result of having matching shared secret keys used by IPSec encryption algorithms.

- Authenticates and protects the identities of the IPSec peers.

- Sets up a secure tunnel to negotiate IKE Phase 2 parameters.

IKE Phase 1 occurs in two modes: main mode and aggressive mode.

IKE Phase 1 Main Mode

Main mode has three two-way exchanges between the initiator and the receiver:

1 In the first exchange, the algorithms used to secure the IKE communications are agreed upon in matching IKE SAs in each peer.

2 The second exchange uses a Diffie-Hellman exchange to generate shared secret keying material used to generate shared secret keys, and to pass nonces (random numbers sent to the other party), sign them, and return them to prove their identity.

3 The third exchange verifies the other side's identity. The identity value is the IPSec peer's IP address in encrypted form.

The primary outcome of main mode is matching IKE SAs between peers to provide a protected pipe for subsequent IKE exchanges. The IKE SA specifies values for the IKE exchange: the authentication method used, the encryption and hash algorithms, the Diffie-Hellman group used (two are available), the lifetime of the IKE SA in seconds or kilobytes, and the shared secret key values for the encryption algorithms. The IKE SA in each peer is bidirectional.

IKE Phase 1 Aggressive Mode

In aggressive mode, fewer exchanges are done with fewer packets, with a resulting decrease in the time it takes to set up the IPSec session. The exchanges occur as follows:

1 On the first exchange, almost everything is squeezed into the proposed IKE SA values, the Diffie-Hellman public key, a nonce that the other party signs, and an identity packet that can be used to verify the other party's identity via a third party.

2 The receiver sends back everything that is needed to complete the exchange. The only thing left is for the initiator to confirm the exchange.

The disadvantage of using aggressive mode is that both sides exchange information before a secure channel is set up. Therefore, it is possible to sniff the wire and discover who formed the new SA. However, it is faster than main mode. Aggressive mode generally is not used by Cisco products to initiate an IKE exchange. Cisco routers and PIX Firewalls can respond to an IPSec peer originating an aggressive-mode exchange.

Step 3: IKE Phase 2

The purpose of IKE Phase 2 is to negotiate IPSec SAs to set up the IPSec tunnel. IKE Phase 2 performs the following functions:

- Negotiates IPSec SA parameters protected by an existing IKE SA
- Establishes IPSec SAs
- Periodically renegotiates IPSec SAs to ensure security
- Optionally performs an additional Diffie-Hellman exchange

IKE Phase 2 has one mode, quick mode, which occurs after IKE has established the secure tunnel in Phase 1. It negotiates a shared IPSec policy, derives shared secret keying material used for the IPSec security algorithms, and establishes IPSec SAs. Quick mode exchanges nonces that provide replay protection. The nonces are used to generate fresh shared secret key material and to prevent replay attacks from generating bogus security associations.

Quick mode is also used to renegotiate a new IPSec SA when the IPSec SA lifetime expires. Base quick mode is used to refresh the keying material used to create the shared secret key based on the keying material derived from the Diffie-Hellman exchange in Phase 1. IPSec has an option called Perfect Forward Secrecy (PFS) that increases keying material security. If PFS is specified in the IPSec policy, a new Diffie-Hellman exchange is performed with each quick mode, providing keying material that has greater entropy (key material life) and thereby greater resistance to cryptographic attacks. Each Diffie-Hellman exchange requires large exponentiations, thereby increasing CPU utilization and exacting a performance cost.

The identities of the SAs negotiated in quick mode are the IP addresses of the IKE peers.

IPSec Transforms Negotiated in Phase 2

IKE negotiates IPSec transforms (IPSec security algorithms) during Phase 2. IPSec consists of two main security protocols and a variety of supporting protocols. The IPSec transforms and associated encryption algorithms are summarized as follows:

- **Authentication Header (AH)**—A security protocol that provides authentication and optional replay-detection services. AH acts as a digital signature to ensure that data in the IP packet has not been tampered with. AH does not provide data encryption and decryption services. AH can be used either by itself or with Encapsulating Security Payload.

- **Encapsulating Security Payload (ESP)**—A security protocol that provides data confidentiality and protection with optional authentication and replay-detection services. Cisco products supporting IPSec use ESP to encrypt the data payload of IP packets. ESP can be used either by itself or in conjunction with AH.

- **Data Encryption Standard (DES)**—An encryption algorithm used to encrypt and decrypt packet data. DES is used by both IPSec and IKE. DES uses a 56-bit key, ensuring high performance yet secure encryption. DES is a symmetrical algorithm, requiring identical secret encryption keys in each IPSec peer. Diffie-Hellman is used to establish the symmetrical keys. IKE and IPSec use DES for message encryption.

- **Triple DES (3DES)**—3DES is a variant of DES that iterates three times with three separate keys, effectively tripling the strength of DES. 3DES is used by IPSec to encrypt and decrypt data traffic. 3DES uses a 168-bit key, ensuring strong encryption. IKE and IPSec use 3DES for message encryption.

IPSec transforms also use two standard hashing algorithms to authenticate data:

- **MD5 (Message Digest 5)**—MD5 is a hash algorithm used to authenticate packet data. Cisco products use the MD5 hashed message authentication code (HMAC) variant, which provides an additional level of hashing. A hash is a one-way encryption algorithm that takes an input message of arbitrary length and produces a fixed-length output message. IKE, AH, and ESP use MD5 for authentication.

- **Secure Hash Algorithm-1 (SHA-1)**—SHA is a hash algorithm used to authenticate packet data. Cisco products use the SHA-1 HMAC variant, which provides an additional level of hashing. IKE, AH, and ESP use SHA-1 for authentication.

IKE uses Diffie-Hellman to establish symmetrical keys using DES, 3DES, MD5, and SHA. Diffie-Hellman is a public-key cryptography protocol. It lets two parties establish a shared secret key over an insecure communications channel. Shared secret keys are required for DES and the HMAC algorithms. Diffie-Hellman is used within IKE to establish session keys. 768-bit and 1024-bit Diffie-Hellman groups are supported in Cisco products. The 1024-bit group is more secure.

Each IPSec SA is assigned a security parameter index (SPI), a number used to identify the IPSec SA. The SA specifies the IPSec transform used (ESP and/or AH and associated encryption and hash algorithms), the lifetime of the IPSec SA in seconds or kilobytes, whether PFS is specified, the IP addresses of the peers, the shared secret key values for the encryption algorithms, and other parameters. Each IPSec SA is unidirectional. A single IPSec SA negotiation results in two SAs—one inbound and one outbound.

IPSec AH and ESP can operate in either tunnel or transport mode. Tunnel mode is used between IPSec gateways and causes IPSec to build an entirely new IPSec header. Transport mode is generally used between a VPN client and a server and uses the existing IP header.

Step 4: Data Transfer

After IKE Phase 2 is complete and quick mode has established IPSec SAs, information is exchanged via the IPSec tunnel between IPSec peers. Packets are encrypted and decrypted using the encryption algorithms and keys specified in the IPSec SA. The IPSec SA contains a lifetime that measures traffic kilobytes or seconds. The SA contains a counter that counts down each second or each kilobyte of traffic transmitted.

Step 5: IPSec Tunnel Termination

IPSec SAs terminate because they are deleted or their lifetime expires. When the SAs terminate, the keys are also discarded. When subsequent IPSec SAs are needed for a flow, IKE performs a new Phase 2 and, if necessary, a new Phase 1 negotiation. A successful negotiation results in new SAs and new keys. New SAs can be established before the existing SAs expire so that a given flow can continue uninterrupted. Typically, Phase 2 renegotiations happen more frequently than Phase 1 renegotiations.

Technologies Used in IPSec

Let's examine the technologies that make up IPSec in more detail. The standards IPSec uses are complex, so we will consider each of the key technologies in more detail in this section. IPSec uses the following technologies:

- Authentication Header
- Encapsulating Security Payload
- Digital Encryption Standard
- Triple Digital Encryption Standard
- Internet Key Exchange
- Diffie-Hellman key agreement
- Hashed message authentication codes
- RSA security
- Certificate authority

Authentication Header

AH provides data authentication and integrity for IP packets passed between two systems. AH does not provide data confidentiality (that is, encryption) of packets. Authentication is achieved by applying a keyed one-way hash function to the packet to create a message digest. Changes in any part of the packet that occur during transit are detected by the receiver when it performs the same one-way hash function on the packet and compares the value of the message digest that the sender has supplied. The fact that the one-way hash also involves the use of a secret shared between the two systems means that authenticity is guaranteed. AH works as shown in Figure 15-2. Here are the details:

1 The IP header and data payload are hashed.

2 The hash is used to build a new AH header, which is attached to the original packet between the new AH header and the data payload.

3 The new packet is transmitted to the IPSec peer.

4 The peer hashes the IP header and data payload, extracts the transmitted hash from the AH header, and compares the two hashes. The hashes must match exactly. If even one bit is changed in the transmitted packet, the hash output on the received packet will change, and the AH header will not match.

Figure 15-2 *Authentication Header Hashing*

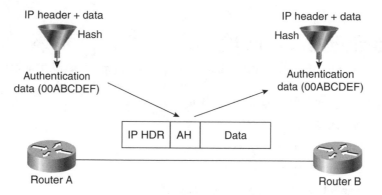

AH provides authentication for as much of the IP header as possible as well as for upper-level protocol data. However, some IP header fields are mutable, meaning that they change in transit. The value of the mutable fields, such as the time-to-live (TTL) field, changes as the packet transits intermediate network devices, and it might not be predictable by the sender. The values of mutable fields cannot be protected by AH. Thus, the protection provided to the IP header by AH is somewhat limited. AH may also provide optional anti-replay protection by using a sequence number in the IP packet header. RFC 2402 describes AH completely.

Encapsulating Security Payload

ESP is a security protocol used to provide confidentiality (that is, encryption), data origin authentication, integrity, optional anti-replay service, and limited traffic flow confidentiality by defeating traffic flow analysis.

ESP provides confidentiality by performing encryption at the IP packet layer. It supports a variety of symmetric encryption algorithms. The default algorithm for IPSec is 56-bit DES. This cipher must be implemented to guarantee interoperability among IPSec products. Cisco products also support the use of 3DES for strong encryption. Confidentiality may be selected independently of all other services.

Data origin authentication and connectionless integrity work together and are optional. They can also be combined with confidentiality.

The anti-replay service may be selected only if data origin authentication is selected, and its election is solely at the discretion of the receiver. Although the default calls for the sender to increment the sequence number used for anti-replay, the service is effective only if the receiver checks the sequence number. Traffic flow confidentiality requires the selection of tunnel mode. It is most effective if implemented at a security gateway, where traffic aggregation might be able to mask true source-destination patterns. Note that, although both confidentiality and authentication are optional, at least one of them must be selected.

The set of services provided by ESP depends on options that are configured during IPSec implementation and that are selected when an IPSec SA is established. However, use of confidentiality without integrity/authentication (either in ESP or separately in AH) might subject traffic to certain forms of active attacks that could undermine the confidentiality service.

The ESP header is inserted after the IP header and before the upper-layer protocol header (transport mode) or before an encapsulated IP header (tunnel mode). RFC 2406 covers ESP completely.

ESP Encryption with a Keyed HMAC

ESP can also provide packet authentication with an optional field for authentication. Cisco IOS Software and the PIX Firewall refer to this service as *ESP HMAC*. Authentication is calculated after the encryption is done. The current IPSec standard specifies SHA1 and MD5 as the mandatory HMAC algorithms.

The main difference between the authentication provided by ESP and that provided by AH is the extent of the coverage. ESP does not protect any IP header fields unless they are encapsulated by ESP (tunnel mode). Figure 15-3 illustrates the fields protected by ESP HMAC.

Figure 15-3 *ESP HMAC Protecting the Data Payload and ESP Header*

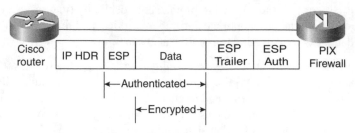

Note that encryption covers only the data payload, and the ESP header with the ESP HMAC hash covers only the ESP header and the data payload. The IP header is not protected. ESP HMAC cannot be used alone. It must be combined with an ESP encryption protocol.

IPSec Tunnel and Transport Modes

IPSec operates in either tunnel or transport mode. Figure 15-4 illustrates tunnel mode. In tunnel mode, the entire original IP datagram is encrypted, and it becomes the payload in a new IP packet with a new IP header (HDR in Figure 15-4) and the addition of an IPSec header. Tunnel mode allows a network device, such as a PIX Firewall, to act as an IPSec gateway or proxy, performing encryption on behalf of the hosts behind the PIX. The source's router encrypts packets and forwards them along the IPSec tunnel. The destination PIX Firewall decrypts the IPSec packet, extracts the original IP datagram, and forwards it to the destination system. The major advantage of tunnel mode is that the end systems do not need to be modified to enjoy the benefits of IPSec. Tunnel mode also protects against traffic analysis. With tunnel mode, an attacker can determine only the tunnel endpoints, not the true source and destination of the tunneled packets, even if they are the same as the tunnel endpoints.

Figure 15-4 *Tunnel Mode Packets*

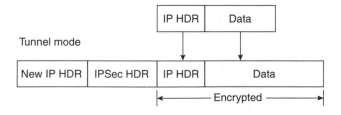

Figure 15-5 illustrates transport mode. In transport mode, only the IP payload is encrypted, and the original IP headers are left intact. An IPSec header is added. This mode has the advantage of adding only a few bytes to each packet. It also allows devices on the public network to see the packet's final source and destination. This capability allows you to enable special processing (for example, quality of service) in the intermediate network based on the information in the IP header. However, the Layer 4 header is encrypted, limiting the examination of the packet. Unfortunately, by passing the IP header in the clear, transport mode allows an attacker to perform some traffic analysis. For example, an attacker could see when many packets were sent between two IPSec peers operating in transport mode. However, the attacker would know only that IP packets were sent. He wouldn't be able to determine whether they were e-mail or another application if ESP were used.

Figure 15-5 *Transport Mode*

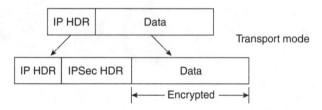

Using Tunnel Mode or Transport Mode

Consider some examples of when to use tunnel or transport mode. Figure 15-6 illustrates situations in which tunnel mode is used. Tunnel mode is most commonly used to encrypt traffic between secure IPSec gateways, such as between the Cisco router and the PIX Firewall, as shown in Example A in Figure 15-6. The IPSec gateways proxy IPSec for the devices behind them, such as Alice's PC and the HR servers in the figure. In Example A, Alice connects to the HR servers securely through the IPSec tunnel set up between the gateways.

Tunnel mode is also used to connect an end station running IPSec software, such as the CiscoSecure VPN client, to an IPSec gateway, as shown in Example B.

In Example C, tunnel mode is used to set up an IPSec tunnel between the Cisco router and a server running IPSec software. Note that Cisco IOS Software and the PIX Firewall set tunnel mode as the default IPSec mode.

Transport mode is used between end stations supporting IPSec, or between an end station and a gateway, if the gateway is being treated as a host. Figure 15-7 shows Example D, in which transport mode is used to set up an encrypted IPSec tunnel from Alice's PC running the Microsoft Windows 2000 client software to terminate at the Cisco VPN 3000 Concentrator, allowing Alice to tunnel L2TP over IPSec.

Figure 15-6 *Use of Tunnel Mode*

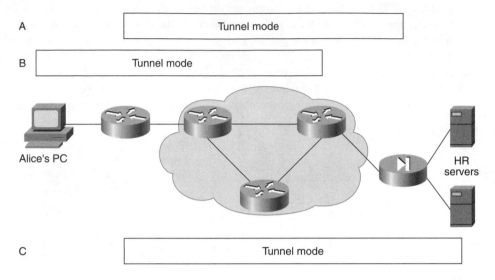

Figure 15-7 *Use of Transport Mode*

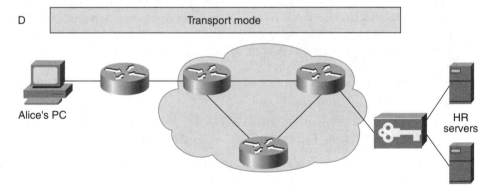

Using AH or ESP

Deciding whether to use AH or ESP in a given situation might seem complex, but it can be simplified to a few rules. When you want to make sure that data from an authenticated source gets transferred with integrity and does not need confidentiality, use the AH protocol. AH protects the upper-layer protocols and the IP header fields that do not change in transit. Protection means that the values cannot be changed without detection, so the IPSec peer will reject any altered IP datagram. AH does not protect against someone sniffing the wire and seeing the headers and data. However, because headers and data cannot be changed without the change being detected, changed packets are rejected.

If you need to keep data private (confidentiality), you use ESP. ESP encrypts the upper-layer protocols in transport mode and the entire original IP datagram in tunnel mode so that neither is readable from the wire. ESP can also provide authentication for the packets. However, when you use ESP in transport mode, the outer IP original header is not protected; in tunnel mode, the new IP header is not protected. Users will probably implement tunnel mode more than transport mode during initial IPSec usage.

Security Associations

An IPSec SA is a connection between IPSec peers that determines which IPSec services are available between the peers, similar to a TCP or UDP port. Each IPSec peer maintains an SA database in memory containing SA parameters. SAs are uniquely identified by an SPI. You need to configure SA parameters and monitor SAs on Cisco products.

The IPSec SAs are set up with a quick mode exchange during IKE Phase 2. Each AH and ESP transform gets its own separate pair of IPSec SAs. Each IPSec peer agrees to set up SAs consisting of policy parameters to be used during the IPSec session. The SAs are unidirectional for IPSec, so Peer 1 will offer Peer 2 a policy. If Peer 2 accepts this policy, it sends that policy back to Peer 1. This establishes two one-way SAs between the peers. Two-way communication consists of two SAs—one for each direction.

Each SA consists of values such as a destination address, an SPI, IPSec transforms used for that session, security keys, and additional attributes such as the IPSec lifetime. The SAs in each peer have unique SPI values that are recorded in the peers' security parameter databases.

Figure 15-8 shows an example of SA parameters for two IPSec peers, Cisco Routers 1 and 2 (R1 and R2). Note that each IPSec SA is unidirectional and that the SA parameters must match on each IPSec peer. The SA parameters are configured by the system administrator, are negotiated during quick mode, and are stored in the SA database.

Figure 15-8 *Examples of IPSec SA Values*

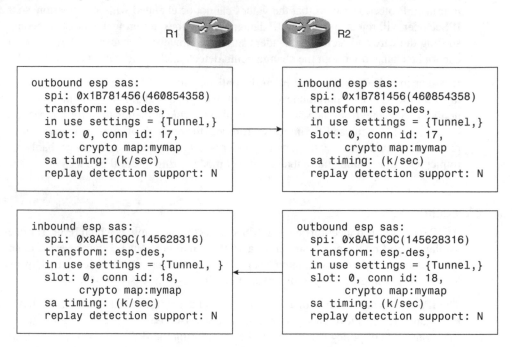

Table 15-1 describes the SA parameters shown in Figure 15-8.

Table 15-1 *Explanation of Sample IPSec Security Association Parameters*

SA Parameter	Description
outbound esp sas: spi: 0x1B781456(460854358)	An SPI that matches inbound SPI in peer for that SA.
transform: esp-des	An IPSec transform of ESP mode to use DES.
in use settings ={Tunnel, }	The IPSec transform mode is tunnel.
slot: 0, conn id: 17, crypto map: mymap	The Cisco IOS crypto engine and crypto map information.
sa timing: (k/sec)	The SA lifetime in KB and seconds.
replay detection support: N	Replay detection that is either on or off.

IPSec Transforms

As mentioned earlier in this chapter, an IPSec transform specifies a single IPSec security protocol (either AH or ESP) with its corresponding security algorithms and mode. The AH transform is a mechanism for payload authentication. The ESP transform is a mechanism for payload encryption. Figure 15-9 illustrates possible transform combinations.

Figure 15-9 *IPSec Transforms*

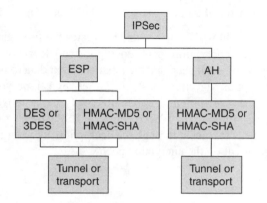

Here are some examples of transforms:

- The AH protocol with the HMAC with MD5 authentication algorithm in tunnel mode is used for authentication.
- The ESP protocol with the 3DES encryption algorithm in transport mode is used for confidentiality of data.
- The ESP protocol with the 56-bit DES encryption algorithm and the HMAC with SHA authentication algorithm in tunnel mode is used for authentication and confidentiality.

Data Encryption Standard

IPSec uses the 56-bit DES algorithm and 168-bit 3DES algorithm for bulk encryption in the ESP protocol and to ensure data confidentiality during IKE exchanges.

The most important feature of a cryptographic algorithm is its security against being compromised. The security of a cryptosystem, or the degree of difficulty for an attacker to determine the contents of the ciphertext, is a function of a few variables. In most protocols, the cornerstone of security lies in the secrecy of the key used to encrypt data. The DES algorithm was built so that it would be too difficult for anyone to determine the cleartext without having this key. In any cryptosystem, great lengths are taken to protect the secrecy of the encryption key.

After two IPSec peers obtain their shared secret key, they can use it to communicate with each other using the DES or 3DES encryption algorithms. Key length is a factor because it is more difficult to guess more digits than fewer. Even DES-encrypted data can be decrypted by an attacker, given enough computing power and time dedicated to finding the key. If a key were to be discovered, every packet that was encrypted with that key would easily be decrypted by the attacker. Frequently changing the shared secret keys makes it less likely that attackers can decrypt the data because there is less time to attack the key, and less data can be deciphered if a key is discovered. DES uses 56- and 168-bit key lengths.

Figure 15-10 shows how DES works and illustrates the following discussion. The components of DES encryption are the encryption and decryption algorithms, the matching shared secret keys on each peer, and the input cleartext data to be encrypted. At the core of DES is the encryption algorithm. A shared secret key is input to the algorithm. Cleartext data is fed into the algorithm in fixed-length blocks and is converted to ciphertext. The ciphertext is transmitted to the IPSec peer using ESP. The peer receives the ESP packet, extracts the ciphertext, runs it through the decryption algorithm, and outputs cleartext identical to that input on the encrypting peer.

Figure 15-10 *DES Operation*

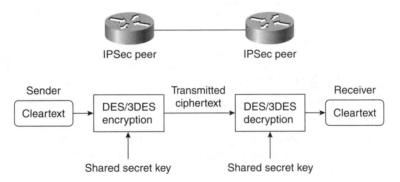

The DES Algorithm

The DES algorithm was designed by IBM in the early 1970s. The National Security Agency (NSA) made some changes to the algorithm, approved it for general use, and published it. DES is believed to be very secure, and no one has been able to disprove this fact thus far. However, it is prudent to periodically change keys.

DES uses a 56-bit key, ensuring high-performance encryption. DES is used to encrypt and decrypt packet data. DES turns cleartext into ciphertext via an encryption algorithm. The decryption algorithm on the remote end restores cleartext from ciphertext. Shared secret keys enable the encryption and decryption. DES is a symmetrical encryption algorithm, meaning that identical 56-bit shared secret keys are required in each IPSec peer.

DES is a block-cipher algorithm, which means that it performs operations on a fixed-length block of 64 bits. Cisco's encryption algorithm incorporates cipher feedback (CFB), which further guarantees the integrity of the data received by using feedback. DES operates as follows:

1 First, DES takes a serial stream of data to be encrypted and forms it into a 64-bit block.

2 DES does a permutation of the block, after which it divides the bits into two 32-bit halves. One of the halves is run through a complex, table-specified substitution that is dependent on the key, and then the output is "exclusive ORed" with the other half of the bits. This function takes place in 16 cycles, called rounds. After each round, the two 32-bit halves are swapped.

3 Following the final round, a final permutation is applied. The resulting ciphertext is a series of bits, each of which depends on every bit of the input and every bit of the key.

The Triple DES Algorithm

3DES is also a supported encryption protocol for use in IPSec on Cisco products. The 3DES algorithm is a variant of the 56-bit DES. 3DES operates similarly to DES in that data is broken into 64-bit blocks. 3DES then processes each block three times, each time with an independent 56-bit key. 3DES effectively triples encryption strength over 56-bit DES. 3DES is a symmetrical encryption algorithm.

Internet Key Exchange

IKE is a hybrid protocol, combining the Oakley and SKEME key exchange methods inside the ISAKMP framework. IPSec uses IKE to authenticate peers, manage the generation and handling of keys used by DES and the hashing algorithms between peers, and negotiate IPSec SAs.

IPSec can be configured without IKE, but IKE enhances IPSec by providing additional features, flexibility, and ease of configuration for the IPSec standard. IKE provides the following benefits:

- It eliminates the need to manually specify all the IPSec SA parameters at both peers.
- It establishes session keys securely for use between peers.
- It allows you to specify a lifetime for the IPSec security association.
- It allows encryption keys to change during IPSec sessions.
- It allows IPSec to provide anti-replay services.
- It permits CA support for a manageable, scalable IPSec implementation.
- It allows dynamic authentication of peers.

IKE Standards

IKE uses the following methods and algorithms to accomplish its purpose:

- **ISAKMP**—A protocol framework that defines payload formats, the mechanics of implementing a key exchange protocol, and the negotiation of a security association.

- **Oakley**—A key exchange protocol that defines how to derive authenticated keying material.

- **SKEME**—A key exchange protocol that defines how to derive authenticated keying material, with rapid key refreshment.

- **DES**—An encryption algorithm that is used to encrypt packet data, ensuring confidentiality of IKE exchanges. IKE uses 56-bit DES and 3DES in Cisco products.

- **Diffie-Hellman**—A public-key cryptography protocol that lets peers establish shared secret keys over an unsecure communications channel. Diffie-Hellman is used within IKE to establish session keys.

- **MD5 and SHA (HMAC variant)**—Hash algorithms used to authenticate packet data during IKE exchanges.

- **RSA signatures and RSA encrypted nonces**—RSA signatures provide nonrepudiation, and RSA encrypted nonces (a random number used in encryption algorithms) provide repudiation. Both are used by IKE to authenticate peers.

- **X.509v3 certificates**—Digital certificates that are used with the IKE protocol when authentication requires public keys. This certificate support allows the protected network to scale by providing the equivalent of a digital ID card to each device. When two devices want to communicate, they exchange digital certificates to prove their identity (thus removing the need to manually exchange public keys with each peer or to manually specify a shared key at each peer).

IKE Phases

IKE negotiates SAs for both IKE and IPSec during two phases, with various modes, as follows:

- **Phase 1**—IKE negotiates IKE SAs during this phase.
- **Phase 2**—IKE negotiates IPSec SAs during this phase.

See the sections "Step 2: IKE Phase 1" and "Step 3: IKE Phase 2" earlier in this chapter for more information on what happens during these phases.

IKE Authentication

Potential peers in an IPSec session must authenticate themselves to each other before IKE can proceed. Peer authentication occurs during the main mode exchange during IKE Phase

1. The IKE protocol is very flexible and supports multiple authentication methods as part of the Phase 1 exchange. The two entities must agree on a common authentication protocol through a negotiation process. At this time, preshared keys, RSA-encrypted nonces, and RSA signatures are the mechanisms implemented in Cisco products:

- **Preshared keys**—The same preshared key is configured on each IPSec peer. IKE peers authenticate each other by computing and sending a keyed hash of data that includes the preshared key. If the receiving peer can independently create the same hash using its preshared key, it knows that both peers must share the same secret, thus authenticating the other peer. Preshared keys are easier to configure than manually configuring IPSec policy values on each IPSec peer, yet preshared keys do not scale well because each IPSec peer must be configured with the preshared key of every other peer it will establish a session with.

- **RSA-encrypted nonces**—Public key cryptography requires that each party generate a pseudorandom number (a nonce) and encrypt it in the other party's RSA public key. Authentication occurs when each party decrypts the other party's nonce with a local private key (and other publicly and privately available information) and then uses the decrypted nonce to compute a keyed hash. This system provides for deniable transactions. In other words, either side of the exchange can plausibly deny that he or she took part in the exchange. Cisco IOS Software is the only Cisco product that uses RSA-encrypted nonces for IKE authentication. RSA-encrypted nonces use the RSA public key algorithm.

- **RSA signatures**—With a digital signature, each device digitally signs a set of data and sends it to the other party. This method is similar to the preceding one except that it provides nonrepudiation. RSA signatures use a CA for authentication and to derive secret key values. RSA signature nonces use the RSA public key algorithm.

IKE Mode Configuration

IKE mode configuration (mode config) is an IPSec feature that allows a gateway to download an IP address (and other network-level configurations) to a client as part of an IKE negotiation. Using this exchange, the gateway gives IP addresses to the IPSec client much as a Dynamic Host Configuration Protocol (DHCP) server assigns IP addresses to a dialup client. The address supplied by mode config is known as the inside IP address and is used in the packet header (TCP or UDP) before encryption. The following steps and Figure 15-11 illustrate how mode config assigns an IP address to the IPSec client:

1 The remote user dials up his or her Internet service provider (ISP). The dialup adapter (or network interface card [NIC]) is assigned an IP address by the ISP via DHCP (address 172.16.2.121).

2 The IPSec client sends traffic to be encrypted and starts an IKE Phase 1 exchange to the IPSec gateway.

3 The IPSec gateway uses mode config to assign an inside IP address of 10.1.1.82 from a pool of IP addresses for clients. The inside address is used to address packets before encryption.

4 The IPSec client encrypts the packet with ESP. The ESP header uses a source address of 172.16.2.121. The destination of the ESP packet is 172.16.1.2, the IPSec gateway or tunnel endpoint.

5 The IPSec gateway receives the packet, decrypts it, and uses the inside address for the decrypted packet's IP header. The decrypted packet is sent to the corporate network destined for an application at 10.1.1.100.

Figure 15-11 *Mode Config Operation*

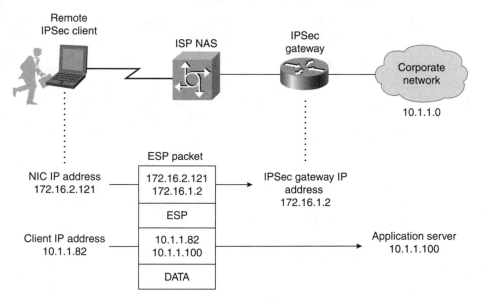

Mode config provides a known IP address for the client, which can be matched against IPSec policy and can be used to connect decrypted traffic to a network inside the enterprise network.

Mode config is supported in Cisco IOS Software, the CiscoSecure PIX Firewall, and the CiscoSecure VPN client. For example, using mode config, you can configure a PIX Firewall to download an IP address to a client as part of an IKE transaction. Mode config is in IETF draft status.

IKE Extended Authentication

The IKE extended authentication (XAuth) feature lets you add user authentication to IPSec for remote users. This feature provides authentication by prompting for user credentials and verifies them with the information stored in a remote security database, providing authentication, authorization, and accounting (AAA) within the VPN.

Two-factor authentication and challenge/response schemes such as SDI's SecureID and RADIUS are forms of authentication that allow a gateway, firewall, or network access server to offload the user administration and authentication to a remote security database such as a Cisco Secure ACS system or a SecureID Ace server.

IKE has no provision for user authentication. XAuth uses IKE to transfer the user's authentication information (name and password) to an IPSec gateway in a secured IKE message. The gateway uses the configured protocol (either RADIUS, SecureID, or a one-time password) to authenticate the user with a remote security database. This allows the administration of usernames and passwords to be offloaded to a remote security database within the private network that the IPSec gateway is protecting.

XAuth is negotiated between IKE Phase 1 and IKE Phase 2 at the same time as mode configuration. Authentication is performed using an existing TACACS+ or RADIUS authentication system. The XAuth feature is enabled with the **crypto map** command.

Diffie-Hellman Key Agreement

The Diffie-Hellman key agreement is a public key encryption method that provides a way for two IPSec peers to establish a shared secret key that only they know, although they are communicating over an insecure channel.

With Diffie-Hellman, each peer generates a public key/private key pair. The private key generated by each peer is kept secret and is never shared. The public key is calculated from the private key by each peer and is exchanged over the insecure channel. Each peer combines the other's public key with its own private key and computes the same shared secret number. The shared secret number is converted into a shared secret key, which is then used to encrypt data using the secret key encryption algorithms specified in the IPSec SAs, such as DES or MD5. The shared secret key is never exchanged over the insecure channel. The following steps summarize how Diffie-Hellman works:

1 The Diffie-Hellman process starts with each peer generating a large prime integer, p or q. Each peer sends the other its prime integer over the insecure channel. For example, Peer A sends p to Peer B. Each peer then uses the p and q values to generate g, a primitive root of p. Table 15-2 shows Step 1 in more detail.

Table 15-2 *Step 1 of the Diffie-Hellman Process*

Peer A Process	Peer B Process
• Generate large integer p	• Generate large integer q
• Send p to Peer B	• Send q to Peer A
• Receive q	• Receive p
• Generate g	• Generate g

2 Each peer generates a private Diffie-Hellman key (peer A: X_a; peer B: X_b) using the p and g values. Table 15-3 shows this step.

Table 15-3 *Step 2 of the Diffie-Hellman Process*

Peer A Process	Peer B Process
Generate private key X_a	Generate private key X_b

3 Each peer generates a public Diffie-Hellman key. The local private key is combined with the prime number p and the primitive root g in each peer to generate a public key, Y_a for Peer A and Y_b for Peer B. The formula for Peer A is $Y_a = g^\wedge X_a$ mod p. The formula for Peer B is $Y_b = g^\wedge X_b$ mod p. The exponentiation is computationally expensive. The $\wedge$ character denotes exponentiation (g to the X_a power), and mod denotes modulus or division. Table 15-4 sums up Step 3 of the process.

Table 15-4 *Step 3 of the Diffie-Hellman Process*

Peer A Process	Peer B Process
Generate the public key: $Y_a = g^\wedge X_a$ mod p	Generate the public key: $Y_b = g^\wedge X_b$ mod p

4 The public keys Y_a and Y_b are exchanged in public, as shown in Table 15-5.

Table 15-5 *Step 4 of the Diffie-Hellman Process*

Peer A Process	Peer B Process
Send public key Y_a to Peer A	Send public key Y_b to Peer B

5 Each peer generates a shared secret number (ZZ) by combining the public key received from the opposite peer with its own private key. The formula for Peer A is $ZZ = (Y_b^\wedge X_a)$ mod p. The formula for Peer B is $ZZ = (Y_a^\wedge X_b)$ mod p. The ZZ values are identical in each peer. Anyone who knows p or g, or the Diffie-Hellman public

keys, cannot guess or easily calculate the shared secret value—largely because of the difficulty in factoring large prime numbers. ZZ is also known as the value SKEYID_d in the IKE RFC 2409. Table 15-6 sums up Step 5 of the process.

Table 15-6   *Step 5 of the Diffie-Hellman Process*

Peer A Process	Peer B Process
Generate the shared secret number: $ZZ = Y_b \char94 X_a \bmod p$	Generate the shared secret number: $ZZ = Y_a \char94 X_b \bmod p$

6 Shared secret keys are derived from the shared secret number ZZ for use by DES or HMACs, as shown in Table 15-7.

Table 15-7   *Step 6 of the Diffie-Hellman process*

Peer A Process	Peer B Process
Generate shared secret key from ZZ (56-bit for DES, 168-bit for 3DES)	Generate shared secret key from ZZ (56-bit for DES, 168-bit for 3DES)

Diffie-Hellman is performed during the IKE Phase 1 main mode to initially generate keying material and to generate nonces for authentication and rekeying. It can optionally be performed during IKE Phase 2 quick mode to generate fresh keying material for IPSec SAs by combining a generated nonce with existing keying material.

The nonces are sent to the IPSec peer for authentication. The nonces are signed and returned to prove their identity (they are signed only if RSA-encrypted nonces or RSA signatures are being used for authentication), thereby providing authentication of the Diffie-Hellman exchange.

Perfect Forward Secrecy

A refresh of shared secret encryption keys occurs during an IKE Phase 2 quick mode exchange. Refreshing involves combining the current key with a random number (nonce) to create a new key using Diffie-Hellman. PFS enforces the recalculation of the shared secret key from scratch using the public key/private key generation and Diffie-Hellman techniques. The reason for the recalculation is to avoid a situation in which a hacker might have derived a particular secret key and compromised all data encrypted with that key. PFS means that a new key can be calculated that has no relationship to the preceding key.

Hashed Message Authentication Codes

IPSec uses HMACs to ensure data integrity and data origin authentication. For example, an HMAC is used to ensure data integrity and authentication during IKE Phase 1 and 2 exchanges and for IPSec AH packets. An HMAC is a mechanism for message authentication using cryptographic hash functions and a private key. A hash function or algorithm condenses a variable-length input message into a fixed-length hash of the message as output. The message hash can then be used as the message's "fingerprint." It is considered computationally infeasible to reverse the hashed value and determine the original message. Hash functions are generally fast, and the results are very secure because one-way functions are difficult if not impossible to reverse. The fundamental hash algorithms used by IPSec are the cryptographically secure MD5 and SHA-1 hash functions.

Hashing algorithms have evolved into HMACs, which combine the proven security of hashing algorithms with additional cryptographic functions. The hash produced is encrypted with the sender's private key, resulting in a keyed checksum as output. Figure 15-12 illustrates how an HMAC works. The hash function takes as input a private key and the variable-length cleartext data that needs to be authenticated. The private key length is the same as the hash's output. The HMAC algorithm is run with a resultant fixed-length checksum as output. This checksum value is sent with the message as a signature. The receiving peer runs an HMAC on the same message data that was input at the sender, using the same private key, and the resultant hash is compared with the received hash, which should match exactly.

Data integrity and data origin authentication depend on the secrecy of the secret key. If only the sender and receiver know the key and the HMAC is correct, this proves that the message must have been sent by the sender.

IPSec specifies that HMAC-MD5 and HMAC-SHA-1 are used as HMACs for IKE and IPSec.

HMAC-MD5-96

IPSec uses the HMAC-MD5-96 (HMAC-MD5) encryption technique to ensure that a message has not been altered. HMAC-MD5 uses the MD5 hash developed by Ronald Rivest of the Massachusetts Institute of Technology and RSA Data Security Incorporated. It is described in RFC 1321.

HMAC-MD5 uses a 128-bit secret key. It produces a 128-bit authenticator value. This 128-bit value is truncated to the first 96 bits. After it is sent, the truncated value is stored in the authenticator field of AH or ESP-HMAC. Upon receipt, the entire 128-bit value is computed, and the first 96 bits are compared to the value stored in the authenticator field.

MD5 alone has recently been shown to be vulnerable to collision search attacks. This attack and other currently known weaknesses of MD5 do not compromise the use of MD5 within HMAC because no known attacks against HMAC-MD5 have been proven. HMAC-MD5 is recommended when the superior performance of MD5 over SHA-1 is important.

Figure 15-12 *HMAC Operation*

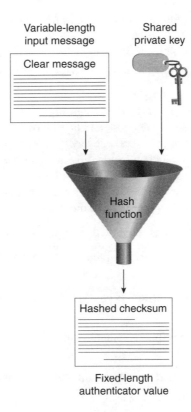

HMAC-SHA-1-96

IPSec uses the HMAC-SHA-1-96 (HMAC-SHA-1) encryption technique to ensure that a message has not been altered. HMAC-SHA-1 uses the SHA-1 specified in FIPS-190-1 combined with HMAC (as per RFC 2104). It is described in RFC 2404.

HMAC-SHA-1 uses a 160-bit secret key. It produces a 160-bit authenticator value. This 160-bit value is truncated to the first 96 bits. After it is sent, the truncated value is stored in the authenticator field of AH or ESP-HMAC. Upon receipt, the entire 160-bit value is computed, and the first 96 bits are compared to the value stored in the authenticator field.

SHA-1 is considered cryptographically stronger that MD5, yet it takes more CPU cycles to compute. HMAC-SHA-1 is recommended when the slightly superior security of SHA-1 over MD5 is important.

RSA Security

IPSec uses the RSA public-key cryptosystem for authentication in IKE Phase 1. RSA was developed in 1977 by Ron Rivest, Adi Shamir, and Leonard Adleman (hence RSA). IKE Phase 1 uses two forms of RSA: RSA signatures for digital signatures used with certificate authorities for scalable IPSec peers, and RSA encrypted nonces used with a small number of IPSec peers.

RSA generates a public key/private key pair in each IPSec peer. The public key can be transmitted over an insecure network and is used by anyone who wants to establish an IPSec session with the peer. The private key is known only to the IPSec peer and is used to decrypt data. Encryption and authentication take place without sharing the private keys: Each person uses only another's public key or his or her own private key. Anyone can send an encrypted message or verify a signed message, but only someone in possession of the correct private key can decrypt or sign a message.

RSA works as follows and is illustrated in Figure 15-13:

1 A cleartext message to be encrypted and the receiver's public key are input to the RSA encryption algorithm.

2 The output of the algorithm is encrypted data (ciphertext), which is transmitted to Peer B.

3 Peer B receives the ciphertext and inputs it and its own private RSA key into the RSA decryption algorithm.

4 The output is cleartext, which should match the input cleartext on Peer A.

Figure 15-13 *RSA Operation*

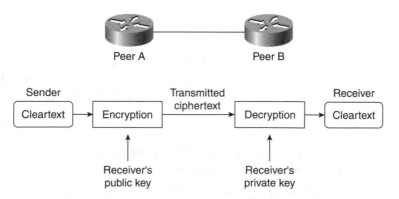

IKE uses the RSA algorithm in Cisco products to authenticate peers via RSA signatures and RSA encryption.

IKE Phase 1 can use preshared keys, RSA signatures, or RSA encryption to authenticate the Phase 1 exchange. Main mode generates keying material from a Diffie-Hellman exchange that must be authenticated. The first two main mode messages negotiate IKE policy, the next two exchange Diffie-Hellman public values and other data such as nonces necessary for the exchange, and the last two messages use RSA to authenticate the Diffie-Hellman exchange. The authentication method is configured in the Cisco product beforehand and is negotiated as part of the initial IKE exchange.

RSA Signatures

An RSA signature uses a nonce value and the IKE identity to exchange ancillary information, and the exchange is authenticated by signing a mutually obtainable hash. Each peer's ability to reconstruct a hash of the nonce and identity authenticates the exchange. RSA signatures work as follows:

1 RSA signature key pairs are generated with configuration commands in each peer. The RSA public keys are exchanged and authenticated, and certificates for each peer are obtained using a CA server.

2 Peer A sends its IKE identity and a signed digital certificate to peer B during IKE Phase 1. Peer B sends the same to Peer A. The signed digital certificate authenticates the IKE exchange.

RSA-Encrypted Nonces

IKE Phase 1 can use RSA-encrypted nonces to authenticate the Phase 1 exchange. Main mode generates keying material from a Diffie-Hellman exchange that must be authenticated. The first two main mode messages negotiate IKE policy, the next two exchange Diffie-Hellman public values and other data such as nonces that are necessary for the exchange, and the last two messages use RSA encryption to authenticate the Diffie-Hellman exchange if RSA encryption is the authentication method negotiated as part of the initial IKE exchange.

Simply put, RSA encryption is used to authenticate the IKE exchange by encrypting a nonce value and the IKE identity and sending it to the peer. Each peer's ability to reconstruct a hash of the nonce and identity authenticates the exchange. Consider the following steps that sum up RSA encryption operation:

1 RSA encryption key pairs are generated with configuration commands in each peer. The RSA public keys are exchanged out-of-band (via disk or e-mail) and are entered into each peer with configuration commands. Note that this manual key generation and exchange limits scalability.

2 Peer A encrypts its nonce and IKE identity with RSA encryption using Peer B's RSA public key and transmits the ciphertext to Peer B.

3 Peer B encrypts its nonce and IKE identity with RSA encryption using Peer A's RSA public key.

4 Both peers exchange the encrypted values.

5 Peer B decrypts the received ciphertext using its private RSA key and extracts Peer A's nonce and identity. It then hashes Peer A's nonce and identity and transmits the hash to Peer A.

6 Peer A decrypts the received ciphertext using its private RSA key and extracts peer B's nonce and identity. It then hashes Peer B's nonce and identity and transmits the hash to Peer B.

7 Peer A hashes its own nonce and identity and compares the hash with the one received from Peer B. The hashes should match, thus authenticating Peer B.

8 Peer B hashes its own nonce and identity and compares the hash with the one received from Peer A. The hashes should match, thus authenticating Peer A.

RSA encryption is very secure because it not only authenticates the IKE exchange but also authenticates the Diffie-Hellman exchange.

Public Key Infrastructure and CA Support

IPSec scalability, the ability to deploy large IPSec networks (those with more than 100 nodes), has been one of the greatest challenges facing implementers of network layer encryption. Digital certificate technology provides the ability for devices to easily authenticate each other in a manner that scales to very large networks.

Many organizations are currently implementing a public key infrastructure (PKI) to manage digital certificates across a wide variety of applications including VPNs, secure e-mail, secure Web access, and other applications that require security. Cisco's implementation of IPSec is interoperable with the products of several leading PKI vendors. This allows you to choose the best PKI for your individual needs while knowing that it will be compatible with Cisco's network security solutions.

CAs allow the IPSec-protected network to scale by providing the equivalent of a digital identification card to each device. When two IPSec peers want to communicate, they exchange digital certificates to prove their identities. The digital certificates are obtained from a CA. CA support on Cisco products uses RSA signatures to authenticate the CA exchange.

With a CA, you do not need to configure keys between all the IPSec peers. Instead, you individually enroll each participating peer with the CA and request a certificate. When the peer has obtained a certificate from the CA, each participating peer can dynamically authenticate all the other participating peers. To add a new IPSec peer to the network, you only need to configure that new peer to request a certificate from the CA instead of making multiple key configurations with all the other existing IPSec peers.

Figure 15-14 illustrates how each IPSec peer individually enrolls with the CA server.

Figure 15-14   *CA Server Fulfilling Requests from IPSec Peers*

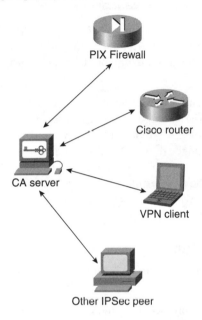

CA servers manage certificate requests and issue certificates to participating IPSec peers. CAs simplify the administration of IPSec peers by centralizing key management. You can use a CA with a network containing multiple IPSec-compliant devices such as PIX Firewalls, Cisco routers, the Cisco Secure VPN client, and other vendors' IPSec products.

Digital signatures, enabled by public key cryptography, provide a way to digitally authenticate devices and individual users. In public key cryptography, such as the RSA encryption system, each user has a key pair that contains both a public key and a private key. The keys are complementary—anything encrypted with one of the keys can be decrypted with the other. In simple terms, a signature is formed when data is encrypted with a sender's private key. The receiver verifies the signature by decrypting the message with the sender's public key. The fact that the message could be decrypted using the sender's public key indicates that the holder of the private key, the sender, must have created the message. This process relies on the receiver having a copy of the sender's public key and knowing with a high degree of certainty that it really does belong to the sender, not to someone pretending to be the sender.

Digital certificates provide this assurance. Digital certificates contain information to identify an IPSec peer. Digital certificates are simply a document in a specified format that contains information such as the name, serial number, company, department, or IP address of the peer and organization. It also contains a copy of the peer's public key. The certificate is itself signed by a CA, a third party that is explicitly trusted by the receiver to validate identities and to create digital certificates.

There is a problem with digital certificates. In order to validate the CA's signature, the receiver must first know the CA's public key. The CA's public key is contained in the CA's root certificate, which is installed in the IPSec peer during certificate configuration and enrollment.

IKE, a key component of IPSec, can use digital signatures to authenticate peer devices before setting up security associations. This provides scalability. When an IPSec peer enrolls with a CA, the CA provides the peer with identity (ID) certificates. The ID certificates are exchanged during IKE Phase 1 and are used to authenticate the peers, much as preshared keys are used. The ID certificate is validated with the public key of the CA itself contained in the root certificate. The certificate infrastructure is made possible by a variety of standards, which are discussed in the next section.

CA Standards Supported

Cisco routers, the Cisco Secure VPN client, and the PIX Firewall support the following open CA standards:

- **IKE**—A hybrid protocol that implements Oakley and SKEME key exchanges inside the ISAKMP framework. IKE provides authentication of the IPSec peers and negotiates IPSec keys and security associations. IKE can use digital certificates to authenticate peers.

- **Public-Key Cryptography Standard #7 (PKCS #7)**—A standard from RSA Data Security, Inc. used to encrypt and sign certificate enrollment messages.

- **Public-Key Cryptography Standard #10 (PKCS #10)**—A standard syntax from RSA Data Security, Inc. for certificate requests.

- **RSA keys**—RSA is the public key cryptographic system developed by Rivest, Shamir, and Adleman. RSA keys come in pairs: one public key and one private key.

- **X.509v3 certificates**—This standard specifies the content format of public key certificates, which are data structures that bind public key values to standard subjects. Certificate support allows the IPSec-protected network to scale by providing the equivalent of a digital ID card to each device. When two devices want to communicate, they exchange digital certificates to prove their identity (thus removing the need to manually exchange public keys with each peer or to manually specify a shared key at each peer). These certificates are obtained from a CA. X.509 is part of the X.500 standard series created by the International Telecommunications Union (ITU). Some subjects in certificates include a unique serial number, a hashing algorithm for signing, an RSA public key, and valid dates.

- **Simplified Certification Enrollment Protocol (SCEP)**—A CA interoperability protocol that permits compliant IPSec peers and CAs to communicate so that the IPSec peer can obtain and use digital certificates from the CA. Using IPSec peers and CA servers that support SCEP provides manageability and scalability for CA support.

- **Certificate revocation lists (CRLs)**—CAs support a CRL, which is a type of certificate that lists IPSec peers that have been revoked and are no longer valid. IPSec peers can obtain the CRL from the CA. The IPSec peer should check the CRL every time an IPSec peer attempts to establish a new IKE SA to ensure that the peer is valid.

- **Registration Authority (RA)**—Some CAs have an RA as part of their implementation. An RA is essentially a server that acts as a proxy for the CA so that CA functions can continue when the CA is offline.

How CA Enrollment Works with SCEP

IPSec peers enroll with a CA using SCEP before they can use IKE configured for digital certificates. Each IPSec peer supporting SCEP contains PKI client software that enrolls with the CA in a client/server relationship using SCEP. The peer-to-CA enrollment process is summarized as follows:

1 The peer administrator configures IPSec and IKE for CA support and creates an RSA public key/private key.

2 The peer obtains the CA's public key (via the CA's own certificate and through manual authentication).

3 The peer sends its public RSA key and identity information to the CA.

4 The peer receives its own public key ID certificate and the CA's certificate from the CA.

5 The peer optionally gets the latest CRL from the CA.

After enrolling with the CA, peers exchange ID certificates via IKE, thereby exchanging their public keys. Each participant verifies the others' certificates with the CA's public key for authenticity and checks its latest copy of the CA's CRL. IPSec Security Associations (SAs) can then be set up by IKE, and a secure tunnel can be created between peers.

CA Server Support

Many vendors offer CA servers either as user-installed and user-managed software or as a managed CA service. Many CA server vendors have developed their products to interoperate with Cisco VPN products by supporting the SCEP protocol. Cisco is using the

Cisco Security Associate Program to test new CA and PKI solutions with the Cisco Secure family of products. More information on the Security Associate Program can be found at www.cisco.com/warp/customer/cc/so/neso/sqso/csap/index.shtml. The following are the vendors that interoperate with Cisco VPN products:

- **Entrust Technologies**—Entrust Technologies makes the Entrust/PKI 4.0, a CA server that supports Cisco VPN products through SCEP. Entrust/PKI 4.0 is software that is installed and administered by the user. Entrust/PKI 4.0 supports Cisco routers, the Cisco Secure VPN client, and PIX Firewalls. Entrust/PKI 4.0 runs on the Windows NT 4.0 (required for Cisco interoperability), Solaris 2.6, HP-UX 10.20, and AIX 4.3 operating systems. Refer to the Entrust Web site at www.entrust.com for more information.

- **VeriSign**—VeriSign offers OnSite 4.5, a service administered by VeriSign. Onsite 4.5 delivers a fully integrated enterprise PKI to control, issue, and manage IPSec certificates for PIX Firewalls and Cisco routers over the public Internet. Users must subscribe to the VeriSign service. Refer to the VeriSign Web site at www.verisign.com for more information.

- **Baltimore Technologies**—Baltimore has implemented support for SCEP in UniCERT (Baltimore's CA server) as well as the PKI Plus toolkit, making it easy for customers to enroll Cisco VPN products. The current release of the UniCERT CA module is available for Windows NT 4.0. Refer to the Baltimore Web site at www.baltimore.com for more information.

- **Microsoft Windows 2000 Certificate Services 5.0**—Microsoft has integrated the SCEP into its CA server through the Security Resource Kit for Windows 2000. This support lets customers utilize SCEP to obtain certificates and certificate revocation information from Microsoft Certificate Services for all Cisco's VPN security solutions. Refer to the Microsoft Web site at www.microsoft.com for more information.

IKE and IPSec Flow in Cisco IOS Software

Cisco IOS Software implements and processes IPSec in a predictable and reliable fashion. A summary of how IPSec works and the commands used to configure it are shown in Figure 15-15. The process shown in the figure assumes that you have already created your own public and private keys and that at least one access list exists. Here is the process:

1 Cisco IOS Software uses extended IP access lists (configured with the **access-list** command) applied to an interface and crypto map to select traffic to be encrypted. Cisco IOS Software checks to see if IPSec SAs have been established. If the SA has already been established by manual configuration using the **crypto ipsec transform-**

set and **crypto map** commands, or if it was previously set up by IKE, the packet is encrypted based on the policy specified in the crypto map and is transmitted out the interface.

2 If the SA has not been established, Cisco IOS Software checks to see if an IKE SA has been configured and set up. If the IKE SA has been set up, the IKE SA governs negotiation of the IPSec SAs as specified in the IKE policy configured by the **crypto isakmp** series of commands. The packet is encrypted by IPSec and is transmitted.

3 If the IKE SA has not been set up, Cisco IOS Software checks to see if CA support has been configured to establish an IKE policy. If CA authentication is configured with the various **crypto ca** and **crypto isakmp policy** commands, the router exchanges its own digital certificate with the peer's certificates. It authenticates the peer's certificate, negotiates and establishes an IKE SA (which in turn is used to establish IPSec SAs), and encrypts and transmits the packet.

Figure 15-15 *IKE and IPSec Operation and Configuration Commands*

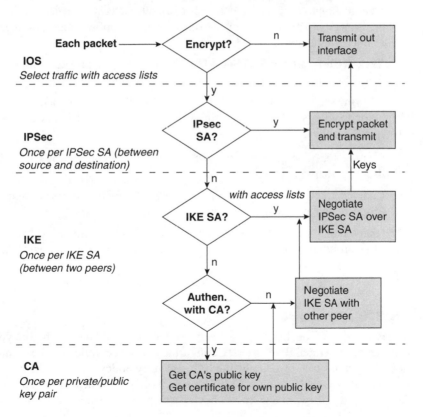

Configuring IPSec Encryption Task Overview

This section presents an overview of the four key tasks involved in configuring IPSec encryption using preshared keys on Cisco routers and the PIX Firewall. This section also discusses the first major task, Task 1: Prepare for IPSec, because it is common to all IPSec configuration methods. Subsequent chapters present the details of how to configure Cisco routers and the PIX Firewall for IPSec:

- **Task 1: Prepare for IPSec**—Preparing for IPSec involves determining the detailed encryption policy, determining how to establish keys between peers, identifying the hosts and networks you want to protect, determining details about the IPSec peers, determining which IPSec features you need, and ensuring that existing access lists used for packet filtering permit IPSec.

- **Task 2: Configure IKE**—Configuring IKE involves enabling IKE, creating the IKE policies, and validating the configuration.

- **Task 3: Configure IPSec**—IPSec configuration includes defining the transform sets, creating crypto access lists (access lists used to determine which traffic to encrypt), creating crypto maps (a template to enact an IPSec policy), and applying crypto maps to interfaces enabling IPSec.

- **Task 4: Test and verify IPSec**—Use **show**, **debug**, and related commands to verify that IPSec encryption works and to troubleshoot problems.

The following section discusses Task 1: Prepare for IPSec in more detail because this task is common to all methods of configuring IPSec. Tasks 2, 3, and 4 are covered in detail in subsequent chapters:

- Chapter 16, "Configuring Cisco IOS IPSec," covers configuring Cisco IOS IPSec using preshared keys.

- Chapter 17, "Configuring PIX Firewall IPSec Support," covers configuring PIX Firewall IPSec using preshared keys.

- Chapter 18, "Scaling Cisco IPSec Networks," covers configuring Cisco IOS and PIX Firewall IPSec using CA support. This chapter covers an additional task, configuring CA support.

Task 1: Prepare for IPSec

Successfully implementing an IPSec network requires that you plan before you begin configuring individual IPSec peers. Configuring IPSec encryption can be complicated. You should begin this task by defining the IPSec security policy based on the overall company security policy. See the sample XYZ Company policy in Appendix B, "An Example of an XYZ Company Network Security Policy." Some planning steps are as follows:

Step 1   Determine an IKE (IKE phase 1) policy between IPSec peers based on the number and location of the peers.

Step 2 Determine an IPSec (IKE Phase 2) policy to include IPSec peer details such as IP addresses and IPSec modes.

Step 3 Check the current configuration by using the **write terminal, show isakmp**, and **show crypto map** commands as well as other **show** commands.

Step 4 Ensure that the network works without encryption.

Step 5 Ensure that existing packet filtering access lists permit IPSec traffic in Cisco routers and the PIX Firewall.

The following sections examine these steps in detail.

Step 1: Determine an IKE Policy

You should determine the IKE policy details to enable the selected authentication method, and then configure it. Having a detailed plan reduces the chances of improper configuration. The planning you do here affects IKE Phase 1, main and aggressive modes. Some planning steps include the following:

- **Determine the key distribution method**—Select a key distribution method based on the numbers and locations of IPSec peers. For a small network, you might want to manually distribute keys. For larger networks, you might want to use a CA server to distribute digital certificates to support scalability of IPSec peers. You must then configure IKE to support the selected key distribution method.

- **Determine the authentication method**—Match the authentication method with the key distribution method. Cisco routers support either preshared keys, RSA-encrypted nonces, or RSA signatures to authenticate IPSec peers. PIX Firewalls support either preshared keys or RSA signatures.

- **Identify IPSec peers' IP addresses and host names**—Determine the details of all the IPSec peers that will use IKE and preshared keys to establish SAs. You will use this information to configure IKE.

- **Determine IKE policies for peers**—An IKE policy defines a combination, or suite, of security parameters to be used during the IKE main mode or aggressive mode negotiation. Each IKE negotiation begins with each peer agreeing on a common (shared) IKE policy. You must determine the IKE policy suites before beginning configuration, and you must configure IKE to support the policy details determined.

NOTE Remember that IKE is synonymous with ISAKMP. Cisco routers and the PIX Firewall have named their IKE commands as ISAKMP commands. For example, you can view IKE policies with the **show isakmp policy** command in the PIX Firewall. Actually, IKE is a newer protocol that uses the older ISAKMP and Oakley protocols.

Creating IKE Policies for a Purpose

IKE negotiations must be protected, so each IKE negotiation begins with each peer agreeing on an identical IKE policy used by each IPSec peer. This policy specifies which security parameters will be used to protect subsequent IKE negotiations.

You can configure multiple IKE policies on each peer participating in IPSec. After the two peers negotiate acceptable IKE policies, the policy's security parameters are identified by an IKE SA established at each peer, and these SAs apply to all subsequent IKE traffic during the negotiation. You can create multiple prioritized policies at each peer to ensure that at least one policy will match a remote peer's policy.

IKE negotiation begins in IKE Phase 1 main mode. IKE looks for a policy that is the same on both peers. The peer that initiates the negotiation sends all its policies to the remote peer, and the remote peer tries to find a match with its policies. The remote peer looks for a match by comparing its own highest-priority policy against the other peer's received policies in its IKE policy suite. The remote peer checks each of its policies in order of its priority (highest-priority first) until a match is found.

A match is made when both policies from the two peers contain the same encryption, hash, authentication, and Diffie-Hellman parameter values and when the remote peer's policy specifies a lifetime less than or equal to the lifetime in the policy being compared. (If the lifetimes are not identical, the shorter lifetime from the remote peer's policy is used.) Assign the most-secure policy the lowest-priority number so that the most-secure policy will find a match before any less-secure policies that are configured.

If no acceptable match is found, IKE refuses negotiation, and IPSec is not established. If a match is found, IKE completes the main mode negotiation, and IPSec security associations are created during IKE Phase 2 quick mode.

Defining IKE Policy Parameters

You can select specific values for each IKE parameter per the IKE standard. You choose a value based on the security level you want and the type of IPSec peer you will connect to. Table 15-8 shows the five parameters to define in each IKE policy as well as the relative strength of each.

Table 15-8 *IKE Policy Parameters*

Parameter	Strong	Stronger
Message encryption algorithm	DES	3DES
Message integrity (hash) algorithm	MD5	SHA-1
Peer authentication method	Preshare	RSA encryption, RSA signature

Table 15-8 *IKE Policy Parameters (Continued)*

Parameter	Strong	Stronger
Key exchange parameters (Diffie-Hellman group identifier)	Diffie-Hellman Group 1	Diffie-Hellman Group 2
IKE-established security association's lifetime	86400 seconds	Less than 86400 seconds

An IKE Policy Parameter Example for Two Peers

Figure 15-16 shows a simplified topology for the XYZ Company used in the examples in this chapter.

Figure 15-16 *XYZ Company Topology for IPSec*

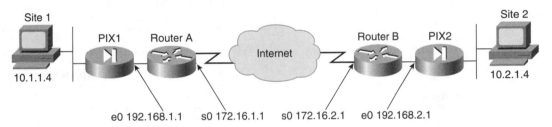

Step 2: Determine IPSec (IKE Phase 2) Policy

Planning for IPSec (IKE Phase 2) is another important step you should complete before actually configuring IPSec on a Cisco router. Policy details to determine at this stage include the following:

- Select IPSec algorithms and parameters for optimal security and performance. You should determine the IPSec encryption algorithms (transforms) that will be used to secure traffic. Some IPSec algorithms require you to make trade-offs between high performance and stronger security.

- Identify IPSec peer details. You must identify the IP addresses and host names of all the IPSec peers you will connect to.

- Determine the IP addresses and applications of hosts to be protected at the local peer and remote peer.

- Select whether security associations are manually established or are established via IKE.

The goal of this planning step is to gather the precise data you will need in later steps to minimize misconfiguration.

An important part of determining the IPSec policy is to identify the IPSec peer that the Cisco router or PIX Firewall will communicate with. The peer must support IPSec as specified in the RFCs supported by Cisco products. Many different types of peers are possible, so you should identify all the potential peers. You should determine IPSec policy details for each peer before configuring IPSec. Possible peers include, but are not limited to, the following:

- Cisco routers
- The PIX Firewall
- The Cisco Secure VPN client
- Cisco VPN 3000 or 5000 series concentrators
- Other vendors' IPSec products that conform to IPSec RFCs

Table 15-9 summarizes possible IPSec policy details that you will have to determine or choose.

Table 15-9 *IPSec Policy Parameters*

IPSec Parameter	Possible Values
Transform set	AH-MD5 or AH-SHA, ESP-DES or ESP-3DES, ESP-MD5-HMAC or ESP-SHA-HMAC
IPSec mode	Tunnel or transport
Hash algorithm	MD5 or SHA-1
SA establishment	**ipsec-isakmp** or **ipsec-manual**
IPSec SA lifetime	**kilobytes** and/or **seconds**
PFS	Group 1 when using ESP-DES, Group 2 when using ESP-3DES
Peer interface	Identify peer interface (hardware or loopback)
Peer IP address or host name	Identify peer device IP address or host name
IP address of hosts to be protected	Identify hosts or networks to protect
Traffic (packet) type to be encrypted	Any traffic specified by extended IP access lists

Step 3: Check the Current Configuration

You should check the current Cisco device configuration to see if any IPSec policies already configured are useful for or might interfere with the IPSec policies you plan to configure. Previously configured IKE and IPSec policies and details can and should be used if possible to save configuration time. However, previously configured IKE and IPSec policies can also interfere with your intended policy. For example, you might add a new IKE policy that is superceded by an existing policy because the old policy has a higher priority. You will need to carefully compare existing policies with your intended new policy to ensure that the new ones fit in.

You can use the **write terminal** (**show running config** in Cisco routers) command to view the current configuration. You can also use the available **show** commands (covered in a moment) to view IKE and IPSec configuration. You can check to see if any IKE policies have previously been configured with the **show crypto isakmp policy** command in Cisco routers (**show isakmp policy** in PIX Firewalls).

Step 4: Ensure That the Network Works

Next you need to ensure that basic connectivity has been achieved between Cisco devices before configuring Cisco IOS IPSec encryption. Although a successful ICMP echo (**ping**) verifies basic connectivity between peers, you should ensure that the network works with any other protocols or ports you plan to encrypt, such as Telnet, FTP, or SQL*NET, before you begin the IPSec configuration. After IPSec is activated, basic connectivity troubleshooting can be difficult because of possible security misconfigurations and the fact that you cannot sniff the encrypted IPSec packets. Previous security settings could result in no connectivity.

Step 5: Ensure That Access Lists Permit IPSec

Perimeter routers typically implement a restrictive security policy with access lists in which only specific traffic is permitted and all other traffic is denied. Such a restrictive policy blocks IPSec traffic, so you need to add specific permit statements to the access list to allow IPSec traffic.

Ensure that access lists are configured so that protocols 50 and 51 and UDP port 500 traffic are not blocked at interfaces used by IPSec. IKE uses UDP port 500. The IPSec ESP is assigned protocol 50, and AH is assigned protocol 51. In some cases, you might need to add a statement to router access lists to explicitly permit this traffic.

A concatenated example showing access list entries permitting IPSec traffic for Router A from Router B only is shown in Example 15-1.

Example 15-1 *An Access List Permitting IPSec Traffic*

```
RouterA# show running-config
!
interface Serial0
 ip address 172.16.1.1 255.255.255.0
 ip access-group 101 in
!
access-list 101 permit ahp host 172.16.2.1 host 172.16.1.1
access-list 101 permit esp host 172.16.2.1 host 172.16.1.1
access-list 101 permit udp host 172.16.2.1 host 172.16.1.1 eq isakmp
```

Note that the protocol keyword **esp** equals the ESP protocol (number 50), the keyword **ahp** equals the AH protocol (number 51), and the **isakmp** keyword equals UDP port 500.

You might need to check your PIX Firewall to ensure that access lists on the outside interface do not block IPSec traffic. You can use the **show access-list** command to view any configured access lists. You might need to add specific access list entries to the PIX Firewall, just as you did to the perimeter router to enable IPSec traffic. A concatenated example showing access list entries permitting IPSec traffic for PIX 1 is shown in Example 15-2. Note that the source address is the peer's outside interface, and the source is PIX 1's outside interface.

Example 15-2 *Access List Entries Permitting IPSec Traffic for PIX 1*

```
access-list 102 permit ahp host 192.168.2.2 host 192.168.1.2
access-list 102 permit esp host 192.168.2.2 host 192.168.1.2
access-list 102 permit udp host 192.168.2.2 host 192.168.1.2 eq isakmp
```

Summary

This section summarizes the main points of this chapter:

- IPSec is a suite of open security protocols that work together to create a secure, scalable VPN.

- The two main protocols used by IPSec are AH, which provides data integrity and authentication with no confidentiality, and ESP, which provides all that AH provides plus data confidentiality via encryption.

- The IKE protocol is used to authenticate IPSec peers and to facilitate the creation of secret keys used by IPSec encryption algorithms.

- IKE consists of two phases. Phase 1 authenticates the IPSec peers, ensures secret key generation, and sets up a secure tunnel for Phase 2, which sets up IPSec SA.

- IPSec SAs are negotiated and established during quick mode during IKE Phase 2.

- IPSec SAs are unidirectional and specify the IPSec parameters and secret keys used for the IPSec sessions. They are stored in an SA database in dynamic memory.

- IKE uses the Diffie-Hellman key exchange agreement during Phase 1 main mode to enable the creation of secure secret keys used by IPSec encryption algorithms.

- The HMACs of HMAC-MD5 and HMAC-SHA-1 are used by IKE and IPSec to ensure data integrity and to authenticate data exchanges.

- IPSec supports RSA signatures, RSA-encrypted nonces, and preshared keys as methods to authenticate IPSec peers during IKE Phase 1.

- Digital signatures, enabled by public key cryptography, provide a means to digitally authenticate IPSec peers, enabling scalability and flexibility of an IPSec network.

Review Questions

Answer the following review questions, which delve into some of the key facts and concepts covered in this chapter:

1 What are the two main IPSec protocols, and what services does each provide?

2 What important IPSec service does AH not provide?

3 What is the difference between how tunnel mode and transport mode are used?

4 What is an IPSec security association, and how is it established?

5 Can IPSec be configured without IKE?

6 What are the benefits of using IKE?

7 What initiates the IKE process?

8 What is the purpose of IKE phase 2?

9 What is the primary purpose of a CA?

10 What are the five overall steps of the IPSec process?

References

This chapter can be considered a starting point in your journey toward understanding IPSec. The topics considered in this chapter are complex and should be studied further to more fully understand them and put them to use. Use the following references to learn more about the topics in this chapter.

RFCs related to IPSec provide detailed definitions for some of the IPSec components. They can be found at the following URL: www.ietf.org/html.charters/ipsec-charter.html.

Internet drafts are working documents of the Internet Engineering Task Force (IETF). Internet drafts define IPSec standards still in the IETF draft phase. Internet drafts can be found at the following URL: www.ietf.org/html.charters/ipsec-charter.html.

IPSec Standards

RFC 2401, S. Kent and R. Atkinson, "Security Architecture for the Internet Protocol," November 1998.

RFC 2402, S. Kent and R. Atkinson, "IP Authentication Header," November 1998.

RFC 2403, C. Madson and R. Glenn, "The Use of HMAC-MD5-96 within ESP and AH," November 1998.

RFC 2404, C. Madson and R. Glenn, "The Use of HMAC-SHA-1-96 within ESP and AH," November 1998.

RFC 2405, C. Madson and N. Doraswamy, "The ESP DES-CBC Cipher Algorithm with Explicit IV," November 1998.

RFC 2406, S. Kent and R. Atkinson, "IP Encapsulating Security Payload (ESP)," November 1998.

RFC 2410, R. Glenn, "The NULL Encryption Algorithm and Its Use with IPSec," November 1998.

RFC 2411, N. Doraswamy, R. Glenn, and R. Thayer, "IP Security Document Roadmap," November 1998.

RFC 2451, R. Pereira and R. Adams, "The ESP 3DES CBC-Mode," November 1998.

Encryption

N. Doraswamy, P. Metzger, and W. A. Simpson, "The ESP Triple DES Transform," July 1997, draft-ietf-ipsec-ciph-des3-00.txt.

FIPS-46-2, "Data Encryption Standard," U.S. National Bureau of Standards Federal Information Processing Standard (FIPS) Publication 46-2, December 1993, www.itl.nist.gov/div897/pubs/fip46-2.htm (supercedes FIPS-46-1).

IKE

M. Litvin, R. Shamir, and T. Zegman, "A Hybrid Authentication Mode for IKE," December 1999, draft-ietf-ipsec-isakmp-hybrid-auth-03.txt.

R. Pereira, S. Anand, and B. Patel, "The ISAKMP Configuration Method," August 1999, draft-ietf-ipsec-isakmp-mode-cfg-05.txt.

R. Pereira and S. Beaulieu, "Extended Authentication within ISAKMP/Oakley (XAUTH)", December 1999, draft-ietf-ipsec-isakmp-xauth-06.txt.

RFC 2407, D. Piper, "The Internet IP Security Domain of Interpretation of ISAKMP," November 1998.

RFC 2408, D. Maughan, M. Schertler, M. Schneider, and J. Turner, "Internet Security Association and Key Management Protocol (ISAKMP)," November 1998.

RFC 2409, D. Harkins and D. Carrel, "The Internet Key Exchange (IKE)," November 1998.

RFC 2412, H. Orman, "The OAKLEY Key Determination Protocol," November 1998.

Hashing Algorithms

FIPS-180-1, "Secure Hash Standard," National Institute of Standards and Technology, U.S. Department of Commerce, April 1995. Also known as 59 Fed Reg 35317 (1994).

RFC 1321, R. Rivest, "The MD5 Message-Digest Algorithm," April 1992.

RFC 2085, R. Glenn and M. Oehler, "HMAC-MD5 IP Authentication with Replay Prevention," February 1997.

RFC 2104, H. Krawczyk, M. Bellare, and R. Canetti, "HMAC: Keyed-Hashing for Message Authentication," February 1997.

Public Key Cryptography

RFC 2437, B. Kaliski and J. Staddon, "PKCS #1: RSA Cryptography Specifications," October 1998.

RFC 2631, E. Rescorla, "Diffie-Hellman Key Agreement Method," June 1999.

Digital Certificates and Certificate Authorities

X. Liu, C. Madson, D. McGrew, and A. Nourse, "Cisco Systems' Simple Certificate Enrollment Protocol (SCEP)," February 2000, draft-nourse-scep-02.txt.

RFC 2314, B. Kaliski, "PKCS #10: Certification Request Syntax Version 1.5," March 1998.

RFC 2315, B. Kaliski, "PKCS #7: Cryptographic Message Syntax Version 1.5," March 1998.

RFC 2459, R. Housley, "Internet X.509 Public Key Infrastructure Certificate and CRL Profile," January 1999.

General Security

"Frequently Asked Questions About Today's Cryptography 4.0," RSA Laboratories, Redwood City, Calif., 1998. This FAQ covers the technical mathematics of cryptography as well as export law and fundamentals of information security.

IPSec, a Cisco Systems, Inc. white paper, located at www.cisco.com/warp/customer/cc/cisco/mkt/security/encryp/tech/ipsec_wp.htm. This URL requires a Cisco Connection Online username and password.

M. Kaeo, *Designing Network Security,* Cisco Press, 1999.

B. Schneier, *Applied Cryptography: Protocols, Algorithms and Source Code in C,* Second Edition, Wiley, 1995.

Upon completing this chapter, you will be able to do the following:

- Describe the commands used to configure Cisco IOS IPSec encryption
- Configure Cisco IOS IPSec encryption using preshared keys for authentication
- Configure Cisco IOS IPSec encryption using RSA-encrypted nonces for authentication
- Test and verify Cisco IOS IPSec encryption

CHAPTER 16

Configuring Cisco IOS IPSec

This chapter shows you how to configure basic IP security (IPSec) in Cisco IOS Software using preshared keys and Rivest, Shamir, and Adleman (RSA) encrypted nonces for authentication. It presents an overview of the Cisco IOS commands used to configure IPSec and then shows you the tasks and steps you must perform to configure IPSec. You should be familiar with IPSec terminology and concepts before reading this chapter. Please review Chapter 15, "Understanding Cisco IPSec Support," if you need a refresher.

This chapter contains two main sections: how to configure IPSec for preshared keys and how to configure RSA-encrypted nonces. The intent of this chapter is to teach the basics of configuring IPSec on Cisco routers by showing you how to use preshared keys for authentication and how to configure RSA-encrypted nonces. After you have mastered these processes, you'll be ready to configure RSA signatures. That topic is covered in Chapter 18, "Scaling Cisco IPSec Networks."

Configuring Cisco IOS IPSec Using Preshared Keys for Authentication

This section covers how to configure IPSec encryption using preshared keys for authentication on Cisco routers. The focus of this section is to configure a Cisco router to become a secure IPSec gateway that will encrypt and protect the traffic flows of networks behind two or more routers. The use of Internet Key Exchange (IKE) preshared keys for authentication of IPSec sessions is relatively easy to configure yet does not scale well for a large number of IPSec peers. Figure 16-1 shows the simplified topology for the XYZ Company used in examples in this chapter.

Figure 16-1 *XYZ Company Topology for Cisco Router IPSec*

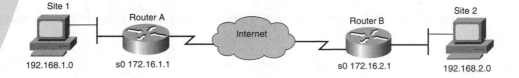

The process for configuring IKE preshared keys in Cisco IOS Software for Cisco routers consists of four major tasks:

- **Task 1: Prepare for IPSec**—Preparing for IPSec involves determining the detailed encryption policy, identifying the hosts and networks you want to protect, determining details about the IPSec peers, determining the IPSec features you need, and ensuring that existing access lists used for packet filtering permit IPSec traffic.

- **Task 2: Configure IKE**—Configuring IKE involves enabling IKE, creating the IKE policies, and validating the configuration.

- **Task 3: Configure IPSec**—IPSec configuration includes defining the transform sets, creating crypto access lists, creating crypto map entries, and applying crypto map sets to interfaces.

- **Task 4: Test and verify IPSec**—Use **show**, **debug**, and related commands to test and verify that IPSec encryption works and to troubleshoot problems.

The following sections discuss each of these configuration tasks in more detail.

Task 1: Prepare for IPSec

Successfully implementing an IPSec network requires planning before you begin configuring individual routers. Configuring IPSec encryption can be complicated. You should begin this task by defining the IPSec security policy based on the overall company security policy. This task is covered in more detail in Chapter 15. Some planning steps are summarized as follows:

Step 1   Determine an IKE (IKE Phase 1) policy between IPSec peers based on the number and location of the peers.

Step 2   Determine an IPSec (IKE Phase 2) policy to include IPSec peer details such as IP addresses and IPSec modes.

Step 3   Check the current configuration by using the **write terminal**, **show crypto isakmp policy**, and **show crypto map** commands as well as other **show** commands.

Step 4   Ensure that the network works without encryption using the **ping** command and by ensuring that unencrypted test traffic is routed to the destination.

Step 5   Ensure that existing packet filtering access lists permit IPSec traffic.

The following sections examine the tasks required to configure IPSec in Cisco routers.

Task 2: Configure IKE for Preshared Keys

The next major task in configuring Cisco IOS IPSec is to configure the IKE parameters gathered earlier. Configuring IKE consists of the following essential steps and commands:

Step 1 Enable or disable IKE with the **crypto isakmp enable** command.

Step 2 Create IKE policies with the **crypto isakmp policy** command.

Step 3 Configure preshared keys with **crypto isakmp key** and associated commands.

Step 4 Verify the IKE configuration with the **show crypto isakmp policy** command.

The following sections describe these steps in detail.

Step 1: Enable or Disable IKE

The first step in configuring IKE is to enable or disable IKE. You can globally enable it with the **crypto isakmp enable** command and disable it with the **no** form of the command. IKE is enabled by default. IKE is enabled globally for all interfaces at the router, so it does not have to be enabled for individual interfaces. You may choose to block IKE access on interfaces not used for IPSec to prevent possible Denial of Service attacks by using an access list statement that blocks UDP port 500 on the interfaces.

Step 2: Create IKE Policies

The next major step in configuring Cisco IOS IKE support is to define a suite of IKE policies and thereby establish IKE between two IPSec peers. IKE policies define a set of parameters to be used during the IKE negotiation.

Table 16-1 summarizes IKE policy details that will be configured in examples in this section.

Table 16-1   *IKE Policy Example for Two Peer Routers*

Parameter	Router A Value	Router B Value
Message encryption algorithm	DES	DES
Message integrity (hash) algorithm	MD5	MD5
Peer authentication method	Preshared key	Preshared key
Key exchange parameters (Diffie-Hellman group identifier)	768-bit Diffie-Hellman group 1	768-bit Diffie-Hellman group 1

continues

Table 16-1 *IKE Policy Example for Two Peer Routers (Continued)*

Parameter	Router A Value	Router B Value
ISAKMP-established security association's lifetime	86400 (default)	86400 (default)
IP address of IPSec peer	172.16.2.1	172.16.1.1

Considering the IKE policy details gathered earlier, you use the **crypto isakmp policy** command to define an IKE policy, and you use the **no** form of the command to delete an IKE policy. The command syntax is as follows:

```
crypto isakmp policy priority
```

The command parameter has the following meaning:

Command Parameter	Description
priority	Uniquely identifies the IKE policy and assigns it a priority. Use an integer from 1 to 10,000, with 1 being the highest priority and 10,000 the lowest.

This command invokes the IKE policy configuration (config-isakmp) command mode, where you can set IKE parameters. If you do not specify one of these commands for a policy, the default value is used for that parameter. While you are in config-isakmp command mode, the keywords shown in Table 16-2 are available to specify the parameters in the policy.

Table 16-2 *config-isakmp Command Mode Keywords*

Keyword	Accepted Values	Default Value	Description
des	56-bit DES-CBC	**des**	Message encryption algorithm.
sha **md5**	SHA-1 (HMAC variant) MD5 (HMAC variant)	**sha**	Message integrity (hash) algorithm.
rsa-sig **rsa-encr** **pre-share**	RSA signatures RSA-encrypted nonces Preshared keys	**rsa-sig**	Peer authentication method.
1 **2**	768-bit Diffie-Hellman or 1024-bit Diffie-Hellman	**1**	Key exchange parameters (Diffie-Hellman group identifier).

Table 16-2 *config-isakmp Command Mode Keywords (Continued)*

Keyword	Accepted Values	Default Value	Description
lifetime *seconds*	Can specify any number of seconds	86,400 seconds (one day)	IKE-established SA's lifetime. You can usually leave this value at the default.
exit			Exits config-isakmp mode.

You can configure multiple IKE policies on each peer participating in IPSec. IKE peers negotiate acceptable IKE policies before agreeing on the SA to be used for IPSec.

An IKE Configuration Example for Two Peers

Consider the example of IKE policies for Router A (Example 16-1) and Router B (Example 16-2). Note that the lifetime value of 43200 seconds equals 12 hours.

Example 16-1 *IPSec Policy Example for Router A*

```
crypto isakmp policy 100
 hash md5
 authentication pre-share
crypto isakmp policy 200
 authentication rsa-sig
 group 2
 lifetime 43200
crypto isakmp policy 300
 authentication rsa-encr
 lifetime 10000
```

Example 16-2 *IPSec Policy Example for Router B*

```
crypto isakmp policy 100
 hash md5
 authentication pre-share
crypto isakmp policy 200
 authentication rsa-sig
 group 2
 lifetime 43200
crypto isakmp policy 300
 authentication rsa-sig
 lifetime 10000
```

Step 3: Configure Preshared Keys

The next major step in configuring Cisco IOS IKE support is to set the IKE identity mode (optional) and configure the preshared keys.

Setting Identity Mode

IPSec peers authenticate each other during IKE negotiations by using the preshared key and the IKE identity. The identity can be either the router's IP address or host name. Cisco IOS Software uses the IP address identity method by default. If you choose to use the host name identity method, you must specify the method with the **crypto isakmp identity** global configuration command. Use the **no** form of this command to reset the IKE identity to the default value (address). The command syntax is as follows:

```
crypto isakmp identity {address | hostname}
```

The command parameters have the following meanings:

Command Parameter	Description
address	Sets the IKE identity to the IP address of the interface that is used to communicate with the remote peer during IKE negotiations. This keyword is typically used when only one interface is used by the peer for IKE negotiations and the IP address is known.
hostname	Sets the IKE identity to the host name concatenated with the domain name (for example, myhost.domain.com). This keyword should be used if more than one interface on the peer might be used for IKE negotiations or if the interface's IP address is unknown (such as with dynamically assigned IP addresses).

NOTE The **crypto isakmp identity address** command does not appear as a separate command in the router configuration because it is the default.

If you use the host name identity method, you need to specify the host name for the remote peer in the router configuration to ensure that it is in the host name table if a DNS server is unavailable for name resolution, as shown in the following example for Router A:

```
RouterA(config)# ip host RouterB.domain.com 172.16.2.1
```

Configuring Preshared Keys

You configure a preshared authentication key with the **crypto isakmp key** global configuration command. You must configure this key whenever you specify preshared keys in an IKE policy. You use the **no** form of this command to delete a preshared authentication key. The command syntax is as follows:

```
crypto isakmp key key-string address peer-address
crypto isakmp key key-string hostname peer-hostname
```

The command parameters have the following meanings:

Command Parameter	Description
key-string	Specifies the preshared key. Use any combination of alphanumeric characters up to 128 bytes. This preshared key must be identical at both peers.
address	Used if the remote peer IKE identity was set with its IP address.
peer-address	Specifies the IP address of the remote peer.
hostname	Used if the remote IKE identity was set with its host name.
peer-hostname	Specifies the host name of the remote peer. This is the peer's host name concatenated with its domain name (for example, myhost.domain.com).

NOTE   The same preshared key must be configured on each pair of IPSec peers when you use preshared keys for IKE authentication. It is highly recommended that a different preshared key be configured on each pair of IPSec peers. Using the same preshared key for more than one pair of IPSec peers is risky and is not recommended.

An IKE Preshared Configuration Example

The configuration example in Example 16-3 shows IKE and preshared keys for Router A and Router B. Note that the keystring of *WhatLighT* matches. The address identity method is specified. The IKE policies are compatible. Default values do not have to be configured.

Example 16-3 *IKE and Preshared Keys for Router A and Router B*

```
RouterA(config)# crypto isakmp key WhatLighT address 172.16.2.1
RouterA(config)# crypto isakmp policy 100
RouterA(config-isakmp)# hash md5
RouterA(config-isakmp)# authentication pre-share
RouterA(config-isakmp)# exit
RouterB(config)# crypto isakmp key WhatLighT address 172.16.1.1
RouterB(config)# crypto isakmp policy 100
RouterB(config-isakmp)# hash md5
RouterB(config-isakmp)# authentication pre-share
RouterB(config-isakmp)# exit
```

Step 4: Verify the IKE Configuration

You can use the **show crypto isakmp policy** command to display configured and default policies. The resultant IKE policy for Router A is shown in Example 16-4; Router B's configuration is identical.

Example 16-4 *Router A's IKE Policy*

```
RouterA# show crypto isakmp policy
Protection suite of priority 100
        encryption algorithm:   DES--Data Encryption Standard (56 bit keys).
        hash algorithm:         Message Digest 5
        authentication method:  Pre-Shared Key
        Diffie-Hellman group:   #1 (768 bit)
        lifetime:               86400 seconds, no volume limit
Default protection suite
        encryption algorithm:   DES--Data Encryption Standard (56 bit keys).
        hash algorithm:         Secure Hash Standard
        authentication method:  Rivest-Shamir-Adleman Signature
        Diffie-Hellman group:   #1 (768 bit)
        lifetime:               86400 seconds, no volume limit
```

Task 3: Configure IPSec

The next major task in configuring Cisco IOS IPSec is to configure the IPSec parameters previously gathered. The general tasks and commands used to configure IPSec encryption on Cisco routers are summarized as follows:

Step 1 Configure transform set suites with the **crypto ipsec transform-set** command.

Step 2 Configure global IPSec security association lifetimes with the **crypto ipsec security-association lifetime** command.

Step 3 Configure crypto access lists with the **access-list** command.

Step 4 Configure crypto maps with the **crypto map** command.

Step 5 Apply the crypto maps to the terminating/originating interface with the **interface** and **crypto map** commands.

Table 16-3 summarizes IPSec policy details that will be configured in the examples in this section. Details about IPSec transforms supported in Cisco IOS Software are covered next.

Table 16-3 *IPSec Policy Example for Two Peers*

Parameter	Peer A Value	Peer B Value
Transform set	AH-MD5, ESP-DES	AH-MD5, ESP-DES
IPSec mode	Tunnel	Tunnel
Hash algorithm	MD5	MD5

Table 16-3 *IPSec Policy Example for Two Peers (Continued)*

Parameter	Peer A Value	Peer B Value
Peer host name	RouterB	RouterA
Peer interface	Serial 0	Serial 0
Peer IP address	172.16.2.1	172.16.1.1
IP address of hosts to be protected	192.168.1.0	192.168.2.0
Traffic (packet) type to be encrypted	TCP	TCP
SA establishment	**ipsec-isakmp**	**ipsec-isakmp**

The following sections discuss each of the IPSec configuration steps in detail.

Step 1: Configure Transform Set Suites

The first major step in configuring Cisco IOS IPSec is to use the IPSec security policy to define a *transform set,* which is a combination of individual IPSec transforms that enact a security policy for traffic. During the IKE IPSec security association, negotiation occurs during IKE Phase 2 quick mode, when the peers agree to use a particular transform set to protect the data flow. Transform sets combine the following IPSec factors:

- Mechanism for payload authentication: Authentication Header (AH) transform
- Mechanism for payload encryption: Encapsulating Security Payload (ESP) transform
- IPSec mode (transport versus tunnel)

You define a transform set with the **crypto ipsec transform-set** global configuration command, which invokes the **crypto-transform** configuration mode. To delete a transform set, use the **no** form of the command. The command syntax is as follows:

```
crypto ipsec transform-set transform-set-name transform1
   [transform2 [transform3]]
```

The command parameters have the following meanings:

Command	Description
transform-set-name	Specifies the name of the transform set to create (or modify).
transform1 *transform2* *transform3*	Specifies up to three transforms, which define the IPSec security protocol(s) and algorithm(s). At least one AH or ESP transform is required.

Up to three transforms can be in a set. The default mode for each transform is *tunnel*. Sets are limited to up to one AH and up to two ESP transforms. When IKE is not used to establish security associations, a single transform set must be used. The transform set is not negotiated.

Cisco IOS Software supports the following IPSec transforms:

- AH transforms:
  - **ah-md5-hmac**—The AH-HMAC-MD5 transform.
  - **ah-sha-hmac**—The AH-HMAC-SHA transform.
  - **ah-rfc1828**—The AH-MD5 transform (RFC1828), used with older IPSec implementations.

NOTE AH is seldom used with ESP because authentication is available with the **esp-sha-hmac** and **esp-md5-hmac** transforms. AH is also incompatible with Network AddressTranslation (NAT) and Port Address Translation (PAT) because they change the IP address in the TCP/IP packet header, breaking the authentication established by AH. AH can be used for data authentication alone, but it does not protect the confidentiality of the packet contents because it does not encrypt. AH is used with ESP when the utmost data security is requested.

- ESP transforms:
  - **esp-des**—An ESP transform that uses DES cipher (56 bits).
  - **esp-3des**—An ESP transform that uses 3DES(EDE) cipher (168 bits).
  - **esp-md5-hmac**—An ESP transform with HMAC-MD5 authentication used with an **esp-des** or **esp-3des** transform to provide additional integrity for ESP packets.
  - **esp-sha-hmac**—An ESP transform with HMAC-SHA authentication used with an **esp-des** or **esp-3des** transform to provide additional integrity for ESP packets.
  - **esp-null**—An ESP transform without a cipher. It may be used in combination with **esp-md5-hmac** or **esp-sha-hmac** if you want ESP authentication with no encryption.

CAUTION Never use **esp-null** alone in a production environment because it does not protect data flows. It can be combined with **esp-sha-hmac** or **esp-md5-hmac** to allow a packet sniffer to see into the IPSec packet for troubleshooting.

— **esp-rfc1829**—An ESP-DES-CBC transform (RFC1829) used with older IPSec implementations.

Transform Set Examples

Examples 16-5 through 16-8 show some of the combinations described in this section.

Example 16-5 *AH Authentication with MD5, ESP Encryption with 56-Bit DES, Tunnel Mode (the Default)*

```
crypto ipsec transform-set SECURE ah-md5-hmac esp-des
```

Example 16-6 *ESP Authentication with MD5, ESP Encryption with 56-Bit DES, Tunnel Mode (the Default)*

```
crypto ipsec transform-set noAH esp-md5-hmac esp-des
```

Example 16-7 *AH Authentication with SHA, ESP Authentication with SHA, ESP Encryption with 3DES, Tunnel Mode (the Default)*

```
crypto ipsec transform-set CPUeater ah-sha-hmac esp-sha-hmac esp-3des
```

Example 16-8 *AH Authentication with SHA, Transport Mode*

```
crypto ipsec transform-set AUTH  ah-sha-hmac
```

The Cisco IOS command parser prevents you from entering invalid combinations. For example, after you specify an AH transform, the parser does not allow you to specify another AH transform for the current transform set.

Editing Transform Sets

Follow these steps if you need to change a transform set:

1 Delete the transform set from the crypto map.

2 Delete the transform set from global configuration.

3 Reenter the transform set with corrections.

4 Assign the transform set in the crypto map.

5 Clear the SA database.

6 Observe the SA negotiation and ensure that it works properly.

An alternative method is to reenter the transform set with the new transforms, as shown in Example 16-9.

Example 16-9 *Transform Set with New Transforms*

```
! Was the following:
crypto ipsec transform-set RouterA esp-des
! Change it to esp-MD5-hmac:
RouterA(config)# interface serial 0
RouterA(config-if)# no crypto map RouterA
RouterA(config-if)# exit
RouterA(config)# no crypto ipsec transform-set RouterA
RouterA(config)# crypto ipsec transform-set RouterA esp-MD5-hmac
RouterA(cfg-crypto-trans)# exit
RouterA(config)# interface serial 0
RouterA(config-if)# crypto map RouterA
RouterA(config-if)# exit
! Now:
crypto ipsec transform-set RouterA esp-MD5-hmac
```

Transform Set Negotiation

Transform sets are negotiated during quick mode in IKE Phase 2, using the transform sets you previously configured. You can configure multiple transform sets and then specify one or more of them in a crypto map entry. You should configure the transforms from most-secure to least-secure, as per your policy. The transform set defined in the crypto map entry is used in the IPSec security association negotiation to protect the data flows specified by that crypto map entry's access list.

During the negotiation, the peers search for a transform set that is the same at both peers, as illustrated in Figure 16-2. When such a transform set is found, it is selected and applied to the protected traffic as part of both peers' IPSec security associations. IPSec peers agree on one transform proposal per SA (unidirectional).

Step 2: Configure Global IPSec Security Association Lifetimes

The IPSec security association lifetime determines how long IPSec SAs remain valid before they are renegotiated. Cisco IOS Software supports a global lifetime value that applies to all crypto maps. The global lifetime value can be overridden within a crypto map entry. The lifetimes apply only to security associations established via IKE. Manually established security associations do not expire. Before a security association expires, a new one is negotiated so that there is no interruption of the data flow.

Figure 16-2 *A Transform Set Negotiated Between IPSec Peers*

You can change global IPSec security association lifetime values by using the **crypto ipsec security-association lifetime** global configuration command. To reset a lifetime to the default value, use the **no** form of the command. The command syntax is as follows:

```
crypto ipsec security-association lifetime
  {seconds seconds | kilobytes kilobytes}
```

The command parameters have the following meanings:

Command	Description
seconds *seconds*	Specifies the number of seconds a security association will live before expiring. The default is 3600 seconds (one hour).
kilobytes *kilobytes*	Specifies the volume of traffic (in kilobytes) that can pass between IPSec peers using a given security association before that security association expires. The default is 4,608,000 kilobytes.

Cisco recommends that you use the default lifetime values. Individual IPSec SAs can be configured using crypto maps, which are covered in the section "Step 4: Create Crypto Maps" later in this chapter.

Step 3: Create Crypto Access Lists

The next step in configuring IPSec is to configure crypto access lists, which are used to define the IP traffic that is or is not protected by IPSec. Crypto access lists perform the following functions for IPSec:

- Select outbound traffic to be protected by IPSec.

- Process inbound traffic to select IPSec traffic.

- Process inbound traffic in order to filter out and discard traffic that should have been protected by IPSec.

- Determine whether to accept requests for IPSec security associations for the requested data flows when processing IKE negotiations.

You must use IP extended access lists to create crypto access lists. The crypto access lists identify the traffic flows to be protected. Although the access list syntax is unchanged from IP extended access lists, the meanings are slightly different for crypto access lists. **permit** specifies that matching packets must be encrypted, and **deny** specifies that matching packets need not be encrypted. Crypto access lists behave similar to an extended IP access list applied to outbound traffic on an interface.

See Appendix C, "Configuring Standard and Extended Access Lists," for a complete description of the TCP and UDP versions of IP extended access lists, showing TCP and UDP port selectors. A limited description of the **access-list** command is provided here:

```
access-list access-list-number {permit | deny} protocol source
    source-wildcard destination destination-wildcard [precedence precedence]
    [tos tos] [log]
```

The command parameters have the following meanings:

Command	Description
permit	Causes all IP traffic that matches the specified conditions to be protected by crypto, using the policy described by the corresponding crypto map entry
deny	Instructs the router to route traffic in the clear
source	Indicates networks, subnets, or hosts
destination	Indicates networks, subnets, or hosts
protocol	Indicates which IP packet type(s) to encrypt

CAUTION Any unprotected inbound traffic that matches a permit entry in the crypto access list for a crypto map entry flagged as IPSec and that does not have a corresponding IPSec SA will be dropped because this traffic was expected to be protected by IPSec.

If you want certain traffic to receive one combination of IPSec protection (authentication only) and other traffic to receive a different combination (both authentication and encryption), create two different crypto access lists to define the two different types of traffic. These different access lists are then used in different crypto map entries that specify different IPSec policies.

CAUTION Cisco recommends that you avoid using the **any** keyword to specify source or destination addresses. The **permit any any** statement is strongly discouraged because it causes all outbound traffic to be protected (as well as all protected traffic sent to the peer specified in the corresponding crypto map entry) and requires protection for all inbound traffic. Then, all inbound packets that lack IPSec protection are silently dropped, including packets for routing protocols, NTP, echo, echo response, and so on.

Try to be as precise as possible when defining which packets to protect in a crypto access list. If you must use the **any** keyword in a **permit** statement, you must preface that statement with a series of **deny** statements to filter out any traffic (that would otherwise fall within that **permit** statement) that you do not want to be protected.

In the next step, you will associate a crypto access list to a crypto map, which in turn is assigned to a specific interface.

Configuring Symmetrical Crypto Access Lists

Cisco recommends that you configure symmetrical or "mirror-image" crypto access lists for use by IPSec. Both inbound and outbound traffic is evaluated against the same "outbound" IPSec access list. The access list's criteria are applied in the forward direction to traffic exiting your router and in the reverse direction to traffic entering your router. When a router receives encrypted packets from an IPSec peer, it uses the same access list to determine which inbound packets to decrypt by viewing the source and destination addresses in the access list in reverse order.

The sample crypto access list pair shown in Example 16-10 illustrates why symmetrical access lists are recommended.

Example 16-10 *Sample Crypto Access List Pair*

```
routerA(config)# access-list 151 permit tcp 192.168.1.0 0.0.0.255
    192.168.2.0 0.0.0.255
routerB(config)# access-list 151 permit tcp 192.168.2.0 0.0.0.255
    192.168.1.0 0.0.0.255
```

Refer to the network diagram shown in Figure 16-1. At Site 1, IPSec protection is applied to traffic between hosts on the 192.168.1.0 network as the data exits Router A's S0 interface en route to Site 2 hosts on the 192.168.2.0 network. For traffic from Site 1 hosts on the 192.168.1.0 network to Site 2 hosts on the 192.168.2.0 network, the access list entry on Router A is evaluated as follows:

- source=hosts on the 192.168.1.0 network
- dest=hosts on the 192.168.2.0 network

For incoming traffic from Site 2 hosts on the 192.168.2.0 network to Site 1 hosts on the 192.168.1.0 network, that same access list entry on Router A is evaluated as follows:

- source=hosts on the 192.168.2.0 network
- dest=hosts on the 192.168.1.0 network

Step 4: Create Crypto Maps

You must create crypto maps to allow IPSec to set up security associations for traffic flows to be encrypted. This section considers the purpose of crypto maps, examines the **crypto map** command, and shows examples of crypto maps. Crypto map entries created for IPSec set up security association parameters, tying together the various parts configured for IPSec, including the following:

- Which traffic should be protected by IPSec (crypto access list) and the granularity of traffic to be protected by a set of SAs
- Where IPSec-protected traffic should be sent (specifies the remote IPSec peer)
- The local address to be used for the IPSec traffic
- What IPSec security type should be applied to this traffic (transform sets)
- Whether security associations are established manually or via IKE
- Other parameters that might be necessary to define an IPSec security association

Crypto Map Parameters

You can apply only one crypto map set to a single interface. The crypto map set can include a combination of Cisco Encryption Technology (CET), IPSec using IKE, and IPSec with manually configured SA entries. Multiple interfaces can share the same crypto map set if you want to apply the same policy to multiple interfaces. See Chapter 14, "Configuring Cisco Encryption Technology," for more details on CET.

You might need to create more than one crypto map set for a given interface. The problem is that you can assign only one crypto map name to an interface. You create multiple sets of crypto map statements per crypto map name by using the sequence number (*seq-num*) of each map entry to group the map entries. The sequence number also ranks the entries by priority: the lower the *seq-num,* the higher the priority. At the interface that has the crypto map set, traffic is evaluated against higher-priority map entries first. You might want to start the numbering at a high enough number (perhaps 100) to allow for higher priorities in the future. You must create multiple crypto map entries for a given interface if any of the following conditions exist:

- Different data flows are to be handled by separate IPSec peers.

- You want to apply different IPSec security to different types of traffic (to the same or separate IPSec peers)—for example, if you want traffic between one set of subnets to be authenticated and traffic between another set of subnets to be both authenticated and encrypted. In this case, the different types of traffic should have been defined in two separate access lists, and you must create a separate crypto map entry for each crypto access list.

- You are configuring IPSec with manual security associations and are not using IKE to establish the security associations, and you want to specify multiple access list entries. You must create separate access lists (one per permit entry) and specify a separate crypto map entry for each access list.

Backup Strategy

You can define multiple remote peers using crypto maps to allow for a backup strategy in case a peer is down. If one peer fails to respond during IKE, there will be an alternative peer. Which peer your router connects to during IKE is determined by the last peer that the router heard from (that received either traffic or a negotiation request) for a given data flow. If the attempt fails with the first peer, IKE tries the next peer on the crypto map list.

You can use dynamic crypto maps so that you do not have to specify all IPSec parameters in a crypto map. For example, if your company has a variety of remote computers running IPSec clients with differing security policies, you can use a dynamic crypto map. Dynamic crypto maps are useful when the establishment of the IPSec tunnels is initiated by the remote peer (such as in the case of an IPSec router fronting a server). They are not useful if the establishment of the IPSec tunnels is locally initiated because the dynamic crypto maps are policy templates, not complete statements of policy. (The access lists in any referenced dynamic crypto map entry are used for crypto packet filtering.) Dynamic crypto maps are covered in more detail in Chapter 18, "Scaling Cisco IPSec Networks."

Configuring Crypto Maps

You use the **crypto map** global configuration command to create or modify a crypto map entry and to enter the crypto map configuration mode. You set the crypto map entries referencing dynamic maps to be the lowest-priority entries in a crypto map set (that is, to have the highest sequence numbers). Use the **no** form of this command to delete a crypto map entry or set. The command syntax is as follows:

```
crypto map map-name seq-num cisco
crypto map map-name seq-num ipsec-manual
```

```
crypto map map-name seq-num ipsec-isakmp [dynamic dynamic-map-name]
no crypto map map-name [seq-num]
```

The command parameters have the following meanings:

Command Parameter	Description
cisco	(Default value) Indicates that CET will be used instead of IPSec to protect the traffic specified by this newly specified crypto map entry.
map-name	Specifies the name assigned to the crypto map set.
seq-num	Specifies the number assigned to the crypto map entry.
ipsec-manual	Indicates that IKE will not be used to establish the IPSec security associations to protect the traffic specified by this crypto map entry.
ipsec-isakmp	Indicates that IKE will be used to establish the IPSec security associations to protect the traffic specified by this crypto map entry.
dynamic	(Optional) Specifies that this crypto map entry references a preexisting static crypto map. If you use this keyword, none of the crypto map configuration commands will be available.
dynamic-map-name	(Optional) Specifies the name of the dynamic crypto map set that should be used as the policy template.

When you enter the **crypto map** command, you invoke the crypto map configuration mode (router(config-crypto-map)# prompt) with the following available commands:

```
match address [access-list-id ¦ name]
set peer [hostname ¦ ip-address]
set pfs [group1 ¦ group2]
set security-association level per-host
set security-association lifetime {seconds seconds ¦ kilobytes kilobytes}
set transform-set transform-set-name [transform-set-name2...transform-set-name6]
set session-key {inbound ¦ outbound} ah ¦ esp
exit
```

The commands available in crypto map configuration mode have the following syntax:

Command Parameter	Description
access-list-id | *name*	Identifies the extended access list used by the crypto map by its number or name. The value should match the *access-list-number* or *access-list-name* argument of a previously defined IP extended access list.
hostname | *ip-address*	Specifies the allowed IPSec peer by IP address or host name. Set multiple peers for redundancy.
group1 | **group2**	(Optional) Specifies that IPSec should use the 768-bit (**group1**) or 1024-bit (**group2**) Diffie-Hellman prime modulus group when performing the new Diffie-Hellman exchange. The default setting is **group1**.
set security-association level per-host	Specifies that separate IPSec security associations should be requested for each source/destination host pair in a crypto access list.
seconds *seconds*	Specifies the number of seconds a security association will live before expiring.
kilobytes *kilobytes*}	Specifies the volume of traffic (in kilobytes) that can pass between IPSec peers using a given security association before that security association expires.
transform-set-name [*transform-set name2 ...transform-set-name6*]	Specifies the list of transform sets in order of priority. For an **ipsec-isakmp** or **dynamic** crypto map entry, you can specify up to six transform sets. Transform sets are negotiated from the lowest priority to the highest priority. Set your strongest transform sets (such as **esp-3des**) to the lowest-priority number.
set session-key {**inbound** | **outbound**} **ah** | **esp**	Sets security association parameters manually, including manual passwords for AH and ESP transforms. Specifies if entered security association values are for **inbound** or **outbound** security associations.
exit	Exits crypto map configuration mode.

After you define crypto map entries, you can assign the crypto map set to interfaces using the **crypto map** (interface configuration) command.

NOTE   Access lists for crypto map entries tagged as **ipsec-manual** are restricted to a single permit entry. Subsequent entries are ignored. The security associations established by that particular crypto map entry are for only a single data flow. To be able to support multiple manually established security associations for different kinds of traffic, define multiple crypto access lists and then apply each one to a separate **ipsec-manual** crypto map entry. Each access list should include one permit statement defining what traffic to protect. Manual IPSec configuration is covered in the *Security Configuration Guide*.

A Crypto Map Example

Example 16-11 illustrates a crypto map with two peers specified for redundancy purposes. If the first peer cannot be contacted, the second peer is used. There is no limit to the number of redundant peers that can be configured.

Example 16-11   *A Crypto Map with Two Peers Specified for Redundancy*

```
RouterA(config)# crypto map mymap 10 ipsec-isakmp
RouterA(config-crypto-map)# match address 151
routerA(config-crypto-map)# set peer 172.16.2.1
routerA(config-crypto-map)# set peer 172.16.3.1
routerA(config-crypto-map)# set pfs group1
routerA(config-crypto-map)# set transform-set mytransform
routerA(config-crypto-map)# set security-association lifetime 2700
routerA(config-crypto-map)# exit
```

Setting Manual Keys

You can configure IPSec SAs manually and not use IKE to set up the SA. Cisco recommends that you use IKE to set up the SAs because it is very difficult to ensure that the SA values match between peers, and Diffie-Hellman is a vastly more secure method to generate secret keys between peers. If you must, you can use the **set security-association** command in crypto map configuration mode to manually specify the IPSec session keys within a crypto map entry.

Security associations established via this command do not expire (unlike security associations established via IKE). Session keys at one peer must match the session keys at the remote peer. If you change a session key, the security association using the key will be deleted and reinitialized.

Step 5: Apply Crypto Maps to the Interfaces

The last step in configuring IPSec is to apply the crypto map set to an interface. Apply the crypto map to the IPSec router's interface connected to the Internet with the **crypto map** command in interface configuration mode. Use the **no** form of the command to remove the crypto map set from the interface. The command syntax is as follows:

```
crypto map map-name
```

The command parameter has the following meaning:

Command Parameter	Description
map-name	Identifies the crypto map set. This is the name assigned when the crypto map was created.

As soon as you apply the crypto map, the SAs are set up in a security association database in system memory. You can observe the initialized SAs with the **show crypto ipsec sa** command. Only one crypto map set can be assigned to an interface. If multiple crypto map entries have the same *map-name* but a different *seq-num,* they are considered part of the same set and are all applied to the interface. The crypto map entry with the lowest *seq-num* is considered the highest priority and is evaluated first.

Example 16-12 shows an application of a crypto map for Router A.

Example 16-12 *An Application of a Crypto Map for Router A*

```
RouterA(config)# interface serial 0
RouterA(config-if)# crypto map RouterAmap
RouterA(config-if)# exit
RouterA(config)#
```

IPSec Configuration Example

Consider the following configuration examples for Router A (Example 16-13) and Router B (Example 16-14). The examples are concatenated to show only commands related to what has been covered in this chapter up to this point.

Example 16-13 *A Configuration Example for Router A*

```
RouterA# show running-config
crypto isakmp policy 100
 hash md5
 authentication pre-share
crypto isakmp key WhatLighT address 172.16.2.1
!
crypto ipsec transform-set RouterAset esp-des esp-md5-hmac
!
 !
 crypto map RouterAmap 100 ipsec-isakmp
 set peer 172.16.2.1
 set transform-set RouterAset
 match address 151
!
interface Serial0
```

continues

Example 16-13 *A Configuration Example for Router A (Continued)*

```
 ip address 172.16.1.1 255.255.255.0
 ip access-group 101 in
 crypto map RouterAmap
!
access-list 101 permit ahp host 172.16.2.1 host 172.16.1.1
access-list 101 permit esp host 172.16.2.1 host 172.16.1.1
access-list 101 permit udp host 172.16.2.1 host 172.16.1.1 eq isakmp

access-list 151 permit ip 192.168.1.0 0.0.0.255 192.168.2.0 0.0.0.255
access-list 151 deny ip any any
```

Example 16-14 *A Configuration Example for Router B*

```
RouterB# show running-config
crypto isakmp policy 100
 hash md5
 authentication pre-share
crypto isakmp key WhatLighT address 172.16.1.1
!
crypto ipsec transform-set RouterBset esp-des esp-md5-hmac
!
 !
 crypto map RouterBmap 100 ipsec-isakmp
 set peer 172.16.1.1
 set transform-set RouterBset
 match address 151
!
interface Serial0
 ip address 172.16.2.1 255.255.255.0
 ip access-group 101 in
 crypto map RouterBmap
!
access-list 101 permit ahp host 172.16.1.1 host 172.16.2.1
access-list 101 permit esp host 172.16.1.1 host 172.16.2.1
access-list 101 permit udp host 172.16.1.1 host 172.16.2.1 eq isakmp
access-list 151 permit ip 192.168.2.0 0.0.0.255 192.168.1.0 0.0.0.255
access-list 151 deny ip any any
```

Task 4: Test and Verify IPSec

The final task in configuring IPSec for preshared keys is to verify that IPSec was configured correctly and to test to ensure that it works properly. Cisco IOS Software contains a number of **show**, **clear**, and **debug** commands that are useful for testing and verifying IKE and IPSec. This topic is considered in the following sections.

IKE Commands

You can use the commands described in the following sections to observe IKE configuration and operation.

The show crypto isakmp policy Command

You can use the **show crypto isakmp policy** EXEC command to view the parameters for each IKE policy, as shown in Example 16-15.

Example 16-15 *Parameters for Router A's IKE Policy*

```
RouterA# show crypto isakmp policy
Protection suite of priority 100
        encryption algorithm:    DES--Data Encryption Standard (56 bit keys).
        hash algorithm:          Message Digest 5
        authentication method:   Rivest-Shamir-Adleman Encryption
        Diffie-Hellman group:    #1 (768 bit)
        lifetime:                86400 seconds, no volume limit
Default protection suite
        encryption algorithm:    DES--Data Encryption Standard (56 bit keys).
        hash algorithm:          Secure Hash Standard
        authentication method:   Rivest-Shamir-Adleman Signature
        Diffie-Hellman group:    #1 (768 bit)
        lifetime:                86400 seconds, no volume limit
```

The show crypto isakmp sa Command

You can use the **show crypto isakmp sa** EXEC command to view all current IKE SAs at a peer, as shown in Example 16-16.

Example 16-16 *All Current SAs for Router A*

```
RouterA# show crypto isakmp sa
    dst            src            state        conn-id   slot
 172.16.1.1    172.16.2.1       QM_IDLE          93       0
```

The clear crypto isakmp Command

You can use the **clear crypto isakmp** global configuration command to clear active IKE connections. The command syntax is as follows:

```
clear crypto isakmp [connection-id]
```

The command parameter has the following meaning:

Command Parameter	Description
connection-id	(Optional) Specifies which connection to clear. If this argument is not used, all existing connections are cleared.

If the *connection-id* argument is not used, all existing IKE connections are cleared when this command is issued. Example 16-17 clears an IKE connection between Router A and Router B and shows the result.

Example 16-17 *The Result of Clearing an IKE Connection*

```
RouterA# show crypto isakmp sa
    dst              src            state        conn-id    slot
 172.16.1.1    172.16.2.1     QM_IDLE          93        0
RouterA# clear crypto isakmp 93
2w4d: ISADB: reaper checking SA,
RouterA# show crypto isakmp sa
    dst              src            state        conn-id    slot
```

The debug crypto isakmp Command

You use the **debug crypto isakmp** EXEC command to display messages about IKE events. The **no** form of this command disables debugging output. The command syntax is as follows:

```
RouterA# debug crypto isakmp
```

IPSec Commands

You can use the commands described in the following sections to observe IPSec configuration and operation.

The show crypto ipsec transform-set Command

You use the **show crypto ipsec transform-set** EXEC command to view the configured transform sets. The command has the following syntax:

```
show crypto ipsec transform-set [tag transform-set-name]
```

The command parameter has the following meaning:

Command Parameter	Description
tag *transform-set-name*	(Optional) Shows only the transform sets that have the specified *transform-set-name*

If no keyword is used, all transform sets configured at the router are displayed.

The show crypto map Command

You can use the **show crypto map** EXEC command to view the crypto map configuration. If no keywords are used, all crypto maps configured at the router are displayed. The command syntax is as follows:

```
show crypto map [interface interface | tag map-name]
```

The command parameters have the following meanings:

Command Parameter	Description
interface *interface*	(Optional) Shows only the crypto map set applied to the specified interface
tag *map-name*	(Optional) Shows only the crypto map set with the specified map name

The show crypto ipsec security-association lifetime Command

You use the **show crypto ipsec security-association lifetime** EXEC command to view the security-association lifetime value configured for a particular crypto map entry. This command has no arguments or keywords.

The show crypto ipsec sa Command

You can use the **show crypto ipsec sa** EXEC command to view the settings used by current security associations. If no keyword is used, all security associations are displayed. The command syntax is as follows:

```
show crypto ipsec sa [map map-name | address | identity] [detail]
```

The command parameters have the following meanings:

Command Parameter	Description
map *map-name*	(Optional) Shows any existing security associations created for the crypto map.
address	(Optional) Shows all the existing security associations, sorted by the destination address and then by protocol (AH or ESP).
identity	(Optional) Shows only the flow information. It does not show the security association information.
detail	(Optional) Shows detailed error counters. The default is the high-level send/receive error counters.

The debug crypto ipsec Command

You use the **debug crypto ipsec** EXEC command to display IPSec events. The **no** form of this command disables debugging output.

The clear crypto sa Command

You use the **clear crypto sa** global configuration command to clear IPSec security associations. The command syntax is as follows:

```
clear crypto sa peer {ip-address | peer-name}
clear crypto sa map map-name
clear crypto sa entry destination-address protocol spi
clear crypto sa counters
```

The command parameters have the following meanings:

Command Parameter	Description
ip-address	Specifies a remote peer's IP address
peer-name	Specifies a remote peer's name as the fully qualified domain name, such as remotepeer.domain.com
map-name	Specifies the name of a crypto map set
destination-address	Specifies the IP address of your peer or the remote peer
protocol	Specifies either the AH or ESP protocol
spi	Specifies a security parameter index (SPI) (found by displaying the security association database with the **show crypto ipsec sa** command)

If the **peer**, **map**, **entry**, or **counters** keywords are not used, all IPSec security associations are deleted.

If the security associations were established via IKE, they are deleted, and future IPSec traffic will require new security associations to be negotiated. (When IKE is used, the IPSec security associations are established only when needed.)

If the security associations are manually established, the security associations are deleted and reinstalled. (When IKE is not used, the IPSec security associations are created as soon as the configuration is complete.)

System Error Messages

Cisco IOS Software can generate many useful system error messages for IKE. Two of these error messages are described in the following sections.

IKE SA with Remote Peer Is Not Authenticated

Example 16-18 shows an example of a system error message for IKE.

Example 16-18 *A System Error Message for IKE*

```
%CRYPTO-6-IKMP_SA_NOT_AUTH: Cannot accept Quick Mode exchange from %15i if SA is not
  authenticated!
```

This message indicates that the IKE security association with the remote peer was not authenticated, yet the peer attempted to begin a quick mode exchange. This exchange must be done only with an authenticated security association. The recommended action is to contact the remote peer's administrator to resolve the improper configuration.

IKE Policy Parameter Mismatch

Example 16-19 shows an example of a system error message for IKE.

Example 16-19 *A System Error Message for IKE*

```
%CRYPTO-6-IKMP_SA_NOT_OFFERED: Remote peer %15i responded with attribute
  [chars] not offered or changed
```

IKE peers negotiate policy by having the initiator offer a list of possible alternative protection suites. This message indicates that the responder responded with an IKE policy that the initiator did not offer. The recommended action is to contact the remote peer's administrator to resolve the improper configuration.

A Debug Example

Example 16-20 shows IKE and IPSec debugging with normal IPSec setup messages (note the inline comments).

Example 16-20 *IKE and IPSec Debugging with Normal IPSec Setup Messages*

```
RouterA# debug crypto ipsec
Crypto IPSEC debugging is on
RouterA# debug crypto isakmp
Crypto ISAKMP debugging is on
RouterA#
*Feb 29 08:08:06.556 PST: IPSEC(sa_request): ,
  (key eng. msg.) src= 172.16.1.1, dest= 172.16.2.1,
    src_proxy= 192.168.1.0/255.255.255.0/0/0 (type=4),
```

continues

Example 16-20 *IKE and IPSec Debugging with Normal IPSec Setup Messages (Continued)*

```
     dest_proxy= 192.168.2.0/255.255.255.0/0/0 (type=4),
     protocol= ESP, transform= esp-des esp-md5-hmac ,
     lifedur= 3600s and 4608000kb,
     spi= 0x0(0), conn_id= 0, keysize= 0, flags= 0x4004
! Interesting traffic from Site1 to Site2 triggers ISAKMP Main Mode.
*Feb 29 08:08:06.556 PST: ISAKMP (4): beginning Main Mode exchange
*Feb 29 08:08:06.828 PST: ISAKMP (4): processing SA payload. message ID = 0
*Feb 29 08:08:06.828 PST: ISAKMP (4): Checking ISAKMP transform 1
  against priority 100 policy
*Feb 29 08:08:06.828 PST: ISAKMP:      encryption DES-CBC
*Feb 29 08:08:06.828 PST: ISAKMP:      hash MD5
*Feb 29 08:08:06.828 PST: ISAKMP:      default group 1
*Feb 29 08:08:06.832 PST: ISAKMP:      auth pre-share
*Feb 29 08:08:06.832 PST: ISAKMP (4): atts are acceptable. Next payload is 0
! The IPSec peers have found a matching ISAKMP policy
*Feb 29 08:08:06.964 PST: ISAKMP (4): SA is doing pre-shared key authentication
! Pre-shared key authentication is identified
*Feb 29 08:08:07.368 PST: ISAKMP (4): processing KE payload. message ID = 0
*Feb 29 08:08:07.540 PST: ISAKMP (4): processing NONCE payload. message ID = 0
*Feb 29 08:08:07.540 PST: ISAKMP (4): SKEYID state generated
*Feb 29 08:08:07.540 PST: ISAKMP (4): processing vendor id payload
*Feb 29 08:08:07.544 PST: ISAKMP (4): speaking to another IOS box!
*Feb 29 08:08:07.676 PST: ISAKMP (4): processing ID payload. message ID = 0
*Feb 29 08:08:07.676 PST: ISAKMP (4): processing HASH payload. message ID = 0
*Feb 29 08:08:07.680 PST: ISAKMP (4): SA has been authenticated with
  172.16.2.1
! Main mode is complete. The peers are authenticated, and secret
! keys are generated. On to Quick Mode!
*Feb 29 08:08:07.680 PST: ISAKMP (4): beginning Quick Mode exchange,
  M-ID of -1079597279
*Feb 29 08:08:07.680 PST: IPSEC(key_engine): got a queue event...
*Feb 29 08:08:07.680 PST: IPSEC(spi_response): getting spi 3658276911d for SA
         from 172.16.2.1     to 172.16.1.1     for prot 3
*Feb 29 08:08:08.424 PST: ISAKMP (4): processing SA payload.
  message ID = -1079597279
*Feb 29 08:08:08.424 PST: ISAKMP (4): Checking IPSec proposal 1
*Feb 29 08:08:08.424 PST: ISAKMP: transform 1, ESP_DES
*Feb 29 08:08:08.424 PST: ISAKMP:    attributes in transform:
*Feb 29 08:08:08.424 PST: ISAKMP:       encaps is 1
*Feb 29 08:08:08.424 PST: ISAKMP:       SA life type in seconds
*Feb 29 08:08:08.424 PST: ISAKMP:       SA life duration (basic) of 3600
*Feb 29 08:08:08.428 PST: ISAKMP:       SA life type in kilobytes
*Feb 29 08:08:08.428 PST: ISAKMP:       SA life duration (VPI) of
  0x0 0x46 0x50 0x0
*Feb 29 08:08:08.428 PST: ISAKMP:       authenticator is HMAC-MD5
*Feb 29 08:08:08.428 PST: ISAKMP (4): atts are acceptable.
*Feb 29 08:08:08.428 PST: IPSEC(validate_proposal_request): proposal part #1,
  (key eng. msg.) dest= 172.16.2.1, src= 172.16.1.1,
    dest_proxy= 192.168.2.0/255.255.255.0/0/0 (type=4),
```

Example 16-20 *IKE and IPSec Debugging with Normal IPSec Setup Messages (Continued)*

```
          src_proxy= 192.168.1.0/255.255.255.0/0/0 (type=4),
          protocol= ESP, transform= esp-des esp-md5-hmac ,
          lifedur= 0s and 0kb,
          spi= 0x0(0), conn_id= 0, keysize= 0, flags= 0x4
*Feb 29 08:08:08.432 PST: ISAKMP (4): processing NONCE payload.
 message ID = -10 79597279
*Feb 29 08:08:08.432 PST: ISAKMP (4): processing ID payload.
 message ID = -1079597279
*Feb 29 08:08:08.432 PST: ISAKMP (4): processing ID payload.
 message ID = -1079597279
! A matching IPSec policy has been negotiated and authenticated.
! Next the SAs are set up.
*Feb 29 08:08:08.436 PST: ISAKMP (4): Creating IPSec SAs
*Feb 29 08:08:08.436 PST:            inbound SA from 172.16.2.1      to 172.16.1.1
       (proxy 192.168.2.0     to 192.168.1.0    )
*Feb 29 08:08:08.436 PST:            has spi 365827691 and conn_id 5 and flags 4
*Feb 29 08:08:08.436 PST:            lifetime of 3600 seconds
*Feb 29 08:08:08.440 PST:            lifetime of 4608000 kilobytes
*Feb 29 08:08:08.440 PST:            outbound SA from 172.16.1.1     to 172.16.2.1
       (proxy 192.168.1.0     to 192.168.2.0    )
*Feb 29 08:08:08.440 PST:            has spi 470158437 and conn_id 6 and flags 4
*Feb 29 08:08:08.440 PST:            lifetime of 3600 seconds
*Feb 29 08:08:08.440 PST:            lifetime of 4608000 kilobytes
*Feb 29 08:08:08.440 PST: IPSEC(key_engine): got a queue event...
*Feb 29 08:08:08.440 PST: IPSEC(initialize_sas): ,
  (key eng. msg.) dest= 172.16.1.1, src= 172.16.2.1,
    dest_proxy= 192.168.1.0/255.255.255.0/0/0 (type=4),
    src_proxy= 192.168.2.0/255.255.255.0/0/0 (type=4),
    protocol= ESP, transform= esp-des esp-md5-hmac ,
    lifedur= 3600s and 4608000kb,
    spi= 0x15CE166B(365827691), conn_id= 5, keysize= 0, flags= 0x4
*Feb 29 08:08:08.444 PST: IPSEC(initialize_sas): ,
  (key eng. msg.) src= 172.16.1.1, dest= 172.16.2.1,
    src_proxy= 192.168.1.0/255.255.255.0/0/0 (type=4),
    dest_proxy= 192.168.2.0/255.255.255.0/0/0 (type=4),
    protocol= ESP, transform= esp-des esp-md5-hmac ,
    lifedur= 3600s and 4608000kb,
    spi= 0x1C060C65(470158437), conn_id= 6, keysize= 0, flags= 0x4
*Feb 29 08:08:08.444 PST: IPSEC(create_sa): sa created,
  (sa) sa_dest= 172.16.1.1, sa_prot= 50,
    sa_spi= 0x15CE166B(365827691),
    sa_trans= esp-des esp-md5-hmac , sa_conn_id= 5
*Feb 29 08:08:08.444 PST: IPSEC(create_sa): sa created,
  (sa) sa_dest= 172.16.2.1, sa_prot= 50,
    sa_spi= 0x1C060C65(470158437),
    sa_trans= esp-des esp-md5-hmac , sa_conn_id= 6
! IPSec SAs are set up and data can be securely exchanged.
RouterA#
```

Configuring Cisco IOS IPSec Using RSA-Encrypted Nonces for Authentication

RSA-encrypted nonces provide a strong method of authenticating the IPSec peers and the Diffie-Hellman key exchange. RSA-encrypted nonces encrypt a nonce (a randomized integer similar to a shared secret key) using RSA encryption. The encrypted nonce value is used to authenticate the IPSec peers, similar to a preshared key.

Some drawbacks to this authentication method include that RSA-encrypted nonces do not provide nonrepudiation, which lets the recipient of the message prove to a third party that the sender really did send the message. RSA signatures provide nonrepudiation. Another problem is that RSA-encrypted nonces are somewhat more difficult to configure.

RSA-encrypted nonces require that peers possess each others' RSA public keys but do not use a certificate authority. Instead, there are two ways for peers to get each others' public keys:

- You manually configure RSA keys.

- You use RSA signatures that were used previously during a successful IKE negotiation with a remote peer.

This section summarizes the differences between configuring RSA encryption and using preshared keys. Refer to the Cisco IOS documentation referenced at the end of this chapter for more details.

The IPSec configuration process for RSA encryption is very similar to that for preshared keys, with some notable exceptions. The tasks involved are summarized as follows:

- Task 1: Prepare for IPSec to determine a detailed security policy for RSA encryption, including how to distribute the RSA public keys.

- Task 2: Configure RSA keys manually.

- Task 3: Configure IKE for IPSec to select RSA encryption as the authentication method in an IKE policy.

- Task 4: Configure IPSec, which is typically done the same as in preshared keys.

- Task 5: Test and verify IPSec, and exercise additional commands to view and manage RSA public keys.

Task 1: Prepare for IPSec

Preparing for RSA encryption includes the following components that are specific to RSA encryption:

- **Determining key distribution methods based on the number and locations of IPSec peers**—The criteria for using RSA encryption is a small number of IPSec peers and the ability to distribute RSA public keys out-of-band.

- **Determining the authentication method**—This step involves choosing RSA encryption based on the need for stronger authentication than preshared keys.

- **Determining IKE policies for peers**—Determine policy details for each peer, especially identifying peer fully qualified domain names and host names, because IKE identity is based on host names for RSA encryption.

- **Identifying IPSec peer router IP addresses and host names**—You need to determine the details of all the IPSec peers that will use IKE to establish SAs, just as you did with preshared keys.

- Checking the current configuration for existing RSA public keys for your router and peer routers.

Task 2: Configure RSA Encryption

This task involves a number of steps that are different from those used with preshared keys. Configuring RSA keys involves five steps:

Step 1   Plan for configuring RSA Encryption to minimize mis-configuration.

Step 2   Configure the router's host name and domain name (if they have not already been configured).

Step 3   Generate the RSA keys.

Step 4   Enter peer RSA public keys. Several substeps are necessary for entering the peer's public keys. Attention to detail is important, because any mistakes made when entering the keys will cause them not to work.

Step 5   Manage RSA keys. Removing old keys is part of the configuration process. Old keys can consume much space.

Step 1: Plan for RSA Keys

You should plan for configuring RSA encryption keys before you begin entering commands. This planning step will help you minimize mistakes in configuration. It includes the following:

- **Identifying peers that will use RSA encryption**—Identify all IPSec peers that use RSA-encrypted nonces. Typically, the peers will be Cisco routers running Cisco IOS Software.

- Determining whether to use general or special-usage RSA keys.

- **Determining RSA key modulus**—Choose the size of the key modulus in the range of 360 to 2048 bits for your RSA keys. A key modulus greater than 512 might take a few minutes to generate. The higher the modulus, the stronger the RSA key.

- **Obtaining peer RSA public keys**—You need to obtain all peers' RSA public keystrings. The keystring is a long hexadecimal number. It should be securely transferred between peers.

Step 2: Configure the Router's Host Name and Domain Name

You must configure the router's host name and domain name because RSA encryption uses them for the IKE identity along with the nonce value. The following steps summarize the commands you must enter to perform this step (refer to the *Security Configuration Guide* and *Security Command Reference* for more details on the commands):

1 Specify the host name for the router with the **hostname** *name* command. The router's host name is used for RSA key generation and IKE identity.

2 Enter the **ip domain-name** *name* command to specify the default domain name used to complete unqualified host names. Do not include the initial period that separates an unqualified name from the domain name. To disable the use of the DNS, use the **no** form of this command.

3 Define a static host name-to-address mapping in the host cache with the **ip host name** *address* command if a domain name server is not available to resolve domain names. To remove the name-to-address mapping, use the **no** form of this command.

Step 3: Generate RSA Keys

Manually configure RSA keys and then view the generated keys as outlined in the following steps:

1 Generate RSA keys with the **crypto key generate rsa [usage-keys]** command. The optional **usage-keys** keyword specifies that two RSA special-usage key pairs should be generated (one encryption pair and one signature pair) instead of one general-purpose key pair.

2 View the generated RSA public key with the **show crypto key mypubkey rsa** privileged EXEC mode command.

By default, RSA key pairs do not exist. RSA keys are generated in pairs—one public RSA key and one private RSA key. If a router already has RSA keys when you issue the **crypto key generate rsa** command, you are warned and are prompted to replace the existing keys with new keys. This command is not saved in the router configuration; however, the keys generated by this command are saved in the private configuration in NVRAM (which is never displayed to the user or backed up to another device).

Special-Usage Keys

If you generate special-usage keys, two pairs of RSA keys are generated. One pair is used with any IKE policy that specifies RSA signatures as the authentication method, and the other pair is used with any IKE policy that specifies RSA-encrypted nonces as the authentication method.

If you plan to have both types of RSA authentication methods in your IKE policies, you might prefer to generate special-usage keys. With special-usage keys, each key is not unnecessarily exposed. (Without special-usage keys, one key is used for both authentication methods, increasing that key's exposure.)

General-Purpose Keys

If you generate general-purpose keys, only one pair of RSA keys is generated, and it is used with IKE policies specifying either RSA signatures or RSA-encrypted nonces. Therefore, a general-purpose key pair might get used more frequently than a special-usage key pair.

Modulus Length

Key generation can be very time-consuming, depending on the router and the length of the key chosen. When you generate RSA keys, you are prompted to enter a modulus length. A longer modulus offers stronger security but takes longer to generate and takes more CPU cycles during the IKE Phase 1 authentication. Cisco recommends using a minimum modulus of 1024 for security strength. Table 16-4 shows examples of how long it takes to generate keys of different modulus lengths.

Table 16-4 *Modulus Lengths*

Router	360 bits	512 bits	1024 bits	2048 bits
Cisco 2500	11 seconds	20 seconds	4 minutes, 38 seconds	Longer than 1 hour
Cisco 4700	Less than 1 second	1 second	4 seconds	50 seconds

An Example of Generating RSA Keys

Example 16-21 shows the command dialogue for the **crypto key generate rsa** command for general-purpose keys.

Example 16-21 *Command Dialogue for the **crypto key generate rsa** Command for General-Purpose Keys*

```
RouterA(config)# crypto key generate rsa
The name for the keys will be: RouterA.cisco.com
Choose the size of the key modulus in the range of 360 to 2048 for
```

continues

Example 16-21 *Command Dialogue for the **crypto key generate rsa** Command for General-Purpose Keys (Continued)*

```
your Signature Keys.
Choosing a key modulus greater than 512 may take a few minutes.
How many bits in the modulus [512]: 512
Generating RSA keys ...
[OK]
% Key pair was generated at: 23:59:59 UTC Feb 29 2000
RouterA# show crypto key mypubkey rsa
Key name: RouterA.cisco.com
 Usage: General Purpose Key
 Key Data:
  305C300D 06092A86 4886F70D 01010105 00034B00 30480241 00A9443B 62FDACFB
  CCDB8784 19AE1CD8 95B30953 1EDD30D1 380219D6 4636E015 4D7C6F33 4DC1F6E0
  C929A25E 521688A1 295907F4 E98BF920 6A81CE57 28A21116 E3020301 0001
```

Step 4: Enter Peer RSA Public Keys

You must manually enter each peer's RSA public keys by completing three steps:

1 Enter the **crypto key pubkey-chain rsa** command.

2 Specify **addressed-key** or **named-key** and enter the address or name. Specify **addressed-key** if the IKE identity is set to **address** and use **named-key** if the IKE identity is set to **hostname**.

3 Enter the peer's RSA public key.

NOTE The IPSec peer must use the same type of keys (named or addressed) as the local system. For example, if you specify **addressed-key**, the IPSec peer must also use **addressed-key**. The same is true for **named-key**.

You can complete the following steps to enter the peer's RSA public keys:

1 Input the **crypto key pubkey-chain rsa** command so that you can enter public key configuration mode. This command invokes config-pubkey-chain mode, where you can manually specify peer RSA public keys. Specify whether the key is an addressed key or a named key and indicate whether it is an encryption or signature key with either of the following commands:

```
addressed-key key-address [encryption ¦ signature]
named-key key-name [encryption ¦ signature]
```

These commands indicate which remote peer's RSA public key you will enter. These commands invoke config-pubkey-key mode. Here are some key points about these commands:

— If the remote peer uses its host name as its IKE identity, use the **named-key** command and specify the remote peer's fully qualified domain name (such as somerouter.domain.com) as the key name.

— If the remote peer uses its IP address as its IKE identity, use the **addressed-key** command and specify the remote peer's IP address as the key address.

— The optional **encryption** keyword indicates that the RSA public key to be specified will be an encryption special-usage key used with RSA encryption.

— The optional **signature** keyword indicates that the RSA public key to be specified will be a signature special-usage key used with RSA signatures.

— If neither the **encryption** nor the **signature** keyword is used, general-purpose keys will be specified.

2 Specify the remote peer's RSA public key by performing the following substeps:

— Enter the **key-string** command. This command invokes config-pubkey mode.

— Input the peer's RSA public keystring (in hexadecimal) copied from the remote peer.

— Enter the **quit** command. The router returns to config-pubkey-key mode.

3 Repeat Steps 2 through 4 to specify the RSA public keys of all the other IPSec peers that use RSA-encrypted nonces in an IKE policy.

4 Exit from pubkey-key mode by entering the **exit** command.

5 Return to global configuration mode by pressing Ctrl+Z.

6 View a list of all the RSA public keys stored on your router, or view details of a particular RSA public key stored on your router, using this command:

```
show crypto key pubkey-chain rsa [name key-name ¦ address key-address]
```

The following sections give examples of configuring peer RSA public keys.

An Example of Configuring a Peer General RSA Public Key Using addressed-key

Example 16-22 shows the commands necessary to configure a general RSA public key using **addressed-key**. You should use the **show crypto key pubkey-chain rsa** command to determine the types of keys previously configured so you can enter the correct key mode with the **crypto key pubkey-chain rsa** command. Note that the usage type here is General because a general key was configured.

Example 16-22 *An Example of Configuring a Peer General RSA Public Key Using addressed-key*

```
RouterA(config)# crypto key pubkey-chain rsa
RouterA(config-pubkey-chain)# addressed-key 172.16.2.1
RouterA(config-pubkey-key)# key-string
Enter a public key as a hexadecimal number ....
RouterA(config-pubkey)# <RouterB's RSA public key string in hexadecimal>
RouterA(config-pubkey)# quit
RouterA(config-pubkey-key)# ^Z
RouterA# show crypto key pubkey-chain rsa
Codes: M - Manually configured, C - Extracted from certificate
Code  Usage   IP-Address      Name
M     General 172.16.2.1
```

An Example of Configuring a Peer Encryption RSA Public Key Using addressed-key

Example 16-23 uses the **encryption** keyword, which makes this key an encryption key only for use with RSA encryption.

Example 16-23 *An Example of Configuring a Peer Encryption RSA Public Key Using addressed-key*

```
RouterA(config)# crypto key pubkey-chain rsa
RouterA(config-pubkey-chain)# addressed-key 172.16.2.1 encryption
RouterA(config-pubkey-key)# key-string
Enter a public key as a hexadecimal number ....
RouterA(config-pubkey)# <RouterB's RSA public key string>
RouterA(config-pubkey)# quit
RouterA(config-pubkey-key)# exit (or ^Z)
RouterA(config-pubkey-chain)# exit
RouterA(config)# quit
RouterA# show crypto key pubkey-chain rsa
Codes: M - Manually configured, C - Extracted from certificate

Code  Usage   IP-Address      Name
M     Encrypt 172.16.2.1
```

An Example of Configuring a Peer General RSA Public Key Using named-key

Example 16-24 uses the **named-key** command. This command should be used only when the router has a single interface that processes IPSec.

Example 16-24 *An Example of Configuring a Peer General RSA Public Key Using named-key*

```
RouterA(config)# crypto key pubkey-chain rsa
RouterA(config-pubkey-chain)# named-key routerB.cisco.com
RouterA(config-pubkey-key)# key-string
Enter a public key as a hexadecimal number ....
```

Example 16-24 *An Example of Configuring a Peer General RSA Public Key Using named-key (Continued)*

```
RouterA(config-pubkey)# <RouterB's RSA public key string>
RouterA(config-pubkey)# quit
RouterA(config-pubkey-key)# exit (or ^Z)
RouterA(config-pubkey-chain)# exit
RouterA(config)# quit
RouterA# show crypto key pubkey-chain rsa
Codes: M--Manually configured, C--Extracted from certificate

Code  Usage    IP-Address        Name
M     General  172.16.2.1        routerb.cisco.com
```

You use the **name** or **address** keywords to display details about a particular RSA public key stored on the router, as shown in Example 16-25.

Example 16-25 *Details About an RSA Public Key Stored on a Router*

```
RouterA# show crypto key pubkey-chain rsa address 172.16.2.1
Key name: routerB.cisco.com
 Usage: General Purpose Key
 Source: Manual
 Data:
  305C300D 06092A86 4886F70D 01010105 00034B00 30480241 00DF6544 9A837659
  C283B198 F57BF7E8 FF1018BC 90826E89 6E20943C E3992543 AF9BF7A0 107911ED
  EBD6302E C134FB9E 6A34DDF2 46FE0921 377B7F63 D8702364 B1020301 0001
```

Step 5: Manage RSA Keys

In managing RSA keys and peer RSA keys, to delete all your router's RSA keys, use the **crypto key zeroize rsa** global configuration command.

NOTE   Using **write erase** on the router does not remove the keys. Use the **crypto key zeroize rsa** command to remove your own public keys.

Deleting Peer RSA Public Keys

Perform the following steps to delete the other peer's RSA public key(s) in your router's configuration:

1 Use the **show crypto key pubkey-chain rsa command** to identify peer RSA key details for the key you want to delete. Details to determine include the key usage type, whether it is a named key or an addressed key, and the key name.

2 Enter public key configuration mode with the **crypto key pubkey-chain rsa** command.

3 Delete the remote peer's RSA public key with the **no named-key** *key-name* [**encryption** | **signature**] or **no addressed-key** *key-address* [**encryption** | **signature**] command. Specify the peer's fully qualified domain name or the remote peer's IP address.

4 Return to global configuration mode with the **exit** command.

Example 16-26 shows how to delete a peer's RSA public key.

Example 16-26 *Deleting a Peer's RSA Public Key*

```
RouterA(config)# crypto key pubkey-chain rsa
RouterA(config-pubkey-chain)# no addressed-key 172.16.2.1
RouterA(config-pubkey-chain)# no named-key routerB.cisco.com encryption
RouterA(config-pubkey-chain)# no named-key routerB.cisco.com signature
```

Task 3: Configure IKE for RSA-Encrypted Nonces

Configuring IKE for RSA encryption includes selecting RSA encryption as the authentication method in the IKE policy. You select RSA encryption using the **crypto isakmp policy** command, which puts you into config-isakmp command mode. You can then specify the authentication method of **rsa-encr**, as shown in Example 16-27.

Example 16-27 *Specifying the Authentication Method of* **rsa-encr**

```
Router(config)# crypto isakmp policy 110
Router(config-isakmp)# authentication rsa-encr
Router(config-isakmp)# exit
```

Note how RSA encryption appears in the crypto policy (the default policy is not shown) in Example 16-28.

Example 16-28 *RSA Encryption in a Crypto Policy*

```
Router(config)# show crypto isakmp policy
Protection suite of priority 110
        encryption algorithm:   DES - Data Encryption Standard (56 bit keys).
        hash algorithm:         Message Digest 5
        authentication method:  Rivest-Shamir-Adleman Encryption
        Diffie-Hellman group:   #1 (768 bit)
        lifetime:               86400 seconds, no volume limit
```

NOTE The rest of the tasks and steps to configure IKE and IPSec are the same as those for configuring preshared keys. See the sections "Task 2: Configure IKE for Preshared Keys," "Task 3: Configure IPSec," and "Task 4: Test and Verify IPSec" in this chapter for more details.

Summary

This section summarizes the main points of this chapter as follows:

- Cisco recommends that you define a detailed crypto security policy for IKE and IPSec before beginning configuration to help minimize errors and so that you have the information you need during the configuration process.

- Some key preliminary steps in configuring IPSec are to check the current configuration for a possible existing IPSec configuration, to identify IPSec peer details, to ensure that network traffic works without encryption, and to ensure that router access lists permit IPSec traffic.

- Transform sets consist of one or more individual IPSec transforms that determine IPSec transform and mode.

- Transform sets can be grouped into supersets in a crypto map to enable transform set negotiation during IKE Phase 2 quick mode.

- Crypto access lists use extended IP access lists to determine traffic to be encrypted.

- Crypto access lists act like outgoing access lists, where permit means encrypt.

- Crypto access lists should mirror each other between peers.

- Crypto maps pull together all IPSec details and are applied to interfaces, enabling IPSec SA setup.

- Use **show** and **debug** commands to test and troubleshoot IPSec.

- Configuring RSA-encrypted nonces for authentication includes configuring RSA key pairs, exchanging RSA public keys, and setting IKE authentication to **rsa-encr**.

Case Study: Configuring Cisco IOS IPSec for Preshared Keys

This case study illustrates how to configure IPSec in the hypothetical XYZ Company. Read the case study scenario, examine the topology diagram, read the security policy, and then analyze the configuration examples to see how the security policy statements are enacted for the Cisco routers.

Case Study Scenario

The XYZ Company needs to ensure the integrity of traffic between the central site and a remote branch. The company would like to use its high-speed reliable connection to the Internet to the remote branch instead of creating a dedicated Frame Relay circuit. The company has decided to create a secure VPN between the campus and the remote branch. It initially prefers to use its existing perimeter router to create the VPN.

Topology

Figure 16-3 illustrates the portion of the XYZ network that will be configured in this case study. Note that the focus here is on the Perimeter 1 routers in each pod pair.

Figure 16-3 *The XYZ Company Perimeter Routers to Be Configured for IPSec*

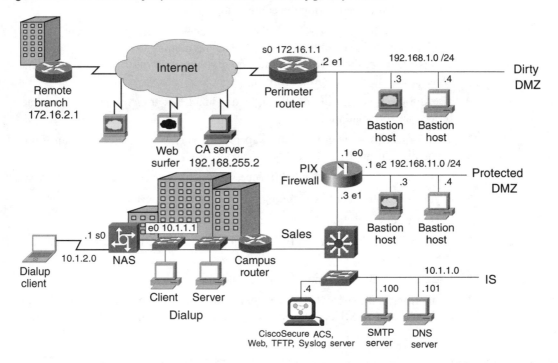

Network Security Policy

The network security policy that XYZ Company wants to implement is as follows:

- Use the Internet to connect a branch office to the corporate network for casual traffic.

- Authenticate data traffic between the corporate network and branch offices over the Internet to ensure that no one is inserting or changing packets in transit.

- Ensure data integrity of traffic between the corporate network and branch offices over the Internet using 56-bit DES encryption.

- Use IKE preshared keys for authentication.

Sample Router Configuration for the Perimeter 1 Router

Examine the configuration example for the Perimeter 1 router of the XYZ Company, shown in Example 16-29. The example implements the network security policy statements related to IPSec network security. One possible configuration of the router for the specified security policy might look as follows. You might have chosen to configure the router differently to enact the same security policy requirements. Note that the sample configurations contain comments showing which router commands enact particular security policy statements. The configuration shown is for a Cisco 1720 router. Unused interfaces and other unrelated commands were deleted for the sake of brevity.

Example 16-29 *Perimeter 1 Router Example for IPSec*

```
Current configuration:
!
version 12.0
!
hostname Perimeter1
!
boot system flash c1700-osy56i-mz_120-3_T3.bin
!
! Use IKE preshared keys for authentication
!
crypto isakmp policy 100
 hash md5
 authentication pre-share
crypto isakmp key mcns address 172.16.2.1
!
! Ensure data integrity of traffic between the corporate network and branch
! offices over the Internet using 56-bit DES encryption.
!
crypto ipsec transform-set 1&2 esp-des esp-md5-hmac
!
 !
 crypto map shared 10 ipsec-isakmp
 set peer 172.16.2.1
 set transform-set 1&2
 match address 151
!
!
interface Serial0
 ip address 172.16.1.1 255.255.255.252
 ip access-group 101 in
 crypto map shared
!
interface Serial1
 no ip address
 no ip directed-broadcast
 shutdown
!
interface FastEthernet0
 ip address 192.168.1.2 255.255.255.0
```

continues

Example 16-29 *Perimeter 1 Router Example for IPSec (Continued)*

```
 ip access-group 102 in
 !
 ip classless
 ip route 0.0.0.0 0.0.0.0 172.16.1.2
 no ip http server
 !
 ! Address 192.168.1.10 points to the PIX static mapped to the NT1
 ! host at 10.1.1.4.
 access-list 1 permit 192.168.1.10
 access-list 16 permit 192.168.255.2
 access-list 16 deny   any log
 ! The following 3 entries permit IPSec
 access-list 101 permit ahp host 172.16.2.1 host 172.16.1.1
 access-list 101 permit esp host 172.16.2.1 host 172.16.1.1
 access-list 101 permit udp host 172.16.2.1 host 172.16.1.1 eq isakmp
 access-list 101 deny   ip 127.0.0.0 0.255.255.255 any log
 access-list 101 deny   ip 255.0.0.0 0.255.255.255 any log
 access-list 101 deny   ip 224.0.0.0 7.255.255.255 any log
 access-list 101 deny   ip host 0.0.0.0 any log
 access-list 101 deny   ip 192.168.1.0 0.0.0.255 any log
 access-list 101 deny   ip 10.0.0.0 0.255.255.255 any log
 access-list 101 deny   udp any any eq snmp
 access-list 101 permit tcp any host 192.168.1.4 eq smtp
 access-list 101 permit tcp any host 192.168.1.3 eq www
 access-list 101 permit tcp any host 192.168.1.3 eq 443
 access-list 101 permit tcp any host 192.168.1.3 eq ftp
 access-list 101 permit tcp any host 192.168.1.3 gt 1023
 access-list 101 permit icmp any 192.168.1.0 0.0.0.255 echo-reply
 access-list 101 permit icmp any host 172.16.1.1 echo-reply
 access-list 101 permit icmp host 192.168.255.2 host 172.16.1.1 echo
 access-list 101 permit udp any host 192.168.1.3 eq domain
 access-list 101 permit tcp host 192.168.255.2 host 192.168.1.3 eq nntp
 access-list 101 permit udp host 192.168.255.2 host 192.168.1.3 eq ntp
 access-list 101 deny   icmp any host 192.168.1.1 echo log
 access-list 101 deny   tcp any host 192.168.1.1 eq telnet log
 access-list 101 deny   tcp any host 172.16.1.1 eq telnet log
 access-list 101 deny   tcp any host 192.168.1.2 eq telnet log
 access-list 101 deny   ip any any log
 access-list 102 permit ip 192.168.1.0 0.0.0.255 any
 access-list 102 deny   ip any any log
 access-list 151 permit ip 192.168.1.0 0.0.0.255 192.168.2.0 0.0.0.255
 access-list 151 deny   ip any any
 no cdp run
 !
 line con 0
  exec-timeout 0 0
  logging synchronous
  login local
  transport input none
 line aux 0
  no exec
  login local
```

Example 16-29 *Perimeter 1 Router Example for IPSec (Continued)*

```
line vty 0 4
 access-class 1 in
 login local
 !
end
```

Review Questions

Answer the following review questions, which delve into some of the key facts and concepts covered in this chapter:

1 What is the default IKE (Phase 1) policy?

2 Why would you choose to use the **show crypto isakmp policy** command to view IKE policies instead of the **show running-config** command?

3 What protocols and ports must be enabled for an interface to use IPSec?

4 How do you enable IKE for one particular interface and not another?

5 How many ESP transforms can be defined at the same time?

6 Where can you configure IPSec security association lifetimes?

7 What command do you use to define the traffic flows to be protected?

8 How do you apply a crypto map to an interface?

9 When are the IPSec SAs initialized with IKE configured?

10 You believe IPSec setup is failing. You have checked your configuration, but you cannot determine where the failure is. What should you do?

References

The topics considered in this chapter are complex and should be studied further to more fully understand them and put them to use. Use the following references to learn more about the topics in this chapter.

Refer to the "IP Security and Encryption Overview" chapter of the *Cisco IOS Release 12.0 Security Configuration Guide* for an overview of how IPSec and related protocols are supported on Cisco routers.

IKE Configuration

In the *Cisco IOS Release 12.0 Security Configuration Guide,* see the "IP Security and Encryption" section of the chapter called "Configuring Internet Key Exchange Security Protocol" for an overview of how to configure IKE on Cisco routers.

In the *Cisco IOS Release 12.0 Security Command Reference,* see the "IP Security and Encryption" section of the chapter called "Router and Network Monitoring Commands" for specific commands you can use to configure general security on Cisco routers.

IPSec Configuration

In the *Cisco IOS Release 12.0 Security Configuration Guide,* see the "IP Security and Encryption" section of the chapter called "Configuring IPSec Network Security" for an overview of how to configure IPSec on Cisco routers.

In the *Cisco IOS Release 12.0 Security Command Reference,* see the "IP Security and Encryption" section of the chapter called "Configuring IPSec Network Security" for specific commands you can use to configure IPSec on Cisco routers.

Extended IP Access Lists

In the *Cisco IOS Release 12.0 Network Protocols Configuration Guide, Part 1,* see the "Filter IP Addresses" section in the "Configuring IP Services" chapter for information on how to configure standard and extended access lists.

In the *Cisco IOS Release 12.0 Network Protocols Command Reference, Part 1,* see the "IP Addressing and Services" section in the "IP Services Commands" chapter for specific standard and extended access list commands.

System Error Messages and Debug References

Refer to the *Cisco IOS Release 12.0 Cisco IOS Software System Error Messages* document for specific information on system error messages.

Refer to the *Cisco IOS Release 12.0 Debug Command Reference* document for specific information on **debug** commands and messages.

Upon completing this chapter, you will be able to do the following:

- Describe the tasks and steps used to configure IPSec support on the PIX Firewall
- Describe the commands used to configure PIX Firewall IPSec encryption
- Configure PIX Firewall IPSec using preshared keys for authentication
- Test and verify PIX Firewall IPSec

CHAPTER 17

Configuring PIX Firewall IPSec Support

This chapter shows you how to configure basic IP security (IPSec) in the PIX Firewall using preshared keys for authentication. It presents an overview of the tasks and steps you must perform to configure IPSec, provides details about IPSec-related commands in the PIX Firewall, and shows command examples. This chapter finishes with a case study based on the XYZ Company case study.

You will notice that the procedural tasks and steps outlined in this chapter are nearly identical to those used to configure preshared keys in Cisco IOS software, which is covered in Chapter 16, "Configuring Cisco IOS IPSec." The commands are very similar between the products as well because the source programming code for IPSec used in Cisco IOS software was ported over to the PIX Firewall.

A nice thing about the PIX Firewall commands is that all commands are entered in configuration mode; none of the PIX Firewall commands have submodes, which simplifies the configuration tasks and steps. Refer to Chapter 16 for more information on how IKE or IPSec works for preshared keys.

The intent of this chapter is to configure PIX Firewalls to become secure IPSec gateways that will encrypt and protect traffic flows of networks behind the PIX Firewalls, using preshared keys for authentication. The use of IKE preshared keys for authentication of IPSec sessions is relatively easy to configure yet does not scale well for a large number of IPSec clients. After you master this process, you will be able to configure Rivest, Shamir, and Adleman (RSA) signatures. This topic is covered in Chapter 18, "Scaling Cisco IPSec Networks."

Figure 17-1 shows the simplified topology for the XYZ Company used in examples in this chapter.

Figure 17-1 *XYZ Company Topology for PIX Firewall IPSec*

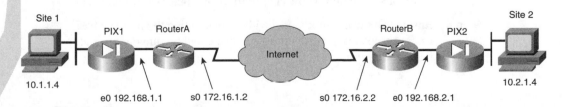

Four key tasks are involved in configuring IPSec encryption using preshared keys on the PIX Firewall:

- **Task 1: Prepare for IPSec**—Preparing for IPSec involves determining the detailed encryption policy, including identifying the hosts and networks you want to protect, choosing an authentication method, determining details about the IPSec peers, identifying the IPSec features you need, and ensuring that existing access lists permit IPSec traffic.

- **Task 2: Configure Internet Key Exchange (IKE) for preshared keys**—Configuring IKE involves enabling IKE, creating the IKE policies, and validating the configuration.

- **Task 3: Configure IPSec**—IPSec configuration includes creating crypto access lists, defining transform sets, creating crypto map entries, and applying crypto map sets to interfaces.

- **Task 4: Test and verify the overall IPSec configuration**—This task involves using **show**, **debug**, and related commands to test and verify that IPSec encryption works and to troubleshoot problems.

The following sections discuss each of these configuration tasks in more detail.

Task 1: Prepare for IPSec

Successfully implementing an IPSec network requires planning before you begin to configure individual PIX Firewalls and other IPSec peers. Configuring IPSec encryption can be complicated. You should begin by defining the detailed IPSec security policy based on the overall company security policy described in Appendix B, "An Example of an XYZ Company Network Security Policy." See Chapter 15, "Understanding Cisco IPSec Support," for more details on how to plan for IPSec. Here are some planning steps in preparing for IPSec:

Step 1 Determine the IKE (IKE Phase 1, or main mode) policy between IPSec peers based on the number and location of the peers.

Step 2 Determine the IPSec (IKE Phase 2, or quick mode) policy, including IPSec peer details such as IP addresses and IPSec transform sets and modes.

Step 3 Check the current configuration by using **write terminal**, **show isakmp**, **show isakmp policy**, **show crypto map**, and other **show** commands.

Step 4 Ensure that the network works without encryption to eliminate basic routing problems using the **ping** command and by running test traffic before encryption.

Step 5 Ensure that existing access lists in the perimeter router and PIX Firewall permit IPSec traffic, or the desired traffic will be filtered out.

Task 2: Configure IKE for Preshared Keys

The next major task in configuring PIX Firewall IPSec is to configure IKE parameters gathered earlier. Note that, in PIX configuration commands, ISAKMP is synonymous with IKE. Configuring IKE consists of the following essential steps and commands, which are covered in subsequent sections in more detail:

Step 1 Enable or disable IKE with the **isakmp enable** command.

Step 2 Create IKE policies with the **isakmp policy** commands.

Step 3 Configure preshared keys with the **isakmp key** and associated commands.

Step 4 Verify the IKE configuration with the **show isakmp [policy]** command.

The following sections describe these steps in detail.

Step 1: Enable or Disable IKE

The first step in configuring IKE is to enable or disable IKE on interfaces used to terminate IPSec tunnels. You enable and disable IKE on individual interfaces by using the **isakmp enable** command. IKE is enabled by default, and you use the **no** form of the command to disable IKE. The command syntax is as follows:

```
isakmp enable interface-name
```

The command parameter has the following meaning:

Command Parameter	Description
interface-name	Specifies the name of the interface on which to enable IKE negotiation

Step 2: Create IKE Policies

The next major step in configuring PIX Firewall IKE support is to define a suite of IKE policies. The goal of defining a suite of IKE policies is to establish IKE peering between two IPSec endpoints. Use the IKE policy details gathered during the planning task.

Table 17-1 summarizes IKE policy details that are configured in examples in this chapter.

Table 17-1 *IKE Policy Example for Peer PIX Firewalls*

Parameter	Peer A Value	Peer B Value
Message encryption algorithm	DES	DES
Message integrity (hash) algorithm	MD5	MD5
Peer authentication method	Preshared key	Preshared key
Key exchange parameters (Diffie-Hellman group identifier)	768-bit Diffie-Hellman group 1	768-bit Diffie-Hellman group 1
IKE-established security association's lifetime	86,400 (default)	86,400 (default)
IP address of IPSec peer	192.168.2.2	192.168.1.2

You use the **isakmp policy** command to define an IKE policy. IKE policies define a set of parameters to be used during the IKE negotiation. Use the **no** form of this command to delete an IKE policy. The command syntax is as follows:

```
isakmp policy priority authentication {pre-share | rsa-sig}
isakmp policy priority encryption {des | 3des}
isakmp policy priority {group1 | group2}
isakmp policy priority hash {md5 | sha}
isakmp policy priority lifetime seconds
```

The command parameters and syntax have the following meanings:

Command Parameter	Description
policy *priority*	Uniquely identifies the IKE policy and assigns it a priority. Use an integer from **1** to **65,534**, with **1** being the highest priority and **65,534** the lowest.
authentication pre-share	Specifies preshared keys as the authentication method.
authentication rsa-sig	Specifies RSA signatures as the authentication method.
encryption des	Specifies 56-bit DES-CBC as the encryption algorithm to be used in the IKE policy. This is the default value.
encryption 3des	Specifies that the Triple DES encryption algorithm is to be used in the IKE policy.

Command Parameter	Description
group1	Specifies that the 768-bit Diffie-Hellman group is to be used in the IKE policy. This is the default value.
group2	Specifies that the 1024-bit Diffie-Hellman group is to be used in the IKE policy.
hash md5	Specifies MD5 (HMAC variant) as the hash algorithm to be used in the IKE policy.
hash sha	Specifies SHA-1 (HMAC variant) as the hash algorithm to be used in the IKE policy. This is the default hash algorithm.
lifetime *seconds*	Specifies how many seconds each security association should exist before expiring. Use an integer from **60** to **86,400** seconds (one day). You can usually leave this value at the default of **86,400**.

If you do not specify one of these commands for a policy, the default value is used for that parameter. You can reset a value to its default by using the **no** form of the command. For example, to reset to **des** the encryption method previously set to **3des**, use the command **no isakmp policy 100 encryption**.

For more details on how IKE policies work, see the section "Internet Key Exchange" in Chapter 15, "Understanding Cisco IPSec Support."

IKE Configuration Example for Two Peers

Examples 17-1 and 17-2 show sample IKE policies for PIX 1 and PIX 2. Note that policy 300 on PIX 1 matches policy 100 on PIX 2. Default values are not shown.

Example 17-1 *Sample IKE Policies for PIX 1*

```
crypto isakmp policy 100
  authentication rsa-sig
crypto isakmp policy 200
  authentication pre-share
crypto isakmp policy 300
  hash md5
  authentication pre-share
```

Example 17-2 *Sample IKE Policies for PIX 2*

```
crypto isakmp policy 100
  hash md5
  authentication pre-share
```

continues

Example 17-2 *Sample IKE Policies for PIX 2 (Continued)*

```
crypto isakmp policy 200
  authentication rsa-sig
  group2
  lifetime 5000
crypto isakmp policy 300
  authentication rsa-sig
  lifetime 10000
```

Step 3: Configure Preshared Keys

The next major step in configuring PIX Firewall IKE support is to optionally set the identity mode and to configure the preshared keys, as discussed in the following sections.

Setting the Identity Mode

IPSec peers authenticate each other during IKE negotiations using the preshared key and the IKE identity. The identity can be either the peer's IP address or its host name. The PIX Firewall uses the IP address identity method by default. If you choose to use the host name identity method, you must specify the method with the **isakmp identity** configuration command. Use the **no** form of this command to reset the IKE identity to the default value (address). The command syntax is as follows:

```
isakmp identity {address ¦ hostname}
```

The command parameters have the following meanings:

Command Parameter	Description
address	Sets the IKE identity to the IP address of the interface that is used to communicate with the remote peer during IKE negotiations for preshared keys.
	This keyword is typically used when only one interface will be used by the peer for IKE negotiations and the IP address is known.
hostname	Sets the IKE identity to the host name concatenated with the domain name (for example, myhost.domain.com).
	This keyword should be used if more than one interface on the peer might be used for IKE negotiations or if the interface's IP address is unknown (such as with dynamically assigned IP addresses).

If you use the host name identity method, you might need to specify the host name for the remote peer if a domain name server (DNS) is not available for name resolution using the **name** command. The command syntax is as follows:

```
name ip_address name
```

The command parameters and syntax have the following meanings:

Command Parameter	Description
ip_address	Specifies the IP address of the host being named.
name	Specifies the name assigned to the IP address. Allowable characters are **a** to **z**, **A** to **Z**, **0** to **9**, and the underscore. The name cannot start with a number. If the name is more than 16 characters long, the **name** command fails.

Example 17-3 shows PIX 1 configuring a name for PIX 2.

Example 17-3 *PIX 1 Configuring a Name for PIX 2*

```
Pix1(config)# name PIX2.domain.com 192.168.2.2
```

Configuring Preshared Keys

You configure a preshared authentication key with the **isakmp key** configuration command. You must configure this key whenever you specify preshared keys in an IKE policy. Use the **no** form of this command to delete a preshared authentication key. The command syntax is as follows:

```
isakmp key keystring address peer-address [netmask mask]
isakmp key keystring hostname peer-hostname
```

The command parameters and syntax have the following meanings:

Command Parameter	Description
keystring	Specifies the preshared key. Use any combination of alphanumeric characters up to 128 bytes. This preshared key must be identical at both peers.
address	Specifies that the remote peer IKE identity was set with its IP address.
peer-address	Specifies the IP address of the remote peer. The address of 0.0.0.0 can be entered as a wildcard, indicating that the key could be used by any IPSec peer with a matching key.

continues

Command Parameter	Description
hostname	Specifies that the remote IKE identity was set with its host name.
peer-hostname	Specifies the host name of the remote peer. This is the peer's host name concatenated with its domain name (for example, myhost.domain.com).
netmask *mask*	(Optional) Specifies the netmask. The netmask 0.0.0.0 can be entered as a wildcard along with an address of 0.0.0.0, indicating that the key could be used for any peer that does not have a key associated with its specific IP address.

A wildcard peer address and netmask of 0.0.0.0 0.0.0.0 may be configured to share the preshared key among many peers. However, Cisco strongly recommends using a unique key for each peer.

NOTE As with any IPSec peer using preshared keys, the same preshared key must be configured on each pair of IPSec peers when using preshared keys for IKE authentication. It is highly recommended that a different preshared key be configured on each pair of IPSec peers. Using the same preshared key for more than one pair of IPSec peers presents a security risk and is not recommended.

Step 4: Verify the IKE Configuration

You can use the **show isakmp [policy]** command to display configured and default policies. The resultant IKE policy for PIX 1 is shown in Example 17-4 (PIX 2's configuration is identical).

Example 17-4 *IKE Policy for PIX 1*

```
Pix1# show isakmp policy
Protection suite of priority 100
      encryption algorithm:   DES - Data Encryption Standard (56-bit keys)
      hash algorithm:         Message Digest 5
      authentication method:  Pre-Shared Key
      Diffie-Hellman group:   #1 (768 bit)
      lifetime:               86400 seconds, no volume limit
Default protection suite
      encryption algorithm:   DES - Data Encryption Standard (56-bit keys)
      hash algorithm:         Secure Hash Standard
```

Example 17-4 *IKE Policy for PIX 1 (Continued)*

```
        authentication method:   Rivest-Shamir-Adleman Signature
        Diffie-Hellman group:    #1 (768 bit)
        lifetime:                86400 seconds, no volume limit
```

The **show isakmp** command displays configured policies much as they would appear with the **write terminal** command, as shown in Example 17-5.

Example 17-5 *Policies Configured with **show isakmp***

```
Pix1# show isakmp
isakmp enable outside
isakmp policy 100 authentication rsa-sig
isakmp policy 100 encryption 3des
isakmp policy 100 hash sha
isakmp policy 100 group 1
isakmp policy 10 lifetime 86400
```

The **write terminal** command displays configured policies. Example 17-6 is a concatenated example.

Example 17-6 *Policies Configured with **write terminal***

```
Pix1# write terminal
hostname Pix1
isakmp enable outside
isakmp key cisco1234 address 192.168.2.2 netmask 255.255.255.255
isakmp policy 100 authentication pre-share
isakmp policy 100 encryption des
isakmp policy 100 hash sha
isakmp policy 100 group 1
isakmp policy 100 lifetime 86400
```

Here the preshared key is cisco1234, and the peer is PIX 2 at 192.168.2.2.

Task 3: Configure IPSec

The next major task in configuring PIX Firewall IPSec is to configure the IPSec parameters previously gathered. This section presents the steps used to configure IPSec. The general tasks and commands used to configure IPSec encryption on PIX Firewalls are summarized as follows. Subsequent sections discuss each configuration step in detail.

Step 1   Configure crypto access lists with the **access-list** command.

Step 2   Configure transform set suites with the **crypto ipsec transform-set** command.

Step 3   (Optional) Configure global IPSec security association lifetimes with the **crypto ipsec security-association lifetime** command.

Step 4 Configure crypto maps with the **crypto map** command.

Step 5 Apply crypto maps to the terminating/originating interface with the **crypto map** *map-name* **interface** *interface* command.

Step 6 Verify IPSec configuration with the variety of available **show** commands.

Table 17-2 summarizes IPSec encryption policy details that will be configured in examples in this chapter.

Table 17-2 *IPSec Policies for Two Peers*

Parameter	Peer A Value	Peer B Value
Transform set	Authentication Header (AH)-MD5, Encapsulating Security Payload (ESP)-DES	AH-MD5, ESP-DES
IPSec mode	Tunnel	Tunnel
Hash algorithm	MD5	MD5
Peer host name	PIX 2	PIX 1
Peer interface	Ethernet 0 (outside)	Ethernet 0 (outside)
Peer IP address	192.168.2.2	192.168.1.2
IP address of hosts to be protected	10.1.1.0	10.2.1.0
Traffic (packet) type to be encrypted	TCP	TCP
SA establishment	**ipsec-isakmp**	**ipsec-isakmp**

Step 1: Create Crypto Access Lists

Crypto access lists are used to define which IP traffic is or is not protected by IPSec. Crypto access lists perform the following functions for IPSec:

- Indicate the data flow to be protected by IPSec
- Select outbound traffic to be protected by IPSec
- Process inbound traffic in order to filter out and discard traffic that should have been protected by IPSec
- Determine whether to accept requests for IPSec security associations for the requested data flows when processing IKE negotiations

You must use access lists to create crypto access lists. The crypto access lists identify the traffic flows to be protected. Although the crypto access list syntax is the same as that for regular access lists, the meanings are slightly different for crypto access lists: **permit** specifies that matching packets must be encrypted, and **deny** specifies that matching packets need not be encrypted. Crypto access lists behave similar to an access list applied to outbound traffic on a PIX Firewall interface.

You can configure interesting traffic with crypto access lists. You define a crypto access list with the **access-list** configuration command. To delete an access list, use the **no** form of the command. The command syntax is as follows:

```
access-list acl_name [deny | permit] protocol src_addr src_mask
   [operator port [port]] dest_addr dest_mask [operator port [port]]
```

The command parameters and syntax have the following meanings:

Command Parameter	Description
acl_name	Specifies the name or number of an access list.
deny	Does not select a packet for IPSec protection. Prevents traffic from being protected by crypto in the context of that particular crypto map entry.
permit	Selects a packet for IPSec protection. Causes all IP traffic that matches the specified conditions to be protected by crypto, using the policy described by the corresponding crypto map entry.
protocol	Specifies the name or number of an IP protocol. It can be one of the keywords **icmp**, **ip**, **tcp**, or **udp**, or an integer representing an IP protocol number, or an integer in the range 1 to 254 representing an IP protocol number. To match any Internet protocol, use the keyword **ip**.
src_addr *dest_addr*	Specifies the address of the network or host from which the packet is being sent or from where the packet was received. There are three other ways to specify the source or destination: • Use a 32-bit quantity in four-part, dotted-decimal format. • Use the keyword **any** as an abbreviation for a *source* and *source-netmask* or *destination* and *destination netmask* of 0.0.0.0 0.0.0.0. This keyword is normally not recommended for use with IPSec. • Use **host** *source* or **host** *destination* as an abbreviation for a *source* and *source-netmask* of 255.255.255.255 or a *destination* and *destination-netmask* of destination 255.255.255.255.

continues

Command Parameter	Description
src_mask *dest_mask*	Specifies the netmask bits (mask) to be applied to source or destination. There are three other ways to specify the source or destination netmask: • Use a 32-bit quantity in four-part, dotted-decimal format. Place zeroes in the bit positions you want to ignore. • Use the keyword **any** as an abbreviation for a *source* and *source-netmask* or *destination* and *destination-netmask* of 0.0.0.0 0.0.0.0. This keyword is not recommended. • Use **host** *source* or **host** *destination* as an abbreviation for a *source* and *source-netmask* of source 255.255.255.255 or a *destination* and *destination-netmask* of destination 255.255.255.255.
operator	(Optional) Specifies a port or a port range to compare source or destination ports. Possible operands include **lt** (less than), **gt** (greater than), **eq** (equal), **neq** (not equal), and **range** (inclusive range). The **range** operator requires two port numbers. Each of the other operators requires one port number.
port	IP service(s) you permit based on TCP or UDP protocol. Specify ports by either a literal name or a number in the range of 0 to 65535. You can specify all ports by not specifying a port value.

Here are some additional details for access lists:

- PIX Firewall version 5.0 supports the IP protocol only with granularity to the network, subnet, and host level.

- PIX Firewall version 5.1 supports granularity to either the TCP or UDP protocol and corresponding port.

- The use of port ranges can dramatically increase the number of IPSec tunnels that PIX can originate or terminate. A new tunnel is created for each port.

Any unprotected inbound traffic that matches a permit entry in the crypto access list for a crypto map entry flagged as IPSec will be dropped.

If you want certain traffic to receive one combination of IPSec protection (for example, authentication only) and other traffic to receive a different combination of IPSec protection (for example, both authentication and encryption), you need to create two different crypto access lists to define the two different types of traffic.

CAUTION Cisco recommends that you avoid using the any keyword to specify source or destination addresses. The **permit any any** statement is strongly discouraged because it causes all outbound traffic to be protected (as well as all traffic sent to the peer specified in the corresponding crypto map entry) and requires protection for all inbound traffic. Then, all inbound packets that lack IPSec protection are silently dropped. Also, you might experience increased CPU utilization and accompanying network throughput degradation.

Try to be as precise as possible when defining which packets to protect in a crypto access list. If you must use the **any** keyword in a **permit** statement, you must preface that statement with a series of **deny** statements to filter out any traffic (that would otherwise fall within that **permit** statement) that you do not want to be protected.

See the "Step 3: Create Crypto Access Lists" section of Chapter 16 for more details on how to configure crypto access lists.

Configure Symmetrical Crypto Access Lists

Cisco recommends that you configure mirror-image crypto access lists for use by IPSec. The crypto access lists on each peer should be symmetrical. For example, the source criteria of PIX 1 should be exactly the same as the destination criteria of PIX 1, and the destination criteria of PIX 1 should be exactly the same as the source criteria of PIX 2. On each PIX Firewall, both inbound and outbound traffic is evaluated against the same outbound IPSec access list. The access list's criteria are applied in the forward direction to traffic exiting the PIX Firewall and are applied in the reverse direction to traffic entering the PIX Firewall. When a PIX Firewall receives encrypted packets from an IPSec peer, it uses the same access list to determine which inbound packets to decrypt by viewing the source and destination addresses in the access list in reverse order.

Example 17-7 shows a crypto access list pair and illustrates why symmetrical access lists are recommended (refer to Figure 17-1 for a network diagram).

Example 17-7 *A Crypto Access List Pair*

```
Pix1(config)# show static
static (inside,outside) 192.168.1.9 10.1.1.4 netmask 255.255.255.255 0 0
pix1(config)# show access-list
access-list 110 permit ip host 192.168.1.9 host 192.168.2.9

Pix2(config)# show static
static (inside,outside) 192.168.2.9 10.2.1.4 netmask 255.255.255.255 0 0
Pix2(config)# show access-list
access-list 101 permit ip host 192.168.2.9 host 192.168.1.9
```

In the example for Site 1, IPSec protection is applied to traffic between the hosts at Site 1 and Site 2. Network address translation is configured on the PIX Firewalls. The host at Site 1 of 10.1.1.4 is statically mapped to global address 192.168.1.10 on PIX 1. The host at Site 2 of 10.2.1.4 is statically mapped to global address 192.168.2.10 on PIX 2. The access lists use the global address in the static command to specify interesting traffic. For traffic from the Site 1 host to the Site 2 host, the access list entry on PIX 1 is evaluated as follows:

- The source is host 192.168.1.10 (statically mapped to 10.1.1.4).
- The destination is host 192.168.2.10 (statically mapped to 10.2.1.4).

For incoming traffic from the Site 2 host to the Site 1 host, the same access list entry on PIX 1 is evaluated as follows:

- The source is host 192.168.2.10 (statically mapped to 10.2.1.4).
- The destination is host 192.168.1.10 (statically mapped to 10.1.1.4).

Step 2: Configure Transform Set Suites

The next major step in configuring PIX Firewall IPSec is to use the IPSec security policy to define a transform set. A *transform set* is a combination of individual IPSec transforms that enact a security policy for traffic. During the IKE IPSec security association, negotiation occurs during quick mode in IKE Phase 2, when the peers agree to use a particular transform set for protecting a particular data flow. Transform sets combine the following IPSec factors:

- A mechanism for payload authentication—the AH transform
- A mechanism for payload encryption—the ESP transform
- The IPSec mode, either transport or tunnel

You define a transform set with the **crypto ipsec transform-set** configuration command. To delete a transform set, you use the **no** form of the command. The command syntax is as follows:

```
crypto ipsec transform-set transform-set-name transform1
  [transform2 [transform3]]
```

The command parameters and syntax have the following meanings:

Command Parameter	Description
transform-set-name	Specifies the name of the transform set to create (or modify).
transform1 *transform2* *transform3*	Specify up to three transforms. Transforms define the IPSec security protocol(s) and algorithm(s). Each transform represents an IPSec security protocol (ESP, AH, or both) plus the algorithm you want to use.

Up to three transforms can be in a set. The default mode for each transform is tunnel. Sets are limited to up to one AH and up to two ESP transforms. Make sure you configure matching transform sets between IPSec peers.

When IKE is not used to establish security associations, a single transform set must be used. The transform set is not negotiated. If you specify an ESP protocol in a transform set, you can specify just an ESP encryption transform or both an ESP encryption transform and an ESP authentication transform.

The PIX Firewall supports the IPSec transforms shown in Table 17-3.

Table 17-3   *PIX-Supported IPSec Transforms*

Transform	Description
ah-md5-hmac	AH-HMAC-MD5 transform used for authentication
ah-sha-hmac	AH-HMAC-SHA transform used for authentication
esp-des	ESP transform using DES cipher (56 bits)
esp-3des	ESP transform using 3DES(EDE) cipher (168 bits)
esp-md5-hmac	ESP transform with HMAC-MD5 authentication used with an **esp-des** or **esp-3des** transform to provide additional integrity of ESP packets
esp-sha-hmac	ESP transform with HMAC-SHA authentication used with an **esp-des** or **esp-3des** transform to provide additional integrity for ESP packets

Choosing Transforms

Choosing IPSec transform combinations can be complex. The following tips might help you select transforms that are appropriate for your situation:

- If you want to provide data confidentiality, include an ESP encryption transform.
- Also consider including an ESP authentication transform or an AH transform to provide authentication services for the transform set.
- To ensure data authentication for the outer IP header as well as the data, include an AH transform.
- To ensure data authentication (using either ESP or AH), you can choose from the MD5 or SHA (HMAC keyed hash variants) authentication algorithms.
- The SHA algorithm is generally considered stronger than MD5, but it is slower.

Transform Set Examples

Transform sets are limited to one AH transform and one or two ESP transforms. Some suggested combinations are shown in Examples 17-8 and 17-9.

Example 17-8 *ESP Encryption with 56-bit DES, and ESP with SHA-1 for Authentication in Tunnel Mode (the Default) to Give Strong Security and Higher Performance*

```
esp-des and esp-sha-hmac
```

Example 17-9 *ESP Encryption with 3DES, and ESP with SHA-1 for Authentication in Tunnel Mode (the Default) to Give Stronger Security*

```
esp-3des esp-sha-hmac
```

NOTE   As with Cisco routers, AH is seldom used with ESP because authentication is available with the **esp-sha-hmac** and **esp-md5-hmac** transforms. AH is also incompatible with network address translation (NAT) and port address translation (PAT) because they change the IP address in the TCP/IP packet header, breaking the authentication established by AH. AH can be used for data authentication alone, but it does not protect the confidentiality of the packet contents because it does not encrypt.

Transform Set Negotiation

Transform sets are negotiated during quick mode in IKE Phase 2 using previously configured transform sets. You can configure multiple transform sets and then specify one or more of the transform sets in a crypto map entry. You should configure the transforms from most-secure to least-secure as per your policy. The transform set defined in the crypto map entry is used in the IPSec security association negotiation to protect the data flows specified by that crypto map entry's access list.

During the negotiation, the peers search for a transform set that is the same at both peers, as shown in Figure 17-2. When such a transform set is found, it is selected and is applied to the protected traffic as part of both peers' IPSec security associations. IPSec peers agree on one transform proposal per SA (unidirectional).

Step 3: Configure Global IPSec Security Association Lifetimes

The IPSec security association lifetime determines how long IPSec SAs remain valid before they are renegotiated. The PIX Firewall supports a global lifetime value that applies to all crypto maps. The global lifetime value can be overridden within a crypto map entry. The lifetimes apply only to security associations established via IKE. Manually established security associations do not expire. When a security association expires, a new one is negotiated without interrupting the data flow.

Figure 17-2 *A Transform Set Negotiated Between IPSec Peers*

You can change global IPSec security association lifetime values by using the **crypto ipsec security-association lifetime** configuration command. To reset a lifetime to the default value, use the **no** form of the command. The command syntax is as follows:

```
crypto ipsec security-association lifetime {seconds seconds |
  kilobytes kilobytes}
```

The command parameters and syntax have the following meanings:

Command Parameter	Description
seconds *seconds*	Specifies the number of seconds a security association will live before it expires. The default is 28,800 seconds (8 hours).
kilobytes *kilobytes*	Specifies the volume of traffic (in kilobytes) that can pass between IPSec peers using a given security association before that security association expires. The default is 4,608,000 KB (10 MBps for 1 hour).

Cisco recommends that you use the default lifetime values. Individual SAs can be configured using crypto maps, which are covered the section "Configuring Crypto Maps" later in this chapter.

Global IPSec SA Lifetime Examples

A general principle in cryptanalysis is that, given enough time or enough traffic protected under a single key, an attacker can break that key. Over time, a key's effective lifetime is reduced by advances made in cryptanalysis. The PIX Firewall allows you to fine-tune the key lifetime with the **crypto ipsec security-association lifetime** command. Consider the sample global IPSec security association lifetime shown in Example 17-10.

Example 17-10 *Sample Global IPSec Security Association Lifetime*

```
crypto ipsec security-association lifetime kilobytes 1382400
```

This lifetime is about 3 MBps for one hour, adequate for a PIX Firewall behind a perimeter router with an E1 wide-area network (WAN) interface to an ISP at 2.048 MBps. Example 17-11 shows a lifetime of 15 minutes, which is rather short but provides less time for breaking a key.

Example 17-11 *Sample Lifetime of 15 Minutes*

```
crypto ipsec security-association lifetime seconds 900
```

Before a key expires, IKE negotiates another one based on the IPSec SA lifetime value to allow for a smooth transition from key to key without having to tear down connections.

Step 4: Create Crypto Maps

Crypto map entries must be created for IPSec to set up SAs for traffic flows that must be encrypted. Crypto map entries created for IPSec set up security association parameters, tying together the various parts configured for IPSec, including the following:

- Which traffic should be protected by IPSec (crypto access list)
- The granularity of the traffic to be protected by a set of security associations
- Where IPSec-protected traffic should be sent (who the remote IPSec peer is)
- The local address to be used for the IPSec traffic
- What IPSec security type should be applied to this traffic (transform sets)
- Whether security associations are established manually or via IKE
- IPSec security association lifetime
- Other parameters that might be necessary to define an IPSec security association

The following sections consider crypto map parameters, examine the **crypto map** command, show how to configure crypto maps, and consider examples of crypto maps.

Crypto Map Parameters

You can apply only one crypto map set to a single interface. The crypto map set can include a combination of IPSec using IKE and IPSec with manually configured SA entries. Multiple interfaces can share the same crypto map set if you want to apply the same policy to multiple interfaces.

If you create more than one crypto map entry for a given interface, use the sequence number (*seq-num*) of each map entry to rank the map entries: the lower the *seq-num,* the higher the priority. At the interface that has the crypto map set, traffic is evaluated against higher-priority map entries first. You must create multiple crypto map entries for a given interface if any of the following conditions exist:

- Different data flows are to be handled by separate IPSec peers.

- You want to apply different IPSec security to different types of traffic (to the same or separate IPSec peers)—for example, if you want traffic between one set of subnets to be authenticated and traffic between another set of subnets to be both authenticated and encrypted. In this case, the different types of traffic should have been defined in two separate access lists, and you must create a separate crypto map entry for each crypto access list.

- You are not using IKE to establish a particular set of security associations, and you want to specify multiple access list entries. You must create separate access lists (one per permit entry) and specify a separate crypto map entry for each access list.

Backup Gateways

You can define multiple remote peers by using crypto maps to allow for gateway redundancy. If one peer fails, there will still be a protected path. The peer that packets are actually sent to is determined by the last peer that the PIX Firewall heard from (received either traffic or a negotiation request from) for a given data flow. If the attempt fails with the first peer, IKE tries the next peer on the crypto map list.

If you are not sure how to configure each crypto map parameter to guarantee compatibility with other peers, you might consider configuring dynamic crypto maps. Dynamic crypto maps are useful when the establishment of the IPSec tunnels is initiated by the remote peer (such as in the case of an IPSec PIX Firewall fronting a server). They are not useful if the establishment of the IPSec tunnels is locally initiated because the dynamic crypto maps are policy templates, not complete statements of policy. (The access lists in any referenced dynamic crypto map entry are used for crypto packet filtering.)

A dynamic crypto map entry is essentially a crypto map entry without all the parameters configured. It acts as a policy template in which the missing parameters are later dynamically configured (as the result of an IPSec negotiation) to match a peer's requirements. This allows peers to exchange IPSec traffic with the PIX Firewall even if the PIX Firewall does not have a crypto map entry specifically configured to meet all the peer's requirements.

Configuring Crypto Maps

You use the **crypto map** configuration command to create or modify a crypto map entry. You set the crypto map entries referencing dynamic maps to be the lowest-priority entries in a crypto map set (that is, to have the highest sequence numbers). You use the **no** form of this command to delete a crypto map entry or set. The command syntax is as follows:

```
crypto map map-name seq-num {ipsec-isakmp | ipsec-manual}
  [dynamic dynamic-map-name]
crypto map map-name seq-num match address acl_name
crypto map map-name seq-num set peer {hostname | ip-address}
crypto map map-name seq-num set pfs [group1 | group2]
crypto map map-name seq-num set security-association lifetime {seconds seconds ¦
  kilobytes kilobytes}
crypto map map-name seq-num set transform-set transform-set-name1
  [transform-set-name6]
crypto map map-name client authentication aaa-server-name
crypto map map-name client configuration address {initiate | respond}
```

The command parameters and syntax have the following meanings:

Command Parameter	Description
map-name	Assigns a name to the crypto map set.
seq-num	Assigns a number to the crypto map entry.
ipsec-manual	Indicates that IKE will not be used to establish the IPSec security associations for protecting the traffic specified by this crypto map entry.
ipsec-isakmp	Indicates that IKE will be used to establish the IPSec security associations for protecting the traffic specified by this crypto map entry.
acl_name	Identifies the named encryption access list. This name should match the name argument of the named encryption access list being matched.
match address	Specifies an access list for a crypto map entry.
set peer	Specifies an IPSec peer in a crypto map entry. Specify multiple peers by repeating this command. The peer is the terminating interface of the IPSec peer.
hostname	Specifies a peer by its host name. This is the peer's host name concatenated with its domain name, such as myhost.example.com.
ip-address	Specifies a peer by its IP address.

Command Parameter	Description
set pfs	Specifies that IPSec should ask for perfect forward secrecy (PFS). With PFS, every time a new security association is negotiated, a new Diffie-Hellman exchange occurs. PFS provides additional security for secret key generation at a cost of additional processing.
group1	Specifies that IPSec should use the 768-bit Diffie-Hellman prime modulus group when performing the new Diffie-Hellman exchange. Used with the **esp-des** transform.
group2	Specifies that IPSec should use the 1024-bit Diffie-Hellman prime modulus group when performing the new Diffie-Hellman exchange. Used with the **esp-3des** transform.
set transform-set	Specifies which transform sets can be used with the crypto map entry. List multiple transform sets in order of priority, with the highest-priority (most secure) transform set first.
transform-set-name	Specifies the name of the transform set. For an ipsec-manual crypto map entry, you can specify only one transform set. For an ipsec-isakmp or dynamic crypto map entry, you can specify up to six transform sets.
kilobytes *kilobytes*	Specifies the volume of traffic (in kilobytes) that can pass between peers using a given security association before that SA expires. The default is 4,608,000 KB. The security association lifetime in a crypto map entry overrides the global security association lifetime value.
seconds *seconds*	Specifies the number of seconds a security association will live before it expires. The default is 3,600 seconds (one hour).
dynamic	(Optional) Specifies that this crypto map entry references a preexisting static crypto map. If you use this keyword, none of the crypto map configuration commands will be available.
dynamic-map-name	(Optional) Specifies the name of the dynamic crypto map set that should be used as the policy template.

continues

Command Parameter	Description
aaa-server-name	Specifies the name of the AAA server that will authenticate the user during IKE authentication. The two AAA server options available are TACACS+ and RADIUS.
initiate	Indicates that the PIX Firewall attempts to set IP addresses for each peer.
respond	Indicates that the PIX Firewall accepts requests for IP addresses from any requesting peer.

Here are some additional guidelines for configuring crypto maps:

- Identify the crypto map with a unique crypto map name and sequence number.
- Use *ipsec-isakmp* for CA server support.
- After you define crypto map entries, you can assign the crypto map set to interfaces using the **crypto map** *map-name* **interface** *interface-name* command.

NOTE　Access lists for crypto map entries tagged as **ipsec-manual** are restricted to a single permit entry, and subsequent entries are ignored. The security associations established by that particular crypto map entry are only for a single data flow. To be able to support multiple manually established security associations for different kinds of traffic, define multiple crypto access lists and then apply each one to a separate **ipsec-manual** crypto map entry. Each access list should include one permit statement defining what traffic to protect.

Example 17-12 illustrates a crypto map with two peers specified for redundancy purposes.

Example 17-12　*A Crypto Map with Two Peers Specified for Redundancy*

```
Pix1(config)# crypto map mymap 10 ipsec-isakmp
Pix1(config)# match address 151
Pix1(config)# set peer 192.168.2.2
Pix1(config)# set peer 192.168.3.2
Pix1(config)# set pfs group1
Pix1(config)# set transform-set mytransform
Pix1(config)# set security-association lifetime 2700
```

If the first peer cannot be contacted, the second peer will be used. There is no limit to the number of redundant peers that can be configured.

Setting Manual Keys

You can configure IPSec SAs manually and not use IKE to set up the SA. Cisco recommends that you use IKE to set up the SAs because it is very difficult to ensure that the SA values match between peers, and D-H is a vastly more secure method to generate secret keys between peers. If you must, you can use **crypto map** commands to manually specify the IPSec session keys and other SA parameters within a crypto map entry.

Security associations established via the **crypto map** command do not expire (unlike security associations established via IKE). Session keys at one peer must match the session keys at the remote peer. If you change a session key, the security association using the key will be deleted and reinitialized. See the "Configuring Manual IPSec" section of the "Configuring IPSec" chapter of the *Configuration Guide for the Cisco Secure PIX Firewall* for more details on manual IPSec.

Step 5: Apply Crypto Maps to Interfaces

The last step in configuring IPSec is to apply the crypto map set to an interface. You apply the crypto map to the PIX Firewall's interface connected to the Internet with the **crypto map** command in interface configuration mode. Use the **no** form of the command to remove the crypto map set from the interface. The command syntax is as follows:

```
crypto map map-name interface interface-name
```

The command parameters have the following meanings:

Command Parameter	Description
map-name	The name of the crypto map set.
interface *interface-name*	Specifies the identifying interface to be used by the PIX Firewall to identify itself to peers. If IKE is enabled and you are using a CA to obtain certificates, this should be the interface with the address specified in the CA certificates.

IPSec tunnels can be terminated on any PIX Firewall interface. This does not mean you terminate traffic coming from the outside on the inside interface. Traffic terminated on the inside interface is traffic from the inside network. Traffic terminated on the outside is traffic from the outside. Traffic terminated on a DMZ is traffic from the DMZ.

As soon as you apply the crypto map, the security association database should initialize in system memory. The SAs are available for setup when traffic defined by the crypto access list is transmitted or received.

Only one crypto map set can be assigned to an interface. If multiple crypto map entries have the same *map-name* but a different *seq-num,* they are considered part of the same set and are all applied to the interface. The crypto map entry with the lowest *seq-num* is considered the highest priority and is evaluated first.

Example 17-13 is an example of applying a crypto map to an outside interface.

Example 17-13 *An Example of Applying a Crypto Map to an Outside Interface*

```
crypto map mymap interface outside
```

Step 6: Verify IPSec Configuration

The last step in configuring IPSec on the PIX Firewall is to verify the IPSec configuration using available **show** commands.

You can view all configured access lists with the **show access-list** command. In Example 17-14, the hitcnt=0 value shows that no traffic has been evaluated against this access list.

Example 17-14 *Showing Configured Access Lists with the **show access-list** Command*

```
Pix2# show access-list
access-list 101 permit ip host 192.168.2.9 host 192.168.1.9 (hitcnt=0)
```

You can view the currently defined transform sets with the **show crypto ipsec transform-set** command. This command has the following syntax:

```
show crypto ipsec transform-set [tag transform-set-name]
```

The command parameter has the following meaning:

Command Parameter	Description
tag *transform-set-name*	(Optional) Shows only the transform sets with the specified *transform-set-name*

If no keyword is used, all transform sets configured at the PIX Firewall are displayed. Example 17-15 shows the transform sets with the names mine and vrysecure.

Example 17-15 *Transform Sets with the Names mine and vrysecure*

```
Pixfirewall# show crypto ipsec transform-set
Transform set mine: { esp-des  }
will negotiate = { Tunnel,  },
Transform set vrysecure: { esp-3des ah-sha-hmac
esp-sha-hmac }
will negotiate = { Tunnel,  },
```

You can use the **show crypto ipsec security-association lifetime** command to view the current global IPSec SA lifetime. In Example 17-16, the global ipsec security-association lifetime is 2305000 KB and 3600 seconds.

Example 17-16 *A Global ipsec security-association lifetime of 2305000 KB and 3600 Seconds*

```
Pix1# show crypto ipsec security-association lifetime
Security-association lifetime: 2305000 kilobytes/3600 seconds
```

You can use the **show crypto map** command to view the crypto map configuration. If no keywords are used, all crypto maps configured at the PIX Firewall arc displayed. The command syntax is as follows:

```
show crypto map [interface interface | tag map-name]
```

The command parameters and syntax have the following meanings:

Command Parameter	Description
interface *interface*	(Optional) Shows only the crypto map set applied to the specified *interface*
tag *map-name*	(Optional) Shows only the crypto map set with the specified *map-name*

Example 17-17 shows an example of crypto maps for PIX 1 and PIX 2. Note how the crypto map pulls together the six IPSec-related values.

Example 17-17 *Crypto Maps for PIX 1 and PIX 2*

```
Pix1(config)# show crypto map
Crypto Map "peer2" 10 ipsec-isakmp
   Peer = 192.168.2.2
   access-list 101 permit ip host 192.168.1.9 host 192.168.2.9 (hitcnt=0)
   Current peer: 192.168.2.2
   Security association lifetime: 4608000 kilobytes/28800 seconds
   PFS (Y/N): N
   Transform sets={ pix2, }

Pix2(config)# show crypto map
Crypto Map "peer1" 10 ipsec-isakmp
   Peer = 192.168.1.2
   access-list 101 permit ip host 192.168.2.9 host 192.168.1.9 (hitcnt=0)
   Current peer: 192.168.1.2
   Security association lifetime: 4608000 kilobytes/28800 seconds
   PFS (Y/N): N
   Transform sets={ pix1, }
```

Task 4: Test and Verify the Overall IPSec Configuration

The final step in configuring IPSec for preshared keys is to verify that all the IKE and IPSec values were configured correctly and to test it to ensure that it works properly. The PIX Firewall contains a number of **show**, **clear**, and **debug** commands that are useful for testing and verifying IKE and IPSec, which are summarized in this section.

Test and Verify IKE Configuration

You can use the commands summarized in Table 17-4 to observe IKE configuration and operation.

Table 17-4 *Commands Used to Observe IKE*

Command	Description
show isakmp	Displays configured IKE policies in a format similar to a **write terminal** command
show isakmp policy	Displays default and any configured IKE policies

Test and Verify IPSec Configuration

You can test and verify IPSec configuration on the PIX Firewall with the commands listed in Table 17-5.

Table 17-5 *Commands Used to Observe IKE*

Command	Description
show access-list	Lists the **access-list** command statements in the configuration. Used to verify that crypto access lists select interesting traffic. Displays the number of packets that match the access list.
show crypto map	Displays crypto access lists assigned to a crypto map. Displays configured crypto map parameters.
show crypto ipsec transform-set	Displays configured IPSec transform sets.
show crypto ipsec security-association lifetime	Displays correct global IPSec SA lifetime values.

Monitor and Manage IKE and IPSec Communications

You can observe IKE and IPSec setup and monitor and manage IKE and IPSec communications between the PIX Firewall and IPSec peers with the commands listed in Table 17-6.

Table 17-6 *Commands Used to Observe IKE*

Command	Description
show isakmp sa	Displays the current status of IKE security associations.
show crypto ipsec sa	Displays the current status of IPSec security associations. Useful for ensuring that traffic is being encrypted.
clear crypto isakmp sa	Clears IKE security associations.
clear crypto ipsec sa	Clears IPSec security associations.
debug crypto isakmp	Displays IKE communications between the PIX Firewall and IPSec peers.
debug crypto ipsec	Displays IPSec communications between the PIX Firewall and IPSec peers.

The **show isakmp sa** command is useful for viewing all current IKE SAs at a peer, as shown in Example 17-18.

Example 17-18 *The show isakmp sa Command, Used to View All Current IKE SAs at a Peer*

```
Pix1# show isakmp sa
    dst            src            state       conn-id   slot
  192.168.1.2    192.168.2.2     QM_IDLE          93      0
```

The **clear isakmp** command clears active IKE connections, as shown in Example 17-19.

Example 17-19 *The clear isakmp Command, Used to Clear Active IKE Connections*

```
Pix1# show crypto isakmp sa
    dst            src            state       conn-id   slot
  192.168.1.2    192.168.2.2     QM_IDLE          93      0
Pix1# clear crypto isakmp 93
2w4d: ISADB: reaper checking SA,
Pix1# show crypto isakmp sa
    dst            src            state       conn-id   slot
```

Summary

This section summarizes the main points of this chapter:

- Determine the types of traffic that will be encrypted and the hosts or networks that will be protected, and specify the IPSec gateways that will terminate the tunnels as part of planning for IPSec.

- You use the **isakmp policy** command to specify preshared keys for authentication and to configure IKE policy parameters.

- Some IPSec transforms require you to make trade-offs between high performance and stronger security.

- IPSec transforms are grouped into sets, and the sets can be grouped into supersets in crypto maps, where you place the strongest security transform sets first.

- Crypto access lists act like outgoing access lists, where permit means encrypt.

- Crypto access lists should mirror each other between peers.

- Crypto maps pull together all IPSec details and are applied to interfaces, enabling IPSec SA setup.

- The PIX Firewall can terminate IPSec tunnels on any interface from traffic coming in on that interface.

- The **show crypto map** command shows a summary of all IPSec parameters used to set up IPSec SAs.

- The configuration procedures and commands are nearly identical between the PIX Firewall and Cisco routers. A key difference is that the PIX Firewall commands do not have a hierarchy with submodes.

Case Study: Configuring PIX Firewall IPSec for Preshared Keys

This case study illustrates how to configure IPSec as taught in this chapter in the hypothetical XYZ Company. Read the case study scenario, examine the topology diagram, and read the security policy. Then analyze the sample configuration to see how the security policy statements are enacted for the PIX Firewalls.

Case Study Scenario

XYZ Company wants to use PIX Firewalls to create a secure VPN over the Internet between sites. The company wants you to configure a secure VPN gateway using IPSec between two PIX Firewalls to use preshared keys and allow access to the Web server.

Topology

Figure 17-3 illustrates the portion of the XYZ network that is configured in this case study. Note that the focus here is on the PIX Firewall at each site.

Figure 17-3 *XYZ Company Configures a Secure VPN Gateway Between PIX Firewalls*

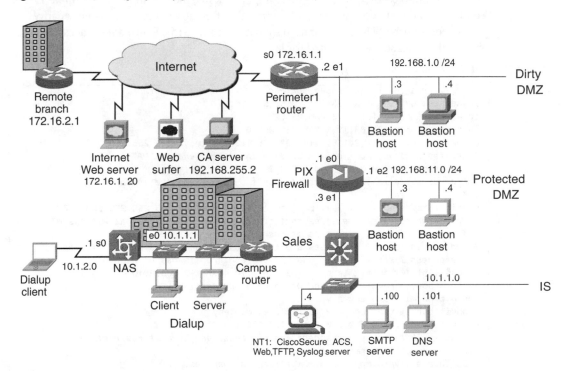

Network Security Policy

The network security policy that XYZ Company wants to implement is as follows:

- Use the Internet to connect a branch office to the corporate network for casual traffic.
- Authenticate data traffic between the corporate network and branch offices over the Internet to ensure that no one is inserting or changing packets in transit.
- Use IKE preshared keys and MD5 for authentication.
- Ensure data integrity of traffic between the corporate network and branch offices over the Internet using 56-bit DES encryption.
- Encrypt Web traffic between internal NT servers at each site.

Sample Configuration for the PIX 1 Firewall

Examine the configuration example shown in Example 17-20 for the PIX 1 and PIX 2 Firewalls of the XYZ Company. The examples implement the network security policy statements related to IPSec network security. One possible configuration of the PIX Firewall for the specified security policy might look like the one shown in Example 17-20. You might choose to configure the PIX Firewall differently to enact the same security policy requirements. The configuration shown is for PIX 515s. Unused interfaces and other unrelated commands were deleted for brevity.

Example 17-20 *PIX 1 Configuration Example*

```
! Configures the IP addresses for each PIX Firewall interface.
ip address outside 192.168.1.1  255.255.255.0
ip address inside 10.1.1.3 255.255.255.0
ip address dmz 192.168.11.1 255.255.255.0
global (outside) 1 192.168.1.10-192.168.1.254 netmask 255.255.255.0
! Creates a global pool on the outside interface, enables NAT.
nat (inside) 1 10.0.0.0 255.0.0.0 0 0
! Creates a static translation between the global and the inside
! Windows NT server.
static (inside,outside) 192.168.1.10 10.1.1.4 netmask 255.255.255.255 0 0
! Crypto access list specifies that traffic between the internal Windows NT
! servers behind PIX Firewalls is encrypted. The source
! and destination IP addresses are the global IP addresses of the statics.
! The access lists for PIX 1 and PIX 2 are mirror images of each other.
access-list 101 permit ip host 192.168.1.10 host 192.168.2.10
! The conduits permit ICMP and Web access for testing.
conduit permit icmp any any
conduit permit tcp host 192.168.1.10 eq www any
route outside 0.0.0.0 0.0.0.0 192.168.1.2 1
! Enables IPSec to bypass access list, access, and conduit restrictions.
sysopt connection permit-ipsec
! Defines a crypto map transform set to use esp-des.
crypto ipsec transform-set pix2 esp-des
crypto map peer2 10 ipsec-isakmp
! Defines the crypto map.
crypto map peer2 10 match address 101
! Defines the crypto map to point to the peer by specifying the peer PIX's
! outside interface IP address.
crypto map peer2 10 set peer 192.168.2.1
! Defines the crypto map to use the transform set.
crypto map peer2 10 set transform-set pix2
! Assigns the crypto map set to the outside PIX interface.
! As soon as the crypto map is assigned to the interface, the IKE and IPSec
! policy is active.
crypto map peer2 interface outside
! Enables IKE on the outside interface.
isakmp enable outside
! Defines the preshared IKE key.
isakmp key cisco123 address 192.168.2.1 netmask 255.255.255.255
! Defines the IKE policy to use preshared keys for authentication.
isakmp policy 10 authentication pre-share
```

Example 17-20 *PIX 1 Configuration Example (Continued)*

```
isakmp policy 10 encryption des
isakmp policy 10 hash sha
! Specifies use of D-H group 1. Could have used D-H group 2 for stronger security
! along with translation esp-3des, but would require more CPU time to execute.
isakmp policy 10 group 1
! Specifies the IKE lifetime.
isakmp policy 10 lifetime 86400
```

Sample Configuration for the PIX 2 Firewall

The example shown in Example 17-21 is a summary of the configuration for PIX 2.

Example 17-21 *PIX 2 Configuration Example*

```
! Configures the IP addresses for each PIX Firewall interface.
ip address outside 192.168.2.1  255.255.255.0
ip address inside 10.2.1.3 255.255.255.0
ip address dmz 192.168.12.1 255.255.255.0
global (outside) 1 192.168.2.10-192.168.2.254 netmask 255.255.255.0
! Creates a global pool on the outside interface, enables NAT.
nat (inside) 1 10.0.0.0 255.0.0.0 0 0
! Creates a static translation between the global and inside Windows NT server.
static (inside,outside) 192.168.2.10 10.2.1.4 netmask 255.255.255.255 0 0
! Crypto access list specifies that traffic between the internal Windows NT
! servers behind PIX Firewalls is encrypted.
! The source and destination IP addresses are the global IP addresses of the
! statics. The access lists for PIX 2 and PIX 1 are mirror images of each other.
access-list 101 permit ip host 192.168.2.10 host 192.168.1.10
! The conduits permit ICMP and Web access for testing.
conduit permit icmp any any
conduit permit tcp host 192.168.2.10 eq www any
route outside 0.0.0.0 0.0.0.0 192.168.2.2 1
! Enables IPSec to bypass access list, access, and conduit restrictions.
sysopt connection permit-ipsec
! Defines a crypto map transform set to use esp-des.
crypto ipsec transform-set pix1 esp-des
crypto map peer1 10 ipsec-isakmp
! Defines the crypto map.
crypto map peer1 10 match address 101
! Defines the crypto map to point to the peer by specifying the peer PIX's
! outside interface IP address.
crypto map peer1 10 set peer 192.168.1.1
! Defines the crypto map to use the transform set.
crypto map peer1 10 set transform-set pix1
! Assigns the crypto map set to the outside PIX interface. As soon as the
! crypto map is assigned to the interface, the IKE and IPSec policy is active.
crypto map peer1 interface outside
! Enables IKE on the outside interface.
isakmp enable outside
! Defines the preshared IKE key.
isakmp key cisco123 address 192.168.2.2 netmask 255.255.255.255
```

continues

Example 17-21 *PIX 2 Configuration Example (Continued)*

```
! Defines the IKE policy to use preshared keys for authentication.
isakmp policy 10 authentication pre-share
isakmp policy 10 encryption des
isakmp policy 10 hash sha
! Specifies use of D-H group 1. Could have used D-H group 2 for stronger security
! along with translation esp-3des, but would require more CPU time to execute.
isakmp policy 10 group 1
! Specifies the IKE lifetime.
isakmp policy 10 lifetime 86400
```

Review Questions

Answer the following review questions, which delve into some of the key facts and concepts covered in this chapter:

1 Name an advantage and a disadvantage of using preshared keys for authentication.

2 What command do you use to enter a preshared key?

3 How do you view IKE policies in the PIX's configuration?

4 How do you enable IKE for one interface and not for another?

5 How many transforms can be defined in a transform set?

6 How do you configure IPSec security association lifetimes on the PIX Firewall?

7 What command do you use to define the traffic flows to be protected?

8 When are the IPSec SAs initialized with IKE configured?

9 How can you view IKE events as they occur between IPSec peers?

10 Why does IKE fail for preshared keys in the following sample configurations?

Example 17-22 *PIX1*

```
crypto isakmp policy 100
  authentication rsa-sig
  group 2
  lifetime 5000

crypto isakmp policy 200
  hash md5

  authentication pre-share
crypto isakmp policy 300
  authentication rsa-encr
  lifetime 10000
```

Example 17-23 *PIX2*

```
crypto isakmp policy 100
  authentication rsa-sig
  group 2
  lifetime 5000

crypto isakmp policy 200
  authentication rsa-sig
  lifetime 10000

crypto isakmp policy 300
 hash sha
 authentication pre-share
```

References

The topics considered in this chapter are complex and should be studied further to more fully understand them and put them to use. Use the following references to learn more about the topics in this chapter.

Refer to the *Configuration Guide for the Cisco Secure PIX Firewall, PIX Firewall Release 5.1,* to learn how to configure IPSec on the PIX Firewall. You will find the following chapters most informative:

- **Configuring IPSec**—Presents an overview of how to configure IPSec and presents the procedure to do so
- **Command Reference**—Contains details on each PIX Firewall command
- **Configuration Examples**—Shows sample configurations for PIX Firewall IPSec

Upon completing this chapter, you will be able to do the following:

- Describe the tasks, steps, and commands used to configure CA support in Cisco routers and on the PIX Firewall

- Configure CA support in Cisco routers and on the PIX Firewall

- Verify CA support

- Configure dynamic crypto maps on Cisco routers and the PIX Firewall

- Configure IPSec mode configuration on Cisco routers and the PIX Firewall

- Configure IPSec extended authentication on the PIX Firewall

- Configure tunnel endpoint discovery in Cisco routers

CHAPTER 18

Scaling Cisco IPSec Networks

This chapter describes how to configure Cisco IPSec networks consisting of Cisco routers and PIX Firewalls using IPSec so that they can scale to support multiple IPSec peers while maintaining security. The chapter starts by covering how to configure certification authority (CA) support so that Rivest, Shamir, and Adleman (RSA) digital signatures can be used for Internet Key Exchange (IKE) peer authentication. This chapter also covers how to configure Cisco routers and PIX Firewalls to support remote access via CiscoSecure VPN clients. The chapter concludes with how to configure tunnel endpoint discovery.

Configuring CA Support in Cisco Routers and the PIX Firewall

This section presents how to configure CA support in Cisco routers and the PIX Firewall. The overall procedure for configuring certificate authority support is similar in both products, with some differences in commands and command syntax.

Many tasks and steps are identical, regardless of the authentication method chosen. This chapter summarizes procedures that are covered in other chapters of this book and describes in more detail steps that are unique or different for CA support.

Refer to the "Public Key Infrastructure and CA Support" section of Chapter 15, "Understanding Cisco IPSec Support," for an overview of how CA servers work.

The IPSec configuration process for CA support can be summed up in five major tasks:

- **Task 1: Prepare for IPSec**—Preparing for IPSec involves determining the detailed encryption policy: selecting an authentication method, identifying CA server details, identifying the hosts and networks you want to protect, determining details about the IPSec peers, determining which IPSec features you need, and ensuring that existing access lists permit IPSec traffic.

- **Task 2: Configure CA support**—Configuring CA support involves setting the Cisco device's host name and domain name, generating the keys, declaring a CA, and authenticating and requesting your own certificates.

- **Task 3: Configure IKE for IPSec**—Configuring IKE involves enabling IKE, creating the IKE policies, and validating the configuration. Then IKE can set up IPSec SAs, enabling IPSec sessions.

- **Task 4: Configure IPSec**—IPSec configuration includes defining the transform sets, creating crypto access lists, creating crypto map entries, and applying crypto map sets to interfaces. The steps are identical regardless of the authentication method chosen and are not covered in this chapter.

- **Task 5: Verify VPN configuration**—Use **show, debug,** and related commands to verify that IPSec encryption works and to troubleshoot problems.

The following sections discuss each configuration task in more detail.

Task 1: Prepare for IPSec

Successfully scaling a Cisco IPSec VPN network requires advance planning before you begin to configure individual Cisco routers, PIX Firewalls, and other IPSec peers for CA support. Configuring IPSec encryption can be complicated. You should begin by defining the detailed IPSec security policy based on the overall company security policy. Here are some planning steps:

Step 1 **Determine IKE (IKE Phase 1, main mode) policy**—Determine the IKE policies between IPSec peers based on the number and location of the peers.

Step 2 **Plan for CA support**—Determine the CA server details. This includes variables such as the type of CA server to be used, the IP address, and the CA administrator contact information.

Step 3 **Determine IPSec (IKE Phase 2 quick mode) policy**—Identify IPSec peer details such as IP addresses and IPSec modes. You then configure crypto maps to gather all IPSec policy details together.

Step 4 **Check the current configuration**—Use appropriate commands on the Cisco router or PIX Firewall to view the current configuration. Some common commands include **write terminal, show isakmp [policy],** and **show crypto map**.

Step 5 **Ensure that the network works without encryption**—Ensure that basic connectivity has been achieved between IPSec peers using the desired IP services before configuring IPSec. You can use the **ping** command to check basic connectivity.

Step 6 **Ensure that access lists are compatible with IPSec**—Ensure that perimeter routers and the IPSec peer router interfaces permit IPSec traffic. In this step, you need to enter the **show access-lists** command.

You should determine IKE policy details for each peer before configuring IKE. Figure 18-1 shows the simplified topology for the XYZ Company used in examples in this chapter.

Figure 18-1 *XYZ Company Topology Used in the Examples*

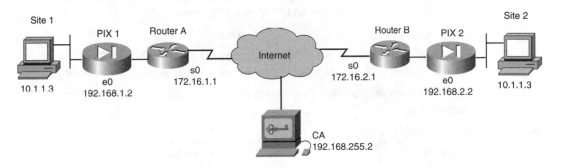

Table 18-1 summarizes IKE policy details that will be configured in examples in this chapter.

Table 18-1 *IKE Policy Example for Cisco Router and PIX Firewall*

Parameter	Peer A Value	Peer B Value
Message encryption algorithm	DES	DES
Message integrity (hash) algorithm	MD5	MD5
Peer authentication method	RSA Signature	RSA Signature
Key exchange parameters (Diffie-Hellman group identifier)	768-bit DH group 1	768-bit DH group 1
IKE-established security association's lifetime	86400 (default)	86400 (default)
IP address of peer Cisco router	192.168.2.2	192.168.1.2
IP address of peer PIX Firewall	172.16.2.1	172.16.1.1

Step 2: Plan for CA Support

Planning for CA support is unique to configuring CA support. It is best to plan ahead and identify CA support details so that you will be ready for CA support configuration. Here are some planning steps:

- Determine the type of CA server to use. CA servers come in a multitude of configurations and capabilities. You must determine which one fits your needs in advance of configuration. Requirements include (but are not limited to) RSA key type required, CRL capabilities, and support for RA mode.

- Identify the CA server IP address, host name, and URL.

- Identify the CA server administrator contact information. You will need to have arranged for your certificates to be validated if the process is not automatic.

Table 18-2 shows an example of CA server details that will be configured in examples in this chapter.

Table 18-2 *CA Server Detail Example*

Parameter	CA Server Detail
Type of CA server	Entrust
Host name	entrust-ca
IP address	192.168.255.2
URL	www.entrust-ca.com
Administrator contact	1-800-555-1212

NOTE   Steps 3 through 6 of Task 1 are identical to those used for configuring preshared keys. See the "Task 1: Prepare for IPSec" sections in Chapter 16, "Configuring Cisco IOS IPSec," and Chapter 17, "Configuring PIX Firewall IPSec Support," for more details on these steps.

Task 2: Configure CA Support

The next major task in configuring IPSec for CA support is to enter the unique commands that enable CA support with parameters based on details gathered in the planning task. This section breaks down each step required to configure CA support, presenting a brief overview of the step and then detailing how to perform the step for Cisco routers and the PIX Firewall. Configuring CA support on Cisco routers and the PIX Firewall consists of the following essential steps and commands. They are covered in subsequent sections.

Be sure that the Cisco router and PIX Firewall clock are set to the current time, month, day, and year before configuring CA. Otherwise, the CA might reject or allow certificates based on an incorrect time stamp. Cisco's PKI protocol uses the clock to make sure that a CRL is not expired. Set the Cisco router's calendar and clock with the **clock timezone** global configuration command and **clock set** privileged EXEC command. You can optionally configure a Cisco router to use a Network Time Protocol (NTP) server to set the clock. Set the PIX Firewall's calendar and clock with the **clock set** configuration command.

Step 1 **Manage nonvolatile memory usage (optional)**—Certificates and CRLs can take up significant NVRAM in Cisco routers and Flash memory in PIX Firewalls. This memory might need to be managed.

Step 2 **Configure Cisco router or PIX Firewall host name and domain name**—The device host name and domain name are used with IKE identity, RSA key generation, and certificates, and they must be correctly specified.

Step 3 **Generate an RSA key pair**—RSA keys are used to authenticate the remote IPSec peer.

Step 4 **Declare a CA**—To declare the CA your Cisco device should use, use the **crypto ca identity** global configuration command. Use the **no** form of this command to delete all identity information and certificates associated with the CA.

Step 5 **Authenticate the CA**—The Cisco device needs to authenticate the CA. It does this by obtaining the CA's self-signed certificate that contains the CA's public key.

Step 6 **Request your own certificate(s)**—Complete this step to obtain your router's certificate(s) from the CA.

Step 7 **Save the configuration**—After configuring the Cisco device for CA support, you should save the configuration.

Step 8 **Monitor and maintain CA interoperability (optional)**—This step is optional, depending on your particular requirements.

Step 9 **Verify CA support configuration**—The commands detailed in this section allow you to view your and any other configured CA certificates.

Step 1: Manage Memory Usage

Certificates, RSA keys, and CRLs can take up a significant amount of Cisco router NVRAM or PIX Firewall Flash memory.

In some cases, storing certificates and CRLs locally does not present a problem. However, in other cases, memory can become an issue—particularly if your CA supports an RA and a large number of CRLs end up being stored on your Cisco router or PIX Firewall.

To save memory space, you can specify that certificates and CRLs should not be stored locally but should be retrieved from the CA or from a Lightweight Directory Access Protocol (LDAP) server. Certificates and CRLs are used every time a new security association is set up or renewed. This saves memory space but can result in a slight performance impact.

To specify that certificates and CRLs should not be stored locally on your Cisco router but should be retrieved from a CA or LDAP server, turn on query mode by using the **crypto ca certificate query** command in global configuration mode.

Step 2: Configure Host Name and Domain Name

You must configure the Cisco router or PIX Firewall's host name and IP domain name for CA support if this has not already been done. This is required because the Cisco device assigns a fully qualified domain name (FQDN) to the keys and certificates used by IPSec, and the FQDN is based on the host name and IP domain name configured. For example, a certificate is named pix1.xyz.com based on a PIX host name of pix1 and a PIX IP domain name of xyz.com. Use the commands in the following sections to configure the host name and IP domain name for Cisco routers and the PIX Firewall.

You can also optionally define a static host name-to-address mapping in the host cache if a Domain Name Server (DNS) is not available to resolve the peer's host name. The names you define become like a host table local to the Cisco router or PIX Firewall.

Host Name and Domain Name Cisco Router Configuration

You can use the **hostname** global configuration command to specify or modify the host name for the Cisco router. The command syntax is as follows:

```
hostname name
```

The command parameter has the following meaning:

Command Parameter	Description
name	Specifies the new host name for the Cisco router

You can define a default domain name that the Cisco IOS Software uses to complete unqualified host names (names without a dotted-decimal domain name) using the **ip domain-name** global configuration command. To remove the use of the default domain name, use the **no** form of this command. The command syntax is as follows:

```
ip domain-name name
```

The command parameter has the following meaning:

Command Parameter	Description
name	Specifies the default domain name used to complete unqualified host names. Do not include the initial period that separates an unqualified name from the domain name.

You can optionally use the **ip host** global configuration command to define a static host name-to-address mapping in the host cache if a DNS server is not available to resolve the peer's host name. To remove the name-to-address mapping, use the **no** form of this command. The command syntax is as follows:

```
ip host name address1 [address2...address8]
```

The command parameters have the following meanings:

Command Parameters	Description
name	Specifies the name of the host. The first character can be either a letter or a number. If you use a number, the operations you can perform are limited.
address1	Specifies an associated IP address.
address2...address8	(Optional) Specifies an additional associated IP address. You can bind up to eight addresses to a host name.

The sample configuration shown in Example 18-1 is based on the commands in this section that the XYZ Company would use.

Example 18-1 *Host Name and Domain Name Cisco Router Configuration*

```
Router(config)# hostname routerA
routerA(config)# ip domain-name xyz.com
routerA(config)# ip host xyzcaserver 192.168.255.2
```

Host Name and Domain Name PIX Firewall Configuration

You can use the **hostname** command to configure the PIX Firewall's host name. The command syntax is as follows:

```
hostname newname
```

The command parameter has the following meaning:

Command Parameter	Description
newname	Specifies the new host name for the PIX Firewall prompt. This name can be up to 16 alphanumeric characters and can be mixed case.

You can use the **domain-name** command to change the IPSec domain name. The command syntax is as follows:

```
domain-name name
```

The command parameter has the following meaning:

Command Parameter	Description
name	Configures the PIX's IP domain name

You can use the **name** command to identify a host by a text name. The names you define become like a host table local to the PIX Firewall. The command syntax is as follows:

```
name ip_address name
```

The command parameters have the following meanings:

Command Parameters	Description
ip_address	Specifies the IP address of the host being named.
name	Specifies the name assigned to the IP address. Allowable characters are a to z, A to Z, 0 to 9, and an underscore. The name cannot start with a number. If the name is more than 16 characters long, the **name** command fails.

The sample configuration shown in Example 18-2 is based on the commands in this section that the XYZ Company would use.

Example 18-2 *Host Name and Domain Name PIX Firewall Configuration*

```
Pixfirewall(config)# hostname PIX1
PIX1(config)# domain-name xyz.com
PIX1(config)# name xyzcaserver 192.168.255.2
```

Step 3: Generate an RSA Key Pair

You need to generate RSA key pairs in Cisco routers and PIX Firewalls to make CA support work. RSA key pairs are used to sign and encrypt IKE key management messages and are required before you can obtain a certificate for your Cisco router or PIX Firewall.

By default, RSA key pairs do not exist. If your Cisco router or PIX Firewall already has RSA keys when you issue the command to generate them, you are warned and prompted to replace the existing keys with new keys.

RSA keys are generated in pairs—one public RSA key and one private RSA key. The public RSA key is sent to the CA server when you enroll with it. The private key is stored in NVRAM (Cisco router) or Flash (PIX Firewall) memory.

Before you issue the command to generate an RSA key pair, make sure your Cisco router or PIX Firewall has a host name and IP domain name configured. You will be unable to generate the key pair without a host name and IP domain name. The command used to generate the RSA keys is not saved in the Cisco router or PIX Firewall configuration. However, the keys generated by this command are saved in the private configuration in NVRAM on Cisco routers and in the persistent data file in Flash memory on the PIX Firewall (which is never displayed to the user or backed up to another device).

There are two mutually exclusive types of RSA key pairs: special-usage keys and general-purpose keys. When you generate RSA key pairs, you can indicate whether to generate special-usage keys or general-purpose keys. See the section "Step 3: Generate RSA Keys" in Chapter 16 for more information on the RSA key pair types. Note that an Entrust CA requires that signature and encryption key pairs be generated, even though the encryption keys are not used for CA support.

RSA Key Pair Cisco Router Configuration

You use the **crypto key generate rsa** global configuration command to generate RSA key pairs. The command syntax is as follows:

```
crypto key generate rsa [usage-keys]
```

The command parameter has the following meaning:

Command Parameter	Description
usage-keys	(Optional) Specifies that two RSA special-usage key pairs should be generated (that is, one encryption pair and one signature pair). If this is omitted, a general-purpose key pair is generated.

When you enter the **crypto key generate rsa** command, you are prompted to select a key modulus size from 512 to 2048 bytes in length. Larger key modulus sizes take more time to generate yet are more secure.

See the section "Step 3: Generate RSA Keys" in Chapter 16 for more information on the **crypto key generate rsa** command and for a configuration example.

RSA Key Pair PIX Firewall Configuration

You can use the **ca generate rsa** configuration command to generate RSA key pairs. The command syntax is as follows:

```
ca generate rsa {key | specialkey} key_modulus_size
```

The command parameters have the following meanings:

Command Parameters	Description
key	Specifies that one general-purpose RSA key pair will be generated.
specialkey	Specifies that two special-purpose RSA key pairs will be generated instead of one general-purpose key.
key_modulus_size	Specifies the size of the key modulus, which is between 512 and 2048 bits. Choosing a size greater than 1024 bits might cause key generation to take a few minutes.

Example 18-3 is an example of generating an RSA general-purpose key.

Example 18-3 *An Example of Generating an RSA General-Purpose Key*

```
Pixfirewall(config)# ca generate rsa key 512
```

Step 4: Declare a CA

The next step in configuring CA support is to declare a CA server, which consists of assigning a name to the CA server and configuring parameters used to communicate with the CA server. After you enter the commands to declare a CA, the Cisco router or PIX Firewall requests the CA's RSA public key and enrolls with the CA using SCEP. The commands and procedure to configure a Cisco router or a PIX Firewall differ slightly. Each CA server vendor that supports Cisco system products requires different parameters.

CA Declaration Cisco Router Configuration

On a Cisco router, you enter the **crypto ca identity** global configuration command to declare a CA. The command assigns a name to the CA server and puts you in the CA-identity configuration mode, where you can enter communication parameters specific to the CA server type. Use the **no** form of the command to delete all identity information and certificates associated with the CA. The command syntax is as follows:

```
crypto ca identity name
```

The command parameter has the following meaning:

Command Parameter	Description
name	Creates a name for the CA. (If you previously declared the CA and you just want to update its characteristics, specify the name you previously created.) The CA might require a particular name such as its domain name. The name is only significant locally. It does not have to match the identity defined on any of the VPN peers. It is referenced by other CA commands.

Using the **crypto ca identity** command puts you into the CA-identity configuration mode, where you can specify characteristics for the CA with the following commands:

Command	Description
enrollment url	Specifies the URL of the CA. Always required.
enrollment mode ra	Specifies RA mode. Required only if your CA system provides an RA. Entrust CA requires RA mode.
query url	Specifies the URL of the Lightweight Directory Access Protocol (LDAP) server. Required only if your CA supports an RA and the LDAP protocol.
enrollment retry-period	(Optional) Specifies how long the router should wait between sending certificate request retries.
enrollment retry-count	(Optional) Specifies how many certificate request retries your router will send before giving up.
crl optional	(Optional) Specifies that your router can still accept other peers' certificates if the CRL is inaccessible.

Example 18-4 is an example of using the **crypto ca identity** command and entering the CA-identity configuration mode, showing a list of CA-identity mode subcommands.

Example 18-4 *An Example of Using the* **crypto ca identity** *Command and Entering the CA-Identity Configuration Mode*

```
Router(config)# crypto ca identity mycaserver
Router(ca-identity)# ?
CA identity configuration commands:
  crl            CRL option
  default        Set a command to its defaults
  enrollment     Enrollment parameters
  exit           Exit from certificate authority identity entry mode
  no             Negate a command or set its defaults
  query          Query parameters
router(ca-identity)#enrollment ?
  http-proxy     HTTP proxy server for enrollment
  mode ra        Mode supported by the Certificate Authority
  retry          Polling parameters
  url            CA server enrollment URL\
```

Example 18-5 declares a CA and identifies its characteristics. The name mycaserver is created for the CA, which is located at http://my_ca_server. This example also declares a CA using an RA. The CA's scripts are stored in the default location, and the CA uses SCEP instead of LDAP. This is the minimum possible configuration required to declare a CA that uses an RA, and it is an example of configuring for an Entrust CA server. An Entrust CA requires that the IPSec peer transact with an RA, which then forwards the requests through to the CA itself.

Example 18-5 *An Example of Declaring a CA*

```
router(config)# crypto ca identity mycaserver
router(ca-identity)# enrollment url http://my_ca_server
router(ca-identity)# enrollment mode ra
router(ca-identity)# exit
```

An example of defining Verisign CA server-related commands is shown in Example 18-6. The IP address of the onsiteipsec.verisign.com server is 172.31.0.2. Note that CA mode is required and configured, yet it is not specified because it is the default mode. In this example, an optional LDAP server inside the XYZ network with a URL of dirserv.xyz.com is used to store certificates.

Example 18-6 *An Example of Defining Verisign CA Server-Related Commands*

```
router(config)# crypto ca identity myvscaserver
router(ca-identity)# enrollment retry count 100
router(ca-identity)# enrollment url http://onsiteipsec.verisign.com
router(ca-identity)# query url ldap://dirserv.xyz.com
! The LDAP server contains the certificates.
router(ca-identity)# crl optional
```

CA Declaration PIX Firewall Configuration

Declaring a CA on the PIX Firewall consists of two substeps: declaring a CA and configuring CA communication parameters. The PIX Firewall does not have submodes, so the equivalent **crypto ca identity** command on Cisco routers is broken into two commands: **ca identity** and **ca configure**.

Step 4A: Declare a CA for the PIX Firewall   You declare one CA to be used by your PIX Firewall with the **ca identity** command in configuration mode. You can optionally specify the location of the CA server's CGI script and the LDAP IP address if it is used. The command syntax is as follows:

```
ca identity ca_nickname ca_ipaddress[:ca_script_location] [ldap_ip_address]
```

The command parameters have the following meanings:

Command Parameters	Description
ca_nickname	The CA's name. Enter any string you want. (If you previously declared the CA and you just want to update its characteristics, specify the name you previously created.) The CA might require a particular name such as its domain name.
ca_ipaddress	The CA's IP address.

Command Parameters	Description
:ca_script_location	The default location and script on the CA server is /cgi-bin/pkiclient.exe. If the CA administrator has not put the CGI script in this location, provide the location and the name of the script in the **ca identity** command.
ldap_ip_address	(Optional) Specifies the IP address of the LDAP server. By default, querying of a certificate or a CRL is done via Cisco's PKI protocol. If the CA supports LDAP, query functions may also use LDAP.

Example 18-7 is an example of using a **ca identity** command.

Example 18-7 *An Example of Using a **ca identity** Command*

```
Pixfirewall(config)# ca identity ca.xyz.com 192.168.255.2
```

Step 4B: Configure CA Communication Parameters for the PIX Firewall   You configure CA communication parameters with the **ca configure** command in configuration mode. You can use this command to indicate whether to contact the CA or an RA to obtain a certificate. Use different parameters for each type of supported CA. The command syntax is as follows:

ca configure *ca_nickname* {**ca** | **ra**} *retry_period retry_count* [**crloptional**]

The command parameters have the following meanings:

Command Parameters	Description
ca_nickname	Specifies the CA's name. Use the nickname entered with the **ca identity** command.
ca or **ra**	Indicates whether to contact the CA or RA when using the **ca configure** command. Some CA systems provide an RA, which the PIX Firewall contacts instead of the CA.
retry_period	Specifies how long (in minutes) the PIX Firewall waits before resending a certificate request to the CA when it does not receive a response to its previous request from the CA. Values can range from 1 to 60 minutes. By default, the firewall retries every minute.
retry_count	Specifies how many times the PIX Firewall will resend a certificate request when it does not receive a certificate from the CA from the previous request. Values can range from 1 to 100. The default is 0, which indicates that there is no limit to the number of times the PIX Firewall should contact the CA to obtain a pending certificate.

continues

Command Parameters	Description
crloptional	Allows other peers' certificates to be accepted by your PIX Firewall even if the appropriate CRL is inaccessible to your PIX Firewall. The default is without **crloptional**.

An example of defining Verisign CA server-related commands is shown in Example 18-8.

Example 18-8 *An Example of Defining Verisign CA Server-Related Commands*

```
Pixfirewall(config)# ca onsiteipsec.verisign.com 172.31.0.2
Pixfirewall(config)# ca configure ca.xyz.com ca 1 20 crloptional
```

The IP address of the onsiteipsec.verisign.com server is 172.31.0.2. Note that CA mode is specified.

An example of defining Entrust CA server-related commands is shown in Example 18-9.

Example 18-9 *An Example of Defining Entrust CA Server-Related Commands*

```
Pixfirewall(config)# ca identity ca.xyz.com 192.168.255.2 192.168.255.2
Pixfirewall(config)# ca configure ca.xyz.com ra 1 20 crloptional
```

The IP address of the CA server is 192.168.255.2. Note that RA mode is specified. The second IP address is for an LDAP query server running on the same host.

Step 5: Authenticate the CA

The next step in configuring CA support is to authenticate the CA server to ensure that it is valid. This step consists of two substeps:

1 Enter a command that obtains the CA's self-signed certificate, which contains the CA's public key (to ensure that the key is valid).

2 Manually authenticate the self-signed certificate by contacting the CA administrator to compare the CA certificate's fingerprint (a hash of the certificate).

CA Authentication Cisco Router Configuration

You can use the **crypto ca authenticate** command in global configuration mode to get the CA's public key. If you are using RA mode (using the **enrollment mode ra** command) when you issue the **crypto ca authenticate** command, RA signing and encryption certificates will be returned from the CA as well as the CA certificate. The command syntax is as follows:

```
crypto ca authenticate name
```

The command parameter has the following meaning:

Command Parameter	Description
name	Uses the same name as specified in the **crypto ca identity** command

After entering the **crypto ca authenticate** command, you should manually authenticate the CA's public key by contacting the CA administrator to compare the CA certificate's fingerprint.

An example of entering the **crypto ca authenticate** command is shown in Example 18-10.

Example 18-10   *An Example of Entering the **crypto ca authenticate** Command*

```
Router(config)# crypto ca authenticate mycaserver
Certificate has the following attributes:
Fingerprint: 1A5416D6 2EEE8943 D11CCEE1 3DEE9CE7
% Do you accept this certificate? [yes/no]: y
```

The command displays the fingerprint of the CA certificate and asks if you accept the certificate. You manually verify the fingerprint with the CA server administrator before answering yes.

CA Authentication PIX Firewall Configuration

You authenticate the CA to verify that it is legitimate by obtaining its public key and its certificate with the **ca authenticate** command in configuration mode. After entering the command, manually authenticate the CA's public key by contacting the CA administrator to compare the CA certificate's fingerprint. An RA, if used (as in the Entrust CA), acts as a proxy for a CA. The command syntax is as follows:

ca authenticate *ca_nickname* [*fingerprint*]

The command parameters have the following meanings:

Command Parameters	Description
ca_nickname	Specifies the CA's name. You use the nickname entered with the **ca identity** command.
fingerprint	Specifies a key consisting of alphanumeric characters that the PIX Firewall uses to authenticate the CA's certificate. The fingerprint is optional and is used to authenticate the CA's public key within its certificate.

The PIX Firewall discards the CA certificate if the fingerprint that you included in the command statement is not equal to the fingerprint within the CA's certificate.

Depending on which CA you are using, you might need to ask your local CA administrator for this fingerprint.

You also have the option of manually authenticating the public key by simply comparing the two fingerprints after you receive the CA's certificate rather than entering it within the command statement.

An example of authenticating a CA is shown in Example 18-11.

Example 18-11 *An Example of Authenticating a CA*

```
Pixfirewall(config)#crypto ca authenticate ca.xyz.com
```

Step 6: Request Your Own Certificate(s)

The next step in configuring CA support is to request certificates for your IPSec device from the CA server. This task is also known as enrolling with the CA.

You can enroll Cisco routers with the **crypto ca enroll** command. You can enroll PIX Firewalls with the **ca enroll** command. During the enrollment process, you are prompted for a challenge password, which can be used by the CA administrator to validate your identity. It is stored with your certificate enrollment on the CA server. The password is required in the event that your certificate needs to be revoked, so it is crucial that you remember this password. Note it and store it in a safe place.

The enrollment command requests as many certificates as there are RSA key pairs. You need to use this command only once, even if you have special-usage RSA key pairs. Your Cisco device needs a signed certificate from the CA for each of its RSA key pairs. If you previously generated general-purpose keys, this command obtains the one certificate corresponding to the one general-purpose RSA key pair. If you previously generated special-usage keys, this command obtains two certificates corresponding to each of the special-usage RSA key pairs. If you already have a certificate for your keys, you will be unable to complete this command; instead, you will be prompted to remove the existing certificate first.

If your Cisco device reboots after you issue the respective enrollment command but before you receive the certificate(s), you must reissue the command.

Before entering this command, contact your CA administrator because he will have to authenticate your Cisco device manually before granting its certificate(s). After entering the respective enrollment command, establish contact with your CA administrator and have that person manually authenticate the CA certificate of your Cisco device. The enrollment command is not saved in the Cisco device configuration.

Certificate Request Cisco Router Configuration

You request signed certificates from your CA for all your Cisco router's RSA key pairs using the **crypto ca enroll** global configuration command. Use the **no** form of this command to delete a current enrollment. The command syntax is as follows:

```
crypto ca enroll name
```

The command parameter has the following meaning:

Command Parameters	Description
name	Specifies the name of the CA. Use the same name as when you declared the CA using the **crypto ca identity** command.

When you issue the **crypto ca enroll** command, you are prompted a number of times. First you are prompted to create a challenge password. This password can be up to 80 characters in length. This password is necessary in the event that you need to revoke your router's certificate(s). When you ask the CA administrator to revoke your certificate, you must supply this challenge password as a protection against fraudulent or mistaken revocation requests. This password is not stored anywhere, so you need to remember it. If you lose the password, the CA administrator might still be able to revoke the router's certificate, but he will require further manual authentication of the router administrator identity.

You are also prompted to indicate whether your router's serial number should be included in the obtained certificate. The serial number is not used by IPSec or IKE, but it may be used by the CA to either authenticate certificates or to later associate a certificate with a particular router. (Note that the serial number stored is the serial number of the internal board, not the one on the enclosure.) Ask your CA administrator if serial numbers should be included. If you are in doubt, include the serial number. Normally, you would not include the IP address because it binds the certificate more tightly to a specific entity. Also, if the router is moved, you would need to issue a new certificate. Finally, a router has multiple IP addresses, any of which might be used with IPSec.

If you indicate that the IP address should be included, you are prompted to specify the interface of the IP address. This interface should correspond to the interface that you apply your crypto map set to. If you apply crypto map sets to more than one interface, specify the interface that you name in the **crypto map local-address** command. An example of enrolling with a CA is shown in Example 18-12.

Example 18-12 *An Example of Enrolling with a CA*

```
Router(config)# crypto ca enroll mycaserver
% Start certificate enrollment ..
% Create a challenge password. You will need to verbally provide this
   password to the CA Administrator in order to revoke your certificate.
   For security reasons your password will not be saved in the configuration.
   Please make a note of it.
```

continues

Example 18-12 *An Example of Enrolling with a CA (Continued)*

```
Password: <mypassword>
Re-enter password: <mypassword>

% The subject name in the certificate will be: routerA.cisco.com
% Include the router serial number in the subject name? [yes/no]: y
% The serial number in the certificate will be: 11365470
% Include an IP address in the subject name? [yes/no]: n
Request certificate from CA? [yes/no]: y
% Certificate request sent to Certificate Authority
% The certificate request fingerprint will be displayed.
% The 'show crypto ca certificate' command will also show the fingerprint.
Router(config)#
```

Some time later, the router receives the certificate from the CA and displays the confirmation message shown in Example 18-13.

Example 18-13 *An Example of a CA's Confirmation Message*

```
Router(config)#  Fingerprint: 01234567 89ABCDEF FEDCBA98 75543210
%CRYPTO-6-CERTRET: Certificate received from Certificate Authority
Router(config)#
```

If necessary, the router administrator can verify the displayed fingerprint with the CA administrator.

Certificate Request PIX Firewall Configuration

You request signed certificates from your CA for all your PIX Firewall's RSA key pairs using the **ca enroll** command. The command syntax is as follows:

ca enroll *ca_nickname challenge_password* [**serial**] [*ip_address*]

The command parameters and syntax have the following meanings:

Command Parameters	Description
ca_nickname	Specifies the CA's name. You use the nickname entered with the **ca identity** command.
challenge_password	Specifies a required password that gives the CA administrator some authentication when a user calls to ask for a certificate to be revoked. It can be up to 80 characters in length.
serial	(Optional) Specifies the PIX Firewall's serial number.
ip_address	Specifies the PIX Firewall's IP address.

If you want to cancel the current enrollment request, use the **no ca enroll** command.

The required challenge password is necessary in the event that you need to revoke your PIX Firewall unit's certificate(s). When you ask the CA administrator to revoke your certificate, you must supply this challenge password as a protection against fraudulent or mistaken revocation requests. This password is not stored anywhere, so you need to remember it. If you lose the password, the CA administrator might still be able to revoke the PIX Firewall's certificate, but he will require further manual authentication of the PIX Firewall administrator identity.

The PIX Firewall unit's serial number is optional. If you provide the *serial* option, the serial number will be included in the obtained certificate. The serial number is not used by IPSec or IKE, but it may be used by the CA to either authenticate certificates or to later associate a certificate with a particular device.

The PIX Firewall unit's IP address is optional. If you provide the *ipaddress* option, the IP address will be included in the obtained certificate. Normally, you would not include the *ipaddress* option because the IP address binds the certificate more tightly to a specific entity than not specifying the option does. Also, if the PIX Firewall is moved, you would need to issue a new certificate.

When configuring IKE for certificate-based authentication, it is important to match the IKE identity type with the certificate type. The **ca enroll** command used to acquire certificates will, by default, get a certificate with the identity based on host name. The default identity type for the **isakmp identity** command is based on address instead of host name. If the identity is based on address and you are using RSA signatures for authentication, the IKE main mode authentication will fail. You can reconcile this disparity of identity types by using the **isakmp identity hostname** command. Then, during IKE Phase 1 main mode, the peers will authenticate using host name-based identities.

An example of authenticating a CA is shown in Example 18-14. The keyword **mypassword1234567** in the example is a password, which is not saved with the configuration but is registered with the CA server.

Example 18-14 *An Example of Authenticating a CA*

```
Pixfirewall(config)#ca enroll ca.xyz.com mypassword1234567
```

After entering this command, have the CA administrator manually authenticate your PIX Firewall's CA certificate.

Step 7: Save the Configuration

The next step in configuring CA support is to save the configuration to memory. Cisco routers and the PIX Firewall each require a different procedure to accomplish this:

- **Cisco router configuration**—After you configure a Cisco router for CA support, you should save the configuration using the **copy running-config startup-config** command. This command saves the router's running configuration to NVRAM.

- **PIX Firewall configuration**—Save your PIX Firewall's CA configuration with the **ca save all** and **write memory** commands. The **ca save all** command allows you to save the PIX Firewall's RSA key pairs; the CA, RA, and PIX Firewall's certificates; and the CA's CRLs in the persistent data file in Flash memory between reloads. The **no ca save** command removes the saved data from PIX Firewall's Flash memory. The **ca save** command itself is not saved with the PIX Firewall configuration between reloads. The **write memory** command stores the current CA configuration in Flash memory.

Step 8: Verify CA Support Configuration

The next step in configuring CA support is to verify that you have correctly configured your Cisco device and that you have successfully enrolled to the CA server. Cisco routers and PIX Firewalls contain a number of **show** commands that are useful for verifying CA support configuration. These commands are summarized in this section.

Verifying CA Support in the Cisco Router Configuration

You can use two commands to verify CA support configuration on Cisco routers. The **show crypto ca certificates** command displays information about your certificate, the CA's certificate, and any RA certificates, and the **show crypto key mypubkey** command lets you view RSA keys for your router and other IPSec peers enrolled with a CA.

Example 18-15 illustrates the result of using the **show crypto ca certificates** command.

Example 18-15 *The Result of Using the **show crypto ca certificates** Command*

```
router# show crypto ca certificates
Certificate
  Subject Name
    Name: routerA.xyz.com
        IP Address: 172.16.1.1
    Status: Available
  Certificate Serial Number: 0123456789ABCDEF0123456789ABCDEF
  Key Usage: General Purpose

CA Certificate
  Status: Available
  Certificate Serial Number: 3051DF7123BEE31B8341DFE4B3A338E5F
  Key Usage: Not Set
```

Example 18-16 is sample output from the **show crypto key mypubkey rsa** command. Special-use RSA keys were previously generated for this router using the **crypto key generate rsa** command.

Example 18-16 *Sample Output from the **show crypto key mypubkey rsa** Command*

```
router# show crypto key mypubkey rsa
% Key pair was generated at: 06:07:49 UTC Feb 29 2000
Key name: routerA.xyz.com
  Usage: Signature Key
  Key Data:
  005C300D 06092A86 4886F70D 01010105 00034B00 30480241 00C5E23B 55D6AB22
  04AEF1BA A54028A6 9ACC01C5 129D99E4 64CAB820 847EDAD9 DF0B4E4C 73A05DD2
  BD62A8A9 FA603DD2 E2A8A6F8 98F76E28 D58AD221 B583D7A4 71020301 0001
% Key pair was generated at: 06:07:50 UTC Feb 29 2000
Key name: myrouter.domain.com
  Usage: Encryption Key
  Key Data:
  00302017 4A7D385B 1234EF29 335FC973 2DD50A37 C4F4B0FD 9DADE748 429618D5
  18242BA3 2EDFBDD3 4296142A DDF7D3D8 08407685 2F2190A0 0B43F1BD 9A8A26DB
  07953829 791FCDE9 A98420F0 6A82045B 90288A26 DBC64468 7789F76E EE21
```

Example 18-17 is sample output from the **show crypto key pubkey-chain rsa** command.

Example 18-17 *Sample Output from the **show crypto key pubkey-chain rsa** Command*

```
router# show crypto key pubkey-chain rsa
Codes: M - Manually Configured, C - Extracted from certificate
Code     Usage        IP-address          Name
M        Signature    172.16.3.1          routerC.xyz.com
M        Encryption   172.16.3.1          routerC.xyz.com
C        Signature    172.16.2.1          routerB.xyz.com
C        Encryption   172.16.2.1          routerB.xyz.com
C        General      172.16.4.1          routerD.xyz.com
```

Example 18-17 shows two manually configured special-usage RSA public keys for peer routerC. This example also shows three keys obtained from peers' certificates: special-usage keys (encryption and signature) for peer routerB and a general-purpose key for peer routerD. The peer's keys derived from certificates show C in the code column. Manually configured keys show M in the code column. After you authenticate with a peer using RSA signatures, the peer's public RSA key should appear in the public keychain with a code of C.

Example 18-18 displays a concatenated version of the running configuration of a router properly configured for CA support.

Example 18-18 *A Concatenated Version of the Running Configuration of a Router Properly Configured for CA Support*

```
routerA# show running-config
!
hostname routerA
!
ip domain-name xyz.com
!
crypto ca identity mycaserver
 enrollment mode ra
 enrollment url http://xyzcaserver:80
 query url ldap://xyzcaserver
 crl optional
crypto ca certificate chain entrust
 certificate 37C6EAD6
  30820299 30820202 A0030201 02020437 C6EAD630 0D06092A
  864886F7 0D010105
  (certificates concatenated)
```

Verifying CA Support in the PIX Firewall Configuration

You can use the commands outlined in Table 18-3 to verify CA support configuration on the PIX Firewall.

Table 18-3 *Commands to Verify PIX Firewall CA Support*

Command	Description
show ca identity	Shows the current CA identity settings stored in RAM.
show ca configure	Shows the CA communication parameter settings.
show ca certificate	Shows the PIX Firewall, CA, and RA certificates. Use to verify that the CA enrollment process succeeded.
show ca mypubkey rsa	Shows the PIX Firewall's RSA public key pair(s).

Example 18-19 is an example of the display after the **show ca mypubkey rsa** command is used.

Example 18-19 *An Example of Using the **show ca mypubkey rsa** Command*

```
Pixfirewall# show ca mypubkey rsa
% Key pair was generated at: 15:34:55 Feb 29 2000

    Key name: ca.xyz.com
     Usage: General Purpose Key
     Key Data:
      305c300d 06092a86 4886f70d 01010105 00034b00 30480241 00c31f4a ad32f60d
      6e7ed9a2 32883ca9 319a4b30 e7470888 87732e83 c909fb17 fb5cae70 3de738cf
      6e2fd12c 5b3ffa98 8c5adc59 1ec84d78 90bdb53f 2218cfe7 3f020301 0001.
```

Example 18-20 shows a concatenated version of the configuration of a PIX Firewall properly configured for CA support.

Example 18-20   *An Example of a PIX Firewall Properly Configured for CA Support*

```
Pix1# write terminal
!
hostname Pix1
domain-name xyz.com
!
ca identity ca.xyz.com 192.168.255.2:cgi-bin/pkiclient.exe 192.168.255.2
ca configure ca.xyz.com ra 1 100 crloptional
```

Step 9: Monitor and Maintain CA Interoperability

After you configure CA support on a Cisco router or PIX Firewall, you might need to perform optional maintenance tasks that will ensure continued smooth operation. This section covers the following optional steps for both Cisco routers and the PIX Firewall:

- Request a certificate revocation list.
- Delete your router or PIX Firewall's RSA keys.
- Delete certificates from the configuration.
- Delete the peer's public keys.

The following sections describe these steps.

Requesting a CRL

You might periodically need to request a CRL from the CA to obtain an updated CRL. If your Cisco device has a CRL that has not yet expired, but you suspect that the CRL's contents are out of date, you need to request that the latest CRL be immediately downloaded to replace the old CRL with the **crypto ca crl request** command in a Cisco router or the **ca crl request** command in a PIX Firewall. Manually request a CRL only if your CA does not support an RA.

A CRL lists all the network devices' certificates that have been revoked. Revoked certificates will not be honored by your Cisco device; therefore, any IPSec device with a revoked certificate cannot exchange IPSec traffic with your Cisco device.

The first time your Cisco device receives a certificate from a peer, it downloads a CRL from the CA. Your Cisco device then checks the CRL to make sure that the peer's certificate has not been revoked. If the certificate appears on the CRL, it will not accept the certificate and will not authenticate the peer.

A CRL can be reused with subsequent certificates until the CRL expires. If your Cisco device receives a peer's certificate after the applicable CRL has expired, it automatically downloads the new CRL. The CRL request command is not saved to the configuration.

CRL Request Cisco Router Configuration   To request that a new CRL be obtained immediately from the CA, use the **crypto ca crl request** command in global configuration mode. Use this command only when your CA does not support an RA. The command syntax is as follows:

```
crypto ca crl request name
```

The command parameter has the following meaning:

Command Parameter	Description
name	Specifies the name of the CA. You use the same name as when you declared the CA using the **crypto ca identity** command.

Example 18-21 immediately downloads the latest CRL to a router.

Example 18-21   *An Example of Downloading the Latest CRL to a Router*

```
Router(config)# crypto ca crl request mycaserver
```

CRL Request PIX Firewall Configuration   The PIX Firewall requests a CRL the same way a Cisco router does, except that a PIX Firewall automatically requests a CRL from the CA at various times, depending on whether the CA is in RA mode. If the CA is not in RA mode, a CRL is requested whenever the system reboots and finds that it does not already contain a valid (that is, unexpired) CRL. If the CA is in RA mode, no CRL can be obtained until a peer's certificate is sent via an IKE. This is because the certificate itself contains the location where the PIX Firewall must query to get the appropriate CRL. When a CRL expires, the PIX Firewall automatically requests an updated one. Until a new valid CRL is obtained, the PIX Firewall will not accept peers' certificates.

To request that a new CRL be obtained immediately from the CA to a PIX Firewall, use the **ca crl request** command in configuration mode. The command syntax is as follows:

```
ca crl request ca_nickname
```

The command parameter has the following meaning:

Command Parameter	Description
ca_nickname	Specifies the name of the CA. You use the same nickname as when you declared the CA using the **ca identity** command.

Example 18-22 indicates that the PIX Firewall will obtain an updated CRL from the CA with the name mycaserver.

Example 18-22 *An Example of Obtaining an Updated CRL from the CA*

```
Pixfirewall(config)# ca crl request mycaserver
```

Deleting Your Own Device's RSA Keys and Certificates

There might be circumstances in which you want to delete your Cisco router's or PIX Firewall's RSA keys. For example, if you believe the RSA keys were compromised in some way and should no longer be used, you should delete them. Or you might need to change the Cisco device's host name, which causes the change of the fully qualified domain name on which the RSA keys are based. If you delete your RSA keys, you also need to delete the Cisco device's certificates, regenerate the RSA keys, reconfigure CA support, and reenroll with the CA server, as described in the following two sections.

Deleting RSA Keys and CA Certificates for Cisco Routers   You can use the following procedure to delete RSA keys and CA certificates for a Cisco router:

1 Delete all your Cisco router's RSA keys with the **crypto key zeroize rsa** command in global configuration mode. If you issue this command, you must also delete your CA certificates.

2 Manually remove the router's certificates from the router configuration. To delete your router's certificate or RA certificates from your router's configuration, use the following commands in global configuration mode:

   — **show crypto ca certificates**—Views the certificates stored on your router and notes the serial number of the certificate you want to delete

   — **crypto ca certificate chain** *name*—Enters certificate chain configuration mode

   — **no certificate** *certificate-serial-number*—Deletes the certificate using the serial number you noted previously

---

NOTE   You can also remove the entire CA identity, which removes all certificates associated with the CA—your router's certificate, the CA certificate, and any RA certificates. To remove a CA identity, you use the **no crypto ca identity** *name* command in global configuration mode.

---

3 Ask the CA administrator to revoke your router's certificates at the CA. You must supply the challenge password you created when you originally obtained the router's certificates with the **crypto ca enroll** command.

Deleting RSA Keys and CA Certificates for PIX Firewalls   You can use the following procedure to delete RSA keys and CA certificates for a PIX Firewall:

1 Delete all your PIX Firewall's RSA keys with the **ca zeroize rsa** command in configuration mode. This command deletes all RSA keys that were previously generated by your PIX Firewall. If you issue this command, you must also perform the following two additional tasks in order to delete your CA certificates.

2 Manually remove the PIX Firewall's certificates from the configuration with the **no ca identity command**. This deletes all the certificates issued by the CA and deletes the CA identity.

3 Ask the CA administrator to revoke your PIX Firewall's certificates at the CA. Supply the challenge password you created when you originally obtained the PIX Firewall's certificates using the **crypto ca enroll** command.

NOTE   You can remove all RSA key pairs; the CA, RA, and PIX Firewall's certificates; and the CA's CRLs from the persistent data file in Flash memory with the **no ca save** command in configuration mode.

Deleting Public RSA Keys

There might be circumstances in which you want to delete other peers' RSA public keys from your Cisco router's configuration. For example, if you no longer trust the integrity of a peer's public key, you should delete it. Refer to the "Deleting Peer RSA Public Keys" section of Chapter 16 for the steps required to delete a peer's RSA public key.

Task 3: Configure IKE for IPSec

The next major task in configuring IPSec for CA support is to configure IKE parameters gathered earlier. This section presents the steps used to configure IKE policies. Note that the IKE tasks are identical to configuring preshared keys except for configuring the authentication method.

Configuring IKE consists of the following essential steps and commands:

Step 1   Enable or disable IKE with the **crypto isakmp enable** command on Cisco routers or the **isakmp enable** command on PIX Firewalls.

Step 2   Create IKE policies with the **crypto isakmp policy** command on Cisco routers or the **isakmp policy** command on PIX Firewalls to support RSA signatures. This is the only unique step in configuring IKE for CA support. Configure CA support by specifying RSA signatures as the IKE authentication method as follows:

— For Cisco routers, enter the **authentication rsa-sig** command in a crypto IKE policy.

— For PIX Firewalls, enter the **isakmp policy** *priority* **authentication rsa-sig** command for an IKE policy.

Step 3 Verify the IKE configuration with **show** and **debug** commands, as is done with preshared keys.

For more information on configuring IKE for Cisco routers and PIX Firewalls, see the following sections and chapters: For Cisco routers, see the section "Task 3: Configure IPSec" in Chapter 16; for PIX Firewalls, see the section "Task 3: Configure IPSec" in Chapter 17.

Task 4: Configure IPSec

IPSec configuration includes defining the transform sets, creating crypto access lists, creating crypto map entries, and applying crypto map sets to interfaces. The steps are identical regardless of the authentication method chosen (as long as IKE is used) and are therefore not duplicated here. They are covered for Cisco routers in the section "Task 3: Configure IPSec" in Chapter 16 and for PIX Firewalls in the section "Task 3: Configure IPSec" in Chapter 17.

Task 5: Verify VPN Configuration

The last major task in configuring CA support is to verify that the CA, IKE, and IPSec configurations were accomplished accurately in the previous tasks. This section summarizes the methods and commands used to verify the CA support portion of the VPN configuration. The commands and procedures for IKE and IPSec configuration are identical regardless of the authentication method and are not duplicated in this chapter.

Verify Cisco Router CA Support Configuration

This section summarizes commands you can use on Cisco routers to verify CA support.

You can verify CA configuration and certificates with the commands outlined in Table 18-4.

Table 18-4 *Commands to Verify Cisco Router CA Configuration and Certificates*

Command	Description
show crypto ca certificates	Displays information about your certificate, the CA's certificate, and any RA certificates
show crypto key mypubkey	Shows RSA keys for your router and other IPSec peers enrolled with a CA server

You debug CA messages with the command shown in Table 18-5.

Table 18-5 *Command to Debug Cisco Router CA Enrollments*

Command	Description
debug crypto pki	Displays SCEP communications between the router and the CA server

You delete RSA keys and CA certificates with the commands listed in Table 18-6.

Table 18-6 *Commands to Delete Cisco Router RSA Keys and CA Certificates*

Command	Description
crypto key zeroize rsa	Deletes all RSA keys that were previously generated by your router. If you issue this command, you must also enter the **no crypto ca identity** command to delete CA certificates and ask the CA administrator to revoke your router's certificates at the CA.
no crypto ca identity *name*	Manually removes the router's certificates from the configuration and deletes all the certificates issued by the CA.

Verify PIX CA Support Configuration

This section summarizes commands you can use on the PIX Firewall to verify PIX Firewall CA support.

You can verify CA configuration with the commands listed in Table 18-7.

Table 18-7 *Commands to Verify PIX Firewall CA Configuration and Certificates*

Command	Description
show ca identity	Displays the CA your PIX Firewall will use
show ca configure	Displays the parameters for communication between the PIX Firewall and the CA
show ca mypubkey rsa	Displays the PIX Firewall's public RSA keys
show ca certificate	Displays the current status of requested certificates as well as relevant information for received certificates such as CA and RA certificates

You debug CA messages with the command listed in Table 18-8.

Table 18-8   *Command to Debug PIX Firewall CA Enrollment*

Command	Description
debug crypto ca	Displays communications between the PIX Firewall and the CA server

You delete RSA keys and CA certificates with the commands listed in Table 18-9.

Table 18-9   *Commands to Delete PIX Firewall RSA Keys and CA Certificates*

Command	Description
ca zeroize rsa	Deletes all RSA keys that were previously generated by your PIX Firewall. If you issue this command, you must also enter the **no ca identity** command to delete CA certificates and ask the CA administrator to revoke your PIX Firewall's certificates at the CA.
no ca identity	Manually removes the PIX Firewall's certificates from the configuration and deletes all the certificates issued by the CA.

Scaling Cisco VPNs

Cisco routers, PIX Firewalls, and the CiscoSecure VPN client can be used to create remote access VPNs using IPSec. Dynamic crypto maps, IKE mode configuration, and IPSec extended authentication are all IPSec features that can be used to create remote access VPNs.

Site-to-site VPNs can also be configured to scale to larger, more complex networks with the tunnel endpoint discovery feature on Cisco routers.

This section is an overview of how to configure features that support remote access networks and site-to-site scalability. After a brief overview of each feature, a summary of how to configure the feature on Cisco routers or the PIX Firewall (as supported by each device) is outlined. You might need to review the documents specified in the "References" section for more details.

Configure Dynamic Crypto Maps

Dynamic crypto maps are supported in Cisco routers and the PIX Firewall. Dynamic crypto maps can ease IPSec configuration and are recommended for use with networks where the peers are not always predetermined. An example of this is mobile users (VPN clients), who obtain dynamically assigned IP addresses. First, the mobile clients need to authenticate themselves to the local Cisco router or PIX Firewall using IKE by something other than an IP address, such as a fully qualified domain name. After authentication, the security association request can be processed against a dynamic crypto map that is set up to accept requests (matching the specified local policy) from previously unknown peers.

Dynamic crypto maps are available only for use by IKE. A dynamic crypto map entry is essentially a crypto map entry without all the parameters configured. It acts as a policy template in which the missing parameters are later dynamically configured (as the result of an IPSec negotiation) to match a peer's requirements. This allows peers to exchange IPSec traffic with the Cisco device even if the Cisco device does not have a crypto map entry specifically configured to meet all the peer's requirements.

Dynamic crypto maps are used by Cisco devices when a peer tries to initiate an IPSec security association with the Cisco device.

Dynamic Crypto Map Router Configuration

Configuring dynamic crypto maps on Cisco routers consists of the following four steps:

Step 1 Enter the **crypto dynamic-map** *map-name seq-num* command, which puts you into config-dynamic-crypto-map mode.

Step 2 Configure dynamic crypto map parameters. Only the **set transform-set** command is required within each dynamic crypto map entry. Normally, the **set peer** command is not used because the peer is unknown.

Step 3 Assign the dynamic crypto map to a regular crypto map with the **crypto map** *map-name seq-num* **ipsec-isakmp** [**dynamic** *dynamic-map-name*] command.

Step 4 Assign the crypto map to an interface by entering interface configuration mode and enter the **crypto map** *map-name* command.

Example 18-23 shows a dynamic crypto map on a Cisco router.

Example 18-23 *A Dynamic Crypto Map on a Cisco Router*

```
crypto ipsec transform-set mine esp-3des
!
crypto dynamic-map dynomap 210
 set transform-set mine
 match address 110
!
crypto map mymap 30 ipsec-isakmp dynamic dynomap
!
interface Serial0
 crypto map mymap
!
access-list 110 permit tcp 10.0.1.0 0.0.0.255 10.0.2.0 0.0.0.255
```

Dynamic Crypto Map PIX Firewall Configuration

Configuring dynamic crypto maps on PIX Firewalls consists of the following three steps:

Step 1   Specify which transform sets are allowed for this dynamic crypto map entry. List multiple transform sets in order of priority, with the highest priority first. Use the **crypto dynamic-map** *dynamic-map-name dynamic-seq-num* **set transform-set** *transform-set name1*, [*transform-set name2, transform-set name9*] command to specify the transform set. You can optionally set an access list, a peer, IPSec lifetime, and PFS parameters with the **crypto dynamic-map** series of commands.

NOTE   You can optionally use the **nat** (*if_name*) **0 access-list** *acl_name* command to exempt traffic that is matched by the **access-list** command statements from Network Address Translation (NAT) services. The accompanying **access-list** command cannot specify port selectors.

Step 2   Add the dynamic crypto map set to a static crypto map set using the **crypto map** *map-name seq-num* **ipsec-isakmp dynamic** *dynamic-map-name* command. Be sure to set the crypto map entries referencing dynamic maps to be the lowest-priority entries (the highest-sequence numbers) in a crypto map set.

Step 3   Apply a crypto map set to an interface on which the IPSec traffic will be evaluated using the **crypto map** *map-name* **interface** *interface-name* command.

Example 18-24 shows an example of configuring a dynamic crypto map on the PIX Firewall, setting an access list.

Example 18-24   *An Example of Configuring a Dynamic Crypto Map on the PIX Firewall, Setting an Access List*

```
crypto ipsec transform-set myset1 esp-3des esp-md5-hmac
crypto dynamic-map dynomap 10
match address 110
crypto dynamic-map dynomap 10
set transform-set myset1
crypto map mymap 200 ipsec-isakmp dynamic dynomap
crypto map mymap interface outside
access-list 110 permit ip 10.1.1.0 0.0.0.255 10.2.1.0 0.0.0.255
nat (outside) 0 access-list 110
```

Configure IKE Mode Configuration

IKE Mode Configuration (IKE mode config) is a feature that allows a security gateway (a Cisco router or a PIX Firewall) to download an IP address (and other network-level configuration) to a VPN client (peer) as part of an IKE negotiation. Using this exchange, the security gateway gives an IP address to the IKE client to be used as an "inner" IP address encapsulated under IPSec, similar to Dynamic Host Configuration Protocol (DHCP) for dialup clients. This provides a known IP address for a VPN client, which can be matched against the IPSec policy. There are two types of IKE mode configuration:

- **Gateway initiation**—The gateway initiates the configuration mode with the client. After the client responds, the IKE modifies the sender's identity, the message is processed, and the client receives a response.

- **Client initiation**—The client initiates the configuration mode with the gateway. The gateway responds with an IP address it has allocated for the client.

IKE Mode Router Configuration

The Cisco router needs to be configured for IKE mode config using a dynamic crypto map. Configuring IKE mode config on Cisco routers consists of the following seven steps in global configuration mode:

Step 1   Define a pool of IP addresses to be assigned to the VPN client with the **ip local pool** *pool-name start-address end-address* command.

Step 2   Reference the local address pool in the IKE policy using the **crypto isakmp client configuration address-pool local** *pool-name* command.

Step 3   Configure a dynamic crypto map for IKE mode config with the **crypto dynamic-map** *dynamic-map-name dynamic-seq-num* command. This command puts you into config-dynamic-crypto-map mode.

Step 4   Configure dynamic crypto map parameters and then exit. Only the **set transform-set** command is required within each dynamic crypto map entry.

Step 5   Configure IKE mode config to initiate and/or respond to requests with the **crypto map** *tag* **client-configuration address** {**initiate** | **respond**} command.

Step 6   Assign the dynamic crypto map that uses IKE mode config to a global IPSec crypto map with the **crypto map** *map-name seq-num* **ipsec-isakmp** [**dynamic** *dynamic-map-name*] command.

Step 7   Finally, assign the crypto map to an interface by entering interface configuration mode and then using the **crypto map** *map-name* command.

An example of a configuration for IKE mode config on a Cisco router is shown in Example 18-25.

Example 18-25 *An Example of a Configuration for IKE Mode Config on a Cisco Router*

```
crypto ipsec transform-set myset1 esp-3des esp-md5-hmac
crypto isakmp client-config address-pool local site1clients
crypto dynamic-map dynomodecfg 1
set transform-set myset1
crypto map modecfg client-configuration address initiate
crypto map modecfg client-configuration address respond
crypto map modecfg 1 ipsec-isakmp dynamic dynomodecfg
ip local pool site1clients 10.1.1.1 10.1.1.254
```

IKE Mode PIX Firewall Configuration

To configure IKE mode configuration on your PIX Firewall, perform the following seven steps after configuring IKE:

Step 1 Define the pool of IP addresses with the **ip local pool** *pool-name start-address* [*end-address*] command.

Step 2 Reference the defined pool of IP addresses in the IKE configuration with the **isakmp client configuration address-pool local** *pool-name* [*interface-name*] command.

Step 3 Configure a dynamic crypto map for IKE mode config with the **crypto dynamic-map** *dynamic-map-name dynamic-seq-num* command.

Step 4 Configure a dynamic crypto map with the **crypto dynamic-map** *dynamic-map-name dynamic-seq-num* **set transform-set** *transform-set-name1* [*transform-set-name9*] command. You can optionally set other crypto dynamic-map commands such as **match address**.

Step 5 Define which crypto maps should attempt to configure clients with the **crypto map** *map-name* **client configuration address** {**initiate** | **respond**} command.

Step 6 Assign the dynamic crypto map that uses IKE mode config to a global IPSec crypto map with the **crypto map** *map-name seq-num* **ipsec-isakmp** [**dynamic** *dynamic-map-name*] command.

Step 7 Finally, assign the crypto map to an interface with the **crypto map** *map-name* **interface** *interface-name* command.

Example 18-26 is a partial configuration that shows a PIX Firewall that has been configured to both set IP addresses to clients and respond to IP address requests from clients whose packets arrive on the outside interface using a dynamic crypto map without explicitly specifying the peer.

Example 18-26 *An Example of Using a Dynamic Crypto Map Without Explicitly Specifying the Peer*

```
ip local pool remoteclient 172.30.1.1-172.30.1.254
crypto isakmp client configuration address-pool local remoteclient outside:
crypto ipsec transform-set pc esp-des esp-md5-hmac
crypto dynamic-map dyno 10
set transform-set pc
crypto map dyno client configuration address initiate
crypto map dyno client configuration address respond
crypto map dynmap 10 ipsec-isakmp dynamic dyno
crypto map dynmap interface outside
```

Configure IPSec Extended Authentication

The PIX Firewall supports the Extended Authentication (Xauth) feature within the IKE protocol. Xauth lets you add user authentication to your IPSec VPN against a remote security database running TACACS+ or RADIUS. The Xauth feature is designed for VPN clients. It requires user authentication by prompting the user for a username and password and verifies them with the information stored in your TACACS+ or RADIUS database. XAuth is negotiated between IKE Phase 1 (the IKE device authentication phase) and IKE Phase 2 (the IPSec SA negotiation phase). If the Xauth fails, the IPSec security association is not established, and the IKE security association is deleted.

IPSec Extended Authentication PIX Firewall Configuration

To configure Xauth on your PIX Firewall, perform the following four steps after configuring IKE:

Step 1 Set up a basic AAA Server with the **aaa-server** *group_tag* (*if_name*) **host** *server_ip key* command.

Step 2 Enable Xauth with the **crypto map** *map-name* **client authentication** *aaa-group-tag* command. Be sure to specify the same AAA server group tag within the **crypto map client authentication** command statement that was specified in the **aaa-server** command statement.

Step 3 You can optionally allow the PIX Firewall to make an exception to the XAuth feature for remote IPSec clients not requiring XAuth that share the same interface as VPN client(s) that do. Use the **isakmp key** *keystring* **address** *ip-address* [**no-xauth**] command to make an XAuth exception when the PIX Firewall is configured to use preshared keys, or use the **isakmp peer fqdn** *fqdn* [**no-xauth**] command to make an XAuth exception when the PIX Firewall is configured to use RSA signatures.

Example 18-27 is a partial configuration that shows a PIX Firewall that has been configured to authenticate VPN clients using XAuth against a TACACS+ security server at address 10.1.1.4.

Example 18-27 *A PIX Firewall That Has Been Configured to Authenticate VPN Clients Using XAuth Against a TACACS+ Security Server*

```
aaa-server TACACS+ outside host 10.1.1.4 secret123
crypto map mymap client authentication TACACS+
isakmp key cisco1234 address 172.16.2.2 255.255.255.255 no-xauth
isakmp peer fqdn site2.xyz.com no-xauth
```

The PIX Firewall will not perform XAuth against IPSec clients using preshared keys at address 172.16.2.2 or using RSA signatures from the fully qualified domain name of site2.xyz.com.

Configure Tunnel Endpoint Discovery

Dynamic Tunnel Endpoint Discovery (TED) is an enhancement to IPSec that allows Cisco routers configured with dynamic crypto maps to initiate IPSec sessions with peers that are not preconfigured.

TED is useful in large Enterprise IPSec deployments when there are many sites in a fully meshed topology that need to establish security associations with each other. With TED, IPSec can scale to a complex topology without having to predefine all possible IPSec peers in crypto map statements on each router.

TED extends the benefits of dynamic crypto maps by allowing any peer with the TED-based dynamic crypto map to initiate an IPSec SA with a peer that has not been predefined as a peer in a crypto map, easing network-wide configuration.

TED operates by sending a discovery probe from the initiator to determine which IPSec peer is responsible for a desired destination host or subnet. After the address of that peer is learned, the initiator proceeds with IKE Phase 1 (main mode) in the normal way. The TED discovery probe is a special IKE packet (UDP port 500) that is sent from the initiating peer toward the destination network or host that the original traffic was destined to as specified in the crypto access list. The responding peer router recognizes the TED probe and returns its address as the destination tunnel endpoint rather than forwarding it to the actual destination. The responding peer also learns the address of the initiating peer via the probe.

TED has the following restrictions:

- It is available only with dynamic crypto maps.
- Load balancing cannot be implemented between peers using TED.

To create a dynamic crypto map entry with TED configured, use the following commands, beginning in global configuration mode:

Step 1 Configure a dynamic crypto map that will use TED with the **crypto dynamic-map** *dynamic-map-name dynamic-seq-number* command. This command puts you in config-dynamic-crypto-map mode.

Step 2 Configure dynamic crypto map parameters and then exit. Specify a transform set with the **set transform-set** command and specify an access list with the **match address** command.

Step 3 Add the dynamic crypto map to a static crypto map set with the **crypto map** *map-name seq-number* **ipsec-isakmp dynamic** *dynamic-map-name* [**discover**] command. The **discover** keyword enables TED.

Example 18-28 is a partial configuration that shows a Cisco router configured for TED for traffic from the 10.1.0.0 network behind the router to the 10.2.0.0 network on an undefined peer router.

Example 18-28 *A Cisco Router Configured for TED*

```
interface Serial 0
 crypto map ted
crypto ipsec transform-set myset1 esp-3des esp-md5-hmac
crypto dynamic-map probe 1
 set transform mymap1
 match address 103
crypto map ted 1 ipsec-isakmp dynamic probe discover
access-list 103 permit ip 10.1.0.0 0.0.255.255 10.2.0.0 0.0.255.255
```

Summary

This section summarizes the main points of this chapter:

- CAs let IPSec networks scale by providing a trusted source for IPSec peers to authenticate each other during an IKE exchange without having to manually configure keys between peers.

- CAs are offered by security vendors either as software that is purchased, installed, and administered by the end user or as a managed service that the end user can subscribe to.

- Most of the tasks and steps for configuring Cisco routers and PIX Firewalls for CA support match those for configuring preshared keys, with some unique tasks and steps to include planning for CA and configuring CA support, and configuring IKE for RSA signature authentication.

- You should configure CA server details before configuring IKE.

- Cisco devices must enroll to a CA server using SCEP, a protocol for automating CA enrollment.
- Each CA server that supports Cisco IPSec devices requires a slightly different configuration process in the devices.
- Use the RSA signatures authentication method for IKE when using CA support on both Cisco routers and the PIX Firewall.
- The IPSec configuration process is the same as that used for preshared and RSA encrypted nonces authentication.
- Cisco routers and PIX Firewalls support remote access features including dynamic crypto maps, extended authentication, and IKE mode configuration.
- Cisco routers support tunnel endpoint discovery, which can simplify the configuration of complex meshed IPSec VPNs.

Review Questions

Answer the following review questions, which delve into some of the key facts and concepts covered in this chapter:

1 What is the advantage of using a CA to authenticate IPSec peers?

2 What are some CA server vendors that can interoperate with Cisco VPN devices using SCEP and that offer software that the end user installs and administers?

3 Which IKE authentication method is used for CA support?

4 How do you view CA certificates in the router's configuration?

5 Is any special IPSec configuration required for CA support?

6 When should you principally use dynamic crypto maps?

7 What is the general procedure for configuring dynamic crypto maps on a PIX Firewall?

8 When should you use IKE mode configuration?

9 How is using IKE extended authentication beneficial in a VPN client-initiated remote access topology?

10 What command do you use to configure tunnel endpoint discovery?

References

The topics considered in this chapter are complex and should be studied further to more fully understand them and put them to use. Use the following references to learn more about the topics in this chapter.

CA Standards and Overviews

Cisco white paper, "Certificate Authority Support for IPSec Overview," November 1999, located at www.cisco.com/warp/public/cc/cisco/mkt/security/encryp/prodlit/821_pp.htm.

Cisco white paper, "Cisco Systems' Simple Certificate Enrollment Protocol," January 2000, located at www.cisco.com/warp/public/cc/cisco/mkt/security/tech/scep_wp.htm.

Configuring CA for Cisco IOS Software

Refer to the *Cisco IOS Security Configuration Guide, Release 12.1*, in the chapter "Configuring Certification Authority Interoperability," for an overview of how to configure CA support on Cisco routers.

Refer to the *Cisco IOS Security Command Reference, Release 12.1*, in the chapter "Certification Authority Interoperability Commands," for details on commands used to configure CA support on Cisco routers.

CA for the PIX Firewall

Refer to the *Configuration Guide for the PIX Firewall, Version 5.1*, to see how to configure IPSec CA support on the PIX Firewall. You will find the following chapters most informative:

- **Configuring IPSec**—Presents an overview of how to configure IPSec CA support and presents the procedure to do so
- **Command Reference**—Contains details on each PIX Firewall command
- **Configuration Examples**—Shows sample configurations for PIX Firewall IPSec with CA support

IPSec Standards and RFC Documents

draft-nourse-scep-02.txt, Xiaoyi Liu, Cheryl Madson, David McGrew, and Andrew Nourse, "Cisco Systems' Simple Certificate Enrollment Protocol (SCEP)," February 2000.

RFC 2314, B. Kaliski, "PKCS #10: Certification Request Syntax Version 1.5," March 1998.

RFC 2315, B. Kaliski, "PKCS #7: Cryptographic Message Syntax Version 1.5," March 1998.

RFC 2459, R. Housley, W. Ford, W. Polk, and D. Solo, "Internet X.509 Public Key Infrastructure Certificate and CRL Profile," January 1999.

Security Associates Program

The following URL is for the Security Associates Program, which lists public key infrastructure and CA products that are compatible with Cisco products. The following URL requires a CCO username and password: www.cisco.com/warp/customer/cc/so/neso/sqso/csap/index.shtml.

PART VII

Appendixes

Appendix A XYZ Company Case Study Scenario

Appendix B An Example of an XYZ Company Network Security Policy

Appendix C Configuring Standard and Extended Access Lists

Appendix D Answers to Review Questions

XYZ Company Case Study Scenario

The XYZ Company network scenario described in this appendix is used throughout the book to tie together all the network security concepts and implementation procedures you will learn and perform. All the IP addresses and networking devices used throughout this book are consistent with the XYZ Company case study scenario.

This appendix presents an overview of the hypothetical XYZ Company. It shows the beginning state of the company before systematic network security methods are applied. Each chapter of this book shows you how to implement a particular Cisco network security technology so that XYZ's network is progressively more secure with each chapter.

This appendix finishes up by showing the secured XYZ Company network that will be achieved in this book. This appendix also relates the XYX case study to the actual equipment used for labs in the Managing Cisco Network Security (MCNS) course.

XYZ Company Overview

XYZ Company is a Silicon Valley growth company that has historically had a trusting, open environment with full network access to all. Recently, the company has experienced numerous network intrusions that have been discovered or are suspected by the Information Systems (IS) department.

The company now realizes that it is vulnerable to network intruders and is eager to implement secure networking using Cisco network and security products. The company is already a strong Cisco customer and is using TCP/IP networking. The company has three primary network environments to secure: campus, dialup, and Internet access.

XYZ wants to limit access to sensitive data on servers by internal and external users, limit outbound traffic, and improve authorization, authentication, and accounting practices. Company management has heard about IPSec and VPNs. They want advice on how to identify threats and select appropriate security policies, and they want configuration expertise to try out the Cisco security management offerings.

The IS department is responsible for maintaining the entire network. The campus applications and file servers run on Windows NT servers that support the overall company, the Engineering and Sales organizations, and partners. The IS group also has a network management system (NMS) running Windows NT server and network management software. The campus network consists of Cisco routers and Ethernet switches.

XYZ wants to limit access to sensitive data on servers in the Sales and Engineering subnets by internal and external users. XYZ is concerned that unauthorized persons have accessed product sales and engineering data on those servers. The unsecured state of the network before Cisco security technologies are applied is shown in Figure A-1. As you can see, even the perimeter router is not configured to secure the inside network.

Figure A-1 *The XYZ Company Network Diagram, Showing the Existing, Unsecured Network*

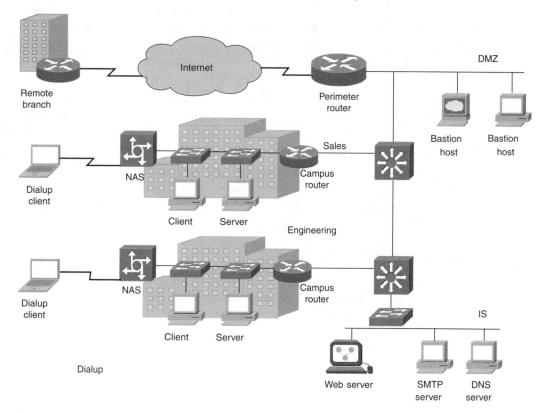

Dialup Access

XYZ Company has a small force of mobile users (sales representatives and system engineers) who have laptop computers running Windows 95/NT. They need to access servers in their departments. Some XYZ employees regularly telecommute using PCs running Windows 95/NT. The company also has several remote branch offices with Cisco 1720 routers, using dial-on-demand routing to connect to the campus site. The company plans to allow suppliers to connect to its campus network via the Engineering dialup network. XYZ uses Cisco 3640 network access servers for dialup networking, connected to Catalyst Ethernet switches and Cisco 4700 campus routers.

XYZ is worried that unauthorized people have accessed the network via the dialup network access servers. Company officials want to control dialup access, which is currently uncontrolled.

Internet Access

XYZ has a high-speed connection to an Internet service provider (ISP). The ISP circuit connects to a Cisco 1720 perimeter router on campus. External Internet users include customers and employees who access the corporate bastion host, which runs a Web server containing product information and an FTP server containing demonstration software and product documentation. The company's intent is to limit external Internet access to the bastion host. Internal Internet users are employees who need to access the Internet for research. The company intends to allow unrestricted use of the Internet to employees. Internal and external users can send each other e-mail. However, due to the fact that e-mail attachments and unauthorized applications have introduced problems, the company wants better SMTP mail controls.

XYZ suspects, yet has no proof, that people with malicious intent have accessed the company network via the Internet. The company Web site was vandalized. The Internet router was attacked to the extent that intended users could not access the Internet at all.

The Departments Involved

The three main groups involved with network usage and security are the IS, Sales, and Engineering departments.

The IS Department

The IS department has one Windows NT server that centralizes network management. It is responsible for administrative oversight and connectivity to the network infrastructure, servers, and workstations, and it can access all network devices via Telnet.

The Sales Department

The following are true of the Sales department:

- On-site sales workstations are PCs running Windows 95/NT.
- A mobile workforce of sales representatives and sales engineers use laptop computers running Windows 95.
- Remote sales branches use Cisco 1720 routers via dial-on-demand routing to the campus site.
- Windows NT servers run sales support applications, sales databases, and a file server.
- Remote users use a Cisco 3640 network access server with modems and analog dialup lines.
- The Sales department is connected to the rest of the corporate campus via a Catalyst Ethernet switch and a Cisco 4700 router Ethernet port.
- Sales employees need to access only their own Windows NT servers.

The Engineering Department

The following are true of the Engineering department:

- On-site workstations consist of UNIX workstations and PCs running Windows NT.
- Telecommuting engineers have PCs and laptops running Windows NT.
- Remote users use a Cisco 3640 network access server with modems and analog dialup lines.
- The Engineering department has its own Windows NT servers with engineering and product information that must be secured from other users.
- The Engineering department is connected to the rest of the corporate campus via a Catalyst Ethernet switch and a Cisco 4700 router Ethernet port.

XYZ's Network Security Goal

XYZ Company ultimately wants to create a secure network environment with Cisco technologies. It hopes to implement the secure network shown in Figure A-2.

XYZ Company has a remote branch site that is nearly a mirror image of the corporate site, with different IP addresses. The secure network topology for this branch is shown in Figure A-3.

Figure A-2 *The XYZ Company Secure Network*

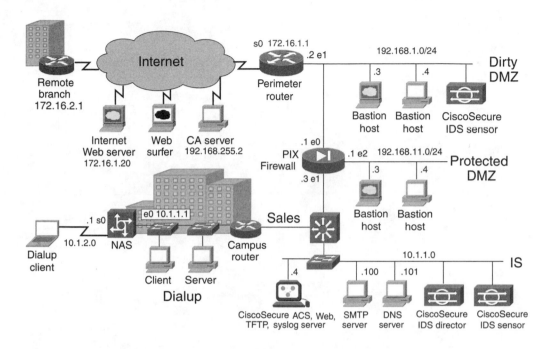

Figure A-3 *The XYZ Company Branch Site, a Mirror Image of the Corporate Site*

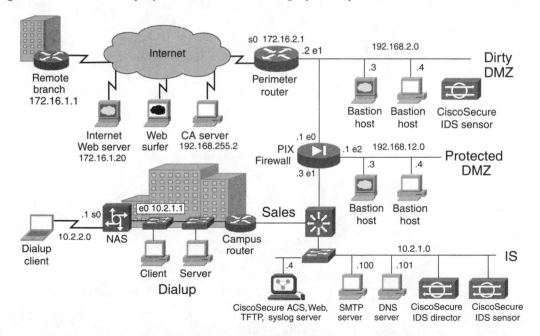

APPENDIX B

An Example of an XYZ Company Network Security Policy

This appendix contains an example of a network security policy for the XYZ Company network. The policy statements contained in this appendix cover the major issues of enterprise network security for XYZ Company. It is not intended to be a critique of, or a standard for, a security policy for a real enterprise.

Statement of Authority and Scope

As an authorized user of the XYZ Company internal network, each employee has access to information with a wide range of sensitivity levels. Familiarity with and observance of XYZ's Network Security Policy ("the policy") is important so that every employee can contribute to ensuring network security and information integrity. XYZ Company follows the "need to know" principle by deliberately avoiding disclosure of information that the employee does not need to know for job performance.

Intended Audience

The policy was written for the following intended audience:

- Network users expected to comply with the security policy
- System support personnel who implement and support the policy
- Managers who are concerned about protection of data and the associated cost of the policy
- Company executives who want to ensure network integrity balanced with ease of use and cost of implementation
- Company lawyers and auditors who are concerned about the company's reputation and responsibility to clients and customers

Scope of Security Policy

The policy is a part of "XYZ's Commitment to Security," a top-level document outlining XYZ Company's commitment to security of all types. The policy outlines the security guidelines for online access to XYZ Company corporate information by company employees and subcontractors and by any other business, including (but not limited to) business partners, vendors, and customers.

Legal Authority of the XYZ Network Security Policy

The XYZ Company board of directors and senior executive staff have been empowered by the company shareholders to create, implement, enforce, and maintain the policy in accordance with applicable local, national, and international laws. The XYZ information security officer and corporate attorney are responsible for enforcing the policy.

Policy Stakeholders

It is the responsibility of all XYZ Company users, system administrators, and information system operations and maintenance personnel to help ensure that the integrity of corporate network and computing resources, as well as the integrity and confidentiality of information processed and stored on those resources, is protected in accordance with sound security practices as outlined in the policy.

The following personnel are responsible for drafting, maintaining, and enforcing the policy:

- Vice president of information systems and chief information officer
- Vice president of central engineering
- Vice president of sales and marketing
- Information security officer
- Director of networking and telecommunications in the information systems organization
- Senior manager of IS operations
- Corporate controller
- Corporate attorney

System Administrator Responsibilities

System administrators for network equipment and multiuser hosts are responsible for ensuring compliance with the following guidelines:

- Assign accounts only to individuals.

- Within XYZ Company, account names and other machine-based representations of a user's account (such as UNIX UIDs) should be globally unique. For example, throughout the entire company, only one individual must be associated with the login ID "jdoe". If any given account name appears on multiple hosts, that name should always represent the same person.

- Security patches and updated network equipment images recommended by the information security officer or designee should be installed on a priority basis agreed upon for the severity of each patch.

- Implement username and password management as outlined in this Network Security Policy.

- Deactivate user accounts upon termination.

- Store system configuration files on a secure TFTP server. Do not share the files or make them publicly available. Consider the use of kerberized rcp between Cisco routers and the TFTP host.

- Review the system log files on a daily basis. Report signs of a possible major security incident to the information security officer or designee immediately. Send a report of minor security breaches (such as multiple failed login attempts) to the information security officer on a weekly basis as appropriate.

- Run network security management tools designed to help system administrators find weak passwords and network vulnerabilities and check file integrity and system configurations (such as CiscoSecure Scanner, CiscoSecure Intrusion Detection System [IDS], Cisco Netsys, Crack, COPS, Tiger, or Tripwire) on a regular basis.

Security Policy Maintenance Procedure

The company stakeholders shall review and update the policy at least once a year.

The IS department must conduct random system audits with little or no advance notice under the direction of the information security officer and document the results of the audit checks.

Implementation Procedure

The director of networking and telecommunications shall create a network design that specifies the exact network topology and network equipment that will be used to implement the policy.

Audits shall be conducted when new network equipment and host systems are connected to the network to establish a baseline of operation and to ensure that it conforms to the policy.

User Education

Policy awareness must be incorporated as part of employee orientation. Users are required to read and sign the Acceptable Use Policy annually as a condition of employment.

Social Engineering Awareness Prevention

Employees shall use discretion when discussing business matters with nonemployees. Establish a need to know before discussing anything that might be used to construct a concept of how the company manages its affairs.

Acceptable Use Policy

The Acceptable Use Policy defines what the company will and will not tolerate regarding internal and external access, use of software and hardware, and any additional constraints required by federal, state, or local laws, regulations, or ordinances.

Acceptable Uses of the Network

Individuals and groups within XYZ Company who are responsible for establishing or maintaining connections between XYZ's network and other businesses should take appropriate measures to minimize the risk of these connections being used to compromise XYZ's information security.

Unacceptable Uses of the Network

Users are not allowed to access or make copies of system configuration files from network equipment or network servers (such as /etc/passwd or router configuration files) unless they are system administrators.

Users are not allowed to gain, or attempt to gain, EXEC or root access or the equivalent to network equipment and hosts that make up the XYZ Company network and IS infrastructure unless their job tasks permit such access.

Compliance Requirements

Users must comply with the directives contained in this policy and any revisions or modifications made to it. Access to the company's infrastructure and data that it contains is a privilege associated with employment; it is not a right. As such, the company may change a user's access privileges at its discretion at any time. Failure to comply with the company's requirements regarding use of its data infrastructure can result in disciplinary action up to and including dismissal.

Identification and Authentication Policy

The Identification and Authentication Policy defines the technical and procedural methods used for identification and authorization.

Password Management Guidelines

The following guidelines govern the selection and use of passwords:

- Passwords, if possible, should use a mixture of dictionary-based words containing uppercase and lowercase letters, should use a mixture of special and numeric characters, and should be at least eight characters long (for example, deltA9Cog, china&fish, or run7w00deN).
- Change passwords quarterly (every three months).
- Create unique passwords for each account a user possesses.
- Do not record passwords in written form.
- Do not disclose passwords to anyone, even to coworkers.

Authentication Guidelines

XYZ Company will use a remote security database running the TACACS+ protocol for policy enforcement of authentication.

Internet Access Policy

XYZ Company realizes that a connection to the Internet is important to company business, yet having such a connection creates security risks. The Internet Access Policy defines guidelines for accessing the Internet as follows.

Acceptable Use

Outbound access to the Internet can be openly used by XYZ Company employees for company research. Dial-in users can gain outbound access to the Internet. Reasonable constraints on total logon time and idle time should be determined and implemented.

Firewall Policy

A firewall system consisting of a perimeter router and bastion host at a minimum must be used to prevent unauthorized access to the campus network from the Internet. Packet filtering rules should be developed to control access to and through the perimeter, with logging of violations of the rules to a syslog server.

Public Services Policy

Inbound access from the Internet to the campus network will be severely restricted unless network layer encryption is employed over the Internet. Inbound Internet access shall be restricted to the bastion host for e-mail, HTTP, FTP, and other required Internet traffic.

Campus Access Policy

The Campus Access Policy defines the process of assigning levels of access to each user.

Trust Relationship

Access to campus hosts is permitted to all company employees based on the trust level assigned by the employee's manager. The XYZ Company seeks to balance transparent user access with network security. XYZ Company has established five trust levels. Each employee is assigned a trust level based on the person's need to access network services to perform job tasks. Technical controls shall be established and enforced to ensure that trust relationships are maintained.

Access to campus hosts by external parties is denied unless specifically authorized by the IS department and the affected department manager.

Network Equipment Security

EXEC or root access to network equipment is denied except to IS department employees specified by the senior manager of IS Operations. Employ network layer encryption to secure vital traffic flows between internal servers.

Remote Access Policy

Personnel who access XYZ's corporate network from home-based offices or via dialup lines must clearly understand and accept the security responsibilities that accompany remote access privileges.

Remote access is a literal extension of XYZ's internal network, providing a potential path to the company's most sensitive information. It is therefore of paramount importance that people with remote access privileges take extreme care in ensuring that only employees and authorized contractors can gain access to the internal network.

Any computer used to access the XYZ Company internal network shall be password-protected or shall be configured in such a way that an unauthorized user cannot launch the communications software package that initiates a connection to the XYZ Company network. The XYZ Company IS department shall specify which type of machine or file protection utility is used, and it should not be possible for password protection to be easily bypassed (for example, by rebooting the machine).

Remote access connections must be authenticated with TACACS+ or token cards and servers.

Mobile Computing

XYZ employees who have a need shall be allowed to gain access to the campus network only via network access servers controlled by the IS department. Employees must use IS-supported Windows 95, Windows 98, Windows 2000, or Apple Macintosh computers with remote access software approved by the IS department.

XYZ Company employees and authorized third parties (such as customers and vendors) can use dialup connections to gain access to the corporate network. Dialup access should be strictly controlled using one-time password authentication.

It is the responsibility of employees with dialup access privileges to ensure that a dialup connection to XYZ Company is not used by nonemployees to gain access to company information system resources.

Home Access

XYZ Company employees who want to set up home-based offices may use remote connections to link their home computers to the corporate network. When possible, remote connections to the corporate network must use CHAP authentication.

Telecommuter Agreement

Users granted remote access privileges will be required to sign a document indicating their understanding of the importance of protecting XYZ Company information from unauthorized disclosure. The document shall also indicate their acceptance of the security requirements set forth in this document and in the top-level security policy.

Branch Office Access

The IS department must approve all remote branch office access to the campus network to ensure network security.

Business Partner (Extranet) Access

The IS department must approve all remote business partner access to the campus network to ensure network security. A firewall must be employed to control such access.

Encryption Policy

An encryption program shall be used for all remote access transactions. The encryption algorithm chosen shall balance the security needs of the transaction in question against the required data throughput.

Incident-Handling Procedure

The XYZ Company security policy stakeholders must develop a detailed incident-handling procedure containing contingency plans designed to handle all possible security incidents. The incident-handling procedure must be written in a "cookbook" approach to ensure that incidents can be managed in a predictable way by on-duty IS personnel at any time. The incident-handling procedure must address the points in this section.

Intrusion Detection Requirements

Intrusion detection software (IDS), such as the CiscoSecure IDS system, should be deployed to provide vital information about the status of the security perimeter. A real-time, enterprise-scale IDS designed to detect, report, and terminate unauthorized activity in the DMZ portion of the perimeter network should include the following capabilities:

- IDS must have scalability and performance to allow the administrators to centrally monitor network activity at the DMZ.

- IDS must be implemented in a multitiered hierarchy, allowing the administrators to quickly add IDS monitor systems as the network grows.

- The central management station also must remotely control the configuration of the remote IDS systems via an intuitive GUI integrated into a network management system, allowing the organization to monitor the security of its connections from one centralized location. This ensures consistent security policy enforcement enterprise-wide.

- The management station must also feed alarm information into an adjacent database archive. Information such as the origin, type, destination, and time of attacks must be logged for trend analysis.

Incident Response Procedure

A detailed Incident Response Procedure must be written as an operational document by the senior manager of IS operations and must be updated quarterly or within one week after a major incident. The Vice President of IS and the Information Security Officer must approve the procedure document. The Incident Response Procedure must structure the company's response to an attack so that, when an incident occurs, the available resources are applied to solving the problem instead of deciding how to solve it. The procedure must address the following requirements:

1 Prepare and plan for incidents—IS operations personnel must receive a minimum of 16 hours of training per year on how to identify incidents and how to implement the Incident Response Procedure. The procedure document must specify the type and duration of training.

2 Identify an incident—System administrators must monitor the IDS system throughout the day to identify incidents. System log files should be monitored hourly and analyzed at the end of the day. The senior system administrator on duty at the time of an incident is responsible for identifying an incident. The Incident Response Procedure must specify priority levels of incidents as suggested in RFC 2196, "Site Security Handbook."

3 Handle the incident—The Incident Response Procedure must specify how system administrators must handle an incident. The following procedure is an outline of the steps to take and document:

— Identify the attack's type and priority.

— Identify the attack's start and stop times.

— Identify the attack's point of origin.

— Specify the impacted computer or network systems.

— Trace the attack back to its origin without trespassing on other networks or computer systems.

— Attempt to thwart the attack or mitigate damage. Isolate the system under attack.

— Notify appropriate points of contact.

— Protect evidence of the attack (such as log files).

— Restore IS services when appropriate.

4 Document and apply lessons learned—An incident report should be written under the guidance of the senior manager of IS operations and should address the following points:

— An inventory should be taken of the attacked systems' assets.

— A description of lessons learned should be written.

— The Network Security Policy should be revised if required.

— The attack perpetrators should be investigated and prosecuted.

Points of Contact

Table B-1 lists the members of the incident response team, which is responsible for implementing the company's security policy when an incident occurs.

Table B-1 *The Members of the Incident Response Team*

Point of Contact	Roles
Senior system administrator on duty when an incident occurs	• Primary point of contact to identify and respond to an incident • Documents the incident in a report
Senior manager of IS operations	• Primary management point of contact • Determines how to respond to the incident • Coordinates system administrators during serious incidents • Must be able to be reached by pager or cell phone 24 hours a day • Contacts the next person in the chain of command
Information and security officer	• Escalates the incident to a computer incident response team such as CERT • Involves law enforcement
Vice president of IS and CIO	• Works with the executive team to handle communications inside and outside the company • Is the only person authorized to talk to news agencies and any entities external to the company • Ensures that the incident response is documented and that appropriate changes in procedures are implemented to prevent further occurrences
Corporate attorney	• Coordinates the prosecution of perpetrators • Approves external communications

Configuring Standard and Extended Access Lists

This appendix presents an overview of configuring standard and extended IP access lists in Cisco IOS Software. This appendix is included in this book because many Cisco security features in Cisco IOS Software use standard or extended IP access lists, and you might need a refresher or reference on access list fundamentals.

An *IP access list* is a sequential collection of permit and deny conditions that apply to IP addresses and optionally to IP protocols and TCP and UDP ports. Access lists permit or deny packets from entering or leaving specified interfaces. Cisco IOS Software supports the following types of access lists for IP:

- Standard IP access lists use source addresses for matching operations.

- Extended IP access lists use source and destination addresses for matching. They also allow optional matching of IP protocol and TCP or UDP port, allowing finer granularity of control.

- Dynamic extended IP access lists grant per-user access from a specific source to a specific destination through a user authentication process.

- Reflexive access lists allow IP packets to be filtered based on session-backflow information.

IP access lists provide two primary uses for implementing network security: packet filtering and traffic selection.

Packet filtering helps control packet movement through the network, helping limit network traffic and restricting network use by certain IP addresses or networks across Cisco router interfaces. For example, packet filtering is useful on a perimeter router to allow only traffic from the public Internet to access a bastion host, or to prevent IP address spoofing. Packet filtering using access lists can also be used to control access to the network and to network equipment. For example, a standard IP access list can control which remote IP addresses can perform router or Ethernet switch administration via Telnet access.

Traffic selection determines "interesting" traffic that will invoke a desired security operation. For example, extended IP access lists are used in crypto maps to determine interesting traffic that will be encrypted with Cisco Encryption Technology (CET) and IPSecurity (IPSec) in Cisco IOS Software.

The types of access lists and the available list numbers for IP are described in Table C-1.

Table C-1 *Types of Access Lists and Their Numbers*

Type of Access List	List Number Range
IP standard	1 to 99
IP extended	100 to 199
Bridging access list for filtering protocol type code	200 to 299
AppleTalk access list	600 to 699
Bridging access list for filtering 48-bit MAC address or vendor code	700 to 799
IPX standard	800 to 899
IPX extended	900 to 999
IPX SAP	1000 to 1099
Extended bridging access list for filtering 48-bit MAC address or vendor code	1100 to 1199
IPX summary address access list	1200 to 1299
IP standard access list (expanded range)	1300 to 1999
IP extended access list (expanded range)	2000 to 2699
Simple rate-limit access list for quality of service policies uses **access-list rate limit** command.	1 to 99 or 100 to 199

IP Addressing and General Access List Concepts

This section presents a review of IP addressing and network and subnet masks. It also covers concepts common to both standard and extended IP access lists, such as wildcard masks, explicit deny all masks, implicit masks, and general access list configuration and design principles. This review section is included because you should thoroughly understand IP addressing in order to create effective access lists.

IP Addressing

An IP address is 32 bits in length and is divided into two parts. The first part designates the network portion of the address, and the second part designates the host address portion. The host address can optionally be partitioned into a subnet address and a host address. A subnet address lets a network address be divided into smaller networks.

IP addresses use dotted-decimal notation to represent a binary number up to 32 bits in length. Each decimal digit represents an 8-bit binary number, or an octet. An example of an address is 192.168.20.204, which represents the binary number 11000000.10101000.00010100.11001100.

Each of the 8 bits in an octet has an equivalent decimal weight, as shown in Table C-2. Going from right to left, the bit weight is 1, 2, 4, 8, 16, 32, 64, 128. The minimum value for an octet is 0; it contains all 0s. The maximum value for an octet is 255; it contains all 1s. If a value of 255 occurs in the host portion of an IP address, it is reserved for broadcast messages to all hosts on a network.

Table C-2   *Decimal Weight of Each Bit in an Octet*

Bit Weight	128	64	32	16	8	4	2	1	Decimal Equivalent
Bits in Octet	0	0	0	0	0	0	0	0	0
Bits in Octet	1	1	1	1	1	1	1	1	255

The allocation of IP addresses is managed and administered by the Internet Network Information Center (InterNIC), a central authority. InterNIC is also the main repository for Requests For Comments (RFCs), which specify how Internet protocols work.

Network Classes

IP addressing supports five different network classes. The far leftmost bits of an IP address indicate the network class, which can be one of the following:

- Class A networks are intended mainly for use with a few very large networks because they provide only 7 bits for the network address field. Each Class A network can have over 16 million hosts. All Class A IP addresses have been assigned.

- Class B networks allocate 14 bits for the network address field and 16 bits for the host address field. This address class offers a good compromise between network and host address space.

- Class C networks allocate 22 bits for the network address field. Class C networks provide only 8 bits for the host field, however, so the number of hosts per network might be a limiting factor.

- Class D addresses are reserved for multicast groups, as described formally in RFC 1112. In Class D addresses, the four highest-order bits are set to 1, 1, 1, and 0.

- Class E addresses are also defined by IP but are reserved for future use. In Class E addresses, the four highest-order bits are all set to 1.

Table C-3 summarizes address ranges and standard network masks for Class A, B, and C networks, which are the most commonly used. The high-order bits of the first octet determine the address range for each class.

Table C-3   *Class A, B, and C Subnets and Addresses*

Class	High-Order Bits	First Octet	Standard Mask
A	0	1.0.0.0 to 126.0.0.0	255.0.0.0
B	10	128.1.0.0 to 191.254.0.0	255.255.0.0
C	110	192.0.1.0 to 223.255.254.0	255.255.255.0

Figure C-1 shows the address formats for Class A, B, and C IP networks. Each network address in the overall IP address consists of one or more octets, and each network address falls on an even octet boundary. The rest of the IP address consists of the host octets, which specify addresses for individual hosts in the network address.

Figure C-1   *Network and Host Fields for Class A, B, and C Networks*

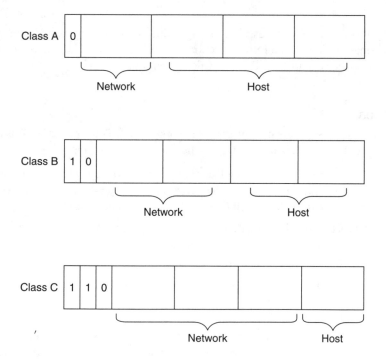

Subnet Addresses

IP networks can also be divided into smaller units, called *subnets*. Subnets allow you to "carve up" your assigned IP schema into smaller units within your enterprise. Subnets are created by borrowing bits from the leftmost (higher-order) bits in the host field of the IP address and using them as a subnet field, as shown in Figure C-2. A subnetted IP address consists of an address field, a subnet field, and a host ID field. If you chose to use 8 bits of subnetting in a Class B IP address, the third octet provides the subnet number. Subnets are useful for dividing up an organization's network structure, for hiding the internal complexity of an organization from the open Internet, and for making more efficient use of the host ID field of IP addresses. A subnet mask is used to differentiate the host address from the network address.

Figure C-2   *Example of Subnetting a Class B Network Address, in Which 8 Bits Borrowed from the Host Field Enables up to 16 Subnets of the Network Address*

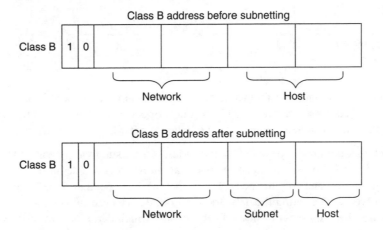

Subnet bits come from the high-order bits of the host field. To determine a subnet mask for an address, add up the decimal values of each position that has a 1 in it. Here's an example:

$224 = 128 + 64 + 32 = 11100000$

Because the subnet mask is not defined by the octet boundary but by bits, you need to convert dotted-decimal addresses to binary and back into dotted-decimal. Table C-4 is a handy reference for converting a binary octet to its decimal equivalent.

Table C-4   *Decimal Weight of Each Bit in a Subnet Mask*

Bit Weight	128	64	32	16	8	4	2	1	Decimal Equivalent
Bits in Octet	1	0	0	0	0	0	0	0	128
Bits in Octet	1	1	0	0	0	0	0	0	192
Bits in Octet	1	1	1	0	0	0	0	0	224

continues

Table C-4 *Decimal Weight of Each Bit in a Subnet Mask (Continued)*

Bit Weight	128	64	32	16	8	4	2	1	Decimal Equivalent
Bits in Octet	1	1	1	1	0	0	0	0	240
Bits in Octet	1	1	1	1	1	0	0	0	248
Bits in Octet	1	1	1	1	1	1	0	0	252
Bits in Octet	1	1	1	1	1	1	1	0	254
Bits in Octet	1	1	1	1	1	1	1	1	255

Table C-5 contains a reference to help you determine subnet addresses for Class B and Class C addresses. Subnetting Class A networks is especially useful to make the most use of the large host field (three octets) of Class A networks.

Network administrators create subnet addresses by subdividing part of the host field of an IP address with a subnet mask. Network administrators decide the size of subnets based on organization and growth needs. The subnet mask is coded into the network equipment involved with creating the network. Network devices use subnet masks to identify which part of the address is considered network and which part to use for host addressing. The network equipment compares the IP address of packets with the subnet mask to determine the network, subnetwork, and host fields when receiving or transmitting packets. The lengths of the network, subnet, and host fields are all variable.

Table C-5 *Class B and C Subnets and Hosts*

Class B Subnetting		
Subnet Mask	Number of Subnets	Number of Hosts
255.255.192.0	2	16,382
255.255.224.0	6	8,190
255.255.240.0	14	4,094
255.255.248.0	30	2,046
255.255.252.0	62	1,022
255.255.254.0	126	510
255.255.255.0	254	254
255.255.255.128	510	126
255.255.255.192	1,022	62

Table C-5   *Class B and C Subnets and Hosts (Continued)*

	Class B Subnetting	
Subnet Mask	**Number of Subnets**	**Number of Hosts**
255.255.255.224	2,046	30
255.255.255.240	4,094	14
255.255.255.248	8,190	6
255.255.255.252	16,382	2

	Class C Subnetting	
Subnet Mask	**Number of Subnets**	**Number of Hosts**
255.255.255.192	2	62
255.255.255.224	6	30
255.255.255.240	14	14
255.255.255.248	30	6
255.255.255.252	62	2

Wildcard Masks

Both standard IP and extended IP access lists use wildcard masks to determine if a packet matches an access list entry. Wildcard masks are like network and subnet masks in that they are written in 32-bit dotted-decimal format.

A wildcard mask works as follows: A 0 in a bit position of the wildcard mask indicates that the corresponding bit in the address is checked against the rules in the access list; a 1 in a bit position of the wildcard mask indicates that the corresponding bit in the address is not "interesting" and can be ignored.

For this reason, the 0 bits in the mask are sometimes called "do-care" bits, and the 1 bits are called "don't-care" bits. Table C-6 contains examples of wildcard masks in decimal and binary form.

Table C-6   *Examples of Wildcard Masks*

	Octet Bit Position								
Decimal Octet	**128**	**64**	**32**	**16**	**8**	**4**	**2**	**1**	**Example**
0	0	0	0	0	0	0	0	0	Check all address bits
15	0	0	0	0	1	1	1	1	Check the first four address bits

continues

Table C-6 *Examples of Wildcard Masks (Continued)*

Decimal Octet	Octet Bit Position								Example
	128	64	32	16	8	4	2	1	
252	1	1	1	1	1	1	0	0	Check the last two address bits
255	1	1	1	1	1	1	1	1	Do not check the address

By carefully setting wildcard masks, an administrator can select a single or several IP addresses for permit or deny tests.

An access list can contain an indefinite number of actual and wildcard addresses. A wildcard address has a nonzero address mask and thus potentially matches more than one actual address. Remember that the order of the access list statements is important because the access list is not processed further after a match is found. Table C-7 contains examples of IP addresses and corresponding access list masks and the resulting matches for each example. When considering Tables C-6 and C-7, remember the following rules used to find a matching address with a wildcard mask:

- 0 bit = must match bits in addresses
- 1 bit = no need to match bits in addresses

Table C-7 *Examples of Access List Wildcard Masks and Matches*

Address	Wildcard Mask	Matches
0.0.0.0	255.255.255.255	Any address
131.108.0.0	0.0.255.255	Network 131.108.0.0
131.108.7.8	0.0.0.0	Host or subnet address
255.255.255.255	0.0.0.0	Local broadcast
131.120.121.5	0.0.7.255	Only subnet 131.120.121.0, assuming a subnet mask of 255.255.248.0

General Access List Configuration Tasks

You need to complete two general tasks to create standard IP or extended IP access lists—create the access list and apply the access list to an interface or terminal line:

1 Create an access list in global configuration mode by specifying an access list number and access conditions. Refer to Table C-1 for the access list number.

Define a standard IP access list using a source address and wildcard.

Define an extended IP access list using source and destination addresses, a protocol identifier, and optional port-type information on some protocols for finer granularity of control.

Use the context-sensitive help feature by entering **?** in the Cisco IOS user interface to verify available names and proper command syntax.

2 Apply the access list to interfaces or terminal lines in interface configuration mode.

After an access list is created, you can apply it to one or more interfaces or terminal lines. Access lists can be applied on either outbound or inbound interfaces.

Access List Configuration Principles

Following these general principles helps ensure that the access lists you create have the intended results:

- **Top-down processing**—Organize your access list so that more-specific references in a network or subnet appear before more-general ones. For example, filter on IP addresses from specific to general: hosts first, then subnets, then specific networks, then any networks. If a specific entry appears after a general entry and they are related conditions, the specific entry will never be processed. For example, if you want to filter a specific host address and then permit all other addresses, make sure your entry about the specific host appears first.

- **Occurrence precedence**—Place more frequently occurring conditions before less-frequent conditions so that less CPU processing is done by the access list, but do not violate the specific-to-general rule.

- **Implicit deny any**—Unless you end your access list with an explicit permit any, it will deny by default all traffic that fails to match any of the access list lines.

- **New lines added to the end**—Subsequent additions are always added to the end of the access list. You cannot selectively insert or delete lines when using numbered access lists, but you can selectively delete lines when using IP named access lists. (This is a Cisco IOS Release 11.2 feature that is discussed further in the "Named IP Access Lists" section of this appendix.) You can use a text editor to edit, delete, and then reapply an access list, or you can use the Access List Manager software from Cisco Systems to manage complex access lists.

- **Undefined access list equals permit any**—If you apply an access list to an interface with the **ip access-group** command before any access list lines have been created, the result is to permit any traffic. The list goes "live" when you apply the access to an interface. If you were to enter only one host-specific permit line, the list would go from a permit any to a "deny most" (because of the implicit deny any) as soon as you press Enter. For this reason, you should create your complete access list before you apply it to an interface.

Configuring Standard IP Access Lists

This section covers how to configure standard IP access lists. Standard IP access lists permit or deny packets based only on the packet's source IP address. The access list number range for defining standard IP access lists is 1 to 99. Standard IP access lists are easier to configure than extended IP access lists, yet they are less powerful because they cannot be used to filter on traffic types or destination addresses. Figure C-3 shows that a standard IP access list could be used to deny access to a network based on the source address.

Figure C-3 *Standard IP Access Lists Permit or Deny Packets Based on the Packet's Source IP Address—The Access List Here Denies Access to a Network*

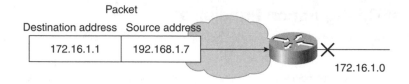

CAUTION Cisco IOS Software Release 11.1 and later have introduced substantial changes to IP access lists. The extensions in Release 11.1 and later are compatible with previous releases; migrating from a release earlier than Release 11.1 to the current image converts your access lists automatically. However, previous releases are not upwardly compatible with these changes. Thus, if you save an access list with the current image and then use older software, the resulting access list will not be interpreted correctly. This could cause severe security problems. Save your old configuration file before booting Release 11.1 or later images.

Standard IP Access List Processing

A standard IP access list is a sequential collection of permit and deny conditions that apply to source IP addresses. The router tests addresses against the conditions in an access list one by one. The first match determines whether the router accepts or rejects the packet. Because the router stops testing conditions after the first match, the order of the conditions is critical. If no conditions match, the router rejects the packet. Standard IP access lists process packets differently for inbound and outbound traffic filtering, which is considered next.

Inbound Traffic Processing

Let's discuss processing for standard IP access lists intended to filter inbound traffic. This process is illustrated in Figure C-4. Upon receiving a packet, the router checks the packet's source address against entries in the access list. If the access list permits the source address, the router exits the access list and continues processing the packet according to the router configuration. If the access list rejects the address, the router discards the packet and returns an ICMP Host Unreachable message.

Figure C-4 *Inbound Traffic Processing for Standard IP Access Lists*

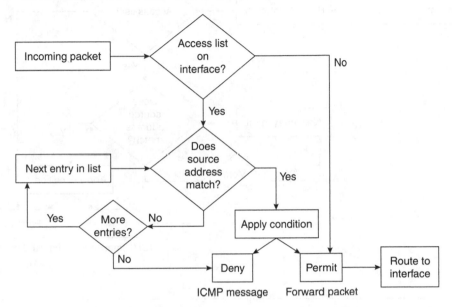

Note that, if no more entries are found in the access list, the packet is denied. This highlights an important rule to remember when creating access lists. The last entry in an access list is known as an *implicit deny any*. It is embedded in Cisco IOS Software and is not listed in the router configuration. All traffic not explicitly permitted is implicitly denied. The implicit deny any rule is useful in implementing a security policy because access lists default to a closed security policy, and you do not have to specify every deny condition. Make sure you have explicit permit statements for traffic you want to allow across the interface, or you will cut off desired traffic. The implicit deny any rule applies to both standard and extended IP access lists.

Outbound Traffic Processing

Next, let's consider processing for standard IP access lists intended to filter outbound traffic. This process is illustrated in Figure C-5. For standard IP access lists applied to outbound traffic, after receiving and routing a packet to a controlled interface, the router checks the packet's source address against the access list. If the access list permits the address, the router transmits the packet. If the access list denies the address, the router discards the packet and returns an ICMP Host Unreachable message.

Figure C-5 *Outbound Traffic Processing for Standard IP Access Lists*

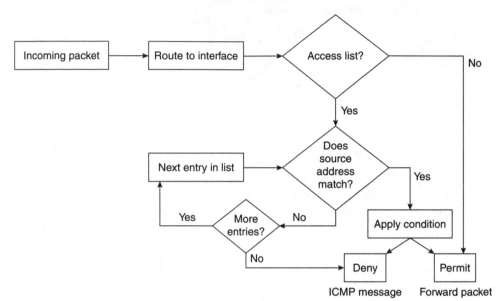

NOTE The primary difference between a standard IP access list and an extended IP access list is that the latter checks information other than the source address in the packet against the access list.

Standard IP Access List Commands

You use the **access-list** command to create an entry in a standard traffic filter list. The command syntax for the **access-list** command used in a standard IP access list is as follows:

```
access-list access-list-number {deny ¦ permit} {source [source-wildcard] ¦ [log]}
```

The following are the parameters for this syntax:

Command Parameter	Description
access-list-number	Identifies the list to which the entry belongs. A number from 1 to 99.
deny ǀ permit	Indicates whether this entry allows or blocks traffic from the specified address.
source	Identifies the source IP address.

Command Parameter	Description
source-wildcard	(Optional) Indicates the wildcard bits to be applied to *source,* as follows: • Use a 32-bit quantity in four-part dotted-decimal format. Place 1s in the bit positions to be ignored by the access list entry. • Use the keyword **any** as an abbreviation for *source* and a *source-wildcard* of 0.0.0.0 255.255.255.255. • If this field is omitted, the mask 0.0.0.0 is assumed.
log	(Optional) Generates an informational syslog message about the packet that matches the entry to be sent to the console or to a syslog server. (The level of messages logged to the console is controlled by the **logging console** command.)

You use the **ip access-group** command in interface configuration mode to apply an existing access list to an interface. Each interface may have both an inbound and an outbound access list (provided that they are both standard or extended). The command syntax for the **ip access-group** command is as follows:

```
ip access-group access-list-number {in ¦ out}
```

The following are the parameters for this syntax:

Command Parameter	Description
access-list-number	Identifies the list to which the entry belongs. A number from 1 to 99.
in	Filters on inbound packets.
out	Filters on outbound packets.

You can delete the entire list from the configuration by entering the **no access-list** *access-list-number* command in global configuration mode. You can remove the application of an access list to an interface or line with the **no ip access-group** *access-list-number* command in interface configuration mode.

Implicit Masks

You can use the implicit mask feature of standard IP access lists to reduce typing and simplify configuration. The implicit mask makes it easier to enter a large number of individual addresses. You use implicit masks by not coding a wildcard mask into the access list entry. You apply an implicit wildcard mask of 0.0.0.0 to the IP address entered as source, and all bits of the address are used to permit or deny traffic. One restriction of implicit masks is that the source IP address must specify a host address, not a network or subnet address. Consider the following three examples of standard IP access lists with implicit masks:

```
access-list 1 permit 10.1.1.3
access-list 1 permit 172.16.21.3
access-list 1 permit 192.168.244.196
```

The first line is an example of a specific host configuration for a Class A IP address. Because no mask is specified, the mask is assumed or implied to be 0.0.0.0 so that all bits in the IP address are used in the access list. The implicit mask makes it seem as if the access list entry is really **access-list 1 permit 10.1.1.3 0.0.0.0**. The second and third lines are examples of implicit masks for a Class B and a Class C address.

Location of Standard Access Lists

Access list location can be complex, but you should generally place standard IP access lists as close to the destination router as possible to exercise the most security control while enabling the greatest flexibility of access. Some general guidelines that are useful for access list placement are shown in the sample configuration in Figure C-6.

Figure C-6 *Sample Topology Showing Where Standard IP Access Lists Should Be Placed*

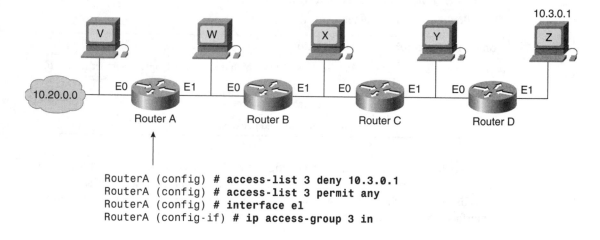

```
RouterA (config) # access-list 3 deny 10.3.0.1
RouterA (config) # access-list 3 permit any
RouterA (config) # interface el
RouterA (config-if) # ip access-group 3 in
```

If the policy goal is to deny Host Z access to Host V and not to change any other access policy, on which router should the access list shown be configured and on which interface of that router? The access list would be placed on Router A. The reason is that the standard IP access list can specify only the source address. Wherever in the path the traffic is denied, no hosts beyond can connect.

The access list could be configured as an outbound list on E0, but it would most likely be configured as an inbound list on E1 so that packets to be denied would not have to be routed first.

What would be the effect of placing the access list on other routers? The answer follows:

- **Router B**—Host Z could not connect with Hosts V and W.
- **Router C**—Host Z could not connect with Hosts V, W, and X.
- **Router D**—Host Z could not connect with hosts V, W, X, and Y.

Common Errors in Standard IP Access Lists

Consider the example of errors in coding standard IP access lists in the following lines:

```
access-list 1 permit 172.16.129.231
!
access-list 1 permit 0.0.0.0
access-list 1 permit 192.168.0.0
!
access-list 1 deny 0.0.0.0 255.255.255.255
access-list 1 deny any
```

This example of standard IP access lists contains the following errors:

- The IP address in the first line is actually a subnetted address with a subnet mask of 255.255.240.0, so a wildcard mask of 0.0.15.255 should have been used instead of the implicit mask of 0.0.0.0 (see Table C-7).

- **permit 0.0.0.0** would exactly match the address 0.0.0.0 and then permit it. In most cases, this address is illegal, so this list would prevent all traffic from getting through (the implicit deny any).

- **permit 192.168.0.0** is probably a configuration error. The intention is probably 192.168.0.0 0.0.255.255. The exact address 192.168.0.0 is reserved to refer to the network and would never be assigned to a host. Network and subnets are represented by explicit masks. As a result, no traffic would get through with this list, again due to the implicit deny any.

- **deny 0.0.0.0 255.255.255.255** and **deny any** are unnecessary to configure from a strictly technical standpoint because they duplicate the function of the implicit deny any that occurs when a packet fails to match all the configured lines in an access list. Denying any is the same as configuring 0.0.0.0 255.255.255.255. It is considered good configuration practice for system administrators to include a **deny any** statement at the end of an access list, so the last line is actually not in error!

Standard IP Access List Example

Consider the sample configuration for the network shown in Figure C-7. The access list configuration for Router A is shown.

Figure C-7 *Standard Access List Example for Router A*

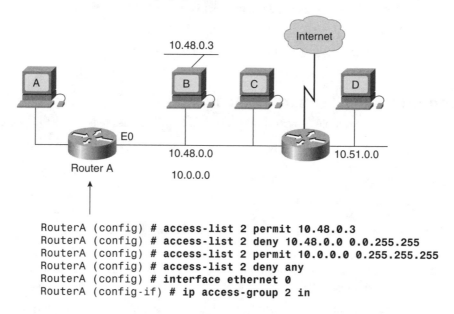

```
RouterA (config) # access-list 2 permit 10.48.0.3
RouterA (config) # access-list 2 deny 10.48.0.0 0.0.255.255
RouterA (config) # access-list 2 permit 10.0.0.0 0.255.255.255
RouterA (config) # access-list 2 deny any
RouterA (config) # interface ethernet 0
RouterA (config-if) # ip access-group 2 in
```

Who can connect to Host A? Can Host B communicate with Host A? Yes. This is permitted by the first line, which uses an implicit host mask.

Can host C communicate with host A? No. Host C is in the subnet denied by the second line.

Can host D communicate with host A? Yes. Host D is on a subnet that is explicitly permitted by the third line.

Can users on the Internet communicate with host A? No. Users outside this network are not explicitly permitted, so they are denied by the **access-list 2 deny any** command.

Configuring Extended IP Access Lists

This section considers how to configure extended IP access lists, which allow more granular control of traffic filtering and selection than do standard IP access lists. After presenting an overview of extended IP access lists, this section examines how extended IP access lists are processed in Cisco IOS Software. This section examines the commands used to configure extended IP access lists, and it then presents several examples. It concludes by discussing where to place extended IP access lists.

Standard IP access lists offer quick configuration and low overhead in limiting traffic based on the source address within a network. Extended IP access lists provide a higher degree of control by enabling filtering based on the transport layer protocol, destination address, and application port number. These features make it possible to limit traffic based on the uses of the network, as illustrated in Figure C-8. In the figure, the perimeter router can control access to internal servers and applications using extended IP access lists on traffic from the Internet. Alternatively, extended IP access lists can be used on internal routers to control access to servers and applications inside the network.

Figure C-8 *Extended IP Access Lists Enable Filtering Based on the Transport Layer Protocol, Source and Destination Address, and Application Port Number*

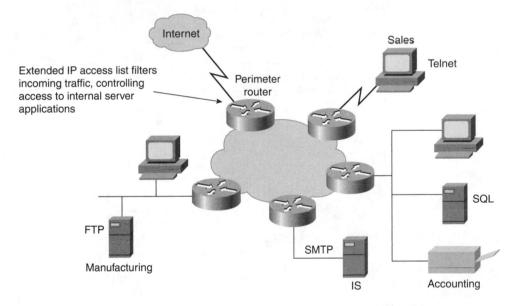

Extended IP Access List Processing

Access list statements operate in sequential, logical order. They evaluate packets from the top down. If a packet header and access list statement match, the packet skips the rest of the statements. If a condition match is true, the packet is permitted or denied. As soon as one parameter or condition fails, the next line in the access list is tested until the end of the access list is reached.

You can use extended IP access lists to check the source address, protocol, and destination address. Depending on the network configuration and protocols used, extended IP access lists provide more protocol-dependent options available for filtering. For example, TCP or UDP ports can be checked, which allows routers to filter at the application layer.

Let's consider packet processing for extended IP access lists, which is illustrated in Figure C-9. The router checks each packet for matches in source address, destination address, protocol, and protocol options. If the conditions are met and the access list is a permit statement, the packet is forwarded. If the conditions are met and the access list is a deny statement, the router discards the packet and returns an ICMP Host Unreachable message.

Figure C-9 *The Extended IP Access List Checks Source Address, Protocol, and Destination Address in the Order Shown*

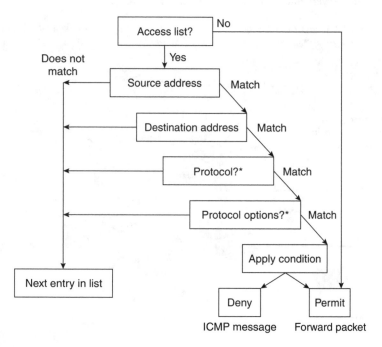

* If present in access list

Extended IP Access List Commands

You use the **access-list** command to create an entry in a complex traffic filter access list.

The command syntax for the **access-list** command used in an extended IP access list is as follows:

```
access-list access-list-number [dynamic dynamic-name [timeout minutes]]
 {deny | permit} protocol source source-wildcard destination destination-wildcard
 [precedence precedence] [tos tos] [log]
```

The following are the parameters for this syntax:

Command Parameter	Description
access-list-number	Identifies the list to which the entry belongs. A number from 100 to 199.
dynamic *dynamic-name*	(Optional) Identifies this access list as a dynamic access list used for lock-and-key security.
timeout *minutes*	(Optional) Specifies the absolute length of time (in minutes) that a temporary access list entry can remain in a dynamic access list used for lock-and-key security. The default is an infinite length of time and allows an entry to remain permanently.
deny | permit	Indicates whether this entry is used to allow or block the specified address(es).
protocol	Specifies the name or number of an IP protocol. It can be one of the protocol keywords: **ahp**, **eigrp**, **esp**, **gre**, **icmp**, **igmp**, **igrp**, **ip**, **ipinip**, **nos**, **ospf**, **pcp**, **tcp**, or **udp**, or an integer in the range 0 to 255 representing an IP protocol number. To match any Internet protocol (including ICMP, TCP, and UDP), use the keyword **ip**. Protocol keywords **icmp**, **tcp**, and **udp** define alternative syntax with protocol-specific options.
source and *destination*	Specify the number of the network or host as a 32-bit quantity in dotted-decimal notation. You can use the keywords **any** and **host** to simplify configuration.
source-wildcard	Specifies the wildcard bits to be applied to *source*. 0s indicate bits that must match, and 1s are "don't-care" bits. There are three alternative ways to specify the source wildcard: • Use a 32-bit quantity in four-part dotted-decimal format. Place 1s in the bit positions you want to ignore. • Use the keyword **any** as an abbreviation for *source* and a *source-wildcard* of 0.0.0.0 255.255.255.255. • Use **host** *source* as an abbreviation for *source* and a *source-wildcard* of *source* 0.0.0.0.

continues

Command Parameter	Description
destination-wildcard	Specifies the wildcard bits to be applied to the *destination*. 0s indicate bits that must match, and 1s are "don't-care" bits. There are three alternative ways to specify the destination wildcard: • Use a 32-bit quantity in four-part dotted-decimal format. Place 1s in the bit positions you want to ignore. • Use the keyword **any** as an abbreviation for *destination* and a *destination-wildcard* of 0.0.0.0 255.255.255.255. • Use **host** *destination* as an abbreviation for *destination* and a *destination-wildcard* of *destination* 0.0.0.0.
precedence *precedence*	(Optional) Specifies the packets that can be filtered by precedence level. Specified by a number from 0 to 7 or by name: • **critical** (**5**) • **flash** (**3**) • **flash-override** (**4**) • **immediate** (**2**) • **internet** (**6**) • **network** (**7**) • **priority** (**1**) • **routine** (**0**)
tos *tos*	(Optional) Specifies the packets that can be filtered by type of service (ToS) level, as specified by a ToS name or number: • **max-reliability** (**2**) • **max-throughput** (**4**) • **min-delay** (**8**) • **min-monetary-cost** (**1**) • **normal** (**0**)
log	(Optional) Generates an informational syslog message about the packet that matches the entry to be sent to the console or to a syslog server. (The level of messages logged to the console is controlled by the **logging console** command.) Exercise caution when using this keyword because it consumes CPU cycles.

Extended Mask Keywords

The keyword **any** in either the source or destination position matches any address and is equivalent to configuring 0.0.0.0 255.255.255.255, as illustrated in the following example:

```
access-list 101 permit ip  0.0.0.0  255.255.255.255  0.0.0.0  255.255.255.255
! alternate configuration follows:
access-list 101 permit ip any any
```

The keyword **host** in either the source or destination position causes the address that immediately follows it to be treated as if it were specified with a mask of 0.0.0.0, as illustrated in the following example:

```
access-list 101 permit ip  0.0.0.0  255.255.255.255 172.16.6.3 0.0.0.0
! alternate configuration follows:
access-list 101 permit ip any host 172.16.6.3
```

ICMP Command Syntax

You use the **access-list icmp** command to create an entry in a complex traffic filter list. The protocol keyword **icmp** indicates that an alternative syntax is being used for this command and that protocol-specific options are available.

The command syntax for the **access-list icmp** command used in an extended IP access list is as follows:

```
access-list access-list-number [dynamic dynamic-name [timeout minutes]]
{deny | permit} icmp source source-wildcard destination
destination-wildcard [icmp-type [icmp-code] | icmp-message]
[precedence precedence] [tos tos] [log]
```

The following are the parameters for this syntax:

Command Parameter	Description
icmp	Specifies the ICMP protocol.
icmp-type	(Optional) Specifies the packets that can be filtered by ICMP message type. The type is a number from 0 to 255.
icmp-code	(Optional) Specifies the packets that have been filtered by ICMP message type that can also be filtered by ICMP message code. The code is a number from 0 to 255.
icmp-message	(Optional) Specifies the packets that can be filtered by a symbolic name representing an ICMP message type or a combination of ICMP message type and ICMP message code.

ICMP Message Names, Types, and Codes

Cisco IOS Release 10.3 and later provide symbolic message names that make configuration and reading of complex access lists easier. With symbolic names, it is not critical to understand the meaning of message 8 and message 0 in order to filter the **ping** command. Instead, the configuration would use **echo** and **echo-reply**.

Table C-8 summarizes the ICMP message names in alphabetical order, showing the ICMP type and, where applicable, the ICMP codes.

Table C-8 *ICMP Message Names, Types, and Codes*

ICMP Message Name	ICMP Type	ICMP Code	Description
administratively-prohibited	3	13	Communication administratively prohibited.
alternate-address	6	None	Alternative address.
conversion-error	31	None	Datagram conversion error.
dod-host-prohibited	3	10	Host prohibited.
dod-net-prohibited	3	9	Net prohibited.
echo	8	None	Echo (**ping**).
echo-reply	0	None	Echo reply.
general-parameter-problem	12	0	Parameter problem. Pointer indicates the error.
host-isolated	3	8	Source host isolated.
host-precedence-unreachable	3	14	Host unreachable for precedence.
host-redirect	5	1	Host redirect.
host-tos-redirect	5	3	Host redirect for ToS.
host-tos-unreachable	3	12	Host unreachable for ToS.
host-unknown	3	7	Host unknown.
host-unreachable	3	1	Host unreachable.
information-reply	16	None	Information replies.
information-request	15	None	Information requests.
log-input	None	None	Log matches against any ICMP message name and associated type, code, or parameter.

Table C-8 *ICMP Message Names, Types, and Codes (Continued)*

ICMP Message Name	ICMP Type	ICMP Code	Description
mask-reply	18	None	Mask replies.
mask-request	17	None	Mask requests.
mobile-redirect	32	None	Mobile host redirect.
net-redirect	5	0	Redirect datagram for network.
net-tos-redirect	5	2	Net redirect for ToS.
net-tos-unreachable	3	11	Network unreachable for ToS.
net-unreachable	3	0	Network unreachable.
network-unknown	3	6	Network unknown.
no-room-for-option	12	2	Parameter required but no room. Bad length.
option-missing	12	1	Parameter required but not present.
packet-too-big	3	4	Fragmentation needed and data fragmentation (DF) bit set.
parameter-problem	12	None	All parameter problems.
port-unreachable	3	3	Port unreachable.
precedence-unreachable	3	15	Precedence cutoff in effect.
protocol-unreachable	3	2	Protocol unreachable.
reassembly-timeout	11	1	Fragment reassembly time exceeded.
redirect	5	None	All redirects.
router-advertisement	9	None	Router discovery advertisements.
router-solicitation	10	None	Router discovery solicitations.
source-quench	4	None	Source quenches.

continues

Table C-8 *ICMP Message Names, Types, and Codes (Continued)*

ICMP Message Name	ICMP Type	ICMP Code	Description
source-route-failed	3	5	Source route failed.
time-exceeded	11	None	All time-exceeded messages.
timestamp-reply	14	0	Timestamp replies.
timestamp-request	13	0	Timestamp requests.
traceroute	30	None	Traceroute.
ttl-exceeded	11	0	TTL exceeded in transit.
unreachable	3	None	All destination unreachables.

NOTE You can log packets that match an ICMP message code with the **log-input** keyword. For example, the following sample access list logs packets of ICMP message type 3 and code 4 (ICMP unreachable, packet too big) for any IP address:

```
router(config)# access-list 101 permit icmp any any log-input 3 4
router# show access-lists 101
Extended IP access list 101
    permit icmp any any packet-too-big log-input
```

TCP Syntax

You use the **access-list tcp** command to create an entry in a complex traffic filter list. The protocol keyword **tcp** indicates that an alternative syntax is being used for this command and that protocol-specific options are available.

The command syntax for the **access-list tcp** command is as follows:

```
access-list access-list-number [dynamic dynamic-name [timeout minutes]]
{deny ¦ permit} tcp source source-wildcard [operator port [port]]
destination destination-wildcard [operator port [port]] [established]
[precedence precedence] [tos tos] [log]
```

The parameters that are unique to this syntax are as follows:

Command Parameter	Description
tcp	Specifies TCP.
operator	(Optional) Specifies a qualifying condition that compares source and destination ports. The keyword can be **lt**, **gt**, **eq**, **neq**, or **range**.

Command Parameter	Description
port	(Optional) Specifies a decimal number from 0 to 65535 or a name that represents a TCP port number. TCP port names can be used only when filtering TCP.
established	(Optional) Establishes a Telnet or another activity in one direction only. A match occurs if the TCP datagram has the ACK or RST bits set.

Reserved TCP Port Keywords and Numbers

IP and TCP extended IP access lists can filter on source and/or destination port number. Cisco IOS Software allows you to filter on any TCP port with the **access-list** command. You can enter either the port number or a keyword in the **access-list** command. Cisco IOS contains convenient keywords you can use in place of the port number. You can use the **?** in place of the port number when entering the command in order to verify the port numbers associated with these protocol names.

Table C-9 lists the TCP keywords, brief descriptions of the TCP ports, and the port numbers for keywords supported in the **access-list** command. See the Assigned Numbers RFC (RFC 1700) for a complete list of assigned ports.

Table C-9 *TCP Well-Known Port Key Names and Numbers*

Keyword	Description	Port Number
bgp	Border Gateway Protocol	179
chargen	Character generator	19
cmd	Remote commands (**rcmd**)	514
daytime	Daytime	13
discard	Discard	9
domain	Domain Name Service	53
echo	Echo	7
exec	Exec (**rsh**)	512
finger	Finger	79
ftp	File Transfer Protocol	21
ftp-data	FTP data connections (used infrequently)	20
gopher	Gopher	70
hostname	NIC host name server	101
ident	IDENT protocol	113
irc	Internet Relay Chat	194

continues

Table C-9 *TCP Well-Known Port Key Names and Numbers (Continued)*

Keyword	Description	Port Number
klogin	Kerberos login	543
kshell	Kerberos shell	544
login	Login (**rlogin**)	513
lpd	Printer service	515
nntp	Network News Transport Protocol	119
pim-auto-rp	PIM Auto-RP	496
pop2	Post Office Protocol version 2	109
pop3	Post Office Protocol version 3	110
smtp	Simple Mail Transport Protocol	25
sunrpc	Sun Remote Procedure Call	111
syslog	Syslog	514
tacacs	TAC Access Control System	49
talk	Talk	517
telnet	Telnet	23
time	Time	37
uucp	UNIX-to-UNIX copy program	540
whois	Nickname	43
www	World Wide Web (HTTP)	80

UDP Syntax

The **access-list udp** command creates an entry in a complex traffic filter list. The protocol keyword **udp** indicates that an alternative syntax is being used for this command and that protocol-specific options are available.

The command syntax for the **access-list udp** command is as follows:

```
access-list access-list-number [dynamic dynamic-name [timeout minutes]]
  {deny | permit} udp source source-wildcard [operator port [port]]
  destination destination-wildcard [operator port [port]]
  [precedence precedence] [tos tos] [log]
```

The parameters that are unique to this syntax are as follows:

Command Parameter	Description
udp	Specifies UDP.

Command Parameter	Description
operator	(Optional) Specifies a qualifying condition that compares source and destination ports. The keyword can be **lt**, **gt**, **eq**, **neq**, or **range**.
port	(Optional) Specifies a decimal number from 0 to 65535 or a name that represents a UDP port number. UDP port names can be used only when filtering UDP.

Reserved UDP Port Keywords and Numbers

IP and UDP extended access lists can filter on source or destination port number. Cisco IOS allows you to filter on any UDP port with the **access-list** command. You can enter either the port number or a keyword in the **access-list** command. Cisco IOS contains convenient keywords you can use in place of the port numbers. You can use the **?** in place of the port number when entering the command in order to verify the port numbers associated with these protocol names. Table C-10 lists the UDP keywords, a brief description of the UDP port, and the port numbers for keywords supported in the **access-list** command. See the Assigned Numbers RFC (RFC 1700) for a complete list of assigned ports.

Table C-10 *Extended IP Access List Fields for Reserved UDP*

Keyword	Description	Port Number
biff	Biff (mail notification, comsat)	512
bootpc	Bootstrap protocol (BOOTP) client	68
bootps	BOOTP server	67
discard	Discard	9
dnsix	DNSIX security protocol auditing	195
domain	Domain Name Service (DNS)	53
echo	Echo	7
isakmp	Internet Security Association and Key Management Protocol	500
mobile-ip	Mobile IP registration	434
nameserver	IEN116 name service (obsolete)	42
netbios-dgm	NetBIOS datagram service	138
netbios-ns	NetBIOS name service	137
ntp	Network Time Protocol	123
pim-auto-rp	PIM Auto-RP	496
rip	Routing Information Protocol (**router** UDP keyword)	520

Table C-10 *Extended IP Access List Fields for Reserved UDP (Continued)*

Keyword	Description	Port Number
snmp	Simple Network Management Protocol	161
snmptrap	SNMP Traps	162
sunrpc	Sun Remote Procedure Call	111
syslog	System Logger	514
tacacs	Terminal Access Controller Access Control System	49
talk	Talk	517
tftp	Trivial File Transfer Protocol	69
time	Time	37
who	Who service (**rwho**)	513
xdmcp	X Display Manager Control Protocol	177

Location of Extended IP Access Lists

Because extended IP access lists can filter on more than source address, location is no longer a constraint. Frequently, policy decisions and goals are the driving force behind extended IP access list placement.

If your goal is to minimize traffic congestion and maximize performance, you might want to deploy access lists on the network's perimeter routers to minimize cross traffic and host unreachable messages. If your goal is to maintain tighter control of access to specific internal hosts as part of your network security policy, you might want to place your access lists on routers closest to the protected hosts. You should avoid placing access lists on core or backbone routers because this can cause additional latency. Notice how changing network goals affects access list configuration.

Here are some suggestions and considerations regarding access list placement:

- Minimize the distance traveled by traffic that will be denied (and ICMP unreachable messages).
- Keep denied traffic off the backbone.
- Size the router to handle the CPU overhead from access lists.
- Place access lists on the correct interfaces to protect traffic as efficiently as possible.
- Complex access lists can be difficult to maintain. Carefully review changes to access lists before applying them to your production network.
- Consider network growth impacts on access list maintenance.

Extended IP Access List Example 1

Consider an example of an extended IP access list designed to enable and protect Internet mail traffic. Figure C-10 illustrates the network and contains the partial configuration of Router B.

Figure C-10 *Using an Extended IP Access List in Router A Enables Yet Protects Internet Mail Traffic*

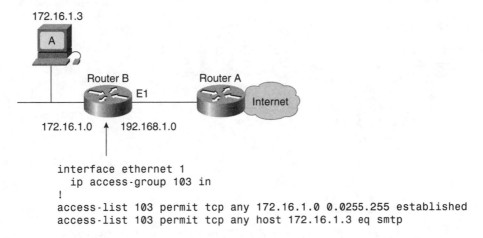

```
interface ethernet 1
  ip access-group 103 in
!
access-list 103 permit tcp any 172.16.1.0 0.0255.255 established
access-list 103 permit tcp any host 172.16.1.3 eq smtp
```

In this example, Ethernet interface 1 is part of a Class B network at 172.16.0.0, and the mail host's address is 172.16.1.3. The keyword **established** is used only for the TCP protocol to indicate an established connection. A match occurs if the TCP packet has the ACK or RST bits set, which indicates that the packet belongs to an existing connection. If the SYN bit is set, indicating session initialization, the packet does not match and is discarded.

NOTE   TCP hosts must establish a connection-oriented session with one another. To ensure reliable transport services, connection establishment is performed by using a *three-way handshake* mechanism. The three-way handshake is accomplished using two flag bits in the TCP packet header. The synchronization (SYN) bit is used to initiate the connection, and the acknowledge (ACK) bit is used to acknowledge the SYN. The three-way handshake proceeds in the following manner:

1 The first host (Router A in Figure C-10) initiates a connection by sending a packet with the SYN bit set to indicate a connection request.

2 The second host (Router B) receives the SYN and replies by acknowledging the SYN with an ACK bit.

3 The first host (Router A) replies with an ACK bit also. Data transfer can then begin.

Extended IP Access List Example 2

Consider the example of an extended IP access list that permits name/domain server packets and ICMP echo and echo-reply packets. Figure C-11 illustrates this network and contains the partial configuration of Router B.

Figure C-11 *An Extended IP Access List That Permits Name/Domain Server Packets and ICMP Echo and Echo-Reply Packets*

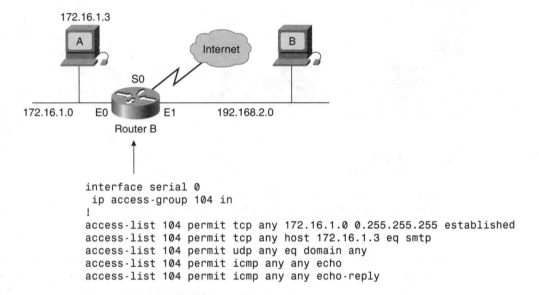

```
interface serial 0
 ip access-group 104 in
 !
access-list 104 permit tcp any 172.16.1.0 0.255.255.255 established
access-list 104 permit tcp any host 172.16.1.3 eq smtp
access-list 104 permit udp any eq domain any
access-list 104 permit icmp any any echo
access-list 104 permit icmp any any echo-reply
```

Verifying Access List Configuration

This section covers how to verify access list configuration. A variety of commands useful for verifying access list configuration are at your disposal. They include the **show access-lists**, **clear access-list counters**, and **show line** commands. The **show running-config** command is very useful for displaying currently configured access lists. Each of these commands is entered in privileged EXEC mode.

You use the **show access-lists** command to display access lists from all protocols. You use the **show ip access-list** command to display all configured IP access lists. You use the **show ip access-list** [*access-list-number | name*] command to examine a specific access list. You can also use the **show running-config** command to display the access lists that you have created.

The system counts how many packets pass each line of an access list; the counters are displayed by the **show access-lists** command. These counters are useful for troubleshooting an access list to determine which line of the list is causing a packet to be permitted or denied. They are also useful for maintenance to determine which lines of an access list are used the most. You use the **clear access-list counters** command in EXEC mode to clear an access list's counters. You use the **clear access-list counters** {*access-list-number | name*} command to clear a specific access list.

You use the **show line** command to display information about terminal lines.

The output from the **show ip access-list** command displays the contents of currently defined IP access lists. Consider the following example of the **show access-lists** command, noting the matches shown for the access list:

```
p1r1#show access-lists
Extended IP access "list" 100
    deny tcp host 10.1.1.2 host 10.1.1.1 eq telnet (3 matches)
    deny tcp host 10.1.2.2 host 10.1.2.1 eq telnet
    permit ip any any (629 matches)
```

Named IP Access Lists

You use the **ip access-list** command to configure a named IP access list as opposed to a numbered IP access list. Named access lists are used to configure reflexive access lists and context-based access control. Named access lists are entered in global configuration mode. The **ip access-list** command first appeared in Cisco IOS Release 11.2.

The **ip access-list** command takes you into access-list configuration mode, where you must define the denied or permitted access conditions with **deny** and **permit** commands. Specifying **standard** or **extended** with the **ip access-list** command determines the prompt and options you get when you enter access list configuration mode.

You use the **ip access-group** command to apply the access list to an interface.

The command syntax for the **ip access-list** command is as follows:

```
ip access-list {standard | extended} name
```

The parameters of this syntax are as follows:

Command Parameter	Description
standard	Specifies a standard IP access list.
extended	Specifies an extended IP access list.
name	Specifies the name of the access list. Names cannot contain a space or quotation mark, and they must begin with an alphabetic character to prevent ambiguity with numbered access lists.

NOTE   Named access lists are not recognized by or compatible with any software release prior to Cisco IOS Release 11.2.

Consider the following captured session, which shows **ip extended access-list** command options:

```
p2r1(config)#ip access-list extended AccessList
p2r1(config-ext-nacl)#?
Ext Access List configuration commands:
  default   Set a command to its defaults
  deny      Specify packets to reject
  dynamic   Specify a DYNAMIC list of PERMITs or DENYs
  evaluate  Evaluate an access list
  exit      Exit from access-list configuration mode
  no        Negate a command or set its defaults
  permit    Specify packets to forward
  remark    Access list entry comment

p2r1(config-ext-nacl)#permit ?
  <0-255>  An IP protocol number
  ahp      Authentication Header Protocol
  eigrp    Cisco's EIGRP routing protocol
  esp      Encapsulation Security Payload
  gre      Cisco's GRE tunneling
  icmp     Internet Control Message Protocol
  igmp     Internet Gateway Message Protocol
  igrp     Cisco's IGRP routing protocol
  ip       Any Internet Protocol
  ipinip   IP in IP tunneling
  nos      KA9Q NOS compatible IP over IP tunneling
  ospf     OSPF routing protocol
  pcp      Payload Compression Protocol
  pim      Protocol Independent Multicast
  tcp      Transmission Control Protocol
  udp      User Datagram Protocol

p2r1(config-ext-nacl)#permit ip ?
  A.B.C.D  Source address
  any      Any source host
  host     A single source host

p2r1(config-ext-nacl)#permit ip any any ?
  log        Log matches against this entry
  log-input  Log matches against this entry, including input interface
  precedence Match packets with given precedence value
  reflect    Create reflexive access list entry
  time-range Specify a time-range
  tos        Match packets with given TOS value

p2r1(config-ext-nacl)#permit tcp ?
  A.B.C.D  Source address
  any      Any source host
  host     A single source host

p2r1(config-ext-nacl)#permit tcp any any ?
  ack         Match on the ACK bit
  eq          Match only packets on a given port number
  established Match established connections
  fin         Match on the FIN bit
  gt          Match only packets with a greater port number
  log         Log matches against this entry
  log-input   Log matches against this entry, including input interface
  lt          Match only packets with a lower port number
  neq         Match only packets not on a given port number
  precedence  Match packets with given precedence value
  psh         Match on the PSH bit
```

```
  range         Match only packets in the range of port numbers
  reflect       Create reflexive access list entry
  rst           Match on the RST bit
  syn           Match on the SYN bit
  time-range    Specify a time-range
  tos           Match packets with given TOS value
  urg           Match on the URG bit

p2r1(config-ext-nacl)#permit tcp any any eq ?
  <0-65535>     Port number
  bgp           Border Gateway Protocol (179)
  chargen       Character generator (19)
  cmd           Remote commands (rcmd, 514)
  daytime       Daytime (13)
  discard       Discard (9)
  domain        Domain Name Service (53)
  echo          Echo (7)
  exec          Exec (rsh, 512)
  finger        Finger (79)
  ftp           File Transfer Protocol (21)
  ftp-data      FTP data connections (used infrequently, 20)
  gopher        Gopher (70)
  hostname      NIC hostname server (101)
  ident         Ident Protocol (113)
  irc           Internet Relay Chat (194)
  klogin        Kerberos login (543)
  kshell        Kerberos shell (544)
  login         Login (rlogin, 513)
  lpd           Printer service (515)
  nntp          Network News Transport Protocol (119)
  pim-auto-rp   PIM Auto-RP (496)
  pop2          Post Office Protocol v2 (109)
  pop3          Post Office Protocol v3 (110)
  smtp          Simple Mail Transport Protocol (25)
  sunrpc        Sun Remote Procedure Call (111)
  syslog        Syslog (514)
  tacacs        TAC Access Control System (49)
  talk          Talk (517)
  telnet        Telnet (23)
  time          Time (37)
  uucp          Unix-to-Unix Copy Program (540)
  whois         Nickname (43)
  www           World Wide Web (HTTP, 80)
```

Summary

This appendix presented a review of standard and extended IP access lists supported in Cisco IOS Software for controlling traffic and identifying interesting traffic on Cisco routers.

References

The topics considered in this appendix are complex and should be studied further to more fully understand them and put them to use. You can use the following references to learn more about the topics in this appendix.

Configuring IP Access Lists

Refer to the *Cisco IOS Release 12.0 Network Protocols Configuration Guide, Part 1,* in the "Filter IP Packets" section of the "Configuring IP Services" chapter, for more information on configuring IP access lists.

Refer to the *Cisco IOS Release 12.0 Network Protocols Command Reference, Part 1,* in the "IP Services Commands" chapter, for information on specific IP access list commands.

IP Protocol and Addressing Information

Cisco Connection CD, "Technology Information" section, Internetworking Technology Overview, "Internet Protocols" section. Cisco Systems, Inc., 1999.

RFC 950, J. Postel and J. Mogul, "Internet Standard Subnetting Procedure," August 1985. This RFC describes how to subnet IP addresses.

RFC 1700, J. Postel and N. Haller, "Assigned Numbers," October 1994. This RFC is a summary of the ongoing process of the assignment of protocol parameters for the Internet protocol suite.

Answers to Review Questions

This appendix contains answers to each chapter's review questions.

Chapter 1

1 What are two characteristics of the network security problem facing businesses today?

Sophisticated security defenses are required to keep up with the latest hacker techniques and to reduce business vulnerability.

Security is complicated to implement because a comprehensive solution must be cobbled together from a vast assortment of various "point products."

2 List five driving factors in the growth of network security.

Increased network traffic

Explosive growth in the number of Internet connections

Growth in the number of network-enabled applications

Increased losses due to security breaches

An increase in reported network intrusions

3 What are the three primary reasons for network security issues?

Technology weaknesses

Configuration weaknesses

Policy weaknesses

4 What are some security policy weaknesses?

Lack of a written security policy.

Internal politics and lack of business continuity, hindering the ability to enact and enforce a security policy.

Logical access controls to network equipment are not applied.

Security administration is lax, including monitoring and auditing.

Software and hardware installation and changes do not follow the policy, permitting vulnerabilities.

Security incident and disaster recovery procedures are not in place.

5 Who typically carries out internal attacks?

Current employees (inside threats), who might deliberately or accidentally carry out network security attacks

Employees who mismanage the environment by misusing or misconfiguring equipment

6 How is a packet sniffer used to carry out reconnaissance attacks?

Sniffers can be physically placed inside an organization at the wiring closet or some other access point.

Sniffer software can be placed in network hosts surreptitiously.

Sniffers can be used in the open Internet to intercept transmissions and retrieve usernames and passwords or even steal information.

7 List the four stages of unauthorized access attacks.

(1) Obtain initial access by attempting to log in with a guessed password or a captured username and password.

(2) Gain privileged or root access to gain trusted access to network equipment.

(3) Place a "back door" to allow secondary access for later unauthorized access.

(4) Conceal any evidence of the remote access.

8 Why are DoS attacks so prevalent?

DoS attacks are relatively easy to carry out because the IP protocol is vulnerable to them, and network intruders enjoy "vandalizing" networks.

9 What is the most common data manipulation attack?

IP spoofing

10 How can an organization benefit from having network engineers and system administrators with network security expertise?

The organization can implement end-to-end network security measures that enable more secure networked commerce.

Chapter 2

1 What two elements of network security must be balanced against each other?

The cost of implementing network security measures versus the potential cost of network security exposures

2 What are the five components of the Security Wheel?

Secure, monitor, test, improve, and the security policy itself

3 What is a network security policy?

According to the Site Security Handbook (RFC 2196), "A security policy is a formal statement of the rules by which people who are given access to an organization's technology and information assets must abide." It further states that "a security policy is essentially a document summarizing how the corporation will use and protect its computing and network resources."

4 Why should an organization expend the time and energy to create a workable network security policy?

A security policy does the following:

- **Provides a process to audit existing network security**

- **Provides a general security framework for implementing network security**

- **Defines which behavior is and is not allowed**

- **Often helps determine which tools and procedures are needed for the organization**

- **Helps communicate consensus among a group of key decision makers and define responsibilities of users and administrators**

- **Defines a process for handling network security incidents**

- **Enables global security implementation and enforcement: computer security is now an enterprise-wide issue, and computing sites are expected to conform to the network security policy**

- **Creates a basis for legal action if necessary**

5 What are some key sections of a network security policy?

The following are some key sections of a network security policy:

- **Statement of authority and scope**

- **Acceptable use policy**

- **Identification and authentication policy**

- **Internet access policy**

— **Campus access policy**

— **Remote access policy**

— **Incident handling procedure**

6 How can you use a network security policy?

You use a network security policy to define what is vital to protect, identify known threats to protect against, document a general implementation plan, and educate users about acceptable and unacceptable network behavior.

7 How can a network security policy help you test and audit the network security implementation?

The policy document can specify details of how and when to conduct testing and auditing of the implementation. The policy should specify procedures used to audit and maintain the secure network.

8 What are some Cisco tools that are useful for security testing and auditing?

CiscoSecure Scanner automates the process of auditing a network's security posture through comprehensive network mapping and vulnerability scanning. Cisco Secure IDS is a real-time intrusion-detection system that is transparent to legitimate traffic and network usage.

9 Where can you report a serious network intrusion that has not yet been reported and resolved?

You can use the Computer Incident Advisory Capability (CIAC) at www.ciac.llnl.gov.

10 What is the defining characteristic of a closed security policy?

That which is not explicitly permitted is denied.

Chapter 3

1 What are some advantages of taking the time to ensure that the equipment that makes up your network infrastructure is as secure as possible?

There could be many people inside and outside any establishment who want to impact campus security. Campus network equipment has features and interfaces that are vulnerable to intrusions yet can be readily made more secure. You do not have to purchase any new network equipment to gain significant increases in network security for the network infrastructure.

2 What two Cisco IOS commands would you use to configure console and Telnet login passwords?

The line console or line vty command and then the enable password command

3 What are some key commands useful for securing the administrator interface in line configuration mode?

exec-banner to enable the display of the EXEC banner

exec-timeout to set the EXEC timeout

login to enable password checking

motd-banner to enable the display of the MOTD banner

privilege to change the privilege level for line

session-timeout to close the connection when there is no input traffic

4 What command would you use to create hierarchical levels of administrator privileges?

The privilege command

5 What three Cisco IOS commands would you enter to restrict Telnet access to a router with five configured vty ports to a host with an address of 10.2.4.1?

```
router(config)#access-list 30 permit 10.2.4.1
router(config)#line vty 0 4
router(config-line)#access-class 30
```

6 How can you prevent an intruder NMS from accessing an SNMP agent?

Use the snmp-server community string command to set a community string to match that of approved NMS systems only and use access lists to control SMNP NMS access.

7 What Cisco IOS feature would you use to secure routing updates from spoofing attacks for the EIGRP routing protocol?

The neighbor routing authentication feature using MD5 for authentication

8 What are four methods and their commands used to control router broadcast or the processing of routing updates?

(1) Suppress routes from being advertised in routing updates with standard access lists and the distribute-list command.

(2) Suppress routes received in updates from being processed with standard access lists and the distribute-list command.

(3) Suppress routing updates through an interface with the passive-interface command.

(4) Filter sources of routing information with the distance *weight* command.

9 What three Cisco IOS commands would you enter to prevent the broadcast of IGRP (autonomous system 100) routing updates on an Ethernet 0 interface from a 16.17.1.0 network on an Ethernet 1 interface?

```
router(config)#access-list 45 deny 10.17.1.0 0.0.0.255
router(config)#router igrp 100
router(config-router)#distribute-list 45 out ethernet 0
```

10 What are two methods used to control Ethernet switch security?

You control Ethernet switch access using secure port filtering with the set port security command, and you control administrator access with the set ip permit command.

Chapter 4

1 AAA protects which modes of network access?

AAA protects the following modes of access: character mode or line mode traffic, such as that used for console or vty access, and packet mode traffic, such as that used for PPP or ARA access.

2 An authentication method should be selected based on what criteria or standard?

The authentication method should be selected based on the guidelines established in the network security policy, which should specify the needed balance between security and ease of use.

3 What are the parts of the CHAP three-way handshake?

(1) The network access server sends a challenge to the remote client.

(2) The remote client responds with a one-way hash.

(3) The network access server checks the received hash value.

4 Network managers use authorization to accomplish what tasks?

Authorization is used to control the network services that are available to each user.

5 When should a local security database be used?

A local security database should be used when a small number of users access one or two network access servers and the expense of a remote security database is not justified.

6 Which security server protocols does Cisco IOS Software support?

Cisco IOS software supports TACACS+, RADIUS, and Kerberos.

7 What are the chief characteristics of TACACS+?

TACACS+ uses the TCP protocol, supports the AAA architecture, encrypts the body of each packet, and supports PAP and CHAP.

8 What is a strength of RADIUS compared with TACACS+?

RADIUS has extensible attributes that vendors can modify.

9 Which Cisco IOS Software services have been Kerberized?

Telnet, rlogin, rsh, and rcp

10 When should CiscoSecure ACS for Windows NT be used?

CiscoSecure ACS for Windows NT should be used when a company prefers to use Windows NT in its networking environment, to centralize network access control, and when a company wants to allow the use of single login by leveraging the use of an existing NT user database.

Chapter 5

1 What would you use the **service password-encryption** command for when preparing to implement AAA configurations?

To secure privileged EXEC mode on the NAS

2 Which two network access server modes can be secured by AAA commands?

Character (line mode) with tty, vty, aux, and cty ports; and packet (interface mode) with async, group-async, BRI, and serial (PRI) ports

3 Why is the **local** parameter needed in the command **aaa authentication ppp sales if-needed local**?

If the if-needed method fails, the local database method is used for PPP authentication.

4 Which AAA commands would be useful to enable AAA globally and instantly secure all access lines?

aaa new-model and aaa authentication login default enable

5 What does the **aaa authorization network risible local none** command do?

The aaa authorization network risible local none command uses the local database to authorize the use of all network services such as SLIP, PPP, and ARAP. If the local server is not available, no authorization is performed, and the user can use all network services.

6 What EXEC command can be used to monitor information on accountable events as they occur?

debug aaa accounting

7 What three steps are used to define method lists?

(1) Specify the service (PPP, ARAP, or NASI).

(2) Identify a list name or default.

(3) Specify the authentication method.

8 What command might you use to ensure a proper time reference for messages as you begin a **debug aaa authentication** session?

service timestamps debug datetime msec. This command should be coupled with the proper reference to an authoritative NTP server for more useful timestamps.

9 What does the **aaa accounting exec start-stop local** command do?

It sends a start record notice when the EXEC process begins and a stop record when the EXEC process ends.

10 When using the **aaa authentication** command to define an authentication method list, how many authentication methods can be specified?

Up to four

Chapter 6

1 List the pros and cons of using the Windows NT User Database with CSNT.

Pros:

— **A single database simplifies administration and allows for ease of login for the user, who needs only one username/password combination.**

— **Can reuse existing username and password entries in the database.**

— **Enables single login for users.**

Cons:

— **Cannot repopulate another database with usernames and passwords located in the NT SAM hive.**

— **Cannot store third-party passwords such as CHAP passwords.**

— **Cannot run token card algorithm in the NT SAM hive.**

2 What do you need in order to configure CSNT in the Windows NT User Manager?

Username and password pairs in the NT User Database.

The user group must include the policy "Log on Locally."

The user profile must not have "Change password at next login" or "Disable account" selected.

Enable "Grant dialin permissions" from the dialup menu if you want to optionally control user login privileges from within NT.

The callback number should not be configured.

3 What is configured using the CiscoSecure ACS Web interface?

User profiles; group profiles; NAS information, including authorization parameters; CiscoSecure ACS services; token server configuration; remote administrators; and viewing of online documentation

4 How is AAA accounting information reported in CiscoSecure ACS?

Accounting information can be viewed under "Reports and Activity" via the Web browser interface. Report files in .csv format can be imported into other database and spreadsheet applications for evaluation.

5 Where should you start when troubleshooting CiscoSecure ACS problems?

Review the "Failed Attempts Report" under "Reports and Activity" via the Web browser interface.

6 Name and describe the features of CiscoSecure ACS for NT that make it valuable in a distributed security system.

Authentication forwarding allows one CSNT server to automatically forward an authentication request from a NAS to another CSNT server.

Fallback on Failed Connection allows you to configure the order in which remote CSNT servers are checked if the network connection to the primary CSNT server fails.

Remote and Centralized Logging allows for the configuration of remote CSNT servers to forward all logs to one CSNT server acting as a centralized repository.

7 CiscoSecure ACS for NT supports which three types of token servers?

CRYPTOCard, Security Dynamics Inc., and Axent

8 What is the purpose of the **tacacs-server key** *your_key_string* command?

The tacacs-server key *your_key_string* command specifies a shared secret text string used between the access server and the TACACS+ server. This text string is used to encrypt passwords and exchange responses.

9 List the three basic steps of NAS configuration for a RADIUS security server.

(1) Configure communication between the router and the RADIUS server.

(2) Use the AAA commands to define method lists containing RADIUS to define authentication and authorization methods.

(3) Use line and interface commands to cause the defined method lists to be used.

10 What are the two stages of Double Authentication authentication/authorization?

In the first stage, CHAP (or PAP) authenticates the remote host, and then PPP negotiates with AAA to authorize the remote host (this assigns network access privileges). In the second stage, the remote user must Telnet to the local host (NAS), log in, and be authenticated with AAA login authentication. The user then must enter the access-profile command to be reauthorized using AAA.

Chapter 7

1 List three purposes of a perimeter security system.

It secures the edge of the network, it implements the outside security policy, and it controls traffic using firewalling technology.

2 List the components that make up a perimeter security system and briefly identify the functions they perform.

The perimeter router is the first line of defense. A DMZ enabled by the perimeter router creates a semisecure area. One or more bastion hosts provide Web, FTP, proxying e-mail, and other services.

3 What is the purpose of a Cisco perimeter router?

It acts as a first line of defense against attacks, it defines the DMZ, it protects the bastion hosts on the DMZ, it protects the firewall from directed attacks and acts as an alarm system for the perimeter system, it has a flexible configuration to adapt to new security threats and new Internet applications, and it harnesses the power of Cisco IOS software, including specific firewall and perimeter security features.

4 Consider the following IOS command: **ip route 0.0.0.0 0.0.0.0 172.16.100.2**. Where and why would you use this command on a perimeter security system?

The ip route command can be used in a perimeter router to create a default (static) route to the ISP's point of presence, preventing rerouting attacks and eavesdropping on a dynamic routing protocol.

5 Which Cisco IOS Software commands would you use to control TCP/IP services on a perimeter router to block echo and finger inquiries from the Internet?

no service tcp-small-servers and no service udp-small-servers

6 Which Cisco IOS command could be used to prevent a perimeter router from becoming a broadcast amplifier in a distributed DoS attack?

The no ip directed-broadcast command could be used to turn off IP directed broadcasts.

7 What types of IP address spoofing would you filter on the incoming traffic of a perimeter router?

RFC 1918 public addresses; addresses with inside addresses as source; any service or port that you specifically want to disallow, such as SNMP, traceroute, or TFTP; and addresses specified in RFC 2827

8 What type of access list is used with lock-and-key security?

Dynamic access lists

9 List the six commands you would use to set up dynamic NAT on a perimeter router.

ip nat pool *name start-ip end-ip*

access-list

ip nat *inside source list*

interface *type number*

ip nat inside (*interface command*)

ip nat outside (*interface command*)

10 Why is it important to log perimeter router events to a syslog server?

To gather data that can be used to analyze an attack and to record data that can indicate an attack

Chapter 8

1 What are four features of CBAC?

Any four of the following: secure per-application filtering, support for advanced protocols, control of downloading of Java applets, DoS detection and prevention, real-time alerts, TCP/UDP transaction logs, and administration

2 What are the steps in the CBAC configuration process?

(1) Pick an interface.

(2) Configure IP access lists at the interface.

(3) Configure global timeouts and thresholds.

(4) Define an inspection rule.

(5) Apply the inspection rule to an interface.

(6) Test and verify CBAC.

3 What command would you use to verify application protocol inspection of packets?

debug ip inspect protocol

4 Is CBAC capable of inspecting TCP, UDP, and ICMP IP protocol traffic?

No. CBAC is available only for TCP and UDP IP protocol traffic.

5 What command would you use to turn on audit trail messages that will be displayed on the console after each CBAC session closes?

ip inspect audit-trail

6 Does CBAC block malicious Java applets that are in .jar format?

No. CBAC cannot block any Java applet that is encapsulated or wrapped in a .zip or .jar format.

7 Are inspection rules mandatory components of CBAC?

Yes. If a protocol (or Java) does not have an inspection rule created for it, CBAC ignores it.

8 What command would you use to define the number of half-open sessions (250, for example) that would cause CBAC to start deleting half-open sessions above this number?

ip inspect max-incomplete high 250

9 What three categories of **debug** commands are typically used to debug CBAC?

Generic, transport level, and application level

10 If CBAC is installed on a firewall located between two routers that are IPSec endpoints, can CBAC inspect the IPSec packets?

CBAC will not inspect the packets because the protocol number in the IP header of the IPSec packet is not TCP or UDP (CBAC inspects only TCP and UDP packets).

Chapter 9

1 What is stateful filtering?

Stateful filtering is a secure method of analyzing data packets that places extensive information about a data packet in a table.

2 What kind of operating system does the PIX Firewall use?

The PIX Firewall uses a secure, real, embedded operating system.

3 What internal processor does the PIX Firewall use?

An Intel-based Pentium-class processor

4 What happens to inbound connections on a PIX Firewall?

Inbound connections on a PIX Firewall are denied unless they are specifically authenticated or mapped.

5 Why is cut-through proxy user authentication better than standard proxy servers?

Cut-through proxy user authentication is better and faster than traditional proxy server authentication because of the ASA's ability to shift session flow to the network layer after authentication.

6 What does ASA stand for?

Adaptive Security Algorithm

7 How many interfaces can a PIX Firewall have?

It depends on the model and the licensing plan.

8 What operation are you trying to perform if you type the following commands?

```
PIXx(config)# interface ethernet0 auto
PIXx(config)# interface ethernet1 auto
PIXx(config)# interface ethernet2 auto
```

You are trying to configure three Ethernet interfaces for 10/100 automatic speed sensing.

9 Which command mode allows you to issue the **show version** command?

This is somewhat of a trick question. Both unprivileged and privileged mode allow this command to run. All unprivileged mode commands work in privileged mode also. Configuration mode also allows this command.

10 An interface with the lowest security value in a pair is considered to be what?

An outside interface

Chapter 10

1 The PIX Firewall NAT feature allows networks connected to the Internet to be which of the following?

   a. Free from Internet port limitations

   b. Free from Internet address limitations

   c. Independent networks

   d. Totally stealthy and secure

   b. Free from Internet address limitations

2 All internal network addresses in the 10.1.0.0 network are translated to global addresses specified by which set of commands?

   a. global (outside) 1 192.168.1.128-192.168.1.254 netmask 255.255.255.0
      nat (inside) 1 10.1.0.0 255.255.0.0

   b. global (inside) 1 192.168.1.128-192.168.1.254
      nat (outside) 1 10.1.0.0 255.255.0.0

   c. inside 1 192.168.1.128-192.168.1.254
      nat 1 10.1.0.0 255.255.0.0

   d. outside 1 192.168.1.128-192.168.1.254
      inside 1 10.1.0.0 255.255.0.0

   **a. global (outside) 1 192.168.1.128-192.168.1.254 netmask 255.255.255.0
   nat (inside) 1 10.1.0.0 255.255.0.0**

3 What does the **nat 0** command allow you to do?

   Disable address translation so that inside IP addresses are visible on the outside without address translation

4 Should you use PAT when you run multimedia applications through a PIX Firewall?

   No

5 How is NetBIOS translation different from TCP/IP address translation?

   It has no numeric source address.

6 What does the **established** command do?

   It allows connections to be initiated to internal hosts from the outside for specific source ports.

7 What does the **static** command do?

   It creates a permanent mapping (called a static translation slot or "xlate") between a global (outside) IP address and a local (inside) IP address.

8 What command limits the number of partially completed connections allowed?

em_limit

9 What does the **conduit** command do?

It permits or denies connections from outside the PIX Firewall to access TCP and/or UDP port services on hosts inside the network.

10 In what order are **conduit permit** and **deny** statements processed?

a. In the order listed in the PIX Firewall configuration

b. In numerical order based on IP address

c. In numerical order based on port address

d. None of the above

a. In the order listed in the PIX Firewall configuration

Chapter 11

1 What are two advantages of using multiple perimeter interfaces?

Platform extensibility and security policy enforcement

2 What command replaced the **aaa-tacacs** and **aaa-radius** commands?

aaa-server

3 How many group tags does the PIX Firewall software allow, and how many servers are allowed in each AAA group?

16 group tags, 16 servers in each group tag

4 When adding, changing, or removing a global statement, what is the next command to enter after saving the configuration?

clear xlate

5 How many **conduit** statements can the PIX Firewall support?

8,000

6 What protocol and port number are syslog messages sent to in a default configuration?

UDP, port 514

7 How many different types of ICMP packets does the PIX Firewall allow filtering on?

18

8 Where are log messages sent by default?

Console port

9 How many different security levels are there to be assigned to interfaces?

101, ranging from 0 to 100

10 When users outside on the Internet initiate a "ping scan" of a network, what type of packet is seen (and perhaps denied) coming in through the PIX Firewall?

An ICMP echo packet

Chapter 12

1 What is the name for TCP connections that have not completed the three-way handshake?

Embryonic

2 How do you upgrade a PIX Firewall model 515's software image for Release 5.1.2 and later?

Obtain the PIX Firewall 515 software image from CCO, place the image on a TFTP server, and enter the copy tftp flash command.

3 Does WebSENSE allow FTP filtering?

No

4 What security level is listed for URL and FTP syslog messages?

Security level 7

5 How often do PIX Firewall failover units send hello messages?

Every 15 seconds

6 What three things are required to make stateful failover work between two PIX Firewall units?

A software license, a PIX Firewall failover serial cable, and a dedicated Fast Ethernet interface for control messages

7 Which version of PIX Firewall software first supported IPSec VPN tunnels?

5.0

8 What two port numbers do SNMP packets use?

TCP/161 for configuration/get requests and UDP/162 for traps and return messages

9 What conduit permission(s) is/are necessary to permit PPTP sessions to pass through the PIX Firewall to a Microsoft Windows NT Server inside?

A conduit permitting TCP/1723 for control messages and a conduit permitting Generic Routing Encapsulation (GRE) packets

10 How many different protocols are covered by the **fixup** feature? What are they?

Six protocols at this time: FTP, HTTP, H323, RSH, SMTP, and SQLNET

Chapter 13

1 What are two security problems that encryption technology helps solve?

Eavesdropping and associated information gathering and information theft attacks, and data manipulation and associated session hijacking and repudiation attacks

2 What four essential elements make up encryption?

Data to be encrypted, encryption and decryption algorithms, encryption keys, and data to be decrypted

3 How does encryption technology enable secure communications over the Internet, an extranet, or an intranet?

Encryption technology enables secure communications over a shared infrastructure such as the Internet, ensuring data privacy, integrity, and nonrepudiation.

4 What three features does encryption provide?

Data privacy through encryption and decryption, data integrity to provide data and device authentication, and nonrepudiation to prove communication actually occurred

5 What four encryption technologies does Cisco use to make up CET?

DES for data privacy, DSS for data integrity and nonrepudiation, MD5 hashing algorithm for data integrity, and Diffie-Hellman for secure key establishment

6 What is the purpose of DES in CET?

DES, a standard encryption algorithm, is the primary encryption method used to encrypt and decrypt bulk data.

7 What DES key lengths are supported in CET, and why is key length important?

CET supports 40-bit and 56-bit DES key lengths. The longer the key length, the more secure the data.

8 How is the MD5 message hash used in Cisco products?

MD5 is used to provide data authentication. It is a message hashing algorithm used by DSS.

9 How is DSS used in CET?

DSS is used to authenticate data exchanges and to authenticate peer encrypting routers to prevent data manipulation attacks.

10 How is Diffie-Hellman used in CET?

Diffie-Hellman is used to establish the shared secret keys used by DES in each peer. The keys are securely established by Diffie-Hellman without sending the keys over the wire.

Chapter 14

1 What are the three types of encryption engines used in Cisco routers?

Cisco IOS crypto engine, VIP2-40 crypto engine, and ESA crypto engine

2 What command is used to generate the peer router's public and private keys?

crypto key generate dss

3 Which of the following commands should be entered first on peer routers when exchanging DSS public keys?

```
crypto key exchange dss ip-address key-name [tcp-port]
crypto key exchange dss passive
```

Enter the crypto key exchange dss passive command on the passive-side router when exchanging DSS public keys.

4 What command do you use to define global encryption policy?

crypto cisco algorithm des | 40-bit-des

5 Which of the following commands defines and controls per-session encryption policy?

```
crypto key generate dss
crypto key exchange dss
crypto map
access-list
```

The crypto map command controls per-session encryption policy.

6 How do you control the traffic, hosts, and subnets that trigger an encrypted session?

Traffic selection is accomplished with crypto access lists (extended IP access lists) applied to crypto maps.

7 What command would you use to test encrypted connection setup between routers?

test crypto initiate session

8 What command would you use to verify that packets are actually being encrypted?

show crypto engine connections active

9 What command should you use to examine the DSS key hexadecimal values of public DSS keys in a router?

show crypto key pubkey-chain dss name *key-name*

10 What three debug commands are available for CET?

debug crypto key-exchange, debug key-exchange, and debug crypto sesmgmt

Chapter 15

1 What are the two main IPSec protocols, and what services does each provide?

AH provides data authentication, integrity, and limited replay detection, and ESP provides data confidentiality, authentication, integrity, and limited replay detection.

2 What important IPSec service does AH not provide?

AH does not provide data confidentiality, because it sends packet contents in cleartext and does not encrypt the data payload.

3 What is the difference between how tunnel mode and transport mode are used?

Tunnel mode is primarily used between IPSec gateways or between an IPSec host and an IPSec gateway. Transport mode is usually used between IPSec hosts.

4 What is an IPSec security association, and how is it established?

An IPSec SA is a connection between IPSec peers that determines the IPSec services available between the peers. IPSec SAs are set up during IKE Phase 1, quick mode.

5 Can IPSec be configured without IKE?

Yes, IPSec security association parameters can be configured manually, but this is not recommended because it is difficult and cannot scale.

6 What are the benefits of using IKE?

IKE provides the following benefits:

— **Allows dynamic authentication of peers**

— **Eliminates the need to manually specify all the IPSec SA parameters at both peers**

— **Establishes session keys**

— **Allows encryption keys to change during IPSec sessions**

— **Allows IPSec to provide antireplay services**

— **Permits CA support for a manageable, scalable IPSec implementation**

7 What initiates the IKE process?

IKE (and the IPSec process) is initiated when traffic to be encrypted as specified in the IPSec security policy is transmitted.

8 What is the purpose of IKE Phase 2?

IKE Phase 2 uses quick mode to negotiate and then set up IPSec security associations, to periodically renegotiate security associations and keying material, and to optionally do a Diffie-Hellman exchange during security association renegotiation.

9 What is the primary purpose of a CA?

A CA is a third party that is used to verify individual IPSec peers' public keys.

10 What are the five overall steps of the IPSec process?

(1) Interesting traffic initiates the IPSec process.

(2) IKE Phase 1.

(3) IKE Phase 2.

(4) Data transfer.

(5) IPSec tunnel termination.

Chapter 16

1 What is the default IKE (Phase 1) policy?

Encryption algorithm = DES

Hash algorithm = Secure Hash Standard

Authentication method = Rivest Shamir Adleman Signature

Diffie-Hellman Group = #1 (768 bit)

Lifetime = 86400 seconds, no volume limit

2 Why would you choose to use the **show crypto isakmp policy** command to view IKE policies instead of the **show running-config** command?

The show crypto isakmp policy command displays configured and default policies and values, and the show running-config command shows only configured values, not default values.

3 What protocols and ports must be enabled for an interface to use IPSec?

Protocol 50 for ESP, protocol 51 for AH, and UDP port 500 for IKE

4 How do you enable IKE for one particular interface and not another?

You cannot enable or disable IKE on each individual interface. IKE is enabled or disabled for all interfaces at the same time. You can deny IKE communications on an interface by configuring an access list to deny UDP port 500 traffic.

5 How many ESP transforms can be defined at the same time?

You can define up to two ESP transforms in a transform set.

6 Where can you configure IPSec security association lifetimes?

You can configure IPSec security association lifetimes globally with the crypto ipsec security association lifetime command, or you can configure them in crypto maps with the set security-association lifetime command.

7 What command do you use to define the traffic flows to be protected?

Use extended IP access lists with the access-list command applied to crypto maps.

8 How do you apply a crypto map to an interface?

Enter interface configuration mode and apply the crypto map map-name command.

9 When are the IPSec SAs initialized with IKE configured?

When the crypto map is applied to the interface with the crypto map command

10 You believe IPSec setup is failing. You have checked your configuration, but you cannot determine where the failure is. What should you do?

Turn on IKE and IPSec debug commands and observe where the failure is occurring.

Chapter 17

1 Name an advantage and a disadvantage of using preshared keys for authentication.

An advantage of using preshared keys is simplicity of configuration. A disadvantage is lack of scalability because you must code the preshared key value in each IPSec peer.

2 What command do you use to enter a preshared key?

isakmp key *key-string*

3 How do you view IKE policies in the PIX's configuration?

With the write terminal, show isakmp, or show isakmp policy commands

4 How do you enable IKE for one interface and not for another?

You can enable IKE on specific interfaces with the crypto map *map-name* interface *interface-name* command.

5 How many transforms can be defined in a transform set?

You can define up to one AH and up to two ESP transforms in a transform set.

6 How do you configure IPSec security association lifetimes on the PIX Firewall?

You can configure IPSec security association lifetimes globally with the crypto ipsec security association lifetime command, or you can configure them using the crypto map command with the set security-association lifetime command option.

7 What command do you use to define the traffic flows to be protected?

Use the access list command to select interesting traffic, which becomes crypto access lists when applied to a crypto map.

8 When are the IPSec SAs initialized with IKE configured?

When the crypto map is applied to the interface with the crypto map *map-name* interface *interface-name* command

9 How can you view IKE events as they occur between IPSec peers?

Use the debug crypto isakmp command to view IKE events.

10 Why is IKE failing for preshared keys in the following sample configurations?

PIX1	PIX2
crypto isakmp policy 100	crypto isakmp policy 100
authentication rsa-sig	authentication rsa-sig
group 2	group 1
lifetime 5000	lifetime 5000
crypto isakmp policy 200	crypto isakmp policy 200
hash md5	authentication rsa-sig
authentication pre-share	lifetime 10000
crypto isakmp policy 300	crypto isakmp policy 300
authentication rsa-sig	hash sha
lifetime 10000	authentication pre-share

The peers have no matching IKE policies.

Chapter 18

1 What is the advantage of using a CA to authenticate IPSec peers?

An advantage of using a CA server is to enable scaling of multiple IPSec peers without having to manually enter each peer's encryption keys.

2 What are some CA server vendors that can interoperate with Cisco VPN devices using SCEP and that offer software that the end user installs and administers?

Entrust, Baltimore, and Microsoft

3 Which IKE authentication method is used for CA support?

RSA signatures on both Cisco routers and PIX Firewalls are the IKE authentication method used for CA support.

4 How do you view CA certificates in the router's configuration?

With the show crypto ca certificates command

5 Is any special IPSec configuration required for CA support?

None other than configuring ipsec-isakmp to enable the use of IKE for authentication

6 When should you principally use dynamic crypto maps?

Use dynamic crypto maps on a Cisco router or PIX Firewall used to terminate many remote access VPN clients.

7 What is the general procedure for configuring dynamic crypto maps on a PIX Firewall?

Configure dynamic map properties such as setting the transform set and an access list, apply the dynamic map to a static crypto map, and apply the static crypto map to an interface.

8 When should you use IKE mode configuration?

Use IKE mode configuration on a Cisco router or PIX Firewall used to terminate many remote access VPN clients when the VPN clients need to have their IP addresses dynamically assigned by a remote server.

9 How is using IKE extended authentication beneficial in a VPN client-initiated remote access topology?

IKE extended authentication improves security by adding user authentication to the IKE process.

10 What command do you use to configure tunnel endpoint discovery?

After configuring a dynamic crypto map, use the crypto map *map-name seq-number* ipsec-isakmp dynamic *dynamic-map-name* [discover] command.

Symbols

Numerics

3DES (Triple DES) encryption algorithm, 526

A

AAA (authentication, authorization, and
    accounting) architecture, 111, 157, 408–412
    access traffic, 112
    accounting, 112, 126–127
        configuring, 168
    authentication, 111
        CHAP (Challenge Handshake
            Authentication Protocol), 121–122,
            124–125
        methods, 114–125
        PAP (Password Authentication
            Protocol), 121–125
        passwords, 114–117
        S/Key, 117–120
        token cards, 120
        token servers, 120
        usernames, 114, 116–117
    authentication profiles, configuring, 163
    authorization, 111
        configuring, 166
    character-mode traffic, 113
    configuring, 205
        debugging, 169
    enabling, 205
    local security databases, 127
    NAS (Network Access Server), 158–174
        globally enabling, 162
        privileged EXEC (enable) mode, 160
    network access
        securing, 111–114
        packet-mode traffic, 114
        PIX Firewall, configuring, 401–412
        remote security databases, 128–130
            CiscoSecure ACS, 148
            Kerberos, 142–151
            RADIUS, 136–142
            standards, 130–151
            TACACS+, 131–136
        security servers, 127–151
aaa authentication command, 197, 199
aaa authentication login command, 147
aaa authentication ppp command, 146
AAA configuration commands, 199
aaa new-model command, 159, 197
Acceptable Use Policy, 696–697
access
    administrative interfaces, console, 70–76
    HTTP, controlling, 95–96
    perimeter routers, controlling, 234–237
    physcial access, securing, 69–70
    securing, AAA architecture, 111–114
    SNMP, controlling, 81–86
    Telnet, controlling, 80–81
access lists
    configuring, 713
        verifying, 734–735
    IP access lists, extended IP access lists,
        714–734
    named IP access lists, 735–737
    references, 106
    SNMP, 85
access traffic, AAA architecture, 112
access-list command, 552, 716, 722
access-list icmp command, 725
access-list tcp command, 728
access-list udp command, 730
accounting, AAA architecture, 112, 126–127,
    168
Adaptive Security Algorithm. See ASA
    (Adaptive Security Algorithm)
administration
    Cisco IOS Firewall, 277–279

B-C

interoperability, managing, 667
IPSec, 548–552
PIX Firewall, configuring, 645–673
routers, configuring, 645–673
standards, 550
case studies, network security, 48–60
CBAC (Context-Based Access Control), 259
Cisco IOS Firewall, 260–264
configuring, 266–277
memory, 265
performance, 265
restrictions, 264–265
debugging, 277
global timeouts, configuring, 268–271
inspection rules
applying, 276
defining, 271–276
interfaces, choosing, 266
IP access lists, configuring, 267
monitoring, 276
testing, 276–277
thresholds, configuring, 268–271
verifying, 276–277
CBAC (context-based access control)
perimeter routers, 226
Certificate Revocation Lists. *See* CRLs
(Certificate Revocation Lists)
CET (Cisco Encryption Technology), 241, 453,
471–479
configuration procedures job aid, 512
configuring, 479–505, 510
crypto engines, 471–473
cryptosystems, forming, 460–468
data integrity, 453–460
designing, 508–509
diagnosing, 505–507
DSS keys
generating, 480–483
sending from passive side, 486
DSS public keys
accepting, 486
authenticating, 486
exchanging, 483–490

encryption
testing, 499–505
verifying, 499–505
encryption export policy, 511
encryption job aid, planning for, 511–512
encryption solutions, 453–460
exchange connections
enabling from active side, 485
enabling from passive side, 484
global encryption policies, defining, 490–
493
implementing, 508–510
network layer encryption, 459
per-session encryption policy, configuring,
493–498
references, 469
troubleshooting, 505–507
CHAP (Challenge Handshake Authentication
Protocol), 114
AAA architecture, 121-125
character-mode traffic, AAA architecture, 113
circuit-level gateways, firewalls, 229
Cisco, 137
Cisco ConfigMaker, 259, 278
Cisco Encryption Technology. *See* CET (Cisco
Encryption Technology)
Cisco IOS crypto engine, 472
Cisco IOS Firewall, 259
administration, 277–279
audit trails, 261
authentication proxy, 260
CBAC, 260–264
configuring, 266–277
memory, 265
performance, 265
restrictions, 264–265
configuring, 260–262, 280–284
DoS (denial of eervice), 260
dynamic port mapping, 261
event logging, 261
features, 260–261
firewalls, managing, 261
IDS (Intrusion Detection System), 262

E

no ip unreachable command, 231
no mop enabled command, 231
no service finger command, 230
no service tcp-small-servers command, 230
no service udp-small-servers command, 230
nonprivileged access, SNMP, 84
nonrepudiation, encryption, 455
nonvolatile random-access memory, 75
norandomseq command, 342
notifications, SNMP, 83
NVRAM (nonvolatile random-access memory), 75

O

operating systems, CiscoSecure ACS, 177–178
outbound access control, PIX Firewall, 339–355
    NAT (Network Address Translation), 341–344
outbound command, 323, 419
outbound packet filtering, 235
outboung access, PIX Firewall, controlling, 419–422
outside command, 342
outside global addresses, NAT, 243
outside interfaces, PIX Firewall, 385
    configuring, 392–394
outside local addresses, NAT, 243
overload command, 246
overloading, NAT, 245

P

packet filtering
    firewalls, 229
        inbound packet filtering, 234–235
        outbound packet filtering, 235
packet mode traffic, AAA, 114
packet sniffing, 17
packet-capturing utilities, 17

PAP (Password Authentication Protocol), 52, 114, 180
    AAA architecture, 121–125
password attacks, 24
Password Authentication Protocol. *See* PAP (Password Authentication Protocol)
password-based attacks, 20
password-encryption command, 161
passwords
    authentication, AAA architecture, 114, 116–117
    encryption, administrative interfaces, 73
    line parameters, fine-tuning, 76
    management guidelines, 697
    recovering, PIX Firewall, 440
PAT (Port Address Translation), 242, 339
    configuring, 246
    IP addresses, managing, 242–246
    NAT (Network Address Translation), 340, 347–349
peer router authentication, Cisco IOS Firewall, 261
perimeter routers, 224–228
    access, controlling, 234–237
    CBAC (context-based access control), 226
    Cisco IOS Firewall feature set, 226
    configuring, 248, 250, 252–254
    DMZ (demilitarized zone), 228
    DoS attacks, preventing, 237–240
    events, logging, 247
    features, 225
    inbound packet filtering, 234–235
    IP addresses, managing, 242–246
    lock-and-key security, 235–237
    network-layer encryption, 241–242
    outbound packet filtering, 235
    rerouting attacks, preventing, 232–233
    route advertisement, controlling, 233
    route authentication, 233
    screened subnet architecture, 224
    static routes, 232
perimeter security, 223–230
    bastion hosts, 228

Q-R

W-Z

Cisco Press Solutions

Building Scalable Cisco Networks
Edited by Diane Teare and Catherine Paquet, CCSI

1-57870-228-3 • CCNP/CCDP #640-503

Based on the Cisco BSCN training course, this book addresses tasks that network managers and engineers need to perform when managing access and controlling overhead traffic in growing routed networks. Learn to utilize router capabilities to control multiprotocol traffic over LANs and WANs and to connect corporate networks to Internet service providers. Provides a complete early study resource for the new professional level Routing Exam #640-503 with configuration examples, case studies, and chapter-ending review questions.

Building Cisco Multilayer Switched Networks
Karen Webb, CCIE

1-57870-093-0 • CCNP/CCDP #640-504

Based on the Cisco Systems instructor-led course available worldwide, *Building Cisco Multilayer Switched Networks* teaches you how to build and manage campus networks using multilayer switching technologies. As the replacement for the Cisco LAN Switch Configuration (CLSC) course, BCMSN is one of four courses recommended by Cisco for CCNP and CCDP preparation. If you are pursuing CCNP or CCDP Switching Exam #640-504, this book helps you with strong and accurate early study material.

Building Cisco Remote Access Networks
Edited by Catherine Paquet, CCSI

1-57870-091-4 • CCNP/CCDP #640-505

A compilation from the BCRAN course taught at Cisco-approved training centers worldwide, this book shows you how to design, configure, maintain, and scale a remote access network using Cisco products. Learn how to enable and enhance the on-demand connectivity of a small office, home office, or telecommuter site to a central site while you prepare for CCNP or CCDP Remote Access Exam #640-505.

Cisco Press Solutions

Cisco Internetwork Troubleshooting
Edited by Laura Chappell and Dan Farkas
1-57870-092-2 • CCNP #640-506

With the Cisco CIT course as its foundation, this book covers troubleshooting methodology, routing and routed protocol troubleshooting, campus switch and VLAN troubleshooting, and Frame Relay and ISDN BRI problems. Master standard problem solving using network troubleshooting tools and Cisco diagnostic tools as you prepare for the CCNP Support Exam #640-506.

Cisco Internetwork Design
Revised and Edited by Mathew Birkner, CCIE
1-57870-171-6 • CCDP #640-025

Recommended by Cisco Systems as study material for CCDP candidates, this book is an in-depth and direct compilation from the CID course taught by Cisco-approved training centers. This book contains case studies and exercises covering design issues for LANs, WANs, SNA, TCP/IP, and desktop protocols. Prepare for CCDP certification while mastering the intricacies of internetwork design.

Cisco ATM Solutions
Revised and Edited by Galina Diker Pildush
1-57870-213-5 • CCNP #640-446

Based on the actual Cisco ATM course, this book teaches you how to configure Cisco ATM router interfaces, LightStream 1010 ATM switches, and LAN emulation services. Unlike other ATM books, which can quickly get bogged down in theory and acronyms, this book is a practical introduction to the complex topic of ATM technology and its application in a Cisco environment. Includes extensive lab scenarios and solutions as well as chapter-ending review questions. A great resource for general ATM training or for CCIE or CCNP LAN/ATM Specialization exam preparation.

Cisco Career Certification

Cisco Career Certification

CCNP Support Exam Certification Guide

Amir Ranjbar

0-7357-0995-5 • CCNP #640-506 • CD-ROM

The Cisco Press guide for preparing for the new professional-level Support Exam #640-506. Offers an in-depth reference of key topics, practical scenarios, chapter review questions, and a test simulator on CD-ROM, helping you achieve mastery of all exam topics. The book focuses on review of the concepts involved in diagnosing, isolating, and correcting network problems. Review and practice in five major areas: troubleshooting resources, tools, and methodology; understanding data link layer troubleshooting, fast switching methods, and buffering technologies; network layer protocol troubleshooting; troubleshooting Catalyst 5000 switches; and troubleshooting WAN connections.

CISCO SYSTEMS

CISCO PRESS

www.ciscopress.com

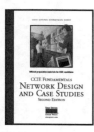

Cisco Interactive Mentor

The Cisco Interactive Mentor product line is a series of e-learning solutions designed to provide entry-level networking professionals with the opportunity to gain practical, hands-on experience through self-paced instruction and network lab simulation exercises. This combination of computer-based training with lab exercises offers users a unique learning environment that eliminates the cost overhead necessary with the actual network devices, while offering the same degree of real-world experience. Current releases include:

Router Basics
1-58720-011-2
$149.95
AVAILABLE NOW

LAN Switching
1-58720-021-X
$199.95
AVAILABLE NOW

IP Routing: Distance-Vector Protocols
1-58720-012-0
$149.95
AVAILABLE NOW

Access ISDN
1-58720-025-2
$149.95
AVAILABLE NOW

Expert Labs: IP Routing
1-58720-010-4
$149.95
AVAILABLE NOW

Voice Internetworking: Basic Voice over IP
1-58720-023-6
$149.95
AVAILABLE NOW

For the latest on Cisco Press resources and Certification and Training guides, or for information on publishing opportunities, visit **www.ciscopress.com**

Cisco Press

Committed to being your **long-term** resource as you grow as a **Cisco Networking professional**

CISCO SYSTEMS

CISCO PRESS

Help Cisco Press **stay connected** to the issues and challenges you face on a daily basis by registering your product and filling out our brief survey. Complete and mail this form, or better yet ...

Register online and enter to win a **FREE** book!

Jump to **www.ciscopress.com/register** and register your product online. Each complete entry will be elIglble for our monthly drawing to win a FREE book of the winner's choice from the Cisco Press library.

May we contact you via e-mail with information about **new releases, special promotions** and customer benefits?

☐ Yes   ☐ No

E-mail address _____

Name _____

Address _____

City _____ State/Province _____

Country _____ Zip/Post code _____

Where did you buy this product?

☐ Bookstore   ☐ Computer store/electronics store
☐ Online retailer   ☐ Direct from Cisco Press
☐ Mail order   ☐ Class/Seminar
☐ Other_____

When did you buy this product? _____ Month _____ Year

What price did you pay for this product?

☐ Full retail price   ☐ Discounted price   ☐ Gift

How did you learn about this product?

☐ Friend   ☐ Store personnel   ☐ In-store ad
☐ Cisco Press Catalog   ☐ Postcard in the mail   ☐ Saw it on the shelf
☐ Other Catalog   ☐ Magazine ad   ☐ Article or review
☐ School   ☐ Professional Organization   ☐ Used other products
☐ Other_____

What will this product be used for?

☐ Business use   ☐ School/Education
☐ Other_____

Cisco Press

How many years have you been employed in a computer-related industry?

❏ 2 years or less   ❏ 3-5 years   ❏ 5+ years

Which best describes your job function?

❏ Corporate Management   ❏ Systems Engineering   ❏ IS Management
❏ Network Design   ❏ Network Support   ❏ Webmaster
❏ Marketing/Sales   ❏ Consultant   ❏ Student
❏ Professor/Teacher   ❏ Other

What is your formal education background?

❏ High school   ❏ Vocational/Technical degree   ❏ Some college
❏ College degree   ❏ Masters degree   ❏ Professional or Doctoral degree

Have you purchased a Cisco Press product before?

❏ Yes   ❏ No

On what topics would you like to see more coverage?

_____

_____

Do you have any additional comments or suggestions?

_____

_____

Thank you for completing this survey and registration. Please fold here, seal, and mail to Cisco Press.

Managing Cisco Network Security (1-57870-103-1)

Indianapolis, IN 46278-8046
P.O. Box #781046
Customer Registration—CP050227
Cisco Press

Place
Stamp
Here

Cisco Press
201 West 103rd Street
Indianapolis, IN 46290
ciscopress.com

PACKET

Packet magazine serves as the premier publication linking customers to Cisco Systems, Inc. Delivering complete coverage of cutting-edge networking trends and innovations, *Packet* is a magazine for technical, hands-on users. It delivers industry-specific information for enterprise, service provider, and small and midsized business market segments. A toolchest for planners and decision makers, *Packet* contains a vast array of practical information, boasting sample configurations, real-life customer examples, and tips on getting the most from your Cisco Systems' investments. Simply put, *Packet* magazine is straight talk straight from the worldwide leader in networking for the Internet, Cisco Systems, Inc.

We hope you'll take advantage of this useful resource. I look forward to hearing from you!

Jennifer Biondi
Packet Circulation Manager
packet@cisco.com
www.cisco.com/go/packet

☐ **YES!** I'm requesting a **free** subscription to *Packet™* magazine.

☐ No. I'm not interested at this time.

☐ Mr.
☐ Ms.

First Name (Please Print) / Last Name

Title/Position (Required)

Company (Required)

Address

City / State/Province

Zip/Postal Code / Country

Telephone (Include country and area codes) / Fax

E-mail

Signature (Required) / Date

☐ I would like to receive additional information on Cisco's services and products by e-mail.

1.0 Do you or your company:
- A ☐ Use Cisco products
- B ☐ Resell Cisco products
- C ☐ Both
- D ☐ Neither

1. Your organization's relationship to Cisco Systems:
- A ☐ Customer/End User
- B ☐ Prospective Customer
- C ☐ Cisco Reseller
- D ☐ Cisco Distributor
- DI ☐ Non-Authorized Reseller
- E ☐ Integrator
- G ☐ Cisco Training Partner
- I ☐ Cisco OEM
- J ☐ Consultant
- K ☐ Other (specify):

2. How would you classify your business?
- A ☐ Small/Medium-Sized
- B ☐ Enterprise
- C ☐ Service Provider

3. Your involvement in network equipment purchases:
- A ☐ Recommend
- B ☐ Approve
- C ☐ Neither

4. Your personal involvement in networking:
- A ☐ Entire enterprise at all sites
- B ☐ Departments or network segments at more than one site
- C ☐ Single department or network segment
- F ☐ Public network
- D ☐ No involvement
- E ☐ Other (specify):

5. Your Industry:
- A ☐ Aerospace
- B ☐ Agriculture/Mining/Construction
- C ☐ Banking/Finance
- D ☐ Chemical/Pharmaceutical
- E ☐ Consultant
- F ☐ Computer/Systems/Electronics
- G ☐ a. Education (K–12)
- ☐ b. Education (College/Univ.)
- H ☐ Government—Federal
- I ☐ Government—State
- J ☐ Government—Local
- K ☐ Health Care
- L ☐ Telecommunications
- M ☐ Utilities/Transportation
- N ☐ Other (specify):

PACKET